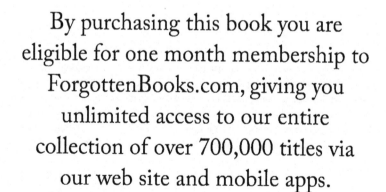

ISBN 978-0-331-53290-6
PIBN 11205043

EXPLANATION OF THE CHART OF HISTORY,

Representing in a Chronological Series, the Rise, Revolutions, and Fall of the principal Empires of the World.—On the plan of Dr, J. Priestley.

It is necessary to notice, that the space allotted to each country is rather according to its relative political importance, than to its geographical extent.—

The spaces between the *vertical* lines which cross the chart, represent *time*, viz., each a century or 100 years; those between the *horizontal* lines represent countries, the names of which are expressed at the end of the chart.

By examining the vertical columns, we ascertain the contemporary state of different nations at the period we fix upon. For instance:—about 1500 years before Christ, we see states forming in Greece; the Israelites in Egypt, (from whence they depart 9 years after;) the Egyptian, Assyrian, Persian, Chinese and other kingdoms had been founded several centuries previous—but their history uncertain and obscure. At the time of Christ, we find the Roman Empire spread over a greater part of the then known world, but the Parthians, Britons, and Germans, as yet unsubdued by them. 700 years after, this empire exists only in Turkey, and its former territories, are under barbarians: the Heptarchy in England; the Lombards in Italy, the Franks in Gaul; the African provinces and a large part of Asia under the Saracens. In 1500 we find the Eastern or Greek Empire fallen under the Turks; the Tartars powerful in Asia; many of the modern states of Europe founded; America discovered by the Europeans, &c. &c.

On the other hand, the revolutions of each country may be seen in continuation by looking along the chart horizontally: The *Persian* empire is founded in remote antiquity; united with that of the Medes, about 600 B. C.; is extended by Cyrus into Assyria, Asia Minor, and Egypt, 536; falls in turn, under the Macedonians, Parthians, Saracens, Turks and Tartars, successively.—The *Israelites* in Egypt from 1706 to 1491 B. C.; in Canaan 1451; under the Judges about 1300; under Kings 1095; Ten Tribes separated, 975; *they* are conquered, 721, and Judah, 588, by the Assyrians; restored by the Persians, 535; under the Macedonians, 330; restored to independence by the Maccabees, 150; conquered by the Romans, 63; by the Saracens, A. D. 622; afterwards by the crusaders, Mamelukes, and Turks, successively.—*England* subdued by the Romans in the first century; relinquished by them, A. D. 410; subdued by the Saxons, 500; by the Danes, 860; by the Normans, (receiving French territories) 1066; united with Ireland, 1170; with Wales, 1280; with Scotland, 1600.—*Italy* in antiquity possessed by several petty tribes; by the Romans from 300-200, B. C. to 480, A. D., then by the Herulii, Ostrogoths, Lombards, and Franks, successively;—in modern times, divided into several small republics and principalities; joined to the French empire about 1800, and now under the sovereignty of Austria.—

"They are rather melancholy reflections which the view of such a chart of history is apt to excite in the minds of persons of feeling and humanity. What a number of revolutions are marked upon it! What torrents of human blood has the restless ambition of mortals shed, and in what complicated distress has the discontent of powerful individuals involved a great part of their species."—*Priestley.*

CHRONOLOGY:

OR AN

INTRODUCTION AND INDEX

TO

Universal History, Biography,

AND

USEFUL KNOWLEDGE.

COMPRISING A CHRONOLOGICAL, CONTEMPORARY, AND ALPHABETICAL RECORD, OF IMPORTANT AND INTERESTING OCCURRENCES, FROM THE EARLIEST PERIOD TO THE PRESENT TIME; WITH COPIOUS LISTS OF EMINENT AND REMARKABLE PERSONS, &C.

TO WHICH ARE ADDED,

VALPY'S POETICAL RETROSPECT;

LITERARY CHRONOLOGY;

AND

THE LATEST STATISTICAL VIEWS OF THE WORLD.

WITH A CHART OF HISTORY.

Intended for the use of Schools, and for general reference.

New-York.

PUBLISHED BY JONATHAN LEAVITT, 182 BROADWAY:
BOSTON; CROCKER & BREWSTER.

1833.

useful to connect the histories you read in such a manner in your own mind, that you may be able to refer from one to the other, and form them all into a whole. For this purpose, it is desirable to observe and retain in your memory certain coincidences, which may link, as it were, two nations together. Thus you may remember that Haroun al Raschid sent to Charlemagne the first *clock* that was seen in Europe. If you are reading the history of Greece when it flourished most, and want to know what the Romans were doing at the same time, you may recollect that they sent to Greece for instruction when they wanted to draw up the laws of the Twelve Tables. Solon and Crœsus connect the history of Lesser Asia with that of Greece. Egbert was brought up in the court of Charlemagne; Philip Augustus of France and Richard I. of England fought in the same crusade against Saladin. Queen Elizabeth received the French ambassador in deep mourning after the massacre of St. Bartholomew.

"That the literary and political history of a nation may be connected, study also biography, and endeavour to link men of science and literature and artists with political characters. Thus Hippocrates was sent for to the plague of Athens; Leonardo da Vinci died in the arms of Francis I. Often an anecdote, a smart saying, will indissolubly fix a date."*

The first division of this book and the accompanying chart, are intended to afford this general, contemporary, view. The columns are varied, in different periods, as may be necessary.

[For an explanation of the arrangement &c., see Introduction.]

The compiler believes that all, or very nearly all, the materially interesting and important facts in the course of universal history, particulary those relating to England and the United States, have been mentioned; but of course there is no space for the details which belong to continued histories.

Particular care has been taken to insert in the contemporary table, the succession of sovereigns; items relating to the progress of literature and the arts; and the names of individuals conspicuous for learning and science, as well as those of military and political characters. In order that each name and subject may he more easily referred to,—copious biographical and other ables have been prepared. The valuable article showing the *literary* character of each age and nation, is taken principally from the *Companion to the British Almanac:* and *Valpy's Poetical Retrospect*, which is appended will materially aid in that difficult task the remembrance of *dates* with their *associations.*

The present extent, population, religions, heads of government, military and naval force, &c., of the different countries on the globe are exhibited in the *Statistical Views.*

Nearly two hundred volumes have been consulted for this compilation—including it is believed, most of the principal modern authorities on the subject. The ancient dates are according to archbishop Usher.

* Mrs. Barbauld.

CONTENTS.

INTRODUCTION.

The word *Chronology*, is derived "from the Greek, χρονολογια; χρονος, time, and λογος, discourse or doctrine." It signifies "the science of time; the method of measuring or computing time by regular divisions or periods, according to the revolutions of the sun, or moon; of ascertaining the true periods or years when past events or transactions took place; and arranging them in their proper order according to their dates."*

THE DIVISION OF TIME

has been most commonly made in all ages and countries according to the apparent or real revolutions of the sun and moon.

The Day, is that portion of time which elapses while the earth performs a complete revolution round its axis; and its length is measured by observing the precise instant when the centre of a star passes the meridian on two successive days. A day thus measured is called the *sidereal day*. A *solar* or natural day, is that portion of time which elapses between the arrival of the sun at the meridian on two successive days. The mean length of the solar day is 24 hours; but owing to the inclination of the earth's axis to the ecliptic, and the unequal motion of the earth in its orbit, the solar days are of unequal length, sometimes exceeding, and sometimes falling short of 24 hours. The hour hand of a well regulated clock performs two complete revolutions on the dial plate in the course of a mean solar day, and twice 365 or 730 revolutions in the course of a year; whereas the shadow of the stile or gnoman, of a sundial, sometimes performs more and sometimes less than one revolution during a mean solar day, but always completes 365 revolutions in the course of one year. The difference between the mean solar time, as shown by a well regulated clock, and the apparent time, as shown by a sundial is called the *equation of time*.

All nations have agreed in adopting the solar day as the unit of their scale for measuring time,—but they have differed from each other in fixing its commencement.—This was reckoned by the Chaldeans, Syrians, Persians, most of the Greeks, Jews (except the Sabbath,) and almost all eastern nations, at sunrise; by the Athenians, Turks, Italians, &c., at sunset; by the Arabians, and by astronomers of all nations, at mid-day; and by the ancient Egyptians, and the principal modern nations, at midnight.

The subdivision of the day has also been various. The Chaldeans, Syrians, Persians, Indians, Jews, and Romans, divided both the day and night into four parts, denominated watches or vigils. The Greeks divided the natural day into 12 *hours*, in imitation of the Babylonians, and this practice was afterwards adopted by the Romans. The division into 24 hours, reckoned twice from 1 to 12 has been adopted by all modern nations, except the Italians Bohemians and Poles, who reckon them from 1 to 24. The Chinese divide the solar day into 12 hours, each of which is of course equal to two of ours.

The Week, or period of seven days, was used by the Jews and most of the oriental nations, and was introduced with Christianity into Europe.—In the Old Testament the term week is occasionally applied to a period of seven *years*; and to this it is necessary to attend, in order to understand the passages wherein the word is used in that sense.

The Month. This period was probably suggested by the phases, or periodical changes of the moon. The *astronomical* month is the time, in which the moon performs a complete revolution round the earth, and is either *periodical*

* Webster's Dictionary.

or *synodical*. The *periodical* month is the time in which the moon moves from one point of the heavens to the same point again, and is equal to 27d 7h 43′ 4″. 7; and the *synodical* month or *lunation*, as it is sometimes called, is that portion of time which elapses between two successive new moons, or between two successive conjunctions of the moon with the sun, and is equal to 29d 12h 44′ 3″. 11. The *solar* month is that portion of time in which the sun moves through one sign of the ecliptic, and is equal at an average to 30d 10h 29′ 5″. The *civil* month, which is formed for the purposes of civil life, consists of a certain number of whole days, and approaches as nearly as possible to the astronomical or to the solar month.

THE JEWISH MONTHS.

No.	Name.	Signification.	Corresponding months in our Calendar.	Days in ea.
1	Tisri		Aug.—Sept.	30
2	Marchesvan	Great Ram	Sept.—Oct.	29
3	Casleau	Stormy weather	Oct.—Nov.	30
4	Tebeth	Hope	Nov.—Dec.	29
5	Shebat	Repose	Dec.—Jan.	30
6	Adar	Purifying fire	Jan.—Feb.	29
7	Nisan, or Abib.	Standard	Feb.—March	30
8	Jiar	Wat. Meadow	Mch.—April	29
9	Sivan	Anim. in past.	Apl.—May	30
10	Tamuz	The Sun	May—June	29
11	Ab	Fruit	June—July	30
12	Elul	Vine press	July—Aug.	29

The Year, is the next and most important period indicated by the celestial motions.

The *solar* or *tropical* year is that period which corresponds to the sun's revolution in the ecliptic from any equinox or solstice to the same again, and consists of 365d 5h 48′ 54″.

The *sidereal* year is that portion of time which corresponds to the revolution of the sun from any fixed star to the same star again, and is equal to 365d 6h 9′ 15″ or 20′ 21″ shorter than the solar year.

The *lunar* year is equal to 12 revolutions of the moon from the sun to the sun again, or from one conjunction with the sun to the next. It contains 354d 8h 48′ 36″ and is 10d 21h 0′ 18″ shorter than the solar year.

The *civil* year is that which is used for the purposes of civil life.

"In the earliest periods of society," says the Edinburgh Encyclopedia," the most barbarous nations could not fail to observe a regular return of the seasons; and the necessity of providing against the inclemency of winter or the burning heat of summer must have compelled them to ascertain in a rude manner, the length of the year. The period in which the seasons returned would probably be measured at first by the motions of the sun and moon, and be reckoned equivalent to 12 of her monthly revolutions. Hence a year of 12 lunations would be formed, each of which consisted of 30 days, forming the luni-solar year of 360 days. This form of the year was adopted by the Chaldeans, Egyptians, and Indians, and was in use among almost all the nations of antiquity. As the true solar year however, exceeded the luni-solar about 5¼ days, the seasons would rapidly deviate from the months to which they at first corresponded, and in the short space of 34 years, the winter would happen in those months which formerly corresponded with the summer."—The Egyptians were early acquainted with the year of 365 days, but the time when the true solar year was discovered is uncertain. The Theban priests claimed the discovery: and it is said to have been known to Plato and Eudoxus.

The Roman year, as regulated by Romulus, and afterwards reformed by Numa was divided into 10 lunar months (or 304 days) of which the first was March. The Decemviri altered this arrangement by introducing the two intercalary months, January and February into the calendar; but owing to the negligence of the pontiffs to whom the duty of intercalation was confided, the supernumerary months were not properly applied; and in the time of Julius Cæsar the civil had receded from the solar year by no less than 90 days. With the assistance and advice of Sosigenes, Julius Cæsar undertook, B. C. 46, the formation of a new calendar. In order to include the 90 days, he formed a year of 445 days or 15 months; and this year, which was called the year of confusion, terminated on the day preceding Jan. 1, B. C. 46, when the Julian year commenced. This consisted of 365 days; but to adjust it to the annual revolution of the earth, 365d 5h 48′ the excess of 6 hours (amounting to one day in four years,) a day was appointed to be intercalated every fourth year in the month of February. Hence the year of 366 days was called *Bissextile* by the Romans; and in England it received the name of the *Leap year*.

This regulation, though extremely simple and ingenious, was still imperfect, as it was founded on the supposition that the solar year consisted of 365 days, 6 hours, instead of 365 days, 5 hours, 48′, 54″. The difference, though at first trifling, amounted to a whole day in 130 years; and at the council of Nice in 325, the vernal equinox, which in the time of Cæsar was on the 25th of March, had receded to the 21st, and in 1582 to the 11th of March. To remedy this growing defect, Pope Gregory XIII. invited the most eminent astronomers and mathematicians to Rome, and in 1582 he effected a complete reformation in the calendar.

That the vernal equinox, might be restored to the 21st of March, he caused 10 days to be taken out of the month of October, (1582,) and to avoid any future deviation, of the civil from the solar year, it was determined instead of every 100th, that every 400th year only should be a leap year. This calculation comes so near the truth, that the only correction it will require is the suppression of 1⅓ days in 5000 years.

The *Gregorian Calendar*, or the *new style* was immediately adopted in Spain Portugal, and a part of Italy. It was introduced into France, Dec. 1582; in the German Catholic states, 1583; in England, 1752. Russia is now the only country in Europe in which the old mode of reckoning is still in use.

COMBINATIONS OF YEARS—of these

The Olympiads, are first in order. They consist of four Grecian years, which elapsed between the celebration of the *Olympic games*, from which they were named. These games, first instituted in honour of Jupiter, 1453 B. C. are only reckoned in chronology from the year 776 B. C.

Cycles.—A Cycle, (derived from the Greek χυχλοζ, a circle,) is a circulating period of time, at the expiration of which certain celestial phenomena return in the same order.

The *Metonic*, or lunar cycle of Meton, is a period of 19 solar years, or 6940 days, in which interval, the sun and moon return to very nearly the same part of the heavens. This cycle was adopted in Greece, on the 16th day of July, 433 B. C. As the scheme of the festivals was inscribed by the Greeks on a marble pillar in letters of gold, the current year of this cycle was called the Golden Number. Meton's system, however, was inaccurate; it was afterwards corrected by Eudoxus, and subsequently by Calippus, whose improvements have been adopted by modern astronomers.

The *Solar Cycle* is a period of 28 years, at the end of which the days of the week correspond to the same days of the month.

The first seven letters of the alphabet, A, B, C, D, E, F, G, have been used by chronologers to make the several days of the week, the first letter standing for the first of January, and so on; and as one of the letters must necessarily stand opposite to Sunday it is called the *dominical letter*, or Sunday letter, and is printed in capitals, to distinguish it from the other six. As a Julian year of 365 days contains 52 weeks and one day, it is obvious that it must begin and end on the same day of the week, and the next year commence on the day following. Had there been only 52 weeks in the common year, without any day remaining, the year would have constantly begun on the same day of the week. When January, therefore, begins on Sunday the dominical letter of that year is A, and as the next year must begin on Monday, Sunday will be the 7th day, to which the letter G is annexed, which will therefore be the dominical letter for that year. The third year will begin on Tuesday, and as Sunday falls on the 6th day, F will be, the dominical letter. Hence it follows that the dominical letters will succeed each other in a retrograde order, viz. G, F, E, D, C, B, A, and if there was no leap year, the same days of the week would in the course of *seven* years return to the same days of the month. But as a leap year contains 52 weeks and 2 days, any one of these beginning on Sunday, will end on Monday, and the following year will begin on Tuesday, the first Sunday of which must fall on the sixth of January, to which the dominical letter F corresponds, and not G, as in common years. As the leap year returns every fourth year, the regular succession of the dominical letter is interrupted, and does not return to its former state till after 7 × 4 or 28 years; when the same days of the week, will correspond to the same days of the month, as formerly.

The *Cycle of Indiction* consists of 15 years. It was established by Constantine, A. D. 312.

The *Julian Period*, a knowledge of which is very important in the study of chronology, is formed by the combination of the three above mentioned cycles—multiplying the numbers 28, 19, and 15, of the cycles of the sun, moon and indiction, into each other, the total of years produced is 7980, of which the Julian period consists. The year 4714 B. C. is the only one in the whole period which presents the numbers for each of three cycles, and is accordingly reckoned as the first of the period. The year of the creation is the year 710 of the Julian period.

COMPARATIVE TABLE

Of the principal Eras, used by Chronologers in fixing the order of Events.

Names.	Remarks.	Abbreviations.	A.M.	Chr'n. Era.	A. U. C.	Olympi.
The Creation	Generally adopted. According to the Hebrew text, ...	A. M. Annus Mundi		4004 B.C.	3251 before	3228 before the 1st
	According to the Septuagint, ...			5872 B.C.		
	According to the Samaritan, ...			4700 B.C.		
Olympiads (first year of)	Used by the Greeks for 1068 years, till A. D. 312, when Constantine substituted in its room, the era of Indiction. .		3228	776 B.C.	23 before	
Founding of Rome	Used by the Romans till A. D. 250. (The Romans formerly marked their years by their consuls.)	A. U. C. Anno Urbis. Conditæ	3251	753 B.C.	0	4 of the sixth
Christian Era	Adopted by the greater number of writers	A. D. Anno Domini B. C. Before Christ.	4004	0	753	1 of the 195th
Hegira	The word Hegira signifies *fled*, and is used to memorialize Mahomet's flight from Mecca to Medina. . . .	Minor Eras.	4626	622 A.D.	1375	3 of the 349th.
Era of Nabonassar	Used by Ptolemy and Censorinus, the chronologist: named from having begun in the reign of Nabonassar. . .		3257	747 B.C.	6	1 of the 8th.
Era of the Seleucidæ	Named from Seleucus Nicanor:—followed by the Syrians and by the Jews in Syria.		3962	312 B.C.	441	4 of the 116th.
Era of Dioclesian	Also called the Era of the Martyrs, and the Era of the Abyssinians began in the reign of Dioclesian.		4288	248 A.D.		

EXPLANATORY REMARKS AND METHOD OF USING THIS BOOK.

The design of the 1st part, is to exhibit in chronological and contemporaneous order, a brief summary of the principal facts, and the names of the ost conspicuous persons recorded in history.

The order of events has been variously ascertained among different nations, from eclipses, public registers, medals, columns, obelisks, pyramids, marbles, inscriptions, &c. The leading eras which serve as landmarks on the great chart of time, have already been noticed.

Ancient chronology, particularly down to the 8th century before Christ, is involved in uncertainty. The era of the Olympiads began 776 B. C.—from this date only, the Grecian story becomes credible and authentic:

"Till then all fable, or with fable mixt."

The history of the early Assyrians and Egyptians, also, is but legendary tradition until the year 747 B. C., when Nabonassar, king of Babylon directed regular annals to be kept of the political and civil concerns of the kingdom, as also of the eclipses, it being in his reign that the study of astronomy was restored, and the science matured to a comparative degree of perfection.

The epocha of the Romans commenced with the building of their city, 753 B. C. These three eras furnish data sufficient to enable us to fix the subsequent events of history with tolerable precision.

The chronology of each country can be easily traced in the columns of the *contemporary* division: the design of the other articles has already been stated. The Poetical Retrospect will serve to relieve the monotonous repetition of dates, while it stereotypes the more important ones in the memory. The Literary Chronology will be found very convenient—especially to bibliographers. Reference to names, &c., in these articles, is facilitated by the *Alphabetical Tables.*—Thus if we wish to know in what period Cicero, for instance, flourished, what was his nation and profession, and who his contemporaries, we refer to his name in the Biographical table;—we find that he was born 105, B. C., and died 43, B. C.—Then turn to the Literary Chronology, Roman, 1st century B. C.—and to the Chronological Table, where some of his public actions, &c., are mentioned; and we can form someidea of the literary and political character of his times.

In the first division, the type is varied, in order that the more important names and events may be conspicuous.

The following are specimens:—

The Deluge.
Cæsar. } This size is used to express the leading epochs, and also the names of those who have effected political revolutions.

Argonautic Expedition.
Louis XV. } Items of the second grade of importance, and the sovereigns of the principal monarchies.

MACEDON. } Kingdoms and States, when founded, or first mentioned.

ALFRED.
WASHINGTON. } Chiefs and rulers, particularly eminent or useful.

Aristides—LaFayette. } Remarkable public men.

Socrates—Newton.
Franklin. } Founders of systems of philosophy, and those who have made important discoveries in science.

Virgil.—Shakspeare. } Authors, particularly celebrated.

Sallust—Pope.
Barlow. } Authors and scientific men generally.

ABBREVIATIONS.

A. M.—year of the world.
A. D.—year after Christ.
Amer.—American.
B. C.—before Christ.
Bp.—bishop.
Brit.—British, Britain.
Dan.—Danish.
E. Ind. or E. I.—East Indies.
Eng.—England, English.
Fr.—France, French.
Gen.—general.
Ger.—Germany, German.
Gr.—Greece, Germany.
Ital.—Italian.
K. or k.—king.
Maced.—Macedonian.
P.—period.
Pers.—Persian.
Port.—Portugal, Portuguese.
Pol.—Poland, Polish.
Prus.—Prussia, Prussian.
Rom.—Roman.
Russ.—Russian.
Sp. or Span.—Spain, Spanish.
Scot.—Scotland, Scottish.
Swe.—Sweden, Swedish.

ERRATA.

" 6. "Judah"; (975) before Abijah, should be 958.
" 8. "Profane"; (164.) Insert *year*, before 3951, and the figures 753, after *April*.
" 15. Running title.—Read *P. V.* 490—356, B. C.
" 29. "Miscel." (164.) Insert "*Antiochus V. succeeds him*, after "the Jews."
" 32. "Miscel."(65.) Insert VII. instead of XII., after *Antiochus*.
" 54. "France and Spain." (628.) For *Spain* read *France*.
" 67. "Miscel. (1068.) Insert *E. Empire* before *Romanus*.
" 71. "France and Spain." (1149.) For *divorcing*, read *divorces*."
" 95. "Miscel." (1512) For *Michael, Angelo*, read *Michael Angelo*.
" 97. do (1522.) For *English*, read *Portuguese*.
" 143. "France." (1789.) Read the *Tiers-Etats* or the *Commons ; the privileged order*, comprising the clergy, nobility, &c.
" 145. do For *Lyons*, read *Toulon*.
" 161. "Miscel." The three last lines should read "American confederation of Venezuela."
" 167. do (1815, June 15.) For *Ling*, read *Ligny*.
" 114. "Britain," (1824, April 19.) For *Eastern*, read *Easter*.
" 180. "U. States." (Aug. 12.) For *Reive* read *Rives*.
" 194. (A. M. 2475.) For *It rages* read *It raged*.
" 326. Seventh administration. Insert *after* John Mc. P. Berrien, attorney general, *Roger B. Taney*, 1831.

TO TEACHERS.

In arranging the following tables, one object has been to render them useful to students of history in schools and academies. Chronology has not been generally introduced as a branch of study—although it is most evidently important that this science should be understood before we can obtain a correct and systematic knowledge of history in general. And it can be rendered an *interesting* subject—notwithstanding the natural antipathy of young persons to columns of names and figures. The following are examples of some of the various questions which arise in reading detached portions of history, and which may be put to the pupil in the course of recitations on that subject.

When was Cicero born? (See biographical Table.) When did he die? Of what country was he? What were some of the events which happened during his life? What sovereigns, &c. were his contemporaries? The same of Moses—Cyrus—Mahomet—Milton—Herodotus—Belisarius—(or any other conspicuous character.) Mention some of the literary men who flourished in England in the reign of George II.?—of Elizabeth?—their contemporaries in foreign parts? Those in the Roman empire during the reign of Augustus—of Nero? Those in Greece about the time of the Persian war? What prophets among the Jews in the days of Pericles and Socrates? Did Plato flourish before or after Aristotle, and how many years? Which was the earliest, the Peloponnesian or the 1st Punic war, and between what nations was the latter? Who were the kings of England and France when Constantinople was taken by the Turks? What important invention was announced a short time previous to this? Was the art of printing invented before the mariner's compass? Name the sovereigns of Europe at the time of Columbus, and the president of the United States when Napoleon became Emperor.

What countries composed the empire of Charlemagne? Who was caliph of the Saracens, and who king of England during his reign? In whose reign did the celebrated Belisarius flourish, and what were some of his exploits?

Page I. The division of Ancient Chronology?—from what two epochs does the first period extend?—Its duration?—for what was it remarkable?

In what year of the world was the deluge? the calling of Abraham? the building of Solomon's Temple? the founding of Rome? the birth of Christ? the discovery of America? the French revolution (A. D. 1789,)?

It will be obvious that questions of this kind may be asked in a great variety of forms, both general and particular on the different periods. The above are set down at random—but they may serve as hints.

CHRONOLOGY:

IN TWO PARTS.

Ancient Chronology, extending from the Creation of the World, 4004 years before Christ, to his Nativity.

Modern Chronology, extending from the Nativity of Christ to the present time.

ANCIENT CHRONOLOGY.

Epochas or *Periods.*

I. From the Creation of the World, to the Deluge,	4004 years B. C. 2348 "		*Antediluvian Period.*
II. From " " to the Calling of Abraham,	" " 1921 "		*Confusion of Languages.*
III. From " " to the Exode of the Israelites,	" " 1491 "		*Egyptian Bondage.*
IV. From " " " " to the Dedication of Solomon's Temple, 1004			*Trojan War.*
V. From " " to the Founding of Rome,	" " 752 "		*Homer and Lycurgus.*
VI. From " " to the Battle of Marathon,	" " 490 "		*Roman Kings.*
VII. From " " to the Birth of Alexander the Great,	" " 356 "		*Grecian Glory.*
VIII. From " " to the Destruction of Carthage.	" " 146 "		*Roman Military Renown.*
IX. From " " to the First Campaign of Julius Cæsar,	" " 80 "		*Marius and Sylla.*
X. From " " to the Commencement of the Christian Era.	" "		*Roman Literature.*

Period I.—(Antediluvian)—1656 years.

B. C.
4004 THE CREATION OF THE WORLD, according to the Heb ew Pentateuch.*
The transgression of **Adam** and **Eve**, and the promise of a Saviour.
3875 The murder of Abel, by Cain his brother, the first born of man.
3074 Adam dies, aged 930 years.
3017 **Enoch** is translated, to heaven, aged 365 years.
2468 The prediction of the Deluge to **Noah**, 120 years before that event took place.
2348 **Methuselah**, the oldest man, dies aged 969 years.
† The Deluge, (in the 600th year of Noah's age,) destroying all the inhabitants of the earth, except Noah and those with him in the ark.

* The *Samaritan Pentateuch* places this epoch B. C. 4700; the *Septuagint*, 5872; *Josephus* 4658; the *Talmudists*, 5344; *Scaliger*, 3950; *Petavius*, 3984; and Dr. *Hales*, 5411 The last named enumerates above 120 various opinions on this subject, the difference between the latest and remotest date of which is no less than 3268. The Hebrew account is followed by *Usher*, and is here adopted as the most generally received standard.

† According to *Hales*, 3154 B. C.

ABBREVIATIONS.

A. M.—year of the world.
A. D.—year after Christ.
Amer.—American.
B. C.—before Christ.
Bp.—bishop.
Brit.—British, Britain.
Dan.—Danish.
E. Ind. or E. I.—East Indies.
Eng.—England, English.
Fr.—France, French.
Gen.—general.
Ger.—Germany, German.
Gr.—Greece, Germany.
Ital.—Italian.
K. or k.—king.
Maced.—Macedonian.
P.—period.
Pers.—Persian.
Port.—Portugal, Portuguese.
Pol.—Poland, Polish.
Prus.—Prussia, Prussian.
Rom.—Roman.
Russ.—Russian.
Sp. or Span.—Spain, Spanish.
Scot.—Scotland, Scottish.
Swe.—Sweden, Swedish.

ERRATA.

" 6. "Judah"; (975) before Abijah, should be 958.
" 8. "Profane"; (164.) Insert *year*, before 3951, and the figures 753, after *April*.
" 15. Running title.—Read *P. V.* 490—356, B. C.
" 29. "Miscel." (164.) Insert "*Antiochus V. succeeds him*, after "the Jews."
" 32. "Miscel."(65.) Insert VII. instead of XII., after *Antiochus*.
" 54. "France and Spain." (628.) For *Spain* read *France*.
" 67. "Miscel. (1068.) Insert *E. Empire* before *Romanus*.
" 71. "France and Spain." (1149.) For *divorcing*, read *divorces*."
" 95. "Miscel." (1512) For *Michael, Angelo*, read *Michael Angelo*.
" 97. do (1522.) For *English*, read *Portuguese*.
" 143. "France." (1789.) Read the *Tiers-Etats* or the *Commons*; the *privileged order*, comprising the clergy, nobility, &c.
" 145. do For *Lyons*, read *Toulon*.
" 161. "Miscel." The three last lines should read "American confederation of Venezuela."
" 167. do (1815, June 15.) For *Ling*, read *Ligny*.
" 114. "Britain," (1824, April 19.) For *Eastern*, read *Easter*.
" 180. "U. States." (Aug. 12.) For *Reiss* read *Rives*.
" 194. (A. M. 2475.) For *It rages* read *It raged*.
" 326. Seventh administration. Insert *after* John Mc. P. Berrien, attorney general, *Roger B. Taney*, 1831.

TO TEACHERS.

In arranging the following tables, one object has been to render them useful to students of history in schools and academies. Chronology has not been generally introduced as a branch of study—although it is most evidently important that this science should be understood before we can obtain a correct and systematic knowledge of history in general. And it can be rendered an *interesting* subject—notwithstanding the natural antipathy of young persons to columns of names and figures. The following are examples of some of the various questions which arise in reading detached portions of history, and which may be put to the pupil in the course of recitations on that subject.

When was Cicero born? (See biographical Table.) When did he die? Of what country was he? What were some of the events which happened during his life? What sovereigns, &c. were his contemporaries? The same of Moses—Cyrus—Mahomet—Milton—Herodotus—Belisarius—(or any other conspicuous character.) Mention some of the literary men who flourished in England in the reign of George II.?—of Elizabeth?—their contemporaries in foreign parts? Those in the Roman empire during the reign of Augustus—of Nero? Those in Greece about the time of the Persian war? What prophets among the Jews in the days of Pericles and Socrates? Did Plato flourish before or after Aristotle, and how many years? Which was the earliest, the Peloponnesian or the 1st Punic war, and between what nations was the latter? Who were the kings of England and France when Constantinople was taken by the Turks? What important invention was announced a short time previous to this? Was the art of printing invented before the mariner's compass? Name the sovereigns of Europe at the time of Columbus, and the president of the United States when Napoleon became Emperor.

What countries composed the empire of Charlemagne? Who was caliph of the Saracens, and who king of England during his reign? In whose reign did the celebrated Belisarius flourish, and what were some of his exploits?

Page I. The division of Ancient Chronology?—from what two epochs does the first period extend?—Its duration?—for what was it remarkable?

In what year of the world was the deluge? the calling of Abraham? the building of Solomon's Temple? the founding of Rome? the birth of Christ? the discovery of America? the French revolution (A. D. 1789,)?

It will be obvious that questions of this kind may be asked in a great variety of forms, both general and particular on the different periods. The above are set down at random—but they may serve as hints.

CHRONOLOGY:

IN TWO PARTS.

Ancient Chronology, extending from the Creation of the World, 4004 years before Christ, to his Nativity.

Modern Chronology, extending from the Nativity of Christ to the present time.

ANCIENT CHRONOLOGY.

Epochas or *Periods.*

I. From the Creation of the World,	4004 years	B. C.	*Antediluvian Period.*
to the Deluge,	2348	"	
II. From " "	"	"	*Confusion of Languages.*
to the Calling of Abraham,	1921	"	
III. From " "	"	"	*Egyptian Bondage.*
to the Exode of the Israelites,	1491	"	
IV. From " " "	"		*Trojan War.*
to the Dedication of Solomon's Temple,	1004		
V. From " "	"	"	*Homer and Lycurgus.*
to the Founding of Rome,	752	"	
VI. From " "	"	"	*Roman Kings.*
to the Battle of Marathon,	490	"	
VII. From " "	"	"	*Grecian Glory.*
to the Birth of Alexander the Great,	356	"	
VIII. From " "	"	"	*Roman Military Renown.*
to the Destruction of Carthage.	146	"	
IX. From " "	"	"	*Marius and Sylla.*
to the First Campaign of Julius Cæsar,	80	"	
X. From " "	"	"	*Roman Literature.*
to the Commencement of the Christian Era.			

Period I.—(Antediluvian)—1656 years.

B. C.
4004 THE CREATION OF THE WORLD, according to the Heb ew Pentateuch.*

The transgression of **Adam** and **Eve**, and the promise of a Saviour.

3875 The murder of Abel, by Cain his brother, the first born of man.

3074 Adam dies, aged 930 years.

3017 **Enoch** is translated, to heaven, aged 365 years.

2468 The prediction of the Deluge to **Noah**, 120 years before that event took place.

2348 **Methuselah**, the oldest man, dies aged 969 years.

† The Deluge, (in the 600th year of Noah's age,) destroying all the inhabitants of the earth, except Noah and those with him in the ark.

* The *Samaritan Pentateuch* places this epoch B. C. 4700; the *Septuagint*, 5872; *Josephus* 4658; the *Talmudists*, 5344; *Scaliger*, 3950; *Petavius*, 3984; and Dr. *Hales*, 5411. The last named enumerates above 120 various opinions on this subject, the difference between the latest and remotest date of which is no less than 3268. The Hebrew account is followed by *Usher*, and is here adopted as the most generally received standard.

† According to *Hales*, 3154 B. C.

Period IV.—487 *Years.*

B. C. SACRED.

1491 The Deliverance of the Israelites from Egypt * under Moses. They pass through the Red Sea, in which their pursuers, Pharaoh and the Egyptian host are drowned. Moses receives *The Law* on Mt. Sinai.

1471 Rebellion of Korah, Dathan, and Abiram.

1452 Moses writes the *Pentateuch*.

1452 —— defeats Sihon, k. of the Amorites, &c. and dies æt. 120.

1451 Entrance of the Israelites into Canaan under **Joshua**, who divides the country among the twelve tribes: leagues with the Gibeonites.

1450 — wars against the kings of Canaan.

1443 — dies.

1405 **Othniel** delivers the Israelites from servitude under the Mesopotamians.

1390 The Benjamites are almost annihilated by the other tribes.

1343 The Israelites relapsing into idolatry, are again enslaved by Eglon, king of Moab.

1325 —liberated by **Ehud**, who kills Eglon.

—— Government of the Judges. ——

1317 **Shamgar** kills 600 Philistines with an ox-goad.

1305 Third servitude of Israel under Jabin, king of Canaan.

1285 **Deborah** and **Barak** defeat the Canaanites under Sisera, who is put to death by Jael, the wife of Heber.

1252 Fourth servitude of the Israelites under the Midianites.

* Acc. to *Hales*, 1648 B. C.

B. C. PROFANE.

1491 Egypt:—Amenophis, king of Egypt, is drowned with his army in the **Red Sea**, while in pursuit of the Israelites.

Sesostris, his son, the great conqueror succeeds; subdues Asia, Ethiopia, and the Scythians.†

1474 Gr. — Danaus usurps the kingdom of Argos.

1459 *Hermes Trismegistus*, flourished.

1457 — The kingdom of Mycene, begins, under Perseus, late k. of Argos.

Egypt:—Pheron succeeds Sesostris.

1453 Gr. — The Olympic games first celebrated at Elis.†

Apollo, the god of **music** and *poetry*.

1438 **Pandion** begins to reign at Athens.

Bacchus, the god of wine.

1400 **Minos** reigns in Crete and frames his *code of laws*.

1397 CORINTH becomes a kingdom under Sisyphus its usurper.

1376 The Isthmian games instituted.

1284 *Orpheus* the father of poetry, and *Linus*, flourished.

1263 The Argonautic Expedition to ‡ Colchis, conducted by **Jason** for the recovery of "the golden fleece."

1257 Gr. **Theseus** unites the cities of Attica into one government.

1259 PHENICIA:—Tyre its capital, founded by Agenor, an Egyptian.

† *Eusebius*, *Usher*, *Playfair*, *Rollin*, and others.

Hales represents Amenophis III. to be the same as **Mœris**, the 17th king after Menes, and the father of Sesostris; but dates his death 340 years after the Exode of the Israelites. Sesostris is variously supposed to be Sesac or Shishak, who took Jerusalem 971 B. C. Sethos, said to have reigned 1376 B. C.; Rameses, at 1722 B. C. &c. &c.

‡ *Newton* says 947. Others 1284, 1293, &c.

B. C. SACRED.

1245 **Gideon,** Judge of Israel, with 300 men, routs the Midianites; restores peace; and is offered, but refuses the crown.

1236 **Abimelech** judges Israel

1223 Tola, — —

1210 Jair, — —

1206 The Israelites, on account of their idolatry, are delivered into the hands of the Philistines and Ammonites.

1188 **Jephtha,** Judge of Israel; defeats the Ammonites;—his rash vow, by which he loses his daughter. *Judges* xi.

1182 Ibzan, Judge of Israel.

1175 Elon, —— ——

1165 Abdon, —— ——

1157 **Eli,** the High Priest, judges Israel.

1156 Sixth servitude under the Philistines.

1152 **Samson** born.

1136 ———— kills 1000 Philistines with a jaw bone.

1117 ———— is betrayed by Delilah and perishes with his enemies in the temple of Dagon.

The Israelites twice defeated, and the ark of God taken by the Philistines.

Death of Eli.

1116 **Samuel** the last judge of Israel.

1096 —— defeats the Philistines at Ebenezer.

1095 The Establishment of Monarchy in Israel.

Saul anointed king by Samuel.

1078 —— gains a victory over the Philistines.

1080 —— destroys the Amalekites, but spares Agag thei king, contrary to God's command.

B. C. PROFANE.

1243 The Arcadians conducted by Evander into Italy.

Museus, a poet, flourished.

1239 Latinus begins to reign in Italy.

1225 Gr.—The Theban war of the Seven Captains against Eteocles.

1222 — **Hercules** (afterwards deified) celebrates the Olympic games.

LYDIA: Argo, its first king mentioned in history.

1216 Gr. —— War of the Epigoni against Thebes.

1213 Helen is carried off from Lacedèmon, by Theseus, king of Athens; is recovered by her brothers Castor and Pollux, and marries Menelaus of the family of the Pelopidæ.

1198 — elopes with Paris, son of Priam, k. of Troy, which causes

1193 The Trojan War, undertaken by the Grecian states for the recovery of Helen: **Agamemnon, Ulysses, Hector,** and **Achilles,** leaders. The fleet consists of 1200 vessels, the army of 100,000 men.

1184 The Taking of Troy by the Greeks, after a siege of ten years.

1182 **Æneas,** son of Priam, k. of Troy, lands in Italy, marries the daughter of Latinus, and begins the Latin kingdom. *Dares Phrygius*, historian.

1176 Salamis in Cyprus founded by Teucer.

1170 EPIRUS:—Pyrrhus Neoptolemus, k.

1152 Alba-Longa built by Ascanius.

1122 China:—The 3d dynasty, Tcheoo.

1104 Gr.—Return of the Heraclidæ, or the descendants of Hercules, to the Peloponnesus, and their usurpation of Sparta, where the two brothers, Eurysthenes and Procles reign together.

1088 — End of the kingdom of Sicyon.

1060 — Athens: Institution of the Archons; Medon, the son of Codrus, is the first.

B. C.	SACRED.	B. C.	PROFANE.
1062	**David** kills Goliath, the Philistine giant.	1069	Gr. Athens : Codrus devotes himself for his country.
1055	Saul falls on his own sword, after the defeat of his army by the Philistines and the death of this three sons on Mount Gilboa		
	David reigns over Judah, and Ishbosheth over the ten tribes.		
1048	David becomes the sole monarch of Israel.		
1043	—— subdues the Philistines, the Moabites, the Ammonites, and the Syrians.	1044	The Ionian colonies migrate from Greece and settle in Asia Minor.
1023	Absalom revolts; he is killed, and his troops are defeated by Joab.		
1012	**Solomon** succeeds his father David. —— lays the foundation of his temple. Flourishing period of the Israelites. Commerce with Tyre and Ophir.	1012	Egypt :—Pharaoh, the reigning king, gives his daughter in marriage to Solomon. (*Script. Hist.*) Phenician commerce with the Israelites. (Vessels open and small.) Hiram king of Tyre.
	Hebrew laws and poetry, (*Moses, David*, and *Solomon*,) during this period.		*Mythology* and *poetry* originated in this period. *Commerce, colonies; cities and works of art.*

Period V.—252 Years.

B. C.	SACRED.	B. C.	PROFANE.
1004	*Dedication of Solomon's Temple.*	986	Samos, in the island of the same name and Utica, in Africa, built about this time.
980	Rehoboam succeeds his father Solomon.		
975	Revolt of the Ten Tribes under Jeroboam, and division of the kingdom.	978	Egypt :—Sesac, (supposed by some to be the same as Sesostris,) begins to reign.

JUDAH. (Jerusalem, the capital.)	ISRAEL.	PROFANE.
— Rehoboam, king.	—Jeroboam king.—	
971 Shishak, king of Egypt, plunders the temple. (II. Chron. xii.)	— encourages idolatry.	971 Sesac, (in Scripture Shishak,) marches with a great army to Jerusalem, and plunders the temple.
975 —— Abijah. ——		
957 —— makes war against Jeroboam, who is defeated and loses 500,000 men, in the great battle of Zemaraim. (II. Chron. xiii.)		
955 —— Asa —— a pious king; abolishes idolatry; defeats Zerah, the Ethiopian; enters into an alliance with Benhadad, k. of Syria.	954 — Nadab, k. — 953 — Baasha, k. — 930 — Elah, k. — 929 — Zimri, k. — — Omri, k, first of a new dynasty and founder of Samaria.	

SACRED.		PROFANE.
B. C. Judah.	B. C. Israel.	B. C.
	918— Ahab, k. — and his queen Jezebel, noted for impiety.	
914 Jehosaphat, k. — pious and prosperous.		907 *Homer* and *Hesiod* flourish.
	907 Benhadad, k. of Syria, besieges Samaria, but is repulsed.	
	897 — Ahaziah, k. —	
	896 — Jehoram, k. —	
	895 *Elijah*, the prophet, translated.	
889 — Jehoram, k. — Revolt of the Edomites. Invasion of the Philistines [and Arabians.		886 Gr. *The Introduction of Homer's Poems* into Greece from Asia,—contributes considerably to the literary taste, spirit, and distinction of the Greeks.
885 — Ahaziah, k. —		
884 — Athaliah, q. — put to death by the high priest Jehoiada.	884 — Jehu, k. — destroys the family of Ahab, and the priests of Baal.	884 — *The Reformation of the Republic of Lacedemon*, by LYCURGUS, whose singular code of laws and regulations has rendered both himself and his country celebrated. The Olympic games restored at Elis, by Lycurgus, Iphitus, k. of Elis, and Cleosthenes.
879 — Joash, k. — falls into idolatry, and is put to death by his servants.	856 — Jehoahaz, k. — is taken prisoner by Hazael, k. of Syria	869 CARTHAGE, founded by **Dido**, a Tyrian princess. (Acc. to others, only enlarged by her, having been built several centuries before.)
839 — Amaziah, k. idolatrous; is taken prisoner by Jehoash, who plunders the temple.	839 — Joash, k. — defeats Benhadad in three battles; takes Amaziah prisoner, &c.	
	825 — Jeroboam II. k. —	814 MACEDON, the kingdom of, founded by **Caranus.** Continues 646 years.
810 — Uzziah, k. —	*Hosea* and *Amos* prophecy.	786 Gr. — Vessels called triremes, invented by the Corinthians.
		779 Abolition of the monarchical government of Corinth, and institution of the *prytanes*, to be elected annually.
	784 —Interregnum.—	776 *The Era of the Olympiads* begins. See 884 B. C.
	773 —Zachariah, k.—	
	— Shallum, k. —	
	772— Menahem, k. —	
	770 Pul, k. of Assyria, invades Israel, and is bribed to depart with 1000 talents.	

SACRED.		PROFANE.
B. C. Judah.	B. C. Israel.	B. C.
	Preaching of Jonah to the Ninevites.	771 Assyria again becomes known, under Phul, or Pul, who makes Israel tributary, and repents upon Jonah's preaching.*
		769 Syracuse built by Archias of Corinth.
	— Pekaiah, k. —	767 Assyria: Sardanapalus, king.
	759 — Pekah, k. —	360 Gr. Institution of Ephori, popular magistrates, at Lacedemon, by Theopompus.
758 — Jotham, k. —		757 Lydia: Hylattes, king.
758 *Isaiah*, prc.h.		754 Gr. — The office of Archon, at Athens, becomes decennial.
		752 **The Founding of Rome by Romulus.** (Acc. to Varro on the 20th April, in the 3961 of the Julian period.)

* *Usher*, and others. The editors of the *Univ. Hist.* consider Pul to be son of Sardanapalus, and the restorer of Monarchy after his death.

Note. The Chronology is continued to 146 B. C. on two pages, contemporary.

Period

SACRED.				GRECIAN.	
B. C.	Judah.	B. C.	Israel.	B. C.	
				747	Xth Olympiad.
				743	The first war between the Messenians and Lacedemonians begins. Continues 20 years.
742	— Ahaz, k. — idolatrous. Pekah, k. of Israel, and the king of Assyria, carry away 200,000 of the children of Judah captive to Samaria.	739	— Hoshea, k. — becomes tributary to Shalmanezer, k. of Assyria, but revolts.	732	A colony of Corinthians build Syracuse in Sicily.
				724	End of the first Messenian war, after the capture of Mythone.
717	—Hezekiah, k.— restores the worship of the Lord which had been subverted by Ahaz.	721	The Captivity of the Ten Tribes, by Shalmanezer, k. of Nineveh, who takes Samaria, and puts an end to the kingdom Israel.		
712	Sennacherib, k. of Nineveh, invades Judah, and takes several cities.			703	Corcyra built by the Corinthians.
711	His army, (185,000 men) destroyed in one night by an angel.			700	XXth Olympiad.
				685	The second Messenian war begins. The *Iambic verse* invented by *Archilochus* the poet. *Tyrtæus* and *Terpander*, poets.
				684	Athens:—the office of Archon becomes annual.
696	—Manasseh, k.—			668	A colony of Messenians build the city of Messina in Sicily.
677	is carried in chains to Babylon, by Esarhaddon, but afterwards returns.			660	XXXth Olympiad.
				659	Corinth: the gov. usurped by Cypselus, who overthrows the Prytanes.
				658	A colony of Argives and Athenians, under Pausanias, build the city of Byzantium.
649	Judah:—Amon, an idolatrous king:—is murdered by his servants.				
641	— Josiah, k. — *Zephaniah*, *Jeremiah*, and *Joel*, proph.				
				630	Cyrene, in Africa, founded by Battus.
627	Ezekiel's *forty years* begin.			626	Corinth governed by Periander the tyrant.
624	The Pentateuch found by Hilkiah the high priest.			624	Draco, archon of Athens, frames his bloody code of laws.

VI.—252 *Years.*

B. C. ROMAN.

752 —— **Romulus,** ——
first king of Rome :—warlike.

750 The rape of the Sabine women.

747 Union of the Romans and Sabines. The *Senate* established. Division of the people into *tribes* and *curiæ.* The *orders* of the *patricians* and *plebeians,* and the relation of *patron* and *client.*

738 Fidenæ taken by Romulus, and made a Roman colony.

715 —— **Numa Pompilius,** ——
2d king—
— institutes religious ceremonies, and the Salii, an order of priests.

672 —— **Tullus Hostilius,** ——
3d king—warlike.
War against the Albanians.

667 Combat between the Horatii and Curiatii; the latter are all killed.

640 —— **Ancus Martius,** ——
4th king :—builds the port of Ostia, and conquers the Latins.

B. C. MISCELLANEOUS.

747 Assyria :—Sardanapalus, the last king of the first Assyrian empire, is besieged in Nineveh, by Arbaces, gov. of Media, and Belesis, gov. of Babylonia, and burns himself in his palace. On the ruins of his empire three others are founded, viz.

1st. BABYLON ;—**Nabonassar,** or Belesis, k. (in Scripture, Baladan.)
Era of Nabonassar.

2d. NINEVEH, or the Assyrian continued;
— Tiglath-Pileser, or Ninus junior.

3d. MEDIA ; governed by Arbaces.

736 Tiglath-Pileser makes himself master of Syria, and of several cities in Israel.
Babylon :—Merodach Baladan.

735 Lydia.— Candaules begins to reign.
Nineveh :—**Shalmanezer** ——

721 —— takes Samaria and carries the ten tribes beyond the Euphrates.

718 Lydia :—Gyges murders Candaules and usurps the throne. (*Herod.*)

717 Nineveh :—**Sennacherib,** king.

712 —— invades Hezekiah, k. of Judah; 185,000 men in his army are destroyed by an angel. He returns and is put to death by his sons.

710 Media becomes a kingdom under **Dejoces I.**

680 Babylon and Nineveh, the empires of united by **Esarhaddon.**

677 who causes Manasseh, k. of Judah, to be brought in chains to Babylon.

670 Egypt :—Psammeticus begins to reign.

658 Byzantium, afterwards Constantinople, built by a Grecian colony under Pausanias.
Media :—Phraortes, the second king.

648 Babylon and Nineveh : Saracus, k.

634 Media : — Cyaxares 1st, 3d k.

626 Babylon and Nineveh—Revolt of Nabopolassar the general of Saracus.

624 The SCYTHIANS invade Media, Lydia, &c. and keep possession of Asia Minor 28 years.

B. C. — SACRED.

609 Josiah is killed at Megiddo, by Pharaoh-Necho, k. of Egypt.

— Jehoahaz, k. —
is deposed by Necho, and carried to Egypt.

— Jehoiakim, k. —

606 The Conquest of Jerusalem, by Nebuchadnezzar, and beginning of the "Babylonian captivity," of 70 years. Jehoiakim is afterwards released.

601 *Daniel* the prophet, one of the captives, interprets Nebuchadnezzar's dream.

598 — Jehoiachim, k. —
reigns 3 mos. and is carried to Babylon a captive.

— Zedekiah, k. —

591 *Ezekiel* begins to prophesy in Chaldea.

588 Nebuchadnezzar razes the walls of Jerusalem, reduces the temple and city to ashes, and carries the king and nearly all the remaining inhabitants to Babylon. End of the kingdom of Judah after it had existed 467 years.

Obadiah prophesies.

553 Daniel's Vision of the four animals.

B. C. — GRECIAN.

606 About this time flourish, *Sappho*, the lyric poetess, and *Alcæus*, poet, both of Lesbos; *Pittacus* of Mitylene, and *Bias* of Pirene, two of the "wise men." *Arion* the musician, &c.

598 *Solon*, archon, and legislator of Athens, *Thales*, of Miletus, *Chilo* and *Myson*, of Lacedemon, four of the "wise men."—*Anacharsis* the Scythian philos.; *Æsop*, the celebrated fabulist, and philos.; *Ibychis*, *Theognis* *Stesichorus*, and *Phocylides*, poets. *Cadmus*, of Miletus, hist.

591 The Pythian games celebrated at Delphi.

580 Lth Olympiad.

562 *Comedies* introduced at Athens; the first acted upon a cart by Susarion and Dolon.

560 Pisistratus the tyrant usurps the sovereignty of Athens.

559 *Anaximenes*, and *Anaximander* of Miletus, philosophers.

Cleobulus, one of the seven wise men.

549 The temple of Apollo at Delphos burnt by Pisistratus.

B. C. ROMAN.

616 —— **Tarquinius Priscus,** —— 5th king.

—— embellishes the city, constructs the cloacæ, and founds the capitol.

578 —— **Servius Tullius,** —— 6th king:—establishes the *census*, to be made every fifth year and closed by a lustrum.

565 First census, 84,700 citizens.

B. C. MISCELLANEOUS

612 Nineveh destroyed by the combined armies of Cyaxares, k. of Media, and Nabopolassar, who had revolted against Saracus.

Babylon is now the sole capital of the Assyrian empire, and **Nabopolassar** ascends the throne.

606 —— His son, **Nebuchadnezzar,** takes Jerusalem and brings the Jews away captives.

604 —— —— becomes king

601 —— his first dream interpreted by Daniel the Jewish prophet.

A solar eclipse which had been predicted * by Thales, separates the Medes and Lydians in battle.

599 Birth of Cyrus, (the Great,) son of Cambyses, k. of Persia, and Mandane, princess of Media.

596 The Scythians are expelled from Asia Minor by Astyages, of Media.

594 Egypt:—Pharaoh Hophra, king.

588 Nebuchadnezzar entirely destroys Jerusalem, and causes Zedekiah and nearly the whole nation to be brought captives to Babylon.

Media:—Astyages succeeds Cyaxares.

572 Nebuchadnezzar takes the famous city of Tyre, after a siege of 13 years.

— invades Egypt.

569 — is reduced to the condition of a beast. (Sac. Hist.)

New Tyre founded, where the commerce of the world centres.

562 Lydia:—Cresus, king, (famous for his riches.) Solon and Æsop at his court

561 Babylon:—Evil Merodach, king; is put to death on account of his cruelty and licentiousness. One of the conspirators,

559 — Neriglissar, succeeds.

Media:—Cyaxares II. (Darius the Mede in Script.)

—— Cyrus the Persian assists his uncle against Neriglissar, k. of Babylon, who is killed in battle.

556 Babylon:—Laborosorarchod, k. (cruel and vicious.)

555 —— Labynit, in Scripture **Belshazzar.**

549 Cyaxares II. conquers Sardis.

* Newton's Chron. 585.

B. C. SACRED.

538 The hand writing appears to Belshazzar, k. of Babylon, at his impious feast. The same night, Babylon is taken by Cyrus, Belshazzar is put to death, and the Assyrian empire ended.

536 The Return of the Jews from captivity under Zerubbabel, according to the edict of Cyrus.

Joshua high priest.

535 Rebuilding of the temple begins.

534 —is obstructed by the Samaritans.

Zechariah and *Haggai* prophesy.

516 Dedication of the second temple. The Passover celebrated.

B. C. GRECIAN.

540 LXth Olympiad.

539 The Phocians emigrate to Gaul, and build the city of Marseilles.

Pythagoras the philosopher, *Anacreon* and *Simonides* poets.

535 *Thespis* performs the first *tragedy* at Athens.

527 Learning encouraged at *Athens*. A *public library* first founded.

521 Athens governed by Hippias and Hipparchus, the Pisistratidæ.

522 Polycrates, the tyrant of Samos, put to death. The Phocians found Massilia.

510 Athens:—The Pisistratidæ expelled, and democracy established. Statues erected to Harmodius and Aristogiton, the leaders in this revolution.

507 Flourished about this time, *Heraclitus*, *Theano*, *Protagoras*, and *Anaxagoras*, philosophers. *Corinna*, poet.

504 The Ionians burn Sardis, which causes the subsequent Persian invasion of Greece.

500 LXXth Olympiad.

493 The port of Piræus built by Themistocles, archon of Athens.

491 Invasion of Greece by the Persians under Dates and Artaphernes.

Civilization and commerce had progressed to a considerable extent. Discoveries in *science* and *philosophy*, *inventions*, &c. The *sages* flourished. Pure *Monotheism* survives only in the deserts and mountains of Asia and Europe. *Polytheism* is established, and monarchy declines.

B. C. ROMAN.

534 —— **Tarquinius Superbus,** —— 7th king—disgusts the people by his tyranny and licentiousness.

509 The rape of Lucrece by Sextus, son of Tarquin the tyrant, causes the expulsion of the Tarquins by Brutus and Collatinus, the **Abolition of the Regal government at Rome,** and the establishment of **Consuls, Brutus** and **Collatinus** being the first.

First alliance with Carthage.

507 War against the Tarquins and their ally Porsenna.

Second census:—120,909 citizens.

498 **Lartius,** the first **dictator,** with sovereign power.

Contests between the patricians and plebeians begin. *Tribunes of the people* created. Saturnalia instituted.

496 **Posthumius** elected dictator.

491 Banishment of **Coriolanus.**

B. C. MISCELLANEOUS.

548 End of the kingdom of Lydia: Cresus being dethroned and taken prisoner by Cyrus the Persian for his uncle Cyaxares. Asia Minor submits to Cyrus.

538 **The Conquest of Babylon by Cyrus** (the Great) and death of Belshazzar. End of the 2d Assyrian empire.

536 The **PERSIAN EMPIRE** is founded by Cyrus, the Great, (after the death of his father Cambyses, and his uncle Cyaxares.) It is composed of Assyria, Media, and Persia. The latter is supposed to have been founded by Elam, son of Shem; but its history hitherto is obscure.

Cyrus releases the Jews from captivity.

529 Cyrus is taken prisoner by the Scythians and beheaded by their queen Tomyris.

Persia:—Cambyses, king.

526 —— conquers Egypt.

522 —— Darius Hystaspes, king.

Confucius, the great Chinese philosopher, flourished.

512 Babylon revolts from Persia, but is recovered 2 years after.

510 PONTUS becomes a kingdom under Artabazes I.

509 Carthage in alliance with Rome.

508 Darius Ochus conquers India.

504 Sardis burned by the Ionians.

498 The Ionians revolt from Persia, but are subdued

491 Darius, king of Persia, after being defeated in an expedition against the Scythians, sends into Greece an army of 500,000, under Dates and Artaphernes, who conquer Thrace, Macedonia, &c.

Period

B.C.	SACRED.	B.C.	GRECIAN.
		490	Battle of Marathon, in Attica; in which the Persians are defeated by the Athenian general Miltiades,
		488	who is afterwards ungratefully imprisoned.
483	Joachim, high priest of the Jews.	483	**Aristides,** the Athenian general, is banished by *ostracism,* through the intrigues of Themistocles.
		480	Fall of Leonidas and his 300 heroic Spartans, who for two days had checked the whole Persian army, (2,000,000 men,) at the pass of Thermopylæ.
			Thémistocles, the Athenian, with only 380 vessels, defeats the Persian fleet of 1200 vessels at Salamis.
			Xerxes leaves Greece. The remainder of his army under
		479	Mardonius destroys Athens.
			Flourished—*Æschylus*, tragic poet; *Pindar*, lyric poet.
			Battle of Platea; the Persian army (300,000) defeated by **Pausanias** and **Aristides,** and Mardonius is killed.
			The same day the Persian fleet is again defeated at Mycale, by **Leotychines** and **Xantippus.**
		476	Themistocles rebuilds Athens. He is accused of a conspiracy and goes over to Xerxes.
		470	Cimon, the son of Miltiades, defeats the Persian army and fleet in two battles on one day, near the Eurymedon.
		469	First quarrel between the Athenians and Lacedemonians.
			Cimon is banished by ostracism.
		465	Third Messenian war.
		463	The Athenians assist the Egyptians against Persia.
		460	LXXXth Olympiad.
		459	The Athenians begin to exercise authority over the other Grecian states.
458	Esther.	458	Deputies arrive from Rome, for a copy of Solon's laws.
457	**Ezra** arrives from Babylon, with a commission from the king, Artaxerxes, to re-establish the government.		Flourished—*Sophocles*, the tragic, and *Plato*, comic poet.
		449	Cimon concludes peace with Persia, glorious for Greece.
		448	First "Sacred War," about the temple of Delphi.
		447	The Athenians are defeated by the Bœotians at Cheronea
		445	*Herodotus* reads his history to the council of Athens, and receives public honours. *Euripides*, tragic poet; *Phidias*, the most famous *sculptor* of antiquity; *Empedocles*, *Parmenides*, *Aristippus*, and *Antisthenes*, philosophers.
453	*Ezra* writes the Books of Chronicles.	444	The Athenians send a colony to Thurium, in Italy
		440	Pericles makes war against the Samians, and takes their capital.
		439	War between Corinth and Corcyra; the latter assisted by the Athenians.
432	*Nehemiah* the prophet rebuilds the walls of Jerusalem, and reforms many abuses.		**Alcibiades** begins to appear in this war, which causes
		431	The Peloponnesian War (between Athens and Sparta, and the allies of each.) Continues 27 years.
			Socrates, the greatest of heathen moralists;
430	*Malachi* prophesies.		*Hippocrates,* of Cos, the father of medicine;
			Thucydides and *Ctesias*, historians;
	End of the Old Testament History.		*Democritus*, the laughing philosopher.
		430	Great plague at Athens for 5 years,—eloquently described by Thucydides.

VII.—134 *years.*

B. C.	ROMAN.	B. C.	MISCELLANEOUS.
488	Coriolanus withdraws the Volsci from Rome.		
		486	Persia:—Xerxes begins to reign.
485	Dissensions respecting the Agrarian law.	481	The expedition of Xerxes into Greece, with an army of about 2,000,000 men, and a fleet of 1200 vessels.
483	Institution of the office of quæstor. War against the Equi and Veiians.		
479	Fabius, the consul, at the head of 306 persons of his own family and 4,000 of their clients, makes war against the Veiians; this little army being surprised two years after, are all killed.	479	Syracuse is governed by Hiero, the tyrant.
471	A law is passed through the influence of Volero, the consul, by which magistrates are to be elected by tribes.		
		469	Etruria founded by the Tuscans.
		464	Persia:—Artaxerxes Longimanus, k.
		463	—— Revolt of the Egyptians under Inarus, assisted by the Athenians, who are defeated.
461	Earthquakes and prodigies at Rome.		
456	The Dictatorship of Cincinnatus, who defeats the Equi and Sabines. The ludi seculares instituted.		
453	Tribunes are increased from 5 to 10.		
451	Decemvirs appointed. *The laws of the twelve tables* compiled.		
449	Virginia violated by a decemvir and killed by her father. The decemvirate abolished.		
445	Intermarriages between the patricians and plebeians begin. Military tribunes created.		
444	Institution of the office of *censor*.		
		441	The battering ram, &c. invented by Artemones.
		433	Persia:—Darius Nothus, k. succeeds Sogdianus and Xerxes II.
		432	Meton begins his *lunar cycle* of 19 years.

JEWISH.	B. C.	GRECIAN.
	420	XCth Olympiad.
	416	The scene of war is transferred to Sicily;—**Nicias**, general of the Athenians.
	414	The Athenians, being terrified by an eclipse, are repulsed before Syracuse.
	412	The Athenians deserted by their allies. Athens governed by the 400.
	410	Thucydides' history ends, and Xenophon's begins.
	405	**Lysander** defeats the Athenians under Conon at Egos-Potomos.
		——— takes Athens and establishes the 30 tyrants.
		End of the Peloponnesian War. Assassination of Alcibiades.
	401	**Thrasybulus** expels the 30 tyrants from Athens. Persecution and death of Socrates. *Philosophy and the Arts.*
		Xenophon, the Athenian, celebrated as a general, historian and philosopher, conducts the 10,000 Greeks from Asia.
	396	**Agesilaus'** (of Sparta) expedition into Asia.
	395	The Corinthian war begun, by the alliance of the Athenians, Thebans, Corinthians, and Argives, against Sparta.
	394	The allies defeated at Coronea by Agesilaus.
	388	About this time flourish—*Plato*, the philosopher; *Philoxenes*, poet.
	387	The Greek cities of Asia made tributary to Persia by the peace of Antalcidas.
	382	Phœbidas, the Spartan, seizes the citadel of Thebes, which is
	380	delivered by **Pelopidas** and **Epaminondas**.
		Cth Olympiad.
	377	The Lacedemonians defeated by Chabrias in a sea-fight at Naxos.
		Flourish—*Diogenes* the Cynic, *Isocrates* and *Isæus*, orators.
	371	Battle of Leuctra, where the Spartans are defeated by the Theban generals, Epaminondas and Pelopidas.
	364	Pelopidas defeats the tyrant of Phœrea, but is killed in the battle.
	362	Agesilaus assists Tachos, k. of Egypt.
	360	The Athenians defeated at Methone, the first battle that Philip, k. of Macedon ever won in Greece.
		Amphipolis, Pydna and Potidea taken by Philip
		War of the allies against Athens.
	357	The 2d Phocian or Sacred War begins.

B. C.	ROMAN.	B. C.	MISCELLANEOUS.
408	The Volsci again defeated.		
406	The Roman troops first receive regular pay.	405	Dionysius, the tyrant, usurps Syracuse.
		404	Persia: Artaxerxes II. (Memnon) k.
		401	Cyrus the younger defeated and killed at Cunaxa by his uncle Artaxerxes. The glorious **Retreat of the 10,000 Greeks under Xenophon.**
397	The lake of Alba drained.		
		396	Syracuse unsuccessfully besieged by the Carthaginians.
391	Veii taken by **Camillus** the Dictator.		
390	**The taking of Rome by the Gauls** under Brennus. They were afterwards routed by Camillus.	388	Flourish—*Damon* and *Pythias*, the Pythagorean philosophers and friends.
383	Manlius Capitolinus thrown down the Tarpeian rock, for having raised a sedition among the plebeians.	383	BITHYNIA becomes a kingdom, under Dydalsus.
376	**Lucius Sextus,** First plebeian consul, Camillus, a fifth time dictator.		
362	**Curtius** leaps into a gulf in the Forum.	362	Revolt of Persian governors in Asia Minor, against Artaxerxes.
	Titus Manlius, (sur. Torquatus,) general in a battle against the Gauls.	361	Persia: Darius Ochus, or Artaxerxes III. (According to Blair, 358.
		360	Macedon: **Philip II.** king.
			CAPPADOCIA becomes a kingdom; Ariarathes I.
			Commerce of Rhodes with Africa and Byzantium.
			Voyages of the Carthaginians under Hanno.
		357	Dionysius the younger expelled from Syracuse by Dion.
		356	The Sidonians besieged by the Persians, burn their city and themselves.

Period

B. C.	JEWISH.	B. C.	GRECIAN.
		353	The Phocians under Onomarchus defeated in Thessaly by Philip.
		348	The Sacred War finished by Philip taking all the Phocian cities.
		346	Philip admitted a member of the Amphictyonic Council.
		343	Flourish—*Aristotle* the logician and philosopher, founder of the Peripatetics; *Æschines*, orator; *Demosthenes*, the prince of orators
		341	**Timoleon** conquers Syracuse.
		340	CXth Olympiad.
		338	The Athenians and Thebans defeated by Philip in the battle of Cheronea. **The subjugation of Greece by Philip.**
		336	Thebes destroyed by Alexander; who preserves, however, the house of Pindar.
		335	Alexander is chosen generalissimo of the Greeks against the Persians.
332	Alexander the Great in Jerusalem; demands the succours usually sent to Persia, which are refused.	330	Æschines the orator banished.
		328	Flourish—*Apelles*, the greatest painter of antiquity; *Callisthenes*, philosopher; *Menander*, the inventor of the new comedy.
		325	Demosthenes banished from Athens.
		323	The Athenians league with the rest of Greece and revolt from Aridæus the successor of Alexander. Demosthenes is recalled from banishment and dies next year.
320	Ptolemy carries 100,000 Jews into Egypt. — Onias I. — high priest.	319	Polysperchon proclaims liberty to the Grecian cities. Flourish—*Theophrastus*, philosopher; *Dinarchus* orator.
		318	**Phocion** put to death by the Athenians. Cassander becomes master of Athens.
		317	Demetrius Phalerius governs Athens for ten years.

VIII.—210 *years.*

B. C. ROMAN.

343 War against the Samnites; lasts 53 years, and leads to the conquest of all Italy.

340 P. Decius devotes himself for his country.

The Latin cities surrender at discretion.

All Campania, with Capua its capital, subdued.

312. The Appian way formed

325 Papirius Cursor, dictator.

321 The Samnites make the Romans pass under the yoke near Caudium.

320 The Samnites submit at Luceria.

MISCELLANEOUS.

356 The birth of Alexander the Great. The same night the temple of Diana at Ephesus was burnt.

Philip conquers the Thracians, Phocians, and Illyrians.

354 Dion put to death and the government of Syracuse usurped by tyrants.

349 Darius Ochus subdues Egypt.

348 Philip of Macedon takes Olynthus.

343 Timoleon the Grecian recovers Syracuse, expels Dionysius the tyrant, and

340 defeats the Carthaginians near Agrigentum. *Icetas*, of Syracuse, philosopher.

338 Philip of Macedon defeats the Greeks at Cheronea.

336 —— murdered by Pausanias, his general.

Macedon:—ALEXANDER the Great, king

—— destroys Thebes, and ravages Greece.

334 —— invades Persia; defeats the Persians in the battle of the Granicus,

333 and of Issus:—conquers Parthia, Bactria, Hyrcania, Sogdiana, and Asia Minor.

332 —— conquers Tyre and Egypt, and builds Alexandria.

—— enters Jerusalem.

331 —— defeats Darius Codomanus in the battle of Arbela, and effects

330 —— the Conquest of the Persian Empire.

328 —— defeats Porus, king of India, and reaches the Ganges: founds several cities.

The voyage of Nearchus from the Indus to the Euphrates.

323 Alexander dies at Babylon, aet. 33.

His brother Aridaeus is declared king in his stead, and Perdiccas regent.

321 Antipater succeeds Perdiccas.

Egypt:—Ptolemy Lagus, (the first of the Ptolemies,) takes possession.

320 —— brings 100,000 Jews captive into Egypt.

Eumenes defeated by Antigonus.

319 Polysperchon succeeds Antipater.

317 Macedon.—Cassander assumes the government.

B. C.	JEWISH.	B. C.	GRECIAN.
		315	Cassander rebuilds Thebes and founds Cassandria.
314	Judea taken from Ptolemy by Antigonus.		
		306	Demetrius Poliorcetes makes himself master of Athens and re-establishes democracy: takes Salamis and Cyprus.
		304	—— besieges Rhodes, but is repulsed.
		303	—— is declared general of the Grecian states.
		300	CXXth Olympiad. Flourish—*Euclid* of Alexandria, the celebrated mathematician; *Bion*, of Borysthenes, a philosopher. *Philosophical sects*; *Zeno*, founder of the Stoic school; *Pyrrho*, of the Skeptics; *Epicurus*, of the Epicurians.
299	Eleazar, high priest.		
		296	Athens retaken by Demetrius Poliorcetes after a year's siege.
		287	The Athenians revolt from Demetrius.
		285	*Theocritus*, the father of *pastoral poetry*, flourished.
284	The sect of the *Sadducees*.	284	The Achæan Republic resumes its ancient form which it had lost under Philip and Alexander. The *Septuagint* at Alexandria.
		281	The Achæan League; or union of the 12 smaller states under Aratus of Sicyon, for reviving the spirit of liberty.
		278	The Gauls under Brennus (the 2d) cut to pieces near the temple of Delphi.
		273	Pyrrhus, after ravaging Greece, is killed at Argos.

B. C. ROMAN.

310 Aqueduct and baths.

308 **Fabius Maximus** defeats the Samnites.

306 The Marsi, Peligni, Fretani, &c. obtain the alliance of Rome.

301 Fabius Maximus and **Valerius Corvus**, dictators.

293 The first *sun dial* erected at Rome by Papirius Cursor, and the time first divided into hours.

290 End of the Samnite war.

Fabius introduces *painting* at Rome.

286 Law of Hortensius, by which the *decrees of the people* are allowed the same force as those of the senate.

281 The Tarentine War begins. (Chariots armed with scythes and *fortified camps* in use.)

280 War with Pyrrhus, ally of the Tarentines.

275 **Curius** defeats Pyrrhus and compels him to leave Italy.

B. C. MISCELLANEOUS.

317 Commerce of Macedon with India through Egypt.

Syracuse and Sicily usurped by Agathocles.

311 SYRIA:—**Seleucus** Nicator; takes Babylon.

Era of the Seleucidæ.

305 EPIRUS: **Pyrrhus I.** king.

The successors of Alexander first take the title of kings.

301 The Battle of Ipsus; where Antigonus is defeated and killed. It is followed by

The division of Alexander's empire between the four victorious princes, viz. Ptolemy, Seleucus, Cassander, and Lysimachus.*

291 Seleucus about this time founds Antioch, Edessa, Laodicea, and other cities in Asia, which he peoples from different nations.

286 Pyrrhus expelled from Macedon by Lysimachus.

285 *Dionysius*, the astronomer, of Alexandria, begins his era. He was the first who found the exact solar year to consist of 365 days, 5 hours, and 49 minutes.

284 *The Septuagint* translation of the Old Testament, begun at Alexandria, by order of Ptolemy-Philadelphus. The Pharos built.

282 PERGAMUS, a kingdom, founded by Philetares.

281 Lysimachus, defeated and killed by Seleucus, and his dominions cease to be a distinct kingdom.

Syria:—Antiochus Soter succeeds Seleucus.

280 Pyrrhus, king of Epirus, goes to Italy to assist the Tarentines.

277 Macedon:—Antigonus Gonatas, king.

275 Antiochus defeats the Gauls in a bloody battle, by which he acquires the name of Soter.

---

* To Ptolemy were assigned Egypt, Lybia, Arabia and Palestine; to Cassander, Macedonia and Greece; to Lysimachus, Bithynia and Thrace; and to Seleucus the remaining territories in Asia as far as the river Indus, which were called the kingdom of Syria.

B. C.	JEWISH.	B. C.	GRECIAN.
		268	Athens taken by Antigonus Gonatus, who keeps it 12 years.
		264	The Chronology of the *Arundelian marbles* composed. *Oratus* Academic philosopher.
		260	CXXXth Olympiad.
		255	The liberty of Athens restored by Antigonus.
253	**Manasseh**, high priest of the Jews.		**Xantippus** is sent by the Lacedemonians to assist the Carthaginians.
		251	Aratus persuades the people of Sicyon to join the Achæan league.
		250	Intercourse with the Romans begins about this time: the Greek treasures of art are gradually carried to Rome.
248	Onias II. high priest.		
		243	The citadel of Corinth taken by Aratus.
		241	**Agis,** king of Sparta, put to death in attempting to settle an *Agrarian law.*
		240	*Cleanthes*, the Stoic philosopher, starves himself.
337	Simon II.		
		233	Original manuscripts of Æschylus, Euripides, and Sophocles, lent by the Athenians to Ptolemy for a pledge of 15 talents.
		228	The Roman ambassadors first appear at Athens and Corinth.
			Cleomenes, king of Sparta, gains a great victory over the Achæans under Aratus.
		225	—— kills the Ephori and restores the Agrarian laws at Sparta.
			Flourished—*Apollonius Rhodius*, poet; *Chrysippus*, Stoic philosopher.
			The Romans send a famous embassy into Greece. They are admitted to a share in the Isthmian games, and granted the freedom of Athens.
		223	Cleomenes takes Megalopolis
		220	The Social War between the Ætolians and Achæans; the latter assisted by Philip III. king of Macedon.
			CXLth Olympiad.
			Cleomenes dies in Egypt.
			Agesipolis and Lycurgus elected kings of Sparta.
		211	Alliance of the Ætolians with the Romans—afterwards joined by the Lacedemonians, and by Attalus, king of Pergamus.

B. C. ROMAN.

272 The Samnites finally subdued.

266 The republic is now mistress of all Italy. Silver money first coined by the Romans. Citizens, 292,224.

264 First Punic War; lasts 23 years.

Appius Claudius goes to Sicily and forces Hiero to retire to Syracuse.

260 The first Roman naval victory gained by **Duillus** over the Carthaginians.

Provincial Quæstors instituted.

256 **Regulus** defeats the Carthaginian fleet.

255 —— is defeated and taken prisoner by the Carthaginians under Xantippus, and is cruelly put to death.

251 **Metellus** gains a great victory over the Carthaginians under Asdrubal.

250 The Romans defeated by Hamilcar, at Liliboeum, and

249 again defeated in the naval battle of Drapanum, by the Carthaginians.

241 End of the first Punic War.

240 *Comedies* first acted at Rome, being those of *Livius Andronicus*.

235 The Temple of Janus shut; Rome being at peace with all nations, for the first time since Numa.

231 Sardinia and Corsica conquered by the Romans.

225 Great victory over the Gauls in Italy.

Fabius Pictor, the first Roman historian.

224 The Romans first cross the Po.

222 Conquest of Cisalpine Gaul, or Insubria, (now the Milanese,) and Liguria, (now Genoa.)

219 The art of *Surgery* introduced.

218 Second Punic War. The Romans defeated by Hannibal, on the Ticinius and at Trebia, and

217 in the battle of the lake of Thrasymenus. (**C. Flaminius.**)

216 Battle of Cannæ; the Romans under **Varro** totally defeated by Hannibal.

Fabius Maximus again dictator.

212 Conquest of Syracuse and Sicily by **Marcellus.**

211 The Carthaginians driven from Capua.

B. C. MISCELLANEOUS.

267 Ptolemy makes a canal from the Nile to the Red Sea.

264 Carthage at war with Rome.

262 Antiochus Soter defeated at Sardis by Eumenes of Pergamus.

256 PARTHIA, a kingdom founded by **Arsaces.**

Berosus, of Babylon, an historian, lived about this time.

255 Fourth imperial dynasty of China begins.

The Carthaginians apply for aid to the Lacedemonians, who send them Xantippus. He gains a victory over the Romans, and takes Regulus prisoner.

246 Syria:—Antiochus II (Theos.)

—— is poisoned by his wife Laodice.

Laodice killed by Ptolemy Euergetes, king of Egypt, who subdues Syria.

241 Pergamus:—**Attilus,** succeeds Eumenes.

238 The Carthaginians end the Lybian war.

237 Hamilcar passes with an army into Spain (with Hannibal his son,) where he is killed, 228.

224 The Colossus of Rhodes thrown down by an earthquake.

Archimedes, of Syracuse, the mathematician.

222 Cisalpine Gaul reduced to a *Roman Province.

221 Egypt:—Ptolemy Philopator, king.

219 Hannibal takes Saguntum in Spain.

—— crosses the Alps. He is victorious at Ticinius and Trebia; at Thrasymenus 217, and at Cannæ 216.

213 Sheehoangtee destroys the records of the Chinese empire.

212 Syracuse taken and Sicily * conquered by the Romans. Archimedes is killed.

211 Syria:—**Antiochus** the Great, king.

* This mark is inserted in several succeeding pages for the purpose of making the progress of the Roman Empire more easily distinguished.

B.C.	JEWISH.	B.C.	GRECIAN.
		208	**Battle between Philip, king of Macedon, and the Ætolians, near Elis.**
203	**Judea conquered by Antiochus the Great.**	206	**Philopœmen, prætor of the Achæans, defeats Machinidas, tyrant of Sparta, at Mantinea.**
			Flourish—*Plautus*, of Umbria, comic poet; *Apollonius*, of Perga, one of the fathers of mathematical science; *Zeno*, of Tarsus, philosopher.
201	**Onias III. high priest**	202	**The Rhodians victorious over Philip, king of Macedon, in a sea-fight off the island of Chios.**
200	***Jesus*, son of Sirach, writes Ecclesiasticus.**	198	**The Achæans, and Nabis, tyrant of Sparta, declare for the Romans against Philip.**
		195	**Flaminius, the Roman general, makes war against Nabis.**
		191	**Nabis is killed. Philopœmen induces the Lacedemonians to join the Achæan league. Antiochus the Great, the ally of the Ætolians, is defeated by the Romans near Thermopylæ.**
		188	**Philopœmen abrogates the laws of Lycurgus in Sparta.**
		183	**—— is defeated and killed by Dinocrates, the tyrant of Messenia. *Bion* and *Moschus*, pastoral poets, flourish.**
176	**Heliodorus in Jerusalem.**		
175	**Jason obtains the high priesthood by corruption.**		
172	**— defeated by Menelaus, h. priest.**		
170	**Jerusalem and the temple plundered by Antiochus Epiphanes, who attempts to abolish the Jewish religion, and commits great cruelties.**	169	***Polybius*, historian of Greece and Rome, flourished.**

B. C. ROMAN.

210 Scipio takes New Carthage, and conquers Asdrubal in Spain.

207 Nero and Livy defeat and kill Asdrubal at Metaurus.

204 Scipio carries the war into Africa and besieges Utica.

203 —— takes in one day the camps of Asdrubal and Syphax.

202 —— defeats Hannibal at Zama:

201 and leads Syphax in triumph to Rome. Peace granted to the Carthaginians; end of the 2d Punic War.

200 The First Macedonian War begins; lasts 4 years.

197 Battle of Cynocephale; the Macedonians defeated by Flaminius.

Two prætors sent to Spain.

Flourished—*Caius Lelius*, the Roman orator.

192 War against Antiochus, king of Syria, 3 years.

190 **Scipio Asiaticus** defeats Antiochus at Magnesia.

187 Scipio Africanus banished from Rome.

Conquest of Syria by Asiaticus.

The luxuries of Asia brought to Rome in the spoils of Antiochus.

183 **Cato**, the elder, censor. The Transalpine Gauls march into Italy.

181 Plague at Rome.

180 Death of Scipio Africanus.

179 *Numa's books* found in a stone coffin at Rome.

171 2d Macedonian War. (king Perseus.)

170 Tiberius and Caius **Gracchus** flourish.

169 The *Comedies of Terence* performed.

168 **Paulus Emilius** defeats Perseus at Pydna and conquers Macedon.

Anicius subjects Illyria.

B. C. MISCELLANEOUS.

210 The Carthaginians in Spain, under Asdrubal, conquered by the Romans, (Scipio.)

207 *Ennius*, of Calabria, poet; *Sotion*, of Alexandria, a grammarian.

205 Egypt:—Ptolemy Epiphanes, king.

203 Antiochus the Great conquers Jerusalem.

The Carthaginians recall Hannibal.

Sophonisba poisoned by Masinissa.

202 Hannibal defeated at Zama.

201 Syphax carried to Rome. Peace obtained by the Carthaginians.

200 *Aristonymus*, 4th librarian of Alexandria

197 The Macedonians, (Philip V.) defeated in the battle of Cynocephale, by the Romans.

Pergamus:—Eumenes, king.

192 Syria: Antiochus the Great at war with the Romans.

190 —— defeated by Scipio in the battle of Magnesia.

187 —— defeated again, and killed in the temple of Jupiter Belus.

Syria becomes a *Roman Province, but remains governed by kings.

185 —— Seleucus IV. king.

183 A comet visible 80 days.

180 Egypt: Ptolemy Philometor.

178 Macedon: Perseus king.

175 —— sends ambassadors to Carthage.

172 Syria: Antiochus IV. (Epiphanes.)

171 —— declares war against Ptolemy Philometor.

Perseus, king of Macedon, at war with Rome.

170 Antiochus Epiphanes conquers Egypt and plunders the temple of Jerusalem. Paper said to be invented in China. An irruption of the Tartars into China.

168 Battle of Pydna: Perseus defeated, and

Macedon becomes a * Roman Province.

B. C.	JEWISH.	B. C.	GRECIAN.
167	Matthias, h. priest	167	The Achæans, suspected of having favoured Perseus, are sent to Rome to give an account of their conduct. The senate banishes them into different towns in Italy. Polybius was of this number.
165	**Judas Maccabeus** expels the Syrians.		
165	— defeats a great army of Antiochus, and purifies the temple.		
163	The government of the *Maccabees* begins.		
161	Judas kills Nicanor.		
	—— succeeded by **Jonathan,**		
158	who compels the Bacchides to withdraw.		
	—— is murdered by Tryphon.	150	Flourish—*Hipparchus* of Rhodes, the greatest of ancient astronomers; *Aristarchus*, of Alexandria, grammarian.
		147	The Achæans defeated by the Romans under Metellus.
		146	Corinth taken and destroyed by Mummius, and Greece becomes a * Roman Province under the name of Achaia.
142	**Simon,** governor and high priest.		[Events relating to Greece, from this date, may be found in the miscellaneous column.]

B. C.	ROMAN.	B. C.	MISCELLANEOUS.
167	The first *library* erected at Rome, consisting of books brought from Macedon. Roman citizens 327,032. Emilius conquers Epirus.	167	Epirus conquered by Paulus Emilius, and becomes a * Roman Province.
		166	Prusias king of Bithynia, goes to Rome.
		164	Antiochus Epiphanes dies while marching to Judea, with a design to exterminate the Jews.
		162	Demetrius Soter, takes possession of Syria, and causes Antiochus to be put to death.
161	The philosophers and rhetoricians banished.		
159	Time measured out by a water machine invented by Scipio Nascia, 134 years after the introduction of sun-dials.		
		152	Macedon:—Andriscus, personating the son of Perseus, assumes the government, but is conquered by Metellus.
		150	Syria;—Alexander Bala puts Demetrius to death and seizes the throne.
149	Third Punic War, lasts 3 years.	149	Bithynia:—Prusias is put to death by his son Nicomedes.
147	War against the Achæans declared on account of their alleged insult to the Roman deputies. Metellus victorious in Greece.		
146	The Subjugation of Greece by Mummius. The Destruction of Carthage by Scipio.	146	Carthage taken and destroyed by the * Romans. The Commerce of the World centres at Alexandria.
		145	Egypt:—Ptolemy Physcon.

Period IX.—66 Years.

B. C.	ROMAN.	B. C.	MISCELLANEOUS	B. C.	JEWISH.
141	The war with Numantia begins. (Continues 8 years.)				
		140	Syria:—Antiochus Sidetes.		
138	The Roman army of 30,000 under Marcinus defeated by 4,000 Numantines.				
136	The famous embassy of Scipio, Metellus, Mummius, and Panœtius into Egypt, Syria and Greece.	137	*Restoration of learning* at Alexandria, and liberal patronage offered to all learned men by Ptolemy Physcon. The age of *Diodorus* and *Satyrus*, the peripatetic philosophers; *Aristobolus*, of Alexandria, the Jewish peripatetic: *Nicander*, physician and poet; *Lucius Accius*, tragic poet, &c.		
135	The Servile War in Sicily begins.	135	War of the Slaves in Sicily, 3 years.	135	The Apocryphal history ends. Jerusalem besieged by Antiochus IV.
133	Numantia taken and destroyed by Scipio Æmilianus. Pergamus annexed to the Roman empire. Tiberius Gracchus put to death. The *equestrian order* now a distinct class.	133	Antiochus IV. besieges Jerusalem. Spain becomes a * Roman Province after the fall of Numantia.		
		133	Attalus dies, and Pergamus becomes a *Roman Province.		
		130	Antiochus IV. defeated and killed. Revival of learning in China.	130	**John Hyrcanus,** first of the Asmoneans, high priest; recovers the towns which had been taken by Antiochus and delivers Judea from the Syrian yoke.
123	War against the pirates of the Belearus.	123	Carthage rebuilt by order of the Roman senate.		
121	Caius Gracchus killed.		Pontus:—**Mithridates** the Great.		
118	Metellus conquers Dalmatia. The consul, Q. M. Rex; plants a colony in Gaul.	118	Dalmatia becomes a *Roman Province.		
116	Flourish—*L. Cœlius Antipater*, historian; *Lucillius*, the first Roman *satirist*.	116	Egypt:—Ptolemy Lathyrus.		

B. C.	ROMAN.	B.C.	MISCELLANEOUS.	B. C.	JEWISH.
		116	Flourish—*Apollodorus*, of Athens, chronologer and grammarian; *Castor*, of Rhodes, chronologer, &c.; *Anthemos*, philosopher.		
112	The Jugurthine War begins.	112	Jugurtha, the usurper of Numidia, at war with Rome.		
110	Famous *sumptuary law*, which limits the expenses of eating every day.			108	Hyrcanus demolishes Samaria.
		109	The Teutoni and Cimbri begin their war against Rome.	107	—— is succeeded by his son. Aristobulus, the first high priest who assumed the title of king.
		107	Egypt:—Alexander I.		
105	**Marius** and **Sylla** conclude the war against Jugurtha, who is defeated and brought to Rome. (Died 103.)	105	Numidia becomes a *Roman Province after the defeat of Jugurtha.	105	**Alex. Jannæus** high priest; engages in war against Egypt; takes Gaza. Rebellion excited by the Pharisees.
104	The Teutoni defeat 80,000 Romans on the banks of the Rhone.				
102	Marius gains a great victory over the Teutoni and Ambrones at Aquæ Sextæ.				
101	Marius and Catullus defeat the Cimbri.	100	CLXXth Olympiad.		
99	Dolabella conquers Lusitania. The Agrarian law revived by Saturnius. Birth of Julius Cæsar.	99	Lusitania becomes a *Roman Province.		
97	Cyrene left to the Romans by Ptolemy.	97	Ptolemy Appion dies, leaving his kingdom of *Cyrene to the Romans.		
91	The Social War, or war of the Italian allies against Rome; (finished by Sylla 3 years after.) Sylla defeats the Marsi, Peligni, &c.	94	Antiochus of Lyricum defeated by Seleucus.		
89	The Mithridatic War, lasts till 66. Sylla commands the Roman army.	89	Pontus:—Mithridates at war with Rome.		
88	Civil War between Marius and Sylla, 6 years.				
87	Cinna, the consul joins the faction of Marius.	86	Athens taken by Sylla, who sends its valuable libraries to Rome;—defeats Archelaus.		
82	Sylla defeats the younger Marius. —is created perpetual dictator. His horrible proscription. The capitol burnt.	82	and plunders the temple of Delphi.		
		81	Egypt:—Alexander II.		

Period X.—80 *Years.*

B. C.	ROMAN.	B.C.	MISCELLANEOUS.	B. C.	JEWISH.
80	Julius Cæsar's first campaign.				
79	Pompey defeats Domitius in Africa. Cicero's first oration for Roscius. The allies first admitted to the rights of citizenship.			79	Alexandra, widow of Janneus governs Judea.
78	Death of Sylla. About this time flourish—*Photius Gallus*, the first Latin *rhetorician*; *Q. Valerius Antias*, Roman historian; *Q. Hortensius*, orator.	78	About this time flourish—*Zeno*, of Sidon, the Epic. philosopher; *Apellicon*, of Athens: *Alexander Polyphistor*, the grammarian, &c.		
77	Sertorius revolts in Spain and defeats Metellus and Pompey				
75	Bithynia left to the Romans by Nicomedes. Sertorius is assassinated by Perperna.	75	Nicomedes king of * Bithynia, dies, leaving his kingdom to the Romans.		
73	The War of Spartacus, the Gladiator, against Rome.				
71	—— ends:—Spartacus defeated by Crassus in Lucania.				
70	The censorship revived. **Pompey** and **Crassus**, consuls.			70	Hyrcanus II. high priest; deposed by his brother,
69	**Lucullus** defeats Mithridates and Tigranes. The capitol rebuilt. Citizens 450,090.	69	Mithridates and Tigranes, defeated by the Romans (Lucullus.)		
66	Metellus subdues Crete after a war of two years. Pompey conquers Mithridates in a night battle and reduces Pontus.	66	Mithridates conquered by Pompey, and Pontus becomes a *Roman Province.	67	Aristobulus, whom he afterwards defeats by the help of Aretas, king of Arabia. The rivals appeal to Pompey, the Roman general.
65	Pompey deposes Antiochus and conquers Syria. Extraordinary honours are decreed to him by the senate at the motion of M. Tullius Cicero, now consul.	65	Syria:—The dynasty of the Seleucidæ ends with Antiochus XII. and Syria, conquered by Pompey, becomes a * Roman Province. Egypt:—Ptolemy Auletes.		
63	Cataline's Conspiracy detected by Cicero and suppressed. Pompey conquers Judea.	63	Mithridates kills himself.	63	Judea becomes a *Roman Province after the taking of Jerusalem by Pompey, who re-
61	—— enters Rome in triumph.				
60	First Triumvirate:—Pompey, Crassus, and Julius Cæsar.	60	Flourish—*Apollonius* of Rhodes, rhetorician; *Aristomedus*, of		

B. C.	ROMAN.	B.C.	MISCELLANEOUS.	B. C.	JEWISH.
	Flourish—Cicero, the famous statesman and orator; *Sallust*, historian; *Varro; Lucretius*, and *Catullus*, poets.		Crete, grammarian; *Andronicus*, of Rhodes, peripatetic philosopher.		stores Hyrcanus to the priesthood, and exacts a tribute; but leaves the treasures in the temple untouched. Gabinius establishes the *Sanhedrim*.
58	Clodius the tribune procures the banishment of Cicero.				
57	Cicero recalled. Sallust expelled from the senate.				
55	Cæsar passes the Rhine; defeats the Germans and Gauls, and invades Britain. Pompey builds a stone theatre for public amusements.	55	Egypt:—Ptolemy, (restored.) The Germans, (Ariovistus,) and the Gauls, defeated by the Romans. (Cæsar.)		
54	Cæsar's second invasion of Britain.				
53	Crassus killed and his army defeated by the Parthians.				
52	Cicero defends Milo, who had quarrelled with Clodius.		The Invasion of Britain by Cæsar. The natives promise a tribute to the Romans.	53	Crassus plunders the temple of 10,000 talents.
51	Cæsar completes the conquest of Gaul.	51	Egypt:—Cleopatra queen. Gaul becomes a *Roman Province.		
49	—— passes the Rubicon; is proclaimed dictator.	49	*Era of Antioch* begins in October.		
48	Civil War between Cæsar and Pompey.				
48	Battle of Pharsalia: Pompey defeated by Cæsar;—flees to Egypt, and is there slain.			48	Antipater, the Idumean, who had aided Hyrcanus, is made lieutenant in Judea by Cæsar.
47	Cæsar takes Alexandria and conquers Egypt.	47	The *Alexandrian Library*, (400,000 vols.) burnt.		
46	The War of Africa. Cato kills himself at Utica. This is called the year of confusion, because the calendar was altered by Sosigenes.	46	Ptolemy Dionysius drowned in the Nile.		
45	Cæsar created perpetual dictator;—reforms the calendar by introducing the *Solar* year instead of the Lunar. *First Julian year* begins January 1. Cæsar subdues the two sons of Pompey in Spain, and acquires the sole power.	45	Battle of Munda. Carthage and Corinth rebuilt by Cæsar.		
44	The Assassination of Cæsar in the senate house. A comet visible 7 days after.	44	A comet seen in China.		
43	2d Triumvirate:—**Octavius Cæsar, Mark Antony, and Lepidus.** Cicero proscribed by the triumvirate and murdered. Flourished—*Cornelius Nepos*, historian. A shower of iron fell in Lucania according to Pliny.	43	Flourish—*Diodorus Siculus*, historian; *Sosigenes*, an Egyptian mathematician.	43	Judea is oppressed by Cassius. Malichus poisons Antipater.
42	Battle of Philippi, in which Antony				

B. C. ROMAN.	B.C. MISCELLANEOUS.	B.C. JEWISH.
and Octavius are victorious over Brutus and Cassius, (the conspirators against Cæsar,) who are both killed.		40 **Herod** the Great, (son of Antipater) defeats his rival Antigonus, and Pacorus the Parthian.
39 **Ventidius** defeats Pacorus, the Parthian general, fourteen years after the disgrace of Crassus.		
36 Octavius subdues Sextus Pompey in Sicily, dispossesses Lepidus of his army and the triumviral power, and gains popularity among all classes.		38 —— takes Jerusalem; marries Mariamne, of the Asmonean family, and is made king of Judea by the Romans.
34 Antony takes possession of Armenia and leads an inglorious expedition against the Parthians.	34 Armenia becomes a *Roman Province, divided by Antony between Cleopatra's children.	
32 Antony quarrels with Octavius and prepares for war.		
31 Battle of Actium: Antony and Cleopatra defeated by Octavius Cæsar. End of the Roman Republic and beginning of the ROMAN EMPIRE;—**Augustus,** (Octavius Cæsar) emperor. *Golden age of Roman Literature.*	30 Alexandria taken by Octavius. Antony and queen Cleopatra put themselves to death. Egypt a *Roman Province.	30 Herod murders Mariamne.
29 Augustus triumphs three days at Rome. Temple of Janus closed. Rome contains 4,101,017 citizens.		
27 The Pantheon built. The title of Augustus and of emperor for 10 years conferred on Octavius.		27 A great earthquake in Palestine. 26 Herod visits Rome, and is confirmed in his government by Augustus.
25 About this time flourish—*Horace, Virgil, Tibullus,* and *Propertius,* poets: *Varius* and *Tucca* critics and editors of the Æneid;—*Livy,* the prince of Roman historians; **Mæcenas,** the minister of Augustus and patron of literature; **Agrippa,** a warrior and patron of the arts.	25 The Egyptians adopt the Julian year. Flourish—*Strabo,* the geographer. *Æmelius Macer,* of Verona, poet.	
Worship of Isis at Rome.	23 Agrippa in Spain.	
22 Conspiracy of Muræna against Augustus.		
21 Augustus recalls Agrippa and gives him his daughter Julia in marriage. —— visits Greece and Asia.		
20 **Tiberius** recovers the Roman ensigns from the Parthians. An embassy from Porus, king of India, soliciting an alliance.	20 Porus, king of India, solicits an alliance with Rome.	
19 Rome in the meridian of her glory. The aqueducts constructed by Agrippa. Secular games.	CXCth Olympiad.	19 The temple of Jerusalem rebuilt by Herod.
16 Lollius defeated by the Germans.	16 The Germans defeat the Romans.	
15 **Drusus** defeats the Rhœti and Vindelenci.	15 Cantabria, Austria, Rhœtia, Vindelencia, and Mœsia successively reduced to * Roman Provinces.	
13 Augustus assumes the office of *pontifex maximus,* and burns 2,000 pontifical books, reserving those of the Sybiline oracles.		

B. C.	ROMAN.	B.C.	MISCELLANEOUS.	B. C.	JEWISH.
12	Tiberius conquers the Pannonians.	12	Pannonia, a * Roman Province.		
11	Drusus conquers several German nations. **Germanicus** victorious in Germany.	11	Several German nations conquered by the * Romans.		
8	The calendar corrected by Augustus.			5	Cyrenius taxes Judea.
	Tiberius goes to Rhodes.				
5	Q. Varrus appointed governor of Syria, and Cyrenius governor of Judea. Augustus orders the empire to be taxed, and a general census taken.	5	Q. Varrus, governor of Syria. Flourish——*Dionysius of Halicarnassus*, historian, and *Dionysius*, the geographer.	4	**Birth of our Saviour, JESUS CHRIST,** 4 years before the vulgar era. Massacre of the infants in Bethlehem.
				3	Archelaus succeeds Herod, with the title of Ethnarch.
2	Julia banished by Augustus, on account of her vices.				

MODERN CHRONOLOGY,

EXTENDS FROM THE CHRISTIAN ERA TO THE PRESENT TIME.

Epochas or *Periods.*

I.	From the Christian Era to the Reign of Constantine the Great,	A.D. 306	*Period of the Ten Persecutions of Christians*
II.	" Extinction of the Western Empire,	" 476	*Northern Invasions.*
III.	" Flight of Mahomet,	" 622	*Justinian and Belisarius.*
IV.	" Crowning of Charlemagne at Rome,	" 800	*Saracen Empire.*
V.	" Battle of Hastings,	" 1066	*New Western Empire.*
VI.	" Founding of the Turkish Empire,	" 1299	*The Crusades.*
VII.	" Taking of Constantinople,	" 1453	*Tamerlane, Wickliffe and Huss*
VIII	" Edict of Nantes,	" 1598	*The Reformation; Discoveries and Inventions.*
IX.	" Death of Charles 12th, of Sweden,	" 1718	*The English Commonwealth, and Wars of Louis XIV.*
X.	" Battle of Waterloo,	" 1815	*American and French Revolutions.*
XI.	" present time, (1832.)		*European Revolutions Literature, and the Arts.*

MODERN CHRONOLOGY.

Period 1.—306 *Years.*

THE CHRISTIAN ERA.

Year of the World, 4004—*CXCVth Olympiad.*

A. D.	ROMAN.	A.D.	MISCELLANEOUS.	A. D.	SACRED.
					Herod (Antipas) tetrarch of Galilee.
1	Caius Cæsar makes peace with the Parthians. Tiberius returns.				
3	Cinna's Conspiracy detected. Caius Cæsar dies.				
				8	Christ reasons with the doctors in the temple.
9	Varrus defeated and killed in Germany. *Ovid*, the poet, banished to Tomos.	9	The Germans under **Arminius**, defeat and kill Varrus, the Roman general.		
10	Augustus dies at Nola, æt. 76, and is succeeded by —— Tiberius, —— a despot;—Sejanus, the instrument of his cruelties. Flourish—*Phædrus*, the fabulist; *Vellius Paterculus.*		*Celsus*, the physician.		
17	Germanicus conquers Cappadocia. Mathematicians and magicians expelled from Rome.	17	Capadocia reduced to a * Roman province.		
19	The Jews banished from Rome by Tiberius. Germanicus is poisoned, and dies at Antioch.		An earthquake destroys 12 cities in Asia.		
21	The theatre of Pompey destroyed by fire.	25	CCIst Olympiad. Here the Olympiads end.		
26	Tiberius retires to Capræa. The Prætorian Guards organized about this time.	26	Thrace, a * Roman Province about this time. The Druids in Germany.	26	*John* the *Baptist* begins his ministry. (beheaded 29.)
				27	Pilate, governor of Judea. Christ baptized by John.
				30	—— at the marriage in Cana.
31	Sejanus disgraced and put to death by Tiberius.			31	Matthew called.
				32	The 12 *Apostles* sent abroad, "two and two."

A. D.	ROMAN.	A.D.	MISCELLANEOUS.	A. D.	SACRED.
33	Conquest of Mauritania.	33	Mauritania becomes a * Roman Province.	33	Lazarus raised from the dead. **The Crucifixion** of our Saviour, Friday, April 3, at 2 o'clock, P. M. Resurrection, Sunday, April 5. Ascension Thursday, May 4.
				33	*St. Peter*; (called the first Pope.)
				35	—— baptizes Cornelius.
				36	*St. Paul*, converted to Christianity.
37	Tiberius dies, æt. 78. In this reign flourished, *Valerius Maximus*, historian. —— Caligula. —— (noted for his profligacy and folly.)	37	*Appion*, of Alexandria, the grammarian, called "The Trumpet of the World."	39	*St. Matthew* writes his gospel.
		40	Petronius, governor of Syria.	40	The disciples of Christ first called *Christians* at Antioch.
41	—— is assassinated by Chereas. —— Claudius, —— (weak.)			41	Herod's persecution. St. Peter imprisoned.
43	—— invades Britain with his general **Plautius.**	43	Britain invaded by the Romans under Claudius.	44	*St. Mark* writes his gospel. Death of *James* the Apostle.
45	**Vespasian,** Roman general in Britain.	45	and Vespasian.	45	Barnabas and Paul preach in Cyprus.
		51	The noble British chief **Caractacus** is carried in chains to Rome. London built by the Romans.	50	Paul preaches in the Areopagus at Athens.
51	Caractacus, the chief of the Britons, is conquered and brought to Rome.			52	Council of the Apostles at Jerusalem.
54	—— Nero, —— a profligate and bloody tyrant.	56	Rotterdam built.		
55	—— poisons Britannicus.			55	Paul preaches at Ephesus, and
				57	pleads at Cæsarea before Felix.
59	—— puts his mother Agrippina to death.				
60	Corbulo subdues Armenia.				ECCLESIASTICAL.
64	Nero sets Rome on fire, and accuses the Christians of the crime. —— persecutes the Christians. *Seneca*, *Lucian*, and others put to death.	61	Britain;——Queen **Boadicea** defeats the Romans under Suetonius.	64	**The First Persecution of the Christians by Nero.**
66	Nero goes to Greece. *Pliny*, the elder, author of the first *natural history*. *Quintius Curtius*, historian; *Persius*, satirist, &c. The Jewish war begins. (Vespasian.)			66	Pope Linus. The Jews at war with the Romans.

A. D. ROMAN.

66 —— Galba, ——
reigns 9 months and is put to death by

69 —— Otho, ——
—— (2 months,) defeated and killed by
—— Vitellius ——
who is defeated by the army of

70 —— Vespasian, ——
Judea subdued by Titus.
an able general and popular emperor.

73 Vespasian conquers Lycia, Rhodes, Byzantium, Samos, Thrace, and Cilicia.

77 Revolt of the Parthians.
A great plague at Rome, 10,000 dying in one day.

79 —— **Titus,** ——
(beneficent.)
Herculaneum and Pompeii destroyed by an irruption of Vesuvius.

80 **Julius Agricola,** conqueror and governor of Britain.

81 —— Domitian, ——
a cruel tyrant. *Quintillian*, orator; *Valerius Flaccus*, poet; *Martial*, epigramist.

88 Capitoline and secular games.
War with Dacia, 15 years.

95 The Christians persecuted at Rome and in the provinces.

96 Domitian put to death by Stephanus.
—— Nerva, ——
well intentioned, but enfeebled by age. *Tacitus*, historian; *Juvenal*, satirist; *Statius*, poet; *Aul. Gellius*.

98 —— **Trajan,** ——
a great sovereign and a warrior. The Roman empire in its greatest extent.
J. Severus, general in Britain.

102 Pliny, proconsul in Bithynia, sends Trajan his account of the Christians.

A.D. MISCELLANEOUS

80 Britain:—the southern parts subdued and governed by Agricola, and the Roman power established.

81 *Apollonius*, Pythagorean philosopher; *Epictetus*, Stoic: *Dio Chrysostom*, Greek rhetorician and philosopher; *Philo-Byblius*.

102 The Victories of Trajan in the East.

A.D. ECCLESIASTICAL.

66 St. Peter crucified.

67 The Jews defeated by Vespasian, and massacred by Florus.
Josephus, the Jewish historian, governor of Galilee.

67 Gamaliel.
Pope St. Clement.

70 The Destruction of Jerusalem by Titus.

77 Pope St. Cletus.

83 Pope Anacletus.
Ignatius and *Papias*, two of the fathers of the church.

95 The second Persecution of the Christians, by Domitian.
St. John writes his gospel and Apocalypse, and is banished to Patmos.

96 Pope Evaristus.

97 Timothy stoned.
St. John returns from exile.

98 Christian Assemblies prohibited by Trajan.

100 St. John dies at Ephesus, æt. 94.

A. D. ROMAN.

103 Conquest of Dacia.
106 Trajan's expedition against the Parthians.
The age of *Suetonius*, *Florus*, *Pliny*, the younger, and *Ælian*, historians.
107 Third persecution of the Christians.
114 Trajan's column erected at Rome.
115 Massacre of the Greeks and Romans by the Jews at Cyrene.
117 —— **Adrian,** —— leads an expedition into Britain.
118 —— persecutes the Christians.
126 —— goes to Asia, and Egypt for 7 years.
130 ——rebuilds Jerusalem, and erects there a temple to Jupiter.
132 ——publishes his perpetual code of laws, compiled by Salvius Julian.
The rebellion of the Jews crushed after a war of 5 years. The Jews banished from Judea; 580,000 had been destroyed in the war.
138 —— **Antoninus Pius,** —— eminent for his virtues and his love of peace.
145 —— defeats the Moors, Germans, and Dacians.
146 —— introduces the worship of Serapis at Rome.
152 —— stops the persecution of the Christians.
161 — **Marcus Aurelius,** (Antoninus)— the stoic philosopher; virtuous.
Escape of the thundering legion.
168 War with the Parthians (3 years.)
A plague over the Roman world.
169 War with the Marcomanni, in which the emperor dies of a pestilence.

A.D. MISCELLANEOUS.

103 Dacia reduced to a * Roman Province.
Plutarch, the Greek biographer.
117 Britain :—Adrian's wall (between the modern Carlisle and Newcastle) built, to prevent the Pictish incursions.
120 Asia :—Nicomedia, and other cities, destroyed by an earthquake.
128 Cæsarea, and Nicopolis, destroyed by an earthquake.
132 The Jews subdued and banished by the Romans after great slaughter.
Ptolemy, the celebrated Egyptian astronomer and geographer;
Arrian, *Appian*, *Maximus Tyrius*, and *Pausanias*, Greek historians; *Lucian*, a satirical writer; *Hermogenes*, a rhetorician of Tarsus.
The Bactrians and Indians submit to Antoninus.
169 The Marcomanni at war with Rome.
169 *Galen*, Greek physician; *Athenæus*, a gramma-

A.D. ECCLESIASTICAL.

107 Third Persecution by Trajan.
108 St. Ignatius devoured by wild beasts.
Pope Alexander I.
117 Pope Sixtus I.
118 Fourth Persecution of the Christians.
126 *Quadratus*, bishop of Athens.
127 Pope Telesphorus.
130 Heresy of Prodicus, chief of the *Adamites*.
134 Heresy of *Marcion*, who acknowledges 3 Gods.
135 Flourished in the reign of Adrian —*Polycarp* and *Aristides*, Christian fathers and writers.
142 Pope Pius I.
Heresy of Valentine.
150 Pope Anicetus.
Canon of Scripture fixed about this time.
162 Pope Soter.
167 Polycarp and Pionices, martyred in Asia.

A. D. ROMAN.

180 —— **Commodus,** ——
profligate and cruel: makes peace with the Germans.

89 The capitol, &c. of Rome destroyed by lightning.
The Romans defeated by the Saracens.
191 Rome nearly destroyed by fire.
192 Commodus assassinated by Martia and Lætus.
193 —— **Pertinax,** ——
proclaimed by the Prætorian guards: —— murdered.
—— **Septimius Severus,** ——
governs with rigour; defeats his competitors Niger and Albinus.
194 —— besieges Byzantium.
202 —— persecutes the Christians.
208 —— and his sons Caracalla and Geta go to Britain, where 50,000 Roman troops died of the plague.
211 Severus dies at York in Britain.
—— **Caracalla** and **Geta** ——
Caracalla murders Geta, and is himself assassinated.
217 —— **Macrinus,** ——
put to death by the soldiers.
218 —— **Heliogabalus,** ——
a monster of vice and cruelty.
222 —— **Alexander Severus,** ——
a beneficent and enlightened prince.
The Romans agree to pay an annual tribute to the Goths, to prevent them from molesting the empire.

226 **The Victory of Severus over the Persians at Tadmor.**
235 Severus is murdered in a mutiny of the army; succeeded by
—— **Maximinus,** ——
who defeats the Dacians and Sarmatians.
236 Maximinus assassinated by his troops near Aquilea.
—— **Balbinus** and **Gordian.** ——

A.D. MISCELLANEOUS.

rian; *Diogenes Laertius*, a Greek historian.
189 **Saracens** defeat the Romans.
Goths in Dacia.

208 Britain:—The wall of Severus between the Forth and the Clyde.
Papinian, the greatest civil lawyer of antiquity.
Julius Africanus, the chronologer.
223 PERSIA:—The new kingdom begun by **Artaxerxes**: (the dynasty of the Sassanidæ.)
226 Parthia tributary to Persia.
235 *Ammonius*, founder of a new school of Platonic philosophy at Alexandria
Dion Cassius, Greek historian.
241 The **Franks** first mentioned in history.

A.D. ECCLESIASTICAL.

171 Pope Eleatherus.
177 The Christians persecuted at Lyons.
Theophilus, *Tatian*, and *Montanus*.
185 Pope Victor I.
St. *Iræneus*.
The Catholic Church.*

197 Pope Zephyrinus.
202 Fifth persecution of the Christians under Severus.
Tertullian, an able defender of Christianity.
Clemens, of Alexandria, and *Minutius Felix* C. F.†
217 Pope Calixtus I.
The Septuagint found in a cask.

228 Pope Urban I.

234 Pope Pontianus.
235 —— Anterus.
Origen, C. F.
Sixth Persecution.

* Ency. Amer.
† Abbreviation for *Christian fathers*.

A. D	ROMAN.	A.D.	MISCELLANEOUS.	A.D.	ECCLESIASTICAL.
242	Gordian defeats the Persians under Sapor;——put to death by	242	Flourished—*Censorinus*, a critic and grammarian.		of the Christians under Maximinus.
244	—— **Philip**, (the Arabian,) —— who succeeds him and makes peace with Sapor.		Persia:—Sapor.	244	*Gregory Thaumaturgus*, and *Dionysius*, of Alexandria, C.F.
247	The Secular games restored.				
249	—— **Decius**, —— persecutes the Christians.	249	*Herodian*, Greek historian.	250	Pope St. Cornelius. Seventh Persecution of the Christians.
251	—— **Gallus**. —— A great pestilence over the empire.	251	*Plotinus*. **Odin** in Scandinavia. **Huns** on the Caspian Sea.	251	*St. Cyprian*, bishop of Carthage.
253	—— **Emilianus**. ——				
254	—— **Valerian**. ——				
258	The empire harassed by 30 tyrants successively. Alliance with Odenatus.		Confederacy of the Franks between the Rhine and Elbe. **Odenatus**, a warlike Arab chief assists the Romans against Sapor.		*Monastic life* originates about this time. Dispute between the churches of Rome and Africa about *baptism*.
260	Valerian, the emperor, is taken prisoner and flayed alive by Sapor, king of Persia. —— **Gallienus**. ——	260	Persia:—Sapor's victory over the Roman emperor. The Temple of Diana at Ephesus burnt.	259	Pope Dionysius.
				262	*Paul*, bishop of Samosatia denies the divinity of Jesus Christ.
		264	Odenatus obtains of the Romans the title of General of the East. He is succeeded by his wife **Zenobia**, who reigns at Palmyra with the titles of Augusta and queen of the East;—conquers Egypt, a part of Armenia, and Asia Minor. *Longinus* flourishes at her court.		
267	Cleodamus and Athenius defeat the Goths and Scythians.				
268	Gallienus killed at Milan. *Paulus*, a Roman poet, flourished. —— **Claudius II.** —— defeats an army of 320,000 Goths.				
270	—— **Aurelian**, —— a great warrior;—			269	Pope Felix 1.
				272	Ninth Persecution, under Aurelian.
273	—— defeats the Goths, and queen Zenobia; takes Palmyra, after meeting with an heroic resistance, and rases a part of it to the ground.	273	Zenobia is defeated at Edessa, by Aurelian, who destroys her magnificent capital and carries her to Rome.		

A. D.	ROMAN.	A.D.	MISCELLANEOUS.	A.D.	ECCLESIASTICAL.
274	The temple of the Sun at Rome burnt. Dacia given up to the barbarians.	274	Dacia possessed by the barbarians.	274	Pope Eutychianes. *Manes*, chief of the heresy of the *Manicheans*.—rejects all the sacraments; refuses allegiance to temporal sovereigns, &c.
275	Aurelian killed near Byzantium.				
	—— Tacitus, —— (a descendant of the historian) reigns with wisdom 6 months.	276	*Porphyry*, the Greek philosopher and opposer of Christianity.		
277	—— Probus, —— obtains several victories over the barbarians.	277	The Franks permitted by Probus to settle in Gaul.		
		280	The Persians defeated by Probus.		
282	—— Carus, —— is killed by lightning.			283	Pope Caius.
	——Carinus and Numerianus,—— (effeminate and cruel.)				
284	—— Dioclesian, —— sends ambassadors to China. The *Era of Dioclesian*, or of the Martyrs, begins August 29.				
286	The empire attacked by the northern barbarians, and several provinces usurped by tyrants. Maximianus, a colleague of the emperor.	286	Britain usurped by Carausius, who reigns 7 years.	286	Hierax, chief of the *Hieraxians*; says that Melchisedec was the Holy Ghost, and denies the resurrection.
290	The Gregorian and Hermogenian codes published.				
291	Division of the empire into four parts under two emperors and two Cæsars. This is the era of its decline.	291	The Franks make themselves masters of Batavi and Flanders.		
		293	The Franks expelled from Batavi.		
296	Britain recovered. Alexandria taken.	296	Britain restored to the emperor. Alexandria taken by Dioclesian. *Monks* in Syria and Egypt.		
		303	Narses, king of Persia.	303	Tenth Persecution of the Christians.
304	Dioclesian and Maximianus resign the empire to ——Constantius and Galerius.—— *Gregory* and *Hermogenes*, the lawyers; *Ælius Spartianus* and *Vopiscus*, historians; *Trebellius Pollo*, &c.			304	*Arnobius*, of Africa, C. F. converted from idolatry.

Period II.—170 *years.*

A. D.	ROMAN.	A.D.	MISCELLANEOUS.	A.D.	ECCLESIASTICAL.
306	—— CONSTANTINE the Great, —— (first Christian emperor,) succeeds his father Constantius, with three colleagues; Licinius, Maximianus, and Maxentius.			306	The Persecution of the Christians stopped by Constantine the Great.
312	Maxentius defeated and killed by Constantine.			310	Pope Eusebius.
314	Civil war with Licinius.			311	—— Malchiades.
319	Constantine favours and tolerates Christianity.			319	Toleration of Christianity, by Constantine the Great.
				320	A dreadful persecution in the East, which lasts 40 years.
321	—— appoints the observance of Sunday.				
322	—— defeats and banishes Licinius, and becomes sole emperor.				
325	—— abolishes the combats of gladiators, and assembles the first general council at Nice.			325	*The first general Council at Nice,* (from June 19 to Aug. 25,) consisting of 318 bishops, who condemn *Arianism.* In the reign of Constantine flourished, *Eusebius,* bishop of Cæsarea; C.F. and ecclesiastical historian; *Lactantius, Athanasius, Arius,* founder of a sect; *Ephraim* and *Basil,* C. F.
328	—— removes the seat of government to Constantinople, (late Byzantium,) which was solemnly dedicated on the 11th of May, 330.	333	Great famine and pestilence in Syria.		
331	Constantine orders all the heathen temples to be destroyed.				
334	Revolt of the Sarmatians.	334	300,000 Sarmatians revolt and are dispersed through the empire. Vandals in Pannonia.		
		340	*Ossian,* the Caledonian bard, supposed to have flourished about this time.	336	Pope Marcus.
337	Death of Constantine, and accession of his three sons, —Constantius, Constantine, and— —— Constans. ——		150 Greek and Asiatic cities destroyed by an earthquake.	337	—— Julius I.
340	Constantine the younger, defeated and killed by Constans, at Aquilea			341	Christianity propagated in Ethiopia by Frumentius.
350	Constans killed in Spain by Magentius.				
354	Gallus put to death by Constantius.			356	Pope Felix II.
357	Julian defeats six German kings at Strasburgh. *Eutropius* and *Marcellinus,* historians.	357	Six German kings defeated by Julian. *Jamblicus* and *Eunapius,* Gr. historians.		*St. Hilary,* C. F.; *Ælius Donatus,* bishop of Carthage, founder of a sect. *Monasteries* in
360	Julian quarrels with Constantius.				
361	Constantius dies at Tarsus. —— Julian, the Apostate, ——				

A. D. ROMAN.	A.D. MISCELLANEOUS.	A.D. ECCLESIASTICAL.
attempts in vain to rebuild the temple of Jerusalem: 365 —— is slain in a war with the Persians. *Aurelius Victor*, flourished. —— Jovian, —— concludes a disadvantageous peace with the Persians. 364 Death of Jovian, and accession of Valentinian and Valens, under whom the empire is divided into two parts, called the Eastern, and Western.		Thebais. *Corruptions of Christianity; ceremonies*, &c. Flourished in Julian's reign—*Gregory Nazianzen*, of Constantinople, C. F.—an eminent writer; *Cyril*, bishop of Jerusalem.

A. D. WESTERN EMPIRE, extending from the Caledonian ramparts to the foot of Mount Atlas.	A. D. EASTERN EMPIRE, extending from the lower Danube to the confines of Persia.
364 —— Valentinian I. —— elected by the army.	364 —— Valens. ——
375 —— Gratian, —— gains a victory over the Germans; succeeds to the Eastern Empire on the death of Valens; Maximus is proclaimed emperor; Gratian is killed at Lyons.	
	379 —— **Theodosius** the Great, —— a zealous supporter of Christianity.
383 —— Valentinian II. —— succeeds his brother Gratian; is dispossessed by Maximus, but restored by Theodosius.	388 Theodosius defeats Maximus, the tyrant of the western empire.
384 Paganism defended in the senate against St. Ambrose.	
The emperor is strangled at Vienna by Arbogastes a Gaul, the commander of the army.	

392 —— Theodosius, ——
becomes sole emperor of the East and West. Complete downfal of paganism. *Prudentius* and *Ausonius*, Latin poets, flourished.
394 Theodosius defeats Eugenius, the usurper of the West, and Arbogastes the Gaul. Final division of the Empire between the two sons of Theodosius.

395 —— Honorius. —— *Claudian*, Latin poet, flourished.	395 —— Arcadius, —— weak; governed by favourites.
403 Stillicho defeats Alaric near Pollentia.	
	408 —— Theodosius II. —— assisted in the administration by his sister Pulcheria, a princess of great genius.
410 The sack and burning of Rome by the Goths under Alaric	
412 Flourished—*Macrobius*, a Platonic philosopher.	
424 —— Valentinian III. ——	425 Theodosius establishes *public schools* and attempts the restoration of learning.
427 Pannonia recovered from the Huns.	
428 **Ætius,** the Roman general, defeated by the Franks and Goths.	
	433 A great part of Constantinople destroyed by fire.

A. D. MISCELLANEOUS.

376 HUNGARY, the ancient Pannonia, invaded by the Huns, from whom it is named.

The Goths, expelled by the Huns, are allowed by Valens to settle in Thrace.

379 The Lombards first leave Scandinavia, and defeat the Vandals.

383 The Huns ravage Mesopotamia.

392 Flourish—*Pappus* and *Theon*, of Alexandria, mathematicians; *Eunapius*, Greek historian.

399 Gainas the Goth, obtains honours from Arcadius.

The Visigoths under Alaric, in Greece.

401 Europe overrun by the Visigoths.

406 The Vandals are permitted by Honorius to settle in Spain and Gaul.

412 The Vandals begin their kingdom in Spain.

413 Burgundian kingdom begins in Alsace.

414 The Visigoths in Thoulouse.

417 The Alani defeated and extirpated by the Goths.

420 Franks:—Pharamond, their first king, on the lower Rhine.

426 Britain finally evacuated by the Romans.

428 Franks:—Clodion, king, extends his conquests to the river Somme.

Ireland, visited about this time by St Patrick, who introduces Christianity.

A. D. ECCLESIASTICAL.

373 The Bible translated into the Gothic language.

379 The prerogatives of the Roman see much enlarged.

381 The second general Council of Constantinople.

384 Symachus pleads in the Roman senate for Paganism, against St. Ambrose.

385 Pope Syricius.

392 Flourish—*St. Chrysostom*, patriarch of Constantinople; *St. Ambrose*, archbishop of Milan; *St. Jerome*, *St. Martin*, and *St. Augustine*, Christian fathers.

Image worship; the Christian *hierarchy* begins.

401 Pope Innocent I.

412 Flourish—*Cyril*, bishop of Alexandria; *Isidore* and *Socrates*, ecclesiastical historians; *Orosius*, a Spanish disciple of St. Augustine; and *Pelagius*, a British monk, who denies the existence of original sin, and the necessity of the grace of God.

416 The Pelagian "heresy" condemned by the African bishops.

417 Pope Zozimus.

418 —— Boniface I.

422 Pope Celestinus.

429 *Nestorius*, bishop of Constantinople, acknowledges two persons in Jesus Christ.

431 Third general Council at Ephesus.

432 Pope Sixtus III.

A. D. WESTERN EMPIRE.

437 Ætius defeats the Goths.

439 The coast of Italy plundered by Genseric, the Vandal.

441 The Roman territories invaded by the Huns, Persians, and Saracens.

443 The Manichæan books burned at Rome.

445 The famous embassy from Britain, soliciting aid against the Picts.

448 The emperor engages to pay a heavy tribute to Attila, king of the Huns.

451 Ætius defeats the Huns.

452 Valentinian is assassinated by

454 —— Petronius Maximus. ——

—— Avitus. ——

Genseric, the Vandal, plunders Rome.

457 —— Majorian. ——

461 —— Severus. ——

467 —— Athemius. ——

(The three last emperors all slain by Ricimer.)

472 —— Olybrius. ——

473 —— Glucerius. ——

474 —— Julius Nepos. ——

475 —— Augustus Romulus. ——

476 Rome taken by Odoacer, king of the Herulii.

End of the Western Empire, 1228 years after the building of Rome: and commencement of the kingdom of Italy under Odoacer. (See Miscellaneous column.)

A. D. EASTERN EMPIRE.

435 The *Theodosian Code* published.

439 The empress Eudocia retires to Jerusalem.

450 —— Marcian, ——

a Thracian, possessed of some abilities; —refuses to pay the annual tribute which had been promised by his predecessor to Attila, king of the Huns.

457 —— Leo I. the Thracian, ——

(the first emperor crowned by the patriarch.)

War with the Goths.

561 Peace with the Goths; Theodric (afterwards king of Italy) is received from them as a hostage.

474 —— Zeno. ——

A turbulent reign, marked with debaucheries and conspiracies.

The Middle, or Dark Ages,

A. D. MISCELLANEOUS.

439 The kingdom of the Vandals in Africa, under **Genseric,** who takes Carthage, and plunders Italy.

445 Britain:—The unsuccessful embassy to Rome for aid against the Picts and Scots.

448 The Franks:—Merovæus, king—1st of the Merovingians.

450 Flourish—*Zozimus* and *Olympiodorus,* Greek historians.

451 The arrival of the Saxons in Britain, under **Hengist** and **Horsa.**

452 The city of Venice beco es known about this time.

454 The Vandals occupy Sicily.

Britain:—The Saxons begin their conquest of Britain.

458 The Franks:—Childeric I. king.

468 Spain:—The Visigoths under Eric establish their kingdom, and expel the Romans.

472 Great eruption of Vesuvius; seen at Constantinople.

476 **Odoacer,** king of the Herulii takes Rome and establishes the kingdom of ITALY.

477 The Alains are conquered in Lusitania, (afterwards Portugal,) by the Visigoths.

A. D. ECCLESIASTICAL.

435 *Nestorianism* prevails in the East.

The Christians persecuted by the Vandals.

440 Pope Leo I. (the Great.)

445 Flavian, patriarch of Constantinople.

447 *Eutyches;* asserts the existence of only one nature in Jesus Christ.

449 Ibus, bishop of Edessa, and Eusebius, bishop of Doryleum, deposed.

450 Flourish—*Sozomen* and *Theodoret,* Ecclesiastical historians; *St. Patrick,* the apostle of Ireland.

451 The fourth general Council at Chalcedon, in which Eutychianism and Nestorianism are solemnly condemned.

457 Persecution by the Vandals in Africa under Genseric.

461 Pope Hilarius.

468 —— Simplicius.

are dated from this Period.

Period

A. D. FRANCE AND SPAIN.

[N. B. All relating to Spain, has an S, or Sp., prefixed.]

481 **Clovis I.** generally considered the founder of the French monarchy, after
485 gaining the battle of Soissons over the Romans. (See 420, A. D.)

491 —— subdues Thuringia.
496 —— is baptized, with 3000 of his subjects, and Christianity is introduced into France.
499 —— concludes an alliance with Theodric in Italy.
500 Burgundy becomes tributary to Clovis.
501 The Burgundian laws published.
507 Clovis defeats and kills Alaric near Poictiers.
510 —— makes Paris his capital.

511 —— **Childebert I.** ——

516 The Christian Era adopted.

532 The kingdom of Burgundy conquered by Childebert.

536 Vitiges, king of the Ostrogoths, surrenders his possessions in Gaul to the French king.

551 The *silk manufacture* introduced from India by the monks.

A. D. EASTERN EMPIRE.

480 An earthquake which lasts 40 days, and destroys the greater part of Constantinople.
481 Zeno makes Theodric general and consul.

491 —— **Anastasius I.** ——

The Green and Blue factions.

The emperor's persecution of the Catholics, and protection of the Manichaeans, occasions a rebellion headed by Vitalianus.

502 The empire ravaged, and the imperial army destroyed by Carbades, king of Persia.

511 A great insurrection in Constantinople.
514 Constantinople besieged by Vitalianus, whose fleet is consumed by the burning mirror of Proclus.

518 Anastasius killed by lightning.

—— **Justin I.** ——

a peasant of Dalmatia.

527 —— **Justinian I.** ——

celebrated for his code of laws, and for the victories of his generals, Belisarius and Narses.

529 **Belisarius** defeats the Persians under Chosroes;
532 —— quells a conspiracy at Constantinople;
534 —— defeats the Vandals in Africa, and ends their kingdom;
535 —— subdues Sicily;

536 —— takes Naples;
537 —— and Rome;
—— defeats the Ostrogoths in Italy;
538 —— the Huns in Thrace:
540 —— and Vitiges at Ravenna.

North Africa, Corsica, and Sardinia, annexed to the empire of the east.

Flourished in this reign—*Proclus*, a learned Platonist.

III.—146 Years.

A. D. MISCELLANEOUS.

484 Huneric, king of the African Vandals.

487 Britain:—The Saxons defeated by prince **Arthur** and Ambrosius.

490 Italy ravaged by the Burgundians.

493 —— conquered by **Theodric**, king of the Ostrogoths.

Odoacer put to death.

499 Thrace ravaged by the Bulgarians.

502 Carbades, king of Persia, invades the Eastern Empire.

507 Alaric defeated and killed by Clovis.

512 The Herulii settle in Thrace.

513 *Boethius*, the Roman poet and philosopher, flourished.

517 Getæ ravages Illyricum, Macedonia, &c.

519 Britain:—Prince Arthur defeated at Charford by Cerdic, who begins the 3d Saxon kingdom, Wessex.

525 Antioch destroyed by fire.

529 **Chosroes II.**, the Great, king of Persia:—defeated by Belisarius,

532 and makes peace with the emperor.

534 **The Defeat of the Vandals in Africa, by Belisarius, and end of their kingdom.**

Carthage taken by Belisarius.

537 **Italy conquered** by Belisarius.

539 —— distressed with war, famine, and pestilence.

—— The city of Milan razed by the Goths.

542 Britain:—Prince Arthur murdered in Cornwall.

550 POLAND, a dukedom, takes its name under Lechus, its first legislator.

A. D. ECCLESIASTICAL.

483 Pope Felix III.

484 Christianity persecuted by Huneric, king of the Vandals.

494 The Roman pontiff asserts his supremacy.

503 The Pope resists the legal magistrate.

504 The Christians persecuted in Africa by the Vandals.

513 Christianity embraced by the Persian king, Carbades.

516 The computation of time by the Christian Era, introduced first by Dionysius.

519 The orthodox bishops restored by Justin.

525 The Arian Bishops deposed.

Pope John I.

526 —— Felix IV.

529 The order of the Benedictine monks instituted at Mount Cassino.

530 Pope Boniface II.

533 —— John II.

535 —— Agapetus.

536 —— Sylvester I.

538 —— Vigilius.

540 The *Monothelites*, who acknowledge only one will in Jesus Christ.

Period

A. D. ENGLAND.

827 The seven kingdoms of the Heptarchy united by Egbert, king of Wessex, into one, under the name of
ENGLAND, or the Land of the Angles.
—— **Egbert I. king.** ——
Invasion of the Danes.
838 —— **Ethelwolf,** ——
a weak prince.
Scotland:—Kenneth, king of Scots defeats and extirpates the Picts, and becomes the sole monarch of Scotland.
The Danes return, ravage England unmolested, and burn the city of London.
Ethelwolf makes a pilgrimage to Rome.

857 —— **Ethelbald** and **Ethelbert,** ——
(sons of the last) reign jointly:—increase the influence of the clergy: succeeded by their brother,
866 —— **Ethelred.** ——
867 The Danes conquer Northumberland.
872 —— ALFRED the Great, ——
defeats the Danes near Wilton.—
879 —— is abandoned by his subjects, and obliged to retire to the Isle of Athelney

A. D. GERMANY, FRANCE, AND SPAIN.

800 **New Empire of the West,** founded by
—— CHARLEMAGNE, ——
who is crowned by the pope at Rome, sovereign of Italy, Germany, and France.
802 —— receives an embassy from Nicephorus, and from Haroun Al Raschid.

814 Western Empire, **Louis I.,** (Debonaire,) an inglorious and turbulent reign.

840 —— —— **Lothario,** emperor. ——
841 —— —— defeated by his brothers. Louis and Charles, in the battle of Fontenoy.
Division of the Empire.
Germany:—**Louis I.** surnamed the German.
Italy:—**Lothario,** with the Imperial dignity.
France:—**Charles I.** the Bald.
—— The Normans sail up the Seine, plunder Rouen, and advance to Paris.
845 —— plunder Hamburgh and penetrate into Germany.
855 Lothario retires to a monastery and dies.
New division of the empire at Mersen;
Louis II. has Italy with the imperial dignity;
—— establishes his court at Pavia.
858 France invaded by Louis the German, who is finally compelled to retire.

868 Lorrain annexed to France.
875 Charles the Bald obtains the imperial crown on the death of Louis II.
877 Germany and France:—**Louis II.** the Stammerer, sovereign of both kingdoms.

V.—266 Years.

EASTERN EMPIRE.	A. D.	MISCELLANEOUS.	A.D.	ECCLESIASTICAL.
	801	DENMARK, becomes a kingdom under Gotricus.		
802 — Nicephorus emperor. —	802	Haroun al Raschid, courts the alliance of Charlemagne with a present of a striking clock.		
811 — Michael I. (Caropaltes.) — at war with the Bulgari.				
813 — Leo V. — (the Armenian.)	813	Al Mamun caliph; a patron of learning.	813	Insurrection at Rome against the pope.
816 Earthquakes, famine, fire &c. ravage the Empire.			816	Pope Stephen III.
			817	Paschal I. The college of cardinals founded.
821 — Michael II. — (Balbus, or the Stammerer.)	823	The Saracens obtain possession of Crete. (naming it Candia,) and	824	Pope Eugene II.
822 Constantinople besieged by the Saracens, and the Bulgarians raise the siege.	827	—— of Sicily, Calabria &c.	827	—— Valentine.
	828	St. Mark's Church at Venice, built.	828	—— Gregory IV. Missionaries sent from France to Sweden.
829 — Theophilus.—				
842 — Michael III.— the Drunkard.			844	Sergius III.* Ignatius, patriarch of Constantinople.
	846	The Saracens destroy the Venetian fleet, and besiege Rome, but	847	Pope Leo IV.
	849	are defeated by the pope's allies.	851	—— John.
	850	Christianity propagated by Auscharius in Denmark, and Sweden.		
851 — Bazil I. — the Macedonian, defeats the Saracens.	851	Sardinia and Corsica ravaged by the Saracens.	858	—— Nicholas I. 1st coronation of a pope.
			859	Eulogius, archbishop of Cordova, martyred.
	856	The coasts of Holland plundered by the Normans.	860	The schism of the Greeks begins.
	862	RUSSIA:—the monarchy supposed to have been founded by Ruric, who builds the city of Lagoda.	869	Pope Adrian II. 8th Council at Constantinople; — *Photius*, the learned patriarch of Constantinople is deposed.
872 *Clocks* brought to Constantinople from Venice.	868	Egypt, throws off its dependence on the caliphs, under Ahmed.		

A. D. ENGLAND.

in the habit of a shepherd, but soon throws off his disguise, assembles a few friends, gains a complete victory over the Danes, expels a part of them from England; and permits the rest to settle in Northumberland on their consenting to embrace christianity.

886 —— founds the *University of Oxford.*
—— establishes a regular *militia and navy*, and the mode of *trial by jury*.

890 —— divides England into shires and counties, and completes his *code of laws*.

891 Another invasion by the Danes.
The first land tax.
Alfred encourages learning, navigation, and commerce; institutes *fairs and markets*, and invents *lanterns*.
Johannes Scotus Erigena, a learned philosophical writer.

901 —— Edward (the Elder.) ——
a prince of martial genius.
War with the Danes continued.

925 —— Athelstan. ——

938 defeats the Scots, Welsh, and Danes in a great battle.
To encourage commerce, he enacts, that any person who shall make two foreign voyages on his own account,

A. D. GERMANY, FRANCE, AND SPAIN.

879 ——Louis III. and Carloman, reign jointly.

881 —— defeat the Normans in a great battle.

884 —— Charles II. the Fat. ——

885 France:—Paris besieged by the Normans, and gallantly defended by bishop Goslin.

886 —— Charles, makes a disgraceful peace with the Normans

887 Germany:—Arnold, emperor. The imperial dignity transferred from France to Germany.

888 France:—Eudes or Eudo, king, (descended from a brother of Charles Martel.)

890 Arnold, Emperor of Germany, takes Rome.

898 France:—Charles III. (the Simple.)

899 Germany:—Louis III. 7 years of age. Invasion of the Hungarians. Contests between the nobles and the bishops.
France:—Hereditary counts and dukes.
Eginhard, the first German historian, and secretary of Charlemagne, flourished in this century.

901 Civil wars in France and Normandy.

905 The Normans make an incursion into France, and

912 establish themselves in Normandy.
Germany:—Conrad I. (The empire becomes *elective*.)

914 —— defeats the Hungarians.
Spain:—Ordogno II, king of Oviedo, transfers the seat of his kingdom to Leon.

919 Germany:—Henry I.(the Fowler.) First of the Saxon line, an able sovereign conquers the neighbouring nations.

921 France:—Robert I. ——
is defeated and killed by his brother Charles at Soissons.

923 —— Rodolph, ——
duke of Burgundy, elected king.

936 Germany:—Otho I. (the Great,) the most powerful sovereign of the age.
France:—Louis IV. (the Stranger.) so called, because he had resided 13 years in England.

A.D. EASTERN EMPIRE.	A.D. MISCELLANEOUS.	A.D. POPES, &c.
		882 Marinus. 884 Adrian III. 885 Stephen VI.
886 — Leo V. — (the philosopher.)	886 The Scythians seize Croatia. The Faroe isles, and Iceland, discovered in this century.	
897 War with the Bulgarians, the Lombards and the Saracens. The latter take the island of Samos.	899 The Hungarians ravage Lombardy.	891 Formosus. 896 Stephen VII. 898 John IX. Veneration of *saints*, and a passion for *relics* prevail.
910 Constantine VII associates his four sons,	901 Republics of VENICE and GENOA, founded about this time. 908 The dynasty of the Fatimides, a Mahometan sect, in Egypt.	904 Sergius III.
	912. The Normans under Rollo established in the Province of Neustria, which is named Normandy.	914 John X.
914 so that there are five emperors at once. 917 Constantinople besieged by the Bulgarians.	Rollo married to the daughter of Charles the Simple, king of France.	
919 — Romanus I. — general of the fleet, usurps the empire with his three sons.	930 Denmark:—Harold VI. the first Christian king. 932 Arnolf of Bavaria, defeated near Verona, by Hugh of Italy. 936 The Saracen empire divided into seven kingdoms.	929 Stephen VIII. 931 John XI.

A. D. ENGLAND.

shall be admitted to the rank of *thane* or *gentleman*.

940 —— Edmund, ——

brother of Athelstan.

946 ——assassinated at a feast by Leolph, a robber.

—— Edred, ——

governed by **Dunstan,** abbot of Glastonbury, who introduces rigid monastic rules.

955 —— Edwy, ——

insulted by Dunstan, and deposed.

959 —— Edgar, ——

—— licentious:—marries the beautiful Elfrida, after the violent death of Athelwold, her lover.

The power of the *Monks* very great.

St. Dunstan, created Archbishop of Canterbury.

Wolves expelled from England and Wales, in consequence of a reward being offered for the purpose by the king.

975 —— Edward (the Martyr.) ——

murdered by his step mother Elfrida.

978 —— Ethelred II. ——

indolent and incapable.

985 Invasion of the Danes under Sweyn.

1002 Great massacre of the Danes throughout England, by order of Ethelred.

1004 Scotland:—Malcolm II.

A. D. GERMANY, FRANCE, AND SPAIN.

941 The figures of *Arithmetic* brought into Europe by the Saracens.

946 Louis is defeated near Rouen, by Hugh the Great, and Richard I. duke of Normandy.

950 Germany;—Bohemia becomes tributary to Otho.

953 —— The Hungarians subdued.

954 France:—Lothaire I. king; confers the dukedoms of Burgundy and Aquitaine on Hugh the Great.

957 Germany:—Otho defeats the Sclavonians in Saxony, and

960 —— marches against the Vandals.

964 Germany:—Italy again united to the empire by Otho.

969 —— Otho expels the Saracens from Italy.

—— is crowned by the pope with the titles of Cæsar and Augustus.

973 —— Otho II. ——

subdues the Bohemians,

979 —— at war with Lothaire.

983 —— Otho III. (3 years of age.) ——

986 France;—Louis V. (the Slothful.) last of the Carlovingians.

988 —— **Hugh Capet,** founder of the 3d or Capetian line of French kings.

996 France:—Robert II. (the Wise.) succeeds his father, Hugh.

998 —— is excommunicated by the pope, for marrying his cousin Bertha.

Spain:—Division of the Mahometan kingdom of Cordova.

1000 —— Sancho III. the Great, king of Navarre, takes the title of emperor.

1002 Germany:—Henry II. (duke of Bavaria,) defeats his rivals, Herman, duke of Suabia, and Ardoin, marquis of Ivrea.

A.D.	EASTERN EMPIRE.	A.D.	MISCELLANEOUS.	A. D.	POPES, &c.
937	Romanus gains a naval victory over the Russians.				
942	Naples annexed to the empire.	942	Naples seized by the Eastern emperor.	946	Agapetus.
945	The empress Helen usurps the throne.				
				956	John XII.
				963	—— is deposed for his crimes, and two popes are elected, one by the council, the other by the inhabitants of Rome.
		958	War between the Normans and Saracens in Italy.		
959	Romanus II.—poisoned by his wife, Theophano, 963.	959	Italy pillaged by Berenger.		
		961	Candia recovered from the Saracens.		
963	Nicephorus.—(Phocas) emperor.	964	Italy again united to the empire of Germany.	965	John XIII.
			—— Tuscany becomes a dukedom.		
967	—— recovers Cyprus and Antioch from the Saracens. —— murdered by	969	The Saracens expelled from Italy by Otho.		
		971	The Russians, Bulgarians &c. defeated on the Danube and the Tigris, by Bardas, the general of the emperor John Zimisces.	972	Benedict VI.
969	John Zimisces. Victories over the Russians and Saracens.			975	Benedict VII.
975	Basil, and Constantine VIII.	983	Venice distracted by violent commotions.	984	John XIV.
		985	Sweyn I. or Sueno, king of Denmark, invades England.	986	—— XV.
980	—— recover Apulia and Calabria, and unite Bulgaria to the empire.			993	First instance of a solemn *canonization*.
				996	Gregory V.
		997	Hungary erected into a kingdom. St. Stephen its first king and legislator.		
				999	Sylvester II. Stephen king of Hungary, embraces Christianity.
1000	Bazil drives the Bulgarians from Thessaly.	1000	Savoy, independent, under Beroald its first count. Poland erected into a kingdom by the emperor Otho III. —— Boleslas I., king.	1003	John XVII.
			Luitprand and *Anastasius*, historians of this century. *Avicenna*, the Arabian physician and philosopher.		
			A fearful expectation of the day of judgment prevails at the close of this century.		
		1002	*PAPER* made of cotton rags—(of linen in 1300.)		

A. D. ENGLAND.

1096 Robert, duke of Normandy, full of the chivalrous spirit of the age, mortgages his dukedom to his brother, the king of England, and joins the multitude in quest of danger and glory in the Crusades.

1097 The king quarrels with Anselm, archbishop of Canterbury, and confiscates his estates, thus incurring the thunders of the pope. Incursions and plunders of the Welch. Robert Mowbray, the powerful earl of Northumberland, is imprisoned for a rebellion. Scotland :—Edgar, nephew of the Atheling, elected king in place of Donald Bane, who is deposed.

1100 William II. is accidentally shot with an arrow in New Forest, by Sir Walter Tyrrel, a Frenchman. He was destitute of the few virtues of his father, and inherited all his vices. Perfidy, tyranny, and cruelty, were the chief ingredients of his character. *Anselm*, the successor of Langfranc, and *Eadmer*, bishop of St. Andrews, an historian.

— Henry I. (Beauclerc, or Scholar ;) — younger brother of William Rufus, crowned in place of Robert, now in Palestine; courts popularity by granting a *charter of liberties*, restoring the *Anglo-Saxon laws*, &c.; reinstates Anselm, as archbishop of Canterbury; marries Matilda, daughter of Malcolm, king of Scotland, and niece of Edgar Atheling, thus uniting the Norman and Saxon interests.

SCOTLAND.
Edgar, d. 1116.
Alexander I, 1124.
David, 1158.

1101 Robert returns, and invades England, as to him of right belonging. An accommodation through the mediation of Anselm; Robert renouncing England for a pension of 3,000 marks, and Henry's castles in Normandy.

1106 Not yet satisfied, Henry invades Normandy, defeats Robert, carries him prisoner to England, and confines him for life in Cardiff-castle.

1110 — defeats the French, who had assisted Robert's son, near Audeley.
His only son William, who had accompanied him to Normandy, is shipwrecked, and perishes, with all his retinue.

A.D.	FRANCE & SPAIN.	A. D.	MISCELLANEOUS.	A. D.	POPES, &c.
			proposition for a general arming against the infidels in the Holy Land, with the unanimous shout "It is the will of God."		
		1096	Peter begins his march at the head of a motley multitude of all ranks and nations, followed soon after by a host of 700,000, led by **Godfrey,** of Bouillon; **Baldwin,** his brother, count of Flanders; **Robert,** duke of Normandy; **Hugh,** count of Vermandois; **Raymond,** count of Toulouse; **Bohemond,** prince of Tarentum; and **Stephen,** Count of Blois.		
			Naples and Sicily taken by the emperor of Germany.		
		1097	Crusaders in Constantinople; they alarm the emperor Alexius by their formidable numbers;—cross into Asia;—take the city of Nice, and twice defeat the Saracens.		
		1098	—— take Antioch, and		
		1099	Jerusalem, and elect Godfrey king of the Christian Empire in Asia.		
1100	*William*, of Poitou, a poet, (the first *troubadour*,) flourished.		*Knights of St. John* instituted. *Anna Commena*, (daughter of Alexius I., eastern emperor,) historian.	1099	Pascal II.
1108	Louis VI. (the Fat,) an able and useful sovereign.				
1109	War against England.				
	Spain:—the Spaniards defeated by Joseph, k. of Morocco, in the "battle of the seven counts," near Badajos.	1102	Baldwin, defeats the Mussulmen near Joppa.		
			William duke of Aquitaine, goes to Palestine with a great army.		
		1103	William's army is massacred at Constantinople.		
	Abelard, the celebrated French scholastic.	1104	Baldwin reduces Ptolemais or Acre.	1105	Council of Mentz.
		1106	Germany:—Death of Henry IV. (He is said to have been present at 66 battles.)		
1119	Battle of Brenneville: the French defeated by the English. Louis corrects the licentiousness of the nobles; establishes the	1111	—Henry V. succeeds:—marries Matilda, daughter of Henry I. of England. —— maintaining the right of investiture, he enters Italy, with a large army, and takes the pope prisoner.	1118	Gelasius II.
		1118.	Eastern Empire:—John Commenus, emperor; able and virtuous.		
			Knights Templars instituted.		

A. D. ENGLAND.

1127 **Matilda, the king's daughter, married to Geoffrey Plantagenet, son of the count of Anjou;—(issue a son, afterwards Henry II.)**

1135 **Henry I. dies. He was accomplished, and brave, but cruel, avaricious, and licentious. *Public* buildings. *Monasteries.* Literature made some progress. *Stealing* and *false coining* punished with *death.***

A *charter* was granted to the city of London in this reign.

—— **Stephen,** (earl of Blois,) ——

grandson of William the Conqueror, usurps the throne in violation of the rights of the heiress Matilda, daughter of Henry I.

1136 **—— grants exorbitant privileges to the nobility and clergy, while great distress prevails among the lower classes.**

David, king of Scotland, invades England in favour of Matilda.

1138 **—— is defeated in the "battle of the Standard," by Thurstan, archbishop of York, and makes peace.**

1139 **Matilda lands in Suffolk; is joined by several barons.**

England is desolated by a civil war.

1141 **Stephen defeated in the battle of Lincoln, taken prisoner, and confined by the earl of Gloucester, in behalf of Matilda.**

1148 Matilda acknowledged queen; but exasperating the people by her haughty conduct, she is driven from London, and after a series of hostilities, returns to Normandy. Henry, her son, invades England, but retires, on having the succession secured to himself.

The clergy and nobility now assume the government in reality, although it is nominally restored to Stephen; and they effectually establish their power by building 1100 *castles*, in which the owners live as *independent princes.*

1154 Stephen dies. London now contains 40,000 inhabitants. The *Saxon* language begins about this time to assume the form of the present *English.*

Flourished in this reign;—*William of Malmesbury,* and *Geoffrey of Monmouth,* historians.—Nicholas Brekespere, who became Pope Adrian IV.

—— Henry II, (First of the family of Plantagenet.) ——

popular and powerful; (his continental dominions are equal to nearly one third of the French monarchy.)—dismisses the foreign mercenaries and demolishes the fortified castles of the barons.—

SCOTLAND.

Malcolm IV. 1163.

William. 1165.

1158 **Thomas a Becket** is introduced to the king's notice by Theobald archbishop of Canterbury. (He was a well educated private citizen; had travelled abroad, and acquired great influence.) He is created chancellor of the realm and preceptor of the prince; lives in extraordinary magnificence; has 1000 *knights* among his vassals.

A.D. FRANCE & SPAIN.

Commons or 3d branch of the legislature: enfranchises the *villains* or *bondmen*, and regulates the *courts of justice*.

1137 **Louis VII.** (le Jeune,) quarrels with the pope: the kingdom put under an interdict.

1147 Louis engages in the second crusade, to atone for having set on fire the town of Vitri, (in which 13,000 persons were burnt.)

1149 —— divorcing his queen Eleanor, who marries Henry Plantagenet, heir of England.

A. D. MISCELLANEOUS.

1119 Baldwin defeats the Turks at Antioch.

1125 Germany:—**Lothaire II.** is opposed by Conrad, of Franconia, and the duke of Suabia.

1132 —— marches into Italy and establishes Innocent II. in the papal chair.

—— introduces the Roman code of laws.

1137 *Pandects of the Roman law*, (Justinian,) discovered at Amalfi.

1138 Germany:—**Conrad III.** (first of the 4th or **Suabian** line.)

1139 Portugal becomes a kingdom under **Alphonso I.** of the house of Burgundy, who defeats 5 Saracen kings.

1141 Germany and Italy:—Dissensions between the *Guelphs* and *Ghibellines*, (or the enemies and adherents of the emperor,) commence.

1143 Eastern Empire:—**Manuel Commenus.**

1147 Second Crusade, excited by *St. Bernard*, and joined by the emperor Conrad III. and his nephew Frederick Barbarossa.

1148 Crusaders repulsed at Damascus, and return.

1150 The *magnetic needle* known in Italy.

1151 The *Canon Law*, collected and digested by the monk *Gratian*.

Peter Lombard, an Italian writer.

1152 Germany:—**Frederick I.** (Barbarossa.)

Denmark becomes a fief of the empire.

1154 Damascus is taken by Nouraddin.

1156 Russia:—The city of Moscow founded.

1157 Baldwin defeats Nouraddin.

Finland conquered by the Swedes.

1158 Germany:—The emperor Frederick, receives the title of king of Bohemia, at the diet of Ratisbon:—conquers Poland and makes i tributary.

A. D. POPES, &c.

1119 Calixtus II.

1124 Honorius II.

1127 —— makes war against Roger, king of Sicily.

Scholastic Theology in vogue; *Abelard*, a teacher of it.

1130 Innocent II.

Schism of Anacletus.

1137 A pretended Messiah in France.

1138 Another in Persia.

1139 Tenth general council.

1143 Ecclesiastical State:—a Senate created and entrusted with the civil administration.

1144 Lucius II.

1145 Eugenius III.

1147 Second crusade.

1153 Anastasius IV.

1154 Adrian IV.

1155 *Arnold* of *Brescia*, Abelard's disciple, condemned and burnt.

A. D. ENGLAND.

1159 He is sent as ambassador to France, and,

1161 —— raised to the See of Canterbury, and the office of *metropolitan*; he now changes his mode of living, affecting rigid austerity, and performing various acts of penance. The king meanwhile had resolved to do away the abuses of the church,—and reform the corrupted character of the ecclesiastics, who, in this age were habitually guilty of the greatest crimes. Becket opposes his proceedings, maintaining that the clergy are not amenable to any civil authority.

1164 Council at Clarendon consisting of the primate, prelates, and nobility, (summoned by the king) in whose decisions, called the *Constitutions of Clarendon*, the line is distinctly drawn between the *civil* and *ecclesiastical jurisdictions*. The pope annuls the constitutions; and Becket repenting his assent retires to France, after being prosecuted and fined by the king for contempt of his authority.

1170 The king dreading the thunders of the pope permits Becket to return.

The prelate again becomes insolent; excommunicates the king's ministers; and is murdered at his own altar, Dec. 29th, by four knights of the royal household.

1171 The king, in order to avert the papal wrath, submits to a scourging by the monks.

An invasion of Ireland had been made in 1169 by Richard, earl of Pembroke, who had reduced Waterford and Dublin.

1172 King Henry now leads an expedition there in person, and meeting with little opposition effects the entire Conquest of Ireland.

1173 Rebellion of the king's sons, Henry, Richard, and Geoffrey, assisted by the kings of France and Scotland.

1174 The king performs *penance* at the tomb of Becket, who is canonized and revered as the most virtuous of saints. The same day the Scots are defeated near Alnwick castle and their king William taken prisoner.—The rebel princes defeated at Rouen, and make peace. The captive William acknowledges Scotland to be a fief of the crown of England. King Henry gives to the Christians of Jerusalem the sum of 50,000 marks.

1188 Henry II. dies. He was an able and useful, but licentious monarch. His death was hastened by grief for the loss of two of his sons, Henry and Geoffrey. They had died while engaged in their rebellion, which was encouraged by their mother Eleanora, on account of the king's intrigue with the fair Rosamond. Two princes, Richard and John, survive.—Foreign literature and improvements in the *arts* are introduced.

Flourished—*John of Salisbury*, *William Little*, and *Henry* of *Huntington*, historians.

ENGLAND	SCOTLAND.
1189 —— Richard I. (Cœur de Lion.) 2d. Plantagenet. —— after unjustly persecuting and plundering the Jews, to obtain money, sets out on the third Crusade, in company with Philip Augustus, king of France, with whom he quarrels on arriving at Messina in Sicily.—Leaving Sicily with a fleet of 53 galleys, he conquers Cyprus; marries Berrengaria daughter of Sancho king of Navarre,—assists the French in the reduction of Acre, a place of great strength; and again excites the jealousy of Philip who returns home.	William I.

A.D.	FRANCE & SPAIN.	A. D.	MISCELLANEOUS.	A. D.	POPES, &c.
1157	Castile and Leon divided under Ferdinand II. and Sancho II.	1158	*Bank* of Venice established. *Fairs* at Leipsic.	1159	Alexander III.
		1162	The emperor Frederick destroys Milan, but preserves the churches.	1160	The *Waldenses* & *Albigenses* begin to appear.
		1163	Raymond (the 2d.) defeated by Nouraddin.		
		1164	The emperor Frederick appoints the first king of Sardinia.	1164	Quarrel between *Henry II. and Becket.*
		1171	Island of Chio is taken by the Venetians End of the Fatimite dynasty in Egypt.	1171	The monastic order of the *Carmelites,* instituted.
		1173	Catania destroyed by an earthquake.		
		1176	The emperor Frederick is defeated by the Milanese, and his fleet by the Venetians.		
			—— Origin of the Venitian ceremony of *wedding the Adriatic.*		
		1177	**Saladin,** nephew of the sultan of Egypt, begins his war against the Christians, and is defeated by Baldwin before Jerusalem.	1178	Eleventh general council against the Albigenses.
1180	**Philip II.** (Augustus,) politic, powerful, and prosperous; confiscates the property of the Jews, and banishes them.	1180	Portugal:—Sancho 1.		
		1181	Eastern Emperor:—Alexius II. Saladin takes Damascus.		
		1183	The inhabitants of Berry massacre 7000 Albigenses.	1183	Lucius III.
			Eastern Empire: Andronicus II.		
		1184	—murders the Latins in Constantinople Isaac Angelus, emperor. —	1185	Urban III.
	Abenezra, a poet, philologist, &c.	1187	Saladin takes Jerusalem, and ends the kingdom of the Crusaders.		
		1188	Third Crusade, agreed upon at the *diet of Mayence* on account of the success of Saladin.		
1189	Philip engages with Richard, king of England in the 3d Crusade.		*Aagesend,* a Danish historian.		
		1190	The emperor Frederick undertakes an expedition to the Holy Land; crosses the Hellespont with a great army; defeats the Turks in several battles; subdues Cilicia; and dies in consequence of bathing in the cold river Cydnus.	1190	The power of granting *Indulgences* to commit crimes for certain sums of money, first assumed by the pope.

A. D. ENGLAND.

1192 Richard defeats Saladin in a great battle, and advances in sight of Jerusalem; but abandoned by his associates, he concludes a truce with Saladin for 3 years.

1193 Returning home through Germany in disguise, Richard is imprisoned by Leopold, duke of Austria, whom he had insulted at Acre. John, the king's brother, endeavours to protract his confinement, and assumes the government.

Richard, after being sold to the emperor, Henry VI., and lodged in chains, is at length ransomed by his subjects for 10,000 marks, returns to England and is joyfully received.

Richard declares war against France; defeats Philip near the river Epte. Riots in London caused by unjust taxes.

1199 Richard is wounded by Vidomar, viscount of Limoges, of whom he had demanded a concealed treasure; dies, and is buried at Fontebrand. His military talents were the most shining part of his character, which has figured, however, in song and romance.

In this age, the *Jews* are the principal *bankers* in all Christian countries; and though spurned and persecuted as the offscouring of the earth, they amassed immense treasures and exacted *usury* from the nobility and from monarchs.

1200 —— John (Lackland) 3d Plantagenet. ——

(The succession belongs to young Arthur, duke of Bretagne, son of Geoffrey, the second brother of John. He is supported by the king of France, but is unfortunately taken prisoner, and inhumanly murdered by his uncle John in the castle of Rouen.)

1205 The king's foreign dominions adjudged forfeited to France, and successively subdued by Philip Augustus. John universally despised; quarrels with the clergy; opposes the election of the arch-bishop of Canterbury by the pope.

1207 The kingdom laid under an *interdict* by the pope. By this sentence religious rites, marriage, mass, and the burial of the dead are suspended.

1213 The pope denounces John as a usurper and commissions the king of France to depose him and take possession of England.

May 13. The king is visited at Dover, by Pandolph the pope's legate, who induces him to resign his dominions to Innocent and his successors, and to hold them as a *vassal of the papal see* for the annual sum of 1000 marks. John then surrenders his crown which is trampled upon by the haughty ambassador, and returned.

1214 War with Philip is continued. John and his allies, the emperor of Germany, and the earl of Flanders, are defeated by the French at Bouvines.

A. D.	FRANCE & SPAIN.	A. D.	MISCELLANEOUS.	A. D.	POPES, &c.
		1190	—— Germany:—**Henry VI.** succeeds Frederick.		
			Teutonic Knights are instituted at Acre,		
		1191	Acre is taken by the Crusaders after a siege of two years and the loss of 300,000 men besides 6 archbishops, 12 bishops, 40 earls, and 500 barons.	1191	Celestinus III.
		1192	Saladin is defeated by Richard Cœur de Lion, in the battle of Ascalon.		
		1195	Eastern Empire:—**Alexius Angelus**, a tyrant.		
		1196	Naples and Sicily, seized by the emperor Henry VI. on the death of Tancred		
		1198	Order of the *Holy Trinity*, instituted in Germany.—*William of Newburgh*, historian.	1198	Innocent III.
1201	War with England in support of prince Arthur.	1199	Germany:—Philip governs, as the guardian of his nephew Frederick.		
				1200	Philip Augustus, king of France, excommunicated.
		1202	Fourth Crusade from Venice, under Baldwin, count of Flanders, who is accompanied by a Venetian fleet under Henry Dandolo, the doge.		
1204	Normandy reunited to France The *Inquisition*, first established in France.	1204	Eastern Empire:—**Alexius IV.** (Murzuphulus.)	1204	The *Inquisition* in France
			The crusaders plunder Constantinople, and their leader usurps the throne, as **Baldwin I.** (first of the Latin emperors.)		
		1205	—— defeats the Bulgarians, near Adrianople.		
		1206	— **Henry I.** (2d Latin emperor.) —— Empires of Nice and Trebisond founded.		
		1208	—— Germany:—**Otho IV.** —— The *silk manufacture* introduced into Germany.	1208	John king of England excommunicated.
1209	The works of Aristotle, imported from Constantinople, condemned by the Council of Paris.	1210	Otho excommunicated by the pope. *Persecution of the Waldenses.*	1209	The order of *Franciscans* instituted. The Albigenses violently persecuted.
		1211	Portugal:—Alphonso II. (king.)		
1214	Spain:—Spithury I. king of Castile and Leon.	1214	Germany:—**Frederick II.** (late king of Sicily.) The Turks defeat the Persians.		

A. D. ENGLAND.

1215 The English barons, exasperated by the tyrannical and licentious conduct of the king have recourse to arms, and demand a reform.—(May 24.) They have a conference with the king at Runnymede near Windsor; where they compel him, after a debate of several days to sign the famous *Magna Charta*, or bill of rights, which grants and secures very important privileges to every order of men in the kingdom; to the barons, the clergy, and the people.

The pope annuls the charter at the request of John who arms against the barons, and ravages the kingdom.

The barons offer the crown to Louis, the dauphin of France, who,

1216 lands in England, but disgusts the people by partiality to his countrymen.

John dies at Newark. His character is a complication of vices equally mean and odious.—*Giraldus Cambrensis*, author of, "A History of the World," flourished.

Henry III. 4th Plantagenet.

The earl of Pembroke protector during the king's minority.

1217 The authority of the young king is acknowledged by the barons, and Louis is obliged to evacuate the kingdom. Dissatisfaction created on account of Henry's profuse favour to foreigners.

1224 Henry's province of Poitou seized by the king of France.

1229 He invades Bretagne, is defeated by the French at Taillebourg, and obliged to give up Normandy, Maine, Anjou, and Poictiers, to France.

1255 The pope offers Henry the sovereignty of Sicily, and drains England of immense sums under that, and other pretences.

The barons excited to an insurrection by the ambitious **Simon de Montfort**, earl of Leicester, and in

1258 extort from the king the *Provisions of Oxford*, extending their power and privileges.

A. D.	FRANCE & SPAIN.	A. D.	MISCELLANEOUS.	A. D.	POPES, &c.
1215	Battle of Bouvines gained by Philip, over the emperor Otho IV. and John, king of England.	1215	Order of the *Knights Hospitallers* founded.	1215	The order of *Dominicans*, instituted. *Auricular confession*, established The word *transubstantiation*.
1216	Louis, the dauphin, is offered the crown of England.	1216	Eastern Empire:—**Peter** and **John Ducas** emperors. (Latin.)	1216	Honorius III.
		1217	Fifth Crusade:—Andrew II. of Hungary.		
		1219	Damietta taken by the Crusaders, under the duke of Austria.		
		1220	*Astronomy and Geography* brought into Europe by the Moors.		
1223	Louis VIII. (the Lion.) Engages in a crusade against the Albigenses	1227	A general expedition from the different states of Europe to Palestine. The TARTARS or Moguls, under Genghis Khan, overrun the Saracen empire.	1227	Gregory IX. excommunicates, the emperor Frederick II.
1226	St. Louis IX. (superstitious.)	1228	Eastern Empire:-Baldwin II. (Latin.)		
1230	Spain:—Castile and Leon united by Ferdinand III., who takes Cordova, Seville, Cadiz, &c., from the Moors.	1230	Teutonic knights subdue Persia.	1229	The Scriptures prohibited to the laity. The Dominicans intrusted with the Inquisition.
		1232	Fire-arms in China and India. Clocks in Egypt.		
		1236	Tartars first penetrate into Russia, Poland, &c. The University of Vienna founded.		
		1241	Swedes and Livonians defeated by the Russians near Narva. The "*Hanseatic league*," between 84 European cities, under a *municipal* form of government, "for their mutual defence against the encroachments of the great lords."	1244	Celestinus IV.
				1243	Innocent IV.
1248	Louis leads the 6th crusade, with his queen, 3 brothers, and a train of French knights.	1248	Sixth Crusade, under Louis IX.	1245	Thirteenth general council. Frederick II. of Germany excommunicated.
		1251	Germany:—Conrad IV.		
		1254	—— Interregnum until 1273. Sweden:—Stockholm founded.	1354	Alexander III. The order of *Augustines* and sect of *Flagellants*.
1252	Spain:—Alphonso X. king of Castile and Leon.	1258	Termination of the Saracen Empire, on the capture of Bagdad, by the Tartars under Halaku.		
		1261	Eastern Empire:—Recovery of Constantinople, by the Greeks, under Michael Paleologus.	1261	Urban IV.

A. D. ENGLAND.

1262 New discontents: the demands of the barons referred to the king of France, who decides against them.

A Civil War. The king joined by Comyn, Bruce, and Baliol, the Scottish lords.

1164 —— defeated at Lewes, and with his son Edward taken prisoner by Leicester, who assumes the government, and summons a new parliament, in which the deputies from the principal boroughs, and two knights from each shire are admitted. This is considered the commencement of the *House of Commons.*

1265 Prince Edward released from prison, assembles an army, defeats and kills Leicester, in the battle of Evesham. King Henry restored.

Scotland:—The Norwegians expelled.

1270 Prince Edward undertakes an expedition to the Holy Land, where he signalizes himself by many gallant exploits, and narrowly escapes assassination.

1271 Henry III. dies. He was gentle and credulous, without vices and without energy; a good man, but a weak monarch. The successive archbishops of Canterbury in this reign, *Stephen Langton, Edmund Rich, Robert Grosseteste,* were able and eminent prelates. The council of nobility and bishops were first called the *Parliament. The manufacture of linen* was introduced. *Glass mirrors, magnifying glasses* and *spectacles,* invented or improved, by that great restorer of science, *Roger Bacon. Matthew Paris,* historian, flourished.

—— **Edward I.** (Longshanks) 5th Plantagenet. ——

1274 Edward having returned from Palestine, begins his reign with wise and vigorous regulations.

1276 Ambitious of the whole sovereignty of Britain, he leads an expedition against Llewellyn, prince of Wales, and compels him to submit.

SCOTLAND.
Alexander, d. 1281.
Margaret, 1290.
Interregnum to 1292.
Baliol, 1296.
Interregnum.
Robert I.

1282 Llewellyn revolts; he is slain in battle, and his countrymen again subdued.

1283 While the king and queen are in Wales, a prince is born, who is created Prince of Wales. Hence the origin of this title (now in use) of the king's eldest son.

In Scotland king Alexander III., queen Margaret, and all their descendants had died, and two principal competitors for the succession appear, viz. Robert Bruce, and John Baliol.*

1286 Edward is chosen umpire between the claimants, by the Scottish parliament, which acknowledges Scotland to be a fief of England

1292 The decision in favour of Baliol, who is declared king, but a vassal of Edward. He soon becomes dissatisfied with this provision, and enters into a secret alliance with the king of France.

* Bruce was the *son* of the *second* daughter, and Baliol *grandson* of the *eldest* daughter of David, earl of Huntingdon, son of David I.

A.D.	FRANCE & SPAIN.	A. D.	MISCELLANEOUS.	A. D.	POPES, &c.
		1265	**Charles,** count of Anjou, is made king of Sicily, which becomes a papal fief.	1264	Clement IV.
				1271	Gregory X. St. *Thomas Aquinas*, the celebrated scholastic.
1267	*Police* established in Paris.	1266	Battle of Benevento, where Manfroi is killed.		
		1668	Antioch taken by the Musselmen. The Tartars invade China.		
1270	The king embarks in a new crusade, and dies while besieging Tunis.	1270	End of the Crusades. Lewis IX. and nearly all his army perish by a pestilence. Flourished—*Nassar Eddin*, a Persian geographer and astronomer. Peter de Vignes, chancellor to Frederic II. *Acropolita*, of Constantinople, historian.		
1271	Philip III. (the Hardy,) is proclaimed in the camp before Tunis, and concludes a truce for 10 years.	1273	Germany :—**Rodolph,** emperor.—(The first of the house of Hapsburgh, or ancient Austria)—wise and brave;—corrects the disorders in Germany and Italy.	1274	Fourteenth general council, for the re-union of the Greek and Latin churches.
1274	Spain :—-Peter III., king of Arragon. —— Hereditary succession.	1974	First commercial treaty between Flanders and England.	1276	Innocent V. Adrian V. John XXI.
		1280	Conquest of China by the Mogul Tartars, who are defeated near Emessa, by the sultan of Egypt.	1277	Nicholas III.
		1281	Marienburg, built by the Teutonic Knights.	1281	Martin IV.
		1282	Sicilian Vespers; when 10,000 Frenchmen are massacred.		
1284	—— Sancho IV. king of Castile and Leon.	1283	Eastern empire—Andronicus I. (Paleologus) emperor.	1285	Honorius IV.
1285	Philip IV. (the Fair.) Spain:—Alphonso III. of Arragon.	1286	Denmark:—Eric V. assassinated near Vibourg.	1288	Nicholas IV.
		1287	The Tartars penetrate into Poland.		
		1288	Tripoli, taken by the Sultan of Egypt.		
1291	—— James II. king of Arragon.	1291	Syria conquered by the Sultan of Babylon. Acre taken by the Turks.		
		1292	Germany:—Adolphus (of Nassau) emperor:—despised for his having received money from England to make war against France.		
1295	—— :—Ferdinand IV. king of Castile.	1295	Eastern Empire:—Michael Andronicus.		
			During this century, society made considerable progress in literature and the arts. The admission of the *commons* into *legislatures*; the *enfranchisement* of the *slaves*; the *aboli-*		

A. D. ENGLAND.

1295 True Era of the regular succession of English parliaments, and of the House of Commons, which is now summoned to provide for war.

1296 Edward's demand for Baliol to appear in the English parliament as his vassal, being refused, he enters and subdues Scotland, takes Baliol prisoner, and sends him to the Tower of London.

1297 The Scots goaded by the tyranny of the English garrisons, rebel and take arms, headed by the heroic **Sir William Wallace,** who is soon joined by **Sir William Douglas, Robert Bruce,** and other chiefs.

1298 Wallace victorious at Stirling over the English under earl Warrenne, but defeated in the battle of Falkirk by king Edward in person. He is declared Regent of Scotland.

Period

A. D. ENGLAND.

1302 English defeated thrice in a day by Comyn and Frazer.

1305 Wallace treacherously betrayed by Sir John Monteith, and executed in London as a rebel.

1306 Robert Bruce elected king by the Scots, and crowned at Scone; encourages the hopes of his countrymen, and expels the English from Scotland.

1307 At the head of 100,000 men, Edward advances towards Scotland; but his project is defeated; he is taken sick, and dies at Carlisle. His persecution of the Jews is a foul blot on the government of Edward. He was however of service to his country, by *regulating* the *jurisdiction* of the several *courts*, and of the *parliament*. By his high character as a legislator, he acquired the title of the "*English Justinian.*" He was an able warrior, but too much governed by ambition and a spirit of revenge. *Clocks* are introduced into England.

Prices.—In 1274, a Bible in 9 vols. fairly written, with a comment, sold for 50 marks, or £33. 6*s*. 8*d*. Wheat 3*s*. 4*d*. a quarter. Labourer's wages, 1½*d* a day.

1307 —— **Edward II.** (Caernarvon.) 6th Plantagenet, (son of Edward I.) relinquishes the conquest of Scotland, after a few feeble efforts, and disgusts his people by his indolence, and his liberality to Piers Gaveston, a foreign minion, who is at length banished at the petition of the barons. Bruce, in the mean time, had nearly recovered Scotland.

SCOTLAND. Robert I.

1314 Edward marches into Scotland with an army of 100,000 men, and is totally defeated in the memorable and bloody **battle of Bannockburn,** which for a time secures the independence of Scotland, and establishes Bruce on the throne.

1315 The Scots ravage the northern provinces of England. Edward Bruce invades Ireland, and is elected king by the natives.

1322 The earl of Lancaster, and twenty other noblemen, are executed.

1324 Isabella, the queen, and Mortimer, her paramour, enter into a conspiracy with the disaffected barons.

A.D.	FRANCE & SPAIN.	A. D.	MISCELLANEOUS.	A. D.	POPES, &c.
			tion of trial by *ordeal*, and *duel*; the establishment of *universities*, and *academical honours*, were some of the characteristics of improvement. But this improvement was as yet but partial. *Chivalry* had exerted a beneficial influence on *manners*,—a spirit of *commercial enterprise* was excited by the *Crusades*.		
1297	Philip declares war against Guy, count of Flanders.				

VII.—154 *Years.*

A.D.	FRANCE & SPAIN.	A. D.	MISCELLANEOUS.	A. D.	POPES, &c.
1300	Guy's dominions are united to the Fr. crown.	1299	Founding of the TURKISH, or Ottoman Empire, in Bithynia, under **Othman I.**		
			Germany:—Albert I.—Persecution of the Jews.		
1301	Philip quarrels with the pope, and is excommunicated.	1302	The *Mariner's Compass*—invented or improved by Flavio Gioia, at Naples.		
	The States-General, or *Parliament*, first summoned at Paris.	1303	Peter Gradenigo, doge of Venice, dies.	1303	Boniface VIII.
		1307	Founding of the SWISS Republics after their revolt from Germany, under **William Tell**, &c.	1304	Benedict XI.
	The order of "*Le tiers-etats.*"		*Dante*, the father of Italian poetry.	1308	The seat of the popes removed to Avignon, where it continues 70 years
1309	Spain:—Ferdinand, king of Castile, and Leon, takes Gibraltar from the Moors.	1308	Germany:—Henry VII. (of Luxembourg.)		
		1309	Naples:—Robert of Taranto, a beneficent and enlightened prince.		
		1310	Knights of St. John take possession of Rhodes.		
		1312	Order of Knights Templars abolished by the council of Vienna.		
1314	Molay, the last grand master of the Knights Templars burned alive in Paris along with several of the Knights.	1314	Germany:—Lewis IV. (of Bavaria,) elected at Frankfort, by five electors, and crowned by the archbishop of Mentz.	1314	The cardinals set fire to the conclave and separate.
1314	— Louis X. —				
1316	— John I. — an infant.	1315	*Lollard*, founder of a sect, suffers martyrdom.		
	Philip V. — (the Long.)	1320	Eastern Empire:—Andronicus II.		
1321	— Charles IV (the Fair.)	1325	First commercial treaty between England and Venice.		
			Abulfeda, a Syrian Geographer.		

A. D. ENGLAND.

1422 Henry VI. 3d of the branch of Lancaster, 11th Plantaganet.
The duke of Bedford regent; allies with the Burgundians; continues the war with the dauphin.
James I. now king of Scotland, released for the sum of 40,000 pounds.

SCOTLAND.
James I. died, 1437.
James II.

1424 Bedford defeats the French and their Scotch allies, in the battle of Verneuil.

1428 —— forms the siege of Orleans; from which his whole army is finally repulsed by the heroic Joan d' Arc.

1430 —— carries over the young Henry, who is crowned at Paris as king of France.

1431 Joan, now called the Maid of Orleans, taken prisoner, and burnt at Rouen as a sorceress.

1435 Death of the duke of Bedford, followed by the loss of all the English possessions on the continent except Calais.

1445 King Henry marries the celebrated Margaret of Anjou.

1447 The duke of Gloucester arrested for treason, and found murdered.

1450 Richard, duke of York, sets up his claim to the throne.

1451 Insurrection of Jack Cade, an Irishman, who assumes the name of Mortimer, and with 20,000 Kentishmen, enters London, but is taken prisoner and put to death.

A.D.	FRANCE & SPAIN.	A.D.	MISCELLANEOUS.	A. D.	POPES, &c.
1422	**Charles VII.** (the Vittorious) an able and popular Sovereign.	1423	F. Foscari, doge of Venice.		
		1427	Academy of Louvain founded.		
1428	**Joan d' Arc,** a country girl, raises the siege of Orleans and causes the king to be crowned at Rheims.	1429	Battles of Herrings and Patay.	1431	Eugenius IV. Amadoeus duke of Savoy, anti-pope, under the name of Felix. V. 18th general council, at Baale.
		1434	Poland:—Ladislaus VI. Florence governed by **Cosmo,** the first of the house of the *Medici.*		
1435	Final expulsion of the English from France, begins this year.	1437	Expedition of the Portuguese into Africa.—Hungary invaded by the Turks	1437	Disputes between Eugenius IV. and the council, of Baale, which deposes him.
		1438	Denmark and Sweden:—Christopher III. Germany:—Albert II. first hereditary emperor of the house of Austria,		
1439	The pragmatic sanction settled in France, regulating the election of bishops and moderating the power of the pope.	1440	Art of *PRINTING,* (at Harlaem 1435, by Costar) at Mentz, by Guttenberg. Germany:—Frederick III.	1439	Council of Ferrara transferred to Florence where a reunion is effected with the Greek Church.
		1444	Amurath II. defeated by John Hunniades, vaivode of Transylvania, and resigns to Mahomet II. Battle of Varna, gained by the Turks.		
		1445	Eastern Empire;—Constantine XII. (Paleologus.) the last of the Greek emperors.		
		1446	Inundation at Dort in Holland, which drowns 100,000 persons.	1447	Nicholas V.
		1447	Turks first defeated by George Castriot, surnamed **Scandeberg** of Albania, and afterwards in 22 battles during several years. Poland:—Casimir IV. *Thomas a Kempis, f.*		
		1448	Denmark and Sweden separated. — Christian I.—Charles VIII., —		
		1450	*Vulgate Bible, the first large book, printed.*		
		1452	Austria erected into an archduchy by Frederick III.		

Period

A. D. ENGLAND. [War of the *Roses.*]

1455 Commencement of the Civil War, between the Houses of York and Lancaster, (the first adopting the emblem of the *white*, the second of the *red* rose.) King Henry defeated by the duke of York at St. Albans, and obliged to resign the government into his hands as protector.

1460 The king restored; again defeated and taken prisoner by the Yorkists under the **Earl of Warwick** at Northampton.

Battle of Wakefield; in which queen Margaret defeats the duke of York, who, together with his second son is slain.

Edward, earl of March, son of the duke of York, enters London, and is received with the cry of "long live king Edward." So ends the reign of Henry VI. who was virtuous and humane, but destitute of energy and fortitude.

In this reign we have the first instance of *debt* contracted upon parliamentary security.

1461 **Edward IV.** 1st of the branch of York, 12th Plantagenet; firmly established on the throne after the battle of Towton, in which the Lancastrians are entirely defeated. Henry and queen Margaret after failing in several bloody battles are forced to take refuge in Scotland. The latter with her army of Scots, defeated at Hexham, 1464, and escapes to France.

SCOTLAND. James II.

1465 King Henry made prisoner, and committed to the Tower.

Edward contrary to his engagement through the earl of Warwick, with the French princess, marries lady Elizabeth Gray. The irritated Warwick joins the Lancastrians and makes a new effort in their favour.—Edward abandoned by his army retires to Holland, and Henry is restored by Warwick.

1471 Edward aided by the duke of Burgundy returns and again defeats the Lancastrians in the battle of Barnet, where Warwick, styled the "king maker," is killed. The desperate battle of Tewksbury in which queen Margaret and her son are defeated and made prisoners. The latter is barbarously murdered.

1475 Edward invades France, and concludes a treaty with Louis XI. who agrees to pay him 75,000 crowns.—The duke of Clarence condemned for treason and witchcraft, and drowned in a butt of Malmsey wine.

1483 Edward IV. dies:—He was accomplished and licentious.

The Art of Printing was introduced into England in this reign, by *William Caxton*, a merchant. He first printed a "History of Troy," and then "The Game of Chess."

VIII.—145 *Years.*

A.D.	FRANCE & SPAIN.	A.D.	MISCELLANEOUS.	A.D.	POPES, &c.
		1453	Constantinople taken by the Turks, and the Turkish Empire in Europe, founded by Mahomet II. (on the ruins of the Eastern Empire of the Romans.)		
		——	*Revival of learning*, in Europe, by the fugitives from Constantinople.		
		1454	Prussians and Poles at war with the Teutonic Knights, for 12 years.		
		1456	Turks repulsed at the siege of Belgrade.	1455	Calixtus III.
		1460	*Wood engraving* invented. (In *Mezzotinto* 1648; *etching* 1512.)	1458	Pius II.
1461	— Louis XI. — tyrannical.		Cape de Verde islands discovered by Cada Mosta, a Portuguese navigator.		
1464	*Post offices* established, Louis attempts to repress the power of the nobles which causes their revolt.	1462	Expedition of the Turks into Wallachia. Russia: Ivan Basilowitz, founder of the Russian greatness.		
1467	Sheep first sent from Spain to England.	1463	War between the Venetians and Turks.		
		1464	League against Louis XI. king of France.		
1469	Spain:—Marriage of the infanta, Isabella of Castile, with Ferdinand prince Arragon.	1466	Second book printed, viz. *Cicero de Officiis.* *Pedal harpsichord*, invented.	1464	Paul II.
1477	Charles the Bold, duke of Burgundy, defeated and killed at Nanci.	1474	Russia: Ivan Basilowitz shakes off the yoke of the Tartars, and conquers Novogorod.	1471	Sixtus IV.
1479	Spain:—Arragon and Castile united into the kingdom of SPAIN, under Ferdinand and Isabella.	1477	*Watches* first made at Nuremburg. (In France 1544: In England 1597.) Burgundy comes into the possession of Austria, on the death of Charles the Bold.		
		1480	Rhodes besieged by the Turks.		
1480	The Inquisition established.	1481	Turkey:—Bajazet II. Portugal:—John II.		
1483	Charles VIII; dissolute but courteous.				

ENGLAND.

ENGLAND	SCOTLAND.
1483 Edward V. 2d, *of* the branch of York; 13th Plantagenet; a minor. His uncle, the duke of Gloucester, a crafty, ambitious and cruel tyrant, is appointed protector; puts to death lords Rivers and Hastings, without trial or accusation; hires the murder of the young king, and his brother the duke of York, in the Tower; and, assisted by the duke of Buckingham, usurps the throne, under the name of	James III.

— Richard III. 3d, *of* York; 14th, and last of Plantagenet. —

Buckingham becomes dissatisfied, and is beheaded.

1485 The usurper soon finds a rival in Henry Tudor, earl of Richmond, the only representative of the house of Lancaster, who lands at Milford Haven, and is soon joined by 40,000 men.

Battle of Bosworth field, where Richard III. is defeated and slain, and his victorious competitor is saluted with the shout of "long live king Henry VII."

ENGLAND	SCOTLAND.
— Henry VII. first of the Tudor line.	
Union of the Houses of York and Lancaster, by the marriage of Henry VII. with Elizabeth, daughter of Edward IV.	James III. —— IV.

The king on the day of his coronation establishes fifty yeomen of the guard, the first *standing army*.

1486 Imposture of Lambert Simnel, a baker's son, who, directed by his tutor Simmons, pretends to be Edward Plantagenet, earl of Warwick; is acknowledged in Ireland; and joined by the earl of Lincoln with 2,000 men, lands in England, is defeated and made prisoner at Stoke, and created a scullion in the royal kitchen.—The Court of the Star Chamber established.

1489 *Maps* and *charts* first brought into England by Bartholomew Columbus.

1492 Perkin Warbeck, a new impostor, assumes the title of "Richard duke of York, son of Edward IV.—escaped from the Tower."

1493 he is received and acknowledged by the duchess of Burgundy, as "The White Rose of England;"—visits Scotland and marries lady Catharine Gordon, sister of the earl of Huntley:—lands in Cornwall under the title of Richard IV. but finally surrenders and is beheaded.

1497 Cabot's (the Venetian) voyage to America, patronized by the king. He discovers Newfoundland, first reaches the continent and explores the coast to Florida.

1500 Great plague in England, which carries off 30,000 people in London, obliging the king and court to remove to Calais.

A. D.	FRANCE & SPAIN.	A. D.	MISCELLANEOUS.	POPES, &c.
1483	Cardinal **Ximenes,** afterwards the prime minister of Ferdinand and Isabella, and patron of learning; **Gonsalvo** the "Great Captain," of Spain.			1484 Innocent VIII.
		1485	Denmark and Sweden again united under John I. Matthias, king of Hungary takes Vienna and expels the emperor. Flourished about this time, *Ariosto* and *Angelo Politian*, poet; *Machiavel*, historian; and *Raphael*, painter, all Italians.	
1491	The king marries Ann of Britany.	1489	Cyprus ceded to the Venetians.	
1492	Spain:—Ferdinand completes the conquest of Granada, from the Moors, who had held it 800 years. — Columbus. —	1492	Discovery of America, by Christopher Columbus, a native of Genoa, under the patronage of Ferdinand and Isabella, of Spain. — Poland:—John Albert I. —	1492 Alexander VI. (Borgia) a rapacious and scandalous tyrant: forms a league with Venice, Castile, Germany &c. against France.
1495	The king of France, conquers Naples; defeats the pope and his allies at Fornova.	1493	Germany:—Maximilian I. emperor. Reuchlin introduces the *Hebrew* and *Greek* languages into Germany.	
		1495	Naples seized by the king of France. Diet of Worms.	
1496	Spain:—Joanna, the heiress of the crown is married to Philip of Austria.	1496	Portugal:—Emanuel I. expels the Jews and Moors.	
		1497	**Vasco de Gama,** a Portuguese navigator, discovers the passage to India, round the Cape of Good Hope.	
1498	Louis XII.—1st, of the house of Orleans.	1498	Poland ravaged by the Wallachians, who carry off 100,000 prisoners, and sell them to the Turks.	
1499	conquers Milan and	1499	Americus Vespucius makes a voyage and gives name to the new world.	
1501	Naples, but is expelled from thence by Gonsalvo de Cordova.	1500	Amer. The Portuguese discover Brazil. —Voyage of John Cabot to Florida. Germany divided into *six circles*, by Maximilian.	

A. D. ENGLAND.

1502 Henry prince of Wales marries Catharine of Arragon, his brother Arthur's widow.

1509 Henry VII. dies. He was an able, but despotic and avaricious sovereign. By means of his iniquitous agents Empson and Dudley, he amassed an enormous treasure on false pretences. He was however useful to the nation; he encouraged industry, commerce, and the arts. *The study of the Greek language* was introduced into England by *William Grocyn.* Henry's Chapel at Westminster, still exists, a monument of his opulence and taste. He left three children;—Henry, his successor, Margaret, queen of Scotland, and Mary, afterwards queen of France.

—— Henry VIII.—2d Tudor, —— ascends the throne in his 18th year with peculiar advantages; possessing the confidence of the nation, which is now peaceful and prosperous. He allies with the pope, the emperor, and the king of Spain against France.

SCOTLAND.

James IV.
—— V.
Mary.

1513 —invades France, and assisted by the emperor Maximilian (who condescends to act under him) defeats the French at Blagny in the "battle of Spurs;" and takes Terouane and Tournay.

The Scots invade England, and are defeated by the earl of Surrey in the battle of Flodden field, where king James IV. and the flower of his nobility are slain.

General pacification;—Mary the king's sister is married to Louis XII. of France.

1515 Rise of the celebrated **Thomas Wolsey,** a clergyman of aspiring views and superior talents, who, ingratiated into the king's favour, fills the offices of archbishop of York, lord chancellor, cardinal, and legate of the pope, and assumes the helm of Europe. Henry's alliance is courted by both the rival candidates for the empire, Charles V. and Francis I.

Retrospective glance at some of the occurrences in the progress of society, &c. (See 13th century.

Navigation and Commerce—up to the 15th century monopolized by the splendid and opulent *Italian cities* (Venice, Genoa, Pisa, Florence, Naples, &c.) under municipal charters—their trade with India and the ports of the Red Sea, the means of introducing into Europe the elegancies and luxuries, as well as the conveniences of life. The extent and importance of navigation vastly increased by the invention of the Mariner's Compass. Portugal, Spain, Flanders and England at length awakened to commercial enterprises. The discovery of America and the passage to India round the Cape of Good Hope. New Era.

Culture of *silk* and *sugar cane* in Italy.

Manufacture of silk, earthen ware and glass in Italy, and of woollen and linen cloths in Flanders.

Fine Arts—Painting—(great perfection) in Italy and Flanders.

Engraving and *Architecture* (progressing) in Italy.

Art of War—material revolution in.—Invention of gunpowder—establishment of standing armies.

Literature.—Learned men dispersed throughout Europe by the fall of Constantinople;—transient revival of letters.

The invention of *Printing*—glorious era in modern history:—the art however yet in its infancy. The few books and MSS. extant, principally in the hands of the churchmen.—The lower classes and the majority even of the nobility, remain entirely illiterate.—(Dante, Petrarch and Bocaccio in *Italy.* Chaucer, Bacon, Wickliffe in *England.*)

Ecclesiastical.—Temporal and spiritual power of the pope; his infallibility undisputed—his decisions absolute. Mendicant orders. The churchmen (with few exceptions) licentious, haughty, tyrannical, rapacious,—under the cloak of their office, and pretended sanctity, they are guilty of the most detestable crimes. Their policy in keeping from the people the means of knowledge. The scriptures strictly forbidden to the laity. Bigotry and superstition hold as extensive sway as ignorance. Abject reverence of the "Holy Church," and submission to her decrees among all ranks. The sale of "indulgences," (or of licenses

A. D.	FRANCE & SPAIN.	A. D.	MISCELLANEOUS.	A. D.	POPES, &c.
1504	Spain:—Joanna, (daughter of Isabella) is succeeded by her husband, Philip I; —1st of the house of Austria.	1501	Venice:—The Inquisitorial tribunal established.		
		1507	Poland:—**Sigismund I.** the Great.	1503	Pius III. Julius II.
		1508	Madagascar discovered by the Portuguese. **League of Cambray** between France, Spain, Germany, and the pope against the power and commerce of **Venice.**		
1507	Louis subdues Genoa.	1510	About 1200 meteoric stones, one of which weighed 120 lbs, fell at Padua.		
1509	Louis defeats the Venetians and subdues Verona, Padua, and Vicentia.	1511	America:—Cuba conquered by the Spaniards. Portuguese commerce and colonies in the East Indies.		
1513	The French defeated in the battle of Spurs, by Henry VIII. and also expelled from Italy.	1512	Turkey: Selim I, emperor. Battle of Novarro, in which the Swiss defeat the French. The latter driven out of Italy. Denmark and Sweden;—Christian II. Flourishing period of the *fine arts; Michael, Angelo Corregio, Titian, Leonardo da Vinci,* the celebrated painters.	1513	Leo X. Foundation of St. Peter's Church, by the proceeds of indulgences.
1515	**Francis I.**—(count of Angouleme)—able and popular; conquers Milan.	1514	War between the Ottoman empire and Persia. *First Polyglot Bible* printed at Alcala, by direction of cardinal Ximenes.		
1516	— Spain: — **Charles I.** (2d of Austria,) afterwards the emperor Charles V. Ximenes dismissed and dies.	1516	The kingdom of Algiers seized by Barbarossa, the Corsair.		
		1517	The Turks supplant the Mamelukes in Egypt. **Commencement of the Reformation** in Germany, by ***Martin Luther,*** an Augustine friar, who writes his essay against the sale of indulgences, and other corruptions of the Romish church; is summoned by Leo to answer for his "crime" at Rome; appears before the Diet of Augsburg, and is denied a hearing by cardinal Cajetan; but protected by Frederick, elector of Saxony; propagates his opinions in	1518	Leo condemns the doctrines of Luther by a bull dated 9th November.
1520	Interview between Francis I. and Henry VIII. in the 'field of the cloth of gold,' near Guisnes. Spain:—The confederacy of the Holy Junta.	1519	Germany, while Zuinglius, his disciple, teaches them in Switzerland.		

A. D. ENGLAND.

to commit crimes of any grade under the sanction of the Church,) revived by Julius II.—These licenses retailed promiscuously from the shops in France and Germany. In opposition to them in particular, and finally to the other corruptions of popery, an able and successful champion at length arises, and the great fabric of ignorance and superstition begins to tremble to its foundation.]

Charles V. visits England.—Execution of the duke of Buckingham.

1521 Wolsey is appointed arbiter between the emperor and Francis.
Alliance of England, Germany, and the pope against France.

525 Henry quarrels with the emperor, and makes peace with France.
—— receives from the pope the title of "*Defender of the Faith*," for his essay, (sent to Rome) against the doctrines of Luther.
—— falling in love with lady Ann Boleyn, a maid of honour to the queen, he applies to the pope for a divorce from Catharine of Arragon, on pretence that his marriage was illegal.

Cardinal Campeggio arrives, as the pope's legate, and holds a conference with Wolsey respecting the divorce; but finally returns without a decision. Wolsey soon loses the favour of his capricious master; is arrested on charge of treason, and dies in a monastery. "Had I but served God," said he on his death-bed, "as diligently as I have served the king, he would not have forsaken me in my grey hairs."

Sir Thomas More, succeeds Wolsey as chancellor and prime minister. After consulting and receiving the sanction of the principal *universities of Europe*, Henry divorces Catharine and marries Ann Boleyn.

Thomas Cranmer, the able advocate of the reformation, is created archbishop of Canterbury.

1534 Henry excommunicated by the pope; who soon pays the price of his conscientiousness, by losing all his authority in England, the *king* being acknowledged by the parliament and many of the clergy as the *Supreme Head of the Church* of England, which is formally separated from the communion of Rome.

Lord **Cromwell** made vicar-general, or the king's vice-gerent. The king suppresses the lesser monasteries, and confiscates their property; commencement of the *Reformation in England*.

1535 Execution of Sir Thomas More, the bishop of Rochester, and others, for refusing to acknowledge the king's supremacy in matters of religion.

A.D. FRANCE & SPAIN.

1521 Cortez conquers Mexico for Spain.

First war between Francis I. and Charles V.; the first endeavouring to reinstate Henry d'Albert in the kingdom of Navarre.

1522 The French lose all their dominions in Italy.

1524 Francis besieges Pavia.

1525 —— defeated and taken prisoner by Charles V.

1526 liberated by the treaty of Madrid.

The *streets* of Paris, (the first in modern Europe) *lighted*.

1529 The French re-enter Italy, but their army is destroyed by pestilence.

1529 Peace concluded with the Emperor at Cambray. Burgundy given up to France.

1532 Spain: Pizarro conquers Peru.

A. D. MISCELLANEOUS.

Germany.—CHARLES V.—(Elected in preference to his rival Francis I.)

[From this era Modern History is sometimes dated.]

1520 War between Prussia and Poland.

Turkey:—**Solyman I.** (the Magnificent.)

South America:—**Montezuma,** emperor of Mexico, dies.

1521 —— Mexico conquered by Cortez, the Spaniard, in two years.

Diet of Worms; summoned by the emperor Charles V. for an investigation of the opinions of Luther, who is present, and begins to be popular with the German princes.

Belgrade taken by the Turks under Solyman the Magnificent.

League between the pope, the emperor, and the king of England.

1522 Island of Rhodes taken from the knights of St. John, by the Turks. First use of *bombs*. The Knights settle in Malta.

First voyage round the world by a ship of Magellan's (Eng.) squadron.

Denmark and Sweden again dis-united.

—— Frederick I.——**Gustavus Vasa.**

1523 Pavia besieged by Francis I.

1525 Battle of Pavia: Francis I. defeated and taken prisoner by the Imperialists under Bourbon and Pascara.

1526 Reformation in Sweden and Denmark.

1527 Rome taken and plundered by the emperor Charles V.

America:—Bermudas discovered. Pizarro and Dalmagio invade Peru.

Revolution in Genoa, by Andrew Doria.

1528 Sweden:—The Roman Catholic religion abolished and Lutheranism established.

1529 Diet of Spires; issues a decree against Luther and the reformers and restores the celebration of mass. Several German princes protest against this and hence are called *Protestants*, the name afterwards common to all Christians opposed to the church of Rome.

Peace of Cambray, between France and Germany. Francis renounces Italy, Flanders, and Artois. Charles renounces Burgundy.

1530 *Confession of Augsburgh*, of the Protestant opinions, drawn up by Melancthon.

1531 Union and league of the Protestants at Smalkald, (Dec. 22.) which begins the Religious War.

1532 Peace between the emperor and the Protestant princes.

America: the conquest of Peru, by Pizarro.

1533 Insurrection of the *Anabaptists:—John of Leyden* their apostle.

Union of Denmark and Norway.

1534 Pope Paul III.

1535 Expedition of Charles V. into Africa. He takes Tunis from Barbarossa, the Moorish prince, and liberates 22,000 Christian slaves.

Society of the *Jesuits* founded by *Ignatius Loyola*, a Spaniard

John of Leyden executed. *Calvin's Institutes of the Christian Religion* published.

A. D. ENGLAND.

1536 Execution of queen Ann Boleyn on accusation of incontinency.

The king marries lady Jane Seymour.

——— receives envoys from the German Lutheran princes, and compiles his "Articles of Doctrine."

William Tyndal, the first publisher of an *English version of the Bible*, is strangled and burnt. Rebellion of the monks caused by the suppression of monasteries.

1537 Queen Jane dies in giving birth to Edward (VI.)

1540 The king marries Anne of Cleves; (who is soon divorced for not being so handsome, as her husband expected.)

—— marries lady Catharine Howard; (who is executed in 1542 for incest.)

Dr. Barnes, sent to the Tower for preaching the doctrine of justification by faith without works. Cromwell executed for heresy and treason.

1542 James V. of Scotland defeated at Solway, and dies, leaving an infant daughter, (the unfortunate Mary.)

1543 Queen Catharine Parr; favours, while the king persecutes the protestants, and all who will not embrace his prescribed creed.

1546 Scotland: Beaton, cardinal of St. Andrews assassinated.

——— Execution of the earl of Surrey, (charged with aspiring to the hand of the princess Mary.)

Henry VIII. dies. In him we have proof that absolute despotism may prevail in a government, and yet the form of a free constitution remain. After the death of Wolsey he became a tyrant; rapacious and prodigal, obstinate and capricious, as fickle in his friendships, as he was merciless in his resentments.

Pins were first used in England by Catharine Howard. *Needles* first made in 1545.

1547 —— Edward VI. 3d Tudor; ——

son of Henry VIII. and Jane Seymour; nine years of age. The duke of Somerset, the king's uncle, chosen protector. The Reformation favoured and forwarded by the protector and archbishop Cranmer. The reformers in Scotland are persecuted by the regent, the earl of Arran. The protector enters Scotland, with an army of 20,000 men, and defeats the Scots in the battle of Pinkney. Their young queen, Mary, sent to France for education, (where she is afterwards married to Francis II.)

1549 Execution of lord Seymour, brother of the Protector.

The English Liturgy is completed and established by act of parliament.

Somerset, through the intrigues of the earl of Warwick, is compelled to resign the protectorship, and soon after is committed to the Tower.

1551 The popish bishops, Bonner, Heath, and Day, imprisoned.

Mary, the heiress apparent, refuses to embrace the reformed religion.

1552 Execution of Somerset, as being guilty of a conspiracy.

The Liturgy and reformed mode of worship introduced into Ireland.

Cranmer publishes a "Collection of the Articles of Religion," and a "Code of Ecclesiastical Constitutions."

1553 Warwick, now the earl of Northumberland, persuades the king to dis-inherit his sisters, and the council to settle the succession on lady Jane Grey (married to Northumberland's fourth son, lord Guilford Dudley.)

Edward VI. dies, aged 16 years. He was amiable, talented, and intelligent.

The eldest sons of peers are first permitted to sit in the house of Commons.

A.D.	FRANCE & SPAIN.	A. D.	MISCELLANEOUS.
1536	Francis leagues with Solyman I. against the emperor.		
		1538	Peace of Nice for four years between Charles V. and Francis I. Rise of the *Antinomians.*
1539	Spain:—The Cortez subverted by Charles V.	1541	Hungary subjected by Solyman the magnificent. Algiers besieged by Charles V.
1544	The count of **Enghien** defeats the imperialists at Cerisoles.	1542	Discovery of Japan.
		1543	League between Charles V. and Henry VIII. against Francis I. America:—California discovered.
		1544	Imperialists defeated by the French in the battle of Cerisoles. Treaty of Crespi between the emperor and Francis.
		1545	*Council of Trent,* the last general council, begins. (Continues 18 years.)
1546	*Genesius de Sepulreda,* the restorer of learning in Spain. *Ignatius Loyola,* the founder of the Jesuits. *Ramus,* a French philosophic writer.	1546	League against the Protestants between the emperor and the pope. Death of Luther. The protestants deserted by Maurice, marquis of Muisni, who invades Saxony. Flourished;—*Melancthon* and *Zuinglius,* the able protestant reformers; *Erasmus,* of Rotterdam, one of the greatest scholars of modern times; *Copernicus,* of Thorn, in Prussia, the reviver of the true *system of the universe,* first discovered by Pythagoras; *Paracelsus; J. C. Scaliger; Vesalius; Vida;* a Latin poet.
1547	Henry II.—king of France.	1547	Elector of Saxony defeated by the emperor at Mulberg, and deposed. Fiesco's conspiracy at Genoa. The landgrave of Hesse, is imprisoned by the emperor.
		1548	The emperor grants an *interim* to the protestants. Reformation forwarded in Poland.
1550	Spain:—Philip conquers Portugal.	1550	Pope Julius III.
		1551	League against the emperor, between Henry II. and Maurice, who declares that his purpose in taking arms is to secure the Protestant religion; to maintain the German constitution; and to liberate the landgrave of Hesse.
		1552	Treaty of Passau by which Charles V. grants religious liberty to the Protestants.
		1553	Servetus executed for heresy by the Council of Geneva.

A. D. ENGLAND.

1553 — Mary, 4th Tudor; —

(daughter of Henry VIII. and Catharine of Arragon.)

Lady Jane Grey proclaimed by Northumberland, and induced to accept the crown; but is soon obliged to resign it to Mary. Northumberland is executed as guilty of high treason. Mary begins her attempts to restore the popish communion; creates bishop Gardiner her prime minister. Cardinal *Reginald Pole* arrives as the pope's legate.

1555 Marriage of the Queen to Philip II. king of Spain, (son of the emperor Charles V.) contrary to the wishes of her parliament, and people.

Insurrection conducted by Sir Thomas Wyatt; suppressed.

Execution of lord Dudley and lady Jane Grey.

The furious Persecution of the Protestants begins, February 4th. John Rogers, the first martyr burnt at the stake in Smithfield.

Bishops *Hooper and Ferrar*, *Saunders*, *Ridley*, *Latimer*, and other eminent reformers successively share the fate of Rogers, rather than abjure their faith.

1556 Cardinal Pole is appointed archbishop of Canterbury. Cranmer arrested, and is persuaded to subscribe to the popish doctrines; but soon after retracts, declaring his faith unchanged, and is martyred like Ridley and Latimer. Bonner bishop of London, a brutal monster, active in the persecution.

1557 War with France; loss of Calais.

1558 Queen Mary dies. Obstinacy, bigotry, and cruelty, were her conspicuous vices;—sincerity her only virtue. The first commercial treaty with Russia was effected in this reign.

— ELIZABETH:—5th Tudor; —

is saluted with the good wishes of the nation;—re-establishes the *Protestant Religion*, and the *Church of England*, in its present form: appoints **Sir William Cecil**, (afterwards lord Burleigh,) her secretary, and principal minister.

1559 The style of "queen of England and Ireland," is assumed by Mary queen of Scots, with the advice of her relatives, of the ambitious house of Guise.

Scotland:—The Protestants, persecuted by the queen-regent, enter into a *Covenant* for their mutual protection, styling themselves the "Congregation of the Lord," and under the guidance of *John Knox*, resist the queen regent's proceedings, break the images in the churches, destroy the monasteries, and assisted by an army from queen Elizabeth, besiege the regent in the castle of Leith.

1560 *Presbyterian* mode of worship established in Scotland by Knox. Queen Mary returns from France, and is joyfully received by her subjects.

1562 Elizabeth sends 6,000 men, to aid the Protestants, or Huguenots in France.

1565 Scotland:—Queen Mary's marriage with lord Darnley, which breaks the harmony between her and Elizabeth.

1566 Darnley, jealous of the queen's secretary David Rizzio, murders him in her presence. Birth of the queen's son, (James VI.) which alarms the jealousy of Elizabeth.

1567 Murder of Darnley; attributed to the earl of Bothwell; who is married to queen Mary. Association of the Scottish nobles against Bothwell. Mary is taken prisoner by them, confined in Lochleven castle; and compelled to sign a resignation of the crown. The earl of Murray is appointed regent; and the infant king proclaimed, as James VI.

1568 Mary escapes from Lochleven; joins the nobles friendly to her cause, and being defeated at Langside, seeks refuge in England. Her case is tried before the commissioners of England and Scotland by order of Elizabeth, as umpire; she is accused by the regent of being guilty of the murder of her husband; denies the charge, and is imprisoned.

A. D. FRANCE & SPAIN.

1555 Spain: Philip II. haughty, bigoted and tyrannical: persecutes the Protestants.

1557 War between Spain and France. Victory of the Spanish duke of Parma, at St. Quentin.

Calais taken from the English.

1559 Francis II. — The duke of Guise, a zealous papist, prime minister.

1560 Charles II. League at Amboise of the Protestants for expelling Guise.

Civil War between the Catholics and the Protestants (called Hugunots,) commences.

Guise and Bourbon parties.

1562 Protestants under Conde, defeated in the battle of Dreux.

1563 Guise assassinated.

1565 A confederacy between the kings of France and Spain, against the Protestants.

1568 Battle of St. Dennis; the Protestants defeated.

A. D. MISCELLANEOUS.

1554 Netherlands invaded by the French.
Russians subdue Astracan.

1555 Pope Marcellus II.
League against the Spaniards between the king of France and the pope.
Portugal:—Sebastian, king.
Peace of Religion, concluded at Augsburg; confirming the Treaty of Passau.

1556 Germany:—Resignation of the emperor Charles V. in favour of his brother,
—— Ferdinand I.
Corsica ravaged by the Turks.

1558 The ex-emperor Charles retires to a monastery and dies.
Flourish—*Camoens*, the most celebrated of the Portuguese poets; *Cardan*, an Italian philosopher and mathematician.

1559 Treaty of Chateau Cambresis; between France, Spain, and Piedmont, (negotiated on the part of France by Montmorency;) Savoy, Piedmont, (Bresse,) and other territories, are restored by France to Emanuel Philbert.
Pope Pius V.
Denmark:—Frederic II.

1560 Sweden Eric XIV. king, on the death of Gustavus Vasa.

1561 Livonia ceded to Poland.

1563 Council of Trent terminates.
War between Denmark and Sweden.

1564 Germany;—Maximilian II. is occupied during the whole of his reign in restoring peace to the empire.

1566 Hungary ravaged by the Tartars.
Turks attack Malta.
Pope Pius V.

A. D. ENGLAND.

1569 Project for the marriage of Mary with the duke of Norfolk, (the most powerful nobleman in England,) discovered and defeated.

Norfolk is committed to the Tower. Unsuccessful attempt of the earls of Northumberland and Westmoreland to liberate the queen of Scots.

1570 Scotland:—Violent death of Murray: the earl of Lennox succeeds him as regent.

1572 Conspiracy in favour of Mary defeated; the duke of Norfolk executed.

Voyage of **Sir Francis Drake,** round the world by the straits of Magellan.

1578 The queen sends troops to assist the revolted provinces of the low countries in gaining their independence.

—— engages to marry the duke of Anjou.

1581 Scotland:—Gowrie's conspiracy against the king.

1583 Plot against the life of queen Elizabeth.

The captive Mary suffers the privations of a rigorous imprisonment.

1585 Elizabeth sends an army under her favourite, the earl of Leicester, to assist the United Provinces, and Sir Francis Drake with a fleet of twenty sail, against the Spaniards in the West Indies.

1586 Leicester recalled for misconduct. Babington and Ballard's conspiracy in favour of Mary and the Catholics discovered, which hastens the "Trial of queen Mary."

1587 Elizabeth signs the death warrant of Mary notwithstanding the remonstrances of the kings of France and Scotland.

February 8. Beheading of Mary Queen of Scots, at Fotheringay. Elizabeth hypocritically affects great sorrow and surprise at the death of her "sister queen."

Cavendish, a successful private adventurer, with three vessels, captures several Spanish merchantmen in the South Seas, and returns by the cape of Good Hope.

Drake destroys 100 vessels in the harbour of Cadiz.

1588 Great preparations made to resist the expected Spanish invasion. The queen on horseback addresses her army at Tilbury.

The Spanish Armada, consisting of 135 vessels of enormous size, arrives in the English Channel, and is defeated by the English fleet of 34 ships, and 137 smaller vessels under **Drake, Hawkins, Frobrisher,** and **Sir Walter Raleigh:** lord **Howard** of Effingham, commander in chief.

The Armada attacked by a violent storm and wrecked on the Hebrides.

Bonfires, illuminations, &c. in England for the defeat of the Armada.

1589 Sir Francis Drake and Sir John Norris capture several vessels at Corunna and take the town of Vigo. (Drake and Hawkins died in America, 1595.)

A.D.	FRANCE & SPAIN	A. D.	MISCELLANEOUS.
1569	Battle of Jarnac; Conde defeated, taken prisoner, and murdered. Coligny, the Protestant leader, defeated at Moncontour.	1570	League of Spain, Venice, and the pope against Turkey.
		1571	Turks take the isle of Cyprus.
			—— defeated by **Don John** of Austria in the naval battle of Lepanto.
1572	"Massacre of St. Bartholomew," (of the Protestants at Paris.)	1572	Pope Gregory XIII.
			Revolt of the provinces of Holland and Zealand, from the Spanish yoke—caused by the tyranny of Philip II. and his barbarous lieutenant, the duke of Alva.
1574	Henry III. — weak and profligate.	1574	Sebastian, king of Portugal, invades the Moors in Africa.
			Pacification of Gheut, by which foreign troops dismissed from the Netherlands, and the Inquisition there abolished.
		1576	Germany:—Rodolph II.
1578	Alexander Farnese, duke of Parma, general of the Spanish forces in the Netherlands.	1578	Long and bloody war between Persia and Turkey.
			Portugal:—Henry I. (Sebastian having been killed in Africa.)
	Catholic League and a new civil war; the Protestants having at their head the prince of Conde, the duke of Alencon and the king of Navarre, all of the royal family.	1579	Commencement of the Republic of HOLLAND by the Union of the Seven Provinces at Utrecht, January 13.
			—— **William,** prince of Orange, Stadtholder.
		1581	Portugal seized by Philip II. of Spain:—first of the Austrian line.
		1582	*Pope Gregory XIIIth's new style introduced in the calendar.*
			Persia acquires power under **Abbas** the Great.
		1584	Holland:—assassination of the prince of Orange. His son **Maurice** elected Stadtholder.
			League of the seven Swiss cantons at Luzerne.
		1585	Greenland discovered by Sir Francis Drake, the English navigator.
			Commerce of Holland and Hamburgh, after the decline of Antwerp and the Rhenish cities.
1588	Spain:—Destruction of the Armada.		
1589	Assassination of Henry III. by Clement, a monk. The king of Navarre succeeds as **Henry IV.** (the Great) 1st of the Bourbons; an able general and popular sovereign.	1590	Pope Urban VII.
			Telescopes, invented in Germany by *Jansen*.
1591	The Jesuits banished from France.	1591	Pope Gregory XIV. excommunicates Henry IV. of France, ineffectually.
			Pope Innocent IX.
		1592	Falkland islands discovered.
			Pope Clement VIII.

A. D. GREAT BRITAIN.

1605 Peace with Spain.

The *Gunpowder Plot*, projected by Robert Catesby, a Roman Catholic; (its object is to destroy the parliament, king, and royal family, at the approaching session)—discovered by an anonymous letter from one of the conspirators to a Roman Catholic lord. Guy Fawkes is arrested in the act of placing the fagots in the vault of the parliament house. Conspirators arrested and executed.

1612 Death of the earl of Salisbury, (R. Cecil,) and prince Henry, the heir apparent.—Robert Carr, a youth of twenty, received into the king's favour, and created earl of Somerset, and prime minister.—Murder of Sir Thomas Overbury.

1615 Disgrace of Somerset, and rise of George Villiers, the cup-bearer, a worthless favourite who is created duke of **Buckingham.**

1616 Sale of the cautionary towns in Holland, (which had been consigned to Elizabeth as security for the payment of her loans,) an unpopular expedient to raise money.

Persecution of the Catholics, Puritans, and Unitarians; Episcopacy only tolerated.

Rise of the *Independents* or *Congregationalists.*

1617 **Sir Francis Bacon** created lord chancellor. The king visits Scotland and unsuccessfully attempts to introduce there the Episcopal form of worship.

Raleigh discharged from the Tower, and receiving authority from the king, embarks to take possession of a gold mine which he pretends he had discovered in Guiana.

1618 Raleigh plunders the town of St. Thomas, returns without finding the expected treasure;—and is beheaded for having disobeyed his orders.

The *circulation of the blood*, discovered by *Harvey*.

1621 Bacon, the chancellor, now lord Verulam, and viscount of St. Albans, is impeached and fined for bribery and corruption.

The king's dispute with the Commons on his *prerogative*: they assert that *freedom of debate* in parliament is the birthright of Englishmen.

1622 The earl of Bristol sent to Spain to negotiate a marriage between prince Charles of Wales, and the infanta.

1623 Secret journey of the prince and the duke of Buckingham to Spain. The latter disgusts even the Spanish court by his licentiousness. The marriage treaty broken off. Bristol committed to the Tower.

1625 James I. dies. He possessed some learning and abilities, but was pedantic and weak.

English settlement at Madras.

Massinger, the dramatist.

A. D.	NORTH AMERICA.	A. D.	FRANCE & SPAIN.	A. D.	MISCELLANEOUS.
1607	English Settlement at Jamestown, Virginia; (the first permanent one in America) by a colony of the London Comp. Captain John **Smith**, its leader, is taken prisoner by the Indians: his life is saved by Pocahontas.	1610	Assassination of Henry IV. by Ravaillac. Louis XIII (9 years old) succeeds under the regency of Mary of Medicis, his mother.	1605	Pope Paul V.
				1609	Holland: A truce with Spain. Independence of the provinces acknowledged. Evangelical Union of the Protestant princes, and league of the Catholic princes in Germany. Theological dispute between *Arminius* and *Gomar*, both professors of Theology at Leyden. *Galileo*, *Harriot*, and *Drebbel*. Sweden:—**Gustavus Adolphus**, king.
1613	The Dutch commence settlements on the Hudson river.			1612	Poles defeated by the Russians in Muscovy. Germany:—Matthias, emperor;—attempts to reconcile the Catholics and Protestants, and
				1615	—concludes an advantageous peace with the Turks.
1616	Raleigh's attempt to colonize Virginia.	1616	The prince of Conde is sent to the Bastile.	1617	Peace between the house of Austria and the Venetians.
				1618	*Synod of Dort*, begins November 21, and continues till April 26, 1619. Germany:—Ferdinand II. —— —— Thirty years War between the Protestants and Catholics, begins, after Frederick V. elector palatine, had accepted the crown of Bohemia, offered him by the Protestant states.
1620	Landing of the Pilgrims at Plymouth, New England, under charter of James I:— **John Carver**, 1st governor.	1620	Navarre annexed to France.	1620	Bohemians defeated by the imperialists at Prague. Frederick, elector palatine and king of Bohemia deposed and loses all his dominions by the treaty of Ulm.
1621	Carver's treaty with Massasoit. Sir F. Wyatt governor of Virginia.	1621	Spain:—Philip V.—Olivares, his minister.	1621	War between Spain and Holland renewed. Pope Gregory XV.
				1622	Heidleburg taken by the emperor, and its library sent to Rome. Pope Urban VIII.
1622	Laconia granted to Gorges and Mason.	1624	Cardinal **Richelieu**, prime minister.	1624	Dutch defeat the Spanish fleet near Lima. *Peter Paul Rubens*, painter.
1624	Royal government in Virginia.	1625	The princess Henrietta married to Charles I. of England.	1625	Breda taken by the Spaniards. Peace between Ferdinand of Hungary, and the sultan. Christian IV. of Denmark becomes the leader of the Protestants.

A. D. GREAT BRITAIN.

1625 —————— Charles I.—2d Stuart, ——————
ascends the throne at the age of 25—disappointed in his plans, by the excessive parsimony of the commons; declares himself a Protestant, and supports Episcopacy; Marries the princess Henrietta of France.

First English settlement in the West Indies, at Barbadoes.

1626 Impeachment of the king's favourite, and director, the duke of Buckingham, for having appropriated public money to his own use, &c. He is supported by the king, who refuses to listen to the charges, and asserts his own *unlimited prerogative*.

War declared against France.

1627 Buckingham fails in attempting to relieve Rochelle: General dissatisfaction.—The Commons frame the "*Petition of right*," praying for redress of various grievances. Charles obliged to pass it, in order to obtain a supply.

1630 Peace with France and Spain. *Laud*, archbishop of Canterbury, persecutes the Puritans, (many of whom embark for America,) and introduces into the church, with the king's consent, many superstitious ceremonies similar to those of Rome.

Murmurings on account of the arbitrary proceedings of the courts of the Star Chamber, and High Commission.

John Hampden, the fearless and patriotic defender of the *rights of the people*, refuses to pay the revived tax of *ship money*, or tonnage and poundage. The matter of *right* in his case, decided before twelve judges, in favour of the *crown*.

Great tumult at Edinburgh on the day appointed for the introduction of a new service book by the king's order; the bishop hooted with the cry of "a pope!" "antichrist!" stone him!

Treaty with the protestant princes of Germany, and their allies.

1638 The Scots being refused their petition against the Liturgy, enter into a new "*Covenant*," or civil and religious convention

1639 and abolish Episcopacy by an act of their general Assembly.

1640 Parliament assembled by the king, after an intermission of 11 years, but refusing to grant supplies until the grievances are redressed, is dissolved.

Scottish covenanters in arms; defeat the English forces at Newburn, and take possession of Newcastle.

Meeting of the *Long Parliament*. Impeachment of the earl of Strafford, (late lieutenant of Ireland,) archbishop Laud, lord keeper Finch, and secretary Windebank, all for high treason.

1641 Strafford makes an able and eloquent defence, but is condemned and executed.

Abolition of the Courts of Star Chamber, and High Commission, and of the tax of ship money.

Rebellion of Roger Moore, in Ireland. Rise of the *Round-heads*, and *Cavaliers*, both of the popular party. Massacre of several thousand Protestants in Ireland by the Catholics.

A. D.	NORTH AMERICA.
1626	Frs. West, governor of Virginia.
1627	Swedes and Fins settle on the Delaware.
1629	New-Hampshire granted to John Mason. Wonter Van Twiller, governor of N. Amsterdam.
1630	Carolina granted to Sir Robt. Heath.
	First permanent settlement in Maine.
1631	Connecticut granted to lords Say and Brook,
1632	and Maryland to lord **Baltimore.**
1636	Rhode Island settled :—(*Roger Williams.*)
1637	*Harvard College* founded.
	New-Hampshire settled.
1637	*Ann Hutchinson's theological disturbances.* Pequod Indians subdued.
1638	Settlement of N. Haven, Conn.
1639	The first *printing office* in America at Cambridge, by Sam'l Green.
	Theoph. Eaton, 1st governor of New-Haven.
	Berkley, governor of Virginia.
1640	Whole number of emigrants to New-England previous to this time is 21,000.
1641	R. Bellingham, governor of Massachusetts.

A.D.	FRANCE & SPAIN.
1627	War with Charles I. who assists the Protestants.
1628	Rochelle surrendered by the Protestants after a memorable siege. Favourable terms are granted them.
1630	France joins the confederacy of Holland, Sweden, and the Protestant princes, against the emperor.
1635	*French Academy* established.
	War against Spain. Treaty with Holland,
1636	and with Sweden.
1640	Spain :—Independence of Portugal.

A.D.	MISCELLANEOUS.
1626	League of the Protestant princes of Germany with Sweden and Holland against the emperor.
	Tilly, general of the Imperialists, gains a victory over Christian IV.
1628	Persia invaded by the Turks.
1629	Peace between Denmark and Germany, and between Poland and Sweden.
	Gustavus Adolphus enters Germany to assist the Evangelical Union.
1630	*Gazettes* first published in Venice.
	England and France join the alliance against the emperor.
	War between Germany and Spain.
	Poland invaded by the Turks.
1631	Imperialists defeated by the Swedes in the battle of Leipsic.
1632	Battle of Lutzen ; the Swedes again victorious, but Gustavus Adolphus is killed.
	Sweden :—Christina, queen.
1633	Galileo condemned by the inquisition.
1634	Swedes defeated by the king of Hungary in the battle of Nordlingen.
1635	Peace of Prague, between the evangelical union and the emperor.
1636	Imperialists defeated by the Swedes at Wistock.
1637	War between the Poles and Cossacks in Ukraine.
	Germany.—Ferdinand III.
	Breda retaken by the prince of Orange.
1638	Bagdad taken by the Turks.
	Saxe-Weimar, duke of, defeats the Imperialists at Rhinfield, and reduces Brisac.
1639	Imperialists defeated in Bohemia by the Swedes under Bannier.
1640	Portugal recovers her independence under John IV. (first of the house of Braganza.)

A. D. GREAT BRITAIN.

1642 The king after a long and violent dispute with his parliament retires to York; resolves to have recourse to the sword; and erects his standard at Nottingham.—Parliament also assembles an army.—Battle of Edghill; (Oct. 24:) the royalists commanded by the king in person, his nephew prince Rupert, and Ruthven, a Swedish general; Parliamentarians by the earl of Essex:—victory doubtful.

1643 Rupert victorious at Calsgrave, where the famous John Hampden is mortally wounded.
Defeat of the Parliamentarians under Sir William Waller.
Battle of Newbury; (Sept. 20.) Essex victorious.
The *Westminster Assembly of Divines.*
"*Solemn League and Covenant,*" between the English and Scottish parliaments

1644 Battle of Marston Moor;—the royalists under Rupert defeated with great slaughter, by lord Fairfax and Oliver Cromwell.
York surrenders to the parliament. Newcastle taken by the Scots.
Disputes between the Presbyterians and the Independents or Congregationalists; the latter favoured by Cromwell, who proposes the *self denying ordinance*, excluding the members of Parliament from all offices, civil, and military. Essex consequently resigns, and the whole military authority under parliament is vested in Sir Thomas Fairfax and Oliver Cromwell.

1645 Trial and execution of archbishop Laud. The king's cause supported in Scotland by James Graham, marquis of Montrose.
Battle of Naseby; the king defeated by Cromwell, loses 5,000 men, and finally every fortress in England.

1646 —— seeks refuge in the Scottish camp at Newark.

1647 —— is delivered up by the Scots to the English parliament, for a stipulated sum.
Quarrel between the army and the parliament, inflamed by Cromwell, Ireton, and Fleetwood. The king seized by Joyce. The army takes possession of London.

1648 The king escapes and is retaken. Col. Pride with a party of Soldiers, expels the Presbyterians from parliament; an act called "Pride's Purge." The house now consisting of but 50 Independents receives the appellation of "*The Rump.*"
Scots under Hamilton, and the English insurgents, subdued by Cromwell. The king sentenced by a court of 133 judges to suffer death, as guilty of high treason in levying war against the parliament.

1649 Beheading of Charles I. on the scaffold erected in the street before Whitehall; "An awful lesson to the possessors of royalty." The Commons proceed to pass an act, abolishing kingly power, and the house of peers, as "useless, burdensome, and dangerous." *Usher, Hobbes, Hammond, Selden, Inigo Jones.*

The Commonwealth.

The Commons order a new seal to be engraved with this legend, "On the first year of freedom, by God's blessing restored." They appoint a Council of State. Cromwell lord lieutenant of Ireland; sends out an army against the marquis of Ormond (who still supports royalty,) and soon after follows in person. Charles the prince of Wales is acknowledged as king, by the Scottish Covenanters.

1650 Cromwell subdues Ireland. In Scotland, the marquis of Montrose is made prisoner, and executed. Prince Charles makes a bargain with the Covenanters on their own terms. Cromwell appointed commander in chief of the forces after the resignation of Fairfax, enters Scotland with an army of 16,000; defeats the royalists at Dunbar, and takes Leith and Edinburgh.

A. D.	NORTH AMERICA.	A. D.	FRANCE & SPAIN.	A. D.	MISCELLANEOUS.
1642	George Wyllis governor of Connecticut.			1642	Swedes defeat the Imperialists of Leipsic, and the French defeat them at Tutelingen.
1643	Confederation of the Colonies of New-England, for mutual defence. J. Endicott, governor of Massachusetts.	1643	Conde defeats the Spaniards at Rocroy. **Louis XIV.** Anne of Austria, queen regent during the king's minority. Cardinal **Mazarine,** succeeds Richelieu and adopts his policy. Royal Academy of *Painting,* founded by the king.	1643	Tartars invade China. *Barometers* invented by Toricelli.
				1644	**Revolution in China by the Tartars;**—Tsong-gate the Tartar prince, becomes emperor of China. Swedes defeat the Imperialists in Bohemia. Pope Innocent X.
		1645	Marshall **Turenne** takes Treves,	1645	Swedes under Torstenson, victorious over the Imperialists at Thabor. The emperor leaves Vienna for Ratisbon. War between the Venetians and Turks. Russia:—Alexius, czar. The first *Russian code of laws* published.
1646	*Thos. Mayhew,* preacher to the Indians, shipwrecked.			1646	Venetians defeated by the Turks near Retimo. A shower of sulphur at Copenhagen.
1647	*Thomas Hooker,* ob. Peter Stuyvesant, governor of New Amsterdam.				
1648	*Cambridge Platform,* adopted.	1648	and is victorious at Augsburg. Dissensions in Paris fomented by cardinal De Retz.	1648	Imperialists defeated by Turenne at Augsburgh. Peace of Munster between Spain and the United Provinces. Oct. 28. **Peace of Westphalia,** signed at Munster, between France, the emperor, and Sweden; the principle of a *balance of power* in Europe is first recognized; Alsace given to France, and a part of Pomerania, and some other districts to Sweden: the civil and political rights of the German States established; the independence of the Swiss Confederation acknowledged by Germany; and the rights of the Protestants confirmed.
1649	**J. Winthrop,** governor of Connecticut, ob.	1649	The populace barricade the streets, and liberate the state prisoners. Mazarine declared by parliament an enemy of the public peace.	1649	League between Denmark and Holland. *Grotius,* an eminent Dutch writer; *Vandyck,* the painter.
1650	First settlement in North Carolina, around Albemarle Sound.	1650	—— regains his authority. Conde, and other princes of the royal blood are arrested.		

A. D. GREAT BRITAIN.

1664 War with Holland, and her allies, France and Denmark.

1665 The duke of York, (the king's brother,) victorious over the Dutch fleet.
The Great Plague in London; carries off 100,000 persons.

1666 Memorable sea-fight of four days off Dunkirk, (June 1,) between the English fleet under Monk, (now duke of Albermarle,) and prince Rupert; and the Dutch under De Ruyter, and the younger Van Tromp. The latter forced to retreat, and insulted in their harbours.
Great Fire in London, Sep. 3, continues 3 days, consuming 13,000 houses.
Insurrection in Scotland of the Presbyterians, who are defeated at Pentland hills.
The Dutch fleet under De Ruyter enters the Thames, and burns several ships at Chatham, causing great consternation in London.

1667 Peace of Breda, by which the Dutch cede to England, the province of New-York.
Banishment of the earl of Clarendon, a man of great abilities and stern integrity.

1668 England a party in the Triple Alliance, through her ambassador, Sir William Temple.

1669 The "Cabal" ministry formed; Clifford, Ashley, Buckingham, Arlington and Lauderdale; an intriguing and dangerous combination.
Secret treaty with France, concluded by the king.

1671 The king shuts the exchequer, and exercises several acts of arbitrary power.

1672 Attack on the Dutch Smyrna fleet, made by Sir Robert Holmes.
War against Holland, declared by England and France.
Sea-fight, (May 28.) between the Dutch fleet under De Witt and De Ruyter, and the combined French and English under the duke of York, the earl of Sandwich, and D'Estrees. The Dutch forced to retire.

1673 Parliament passes the *Test Act.* Indecisive engagements between the Dutch and combined fleets off the Texel.

1674 Peace between England and Holland. (War continued by France,)
Sir William Temple appointed ambassador to the states general of the provinces.

A. D. NORTH AMERICA.

1663 Rhode Island chartered. Carolina granted to the earl of Clarendon.

John Norton ob.

1664 New-Netherlands surrendered by the Dutch to the English;—granted to the duke of York, and named New-York, N. Jersey, granted to Berkley and Carteret.

J. Elliot's *Indian Bible*.

1665 The Colonies of Connecticut & New Haven united.

J. Endicot, ob.

1669 *R. Mather*, ob.

1671 *J. Davenport*, ob.

New Jersey settled.

Charleston (S. C.) founded.

Carolina divided into North and South.

1672 *Charles Chauncey*, minister of the 1st church in Boston ob.

1673 New-York reconquered by the Dutch but

1674 is ceded to England by treaty.

A.D. FRANCE & SPAIN.

1664 Treaty with the pope.

Observatory and Academy for *sculpture* established.

1665 Spain:—CharlesII. (weak;) unsuccessful war with France.

1656 France declares war against England.

Louis XIV. invades the Netherlands, which he claims in right of his queen.

1668 Peace of Aix-la-Chapelle between France and Spain. The former yielding Franche-Compte but retaining her conquests in the Netherlands

1672 Louis passes the Rhine with marshal **Turenne**, having formally declared war against Holland, which is assisted by the Emperor and by Spain.

1674 Victory of Turenne over the Imperialists.

The French first settle in the East Indies.

A. D. MISCELLANEOUS.

1663 Two meteoric stones, one weighing 200, and the other 300 lbs. fell near Verona.

Portuguese defeated by the Spaniards, near Evora.

1664 Holland at war with England;—admiral **De Witt**.

Treaty of Pisa between the king of France and the pope.

War between Germany and the Turks.

1665 The Dutch defeated by the English, near Harwich,

1666 and again off Dunkirk. They ally with Denmark.

Portuguese defeat the Spaniards at Villia.

Antigua settled by the English.

1667 Holland:—Peace of Breda with England.

The Spanish Netherlands invaded by Louis XIV. who terrifies Europe by the progress of his arms.

Pope Clement IX.

1668 Triple Alliance, of Britain, Sweden, and Holland, against France.

Peace between Portugal and Spain, after a war of 26 years:—The former acknowledged independent.

1669 Candia taken by the Turks.

Treaty of the Hague between Holland and Portugal.

1671 Pope Clement X. Cassini discovers the 6th of Saturn's satellites.

1672 War between the Poles and Turks.

Holland:—William III. prince of Orange, stadtholder, and commander in chief.

—— Assassination of the two brothers De Witt, who had assumed the helm of affairs.

—— The prince of Orange nobly rejects the corrupting offers of Louis, and allies with Sweden and Germany.

Poland:—Henry, the first, elective king.

1673 Sea-fight between the Dutch and English.

The Poles defeat the Turks near Chocsin.

1674 Treaty between Holland, Spain, and Britain.

Sicily revolts from Spain.

The Imperialists, defeated by Turenne at Mulhausen and at Turkheim.

A. D. **GREAT BRITAIN.**

1677 Marriage of the lady Mary, daughter of the duke of York, to William III. prince of Orange.

1678 Great consternation in England by the rumour of a "Popish Plot." Titus Oates, the abandoned impostor, affirms on oath, that a horrid conspiracy had been formed by the Jesuits for assassinating the king, restoring Popery, &c. and in proof produces forged letters from prominent Catholics. His story, though contradictory, generally believed, and several peers are in consequence, committed to the Tower. Coleman the queen's secretary, and others are executed. Oates caressed and rewarded as the saviour of his country. Impeachment and committal of the lord-treasurer, Danby.

1679 The *Habeas Corpus Act* passed. Assassination of archbishop Sharpe, of St. Andrews, by the Covenanters, on suspicion of his being hostile to their cause. The Covenanters severely persecuted; have recourse to arms and are defeated by the duke of Monmouth (the king's natural son) at Bothwell bridge.

"The Meal Tub plot."

1680 The slavish doctrines of *passive obedience* and *non-resistance* begin to be inculcated. The epithets of *Whig* and *Tory* in use; the first applied to the country, the latter to the court party. Trial and execution of lord Stafford as concerned in the popish plot.

1681 "Rye-house Plot" for restoring the freedom of the constitution.

Execution of lord Russell and Sir Algernon Sidney, two of the leaders in the conspiracy.

1684 Marriage of lady Anne,* second daughter of the duke of York, to prince George of Denmark.

1685 Charles II. dies suddenly.—He had obtained absolute power.

In this reign the *Royal Society* of London was instituted by *Wilkins*, bishop of Chester, and others. Bombay, E. I., was ceded to England by the Portuguese.

Flourished in this reign: *Dryden* and *Butler*, the poets;—*Barrow*, a divine; *Sir W. Temple*, an eminent writer as well as statesman; *Robert Boyle*, the philosopher.

James II.—4th Stuart,

(late duke of York, and brother of Charles II., who had no legitimate children,) declares his intention of maintaining the established religion while secretly planning its overthrow;—is treated with great complacency by the English and Scotch parliaments.—A conspiracy formed against him in Holland by the duke of Monmouth, natural son of Charles II. and the duke of Argyle. The latter lands in Scotland, is taken prisoner and executed. Monmouth defeated, and made prisoner by the king's forces under the earl of Feversham at Sedgemoor. The rebel prisoners treated with frightful cruelty by Feversham, colonel Kirk, and chief justice Jeffries: 250 of them executed.

1686 The king publicly countenances the Catholics;—receives several into the council;—creates the earl of Tyrconnel lord lieutenant of Ireland.

1687 —— re-establishes the court of High Commissions;—sends an ambassador to Rome;—receives the pope's nuncio;—is warmly opposed in attempting to elevate a papist to the presidency of Magdalen College, Oxford.

*** Afterwards queen.**

A. D.	N. AMERICA.	A. D.	FRANCE & SPAIN.	A. D.	MISCELLANEOUS.
1675	Andros, governor of New-York. King Philip's war in New-England. Population of N. England 60,000.	1677	Treaty with England.	1675	War between Denmark and Sweden. Turenne passes the Rhine and is opposed by Monteculi. Pope Innocent XI.
				1076	The allied fleet defeated by the French at Palermo. Poland, Stephen, king.
1677	Maine purchased by Massachusetts.	1678	Peace with Holland. Louis supports a large army and conducts as sovereign of Europe.	1678	Peace of Nimeguen, between France and Holland, restores tranquillity to Europe. Tartars invade Russia.
1679	New-Hampshire becomes a separate state under royal government.	1682	General assembly of the clergy of France in which the four celebrated propositions about the authority of the pope are enacted.	1679	Peace between Germany and France signed at Nimeguen and between Denmark and Sweden at Fontainbleau. Engagement between the English and Moors at Tangier, which continues eleven days.
1680	Josiah Winslow, ob.				
1682	**Penn** arrives and founds Philadelphia, in Pennsylvania.				
1683	First general assembly in New-York.			1683	Siege of Vienna by the Turks, raised by John **Sobieski** king of Poland.
1684	Massachusetts deprived of her charter. Philadelphia contains 2,000 persons.	1685	*Revocation of the Edict of Nantes.* The protestants violently persecuted, and Louis loses 500,000 of his best subjects. *Le Brun, Menage, Bruyere, Boileau*, &c.	1684	The duke of Lorraine defeats 150,000 Turks at Wertzen.
1686	Sir Edmund Andros, appointed governor of N. England by James II. plays the tyrant. Arrival of French protestants who had left their country on account of the revocation of the Edict of Nantes.	1685	The greatness of Louis XIV. at its height. **Colbert,** prime minister.	1686	The king of Siam sends an embassy to Louis XIV. League of Augsburg against France, between Germany, Holland Britain and Spain; brought about by William, prince of Orange, the inveterate enemy of the powerful and ambitious Louis XIV.
				1687	*Telegraphs* said to have been invented. The crown of Hungary declared hereditary in the house of Austria.

A. D. GREAT BRITAIN.

1688 The king orders a declaration of "Indulgence" to all sects to be read in the Churches.—Sancroft, archbishop of Canterbury, and six bishops petition against the Indulgence and are committed to the Tower; tried and acquitted.

Commencement of the Revolution.—The Whigs and Tories unite to secure the constitution, and invite William, prince of Orange, (married to Mary, daughter of James II.) to accept the crown of England. The prince of Orange, after being driven back by a storm, lands at Torbay with 15,000 men, from a fleet of 600 vessels;—publishes a list of grievances of the people of Great Britain, and his purpose of relieving them; is joined after a long delay by several noblemen, and a part of the army. James sails to France.

1689 The convention of the nobility and prelates, after much dispute, votes the throne vacant, James II. having broken the "original contract," and declares the prince and princess of Orange, king and queen of England.

Prideaux an eminent divine, and author.

— **William III. and Mary,** (5th Stuart.) —

Instrument of settlement passed by parliament.*

War against France declared in alliance with Germany and Holland. The great struggle respecting "*Privilege* and *Prerogative*" finally settled, and the *British Constitution* confirmed. Act of Toleration passed. Presbyterianism re-established in Scotland.

James II. lands in Ireland: his cause supported by Tyrconnel. He raises an army:—is re-inforced by French troops; assembles the Irish parliament which attaints all the Protestants in the island. The Jacobites, or partizans of the Catholic cause in Scotland defeat general Mackay at Killicrankie, but Dundee their leader is killed, and they disperse. James besieges the Protestants in Londonderry; they are relieved after a gallant defence.

1690 King William lands in Ireland. Battle of the Boyne, in which the gallant **Schomberg,** William's general, is killed;—but James is defeated, and returns to France. William repulsed in the siege of Limerick. The earl of Marlborough reduces Cork and Kinsale.

1691 Athlone and Limerick taken by baron Ginckle for William, whose authority is now generally acknowledged in Ireland.

The king dissolves the convention, and assembles a Tory parliament.

1692 Massacre of Glencoe in Scotland. King William takes the command of the allied army in Holland. An invasion of England undertaken by the French, in favour of James.

British fleet under Russell, victorious over the French, (Tourville) who abandons the intended invasion.

1694 Triennial Parliament bill passed. Bank of England incorporated. Queen Mary dies, æt. 33.—Barclay's plot for assassinating the king.

Russell strikes terror along the French coast.—King William retakes Namur.

---

* Anne, daughter of James II. to succeed in default of children of queen Mary.

A. D. NORTH AMERICA.	A.D. FRANCE & SPAIN.	A. D. MISCELLANEOUS.
1688 General suppression of charter governments. 1689 Andros imprisoned. The government of N. York, usurped by Jacob Leisler. Montreal destroyed by the Five Nations.		War of the continental powers against France. 1688 Smyrna nearly destroyed by an earthquake. Imperialists take Belgrade by assault. First *German periodical*, (Thomasius.) French fashions, language, and industry in Germany and England.
Dover, N. H. surprised by the Indians. War between England and France. 1690 The English settlements of Schenectady, N. Y. Casco, Me. and Salmon-Falls, N. H. destroyed by a party of French sent by the governor of Canada. Sir William Phipps reduces Port Royal, Nova Scotia. Unsuccessful expedition against Canada.	1689 War against the allies, Spain, England, Holland and Germany.	1689 Pope Alexander VIII. Turks in alliance with France, defeated in three battles by the Imperialists under prince Louis of Baden. Grand Alliance between England Germany and Holland signed at Vienna; which is afterwards acceded to by Spain and the duke of Savoy.
	1690 Tourville defeats the English and Dutch off Beachyhead. Luxembourg victorious at Fleurus.	1690 Dutch defeated with great slaughter by Luxembourg in the battle of Fleurus. (June 21.) 1691 Mons taken by Louis XIV. Pope Innocent XII.
1691 Schuyler defeats the French at La Prairie. New Hampshire purchased by Allen. N. Y.:—Stoughter, governor. Leisler executed. 1692 Witchcraft superstition in New-England.	1691 Louis takes Mons. 12,000 Irish Catholics arrive in France. 1693 Catinat victorious in Italy. Order of St. Louis instituted. 1694 Noailles defeats the Spaniards.	1693 Dutch and English fleets defeated by the French off St. Vincent. Allies defeated by Luxembourg at Landen. Battle of Massiglia:—the duke of Savoy, general of the allies in Italy, defeated by the marshal de Catinat. 1694 Huy retaken by the allies. Namur by the French.
1693 N. Y.—*Episcopacy* introduced. —— Fletcher, governor. William and Mary's *College* founded.		1696 Russia:—PETER, I. (the Great.)

A. D. GREAT BRITAIN.

1697 Peace of Ryswick.

1699 Visit of Peter the Great, of Russia.

1700 Sir George Rooke, with a British fleet, is sent to assist Charles XII. of Sweden.

Ruin of the Scottish settlements on the isthmus of Darien.

1701 Settlement of the succession to the British throne, (after the princess Anne) on the princess Sophia, dutchess dowager of Hanover.

England a party in another confederacy. (See Misc.) Death of James II. in France. His son James is acknowledged by Louis XIV. as king of Great Britain.

1702 Death of the king.—William was eminent both as a politician and a warrior. He rescued England from Popery and arbitrary power, but laid the foundation of the *National Debt.* System of *private banking* commenced. This was the age of those great luminaries of science, Newton and *Locke.*—*Tillotson,* archbishop of Canterbury.

— **Anne,** (6th Stuart.) —

Marlborough and **Godolphin** chief ministers.

War with France and Spain in consequence of the league of 1701. Marlborough commands the British army; begins his victorious career in Flanders.

Sir George Rooke, and the duke of Ormond fail in an attempt upon Cadiz, but capture Spanish galleons at Vigo.

Defeat of the English admiral Benbow by the French Du Casse, off Carthagena.

1703 Jacobite intrigues. Tory principles ascendant.

1704 Whigs obtain a share in the administration.

Simon Frazer, lord Lovats' conspiracy in favour of " the pretender" James Stuart, son of James II. who styles himself Le Chavalier de St. George.

Marlborough's great victory at Blenheim. He is honoured by the court of Berlin and the States General.

Rooke takes the important Spanish fortress of Gibraltar, hitherto impregnable.

1705 Earl of **Peterborough,** Sir C. **Shovel,** and the archduke Charles take Barcelona.

1706 Marlborough's victories at Ramilies, &c.

Sir John Leake takes the islands of Majorca and Ivica in the Mediterranean.

Legislative Union of England and Scotland, treaty of, signed July 20. Both kingdoms to be represented in one parliament, enjoy equal privileges, &c. Dissatisfaction in Scotland.

A. D. NORTH AMERICA.

1697 Kidd's piracies.

1700 Boston contains 7,000 inhabitants.
R. Island, 10,000
N. Carolina, 6,000
S. Carolina, 5,500

1701 *Yale College* founded.

1702 War of G. Britain with France and Spain.

1703 Apalachian Indians subdued.
Maine, from Casco to Wells, ravaged by the French and Indians.

1704 Deerfield destroyed by the Indians.
Capt. **Church's** expedition against the Indians.
Boston News Letter, the first *American periodical.*

1706 Episcopacy in Connecticut.
Carolina invaded by the French and Spanish.
Samuel Willard, ob.

A. D. FRANCE & SPAIN.

1767 Peace of Ryswick.

1699 North America:—French colony settles in Louisiana.

1700 Spain is transferred to the house of Bourbon, by the will of Chas. II. in favour of the duke of Anjou, grandson of Louis XIV.

1701—Anjou is crowned as
—Philip V.—
League against the allies between France, Spain and Portugal. Philip's title is disputed by Charles archduke of Austria; hence the "war of the Spanish succession." *Fenelon* and *Maintenon*, flourished.

1702 **Tallard, Bouflers, Villeroy, Villars,** and the king of Spain, command the French and Spanish armies.
Bavaria aids France.

1704 Defeat of Tallard at Blenheim.
Spain loses Gibraltar.

1705 Vendome victorious at Cassano.
Spain:—Barcelona taken by the allies.

1706 French defeated at Ramilies

A. D. MISCELLANEOUS.

1697 Battle of Zenta:—prince **Eugene** of Savoy, defeats the Turks under Mustapha.
Peace of Ryswick, September 11, between France and the Allies.
Sweden:—Charles XII.

1698 Peter the Great travels in disguise through Germany and Holland: visits England to learn the art of ship-building, and the science of government; labours in person in the dock yard; and after two years absence introduces among his untutored subjects the arts and customs of civilized society.

1699 Peace of Carlowitz between Russia, Poland, Venice and Turkey.
League against Sweden, (Charles XII.) between Denmark, Poland, and Russia.

1700 Charles XII. invades Denmark, besieges Copenhagen, and obliges the king to sign the treaty of Travendahl.
Battle of Narva: (Russians and Swedes,) Charles victorious.

1701 PRUSSIA becomes a kingdom:—
—— Frederick I.
Another "Grand Alliance" between Germany, Holland and England, "to prevent the union of the crowns of France and Spain," which causes the "war of the Spanish succession."
Leibnitz, the celebrated German philosopher.

1702 War against France declared at London, Vienna, and the Hague, on the same day.
Imperialists take Landau and Venloo.
Charles XII. takes Warsaw, and defeats Augustus II. of Poland at Glissau.

1703 Portugal and Savoy join the Grand Alliance.

1704 Battle of Blenheim; Marlborough and Eugene completely victorious over the French, Spanish and Bavarians.
Peter the Great takes Narva.
Charles XII. again beats Augustus, at Pultausk, and procures his deposition, and the election of **Stanislaus** Leckzinski, to the throne of Poland.

1705 Marlborough victorious at Brabant.—Eugene defeated at Cassano.
Germany:—Joseph I. succeeds his father Leopold.

1706 Battle of Ramilies: Marlborough victorious and conquers Brabant and Spanish Flanders,

1741 Defeat of admiral Vernon before Carthagena, S. A.

Remarkable motion of Lord Somerset in parliament, that "his majesty be requested not to involve these kingdoms in war, to preserve his foreign dominions."

1742 Resignation of Sir R. Walpole, after being created earl of Orford.

New ministry; Cartaret, Sandys, and Pulteny, now earl of Bath.

An army sent over to assist the archduchess of Austria.

Intrepid conduct of commodore Martin in the bay of Naples. He compels the king of Naples to promise neutrality during the war.

1743 King George in person, and the earl of Stair, command the English army which is victorious in the battle of Dettingen.

New intrigues of the Jacobites.

1744 French fleet intended to invade Scotland is driven back.

War declared against France.

Anson returns from his first circumnavigating voyage of three years.

Pelham at the head of a new cabinet, which is called the "broad bottom," as comprising the able and honest of all parties.

1745 Duke of **Cumberland** commands the English at Fontenoy.

Charles Edward, son of James the pretender, lands in Scotland; is joined by Cameron of Lochiel and other highland chiefs; takes possession of Perth, Dundee and Edinburgh, proclaiming 'his father, king of Great Britain;' assembles an army, defeats Sir John Cope at Preston-Pans; enters England, takes Carlisle, reaches Derby; retreats;

1746 —— takes Sterling; beats general Hawley at Falkirk, January 8; is totally defeated in the battle of Culloden, April 16, by the duke of Cumberland; escapes to France his cause is crushed and many of his partisans suffer on the scaffold.

East Indies:—Madras, an English settlement, taken by the French.

1747 Commodores Fox, Anson, Warren, and Hawke, capture French vessels.

1748 Peace of Aix la Chapelle;—England gains nothing for her trouble, but the treaty is welcomed with bonfires and illuminations.

W. Pitt, sen., and **C. J. Fox**, received into the cabinet.

A. D.	N. AMERICA.	A.D.	FRANCE & SPAIN.	A. D.	MISCELLANEOUS.
1740	Oglethorpe invades Florida.			1740	Germany:—On the death of Charles VI. his daughter, Maria Theresa, (married to the duke of Lorraine) succeeds, agreeably to the pragmatic sanction, to the whole Austrian dominions; and receives the homage of Hungary, Bohemia, and Italy. Prussia:—FREDERICK II. (the Great.)
1741	*Moravians* first settle in America at Bethlehem. Conspiracy of the negroes at New-York.	1641	France in league with Prussia against Austria. Mareschals Belleisle and Broglio sent to aid the Bavarians.	1741	—— lays claim to *Silesia*, which begins the eight years war with the house of Austria. Frederick conquers Silesia, and leagues with France to subvert the Austrian power. The elector of Bavaria supported by France, claims the imperial crown. French and Bavarians take Prague.
1742	Spanish fleet invades Georgia, and is repulsed.			1742	Germany:—The elector of Bavaria crowned as Charles VII. Austrian troops expel the French from Bavaria, take Munich, and besiege the French in Prague. Bellisle retreats Treaty of Breslau, between Prussia and Austria: Silesia ceded to Prussia.
		1743	Treaty with Spain at Fountainbleau. Noailles defeated at Dettingen.	1743	Alliance of Austria, Sardinia, Prussia and Britain against France. Battle of Campo Santo, January 17: between the Spanish and Austrians. Battle of Dettingen, June 26; French defeated by the allies. War between Persia and Turkey.
				1744	Treaty between Germany, Prussia and Sweden. Frederick the Great takes Prague but evacuates Bohemia.
1745	Re-conquest of Louisbourg and Cape Breton by the English provincials under Peperell and Warren.	1745	Saxe gains the battle of Fontenoy. An army granted to the English 'pretender.'	1745	Pavia and Milan taken by the French and Spanish. Battle of Fontenoy, April 30; allies under Cumberland, Konigseg, and Waldeck defeated by the French. Germany:—Francis I.—(1st of the house of Lorraine or modern Austria, and husband of Maria Theresa) is elected; France *per contra* notwithstanding.
		1746	Conquest of Flanders, &c. Spain:——Ferdinand VI.	1746	Brussels, Mons, Namur, and finally all Flanders and Brabant, are conquered by the French.
1747	*Benjamin Coleman* and *David Brainerd*, ob.		Forty-six French W. India ships and six frigates taken by the English.	1747	Persian revolution; Kouli Khan murdered.
				1748	Peace of Aix la Chapelle, closing the 8 years war:—Silesia is ceded to Prussia, and the duchies of Parma, Placenza, and Guastalla to the infant don Philip of Spain. Prosperity in Europe after this treaty.

A. D. GREAT BRITAIN.

1750 Death of Frederick prince of Wales. This year remarkable for crimes.
The *New Style*, (Gregory's) introduced; the year hereafter commences Jan. 1.

1751 East Indies:—Mahommed Ally, supported by the English, and Chunda Saheb by the *French*, as nabob of Arcot. War ensues. Clive the English Company's agent subdues Arcot, and takes Saheb prisoner.—A truce.

1752 North America:—Commencement of the dispute between the French and English colonies.
English Ohio Co. formed for the fur trade, which the French had monopolized.
Act passed, naturalizing the Jews in Great Britain.

1753 French commence hostilities in Nova Scotia.
Sir *Hans Sloane's museum*, with the *Harleian Manuscripts*, purchased by parliament.

1754 Death of Mr. Pelham. The duke of Newcastle succeeds him.

1755 North America:—Monckton conquers Nova Scotia.
—— Braddock's expedition against the French fort Du Quesne, cut off by the French and Indians in *ambush*. Dunbar succeeds Braddock.
—— Sir William Johnson's success against the French under Dieskau in Canada.
Failure of the expeditions against Crown Point and Niagara.

1756 "Seven years War" with France begins in form.
Parliament votes £100,000 to relieve the sufferers by the earthquake at Lisbon.
Admiral Byng arrested, for having cowardly yielded Minorca to the French.
North America:-General Abercrombie and lord Loudon command the British forces.
East Indies:—The English fort at Calcutta, taken by the nabob of Bengal.
—— Imprisonment of Holwell, (the English Co's agent) with 146 companions in the "black hole" where all but 23 perish in dreadful tortures.
—— Watson and Clive take the fort of Geriah.
New ministry: Pitt, (now the most popular man in the kingdom) premier.

1757 Execution of Byng. Admiral Knowles takes the isle of Aix.
Pitt and Fox dismissed for opposing an interference in the continental war.
Hanover taken by the French. Cumberland the British general signs the "convention of Closter-seven," which leaves the French in possession of Hanover.
East Indies:—Watson and Clive recover Calcutta, and create Meer Jaffier nabob of Bengal.

1758 Second Convention with Prussia. Pitt and Legge re-instated.
Hanover:—the French expelled by Prince Ferdinand of Brunswick. Three expeditions to the coast of France; admirals Howe, Anson, and Hawke.
Africa:—Senegal, and the French settlements on the isle of Goree, taken by the British.
North America:—General Amherst, and admiral Boscawen, take Louisbourg and Cape Breton.

1759 —— Amherst takes Ticonderoga, and Crown Point.
—— Sir Wm. Johnson reduces the important fortress of Niagara.
—— Gen. Wolfe's expedition against Quebec. He defeats Montcalm on the Plains of Abraham, Sept. 13, but falls in the moment of victory.
—— Quebec taken by the British.
East Indies:—Col. Coote and major Monson, repulse the French at Madras.
—— Surat is taken from the Dutch on account of their hostilities.
Boscawen blockades Toulon, and defeats the French fleet off Cape Lorgos.
Hawke victorious over the grand French fleet, intended to invade England.

A. D. NORTH AMERICA.

1749 English settlement in Nova Scotia.

Peace between France and Britain.

Population of the English colonies 1,046, 000.

1750 French encroachments on English colonies.

1752 *Franklin's* scientific discoveries.

1754 Congress of delegates from 7 provinces at Albany.

Washington's mission to the French.

1755 His intrepid conduct under Braddock.

1756 French War:—Oswego and fort Granby taken by the French.

1757 Expedition against Louisbourg.

Fort Wm. Henry, taken by the French.

1758 Louisbourg taken by Amherst.

Repulse of Abercrombie at Ticonderoga.

General Forbes, takes Fort Du Quesne and names it Fort Pitt.

1759 Crown Point, Ticonderoga, Niagara, and Quebec, taken by the British.

A.D. FRANCE & SPAIN.

1748 Cape Breton restored to France, by the treaty of Aix la Chapelle.

1751 War between the French and English in the East Indies.

1752 Disputes respecting the boundaries of Nova Scotia.

1753 North America:—Hostilities commence.

1755 Nova Scotia conquered by the English.

1756 League against Prussia, which causes a general war.

1757 Damien attempts to assassinate Louis XV. but is arrested.

French take Hanover.

Convention with Britain.

General **Montcalm,** commander in America.

1758 North America:—French success various.

1759 Loss of Quebec, and death of Montcalm.

Two French fleets defeated.

Spain:—Charles III.—**The Family Compact** between France and Spain, or mutual league of the two branches, of the house of Bourbon.

A. D. MISCELLANEOUS.

1749 League of the pope, Venetians, &c. against the corsairs of Algiers and Tunis.

1751 Sweden: Adolphus Frederick, 1st of the house of Holstein.

1755 War between Holland and Algiers.

Quito, (S. A.) destroyed by an earthquake, (April 28.)

Lisbon destroyed by an earthquake, (Nov. 1.)

1756 **Confederacy of France, Germany, Sweden and Russia, against Prussia.**

"Seven years War" begins.

Minorca surrenders to the French.

1757 Frederick the Great, victorious over the Austrians at Prague.

—— repulsed by count **Daun,** in the battle of Colin, June 18.

Verdun and Bremen taken by the French.

Russians defeat the Prussians at Jagersdoff.

Prussians victorious at Rosebeck, Nov. 5, at Lessa, Dec. 5, and at Breslau, Dec. 21, and become masters of Silesia.

1758 Prussia: Ferdinand of Brunswick, takes Minden and defeats the French at Crevelt, Austrians at Frankfort, August 12, and at Hockkirchen, Oct. 14.

Death of marsechal **Keith**.

Russians victorious at Zorndoff, Aug.

Prussians raise the sieges of Leipsic, Colberg, &c.

1759 Battle of Minden, Aug. 1; Prince Ferdinand victor over the French.

Frederick the Great victor at Cunnersdorf, Aug. 12.

Balbec and Tripoli destroyed by earthquakes.

A. D. GREAT BRITAIN.

1760 Elliot repulses the French adventurer Thurot, who with 5 ships had invaded Ireland.
Successful cruizes of Hood, Barrington, Faulkner, Hughes, Parker, &c.
Gaudaloupe, and several French Islands in the West Indies, taken by the British.
The Commons vote 70,000 men for the land service, and 57,000 for the marine.
Spirituous liquors:—bill to "prevent the excessive use of" by "laying additional taxes thereon," passed.
Lord George Sackville disgraced from service in the army, for disobeying orders.
British vessels:—2,531 had been captured by the French:—944 French vessels by British in one year.
Death of George II. Oct. 25; "universally lamented."

In this reign manufactures, commerce, the arts, and society, made very important advances. The following eminent men lived; *Sommerville, C. Pitt, West, Collins, Shenstone, Young, Akenside, Gray, Hill, Carey, Southern*, and *Allan Ramsay*, poets; *Headley, Simpson*, and *Maclaurin*, mathematicians; *Fordyce, Monro, Cheselden*, and *Meade*, anatomists; *Fielding*, and *Richardson*, the celebrated novelists; *Smollet*, the historian and novelist; *Bishops Butler and Lowth; Dr. Doddridge, Dr. Butler, Dr. Leland.*

George III. 3d of Hanover.

son of Frederick, prince of Wales, and Augusta, princess of Saxe-Gothe;
is the most powerful monarch in Europe. The British empire in its greatest extent.
Pitt is retained as premier. Fox, Legge, Newcastle, earl of Bute and lord Anson, ministers.
Royal proclamation for the "encouragement of Piety and virtue," and for "preventing and punishing, vice, profaneness, and immorality."
Supplies £19,616,119.—Civil list fixed at £800,000.

1761 Earl of Bute succeeds Pitt, who had resigned. Resignation of Arthur Onslow, speaker of the Commons.
Marriage of the king with the princess Charlotte of Mecklenburgh-Strelitz.
Published; *Hume's History of England*, 1st part.
Bishop *Sherlock*, ob.

1762 War against Spain.—Monckton and admiral **Rodney** take Martinique, West Indies.
Albermarle and Pococke take Havanna, 13 ships of war, and plunder amounting to £3,000,000.
Preliminaries of Peace, Nov. 3. The notorious Peter Annet sentenced to the pillory, for writing the "Free Inquirer."
Lady Montague, ob.

1763 **Peace of Paris** proclaimed, March 22: Canada and Florida ceded to Britain.
Grenville succeeds Bute.
Tax on cider, imposed. Imprisonment of *Wilkes*, member of parliament, and editor of the "North Briton," for an article in No. 45 of that paper.

1764 Parliament taxes the American Colonies, by imposing additional duties on sugar, molasses, &c.
Voyages and discoveries of admiral **Byron**, in the Pacific.

1765 March 19. Duties imposed on *stamps*, imported into the American colonies, notwithstanding the eloquent opposition of colonel Barre and Mr. Pitt.
East Indies:—Lord Clive is appointed governor general of British India.
Hogarth, the celebrated painter, ob.

1766 New ministry;—the marquis of Rockingham at its head.
American stamp act, and British cider tax, (equally odious,) are repealed. Pitt now earl of Chatham succeeds Rockingham, July 3.

1767 New taxes on the American colonies.
East Indies:—War commenced between the British and their new foe, **Hyder Ally.**
Discoveries by **Wallis** and **Cartaret** in the Pacific.

1768 Resignation of Chatham. Wilkes elected M. P. for Middlesex.

A. D.	NORTH AMERICA.	A.D.	FRANCE & SPAIN.	A. D.	MISCELLANEOUS.
1760	Surrender of Canada to Great Britain, Sept. 8. Massachusetts opposes the "writs of assistance."	1760	Loss of all Canada, New Orleans and a few other settlements, only remain to the French in America. *Rollin, Voltaire, Fontenelle, Montesquieu, and Massillon.*	1760	Allies victorious at Lydorf, July 16, at Warbourg, July 31, at Landshut, June 23, defeated at Corbach, July 10. Russians victorious at Pluffendorf, Aug. 15, in Saxony, Aug. 30, and at Tourgau, Nov. 3. Berlin plundered by the allies, Oct. 9. *Handel*, the great German musical composer.
1761	Cherokees subdued. *Samuel Davies*, ob.			1761	Hanoverians defeated by the French at Grunberg. Belleisle taken by the British, June 7. Allies victorious over the French at Kirckdenckern, July 15, and at Holberg, Sept. 16. Decline of the Power of Frederick the Great.
		1762	Spain: War with England and Portugal. *Jesuits expelled.* France:—preliminaries of peace.	1762	Russia makes peace with Prussia. —— Catharine II.—(Peter III. deposed.) *Antiquities of Herculaneum*;—a 3d vol. presented by the king of Naples to the universities.
1763	Detroit besieged by the Indians. End of the "Old French War."	1763	Treaty of peace with G. Britain at Paris, February 16; France loses Canada. Spain loses Florida.	1763	Peace of Hubertsburg, between Prussia, Austria, and Saxony, Feb. 15. End of the Seven Years War,
1764	*Taxing system* of parliament begins. Philadelphia *Medical School*; 1st in America.	1764	Treaty with Genoa, now at war with Corsica.	1764	Poland:—**Stanislaus Augustus,** succeeds Augustus III. Russia:—murder of Ivan, the heir apparent.
1765	Opposition to the *Stamp Act*, in Massachusetts, Virginia, &c. 1st *Colonial Congress*, at New-York.			1765	Germany:—**Joseph II.** succeeds Francis I. James Stuart the "pretender," to the British throne, died at Rome and was interred as a king.
1766	Repeal of the Stamp Act.	1766	Spain:—Insurrection caused by a royal edict against *long cloaks*.	1766	Holland:—the prince of Orange assumes the government as stadtholder.
1767	Taxes again. *Thomas Clap*, ob.	1767	*J. J. Rousseau.*	1767	Corsicans under **Paoli,** take the isle of Capua. Earthquake at Martinique, West Indies.
1768	British troops stationed at Boston. Measures against oppression, in Massachusetts.	1768	French East India Co. declared bankrupt, and free trade opened.	1768	War between Russia and Turkey; lasts 6 years.

A. D. GREAT BRITAIN.

1768 August, Capt. **James Cook,** sails on his first voyage for discovery.

Royal Academy of Arts, founded, Dec.—*Joshua Reynolds,* its 1st president.

Blackstone's Commentaries on the Laws of England, published.

1769 Wilkes' election to parliament by 1145 votes, is declared "null and void," and Luttrel his opponent, having but 296 votes, "duly elected."

Robertson's Charles V. published. *Secker,* archbishop of Canterbury and *Laurence Sterne,* ob.

1770 Lord **North,** succeeds the duke of Grafton as premier.

Excitement on the affray at Boston, and on the political *Letters of Junius* to the king. Woodfall the publisher is tried for a "seditious libel," but found "guilty of printing and publishing only."

Whitefield, one of the founders of Methodism, ob. (at Newburyport, New England.)

1771 Treaty with Spain, by which the Falkland islands are ceded to Great Britain.

1773 Trial and acquittal of lord Clive, for misdemeanors in India. He commits suicide soon after.

West Indies:—The Caribs of St. Vincent subdued.

Bruce, the English traveller in Africa.

Stanhope earl of *Chesterfield,* and *Dr. J. Hawkesworth,* ob.

1774 January. Account of the "outrage at Boston," received.

Parliament orders the port of Boston to be closed;—annuls a part of the Massachusetts charter; and limits or abolishes, various rights and privileges of the colonies. British troops under Gage sent to Boston.

Cook discovers New California, (Dec.)

Dr. Goldsmith, ob.

1775 Lord North proposes conciliatory measures to the colonies which they reject.

Commencement of the American war by the skirmish at Lexington, where the British troops under Pitcairn, and lord Percy, were fired upon and pursued by the Americans, (April 19.)

Remonstrance of the London citizens against the war.

North America:—British generals **Howe, Pigot, Clinton,** and **Burgoyne,** lose 1,054 men, killed and wounded, out of 3,000, at Bunker's Hill.

—— Montreal surrendered to the Americans by Sir Guy Carleton, and St. Johns by Preston.

Carleton repulses the Americans before Quebec.

A. D.	NORTH AMERICA.	A. D.	FRANCE & SPAIN.	A. D.	MISCELLANEOUS.
				1768	Pope Clement XIV. elected after a conclave of 3 months. He supports the Jesuits.
1769	Non-importation agreements by all the colonies. *American Philosophical Society*, instituted.	1769	Conquest of Corsica.	1769	Russian fleet enters the Mediterranean, The army occupies Wallachia and Moldavia. Paoli flees from Corsica, and that island is subjected to France.
1770	Massacre of citizens at Boston, by the British troops. Duties abolished, except those on *tea*.	1770	Disputes between the king and parliament begin. Marriage of the dauphin with the archduchess Marie Antoinette.	1770	Russians defeat the Turks near Pruth, and take Bender by storm, Sept. 28. Elphinstone destroys the Turkish fleet in the sea of Epidaurus.
1771	Population of Massachusetts, 292,000.			1771	Kaffa, the capital of Crimea, taken by the Turks. Plague breaks out in the Russian army and reaches Moscow. Sweden:—Gustavus III.
1772	Patriotic speeches of **J. Hancock,** and **Saml. Adams,** in Massachusetts **Patrick Henry** in Virginia, &c. Duty on tea, opposed in pupplic meetings.	1773	Madame du Barre rules the king.	1772	1st Partition of Poland, by Russia, Prussia, and Austria; the most unprincipled of public robberies. Revolt and death of Ali Bey, Turkish governor of Egypt.
1773	Three cargoes of tea destroyed at Boston.			1773	Plague carries off 30,000 in Mexico. Jesuits suppressed by a papal bull.
1774	Closing of the port of Boston. *Continental Congress* at Philadelphia. Declaration of rights, &c. *Whigs* and *Tories*, alias, *royalists* and *provincials*.	1774	Death of Louis XV. by small pox. His son -Louis XVI.- succeeds. The ancient parliament restored.	1774	Russia:—rebellion of Puatchepeff, who calls himself the "emperor Peter, escaped from prison." Peace between Russia and Turkey, July 21: Crimea is made independent; Azoph ceded to Russia, and free navigation and commerce on the Black sea guaranteed.

A. D.	NORTH AMERICA.	A. D.	FRANCE & SPAIN.	A. D.	MISCELLANEOUS.
1775	Revolutionary War, of the British Colonies, commences at Lexington, April, 19. American colonels, **Allen,** and Benedict **Arnold,** take Ticonderoga and Crown point, May 10th. Congress at Philadelphia. Battle of Bunker's Hill, June 17; American generals, **Putnam** and **Warren,** (latter killed,) and **Prescott,** with 1000 men—lose 450.	1775	The clergy vote a gift of 20,000,000 livres to the king. **Turgot's** ministry, favourable to reform. Spaniards repulsed in an attack on Algiers.	1775	Turkey:—17 pachas beheaded by order of the grand seignor. The Inquisition abolished at Milan.

A. D. GREAT BRITAIN.

1776 Viscount Pitt, son of the earl of Chatham, resigns his commission, rather than fight against the Americans.

1700 Hessians hired for the service in America.

North America:—British troops evacuate Boston. Canada evacuated by the Americans.

—— American Congress declare the thirteen United States free and independent, July 4.

—— British under Clinton victorious at Flatbush, and enter New-York.

—— Howe and Clinton's engagement with the Americans at White Plains; indecisivet

—— Howe takes forts Washington and Lee, (Nov.)

—— Capture of the Hessians at Trenton, by Washington.

East Indies;—Lord Pigot, governor general, imprisoned by his own council.

1777 North America:—British colonel Bird, and governor Trýon, destroy American stores in New York and Connecticut.

—— Burgoyne takes Ticonderoga. Frazer defeats the Americans at Hubbards town.

—— Defeat of colonel Baum at Bennington.

—— British, general Howe, defeats Washington at Brandywine.

—— Burgoyne vs. Gates, at Stillwater—indecisive.

—— Cornwallis takes Philadelphia.—Howe victorious at Germantown.

—— Sir Henry Clinton takes forts Clinton, Montgomery, &c.

—— Defeat of the British army under Burgoyne, near Saratoga, Oct. 7, and their surrender to the Americans, Oct. 17.

John Horne Tooke, is fined £200 and imprisoned for saying in an advertisement that the king's troops had committed murder at Lexington.

Hume, the philosopher and historian, ob.

1797 Cook discovers Nootka Sound, (Jan.)—Sandwich islands discovered.

French and English ambassadors return to their respective homes, (March.)

A. D.	UNITED STATES.	A. D.	FRANCE & SPAIN.	A. D.	MISCELLANEOUS.
1775	WASHINGTON, elected commander in chief of the American army. **Montgomery** takes St. Johns and Montreal, and falls in a gallant attack on Quebec, Dec. 21. Falmouth and Bristol, burnt by the British.				
1776	Norfolk, Virginia, burnt by the Tories. Washington enters Boston, March 17, and fixes his head quarters at New-York, June 15. **Moultrie** defeats the British at Sullivan's island. **Declaration of Independence,** of the UNITED STATES of America, July 4. Am. (**Sullivan,**) defeated at Flatbush, Long Island, (Aug.) and Arnold defeated on Lake Champlain. New-York possessed by the British, Sept 15. Battle of White Plains, Oct. 28. Washington retreats across New-Jersey: crosses the Delaware; surprises the Hessians at Trenton, and takes 1000 prisoners, Dec. 26, 27.			1776	Russia:—the empress Catharine courts popularity by promoting commerce, education, and the arts. Bassora, (Asia,) surrendered to the Persians after a siege of 12 months. Pope Pius VI.
1777	Washington attempts in the dead of night, Jan. 2. to surprise the British at Princeton, N. J. **Meigs** destroys British stores at Log Harbour. Arrival of the philanthropic and generous La Fayette. Ticonderoga taken by the British, July 5. **Stark** victorious at Bennington Aug. 16. Battle of Brandywine, Sept. 11. Battle of Stillwater—indecisive. Philadelphia taken by the British. Battle of Germantown, Oct. 4. Forts, Clinton and Montgomery, burnt by the British. **Surrender of Burgoyne's** army, to the American gen. **Gates,** Oct. 17. *Articles of confederation* adopted, Nov. 15. Sufferings of the American army—in winter quarters at Valley Forge. Dr. Franklin, **Silas Deane,** and **Arthur Lee,** were this year sent to France, as ambassadors of the U. S.	1777	**La Fayette** sails to America at his own expense, risking his life and fortune to aid the cause of liberty. French ambassador leaves London. Arrival of the American embassy.	1777	Portugal: Maria, Queen. Germany:—The emperor Joseph seizes Bavaria on the death of the elector, Maximilian II. The pope engaged in draining the Pontine marshes.
1778	Alliance with France, Feb. 6. English commissioners sent over to bribe the principal American citizens.			1778	War between Germany and Prussia, Ap. 28. (ended next year.)

A. D. GREAT BRITAIN.

1778 Pitt, earl of Chatham, opposes the duke of Richmond's motion, for acknowledging the independence of the American colonies. He dies in a fit in the house of Peers.

Embargo on all trading vessels, and general press for seamen.

British fleet, admiral Keppel, engages the French, count D'Orvilliers.

Paul Jones, the celebrated adventurer, pillaged the house of lord Selkirk in Scotland, and captured a British ship at Whitehaven.

British take Pondicherry, which annihilates the French power in the East Indies.

1779 North America:—British take Sunbury, which completes the conquest of Georgia.

—— Provost defeats the Americans at Briar Creek, and invests Charleston.

—— Matthews burns towns in Virginia.—Clinton takes Stoney Point, &c.

—— Governor Tryon burns towns in Connecticut.

—— Sea fight between the British fleet, lord Byron, and the French, D'Estaing, (July.)

—— St. Vincent, W. I. taken by the French.

—— British repulse the French and American attack on Savannah.

Duel between C. J. Fox, and W. Adams: Fox wounded.

Garrick, the celebrated actor and dramatist, *bishop Warburton*, and *Armstrong*, the poet ob.

1780 Cook's death at Owhyhee—account of received, Jan. 12.

Burke introduces his economical reform bill.

Dunning's famous resolution in parliament,—that the "influence of the crown has increased, is increasing, and ought to be diminished."

Riots at St. George's fields—June 2; caused by concessions to Roman Catholics.

North America:—British Sir H. Clinton takes Charleston, and establishes the royal government in South Carolina.

—— Lord Rawdon victorious at Camden, South Carolina.

—— Execution of Andre, by the Americans, as a spy. Arnold joins the British.

British, Sir George Rodney captures a squadron of Spanish ships, raises the siege of Gibraltar, and sails to the West Indies.

War with Holland; British capture a Dutch squadron, with Mr. Laurens the American ambassador to Holland.

Petitions for *reform* and *retrenchment*, numerous during this year.

1781 North America:—British lord Cornwallis victorious over Greene at Guilford, N. C.

—— Sea fight off Cape Henry—British fleet, Arbuthnot, vs. French, Destouches; loss equal.

—— Sea fight off the Chesapeake, British fleet, Greaves, vs. French, De Grasse; loss equal.

A. D.	UNITED STATES.	A. D.	FRANCE & SPAIN	A. D.	MISCELLANEOUS.
1778	**La Fayette** defeats a British detachment, May 8. Philadelphia evacuated by the British, June 18. Washington victorious in the battle of Monmouth, June 28. French fleet under D'Estaing arrives, to aid the Americans. Wyoming on the Susquehanna burnt and its inhabitants massacred, by the Tories and savages under Butler, in July. Savannah taken by the British, Dec. 29.			1778	Smyrna nearly destroyed by an earthquake. *Linnæus* a Swede, the most celebrated of modern naturalists, ob.
1779	Sunbury taken, and Georgia reduced by the British. Charleston S. C. invested by the British, May. Norfolk, Gosport, Portsmouth and Suffolk, Va. burnt, and Stoney and Verplanck's points, taken by the British, in June. Fairfield, Norwalk, and Greenwich, Conn. burnt. American gen. **Wayne,** recovers Stoney Point. —— **Lee,** surprises the British at Powles Hook. Sullivan defeats the Indians, Aug. 29. **Paul Jones'** naval victory, on the coast of Scotland, Sep. 23. Rhode Island evacuated by the British. Armed neutrality, in Europe.	1779	French cruisers ordered not to molest capt. Cook. D'Estaing conquers St. Vincent. Spaniards besiege Gibraltar.	1779	*Armed Neutrality,* agreed to by Sweden, Denmark and Holland, to oppose the searching of neutral vessels by the British. Holland: Paul Jones and his prizes sheltered by the government.
1780	Charleston S. C. surrendered to the British, May 12. Massacre of 300 Americans at Waxcaw by the British gen. Tarleton. Arrival of a French squadron and troops, under Rochambeau, to aid the Americans, (May.) Battle near Camden, S. C. Aug. 16, in which baron **De Kalb,** a volunteer in the American army, is killed. Discovery of Arnold's treason at West-Point, July 18,—Andre is executed as a spy. **H. Laurens,** ambassador of the U. S. to Holland, was captured by a British frigate. American privateers successful.	1780	Sea fight between the Fr. and Brit. fleet, off Martinique, April 17. **Rochambeau** sent to aid the Americans. French and Span. fleets capture 50 British W. Indiamen Ag. 9.	1780	Earthquake destroys 15,000 houses in Persia. Hurricane in the W. Indies. Holland at war with Britain. Death of the empress dowager, Maria Theresa.
1781	Revolt of the Pennsylvania troops, caused by want of provisions: it is quelled by the wise and decisive conduct of Washington. **Morgan** defeats the British, at Cowpens, S. C.				

A. D. GREAT BRITAIN.

1781 North America:—Siege of the British army, lord Cornwallis at Yorktown, Va.—while the other division under Clinton, is waiting an attack at New-York.

East Indies:—The British Sir Eyre Coote, effects the overthrew of Hyder Aly.

North America:—Cornwallis surrenders the British army and fleet to the allies, Oct. 17.

Herschel discovers the Georgium Sidus, March 13.

1782 Resignation of lord North. Shelburne succeeds him. Burke's reform bill passed.

British fleet, admiral Rodney, captures the French, De Grasse, April 12.

1783 Great Britain acknowledges the Independence of the United States, by the Treaty of Paris, Sep. 3.

A. D. UNITED STATES.

1783 (continued.) American army disbanded, Nov. 3. New-York evacuated by the British, Nov. 25.

Washington, the Father of his Country, delivers his farewell address to his officers, and retires to Mt. Vernon,—an unstained patriot, the admiration of the world.

Samuel Cooper, D. D., and *Jas. Otis*, ob.

1784 Cities incorporated;—Hartford New-Haven, Norwich, and Middletown, Conn.

Town of Hudson, N. Y. founded.

New-York Chamber of Commerce, inst.

First voyage of an American vessel to China, by the ship Empress, John Green, master, of Boston.

1785 Treaty of commerce with Prussia.

—— with the Cherokees.

A. D. GREAT BRITAIN.

1783 It appears from official returns, that 43,633 British soldiers had either died, or been killed in the American war.

Coalition ministry, formed by Mr. Fox, and lord North, (hitherto opponents in politics,) on the resignation of Shelburne.

East Indies:—Tippoo Saib succeeds his father, Hyder Aly.

H. Home, (lord *Kaimes*,) ob.

1784 **Wm. Pitt**, the younger, premier.

Sunday Schools first established in England, by *Raikes*.

Mail Coaches first in use.

Freedom of London voted to Pitt.

Burke recovers £100 from an editor, for a libel.

Sam'l. Johnson, L. L. D., the colossus of English literature, ob.

1785 Ireland in a state of fermentation, on the subject of reform. Agreements there of non-importation from England.

A. D.	UNITED STATES.	A. D.	FRANCE & SPAIN.	A. D.	MISCELLANEOUS.
1781	**Greene** repulsed at Guilford, S. C. **Marion, Sumpter,** and **Pickens,** gain several advantages in South Carolina. Execution of col. Hayne, as a rebel, by the British. Forts Trumball and Griswold taken, and New-London burnt, by the British, (Arnold.) Greene defeats the British at Eutaw Springs, S. C. American army, gen. Washington, and French army and fleet, Rochambeau, La Fayette, and De Grasse, besiege Cornwallis' army at Yorktown, Sep. 29. **Surrender of Cornwallis,** Oct. 17;—the army, &c. to the Americans,—the fleet to the French.	1781	**Necker,** minister, of France, adopts an economical system but is compelled to resign.	1781	Slavery abolished in Bohemia, Moldavia, and Silesia.
1782	Savannah and Charleston restored to the Americans. Treaty with Holland, concluded by **John Adams, Jay, Franklin** and **Laurens.**	1782	Spaniards take Minorca. Defeat of De Grasse.	1782	The pope visits the emperor to dissuade him from hostilities to the Church. *Metastasio*, ob.
1783	Independence of the U. S. acknowledged by Sweden, Denmark, and Russia. **Treaty of Paris,** Sep. 3.—End of the War. Independence of the United States acknowledged by Great Britain.	1783	Peace of Paris; Tobago and Senegal ceded to France; Florida and Minorca to Spain.		

A. D.	FRANCE & SPAIN.	A. D.	MISCELLANEOUS.
1783	First experiment of *air balloons*, (invented by Montgolphier.) *D'Alembert*, the mathematician, ob.	1783	Earthquakes in Calabria, Sicily, &c;—villages, towns, and multitudes of people, swallowed up. Crimea, the Kuban, and the isle of Tamar, annexed to Russia.
1784	Financial distress of France, at its height. The debt amounts to 6,000,000,000 livres. Spain:—Don Gabriel marries the infanta of Portugal. —— Another attack on Algiers. *Diderot*, first author of the *Encyclopedia*, ob.	1784	Earthquake destroys Achinscan, in Turkey, with 12,000 of its inhabitants. Holland:—the stadtholder suspended from the dignity of commander in chief. —— Anti-Orange league at Utrecht.
		1785	Germany:—Suppression of 2,000 religious houses, by the emperor.

A. D. UNITED STATES.

1785 J. Adams, sent to London, as ambassador of the United States.

Jon. Trumbull, gov. of Conn.; S. Hopkins, and W. Whipple, ob.

1786 Shay's insurrection in Massachusetts. (Scarcity of Money, and heavy taxes.)

Delegates from five of the states, meet at Annapolis to concert an amendment in the government.

Treaty with the Choctaws.

Portland Me. incorporated.

Harrisburgh, Pa. founded.

Printing commenced at Lexington, Ky.

1787 May:—General convention at Philadelphia—(Washington presiding,) frames the Federal Constitution.

Treaty with the emperor of Morocco, concluded by J. Adams, and T. Jefferson.

Published:—A "Defence of the U. S. Constitution," by John Adams.

Bishops:—Rev. Dr. W. White for Pa. and Samuel Prevost rector of Trinity Church, N. Y. consecrated in London.

Baltimore contains 1,959 houses.

1788 *Mass* first performed in Boston by a R. Catholic priest.

Cotton first planted in Georgia by Richard Leake.

Ohio:—the first settlement commenced at Marietta, under the superintendence of gen. Rufus Putnam.

Died; at Grand Cairo, *John Ledyard*, the celebrated American traveller.

1789 *Federal Constitution ratified* by all the states, except Rhode Island and North Carolina.

April 30. — **George Washington,** — inaugurated president of the United States.

— **John Adams,** vice president.

Cabinet:—**Jefferson, Hamilton, Knox, Randolph,** and **Jay.**

Oct. The president visits New England.

First land office, opened at Canandaigua, by Oliver Phelps.

Presbyterian General Assembly, and the *Episcopal Convention* first meet.

Barrell's sound, on the north west coast of America first visited.

A. D. GREAT BRITAIN.

1785 Arrival of John Adams the first ambassador of the U. S. to Gt. Britain.

1786 Impeachment of **Warren Hastings** by Mr. Burke, for high crimes and misdemeanours as gov. general of Bengal.

Colony of negroes sail to Sierra Leone

Lord Cornwallis embarks for India as gov. general.

An attempt to assassinate the king by a female lunatic.

1787 Aug, 11. Nova Scotia erected into a bishop's see.

First settlers of Botany Bay, sail from England.

Herschel discovers the 2d and 4th satellites of the Georgium Sidus.

A bank first established in the E. Indies.

1788 Feb. 13. Trial of Warren Hastings.

July 3. Society formed for exploring the interior of Africa.

Oct. 12. The king becomes insane.

Pitt opposes the election, of the prince of Wales to the Regency.

First motion made for the abolition of the slave trade.

Died; at Rome, Charles Edward C. Stuart, the "Pretender" jun. to the British throne.

1789 February. Rejoicings on the king's recovery.

Herschel gives a catalogue of 2,000 new stars.

May 27. Duel between the duke of York and colonel Lennox.

The eyes of all Europe are now fixed on France.

Published;—*Darwin's Botanic Garden*. *Cullen*, an eminent Scotch physician, ob.

1790 July 14.—The earl of Stanhope, and upwards of 600 gentlemen, meet to celebrate the French Revolution.

The printer of The Times is fined £100, for libels on the prince of Wales, and the duke of Clarence.

A. D.	FRANCE & SPAIN.	A. D.	MISCELLANEOUS.
1786	Treaty of alliance with England. **La Perouse's** voyage of discovery.	1785	Vassallage abolished in Hungary. Russia:—the empress sends two expeditions for discovery: —— *Canals* commenced.
		1786	Jan. 900,000 people die of a plague in the Levant. Cardinal Turlone, the high inquisitor at Rome, murdered by the populace. Prussia:—Death of Frederick II. the Great, æt. 73. He is succeeded by his nephew, Frederick William II. (profligate and weak.)
1787	Plan of taxing the privileged orders proposed. The body of Notables assemble by advice of the minister, **Calonne,** on account of the embarrassment of the finances, but his projects prove unsuccessful and he resigns.—succeeded by **Brienne,** archbishop Toulouse. States-general assembled:—refuse to register the king's stamp duty,—and are dissolved.	1787	War between Turkey and Russia. Holland:—Dispute between the stadtholder and his people. —— The princess of Orange is arrested by armed burghers' while travelling. The king of Prussia demands satisfaction for this insult offered his sister, which being refused, he sends the duke of Brunswick with 40,000 men, who soon restores the stadtholder's authority.
1788	Spain:—**Florida Blanca,** the upright minister, promotes patriotic measures. —— Charles IV. succeeds his father Charles III. France:—The king dissolves the assembly of Notables. M. Necker succeeds Brienne. *Buffon*, the celebrated naturalist, ob.	1788	Asia:—May 4. The island of Formosa shakes off the Chinese yoke. West Indies, Oct. 12.—At St. Lucia 900 persons, lose their lives by an earthquake. Germany:—a contest and bloodshed caused by the emperor's attempt to control the universities.

A. D. — FRANCE AND SPAIN.

1789 — French Revolution. —

May 5—States-General opened at Versailles.

16 —— declare themselves a National Assembly.

Third Estate acquire preponderance:—(Abbe *Sieyes.*)

(Death of the dauphin, Louis Joseph Xavier Benedict.)

June.—Hall of the Assembly being closed, they adjourn to a tennis court, then to a church. Necker again minister.

July 14—The Bastile at Paris taken and destroyed by the populace. The count d' Artois, the prince of Condé, and other nobles leave the country.

July 16.—**La Fayette** elected commander in chief of the National Guards;—Bailly, mayor.

August 4.—National Assembly abolish *privileges*, decree the *liberty of the press*, and declare themselves *permanent*.

October 1.—Disturbances at Versailles; the mob assembles from all quarters.

A. D. MISCELLANEOUS.

1789 Netherlands:—Violent commotions; the Austrian garrisons expelled.

Russia at war with Sweden; some advantages gained over the Turks.

At Borgo-Sepolcro, in Tuscany, the cathedral and 150 houses were destroyed by an earthquake, Sept. 30.

A. D. UNITED STATES.

1789 *Kirby's Reports of the Supreme Court of Connecticut*, the first published in the United States;

"A Dissertation on the *English Language*," by *Noah Webster*; and

"The *American Geography*," by *Jedidiah Morse*, published.

1790 Hamilton's system for funding the national debt, adopted.

Rhode Island accedes to the constitution.

Aug. 7.—Treaty with the Creek Indians.

Sept 30.—General Harmer who had been sent with 1400 men against the hostile Indians is defeated near Chillicothe.

Tennessee erected into a territory.

District of Columbia ceded by Virginia and Maryland to the United States.

Kentucky detached from Virginia and made a separate state.

Population of the U. States, 3,929,326.

Franklin, gen. Putnam, *Bowdoin*, and *Bellamy*, ob.

1791 Vermont admitted into the Union.

Expedition against the Indians on the Miami, defeated, and colonel Butler killed.

Raleigh, N. C., founded.

Revenue of the U. States is $4,771,200

Expenditures, - - 3,797,436

University of Vermont, at Burlington, and the University of Pennsylvania, founded.

Bank of the United States established: capital, $10,000,000.

Duties laid on distilled spirits.

1792 Kentucky admitted into the Union.

U. S. Mint established by congress.

Banks of South Carolina, Pennsylvania, and Union bank, Boston incorporated.

Rev. Dr. Clagget, consecrated at N. York, as Bishop of the Protestant Episcopal Church.

Chemistry:—The first course of lectures in America, on Lavoisier's system delivered at Columbia College by *Dr. Samuel L. Mitchill.*

A. D. GREAT BRITAIN.

1790 Dispute with Spain respecting Nootka Sound, finally compromised. A member of the Commons said that this dispute about a few cat skins, cost the country £3,000,000!

Great Britain is now flourishing in peace:—The national debt reduced. Burke publishes his "Reflections on the French Revolution." Thomas Paine's "Common Sense," and "Rights of Man," are largely circulated.

Howard, the philanthropist;

Adam Smith, L. L. D., author of the "*Wealth of Nations*," &c.;

Rev. *T. Wharton*, D. D., poet laureate, and

Matthew Henry, a learned divine, ob.

1791 Act passed to divide the province of Canada into Upper and Lower; each to have a council and assembly. In the debate on this bill, arose the quarrel between Mr. Burke, and Mr. Fox.

July 14.—On the celebration of the second anniversary of the French revolution a mob destroyed several houses, including that of the Rev. Dr. Priestley, with his library, apparatus, &c.

John Wesley, the founder of the *Methodist Society*, ob.

Published;—*Cowper's translation of Homer;*

Stewart's Philosophy of the Mind.

1792 House of Commons agree to a gradual abolition of the slave trade, April 26.

The people of England are friendly to the reform in France, but the administration hostile to any alteration in the old aristocratical creed.

Sept.—Several thousand emigrants arrive from France.

Thomas Paine found guilty of libels in the "Rights of man."

A. D. FRANCE AND SPAIN.

1789 Nov. 1.—*Lettres de Cachet*, the parliament, and all distinction of *orders* abolished by the Assembly.

Division of parties:—The *Tiers-Etats*, or privileged order comprising the clergy and noblesse: (Maury and Cazalès.) the party of Necker and the ministry, or the moderate party, and the republicans or nationals (**Mirabeau**, La Fayette, Lameth, Duport, &c.)

1790 January.—Nuns and friars turned out of the convents, and the church lands sold.

March 8.—Colonies declared a constituent part of the monarchy.

—— 20.—*Game laws* and *confiscation of goods* abolished.—France divided into 83 *departments*.

April 18.—*Assignats* first issued.

June 23.—The assembly declare that the *nation* alone has the *right* of making peace and war.

—— 28.—*Hereditary nobility*, armorial bearings, and other marks of *distinction* abolished.

July 10.—Estates of the Protestants who fled from France on the repeal of the edict of Nantes are ordered to be restored.

—— 14.—Anniversary of the destruction of the Bastile, celebrated in the Champs de Mars:—600,000 people present.

Sept. 4.—Dismissal of M. Necker, from the ministry.

1791 People divided into *royalists*, *republicans* and *moderate* men. Death of Mirabeau.

March 3.—Silver plate of the *churches* sent to the *mint*.

—— 22.—Act of the assembly, excluding females from the succession to the crown.

April 18.—The king stopped by the populace in going to St. Cloud.

—— 21.—La Fayette resigns the command of the National Guard.

June 8.—The king escapes from Paris, and is arrested at Varennes.

September 14.—Acceptance of the new constitution solemnly sworn to in the Champs Elysees.

—— 29.—Constituent Assembly dissolved, October 4. *Legislative* Assembly opened, October 14. Horrid massacre at Avignon.

Nov.—New ministry: **Dumourier**, for foreign affairs: **Roland**, for the interior.

1792 January 21.—The Assembly declare they will make war only for defence.

March 20. —— declare war against the emperor of Germany: (the army commanded by Rochambeau, La Fayette and Luckner.)

April 28.—French repulsed in Flanders,

(June 19.) —— take Courtnay.

June 25.—All records of nobility burned.

August 19.—La Fayette and 6 companions taken prisoners by the Austrians and sent to the dungeon of Olmutz, Sept. 9. Paris fortified by the revolutionists. —— 20. Meeting of the national Convention:—*Royalty abolished* and France declared a *Republic*.

Titles of *madame*, *monsieur*, &c. set aside.

A. D. MISCELLANEOUS.

1790 Germany:—Death of the emperor Joseph II. His brother Leopold II. (Grand duke of Tuscany,) succeeds.

Turkey:—Ismael taken, and its inhabitants murdered by the Russians, under the savage Suwarrow, Sept. 4.

A fog in Amsterdam, so dense that 230 persons fell into the canals.

1792 Sweden, March 18. The king assassinated by Aukerstworn at a masked ball.

Alliance of Pilnitz, between the emperor Leopold, and the king of Prussia.

Germany:—The emperor dies while preparing for the crusade against the French Revolutionists.

Francis II. succeeds.

Allied army consists of 70,000 Prussians, and 68,000 Austrians, commanded by the duke of Brunswick.

Allies take Longwy (Aug.) and Verdun, (Sept.) but are repulsed at Domperre, and evacuate France.

A. D. UNITED STATES.

1792 *Culture of silk*, progressed. A silk dress made in Connecticut.

Died;—Henry Laurens, Arthur Lee, and (in Paris,) the celebrated John Paul Jones, a captain of the American navy.

1793 Washington re-elected president, and J. Adams, vice-president. American politics affected by the French Revolution; the Republicans approve and the Federalists deprecate it.

French minister to the United States recalled at the request of Washington.

April 22. The president issues a proclamation of neutrality respecting the affairs of France.

Williamstown college, (Mass.) inc.

Port of New-York: entered; 683 vessels from foreign ports, and 1381 coastwise.

Yellow *fever* in Philadelphia, of which 3,645 die.

Wesleyan Methodists in U. S., 60,000;
Baptists, ... 73,471.

Exports of U. S. $26,000,000.

Died; John Hancock, the fearless patriot, and signer of the Declaration of Independence, and governor of Massachusetts. Roger Sherman, signer of the Declaration of Independence. Edward Trowbridge a learned judge.

A. D. GREAT BRITAIN.

1792 East Indies.—The marquis of Cornwallis concludes a treaty with Tippoo Saib, who cedes half his dominions to the English.

Joshua Reynolds, ob.

Published;—*Lavater, on Physiognomy, Priestley's Lectures on History,—Bruce's Travels to the source of the Nile.*

1793 After the execution of the king of France, Great Britain joins the alliance with the emperor.

January 24. French ambassador ordered to leave England.

To carry on the war foreign troops are hired, and an expenditure of upwards of 11 millions voted for this year.—

The ministry supported by a party called the *Alarmists.*

April. Sir Richard Phillips, a bookseller, fined and sentenced to 18 months imprisonment for selling a copy of Paine's Rights of Man.

—— 14. Tobago, and

—— 27. Toulon taken by the British.

September 4. British army under the duke of York, defeated near Dunkirk.

October 12. St. Domingo ceded to Great Britain.

—— 29. The king issues a proclamation to the French nation.

—— First ambassador from the Ottoman Porte arrives.

A. D. FRANCE AND SPAIN.	A. D. MISCELLANEOUS.
French take Spires, Mentz, and Longwy.	
Nov. Dumourier, the French general, subdues Belgium. Savoy annex- to France.	
The *Girondists* or moderate men, and the *Mountainists*, or violent party, divide the revolutionists. Brissot, Petion, Verginreaux, &c. leaders of the first. Danton, Robespierre, &c. of the second.	
Murder of the archbishop of Paris, and two bishops.	
1793 January. Vote of the Convention, that Louis XVI. has been "guilty of a conspiracy against liberty and the safety of the state." Of 721 votes, 366 are for the death, and 321 for the imprisonment of the king.	1793 Second partition of Poland, by which Prussia acquires a territory containing 1,360,000 inhabitants and Russia 3,500,000
Thomas Paine's speech in the Convention against the king's death.	
Jan. 21. Death of Louis XVI. by the guillotine.	
Feb. 1. The Convention declares war against England and Holland.	March 1. Allies under general Clairfoot, defeat the French.
25.—French take Breda.	
28.—The Republic acknowledged by the grand-duke of Tuscany.	
March. War declared against Spain.	Prince of Coburg defeats Dumourier.
April. Desertion of Dumourier.	
May. French defeated near Valenciennes and at St. Armand.	
June. City of Lyons, and the isle of Corsica revolt.	Breda taken by the Allies.
—— Violent tumult at Paris. Triumph of the Mountainists.	
July 12. Royalists successful in La Vendee, but soon after defeated.	Coburg defeats the French at Famars.
—— 14. Marat assassinated by Charlotte Corde.	
Toulon surrenders to the British.	
New Calendar adopted. Eleven armies created by a levy *en masse*.	Aug. 16. The allies invest Cambray and St. Quentin.
Sept. 29. French defeat the king of Sardinia.	Sept. 4. Duke of Brunswick routes the French on the Rhine.
	Coalition against France, consists of the German empire, Great Britain, Prussia, Holland, Portugal, Spain, Sardinia, the Two Sicilies and the pope. Venice acknowledges the Republic.
October 16. Queen Maria Antoinette guillotined.	
—— Girondists totally annihilated by the Mountainists.	
—— *Robespierre's reign of terror*;—revolutionary tribunal; committee of public safety. Women obliged to wear the tricoloured cockade.	
—— **Jourdan** defeats the Austrians at Boufflers.	
Nov. 4. Lyons taken by the revolutionists: 70 persons guillotined, and 68 shot. French defeat the Spanish, and enter Catalonia. **Pichegru** takes possession of Holland.	
—— 6. Duke of Orleans guillotined by the Mountainists.	Oct. 25. **Wurmser** defeats the French, and takes fort Louis, Nov. 15.
—— 8. The celebrated *madame Roland* executed.	
Dec. 4. Royalists totally defeated at Mons.	
—— 23. Toulon re-taken from the English.	
Napoleon Bonaparte, a lieutenant of artillery, first brought into notice.	
Grand festival at Paris on the 30th.	

A. D. UNITED STATES.

1794 Insurrection in Pennsylvania on account of the duties on distilled spirits.

Fire in Boston, July 30th, consuming 7 rope walks and 89 buildings.

Aug. 20. Gen. Wayne defeats the Indians in Ohio.

Nov. 19. Treaty of amity, commerce, and navigation between Great Britain and the United States, signed in London by John Jay and the earl of Grenville.

Colleges founded:—Union, at Schenectady; Greenville, in Tennessee; and Bowdoin at Brunswick, Maine.

Treaties concluded with the Six Nations, the Cherokees, and other Indians.

Mr. Monroe ambassador to France.

Foundation of the American Navy, (March 30,) by an act of Congress, authorising the building of 6 frigates.

Died:—**Richard Henry Lee,** late president of Congress;

John Witherspoon, D. D., LL. D. signer of the Declaration of Independence, and president of Princeton college;

John Sullivan, LL. D., major. gen. in revolution, and late governor of N. Hampshire;

Josiah Bartlett, M. D. signer of Declaration of Independence;

Baron Steuben, maj. gen. in the American Revolutionary army.

A. D. GREAT BRITAIN.

1794 Jan. Preparations for war with France: 165,000 troops voted.

Habeas Corpus suspended.

March 15. Capture of Martinique, and April 22, of Guadaloupe.

Lord Howe defeats the French fleet and takes 7 sail of the line, in the bay of Biscay, June 1.

July 8. Lord Moira joins the army of the duke of York, in Flanders.

Sept. 17. Duke of York defeated at Boxtel, and retreats over the Maese.

Oct. Trial of Messrs. Thomas Hardy, John Horne Tooke, and Thelwall, (members of a reforming society) for treason: the charge opened by the att. general, (afterwards Lord Eldon,) in a speech of 9 hours: Erskine and Gibbs counsel for Hardy: Pitt, a a witness for Tooke: all the accused are acquitted.

Dec. 6. Island of Corsica ceded to Britain.

Died:—*William Russell*, LL. D., author of the History of Modern Europe; *George Colman*, a dramatic author.

Loan of this year was £11,000,000.

1795 Jan. 29. Turkish ambassador made his public entry in great state.

April 5. Prince of Wales married to his cousin, the princess Caroline of Brunswick. His debts are discharged and £125,000 granted him by parliament.

—— 7. Admiral **Hotham** defeats the French fleet in the Mediterranean, and takes two sail of the line.

—— 25. Warren Hastings' trial ended in his acquittal.

Sept. Dusseldorf, cape of Good Hope, Guadaloupe, St. Lucia, St. Vincent, Grenada, and St. Eustatia taken by the British.

A.D. FRANCE & SPAIN.

1794 Jan. Danton and Robespierre, the ferocious leaders of Jacobins, divide the power between themselves.

Slavery abolished. The worship of God commuted for that of the *goddess of reason.*

Feb. 13. 500 royalists shot at Nantes.

March 26. Herbert and his accomplices executed at Paris.

May 29. A decree of the convention that no quarter shall be given to the English and Hanoverians.

The Committee of Public Safety direct affairs.

June 17. Jourdan defeats the allies at Fleuris. (a balloon used to reconnoitre the enemy.)

July. Conquest of Namur, and all Flanders.

—— 27. Robespierre and his partisans executed by order of the Convention.

Aug. 1. French enter Antwerp.

—— 5. —— defeat the Spaniards on the Pyrenees.

20th, re-capture Valenciennes and Corde:

Oct. 6. —— defeat the Austrians near Juliers.

Oct. 18. Jacobin party suppressed.

Nov. 5. Maestricht and Nimeguen taken by the French.

Dec. 6. Figueras with 9,000 Spaniards taken prisoners.

1795 Feb. 12. Free exercise of all religions allowed.

—— Peace concluded with Tuscany.

—— 19. Armistice agreed on in La Vendee.

March 8. In the Convention it is asserted that they had gained 27 victories, taken 116 strong places, 91,000 prisoners, and 3,800 cannon.

April 10. Peace with Prussia.

May 5. Horrid massacre in Paris.

—— 20. Insurrection of the Jacobins quelled.

Louis XVII. dies in prison.

July 28. Louis XVIII. publishes a manifesto that he will not accept the crown of France without the ancient power.

Aug. 4. Peace with Spain and

Sept. 1. with Hesse Cassel.

A. D. MISCELLANEOUS.

1794 Poland, Feb. 22. **Kosciusko,** leader of the Polish patriots, gains possession of Warsaw.

April. Poles gain a victory over the Russians.

May 3. Allies take Landrecy.

June 5. Poles defeated by the Prussians.

—— Revolution in Switzerland, at Geneva.

Oct. 20. The remainder of the Polish army subdued by the Russian savage Suwarrow, who forces an entrance into Warsaw, and massacres 20,000 people. The rest of Poland divided among the three powers, and king Stanislaus sent to prison at Grodna.

1795. Jan. 7. Holland overrun by the French under Pichegru.

—— 24. Prince of Orange and his son flee to England.

Feb. —— Provincial government established by the French. The provinces called Batavia.

—— Prussia makes peace with the French.

June 8. Copenhagen nearly half destroyed by fire.

July 20. Archduke Leopold, palatine of Hungary, killed in making fire-works.

Sept. 20. Wurmser repulses the French near Munheim.

A. D.	UNITED STATES.	A. D	GREAT BRITAIN.
1795	Oct. Treaty with Spain, concluded by Thomas Pinckney.	1795	Herschel completes his celebrated telescope: the tube is forty feet long, and the great mirror 40 inches in diameter.
	Nov. ——— with Algiers, by col. Humphries, and with the western Indians by gen. Wayne.		General scarcity of provisions.
	Conn.—The sum of $1,200,000, the proceeds of the reserve lands, was appropriated for the support of schools in the state.		Lord Cambden succeeds Lord Fitz-William, as governor of Ireland.
	N. York city:—freeholders 36,000.		*Boswell* and *Romaine*, ob.
	Richmond, Va., contains 4,000 inhabitants.		
	Baltimore, Md.:—Amount of exports, $5,000,800.		
	Ohio: a printing press first set up in Cincinnati.		
	Col. Hamilton, secretary of the treasury, resigns: succeeded by Oliver Wolcott, of Connecticut.		
	Col. Pinckney succeeds gen. Knox, in the war office.		
	Dec. 8. The president's speech presents a pleasing view of the national prosperity.		
	Bradford, Marion, and *Stiles*, ob.		
1796	Jan. 1. Tennessee admitted into the Union.	1796	May 6. Motion of Mr. Grey for impeaching the ministry; negotiated.
	Sept. Washington publishes his farewell address, "worthy of the patriot and the statesman:"		July 3. Verdict of £100, given against the proprietor of the Morning Post, for sending a *forged* French paper called L'Clair to the proprietor of the Telegraph.
	Dec. 7.—and makes his last speech to congress.		Aug. 9. British take the isle of Elba.
	Pennsylvania:—An act for establishing public schools.		Oct. 11. Spain declares war against Britain.
	Albany, N. Y., contains 700 houses and 6,021 inhabitants.		—— 13. Lord Malmesbury, sent to negotiate a treaty with France.
	Count Rumford, of Vermont, now residing at Munich, in Bavaria, presented, $5,000 to the American Academy of Arts and Sciences.		—— 22. Corsica evacuated by the British, and the people declare for the French.
	Detroit was delivered up by Britain to the United States.		—— 23. Dutch squadron at the cape of Good Hope with 2,000 troops and their settlements in Ceylon, Malacca, and Cochineal, taken by the British.
	Charleston, S. C., nearly destroyed by fire.		*Macpherson*, *Robert Burns*, & *Sir Wm. Chambers*, ob.
	Savannah:—350 buildings burned.		
	Lynn, (Mass.) annually exports 300,000 pair of shoes.		
	Died: Samuel Huntington, signer of Declaration of Independence;		
	David Rittenhouse, LL. D., F. R. S. an eminent philosopher and astronomer.		

A. D.	FRANCE AND SPAIN.	A. D.	MISCELLANEOUS.
1795	Sept. 20. Manheim taken by the French. Third constitution; The Directory, (5 persons,) the council of the ancients, (250,) and the council of five hundred. Napoleon Bonaparte at the recommendation of Barras, one of the Directory, is elected commander of the army. He first exhibits his intrepidity	1795	Archduke Charles twice victorious over Jourdan. *Goldoni*, an Italian poet, ob.
	Oct. 6. in quelling an insurrection in Paris, which lasts several days.		
	An offensive and defensive alliance with Spain.		
	Treaty concluded with the king of Sardinia.		
1796	Bonaparte is chosen to lead the French army in Italy.	1796	Holland, Feb. 19. A national assembly summoned.
	April 4. He defeats the Austrians at Monte-Notte,	Oct.	Sardinia:—Death of the king, Charles Emmanuel;
	—— 15. and the Piedmontese at Millesimo,		— Edmund V. succeeds.
	—— 18. the Austrians at Mondovi,		Victories of Bonaparte in Italy.
	May 11. and again on the bridge of Lodi.		Russia, Oct. 18:—Death of the empress, Catharine II.
	—— compels the kings of Sardinia and Naples, and the dukes of Parma and Modena to sue for peace.	——	Paul I. emperor; liberates Kosciusko.
	July 7. Jourdan defeats the Austrians at Neckerkercher.		
	—— 17. Moreau defeats the archduke Charles and takes Ettengen.		
	Bonaparte defeats Wurmser, and takes 400 prisoners.		
	—— 25. Moreau defeats the Austrians, and takes Augsburg and Munich.		
	Sept.—again victorious on the Inn.		
	Massena defeats the Austrians near Trent.		
	Bonaparte defeats them at Cavalho, and in 5 days takes 16,000 prisoners.		
	—— 21. Moreau begins his celebrated retreat.	Dec. 1.	Prussia, Saxony, and Hesse agree to a neutrality and withdraw their troops from the allied army.
	Barthelemy, ob.		

UNITED STATES.

A.D.	
	Anthony Wayne, maj. gen. in the Revolution; and,
	Samuel Seabury, bishop of Conn.
1797	—— **John Adams,** —— elected president of the U. S., and Thomas Jefferson, vice-president.
	News received of the capture of several vessels belonging to the U. States by the French.
	Gen. Pickering, and other envoys sent to France to adjust difficulties.
	Exports of the United States amount to $17,000,000.
	Post offices, 480. Revenue of P. O. $46,000.
	Medical Repository, the first work of the kind in the United States was commenced by Drs. S. L. Mitchill, Miller and Smith.
	Frigates launched; the Constitution at Boston, and the Constellation at Baltimore.
	Emigrants: 191 from London, and 140 from Hamburg.
	Treaty concluded with Tripoli.
	Yellow fever in Philadelphia of which 988 die.
	Oliver Wolcott, and Francis Lightfoot Lee, ob.
1798	Dispatches received from the envoys in France announcing the total failure of their mission. Two of them ordered by the directory to leave the country.
	Congress orders preparations for war with France.
	Regular and provisional army organized and Washington appointed commander in chief.
	Transylvania University at Lexington, Kentucky, founded.
	Rhode Island adopts a code of laws.
	Emigrants:—425 arrive in Norfolk, from Ireland.
	The *British Encyclopedia*, the first work of the kind in America, printed in Philadelphia, by Thomas Dobson.
	Jeremy Belknap, D. D., ob.

GREAT BRITAIN.

A.D.	
1797	Feb. 10. Treaty of commerce with Russia.
	—— 14. Sir **John Jervis,** obtains a signal victory over the Spanish fleet off cape St. Vincent.
	—— 21. Trinidad taken by the British.
	—— 27. Bank of England stop payment by order of the council.
	April 16. Petitions to the king against the ministry.
	May 30. Kosciuscko, the Polish patriot arrives in London.
	Oct. 11. Admiral **Duncan** defeats the Dutch fleet off Camperdown.
	Sir Benjamin Hammet fined £100 for refusing to accept the office of lord-mayor of London.
	——19. Thanksgiving for naval victories.
	Edmund Burke, Horace Walpole, Mason, the poet, and *Farmer*, critic, ob.
1798	March. Insurrections and arrests in Ireland.
	April 3. *Wilberforce's* motion for the total abolition of the Slave trade—lost; 87 to 83.
	May 1. Ireland:—1,000 insurgents were killed in a fight with the king's troops.
	April 21. Lord Edward **Fitzgerald,** the Irish Patriot, arrested, and soon after dies.
	—— 25. Havre bombarded by Sir Richard Strachan.
	—— 27. Duel between Mr. Pitt and Mr. Tierney.
	April 1. Lord **Nelson's** victory off the Nile.
	—— 22. French troops land in Ireland, but are soon after expelled.

A. D. FRANCE AND SPAIN.

1797 Jan. 7. Mantua conquered.

—— 14. Bonaparte defeats the Austrians near Mantua and takes 23,000 prisoners.

Feb. 10. —— defeats the army of the pope, and takes 12,000 prisoners.

Feb. 25. —— expels the Austrians from the Venetian states, and takes 20,000 prisoners.

April 1. Hoche gains a victory over the Austrians.

April 7. Bonaparte defeats the archduke Charles in Carinthia.

April 18. Preliminaries of peace at Leoben.

July 15. The banished clergy are permitted to return to France on taking the oaths to the new constitution.

—— 28. French enter Leghorn.

Sept. 4. La Fayette, and his companions released from the prison of Olmutz.

—— 14. Conspiracy discovered: Carnot one of the directors flees; Barthelemi, Pichegru, and several of the deputies imprisoned.

Oct. 17. Treaty of peace with Austria, signed at Campo Formio, by which France retains possession of the Netherlands;

Lombardy is ceded and becomes a part of the new Cisalpine Republic.

Bonaparte chastises the Venetians and establishes in Venice a provincial government on republican principles.

Bonaparte on his return from Italy is received with great distinction by the directory.

1798 Feb. 10. French troops under Berthier, enter Rome, and depose the pope.

Bonaparte's expedition into Egypt:

May 10. He embarks at Toulon in the most formidable and magnificent armament known in modern Europe; (destination kept secret.)

June 12. —— reduces Malta;

July 1. lands in Egypt with 30,000 men;

July 5. takes the city of Alexandria, and

—— 23. Grand Cairo.

Aug. 1. His fleet defeated at Aboukir, near the mouth of the Nile by the English under Lord Nelson; 19 sail of the line taken by the latter, 2 burned, and two escaped.

A. D. MISCELLANEOUS.

1797 Earthquake in South America, Feb, 25, swallowed up 46,000 persons.

Turkey, April 16. Riot at Smyrna; the Janisaries burn the theatre and the houses of the Christians, and kill 12 persons.

Italy, Oct. Cisalpine Republic, established by the French; and Genoa with their assistance overthrows the aristocracy and establishes a provisional government.

Venice made a republic by Bonaparte.

Prussia, November 16:—Frederick William III.

1798 Rome, Jan. 17:—Insurrection:—the French ambassador killed.

Feb. 10. The French take possession of Rome, and abrogate the power of the pope. Pius returns to Vienna.

Roman Republic.

Switzerland, (March 13,) entered by the French troops; and declares in favour of liberty and equality. Swiss lose 7,000 men in combatting the invaders.

Russia, May 29:—Public schools and printing presses suppressed by the emperor Paul.

Swiss are totally defeated by the French, (Sept. 9.) A new constitution formed for them as dictated by the conquerors.

A. D.	UNITED STATES.

1799 French Directory having made proposals for negotiating, the president appoints **Oliver Ellsworth,** (chief justice of U. S.) **Patrick Henry,** (late governor of Va.) and **William Vans Murray,** (the Am. minister at the Hague,) to settle all controversies.

Treaty with Tunis negotiated by Wm. Eaton, and James L. Cathcart; and with Prussia, by **John Quincy Adams,** minister from the U. S. at the court of Berlin.

East India Marine Society at Salem, (Mass.) instituted.

American Review, (the first) was begun at New-York.

Died: at Mount Vernon, George Washington. æt. 63. An oration on this lamented event was delivered at the request of congress by maj. gen. Lee, and the people of the U. S. wore crape on the left arm for 30 days. A marble monument was ordered by congress to be placed in the capitol.

Also, died, Patrick Henry, the distinguished patriot and statesman.

1800 The seat of government transferred to Washington, D. C.

Sept. 30. Treaty with France concluded by the commissioners.

Oct. 1. Louisiana ceded by Spain to France.

Mississippi and Indiana erected into territories.

2nd Census; inhabitants of United States, 5,305,482.

Shipping of United States, amounts to 939,000 tons.

College at Middlebury, Vermont, inc.

Cow-pock inoculation introduced into America by Dr. Benj. Waterhouse of Cambridge.

Ward, Mifflin, and Rutledge, ob.

A. D.	GREAT BRITAIN.

1798 It is estimated that during the troubles in Ireland 30,000 have been killed.

French prisoners in England, 27,000.

Oct. 12. Sir B. Warren, captures a French squadron with troops bound for Ireland.

National debt on the first of January £462,424,9 67.

Navy in commission;—140 sail of the line, 22 of 50 guns, 55 frigates and 317 sloops of war.

1799 Income tax proposed by Mr. Pitt, and passed; (the substance is that assessed taxes are repealed, and a tax of 10 per cent on incomes above £60 a year substituted.)

Jan. 22. The Irish parliament divided 106 to 105, on the question of the proposed union with G. Britain.

East Indies:—War with Tippoo Saib, in consequence of his alliance with France.

—— Seringapatam taken, and Tippoo Sultan killed.

S A:—Aug. 23. Surinam taken from the Dutch.

Aug. 28. Dutch fleet of 12 ships of war and 13 Indiamen, surrender to the British, admiral Mitchill.

Duke of York sent with an army to the Netherlands to assist the allies.

Dec. Peace offered by Napoleon and refused.

German literature begins to be popular in England. Kotzebue's tragedy of Pizarro anglicized by Mr. Sheridan.

Published:—Mungo Park's travels in Africa.

1800 Jan. 25. Act for legislative *Union with Ireland* passed; (takes effect Dec. 31.)—the latter to be represented in the Imperial parliament, by 4 bishops, 28 lords, and 100 commoners.

May 11. The king twice fired upon.

Sept. 5. Malta taken by the British after 2 years siege.

Riots caused by the scarcity of provisions.

Stevens, critic; *Cowper,* poet; and *Dr. Hugh Blair,* ob.

A. D. FRANCE AND SPAIN.

Aug. 6. Bonaparte gains a decisive victory over the Mamelukés.

Sept. Geneva annexed to France.

1799 Feb. 12. French pass the Rhine under Bernadotte and Jourdan, and enter Switzerland under Massena.

March 30. Bonaparte repulsed from before Acre, by the English, under Sir Sidney Smith.

April 9. Austrians defeated by the French, near Cremona in Italy.

Egypt, July 26: Battle of Aboukir, between Bonaparte with the Turks, in which the latter lost 18,000 men.

Sept. 19. French victorious at Bergen and Alkmaer (24th.)

Massena victorious at Zurich.

Oct. 9. Bonaparte and his staff returns from Egypt, and is hailed through France, as the saviour of his country.

Nov. Revolution; The council of 500 abolished: Bonaparte, *first consul:* Sieyes and Duclos, his colleagues.

—— *Marmontel*, ob.

1800 Bonaparte makes friends of all parties and ranks; restores civil and military order;

Ap. 6. assembles the army of reserve at Dijon. Campaign on the Rhine under Moreau. The reserve passes the St. Bernard.

June 14. Battle of Marengo; Bonaparte completely victorious over the Austrians under Milas.

Peace with Austria: the fortresses of Italy surrendered to the French.

Nov. Moreau's victory over the Austrians at Hohenlinden: he took 10,000 prisoners.

Dec. Attempt upon the life of Bonaparte, with the "infernal machine," which killed several persons.

A. D. MISCELLANEOUS.

1799 New coalition against France; between Austria, Russia, Naples, and Turkey.

Jan. 24. Naples taken by the French, after a battle between Mack and Championet.

April 14. Suwarrow with the Russian army in Italy defeats the French near Milan, where 11,000 were either killed or taken prisoners.

April 28. French ambassadors Roberjot and Bonnier, atrociously massacred near Rastadt by an Austrian regiment.

May. Suwarrow's army defeat the French under Moreau on the 17th and 23d, and again,

June 17. on the Trebia, where they lose 18,000 men.

June 20. Cardinal Ruffo enters Naples with an army of Russians and Calabrians, and commits horrid cruelties on the friends of the French.

Neapolitan patriots hung, on board the English squadron.

Aug. 27. British army under gen. Abercrombie, lands in Holland.

Oct. Russia secedes from the coalition, and Suwarrow returns home.

1800 Feb. 14. Pius VII. elected pope, at Venice.

Austrians take Nice.

June 14 Austrians defeated by Bonaparte, in the great battle of Marengo, and lose 18,000 killed.

Aug. Russian colony on the frontiers of China.

Nov. 3. Emperor Paul, now in league with France, lays an embargo on 300 British vessels, &c.

—— Ionian Republic, (consisting of the isles of Corfu, Cephalonia and others lately belonging to Venice,) founded.

A. D. UNITED STATES.

1801 —— **Thomas Jefferson** —— elected president of the United States; Aaron Burr, vice president.

James Madison, secretary of state.

A squadron sent to the Mediterranean to protect the U. States commerce from the Barbary cruisers.

Exports of the U. S. $93,000,000.

Duties $20,000,000.

S. Carolina exported 65,000 barrels of rice and 8,000,000 lb. of cotton.

University of Georgia located at Athens.

Newspapers in United States, 200.

1802 Port of New-Orleans shut against all but Spanish vessels, by the gov. of Louisiana.

Settlements with the Creeks and Choctaws.

Ohio admitted into the Union; it contains 76,000 inhabitants.

Merino sheep; 100 were imported from Spain, by David Humphries.

Jefferson College, Pa. incorporated.

First experiment of *Literary fairs*, for the public sale of books.

Fires:—100 houses burnt in Portsmouth, N. H.—also, Princeton College, N. J.

1803 Purchase of Louisiana for $15,000,000. Gov. Claiborne takes possession.

Lands of the Kaskaskian Indians, ceded to the United States.

Am. frigate Philadelphia, capt. Bainbridge taken by the Tripolitans.

Harmony, Pa. settled by a religious society called Harmonists.

The first American work on *Botany*, an elementary treatise by *Dr. Barton*, published.

Samuel Adams, of Boston, *Samuel Hopkins*, D. D. and William Vans Murray, ob.

1804 Delaware Indians cede to the U. S. their lands east of the Mississippi.

A. D. GREAT BRITAIN.

1801 March 10. Egypt: Aboukir surrendered to the British gen. Abercrombie, after a bloody action.

Battle of Alexandria, 21st: Abercrombie mortally wounded: the French repulsed.

—— 17 change in the ministry: Mr. Pitt and his friends resign, succeeded by **Mr. Addington**, (speaker of the Commons,) and his friends.

Br. fleet under Sir Hyde Parker and lord Nelson, sent to the Baltic.

Nelson's victory at Copenhagen.

May. Horne Tooke expelled from the house of commons, on pretence that clergymen are ineligible to a seat in it.

Aug. 3. Nelson bombards Boulougne.

Sept. 2. Alexandria surrenders to the British.

Published:—Dumont's Translation of Jeremy Bentham, on legislation.

1802 March 25. **Peace of Amiens**, with France:

Britain, of all her conquests, retains only Ceylon and Trinidad. Rejoicings in London. Col. Despard executed for a conspiracy.

Dec. 15. Abolition of the Income Tax.

A telescope which cost £11,000, was made in London, for the royal observatory at Madrid.

1803 The new attempts of Bonaparte for the aggrandisement of France had alarmed the ministry and,

May 12. Lord Whitworth, British minister to France returns, "to relieve Europe from suspense as war is re-commenced."

May French ambassador leaves London, and,

—— 17. War is declared against France.

Dec. French invasion of England expected; standing army increased.

East Indies:—English Co. acquire Delhi, Agra, &c.

War with the Mahrattas.

Hooke, Priestley, and *Beattie*, ob.

1804 Feb. 15. French fleet defeated by the homeward bound East India fleet Captain Dance.

A. D. FRANCE & SPAIN.

1801 French troops evacuate Egypt.

Feb. 9. Peace of Luneville, between France and Austria. The Adige becomes the frontier between the Cisalpine republic and Austria; the left bank of the Rhine and Piedmont remain French.

July 6. Engagement between the French and English fleets, in the bay of Gibraltar.

—— 15. *Concordatum* between Bonaparte and the pope; restoration of the Catholic worship in France.

Expedition of 25,000 French troops to St. Domingo; destroyed by disease and the negroes.

Oct. 9. Peace with Russia and Turkey.

Dec. 24. Bonaparte declines the request of the Parisians, that a statue should be erected to him.

Stereotype printing, in Paris by Didot.

1802 Jan. 25. Bonaparte elected president of the Italian (late Cisalpine) republic.

March 25. Peace of Amiens, with Great Britain.

May 6. Bonaparte made *first consul for life.*

Aug. 21. Mr Fox, the English statesman, visits Paris; received by the council with the highest marks of distinction.

—— 25. The consul forbids the circulation of inflammatory English newspapers.

Sept. 30. —— "mediator" of the Helvetic republic.

Legion of honour, a kind of nobility, instituted.

1803 Orders issued by the consul to arrest all the English of both sexes residing in France, and keep them as hostages. —The number is 7,500.

War declared against England.

June The French take possession of Hanover.

Sept. 6. Havre de Grace blockaded, and Granville and Dieppe bombarded by the British.

Nov. 19. St. Domingo given up to the blacks.

La Harpe, ob.

1804 March 15. Duke d' Enghien, (grandson to the prince of Conde,) arrested, and after a military trial at Paris, shot in the woods of Vincennes by torch light.

A D. MISCELLANEOUS.

1801 Peace of Luneville between the house of Austria and France; the Rhine and the Adige, boundaries of the Fr. republic.

Tuscany ceded to Parma, as the kingdom of Etruria.

March 3. War between Portugal and Spain.

Prussia joins the northern convention.

Russia:—March 23. The emperor Paul found murdered in his bed: his son, Alexander I. emperor and autocrat of Russia.

Georgia a Russian province.

April 2. Copenhagen bombarded and partly destroyed, by the Br. lord Nelson.

The northern confederacy dissolved.

Oct. Peace of Madrid, between Spain and Portugal.

Nov. 10. Massacre of seven beys in Egypt.

West Indies:—Independent republic established at St. Domingo by Toussaint.

1802 Ligurian republic, receives a new constitution.

Switzerland:—July 13. The cantons of Scheveitz, Uri and Underwald seperate themselves from the Helvetic republic.

Sardinia:—the king resigns the crown to his brother.

1803 Holland:—(June 21.) declared the ally of France, by the legislative council.

Wechab, A new prophet in Arabia.

Germany cedes to France 25,000 sq. miles, with 4,000,000 of inhabitants; most of the spiritual principalities abolished; 4 new electors created, viz. Salzburg, Wurtemburg, Baden, and Hesse.

Klopstock, the Milton of Germany, ob.

1804 Ger:—Aug. 11. The emperor Francis II., fearing the ruin of the Germanic constitution assumes the title of emperor of AUSTRIA.

A. D. UNITED STATES.

Feb. 1. Lieut. Stephen **Decatur,** of the United States navy, recaptures and destroys the frigate Philadelphia in the harbour of Tripoli.

Aug. Com. **Preble,** bombards Tripoli.

Published:—*Marshall's life of Washington.*

— Col. Alex. Hamilton, the first secretary of treasury, is killed in a duel by Aaron Burr, late vice pres. of U. S.

Schuyler, and *Linn*, ob.

1805 Jefferson re-elected president, and George Clinton, of New-York, vice-president, of the United States.

Feb. United States troops under gen. Eaton, restore the bashaw of Tripoli to his throne.

Professorship of *Natural History*, founded at Cambridge University.

Botanic gardens opened there; by Dr. Hosack, in N. York, and in Charleston, S. C.

Pennsylvanian *Academy of the Fine Arts*, instituted.

Schuylkill bridge near Philadelphia, completed.

Arthur Brown, and Wm. Moultrie, ob.

1806 Lewis and Clarke, with a company of 45 men sent to explore the Mississippi.

Sabine river agreed upon as the boundary between Louisiana and the Texas.

Treaty of amity and commerce with Great Britain, signed in London by Messrs. Monroe and Pinckney, but not ratified by the American government.

Colleges:—Washington, in Pennsylvania, and Cumberland, at Nashville, Tennessee.

Lehigh coal from the Mauch Chunk mountain, Pennsylvania, first brought into notice.

Cambridge University:—professorship of *rhetoric* founded by N. Boylston, Esq.

A. D. GREAT BRITAIN.

March 7. *British and Foreign Bible Society* instituted, under the auspices of Granville Sharpe.

May 12. New ministry; Mr. Pitt again premier.

Oct. 29. Three Spanish frigates taken, with $300,000 on board.

Dec. 14. *Planet Juno*, discovered.

Potter, the translator, ob.

1805 Jan. 5. War against Spain.

June 26. Lord Melville, a friend of Mr. Pitt, convicted of embezzling public money.

Aug. Duke of Gloucester, next brother of the king, dies, much lamented.

Oct. 21. Lord Nelson defeats the French and Spanish fleets, off Trafalgar; takes and destroys 24 ships, and is killed in the moment of victory.

Nov. 4. French fleet taken by Sir R. Strachan.

Moore, archbishop of Canterbury, and *Dr. Paley*, ob.

1806 Jan. 3. Death of Mr. Pitt.

— 8. Cape of Good Hope conquered by Sir Home Popham.

Feb. 6. French fleet defeated in the West Indies, by Sir Thomas Duckworth.

April 5. War with Prussia.

July 2. Buenos Ayres conquered by the British, but afterwards evacuated.

Sept. 20. Death of Mr. Fox: lord Howick succeeds.

Lord Lauderdale returns from an unsuccessful embassy to France.

Oct 19. Sir S. Hood captures a French squadron.

S. Horsley, D. D., bishop of St. Davids, ob.

A. D.	FRANCE & SPAIN.	A. D.	MISCELLANEOUS.
April 5.	Conspiracy against Bonaparte discovered; Moreau, one of the leaders exiled to America; Pichegru, strangles himself; Georges, and others executed.		W. Indies:—Oct. 8. Dessalines crowned king of St. Domingo, now called Hayti.
	Carnot alone opposing, the senate offer the first consul the imperial crown of France, and,	Nov. 5.	Great hurricane: 24 ships lost on the English islands.
Dec. 2.	He is crowned, and anointed by the pope at Paris, with the title of		
	—— NAPOLEON I., —— *Emperor of the French.*		
1805	May 16. Napoleon crowned king of Italy at Milan. He prepares to invade England.	1805	Ap. 11. Coalition of Russia and Austria, against France.
	Genoa and Parma united to France.		
Sept. 8.	War with Russia and Austria.		
—— 9.	Gregerian calendar restored.		
Oct. 16.	Marshal **Soult** takes 6,000 Austrians prisoners.		
—— 17.	City of Ulm taken and 40,000 prisoners.	Dec. 2.	Great battle of **Austerlitz**: the Austrians and Prussians defeated by Napoleon.
—— 20.	Murat takes Wernick.		
——	War with Sweden.		*Schiller*, the great German dramatist and poet, ob.
Nov. 13.	Napoleon enters Vienna.		
—— 16.	—— defeats the Russians at Gunterdorf; and	Dec. 26.	Peace of Presburg:—Venice, Tyrol, Breisgau, &c. taken from Austria by France.
Dec. 2.	the Austrians and Russians, at Austerlitz.		Hereditary principality of Lucca.
—— 26.	Peace of Presburg;—		Holland: Schimmelpennik, pensionary, with dictatorial power.
	Lucca granted as an hereditary principality, to Napoleon's sister Eliza, and her husband Baccuochi.	1806	Prussia shuts her ports against the British, and the king declares himself sovereign of Hanover. War with Britain.
1806	**Louis Bonaparte,** brother of the emperor, crowned king of Holland, June 5.		Holland:—**Louis I.** (Bonaparte) king.
			Naples:—**Joseph I.** (Bonaparte.)
July 23.	The emperor summons a Jewish Sanhedrim at Paris.	Aug 1.	Confederation of the Rhine, formed by the German States, after the dissolution of the empire;
——	creates his general **Berthier,** sovereign of Neufchateau, and **Talleyrand,** of Benevento; **Joseph,** his brother, king of Naples;		Napoleon the "head and protector."
	Eugene Beauharnais (son of the empress Josephine,) viceroy of Italy;—		BAVARIA becomes a kingdom under Maximilian I.; and,
	Murat, his brother-in-law, grand duke of Berg and Cleves; and,		WURTEMBURG, under Frederick I.
	Paulina, his sister, princess of Guastalla.		Baden:—Charles Frederick, grand duke.
	—— marches into Germany:		Hesse:—Louis grand duke.
Oct. 3.	—— defeats the Prussians in the great battle of Jena, (where 300,000 men were engaged.)		SAXONY detached from Austria and erected into a kingdom by Napoleon.
			Dec. 30. War between Turkey and Russia.

A. D. UNITED STATES.

John Quincy Adams, in the chair.

June 16. Total eclipse of the sun, visible in several places.

During this year, Great Britain invaded the rights of the United States by searching their vessels and impressing their seamen.

Robert Morris, Horatio Gates, *Isaac Backus*, Henry Knox, and George Wythe, ob.

1807 U. S. frigate Chesapeake, commodore Barron, fired upon and captured by the British Ship of war Leopard, for refusing to be searched.

Embargo laid on all the ports of the United States by an act of Congress.

Trial of Col. Burr, late vice president of U. S., for a conspiracy to divide the Union, and erect an independant empire, west of the Mississippi; ends in his acquittal.

Steam Boats: Fulton, makes the first successful trial on the Hudson river.

200th anniversary of the settlement of Jamestown celebrated; no vestige remains of its original site.

A *comet* appears from Sept. 25 to Jan. 30, 1808.

Oliver Ellsworth, and Edward Preble, ob.

1808 *Theological Seminary* at Andover, opened.

Slave trade of the United States abolished by law, January 1.

Bayonne decree, April 17, declaring all American vessels liable to seizure.

Published:—A new *translation of the Scriptures*, by *Charles Thompson*, Sec. of Congress.

Fisher Ames, *James Sullivan*, John Dickinson, and Wm. Shippen, ob.

A. D. GREAT BRITAIN.

1807 Orders in council, prohibiting all commerce with the enemies of Britain.

Feb. 3. Monte Video taken by the British.

March 2. **Percival** chancellor of the exchequer.

Bill for the *abolition of the slave trade*, which had been powerfully advocated by Messrs. Granville Sharpe, Fox, and Wilberforce, is finally passed.

British fleet under Cathcart and Gambier, bombards Copenhagen, which surrenders Sept. 7.

Nov. 1. War declared by Russia against Britain.

Mrs. Charlotte Smith, and *Louis Delolme*, ob.

1808 Island of Madeira taken by the British, (Hood, and Beresford.)

Sicily garrisoned by British troops.

June. Alliance with the patriots in Spain, against the French.

Aug. Louis XVIII. arrives in England under the title of Count de Lille.

£50,000 subscribed to aid the Spanish.

Sir Arthur Wellesley commander of the British forces in Spain; defeats Junot.

Local militia of 200,000 men established to be trained 28 days annually.

The art of *Polyantography*, since called *Lithography*, announced.

Richard Porson, the celebrated Greek scholar, ob.

A. D.	FRANCE & SPAIN.	A. D.	MISCELLANEOUS.
	—— again at Austeradt; enters Berlin, Hamburg, and Warsaw; erects Saxony into a kingdom; defeats the Prussians at Pultusk, and		*Dr. Gall*, a German, publishes a new theory respecting the brain, which he calls *Craniology*.
Dec. 26.	passes the *Berlin Decree*, declaring the British islands in a state of blockade.		
1807	War with Russia.	1807	West Indies:—Christophe president of Hayti, under the name of Henry I. New constitution.
Feb. 8.	Victory at Eylau: the Russians lose 20,000 men.		Turkey, May 29. Revolution in Constantinople; the grand signior deposed.
March 20.	Dantzic surrenders to the French.	June.	The Russian emperor Alexander defeated at Friedland.
June 14.	Napoleon and marshal Ney victorious in the battle of Friedland.		Prussia, by the treaty of Tilsit, loses half her territory which is annexed to Napoleon's new kingdom of Westphalia, under Jerome I. (Bonaparte.)
—— 16.	Marshal Soult takes Koningsburg.		Part of Poland erected into the Duchy of Warsaw.
—— 25.	Interview between Napoleon and Alexander on a raft in the river Niemen: followed by the treaty of Tilsit between France, Russia, and Prussia: the emperor's brothers acknowledged; Jerome presented with the new kingdom of Westphalia; Corfu and several islands ceded to France.		Russia declares war against England.
Nov. 30.	French under Junot enter Lisbon.		Portugal entered by the French. The royal family, alarmed by their threats, sails to Brazil.
Dec. 17.	The emperor issues the Milan decree forbidding commercial intercourse with Great Britain, and permitting the capture of British vessels. *Code Napoleon*, published.		Turkey:—Mustapha IV. emperor.
1808 Jan.	The towns of Kehl, Wessel, Cassel, and Flushing annexed to the French empire.	1808	Denmark, (Feb. 29.) declares war against Sweden. Death of Christian VII.
March 18.	General University established by Napoleon to superintend *national education*.		—— Frederick V. succeeds.
	Spain—had long been declining in power; the government weak; the people ignorant and indolent.—Revolution: Ferdinand, prince of Asturias compels his father, Charles IV. to dismiss Godoy, "the prince of the peace"* from the ministry, and finally to abdicate the throne; he is re		Turkey:—Mahomet VI., or Mahmoud II., emperor.
May 1.	instated and now abdicates in favour of his "Friend and Ally" the emperor of the French. Insurrection and massacre at Madrid.		Naples, July 22. Joachin Murat created king by Napoleon. Joseph transferred to Spain.
25.	Napoleon summons the Notables of Bayonne.		The *Wahabites* spread over Western Asia.

* So called from his having negotiated peace with France.

A. D.	UNITED STATES.
1809	— **James Madison,** — elected president of the U. States: George Clinton, re-elected vice president.
	Embargo repealed and the non-intercourse act, interdicting commercial intercourse with G. Britain passed.
1810	Rambouillet decree of Napoleon (March 18,) ordering all the American vessels in the ports of France to be seized.
Nov. 2.	Intercourse re-opened with France.
	Population of U. S. by the third census, 7,239,903. Kentucky, 406,511.—Pittsburgh, Penn. 4,740. Philadelphia, 90,000.
	Benjamin Lincoln a Revolutionary officer, and *Charles Brockden Brown*, a distinguished novelist, ob.
1811	British government makes reparation for the attack on the Chesapeak.
May 16.	Engagement between the U. States frigate President, capt. **Rogers**, and the British sloop of war Little Belt, capt. Bingham. The L. B. fires first, and loses 11 killed and 21 wounded.
	Gov. **Harrison** with a body of militia defeats the hostile Indians on the Wabash.
	Sugar, wine, and oil, begin to be made in Georgia.
	Merchandise to the amount of $2,950,000 exported from Philadelphia to Canton and Calcutta.
May 16.	The theatre at Richmond, Va. burned, 600 persons present, and nearly 70 perish, among whom were the governor of Virginia, and many respectable citizens.

A. D.	GREAT BRITAIN.
1809	Duke of York, commander in chief of the forces, charged with corrupt practices, and resigns, though acquitted.
July 7.	Senegal and Goree taken by the British.
July 18.	An armament of 75 ships with 40,000 men sent to Walcheren on the continent.
Sept. 22.	Duel between lord Castlereagh, and Mr. Canning, both members of the cabinet; the latter wounded.
1810 April 6.	Riots in London on account of the arrest of Sir Francis Burdett, for a speech in parl. on the Walcheren expedition.
July 9.	*William Cobbet* fined £100 and imprisoned 2 years for a political opinion.
Dec. 2.	Isle of France taken by the British.
18.	Lucien Bonaparte lands at Plymouth.
	Admiral lord **Collingwood** the successor of Nelson, ob.
	Published: *Humboldt's account of New Spain.*
1811 Feb. 3.	The king being in a state of mental incapacity, the prince of Wales is sworn before the privy council as regent.
May 16.	Affair of the Little Belt.
Aug. 7.	Batavia taken by the British.
	The population of Great Britain in 1801 was 10,942,646; this year it is 12,552,144.
	Malone, Cumberland, and *Raikes,* ob.

A. D. FRANCE & SPAIN.

June 6. Napoleon creates his brother Joseph, (late king of Naples,) king of Spain. He is opposed by the majority of the people who conclude an alliance with Great Britain.

Spain:—The French evacuate Madrid, July 27.—Ferdinand VII. ascends the throne.

Aug. 21. —— Battle at Viniera;—French defeated by Sir Arthur Wellesley.

Oct. 12. —— British army under Sir John Moore, and gen. Baird, enter Spain. The Spaniards defeated at Tudela, Nov. 23.

—— The Royal family of Spain imprisoned.

—— The Inquisition and feudal privileges abolished.

1809 —— Jan. 16:—Battle of Corunna; the British compelled to retreat with great loss.

Feb. 17. ——Saragossa taken by the French. Tyrolese in rebellion

29. Oporto taken by the French.

April. War with Austria.

21. Napoleon takes Ratisbon.

May 13. — enters Vienna; annexes Rome to the empire, July 8, defeats the Austrians in the great battle of Wagram, which is followed by the peace of Vienna, Oct. 14. By a secret article Napoleon agrees to divorce Josephine, and marry a princess of Austria. He annexes Valais and the Ionian republic to France: and assumes the dictatorship of Europe.

1810 The emperor is excommunicated by the pope, who is carried to France. Rome becomes the second capital of the empire.

Napoleon repudiates Josephine and marries the archduchess Maria Louisa, of Austria.

War with Algiers declared. French reduce Grenada and Seville, and besiege Cadiz; the Junta flee; the Cortes meet, Sept. 24. Lord Wellington, (late Wellesley,) repulses the French at Busaco.

1811 National Ecclesiastical Council at Paris; cardinal Fesch.

March 20. Birth of the emperor's son who is created king of Rome.

The emperor makes a tour through Holland.

Spain:—Soult victorious at, and takes Badajos.

——The English, (Graham,) victorious at Barrosa, March 6, and enter Cadiz. Wellington and gen. Beresford invest (Badajos, and Almeida, and defeat Soult in the bloody battle of Albuera, May 18.—June 28. Tarragona, and July 24, Montserat surrender to the French, (Suchet.)

Aug. 3. Eight newspapers suppressed at Paris.

The emperor orders all prisoners of war to be employed on public works, and paid for their labour.

A. D. MISCELLANEOUS.

1809 Austria, April 26, declares war against France.

May 2. Austrians victorious in the battle of Asperne, but defeated by Eugene Beauharnais at Leoben, and by Napoleon at Raab & Wagram.

Oct. 14. Peace of Vienna:—Austria loses Illegria;—Western Gallicia ceded to Warsaw; &c.

Sweden: revolution:—Gustavus IV. deposed, succeeded by his uncle Charles XIII.

1810 Holland, July 1. Decree of Trianon; Louis deprived of Holland, which is incorporated with France, as is also the north west of Germany.

Algiers declares war against France.

S. America:—Revolutions commence in Carracas, Mexico, Southern Peru, and Buenos Ayres. The Spanish magistrates deposed, and a union formed under the name of the Venezuela.

American confederation of

A. D.	UNITED STATES.	A. D.	GREAT BRITAIN.
	Robert Treat Paine, and William Williams, ob.		
1812	Feb. 25. Disclosure of the secret mission of John Henry, an agent of the British government, to undermine the union of the States.	1812	Riots of the manufacturers at Leeds, Sheffield, &c.
	April. Embargo on all vessels in the ports of the United States for 90 days.		May 11. Percival, the minister, shot by one Bellingham, who surrenders without resistance.
	June 1. President's war message to Congress, reviewing the hostile acts and intrigues of Great Britain.		Lord **Liverpool** created premier.
	—— 19. **Declaration of War** against Great Britain. The minority on the bill in Congress enter a protest.		Lord Wellington victorious in Spain.
	July. Mob in Baltimore: the office of a newspaper opposed to the war, demolished.		Several British vessels captured by the Americans.
	Gen. Henry **Dearborn**, an officer of the Revolution, is appointed commander in chief.		J. Horne Tooke, ob.
	July 12. American general Hull, invades Canada. A detachment of his army under Van Horn, defeated at Brownstown, Aug. 8.		
	Mackinaw surrenders.		
	Aug. 9. American colonel Miller defeats the British and Indians at Magurga.		
	—— 16. Detroit surrenders to the British on disgraceful terms to the Americans, under Hull.		
	Aug. 13. U. S. frigate Constitution, capt. Isaac **Hull**, captures the British frigate Guerriere, capt. Dacres: the Constitution loses 14 and the Guerriere 22, killed and wounded.		
	Governors of Massachusetts, Connecticut, and Rhode Island refuse to place their militia under the officers of the United States.		
	Connecticut raises troops for her own defence.		
	Oct. 8. Capt. Elliot, captures two British frigates on lake Erie.		
	—— 12. Battle of Queenston; American, capt. Wool, victorious.		
	—— 18. U. S. sloop Wasp, capt. Jones, captures the British sloop Frolic; and, 20th, they are both captured by the British 74, Poictiers.		
	The frigate United States, capt. **Decatur**, captures the British frigate Macedonian.		
	Dec. 29. U. S. frigate Constitution, commodore **Bainbridge** captures the British frigate Java.		
	Louisiana admitted into the Union.		
	American Board of Commissioners for *Foreign Missions* incorporated in Massachusetts.		
	Joel Barlow, George Clinton, and *David Ramsay*, ob.		

A. D. FRANCE & SPAIN.

1812 Spain:—Ciudad and Rodrigo, taken by Wellington; Valencia by the French.

April 6. —— Wellington storms Badajos, and

June 16. takes Salamanca.

War with Russia. Great preparations for the campaign.

May 9. The emperor leaves Paris and proceeds to Dresden; allies with Austria and Prussia;—his army of 500,000 men passes the Niemer under himself, his brother Jerome, Murat, Beauharnais, Powniatowski, marshal Ney, &c.

Spain: French defeated by Wellington in the battle of Salamanca July 23. The latter enters Madrid; Soult abandons Cadiz.

Aug. 17. Napoleon defeats the Russians in the battle of Smolensko.

Sept. 7. Battle of Borodino.

—— 14. Napoleon enters Moscow after it had been set on fire by the Russians, and takes up his abode in the Kremlin.

Oct. 19. French army evacuates Moscow, and begins its disastrous retreat; suffers all the horrors of a Russian winter, without clothing or provisions. Thousands fall victims daily. But 50,000 of the whole vast army repass the Russian frontiers. The French lose 41 generals, 1298 officers, and 1131 pieces of cannon. The empire is now on its decline; discontents and factions at home; and Europe begins to rise in a general combination against the retreating emperor.

A. D. MISCELLANEOUS.

Mar. 2. A volcano appears in the sea near St. Michaels, one of the Azores at 83 fathoms water.

Mahmond Ali, pacha of Egypt.

S. A.—July 5. declaration of Independence of the seven provinces of VENEZULA.

Bogota, (New Granada,) independent. The Indians freed from tribute to Buenos Ayres.

1812 March 29. Russia declares war against France; makes a treaty with G. Britain and Sweden.

July. Poland; Diet at Warsaw. Napoleon declares the Poles again a nation, and appoints a council of state.

Russia: Kutosoff commander in chief.

Sep. 7. Battle of Borodino:—(Russian and French,) 100,000 killed: victory claimed on both sides.

Sept. 16. Burning of Moscow.

Oct. French retreat: Kutosoff victorious over the divisions of Murat, Ney, &c.

A. D. UNITED STATES.

1813 Jan. 22. Battle of Frenchtown; American general Winchester defeated by the British col. Proctor. Americans afterwards massacred by the Indians.

Feb. 22. British, Sir George Prevost, repulsed in an attack on Ogdensburgh, in N. Y.

—— 23. U. S. ship Hornet, capt. **Lawrence**, captures the British ship Peacock, Capt. Peake.

Delaware and Chesapeake bays, blockaded by the British fleet. Admirals Warren and Cockburn.

March 4. James Madison re-inaugurated president, and **Elbridge Gerry**, vice-president.

April 27. York, U. C. surrenders to the American gen. Dearborn. British repulsed at Ft. Meigs.—Fts. Erie and George taken by the Am. Dearborn and Prescott. British repulsed at Sacketts harbour.

June 1. British frigate Shannon, captures the United States frigate Chesapeake, capt. Lawrence, off Boston harbour. Lawrence after losing all his officers, and being wounded himself, cries to the last, "Dont give up the ship."

June 22. British repulsed at Craneys island.

—— 25. Hampton village destroyed by Cockburn.

Aug. 14. British sloop Pelican captures the United States sloop Argus, lieut. Allen.

—— 30. Ft. Mims destroyed and its inhabitants massacred by the Creek Indians.

United States brig Enterprize, lieut. **Burrows**, captures the Br. brig Boxer, capt. Blythe; both commanders are killed.

Sept. 10. **Perry's** glorious victory on Lake Erie.

Battle of the Thames; American gen. Harrison, and col. **R. M. Johnson**, defeat the British and Indians under Proctor and **Tecumseh**, the famous warrior, who is killed.

Oct. 5. Com. **Chauncey**, captures a British flotilla of 7 sail on Lake Ontario.

Nov. 2. Creeks defeated at Tallaschatches, by gen. Coffee.

—— 7. and at Talladega by gen. **Jackson.**

Fort Niagara taken by the British. Buffalo burned.

Mission established at Bombay by the A. B. C. F. M.

Day of public humiliation and prayer was observed Sept. 3d. at the request of congress.

Benjamin Rush, M. D. an eminent physician, chemist, and philanthropist; *Peter R. Livingston*, late chancellor of N. York, an eminent statesman; and *Alexander Wilson*, the celebrated *ornithologist*, ob.

1814 Gen. Jackson defeats the Indians at Tallapoosa.

March 28. British frigate Phœbe, and sloop Cherub, capture, after a severe action, the United States frigate Essex, com. **Porter**, off Valparaiso.

Ap. 21. British frigate Orpheus captured the United States sloop Frolic, com. Bainbridge.

—— 29. United States sloop Peacock, capt. **Warrington**, captures the British brig Epervier.

June 28. United States ship Wasp, capt. **Blakely**, captures the British brig Reindeer.

A. D. GREAT BRITAIN.

1813 March 3. Treaty of alliance with Sweden, and, June 14. with Prussia and Russia.

A new officer,—the vice chancellor of England, is appointed.

Bill in favour of the Catholics, again brought in and lost.

Bills for bettering the condition of the curates and "granting toleration to Unitarians on the subject of the Trinity," &c. are passed.

The E. I. company's charter renewed and trade opened.

Princess of Wales acquitted.

Expenditures this year £ 120,000,000; supplies £ 77,000,000.

Granville Sharpe and *Henry Jas. Pye*, ob.

1814 Jan. 5. Treaty with Murat, king of Naples.

March 25. Deputies from Bordeaux, arrive in London, to invite Louis XVIII. to return to France.

A. D. FRANCE & SPAIN.

1813 Napoleon having returned to his capital, the senate votes him a levy of 350,000 men, to repair his losses.

Jan. 25. The emperor leaves Paris for the camp.

Beauharnais, second in command; Berthier, chief of the staff.

(The allied armies are now at all points of the empire: Austrians in Italy,—Wellington in Spain.)

Victory at Lutzen and Bautzen.

The king of Saxony joins the French.

July 27. Napoleon victorious in the battle of Dresden. Morean dies.

Oct. 8. British army under Wellington, enters France.

Oct. 16. Napoleon with 180,000 men defeated at Leipsic; retreats: leaves his army, and assembles the senate.

Loss of Holland, Hanover, and Dalmatia.

1814 June 8. Napoleon calls out the national guards, and places himself at their head.

Feb. Wellington enters Bordeaux.

—— 17. Fontainbleau entered by the Austrians.

—— 22. The count d' Artois, brother of Louis XVIII. enters France, from Basil.

Feb. 27. Spain:—Soult defeated at Ortheo by the British.

A. D. MISCELLANEOUS.

1813 Warsaw, Berlin, Swedish Pomerania, and Hamburg evacuated by the Fr.

Dutchy of Warsaw dissolved.

Prussia in alliance with Russia, Sweden, and Gt. Britain join the confederacy against France.

May 2. Battle of Lutzen, and

—— 20. —— of Bautzen;—the allies defeated in both; but, victorious,

June 11. In the battle of Vittoria, and,

Aug. 2. Of the Pyrennees.

The grand allied army under **prince Schwartzenburg,** in Switzerland; prince **Blucher,** at Frankfort; Bernadotte, in Belgium.

July 27. Battle of Dresden; the allies defeated.

Oct. 16—19. **Battle of Leipsic,** one of the greatest in history; the French totally defeated.

Bavaria joins the allies.

Holland:—William V. the stadtholder, recalled by the Orange party, and elected sovereign prince.

Kingdom of Westphalia dissolved.

South America:—BOLIVAR drives the Spaniards from Carracas.

Civil war in New Grenada.

1814 Jan. 2. Allied army occupies Coblentz.

—— 17 Denmark joins the allies.

—— 24. Battle of St. Dizier, in Champaigne; allies defeated.

Feb. 17. Murat, king of Naples, joins the allies.

The three allied armies amounting to 380,000 men enter France. Prince Schwartzenberg proclaims the object of the allies to be a sincere and lasting reconciliation with France,

A. D. UNITED STATES.

July 5. Battle of Chippewa: American gens. **Brown, Ripley, Porter,** and **Scott,** victorious over the British gen. Riall. Eastport, and other towns in Maine, taken by the British com. Hardy.

—— 25. Battle of Bridgewater; Brown defeats the Br. Drummond.

Aug. British repulsed from Stonington and fort Erie.

—— 17. Br. fleet, adm. Cochrane, arrives in the Chesapeake.

—— 24. Battle of Bladensburgh:—British gen. Ross, defeats the American gen. Stansbury, col. Munroe, and com. Barney.

Washington, D. C. entered and pillaged by the British.—The capitol and other public buildings burnt.

—— 27. Alexandria, D. C. surrenders to the British.

Sep. 11. **Macdonough's** victory on lake Champlain.

Battle of Plattsburg: American gen. **Macomb,** repulses the British, Sir George Prevost.

Sep. 12. British defeated near Baltimore; at fort M'Henry, 13th, and fort Erie, 18th.

Oct. American Gen. Bissel, defeats the marquis of Tweedale near Chippewa.

Nov. 20. Pensacola surrenders to gen. Jackson.

Dec. 13. British invade Louisiana, and capture a flotilla on lake Borgan.

—— 15. *Hartford Convention* of delegates, from the legislatures of Mass. Conn, and R. I. and from county meetings in N. H. and Vt. to "investigate the state of the country, take measures to redress grievances," &c.

Among the goods of the prize brig Falcon, taken by the America, of Salem, were 900 *bibles*, shipped by the Br. and For. Bible Soc. for the cape of Good Hope.

American Tract Society, instituted.

Elbridge Gerry, vice-president of U. S; William Heath; and *Benjamin Thompson, count Rumford*, a native of Woburn, Mass. who was knighted by the king of England, and was a liberal patron of literature and science, ob.

1815 Jan. 8. **Battle of New Orleans;** gen. Jackson's victory over the British Sir Edward Packenham, who loses 2,600 men, killed and wounded. Americans lose 13.

Jan. 15. British frigate Endymion, captures the United States frigate President.

Feb. 17. Treaty of Peace with Gt. Britain ratified by the president.

—— United States frigate Constitution capt. **Stewart,** captures the British Cyane and Levant, off Madeira.

—— 23 United States sloop Hornet, com. Biddle, captures the British brig Penguin, off Brazil.

A. D. GREAT BRITAIN.

Ap. 20. Louis XVIII. enters London in state, accompanied by the prince-regent, and received with great eclat.

June 7. The emperor of Russia, and king of Prussia, arrive in London, attended by many princes and nobles. The city is illuminated.

—— 9. The two sovereigns are invested with the order of the garter.

July 7. Thanksgiving for peace; the prince regent went in state to St. Pauls.

Dec. 3. Treaty of peace with the United States, signed at Ghent.

By the peace of Paris, Gt. B. retains the Cape of Good Hope, Tobago, St. Lucia, Essequibo, Demarara, Malta, &c.

1815 Feb. 19. Candy, the capital of Ceylon, and Almoro in the E. I. taken by the British, Ap. 25.

A. D. FRANCE & SPAIN.

March 30. Maria Louisa and her son, leave Paris.

—— 31. Battle under the walls of Paris which is entered by the allies.

Ap. 2 Decree of the Senate, that Napoleon Bonaparte and his family, have forfeited the crown of France.

Ap. 4. Napoleon signs his abdication of the crowns of France and Italy, and

—— 18. embarks for the island of Elba, in the British frigate Undaunted.

—— Louis XVIII. (Bourbon :) —— makes a public entry into Paris, and ascends the throne without opposition, May 3.

Spain:–Ferdinand dissolves the Cortes, abolishes the constitution, and restores the Inquisition.

May 30. First peace of Paris: France reduced to nearly her old limits; retains however, Avignon, part of Savoy, and the Netherlands.

A D. MISCELLANEOUS.

March 31. Entrance of the allies into Paris.

May 30. Peace of Paris; the pope, the king of Sardinia, the grand duke of Tuscany, the duke of Modena, the elector of Hesse-Cassel, the dukes of Brunswick, and Oldenburg take possession of their states.

Restoration of the Jesuits by the edict of the pope.

Norway is made a distinct kingdom with a liberal constitution, under the same monarch as Sweden.

Oct. 2. Congress of the allied sovereigns at Vienna.

At Smyrna a plague carries off 35,000 persons.

An explosion of gunpowder at Dresden, destroys nearly 1000 houses.

1815 March 1. Napoleon having escaped from the custody of Sir Neil Campbell at Elba, lands in Provence with less than 1,000 followers; enters Lyons, 10th; is joined by large numbers of his former soldiers.

Great alarm in Paris: Benj. Constant's speech against "the usurper."

Napoleon organizes his cabinet; (Fouche minister of police,)—is joined by marshal Ney; and saluted with the shouts of "Vive Napoleon," by the Bourbon army sent against him.

—— 20. Departure of Louis and his court.

——— Napoleon enters Paris.

June 6. opens the house of peers and deputies.

—— 12 joins his army in Belgium.

1815 March, Europe in consternation, at the news of Napoleon's escape from Elba.

Ap. 21. Murat declares for Napoleon.

——— is defeated, and dethroned by the Austrians. The king of Sicily returns.

March 13. Decrees of the congress of Vienna, that Napoleon is "without the pale of civil and social relations," &c.

Austria and Prussia, return to their state before 1790. Saxony divided, (part to Prussia;) Genoa given to Sardinia; Parma to Maria Louisa; Germanic confederation established.

War of the allies, Austria, Prussia, Russia and Great Britain against Napoleon.

June 15. Prussians under Blucher defeated at Ling.

Period.

A. D. UNITED STATES.

Ap. 6. Barbarous massacre of 63 American prisoners at Dartmoor, England. It is disowned by the British government.

The Algerine government having violated their treaty by hostilities on the American commerce, War against Algiers is declared, and commodores Decatur and Bainbridge, are sent with a squadron to the Mediterranean. They capture two Algerine vessels, June 17, and a treaty of peace is concluded, July 4.

Benj. Smith Barton, M. D.; *Robert Fulton,* the celebrated engineer and benefactor of his country; *Governeur Morris;* and *John Carroll,* D. D. first archbishop of the Roman Catholic Church in the United States, ob.

A. D. GREAT BRITAIN.

June Battle of Waterloo, which although glorious to the British, puts half the nation into mourning. Of the Br. army 600 officers and 15,000 men are killed and wounded.

July 15. Napoleon surrenders to capt. Maitland of the British ship Belerophon,

Aug. 7th and by order of the allied sovereigns sails as prisoner to S Helena in the Northumberland, ad. Cockburn.

Wm. Nicholson, ob.

A. D. UNITED STATES.

1816 Indiana admitted into the Union.

U. S. Bank, established by act of Congress, with a capital of $35,000,000.

Treaties with the Chickasaws, Choctaws, and Cherokees, concluded by gen. Jackson.

Emigrants:—7,122 arrive at N. York from Ireland.

M. Hyde de Neuville, arrives as envoy extraordinary, &c. from Louis XVIII.

American Bible Society, instituted at New-York. *Elias Boudinot,* 1st. president.

Harvard College;—A *law professorship* established; Isaac Parker, LL. D., in the chair; Rumford Professorship; Jacob Bigelow, M. D.

Mission commenced at Ceylon by the American board.

Great fire in New-York, 4th. Dec. Loss $200,000.

James Alexander Dallas, sec. treasury of United States, ob.

A. D. GREAT BRITAIN.

1816 Insurrection of the negroes in Barbadoes quelled: 903 killed and wounded.

May 12. Marriage of the princess Charlotte, (daughter of the regent,) to Leopold prince of Saxe-Coburg.

July 2. Public funeral of *Richard B. Sheridan.*

Aug. 27. British fleet, lord Exmouth, bombards Algiers, and forces the dey to a treaty of peace, by which Christian slavery is abolished.

Lord Amherst and suit sails on an embassy to China.

The *Safety Lamp,* invented by *Sir Humphrey Davy,* to prevent the accidents which happen in coal mines from fire damp.

Adam Ferguson, LL. D., ob.

XI.

A. D.	FRANCE AND SPAIN.	A. D.	MISCELLANEOUS.
— 22.	Napoleon abdicates in favour of his son.	June 18:	—Battle of Waterloo: the English (Wellington) and Prussians (Blucher,) entirely victorious but with immense loss. The French force was 150,000 men, the allied 170,000. Nearly one half of the former remain dead on the field.
July 3.	Paris occupied by the allied army.	Sep. 26.	*Holy Alliance,* of Russia, Austria, Prussia, and France. Monarchs firmly united against the people.
— 5.	Louis XVIII. restored a second time by foreign armies; agrees to maintain 150,000 of the allied troops for 5 years and pay 700,000,000, livres.	Oct. 13.	Murat, King of Naples, returns to Calabria and is shot.
Aug. 16.	Marshal Ney executed, contrary to the treaty of capitulation.		S. America:—United States of Buenos Ayres, declare themselves independent.
Dec. 21.	Lavallette condemned for high treason; escapes from Paris in his lady's clothes.		—— Gen. Morilla lands with a new Spanish army at St. Martha; and conquers Carthagena.
1816	All the relatives of Bonaparte excluded from the kingdom.	1816	Great inundation in Prussia; 119 villages damaged.
	Didier executed as a traitor.		Fire in Constantinople: 1500 houses destroyed.
Aug.	*Chateaubriand,* struck out of the list of ministers of state, for writing a pamphlet against the diminution of the chamber of deputies.		Poland is again enslaved by Russia.
			Empire of Russia succeeds that of Napoleon, in the menacing extent of its resources, and the ambition of its ruler.
			The king of Naples accedes to the Sicilian constitution; feudal rights abolished in both kingdoms.
			The pope abolishes torture, and the forfeiture of goods, by the seizure of the Inquisition.
			S. A:—Independents in Venezuela successful; Bolivar elected commander in chief.
			—— Congress of the provinces of La Plata.
			—— Don Juan Martin de Puyrredo, dictator general.

A. D. UNITED STATES.

1817 —**James Monroe,** president.— **Daniel D. Tompkins,** of New-York, vice president.

Mississippi admitted into the Union.

Amelia island in the St. Marys taken possession of, by the United States government.

Indian lands in Ohio ceded to the United States.

Sandusky city, (Ohio,) laid out.

Rochester, (N. Y.) incorporated

N. Y.:—*First law establishing a Canal Fund*, and directing a canal to be commenced, passed by the Assembly chiefly through the influence of **De Witt Clinton.**

Manufactures and internal improvemt: individual enterprize.

Timothy Dwight, D. D., S. T. D., president of Yale college, ob.

Andrew Pickens, John Morgan, and the Polish patriot, Kosciusko, all officers of the American Revolution, ob.

1818 Illinois admitted into the Union.

War with the Seminole Indians.

Theological seminary at Waterville, Me. inc.

Mission among the Choctaws established.

Arthur St. Clair, æt. 84, a lieutenant under Wolfe at Quebec, and afterwards major general in the American army;

Caspar Wistar, M. D.;

Daniel Boone the first settler of Kentucky; and

Joseph McKean, D. D., LL. D., professor of rhetoric in Bowdoin College, ob.

1819 Alabama admitted into the Union.

Arkansas erected into a territory.

Vandalia, the capital of Illinois, and Catawba, capital of Alabama, are laid out.

First *steam-ship* sails for Europe in May.

William Samuel Johnson, LL. D.;

Hugh Williamson, M. D., LL. D.;

Caleb Strong, LL. D. late governor of Massachusetts;

Jesse Appleton, D. D. president of Bowdoin College; and

Oliver Hazard Perry, the gallant victor on lake Erie, ob.

A. D. GREAT BRITAIN.

1817 The prince-regent fired upon in his carriage, Jan. 28.

Feb. Treaty with the king of Spain, by which he agrees to abolish the slave trade.

— 6. Lord Cochrane presents to the commons two petitions for "Reform and Retrenchment" signed by 54,000 persons. The prince regent gives £50,000 into the treasury.

Mr. Grattan's and Lord Donoughmore's motion in favour of the Catholics, and Sir Francis Burdett's for parliament reform, negatived.

— 30. Charles Manners Sutton, Esq. elected speaker of the commons.

Nov. 4. Death of the princess Charlotte of Saxe-Coburg.

Lithographic art introduced into England by Ackerman and Willich.

Logier's system of musical education.

1818 The principal, and two seconds in a duel imprisoned for two months.

E. I.—Gen. Hislop defeats the 10,000 troops of the Perishu.

April 8. Lord Palmerston fired at in the war-office.

July 13. Marriage of the duke of Clarence to a princess of Saxe Meiningen, and of the duke of Kent to a princess of Saxe Coburg.

Nov. The Isabella and Alexander arrive after an unsuccessful attempt to discover a north west passage.

— 17. *Sir Philip Francis, John Gifford*, and *M. G. Lewis*, ob.

1819 Numerous public meetings in different places on the subject of "reform."—At Smithfield, Mr. Hunt presides: the military are called out to preserve the peace.

Hunt and others arrested.

Sept. 13. He enters London in triumphal procession.

New style of engraving introduced by Perkins, & Co. of Philadelphia, U. S.

John Playfair, D. D. and

Dr. *J. Wolcott*, (Peter Pindar,) ob.

A. D.	FRANCE AND SPAIN.
1817	Spain; Conspiracies against the bigoted and tyrannical government.
	Generals Milau and Lacy implicated; the latter arrested and killed in attempting to escape.
	France; count Mauhreuil tried at Paris for robbing the queen of Westphalia, when it appears that he had been hired to assassinate Napoleon on his journey to Elba.
	Several of the proscribed French officers emigrate to North America.
1818	Congress of the allied sovereigns at Aix-la-Chapelle.
	Law, subjecting journals and periodicals to censorship.
	Prohibition of the slave trade to the French colonies.
	The foreign troops leave France.
June 21.	By a convention, France agrees to pay 14,000,000 francs for debts due to individuals on the continent, and 3,000,000 to British subjects.
	New and liberal ministry.
	Spain:—The king forbids the introduction of foreign publications; decrees the banishment of all who had served Joseph Bonaparte, &c.

A. D.	MISCELLANEOUS.
1817	Russia: *Public schools*, established throughout the empire.
	South America:—**San Martin**, general of the patriots gains a decisive victory over the Spanish Royalists, (Feb.)
	Declaration of the independence of Chili.
	Insurrection of Pernambuco, conducted by Martinez, who with others is taken prisoner and executed.
	The pope issues a bull against Bible Societies.
	Belzoni, the Italian traveller, penetrates the second pyramid of Gheza.
	The ravages of "the CHOLERA" begin at Jessora, India, in August.
1818	Germany:—The petition of several thousand Germans presented to the diet demanding a representative government.
	Sweden, Feb. 5. Death of Charles XIII; **Charles XIV.** (Bernadotte,) first of the new dynasty succeeds.
March.	The dey of Algiers murdered by his soldiers.
	South America:—April 5. Chili entirely freed by San Martin's victory on the Maypo.
	West Indies:—Gen. **Boyer** elected successor to Petion at Port-au-Prince.
Nov. 15.	European plenipotentiaries at Aix la Chapelle, sign a "declaration of public policy."
	The Ionian islands receive a constitution.
	The Prince Leopold obtains one shilling as damages from an Englishman, for shooting on his grounds.
1819	S. America:—Venezuela and Caraccas united under the name of the Republic of COLOMBIA, of which Bolivar is elected president.
April 2.	*Kotzebue*, the popular German dramatist assassinated by a student named Sandt.
	Young Napoleon created duke of Reitchstadt by his grandfather, the emperor of Germany.

A. D. — UNITED STATES.

1820 Maine separated from Massachusetts, admitted as a state into the Union.

Treaty ceding Florida to the United States, ratified by the king of Spain.

Population of the U. S. 9,708,135.

Little Rock, the capital of Arkansas, founded.

Steam boat Comet, the first on the Arkansas arrives at Little Rock from New-Orleans.

Missions among the Cherokees and Osages commenced.

Benjamin West, a celebrated historical painter, (in London;)

William Ellery, a signer of the Declaration of Independence;

Stephen Decatur, a commodore in the United States navy, ob.

A. D. — GREAT BRITAIN.

1820 Jan. 23. Death of H. R. H. the duke of Kent, much lamented;

—— 29. and his majesty George III.

—— 31. Parliament assembled.—The prince of Wales proclaimed as

—— George IV., ——

holds his first court, and takes the usual oaths.

April 27. First parliament of the new reign opened. Rt. Hon. Charles Manners Sutton, re-elected speaker of the commons.

June 5. Arrival of the exiled queen Caroline. She is tried on several charges and acquitted.

Sir *Joseph Banks*, president of the Royal Society; and

William Hayley, ob.

UNITED STATES.

1821 Monroe, re-elected president, and Daniel D. Tompkins, vice president.

Missouri admitted into the Union, which now consists of 24 States.

Indianapolis, the capital of Indiana laid out.

Columbian college at Washington, D. C. organized.

Published:—The *American Medical Botany* by *Jacob Bigelow*, M. D.

Elias Boudinot, LL. D., formerly president of congress; and

Samuel Worcester, D. D., the 1st Sec. A. B. C. for Foreign Missions, ob.

GREAT BRITAIN.

1821 March 30. Advices received of the death of the emperor of China, and that the cholera morbus was making great ravages in that empire.

July 19. Coronation of George IV. The queen repulsed in attempting to gain admittance.

Aug. 7. Death of Queen Caroline.

Gas lights begin to be generally used.

German booksellers:—393 of them have published no less than 3,322 works in the course of 6 months.

In the Russian tongue 8,000 vols. have appeared within the last 20 years; whereas in 1800 only 3000 had ever been published.

John Bonnycastle, *Dr. Vicessimus Knox*, *Mrs. E. Inchbald*, and Admiral *James Burney*, ob.

UNITED STATES.

1822 Florida erected into a territorial government.

Commercial treaty with France.

Ministers sent to the South American republics.

GREAT BRITAIN.

1822 Insurrections in Ireland, caused by the scarcity of provisions.

April. Lord John Russell's motion on the subject of reform—lost, 369—164.

A.D.	FRANCE & SPAIN.	A.D.	MISCELLANEOUS.
			Russia: The emperor Alexander, the most influential sovereign in Europe; actively engaged in improving his empire; augmenting the navy, &c.
			—— The Lancasterian system of education introduced.
1820	Duke of Berri, of the royal family, assassinated.	1820	Jesuits banished from Russia.
	Spain:—Military insurrection in Cadiz; Constitution of the Cortes of 1812 proclaimed; the king obliged to accept it;	July 5.	Naples: Military insurrection; new constitution adopted in consequence.
	Abolition of the Inquisition and of the monastic orders; attention to schools, and liberty of the press, the immediate consequences of the revolution.	Aug.	Portugal:—Military insurrection; new constitution similar to that of Naples and Spain adopted.
		Sept. 5.	Palermo declares itself independent of Naples.
			Saxony:—its first diet opened at Dresden.
		Dec.	Congress of sovereigns at Laybach.
			West Indies:—Henry, emperor of Hayti, dies: Boyer succeeds.
			South America:—Campaign in Peru; siege of Lima.
			—— The possessions of Spain in Colombia reduced to Puerto Cabello, and Maracaibo.
			—— Morillo returns to Spain. Struggle of parties in Buenos Ayres.
			China:—death of the emperor.—Cholera rages.
1821	Jan. 25. A sham plot against the life of the king, and of the duke d'Anjouleme by an explosion of gun powder in the Tuilleries.	1821	Italy, Jan. The Austrian troops enter and enslave Naples, and quell a revolt in Piedmont.
			South America:—The emperor of Brazil consents to establish a representative government, and acknowledges the independence of the South American republics.
	Death of Napoleon at St. Helena, May 5.	April.	Turkey:—Commencement of the Greek revolution. The Greeks of the Peloponnesus rise with one accord against their oppressors, the Turks. The Greek patriarch of Constantinople is executed at the door of his own church.—Great numbers of his countrymen are massacred.
	Discontents and insurrections excited by the restricting and bigoted policy of the king and his new ministry.	May 6.	The congress of Laybach breaks up, after proscribing in a circular all "popular insurrections."
		July 6.	Portugal: John VI. returns from Brazil and adopts the constitution.
			South America:—June 24. The patriots of Colombia victorious at Carababo.
			—— July. Peru and Guatimala independent.
1822	Spain:—Disturbances promoted by the clergy; the insurgents called "the army of the faith."		Insurrection in Moldavia and Walachia by the Hetæria, (Alexander Ypsilanti.) He is defeated at Dragashan, and carried prisoner to Austria.
			Tripolizza taken by the Greeks.
		1822	An imperial ukase, closing all Freemason's lodges in Russia and Poland.

A. D.	UNITED STATES.
	Alarming increase of piracy in the West Indies.
	Boston (Mass.) incorporated as a city: Hon. John Philips first mayor.
	Conspiracy of the negroes at Charleston, S. C.;—35 executed.
	Literature:—Mercantile library at Philadelphia, founded.
	Ex-president Adams, gave to his native town of Quincy, 200 acres of land, the proceeds to be applied to literary purposes.
	Published:—American edition of *Rees' Encyclopedia*, 41 vols.; the boldest enterprise of the kind ever made in the United States.
	William Pinkney, late attorney general, and minister to Russia; and gen. John Stark, ob.
1823	Com. Porter sent with a squadron to the Gulf of Mexico, to subdue the pirates.
	New-York:—The new constitution of this state, goes into operation, Jan.
	Destructive fire in the woods, near Wiscasset, Me. commenced.
1824	New Tariff adopted, affording protection to American manufactures of cotton goods.
March 13.	Convention with Great Britain, against the slave trade.
	Visit of general La Fayette, in compliance with the invitation of Congress, to the "happy land," he had so generously aided in making free. He arrives at New-York, Aug. 13; and is received with acclamations by the assembled multitudes throughout the union, as "the nation's guest."
	Congress votes him the sum of $200,000, and a township of land, as a remuneration in part for his services during the war of the revolution, and as a testimony of their gratitude.

A. D.	GREAT BRITAIN.
May 18.	Lord Westmeath fined and imprisoned 6 months for challenging Mr. Wood.
Aug. 11.	The king's visit to Scotland.
—— 12.	Suicide of the marquis of Londonderry, minister for foreign affairs.
—— 17.	**George Canning** succeeds as minister for foreign affairs.
Oct. 23.	Lord Amherst appointed governor general of India.
Nov. 4.	Hunt's public entry into London, attended by 300,000 people.
	Dr. *E. D. Clarke*, author of Travels, &c., Sir *William Herschel*, the celebrated astronomer, and Dr. *Aikin*, ob.
1823 June.	The Common Council of London vote £2,000 and at another meeting, £6,000 to assist the Greeks and Spaniards in regaining their liberty.
Oct. 18.	Arrival of capt. Parry, from his exploratory voyage to the Polar Seas.
	The English and Italian travellers, (*Denham, Clapperton, Oudeney, Belzoni,*) penetrate into the interior of Africa.
	The Ashantees in Africa, defeated by the British.
	Mrs. Radcliff, Hutton, and *Bloomfield*, ob.
1824	Iturbide ex-emperor of Mexico; San Martin, the Peruvian general; and the king and queen of the Sandwich Islands, arrived this year in London.
	Private and public efforts in favour of the Greeks; Lord Byron's Rochdale manor, sold for £34,000 to aid their cause.
Ap. 19.	Death of lord Byron, at Missolonghi, when the Greeks out of respect, cease their Eastern festivities.
June 19.	John Hunt fined £100 for having published in the Liberal, "a poem reflecting on George III."

A.D. FRANCE & SPAIN.

Royal guards at Madrid declare against the constitution but are overpowered and exiled, July 7.

Insurrections in France. Severe restrictions on the liberty of the press.

Delambre, and *Legendre*, ob.

Hieroglyphics deciphered—(Champollion.)

1823 Spain :—May.—The ministers of the great powers leave Madrid. The Fr. enter 21st. and establish a regency, composed of the bigots of the old system. The patriot Mina maintains a determined resistance against the French in the north. The Cortes conduct the king to Cadiz. The (Fr.) duke of Anjouleme delivers him.

Sep. 23. French bombard Cadiz and re-instate Ferdinand in his despotic authority.

1824 June 16. Death of Louis XVIII. His brother the count d' Artois succeeds as

– Charles X. –

Oct. 4 removes the censorship from the press.

A. D. MISCELLANEOUS.

Turkey, Feb. 2. Ali Pacha taken by the Turks and strangled. Massacre of Christians at Constantinople, and of 15,000 Greeks at Scio, April 12. Turkish fleet destroyed at Scio, by the Greek fire ships. Nauplia taken by the Greeks. Upwards of 800 Greek virgins exposed in the slave markets. Greeks victorious near Thermopylæ.—A Greek congress at Epidaurus.

Jesuits re-established in Austria.

South America:—BRAZIL declared free and independent of Portugal:—Peter I. emperor.

——Bolivar conquers Quito.

MEXICO declares itself independent :—

—— Augustine Iturbide, emperor.

West Indies :—**Boyer** becomes master of St. Domingo.

Europe:—Congress at Verona—(principle of "armed intervention.")

Portugal:—The queen banished for refusing to swear to the constitution.

Oct. 22. Great eruption of Vesuvius.—A new volcano on the island of Oomnak.

An earthquake in Syria, destroys several cities, &c.

1823 Portugal :—Don Miguel encouraged by the success of the French in Spain, plants the standard of despotism in Lisbon.

—— The party of the queen victorious against the liberals: constitution abolished.—Manuel expelled from the chamber of deputies.

Pope Leo XII. (Cardinal Genga) succeeds Pius VII.

S. A.—Mexico :—Iturbide overthrown and banished to Italy :—republic established.

—— In Colombia the last hold of the Spaniards, Puerto Cabello, falls. In Peru, Bolivar acquires the direction of affairs, and is elected commander in chief.

—— Disturbances in Brazil suppressed, and Monte Video, under the name of Cisplatina, forms a part of that great empire.

—— Union of the Mexican provinces.

1824 Turkey :—Revolt of the pacha of Egypt.

—— Greeks take Patros and Lepanto.

Portugal :—Ap. 30. Rebellion of the Infant Miguel at Lisbon, The king escapes on board the British admiral's vessel in the Tagus. Miguel afterwards exiled, and the queen put into a convent.

Netherlands :—The king cedes the Dutch East India colonies to the British, in exchange for Sumatra, and Bencoolen.

Germany :—New prosecutions against the liberals.

South America :—Iturbide returns to Mexico, but is taken and executed.

—— Spaniards drive the republicans from Lima, but their army, in Upper Peru, is defeated at the battle of Ayacucho, Dec. 9.

The emperor of Brazil, swears to the new constitution.

A. D.	UNITED STATES.	A. D.	GREAT BRITAIN.
Oct. 4.	Anniversary of Penn's landing celebrated. Candidates for president: J. Q. Adams, W. H. Crawford, Henry Clay, and Andrew Jackson.		Died; *Rev. Dr. Cartwright*, the oldest poet of his time. *Lord Byron*, "the son of genius, and the friend of freedom."
1825	—— **John Quincy Adams**, —— 6th. pres. [elected by the house of representatives.] **John C. Calhoun**, vice pres. Treaty concluded with the republic of Colombia. Two ministers, (Richard C. Anderson, and John Sergeant,) sent to the congress of Panama.	1825 Feb. 28.	The Kent, East Indiaman, destroyed by fire in the bay of Biscay. Mr. Wilberforce resigns his seat in the House of Commons, having been a member 40 years. A petition 100 feet in length, from the Catholics in Ireland, praying for emancipation, presented by Sir Francis Burdett. In Jan. wool was exported to the United States (N. A.) the first instance in two centuries. Scarcity of money in London and Paris, felt all over Europe and the United States. E. I:—Burmese war continued; Br. take Prome.
June 17.	Celebration of the 50th anniversary of the Battle of Bunker's Hill. Oration on the spot, by the hon. *Daniel Webster*; and the corner stone of the "Bunker Hill Monument," laid by gen. La Fayette.		
Sep. 7.	La Fayette embarks for France, in the U. S. frigate Brandywine, after the farewell address of the president. Treaties concluded with the Creeks, Osages, &c. From Jan. to July, 276 new post offices were established. Died:—Charles Cotesworth Pinckney, aid de camp of Washington. —— John Brooks, M. D. L.L. D. gov. of Mass.		

A. D.	UNITED STATES.	A. D.	SOUTH AMERICA.	A. D.	GREAT BRITAIN.
1826 July 4.	Remarkable coincidence in the death of those distinguished statesmen and patriots, J. Adams and T. Jefferson: Public eulogies on their character and services, in various parts of the Union.	1826	Bolivia:—**Paez** revolts against Bolivar, who enters Caraccas and quiets the country. The credit of the S. Am. republics declines. W. Indian ports closed, by Great Britain.	1826	Canning sends 15,000 men, to assist the regent of Portugal in restoring peace. East Indies:—The rajah of Bhurtpore subjected. The Burmans compelled to conclude a peace with the Br. before their capital, by which Aracan and the S. W coast become British.
Nov. 13.	The Am. minister at London concludes a convention with the Br. Government, by which certain Am. citizens are indemnified, for injuries done them during the late war.				

A. D.	FRANCE & SPAIN.	A. D.	MISCELLANEOUS.
	Spain:—The constitutionalists defeated by the Fr.		
Aug. 19.	Thomas Francis executed at Madrid, for having said, "My sabre is tarnished, I wish I could brighten it in the blood of the king."	1825	Portugal:—Insurrections caused by the ultra party; change of ministers. South America:—Bolivar conquers Cusco. —— Upper Peru declares itself independent, under the title of BOLIVIA. —— Brazil;—Dispute with La Plata, respecting Cisplatina. Independence of Brazil acknowledged by Portugal, Aug. 29. —— Independence of the South American republics, acknowledged by Great Britain, Jan. 1. Russia:—Dec. 1. Death of Alexander I. —— Cesarovitch Constantine, declared emperor, but resigns to his brother, Nicholas I.
	Ferdinand in a public decree ascribes not only the salvation of Spain, but of the whole human race to "the wisdom of the Holy Alliance."		Turkey:—Ibrahim Pacha, son of the pacha of Egypt, devastates the Morea. Reshid Pacha advances to Missolonghi, which is defended with heroism. Greeks victorious by sea.
1825	The civil list, indemnification of emigrants, and three per cents. occupy the Fr. chambers; Villele prevails.		
		1826	Portugal:—Death of John VI; his will appoints the infanta Isabella Maria at the head of the regency, which don Miguel acknowledges, Ap. 7. and the emperor, Pedro I. confirms. The latter renounces the crown of Portugal, in favour of his daughter, Maria da Gloria, (a child 7 years old,) and gives a liberal constitution. The monks and nobility oppose the charter; insurrections. — Miguel is proclaimed absolute king, but swears to observe the constitution, and is contracted to Maria da Gloria. Turks take Missolonghi, Ap. 23. but her heroic defence attracts the attention of all Europe. Congress of Ackerman, settles the disputes between Russia and Turkey. Chinese fight against the revolted Tartars.

A. D. UNITED STATES.

Died :—Mrs. *A. H. Judson*, missionary in India; and *Jedediah Morse*, D. D. the geographer.

1827 The Winnebago Indians having murdered several whites, &c. without provocation, a body of Illinois and Michigan militia is sent against them; they submit and give up the murderers without fighting.

Wm. Tudor appointed charge d'affairs to Brazil, in place of Condy Raguet, who had resigned in consequence of indignities offered by that government.

Rufus King, late minister to England, ob.

1828 May 13. New Tariff passed: (superseded, 1832.)

Died :—Feb. 11, at Albany, Dewitt Clinton, governor and benefactor of New-York;

Feb. 24. Jacob Brown, maj. gen. in the late Am. war;

Sep. 26. *J. G. O. Brainerd* a popular poet.

1829 Feb. 7. General Harrison was recognized at Bogota as minister-plenipotentiary of the U. S.

Feb. 11. Electoral votes opened: Jackson had 178 for president, J. Q. Adams 83 for do. Calhoun 171 for vice president.—Richard Rush 83, Wm. Smith 7, for do.

A. D. SOUTH AMERICA.

1827 Paez submits to the liberator.

Peru :—Counter revolution, which overthrows all the institutions of Bolivar.

1828 Peace between Peru and Bolivia.

Bolivar, dictator of Colombia, June 13: his proclamation of Sept. 13.—Vice president Santander, and general Padilla conspire against him.

Santander taken prisoner.

Mexico :—general Santa Anna, governor of Vera Cruz, declares against Gomer Pedraza, the newly elected president, and in favour of Guerrero, the rival candidate.

1829 Jan. 1. Mexico, Congress opened by a speech from the president Victoria.

Jan. 6. Guerrero chosen president, and Bustamente, vice president.

Colombia, Jan. 18 :—Cordova destroys the Patian faction.

Feb. 27. Battle between the Colombian army of 5000 and the Peruvian of 8000 at Tarqui; the former victorious. The differences are referred to the United States government.

A. D. GREAT BRITAIN.

1827 Canning succeeds Lord Liverpool, as prime minister.

England joins the allies against Turkey,

Aug 8. Death of Canning.

Goderich ministry.

Capt. Parry returns from the North Sea, without having found the desired passage.

Clapperton, the English traveller in Africa, ob.

1828 Wellington's administration.

The queen of Portugal, donna Maria da Gloria arrives in London, Oct. 6; the king receives her as a queen.

London University opened.

Disturbances in Ireland, and the Catholic association resumes its sittings, the act against it having expired.

O'Connel, Shiels.

1829 Feb. 5. Parliament opened.

Feb. 24. Bill for suppressing the Catholic Association, passed.

A. D.	FRANCE & SPAIN.	A. D.	MISCELLANEOUS.
1827	Ministry unpopular. National guards abolished. France sends a fleet to Algiers. The Jesuits (Congregation,) become powerful. Spain:—Carlist insurrection in Tarragona. French fleet at Navarino.	1827	Portugal:—Tranquillity restored by the British army. Persians under Abbas Mirza, in the war with Russia, are defeat-at all points. The Russians conquer Erivan, &c., and, in the peace receive Aran and 18,000,000 rubles. Greece:—Cochrane arrives but cannot prevent the fall of Athens. —— The Greeks in great danger, implore the aid of the European powers.—Treaty of pacification in their favour, between England, Russia, and France. Capo d' Istria is elected president of Hellas. Battle of Navarino, Oct 20;—the English, Russian, and French fleets, destroy the Turkish fleet. Netherlands:—the king signs the concordate with the pope.
1828	Caille returns from Timbuctoo. Dumont d' Urville's voyage of discovery, 1826—29. Dismission of Villele.	1828	Portugal:—Don Miguel arrives, dissolves the chambers, summons the cortes which proclaims him absolute monarch. Protest against his usurpation, by the Brazilian ministers at London and Vienna.—Expedition against Madeira and Terceira, which declare for the emperor Pedro. The former is taken, Aug. 23. Russia:—The cabinet declares it must have satisfaction for itself, from the Porte, but as to Greece it agrees with France and England. —— Declaration of War, Ap. 26.—Russians at first victorious and enter Varna. Their general Wittgenstein establishes his quarters in Jassy. Greece:—French troops land in the Morea, which is evancuated by Ibrahim Pacha, per treaty with Cochrane.
1829	Jan. 27. Opening of the session of the French Chambers. Feb. 24. Cadiz a free port.	1829	Russia and Turkey:—Hostilities recommence, Jan. 9. Jan. 9. Portugal:—Failure of an extensive conspiracy at Lisbon against don Miguel. Feb. 10. Death of pope Leo XII. at Rome. —— 19. Russians under gen. Kumiasoff, defeat a body of Turks. —— 20. Greeks take fort Lithada from the Turks. —— 21. Russia: Diebitsch appointed commander in chief.

A. D. UNITED STATES.

Mar. 4. **Andrew Jackson** inaugurated president.

John C. Calhoun, vice president.

Cabinet :—Van Buren, Eaton, Ingham, Branch, and Berrien.

Mar. 18. Treaty with Brazil.

April 2. Augusta, Georgia ;—183 houses destroyed by fire.

May 2. Extraordinary *hail* storm in Tuscaloosa, Alabama. It fell 12 inches deep.

June 4. Explosion of the magazine of the steam frigate Fulton at Brooklyn, N. Y.—26 persons killed.

July 4. Chesapeake and Delaware canal opened

Aug. 12. Mr. M'Lane, envoy to Great Britain and Mr. Reivs to France embark at N. York.

Deaths.—Jan. 29.—At Salem, Mass. colonel Timothy Pickering, secretary of state under Washington.

March 31. Dr. E. A. Holyoke, æt. 100.

May 17. At Bedford, N. Y., John Jay. (See Biogra. list.)

June 18. Gen.Henry Dearborn.

Oct. 18. At N. York, *Wm. Harris*, D. D., president of Columbia College.

Nov. 26. At Philad., hon. *Bushrod Washington*, judge of the supreme court of U. States.

Dec. 22. At N. Y., *John M. Mason*, D. D.

1830 Jan. 13. Foote's resolution in the senate respecting public lands, which causes a protracted debate.

—14. Virginia:—New Constitution adopted.

A. D. SOUTH AMERICA.

April 3. Guatimala surrenders to the army of St. Salvador under gen. Morazan.

June 6. Revolution at Lima : Gamarra elected president of Peru.

July 5. Spanish invading expedition against Mexico, under Laborde and Barradas, sails from Cuba.

Aug. 22. It is unsuccessfully attacked by the Mexicans, but,

Sep. 12. the whole army surrenders to Santa-Anna, at Tampico.

—22. Peace between Colombia and Peru.

VENEZUELA declared independent of Colombia :—Paez at the head of affairs.

Nov. 9. Yucatan separated from Mexico and united with the Republic of Central America.

Nov. 16. The province of Conception separated from Chili.

Dec. 5. Buenos Ayres :—Rosas succeeds Lavalle as president.

Dec. 14. Civil war in Chili.

1830.

Jan. 20. Colombia : Bolivar resigns his civil and military offices.

March. 22. Chili : Ovalle, president.

April 27. Guatimala nearly destroyed by an earthquake.

A. D. GREAT BRITAIN.

Mar. 21. Duel between the duke of Wellington and the earl of Winchelsea.

—30. *Catholic Emancipation* bill passed the house of commons.

May 30. Capt. Ross sails on a voyage for discovery of a North West passage.

Aug. 4. Severe storm and destructive flood in Scotland.

Dec. 4. East Indies:—Abolition of the Suttee rite, by the British government.

1830.

Feb. 4. Parliament opened.

Prince Leopold elected king of Greece.

—22. Petition of the Jews for the removal of their civil disabilities—rejected.

April. 21. Leopold declines the crown of Greece.

A. D. FRANCE & SPAIN.	A. D. MISCELLANEOUS.
Mar. 21. Earthquake in Spain; 4000 houses and 20 churches destroyed.	March 5. Russia:—Battle with the Turks near the Natonebi. ——6. Portugal:—Moreira and four others hanged for conspiracy. ——22. Greece:—The government, boundaries, &c. fixed by a protocol between Great Britain, France, and Russia.
May 6. The Fr. consul leaves Buenos Ayres, on account of alleged insults to the nation, and the French admiral takes the Buenos Ayerian fleet. French navy:—79 vessels had been added to it in one year.	April 9. Inundation of the Vistula, near Dantzic. A part of that city and 50 villages overflowed; 10,000 cattle drowned. ——22. Lepanto surrendered to the Greeks. May 14. Missolonghi surrendered to the Greeks. ——17. Diebitsch defeats 5,000 Turks in Silistria. ——24. Coronation of the emperor Nicholas of Russia, as king of Poland, at Warsaw. June 11. Russians under Diebitsch gain a great victory over the Turks, near Schumla. The latter lost 6,000 killed. ——12 and 14. Russians again victorious. ——30. ——— take possession of Silistria, with 10,000 prisoners, &c. July 17, 18, and 19. ——— pass the Balkan. ——23. Greek national assembly opened at Argos. Russians take Aidos and several other fortresses. Aug. 11. Portugal:—Unsuccessful attack on the island of Terceira, by the fleet and troops of Don Miguel.
Aug. 9. French ministry changed: the Liberals dismissed and succeeded by prince Polignac and the Ultra-Royalists.	Aug. 20. Russians under Diebitsch take Adrianople. Sept. 14. Treaty of peace between Russia and Turkey signed at Adrianople. ——15. Greece:—Death of Datzel, the Greek general. ——24. ——— Ypsilanti defeats the Turks at Petria. Nov. 26. Inundation of Nile:—30,000 persons drowned. *Frederick von Schlegel*, German author, ob. (Jan. 9.)
1830.	1830
March 2. The Chambers assemble. ——19. —— are prorogued; May 17. — dissolved. ——25. Expedition against Algiers, sails from Toulon. It consists of 11 sail of the line, 19 frigates, 21 sloops, 15 brigs, 2 steam-boats, 280 transports; carrying 34,164 men, under count de Bourmont.	Feb. 4. Greece:—Leopold, prince Cobourg, is elected sovereign prince of Greece, by the plenipotentiaries of Great Britain, France, and Russia, but declines the crown soon after. May 16. Great irruption of Mount Etna:—7 new craters opened, and eight villages destroyed. June 14. Algiers:—landing of the French invading army. ——19. ——— Algerines and Arabs, (50,000,) defeated by the French (25,000.)

A. D. UNITED STATES.

April 6. Assassination of Jos. White, a wealthy merchant, at Salem, Mass.

—27. Bill removing the Indians, passed the senate.

May 7. Treaty with Turkey.

— 31. Tornado in Tennessee.

July 26. Freshet in Vermont.

Aug. 19. *American Institute of Instruction*, organized at Boston.

Fifth census completed. (See "Statistics.")

Sept. 7. Second centenary of the settlement of Boston celebrated.

Oct. 5. Proclamation of the president declaring the ports of the U. States open to British vessels from the W. Indies.

—20. *Literary Convention* at *New-York* for the discussion of the subject of *education* and for establishing a new university.

Dec. 6. Second session of the 21st congress.

Died in 1830:—

Feb. 27. *Elias Hicks.*

March 5. *Bishop Ravenscroft* of North Carolina.

March 9. William Tudor, charge d'Affairs to Brazil.

April 17. Dr. *J. D. Godman.*

July 25. *Isaac Parker*, chief justice S. C. of Mass.

Aug. 24. General Philip Stuart, an officer in the Revolution.

Sep. 20. *Bishop Hobart*, of New-York.

W. B. Giles, late governor of Va.

A. D. SOUTH AMERICA.

May 4. Colombia: Mosquera elected president.

June 1. — Sucre, president of the congress, assassinated.

Aug. 27. Colombia: Revolt at Bogota.

Sept. 18. Bolivar having been re-appointed, accepts the office of president.

Dec. 17. Death of *Bolivar*, the liberator of Colombia, at San Pedro.

A. D. GREAT BRITAIN.

June 26. Death of George IV. at Windsor, æt 68.

—28. His brother, the duke of Clarence, succeeds as

— William IV. —

July 15. Funeral of George IV.

Sept. 15. Liverpool and Manchester railway opened. Rt. hon. W. Huskisson, one of the king's ministers, is killed by the rocket engine. [This work which was commenced in 1826, has [cost £800,000.]

Oct. 26. Opening of the 9th British parliament.—C. M. Sutton, speaker of the Commons.

Nov. 16. Resignation of the Wellington ministry, which is succeeded by the Whigs:—earl **Grey**, premier, *Brougham*, lord chan.

Died:—Jan. 7. *Sir Thomas Lawrence*, president of the Royal academy; one of the most eminent *painters* of the age.

A. D. FRANCE & SPAIN.	A. D. MISCELLANEOUS.
On the dissolution of the (French) chambers, a new election had been ordered which results in the triumph of the Liberals, 220 being re-elected out of 221.	
July 26. "The Revolution of 1830" begins after the publication of the *Three Ordinances.**—All the liberal papers in Paris are suppressed. The editors remonstrate, and call upon the people to resist the ordinances as illegal and tyrannical.	Aug. 25.—Netherlands:—Revolt of Belgium commences at Brussels; the populace destroy several houses belonging to obnoxious individuals.
—— 27. The papers appear as usual; the presses are seized, the editors imprisoned; the citizens assemble in arms; and	Aug. 29. The citizens of Brussels send a deputation to lay their grievances before the king.
—— 28. obtain a complete victory over the king's guards.	Sept. 6. Insurrection at Brunswick:—the duke escapes to England.
	——23. Netherlands:—The royal troops enter Brussels, but are obliged to retreat on the 27th.
	Oct. 4. Independence of Belgium declared by the Central Committee at Brussels; "The province of Belgium, violently separated from Holland, shall constitute, an independent state."

* By the first of these the Chamber of Deputies is again dissolved; 2d the *Liberty of the Press* is suspended: 3d the law of elections is altered.

A. D. FRANCE & SPAIN.	A. D. MISCELLANEOUS.
—— 29. La Fayette elected commander of the National Guards, by the liberal deputies.	Nov. 16. Belgium's independence acknowledged by the king of Netherlands.
—— 31. The king and his family leave St. Cloud.	—— 29 Polish Revolution commences at Warsaw. The tyranical grand duke Constantine is driven from his palace.
Aug. 2. Abdication of Charles X. and the dauphin, in favour of the duke of Bordeaux, as Henry V.	Dec. 18. Polish Diet opened at Warsaw.
Aug. 6. The deputies declare the throne of France vacant—*de facto et de jure.*	—— 24. The emperor Nicholas proclaims his intention of "maintaining entire the rights of his throne," and "denouncing as traitors all who had usurped the government of Poland."
Aug. 7. ——— adopt the new charter, by a vote of 219 to 33, and offer the crown to the duke of Orleans, who accepts it on the 8th as	
— Louis Philippe I., *King of the French.* —	
M. Casimer Perier, and **M. J. Lafitte,** ministers.	
Benjamin Constant, pres. of the Committee of Legislation.	
Treaties with Tunis and Tripoli.	
Aug. 27. Death of prince Bourbon de Conde.	
Oct. 17. Tumults in Paris about a law abolishing the punishment of death for political offences.	
—— 29. Spain: Mina, general of the patriots, is defeated by the royalists near the Pyrenees.	
Dec. 21. The ex-ministers, Polignac, Peyronet, Chantelaure, and Ranville, are sentenced to prison, as guilty of high treason.	
Died in 1830:—B. Constant, member of the cabinet; and *Madame de Genlis*, a distinguished authoress.	

A. D. UNITED STATES.
1831.

Jan. 10. Award of the king of the Netherlands, on the boundary between Maine and New Brunswick.

Feb. 12. *Eclipse of the sun*, visible in several states.

Feb. 16. Publication of vice pres. Calhoun's "Appeal" against president Jackson.

Ap. 5. Commercial treaty with Mexico

Ap. 19. Resignation of the Cabinet at Washington, followed by the appointment of Livingston, Cass, Woodbury, M'Lane, and Taney.

May 29. Fayetteville, N.C. and, June 21. the state house of N. Carolina, burnt.

July 4. Death of James Monroe, 5th. pres. of the U. S., at N. Y.

—— 8. His funeral, when 100,000 persons assembled.

Sep. 13. Treaty with Turkey.

—— 16. Sentence of 3 Christian missionaries, (Butler Trott, and Worcester,) by the supreme court of Geo., to 4 years hard labour in the penitentiary, for residing on the territory occupied by the Cherokees, without taking oath to support the constitution of Georgia.

—— 24. Riot at Providence, R. I.; 4 persons killed and wounded by the military.

—— 28. Nomination of Wm. Wirt, for pres. of the U. S. by the National Anti-Masonic Convention at Baltimore.

A. D. SOUTH AMERICA.
1831.

Feb. 14. Mexico:—Execution of Guerero, the ex-president.

March 18. Venezuela:—the first congress of, meets at Valentia.—It consists of 15 senators, and 23 representatives.

—— 23. Acapulco surrenders to Mexico.

Brazil:—Don Pedro abdicates in favour of his son, who is proclaimed as

— Don Pedro II. —

Aug. 11. W. I:—Tremendous hurricane at Barbadoes:—many lives lost.

Sep. 14. Riot at Pernambuco; about 1400 citizens revolt, take possession of the town, and plunder it. They are defeated by the citizens on the 15th.

Brazil:—Oct. 3; the Chamber of Deputies pass a bill, reforming the constitution: the government is to be a Federative Monarchy with three branches, the executive, legislative, and judiciary; the Deputies and one third of the Senators, are to be elected every two years, and the Council of State is to be suppressed.

A. D. GREAT BRITAIN.
1831.

Mch. 1. Lord John Russel introduces the "*Reform Bill*" into the house of Commons.

Mch. 23. It passes to a second reading.

Apl. 22. Parliament dissolved, in consequence of the rejection of the Reform Bill, on the 19th.

June 21. —— re-opened. The king in his speech declares his intention of effecting reform.

Sep. 22. Passage of the Reform Bill in the house of Commons, and

A. D. FRANCE & SPAIN.	A. D. MISCELLANEOUS.
1831 Feb. Tumults at Paris on the celebration of a funeral mass, for the duke de Berr i.	1831 Jan. 24. Polish diet declares Poland independent, and the throne vacant.
	Feb. 3. Belgians elect the duke of Nemours their king.
	—— 5. Russian army of 150,000 under Diebitsch enters Poland.
	Feb. 14. Poles worsted near Warsaw, and lose 5,500 killed.
Feb. 14. The electoral law altered: all Frenchmen now allowed to vote, who pay 200 francs taxes.	—— 24. Belgians elect De Chokier regent.
	—— 28. Poles appoint Skrzynecki, com. in chief.
	March. 20. Italy; the revolted parts occupied by Austrian troops.
	—— 31. Poles obtain a great victory over the Russians near Braga. (Russians lose 12,000.)
	Ap. 27. Dwernicki, with 5,000 Poles, surrenders to the Russians.
	May 10. Turks defeat 20,000 Albanians.
	June 4. Belgian congress elect prince Leopold of Saxe Cobourg, their king.
June 1. Chambers dissolved.	June 19. Death of the Russian general Diebitsch.
	—— 26. Cholera at St. Petersburg: 2219 deaths in 18 days.
July 11. Fr. fleet enters the Tagus, and compels the Portuguese government to fulfil their engagements.	Aug. 2. Constantinople:—1800 houses burnt.
	Aug. 21. Portugal:—Insurrection at Lisbon in favour of Donna Maria II.
	Sep. 1. Belgium:—Leopold opens his first parliament.
Sep. 19. Riot in Paris on the receipt of the news of the fall of Warsaw.	Sep. 7. Poland:—Fall of Warsaw, after two days hard fighting. Russians lose (killed and wounded) 20,000. The Poles retreat to Modlin; the war terminates soon after; the Russian authority is re-established in Poland, and Paskewitsch, its conqueror, is appointed its governor.

A. D. UNITED STATES.

Oct. 1. "Free trade Convention," at Philadelphia.

— 26. Tariff Convention at New-York, composed of 500 delegates from 13 states:—continues in session till Nov. 1st; and adopts a memorial to Congress.

— 30. Nat. Turner, the leader of the slave insurrection in Southampton Co., Va., taken; (executed, Nov. 11.)

Nov. 1. The United States Literary Convention at New-York, the members of which form themselves into a society called the *National Society of Science, Literature and the Arts.*

Dec. 1. Erie canal closed by ice.

— 5. 1st. session of the 22nd. Congress of the U. S. commences.

Dec. 14. National Republican Convention at Baltimore, nominates Henry Clay for president of the United States.

Died in 1831;—

Ap. 4. At Worcester, Mass. *Isaiah Thomas*, 82, the patriarch of American printers.

May 10. *Jr. Evarts*, cr. sec. of the A.B. Com. for Foreign Missions.

May. *Jno. Trumbull*, author of "M'Fingal."

July 4. *Jms. Monroe.*

— 30. *Richard Varick*, an officer of the Revolution; pres. Am. Bible Society.

Sep. 3. *John H. Rice*, D.D. pres. Union Theological Seminary, Va.

Sep. 8. *Saml L. Mitchill*, M.D. LL. D. a celebrated naturalist.

A. D. SOUTH AMERICA.

Nov. NEW GRANADA, erected into an independent state, by the Bogota convention. Gen. Obando vice pres. in place of Gen. Caicedo, resigned.

Dec. 28. West Indies:—Insurrection of the slaves in Jamaica; 4,000 of them are killed, and $15,000,000 worth of property destroyed.

—31. Great fire at St. Thomas: loss $200,000.

A. D. GREAT BRITAIN.

Oct. 8. its rejection in the house of lords, which causes great riots at Derby and Nottingham.

Oct. 26. "The Cholera" first appears in England, at Sunderland.

— 29, 30, 31, Dreadful riots at Bristol, in consequence of the rejection of the reform bill. Many of the public buildings and an immense amount of property destroyed. In suppressing the riot, 30 persons were killed; 5 were afterwards executed, and many transported.

Nov. 30. Convention between the kings of France and England, for the more effectual suppression of the Slave Trade, signed at Paris.

Dec. 6. Parliament opened. Petition in favour of the Reform Bill, with 140,275 signatures, presented.

Riots and loss of lives in Ireland.

Died in 1831:—

Jan. 14. *Henry Mackenzie.*

Feb. 16. *Andrew Thompson*, D. D., a distinguished minister of the Scotch church.

— 21. *Robert Hall*, an able and celebrated preacher, of the Bapt. church at Bristol.

Ap. 20. *Dr. Abernethy*, eminent surgeon and anatomist.

June 7. *Mrs. Siddons*, a celebrated tragic actress.

— 30. *Wm. Roscoe*, an eminent author.

A. D. FRANCE & SPAIN	A. D. MISCELLANEOUS.
Oct. 18. The bill *abolishing the hereditary rights of the French peerage*, passes in the chamber of Deputies.	Oct. 9. Greece :—Assassination of the president, Capo d' Istrias, by two young Greeks.
Nov. 19. Thirty-six peers created to secure the passage of the peerage bill.	
Nov. 21. Riot at Lyons, in consequence of distress among the working classes. The city is occupied with troops till Dec. 3d; 300 of the rioters killed.	Nov. 1. Belgium:—The chamber of Deputies agree to the terms prescribed by the London conference.
	Dec. 9. Egypt :—Ibrahim Pacha completely defeated before St. Jean d' Acre.
	Died in 1831 :— Oct. 14. At Florence, *Louis Pons*, an eminent astronomer.

A. D. UNITED STATES.

Oct. 22. Gen. Wm. Barton, the captor of the Br. gen. Prescott.

Nov. 5. Gen. Philip Van Courtland, an officer of the Revolution.

Dec. 15. *Miss Hannah Adams*, an authoress.

— 26. *Stephen Girard*, a merchant of Philadelphia, celebrated for his immense wealth.

A. D. SOUTH AMERICA.

A. D. GREAT BRITAIN.

A. D. UNITED STATES.

1832

Jan. 25. The nomination of Martin Van Buren as Minister to England, rejected in the Senate of the U. S. by the casting vote of the vice president.

— 27. The Senate ratifies the Convention of indemnities, negotiated with France.

Feb. 6. The crew of the U. S. frigate Potomac, make an attack on Qualla Battoo, in Sumatra. The town is destroyed and 150 Malays killed; of the Americans 2 killed 14 wounded.

Feb. 10. Great rise of the Ohio, at Pittsburgh, Pa., and shortly after, through the whole course of the river to the Mississippi: many towns on its banks inundated: at Cincinnati, on the 18th, the water rises about 65 feet above high water mark, higher than ever before known: immense destruction of property.

Feb. 22. Centennial celebration of the birthday of Washington.

Mch. 3. Decision of the Supreme Court of the U. S. in the case of the Georgia missionaries, (See Sept. 16, 1831,) that "the law of Georgia, under which they were imprisoned and by which the state assumed jurisdiction over the Indian territory, is contrary to the laws and treaties of the U. S. and therefore null and void."

Ap. 1. War between the Winnebagoes and other Indian tribes, and the United States, begins.

— 2. Treaty with the Creeks, who cede all their lands west of the Mississippi, to the U. States.

— 5. Treaty with Mexico.

A. D. SOUTH AMERICA.

1832

Feb. 22. Mexico:—Bustamente, the vice president, issues a decree closing such ports to foreign commerce as are occupied by rebellious troops.

Mch. 3. —Gen. Santa Anna defeated at Santa Cruz, by the government troops.

Mch. 9. New Granada:—Gen. Santander elected president.

Apl. 15. Unsuccessful revolution at Pernambuco, in favour of the abdicated Don Pedro I.

May 14. Mexico:—the siege of Vera Cruz raised, after a brisk cannonade of eight days by the government troops.

A. D. GREAT BRITAIN.

1832

Feb. 12. The Cholera breaks out in London.

Mch. 23. The Reform Bill (modified,) passes in the house of Commons.

— 26. General *fast* in England, on account of the Cholera.

Ap. 13. Reform Bill passes to a second reading in the house of Lords, (184 to 175.) Wellington, with 75 other peers, enter a protest against it.

— 21. Riot at Montreal, L. Canada, which originates in a contested election: several killed.

May 7. Lord Lyndhurst's amendment in relation to the Reform Bill passes the house of lords; earl Grey and his colleagues soon after resign: great sensation produced throughout England, which subsides on the ministry's being re-instated.

A.D. FRANCE & SPAIN.	A. D. MISCELLANEOUS.
1832.	1832.
	Jan. 28. Austrian troops enter the Roman states, for the purpose of maintaining the papal power.
	Feb. 10. Portugal:—Don Pedro, ex-emperor of Brazil, sails with a squadron from Belleisle for Terceira, on an expedit on for deposing his brother Don Miguel, and restoring the crown of Portugal to his daughter, Maria de Gloria.
Feb. 22. The long pending cause between the princes de Rohan, heirs at law of the duke of Bourbon, as plaintiffs, and the baroness Foucheres and the duke d' Aumale, son of the king, Louis Philippe, as defendants, decided in favour of the latter.	Feb. 22. Italy:—Ancona occupied by French troops.
	Mch. 29. Poland:—the emperor of Russia issues a decree stating that Poland is re-united to the Russian empire, and is to form an inseparable part of it, having a particular administration, as well as a civil and military code.
Mch. 22. The bill banishing the families of Napoleon and of the ex-king, Charles X., passes the house of peers, 80 to 30.	
Mch. 27. The Cholera breaks out in Paris.	Ap. 1. Turkey:—War with the pacha of Egypt, commences.
	—— 12. —— Hussein Pacha proceeds to Egypt to take the command of the Ottoman army.
May 1. A Carlist conspiracy detected and suppressed in the south of France.	—— 18. Belgium:—The 24 articles relating to, agreed upon by the London Conference, are ratified at London by the plenipotentiaries of England, France, Austria and Prussia, and afterwards of Russia.
—— 30. 41 members of the chamber of Deputies, including La-Fayette and Lamarque, publish a manifesto against the policy of Louis Philippe, &c.	May 27. Turkey:—St. Jean d' Acre surrenders to the troops of the pacha of Egypt.

A. D. UNITED STATES.

June 7. Bill for the relief of the Revolutionary soldiers and officers, signed by the president.

June 27. The CHOLERA breaks out at New-York.

—— 28. New Tariff act passes the house of Representatives, (132 to 65,) and the Senate, July 7, (32 to 16.)

July 10. The act extending the charter of the United States Bank, having passed the Senate by a vote of 28 to 20 and Representatives, 105 to 83, is returned by president Jackson to the Senate with his objections to signing it: and less than two thirds voting for its passage, the act is rejected.

July 16. Congress adjourns.

Aug. 27. Capture of the famous Indian chief, 'Black Hawk.'

The Winnebagoes submit to the U. S. army under gen. W. Scott.

Nov. Candidates for president of U. S.; Andrew Jackson, Henry Clay, William Wirt:—for vice president, Martin Van Buren, John Sergeant, and Amos Ellmaker.

Publication of the "Ordinance" of the South Carolina Convention, nullifying the operation of the tariff laws of the United States, in that State.

Dec. 6. 22d Congress, 2d session. The President, in his message, recommends the reduction of the tariff to a revenue standard only.

Dec. 10. Proclamation of the president to the South Carolina nullifiers.

Deaths in 1832:—

Feb. 12. *Elias Cornelius*, D. D., Sec. Am. B. Com. F. Missions.

June 1. Gen. Thomas Sumpter, an officer of the Revolution.

July 30. *John Croes*, D. D., Prot. Episcopal bishop of New-Jersey.

Sept. 25. *E. Fenwick*, D. D., bishop of Cincinnati, Ohio.

Nov. Charles Carroll, the last surviving signer of the Declaration of American Independance.

A. D. SOUTH AMERICA.

June 29. Revolution in Monte Video: Gen. Lavelleja succeeds, by force, gen. Rivera as president.

July 30. Brazil:—The ministry and regency resign, in consequence of the Senate's refusing to dismiss St. Andrade, the tutor of the prince Don Pedro II.

A. D. GREAT BRITAIN.

June 4. *Final passage of the Reform bill* in the house of lords: it receives the royal assent on the 7th, and becomes a law.

—8. Cholera breaks out at Quebec L. Canada, being its first appearance in America.

July 12. The Scotch Reform Bill passes to a third reading in the house of Lords.

—— 30. The Irish Reform bill passes.

Deaths in 1832:

Feb. 8. Rev. *Geo. Crabbe*, an eminent poet.

April 28. (In France,) Rev. *C. C. Colton*, author of 'Lacon.'

May 30. Sir *Jas. Mackintosh*, an eminent author.

June 6. *Jeremy Bentham.*

Aug. 21. *Adam Clarke*, D. D., an eminent oriental scholar and commentator.

A. D. FRANCE & SPAIN.

June 6, 7, 8, and 9.—Dreadful riots in Paris. Skirmishes continue for several days between the Carlists and Republicans united, and the Nat. Guards:—many killed.

The Court of Cassation afterwards pronounces the trial of the rioters by the Court Martial to be illegal.

Deaths in 1832:

Mar. 13. *Champollion*, the celebrated interpreter of Egyptian hieroglyphics.

May 15. Baron *Cuvier*, the celebrated naturalist.

—— 17. M. Casimir Perier.

—— 31. Gen. Lamarque.

A. D. MISCELLANEOUS.

June 4. Belgium:—Protocol of the plenipotentiaries of the 5 great powers, binding themselves to prevent the renewal of hostilities with Holland.

—— 28. Germany:—Date of the Protocol of the German Confederacy for *arresting the progress of liberal principles.*

July 5. —— Resolution of the German Diet, prohibiting the introduction of any foreign periodical, writing or political work, of less than 20 sheets, written in the German language, into any State of the Confederation without the previous consent of government. All foreigners as well as the inhabitants are forbidden to wear ribbons, cockades, or other distinctive marks, except of the country to which the person wearing them belongs. Popular meetings or fêtes, except customary ones, interdicted.

—— 16. The liberty of the press suppressed in Baden.

July 9. Portugal:—Don Pedro with his forces, amounting to 7,500, lands at Metosinhoes, and proceeds to Oporto, which he enters without opposition.

—— 21. Turkey:—The Sultan signs a protocol by which he assents to the extension of the Greek frontier, as required by the London Conference, viz: from the Gulf of Arta to that of Vola.

—— 23. Portugal:—Battle near Coimbra;—Don Miguel's forces, (12,500,) defeated by Pedro's (8,000.)

Oct. 11. ——Engagement off Vigo, between the fleets of Miguel under D. Compos, and of Pedro under Sartorius;—indecisive.

Deaths in 1832:—

Mar. 22. Baron Von *Goethe*, an eminent German author.

July 26. The duke of Reichstadt, son of Napoleon.

Nov. (In Boston, Mass.) *Spurzheim*, a celebrated German phrenologist and naturalist.

POETICAL RETROSPECT

OF

ANCIENT CHRONOLOGY.

[*From the work of Dr. Valpy, with alterations.—Designed to facilitate the remembrance of dates.*]

A. M. **B. C.**

1 4004 Four thousand years and four before the birth
Of our Redeemer was announced to earth;
"Let there be light;" thus spake th' Almighty Lord;
Earth, seas and skies were form'd, by his creating word.

1656 2348 O'er sixteen centuries the revolving sun,
And summers fifty-six his course had run:
When sinful man drew heaven's just vengeance down,
In one wide deluge, the whole earth to drown.

1757 2247 In seventeen fifty-seven, see Babel rise,
In tow'ring pride to emulate the skies!
When God, t' enlarge earth's habitable bounds[a]
Scatters the people, and their tongues confounds.

1801 2203 Eighteen hundred one fierce Nimrod saw,
Then one man's pleasure gave the public law;
Rousing no more the lion from his den,
The hero's task is now the chase of men.
The mighty hunter to a monarch grown,
In rising Babylon exalts his throne.
Now too, proud Nineveh first lifts her head,
And states and cities in the east are spread:
Egyptian Tanis, Memphis, Thebes and Thin;[b]
Here the everlasting pyramids begin.
From earlier date presumptuous China brings
The long succession of her mighty kings.

2083 1921 Two thousand eighty-three, the promised land
The Patriarch seeks, led by Jehovah's hand;

---

a The dispersion of mankind and the increase of population, were the natural consequences of the confusion of tongues, and probably the object of the divine interposition.

b The four states into which Egypt was divided after the reign of Misraim.

A. M. B. C.

2162 1842 Twenty-one sixty-two, Thessalian Jove,[a]
His father Saturn from his kingdom drove,
And on Olympus fix'd his court on high;
Hence superstition raised him to the sky.

2148 1856 Twenty-one forty-eight, (the fable sings,)
Hails Inachus the first of Grecian kings.

2275 1729 Twenty-two hundred sev'nty-five, behold
Joseph to Egypt by his brothers sold.
Tho' long the storms of adverse fortune low'r,
Yet to protect the good, Heaven's gracious pow'r
Can, 'mid the thorns of wo, make roses bloom,
And to a palace change a dungeon's gloom.

2448 1556 Cecrops, in twenty-four and forty-eight
Form'd from thirteen small tribes[b] the Athenian state.
He first to Greece the laws of Egypt brought;
To worship Egypt's gods the Greeks were taught.

2475 1529 What time Deucalion fled th' usurping main;
No general deluge, as the poets feign;
It rages, to narrow Thessaly confined,[c]
Nor dar'd again the ruin of mankind.

2511 1493 Then, too, Phenician Cadmus cross'd the main,
Thebes was the seat of his Bœotian reign.

2513 1491 Israel in twenty-five thirteen were led
From Egypt's land, and in the desert fed,
Spite of the miracles of Moses' rod,
The stiff neck'd people made a calf their God.
Chastis'd, they murmur'd still, their chief revil'd,
And forty years they wander'd in the wild.
Mean time, a colony from Egypt sails,
And o'er the sons of Inachus prevails;
His race no more the Argive sceptre sways,
Argos, Egyptian Danaus obeys.

2553 1451 Now mighty Joshua leads the Hebrew-band
To wars, to triumphs, and the promised land.
Six years their arms are by Jehovah blest:

2559 1445 In twenty-five and fifty-nine they rest.
Oft the ungrateful race their God provoke,
As often bend beneath a foreign yoke;

---

a Jupiter is said to have begun his reign at the age of 62, in Thessaly, where he reigned 60 years. He vanquished the Titans, (the sons of his grandfather Ouranos, who claimed his kingdom) and forced them to fly from Greece. His brother Pluto obtained the command of the west, and Neptune of the sea coast. Jupiter destroyed a band of robbers who infested the country; the greatest instance, in those times, of valour and heroism. His laws were remarkable for their wisdom and strictness. As he kept his court on Mount Olympus in Thessaly, Heaven has been distinguished by that name in classical poetry, since Jupiter obtained the chief place among the divinities of Pagan mythology.

b Univ. Hist. Ch. XVIII. sect. 4.

c The course of the river Peneus being stopped by an earthquake between Ossa and Olympus, an inundation, increased by an uncommon rain, covered the plains of Thessaly. Deucalion and others saved themselves on Mount Olympus.

A. M. B. C.

They mourn, repent, and to their God return,
No longer can Jehovah's anger burn:
He raises *Judges* to assert their cause,
Conduct their battles and dispense their laws;
Brave Othniel frees them from proud Chusan's[a] reign;

2675 1357 Eglon's in twenty-six by Ehud slain,
And seventy-five. When Pelops ruled in peace,
And gave a Phrygian name to Southern Greece;[b]
When Deborah guided Barak's conqu'ring sword,
The son of Bel[c] became Assyria's lord.
Not long ere Tyre rose mistress of the sea;
Rich by her commerce, while by valour free;

2768 1236 And Gideon's son, to fix his impious reign,
His brethren slew; himself by woman slain.
The famous combats of Amphitryo's son;[d]
All the Athenian cantons join'd in one
By Theseus. The great demigods of Greece,[e]
The mighty heroes of the golden fleece;[f]
Orpheus, Musœus, Linus, eldest born
Of Phœbus' sons; the fabled age adorn.

2816 1188 While conqu'ring Jephtha, Israel's cause defends,
And proud Semiramis her power extends;

2820 1184 Lo! twenty-eight and twenty weeps the fall
Of ancient Ilion's long-defended wall.

2886 1118 See twenty-eight and eighty-six declare
The mighty wonders wrought by Samson's hair.

2909 1095 Then Israel, dazzled with an empty show,
Eager the joys of kingly pomp to know,
Disdaining freedom for a tyrant's nod,
Begs to exchange the sceptre of her God.
Yet kings oft merit: Codrus, Athens' pride,

2935 1069 Now, self devoted, for his country died.
A grateful meed to his unrivalled fame,
The Athenians hence suppress the *royal* name.
Jove they declare sole sovereign of the realm,
And place dependent *archons* at the helm:

2949 1055 While humbly great, the royal shepherd sings
Alone the glory of the King of kings.

2988 1016 In twenty-nine and eighty-eight, his son
Arose, the wise, the peaceful Solomon:
Whose pious hands the wondrous temple reared,

---

a King of Mesopotamia. b Peloponnesus.
c Herodotus says that Ninus reigned in Assyria in the year of the world, 2774; but Rollin whose authority we have followed in the Chron. Table, places him A. M., 1345.
d Hercules, son of Jupiter and Alcmena, wife of Amphitryo, king of Thebes.
e Perseus, Theseus, Œdipus, Castor and Pollux, &c. f Jason and Argonauts.

A. M. B. C.
3000 1004 One thousand four years ere our Lord appeared.
But lo! he falls; wise, pious, just no more,
For slaves to women must their god adore.
Yet great Jehovah, by remembrance won,
Of the good sire, almost forgives the son;
Not quite forgives; for now his wide domain
Obeys not Rehoboam—his son's reign.

B. C. A. M.*
975 3029 Nine seventy-five, ten tribes were led
By Jeroboam, and from Judah fled.
The rebel, to sustain a doubtful cause,
Belying Moses' God, retains his laws.
Go, Israel, to thy calves for succour call,

930 3074 Nine hundred thirty, build Samaria's wall;
Yet Shalmanezer shall avenge thy crimes,
And drag thee captive to far distant climes.

907 3097 Now raptur'd Greece hears lofty *Homer* sing
Achilles wrath, of mighty woes the spring.
While Hesiod's humbler muse instructs the swains
In arts of peace, and culture of the plains.

890 3104 Eight hundred ninety,[a] from Phenicia's land
Pygmalion's sister seeks the Lybian strand:
To injured Dido, Carthage owes her date;

884 3120 'Twas then Lycurgus framed the Spartan state.
The strongest walls[b] for her defence he gave;
He made her patient, temperate, firm and brave.

776 3228 Seven hundred seventy-six th' *Olympiad* sees,[c]
At first ordained by godlike Hercules.[d]
Of true record the date by Varro fixt,
Till then all fable, or with fable mixt.

752 3252 Seven hundred fifty-two[e] saw Rome arise:
A vigorous birth; her king was brave and wise.

747 3257 While with the soft Sardanapalus fell
The vast Assyrian realm, and race of Bel.
Three kingdoms from its ruin took their date,
Tiglath renewed the fall'n Assyrian state,
Fam'd Nabonassar reign'd in Babylon:

681 3323 These Esarhaddon joined at length in one.
The Medes, long ranging uncontroll'd and free,
Grown worse than slaves in lawless liberty,
By just restraint true freedom to regain,
Embrace the needful yoke and court the rein;
They choose a king: just Dejoces began
The Median reign, and founded Ecbatan.

---

* From this epoch, the date *before Christ* being more familiar, the columns are transposed.

a Petavius. Usher, (whose authority is followed in the Table in this book,) fixes this event [illegible], B. C.

b Trusting to the valour of the Spartans, Lycurgus ordered that Lacedemon should not be walled, alleging that bravery intrenched was a species of cowardice.

c The Olympic games consisting of coursing, wrestling, and other exercises. See Introduction and Table.

d See Table—B. C. 1453.

e Varro says 753.

B.C. A.M.

606 3398 Six hundred six[a] saw the fam'd sages rise;
Science they taught, and made their hearers wise.
Truths more sublime, yet easier understood,
Confucius taught;[b] he made his hearers good.
Vainly secure in thy stupendous wall;[c]

538 3466 See, Babylon, thy impious monarch's fall:[d],
Envy the captive from thy chain releas'd,
Now slave thyself, who hadst enslaved the east:
The humane victor sets from bondage free
The sons of Judah; such was heav'n's decree.
Full sev'nty years beneath the tyrants nod
The rebel race had groan'd, and learned to fear their God.

536 3468 Five thirty-six, the virtuous and brave
(Who reign'd to bless and conquered but to save,)
Cyrus united with the Median band
Persia's rough sons, not yet by sloth unmann'd.

510 3494 Five hundred ten to Athens freedom brings;
With equal ardour Rome dethrones her kings.
Proud Tarquin's cause Porsenna would maintain,
Hippias' great Darius; both in vain.
'Twixt Greece and Persia vengeful hate ensues;

480 3524 Xerxes' vast host four hundred eighty views;
The sire's defeat repeated by the son,
And Salamis surpassing Marathon.
The victors, mutual jealousy alarms;
Persia's aveng'd of Greece, by Grecian arms.
Thrice nine long years the rival cities fought:

404 3600 Success, four hundred four to Sparta brought;
When in fall'n Athens, who so long maintain'd
The public freedom, thirty tyrants reign'd.
The Spartans now proud Asia's fall design'd
Their ready arms the brave Ten Thousand join;
Who, giv'n by fortune to their foes a prey,
Thro' foes, thro' floods, thro' deserts urg'd their way;
Quell'd adverse force, evaded close deceit,
Greater than conqu'rors by a bold retreat.

400 3604 Four hundred stains the chronologic page,
When the fell pow'r of democratic rage
Doom'd Socrates, the virtuous and the wise,
Blind superstition's patient sacrifice.

396 3608 Agesilaus shook the Persian throne,
'Till call'd to Sparta to defend his own.

395 3609 The Grecians leagu'd, her growing pow'r oppose:
Restor'd by Conon, Athens' walls arose.

---

a See also the Table, 598, B. C.—Grecian. b See ib. Misc. 522, B. C.

c The walls of Babylon were 87 feet in breadth, 350 feet high, and 60 miles in circumference. Nimrod probably founded, but Semiramis, and afterwards Nebuchadnezzar enlarged and adorned this magnificent city.

d See Daniel, Chap. V.

B. C. A. M.

390 3614 Three hundred ninety ras'd the Roman wall,
When brave Camillus drove the victor Gaul.
Henceforth the Roman story truth may boast;
Doubtful before: her annals now were lost.

363 3641 Three hundred sixty three war rages wide,
And Mantinea rolls her bloody tide.
Thebes, crown'd with conquest in the martial strife,
Too dearly purchas'd with her hero's life,
Curses the day when Sparta was undone,
And mourns the battle which she bravely won.
Epaminondas fall'n, her glories fail'd,
While Philip's well conducted arms prevail'd,

335 3669 No more, three hundred thirty-five, she stood:
His son immers'd her in her people's blood.
330 3674 Three hundred thirty, Persia's empire ends;
Great Alexander, Cyrus' throne ascends.
Short was his reign: the eighth returning spring
Stopp'd in mid triumph the victorious king.

One horn cut off, lo! four new horns arise,[a]
301 3703 Three hundred one divides the mighty prize,
While in long war the rival kings contend,
O'er Latium Rome's victorious arms extend.

275 3729 Pyrrhus, two hundred sev'nty-five, retires,
Inflam'd no more by false ambition's fires.
At home by land, now great, Rome turns her eyes
On foreign spoils, and naval victories.
264 3740 With Carthage, rival of her pow'r, contends;
Twice twelve long years the doubtful strife depends;
241 3763 Carthage, two hundred forty-one obey'd:
As Rome advanc'd in glory, Greece decay'd.

Th' Achæan patriot league,[b] of gen'rous fame,
Bore the last heroes of the Grecian name.

218 3786 But Carthage, yet untam'd, the war renew'd.
Hannibal, panting for revenge and blood,
Four times victorious, half unpeopled Rome:
Three heroes sprung up to avert her doom;
Her sword Marcellus, Fabius was her shield,
But Scipio taught the stubborn foe to yield.

202 3802 He cross'd, two hundred two, the Libyan main,
Avenging Cannæ's loss on Zama's plain.

170 3834 Foretold of old,[c] in hundred sev'nty's times,
The king, illustrious only in his crimes,
Rag'd in the blood of Judah's wretched race,
And fix'd his idol in the holy place.

---

a See Daniel, VIII. 8.
b This league was formed B. C. 284, by the inhabitants of Patræ, Dyme, and Pharæ.
c Daniel. VIII. 10.

B. C.	A. M.	
166	3838	But soon the valiant Asmonœans quell
		His impious rage. Then Macedonia fell,[a]
		The mistress once of empire, now become
		A province, vassal to victorious Rome.
146	3858	Corinth shall hundred forty six deplore,
		And mighty Carthage fall to rise no more.
88	3916	Eighty-eight saw, and shuddered at the sight,
		The Roman eagles, self-opposed in fight;
82	3922	Saw Rome by Sylla's impious arms laid low,
		(Arms better used to quell the Pontic foe,)
		Sunk and enslav'd; her haughty spirit broke,
		Tame to the lash and patient to the yoke.
		What tho' the tyrant loos'd her from her chains[b]
		The curs'd example of the deed remains.
49	3955	Forty-nine sees again the dire disgrace,
		Lo, red with slaughter of the Roman race,
48	3956	A new dictator from Pharsalia's plains!
		He triumphs in his country's fall, and reigns.
44	3960	Brutus in vain recalls past liberty;
		For once a slave, Rome dar'd no more be free.
41	3963	With him in forty-one fair freedom fell.
31	3973	In thirty-one, let Actium blushing tell
		How dastard Romans drew their servile swords
		For the base privilege, the choice of lords.
		Unlooked for blessings crown the rising age:
		The havoc of the dire triumvirs' rage
		Augustus' mild paternal sway repays:
		Rome lifts her head, the vanquished world obeys.
		Hush'd is the din of arms, and tumults cease;
0	4004	Four thousand four[c] has given the PRINCE OF PEACE.

a 168, B. C.

b Sylla, having destroyed more than 100,000 Roman citizens, 90 senators and 2,600 knights, and, invested with the title of perpetual dictator, reigned in Rome with absolute authority, abdicated his office and retired to private life.

c From this year of the world the Christian Era takes its rise; but Christ was born in the year 4,000, A. M.

POETICAL RETROSPECT

OF

ENGLISH HISTORY.

NORMAN LINE, (3kings.)

WILLIAM THE CONQUEROR.

21 years.

A. M. A. D.

5070 1066 When years one thousand and three score and six
Had pass'd, since Christ in Bethl'em's manger lay,
Then the stern Norman, red from Hastings' field,
Bruis'd Anglia's realm beneath his iron sway.

WILLIAM RUFUS.

13 years.

5091 1087 One thousand eighty-sev'n, see Rufus king,
That tyrant, who transfix'd by Tyrrel's dart,
No more to spoil and scourge the groaning land,
Bled in the forest like a wounded hart!

HENRY THE FIRST.

34 years.

5104 1100 When centuries eleven had roll'd away,
Henry the first ascended England's throne:
Twice fourteen winters Cardiff's gloomy tow'rs
Heard his poor eyeless captive brother's moan.

HOUSE OF BLOIS,—(1 king.)

STEPHEN.

19 years.

5139 1135 When centuries elev'n, years thirty five,
Were gone, the brave usurper Stephen's hand
The sceptre seiz'd: to keep the glitt'ring prize,
How oft he drench'd in blood the afflicted land!

THE PLANTAGENET RACE, (14 kings.)

HENRY THE SECOND.

35 years.

5158 1154 When centuries elev'n, years fifty-four,
Had pass'd, came second Henry—he whose sword
Made the fierce Cambrian tremble, and compell'd
Hibernia's savage sons to call him lord.

A. M.	A. D.	
		With Rosamunda oft, in fragrant bow'rs, Still by the muse kept verdant and romance, He toy'd the summer's day—O "only weak Against the charms of beauty's powerful glance."

RICHARD I.

10 years.

5193	1189	Years eighty-nine and centuries elev'n, Lo Richard, he who Cœur de Lion hight "Against whose fury and unmatched force" The awless lion could not wage the fight.

JOHN.

17 years.

5203	1199	Since the Redeemer of mankind was born, Now twice six centuries were almost gone, When, to young Arthur due, see England's crown Usurp'd by the detested dastard John. Perfidious, bloody wretch! The glorious band Of barons, arm'd in freedom's sacred cause, Ere long shall make thee, baffled tyrant! know Britons are only subject to the laws.[a]

HENRY THE THIRD.

55 years.

5220	1216	Twelve hundred years and sixteen, then began Third Henry's feeble minion-guided rule: A soft, irresolute, goodnatur'd prince: "Ah, what is mere good-nature, but a fool!"

EDWARD THE FIRST.

34 years.

5276	1272	Not such was Edward; red with Paynim gore, The sun-burnt chief from Syria's parching strand, Is in twelve hundred sev'nty-two call'd home, To sway the sceptre of his native land. How does a breast, black cruelty's abode, Debase the sage's and the hero's name! O ruthless king! through each succeeding age The vengeful ghost of Wallace haunts thy fame.

EDWARD THE SECOND.

20 years.

5311	1307	In thirteen hundred sev'n the fatal crown Encircled second Edward's youthful head. Ah me! how misery scowls behind his throne! Ah me! what fury mounts his bridal bed!

EDWARD THE THIRD.

50 years.

5331	1327	O'er thirteen hundred years and twenty sev'n On rapid pinions time has wing'd his way;

a See Table, 1215, A. D.

A. M. A. D.

Lo, the third Edward reigns; but ah! too fond
Of martial glory and extended sway.

Thy trophies, rear'd on Cressy's crimson field,
Calm reason with undazzled eye surveys:
"Are these the monuments of Edward's fame?"
She cries, "which havoc and injustice raise?"

Death tears his dear Phillippa from his arms,
Low in his grave the sable warrior[a] lies:
Oppress'd with care and grief himself expires,
No friend to soothe his woes, or close his eyes.

RICHARD THE SECOND.

22 years.

5381 1377 In thirteen hundred sev'nty sev'n, the throne
Receives the sable chief's degenerate boy.
His people's rights, which he had sworn to guard,
Misguided prince! he labour'd to destroy.

Though venal *judges* strive to render *law*
The pliant slave of a despotic lord;
Though venal armies page the tyrant's heels,
And round his pomp terrific flames the sword:

What now avails the feast, that wont to roar
With laughter? what the blaze of rich attire?
The jocund dance, and music's melting voice?
And mirth that saw the midnight lamp expire?

BRANCH OF LANCASTER.

HENRY THE FOURTH.

14 years.

5403 1399 In thirteen hundred ninety-nine, the crown
From Richard wrested, the fourth Henry wore.
Soon civil discord calls the dogs of war
To riot lawless on Britannia's shore.

HENRY THE FIFTH.

9 years.

5417 1413 In fourteen hundred thirteen, graceful, young,
Brave, learn'd, and polish'd the fifth Henry reigns:
But ah! with grim attendants, sword and fire,
Ere long to rage on weeping Gallia's plains!

Not such the train, that erst with Harry trod
The flow'ry verge of Isis' classic tide,[b]
When for the student's gown, he deign'd awhile
To throw the purple robe of state aside.

---

a The Black Prince.

b Henry V. was member of Queen's College, Oxford.

A. M. A. D.

Attendant ever on his studious walks
 Was contemplation, tranquil matron there;
The peaceful Muses with their silver lyres,
 And science, with high converse, charm'd his ear!

HENRY THE SIXTH.

39 years.

5426 1422 In fourteen hundred twenty-two, behold,
 Britannia's crown becomes an infant's toy;
'Tis the sixth Harry: how the man shall rue
 The fatal splendours that delight the boy!

BRANCH OF YORK.

EDWARD THE FOURTH.

22 years.

5465 1461 In fourteen hundred sixty-one, the throne
 Fourth Edward mounts, and feasts his brutal eye,
On scaffolds crimsoned with Lancastrian gore,
 And makes the regal dome "a sensual stye."

EDWARD THE FIFTH.

5487 1483 Could not fifth Edward's childhood innocence
 His life, alas! from bloody Richard save?
The year that saw him mount Britannia's throne,
 Saw murder hide him in th' untimely grave!

RICHARD THE THIRD.

2 years.

5487 1483 In fourteen eighty-three, what fiend,
 Mis-shapen, hideous, meets the startled eye?
'Tis the third Richard, drunk with human gore;
 Dogs bay the monster as he passes by.[a]

HOUSE OF TUDOR.—(5 Sovereigns.)

HENRY THE SEVENTH.

24 years.

5489 1485 In fourteen hundred eighty five, the crown
 He won on Bosworth's bloody plain, behold
On the sev'nth Henry's head, demure, severe,
 "Proud, dark, suspicious, brooding o'er his gold."

HENRY THE EIGHTH.

38 years.

5513 1509 Fierce with his pow'r and frolic of his prime,
 Dreadful and gay, in fifteen hundred nine,
The youthful lion, the eighth Harry comes,
 And boasts his high descent from either line.

---

a Dogs bark at me as I halt by them. *Shakspeare's Richard III.*

A. M. A. D.

That gothic church, by superstition reared,
In whose dark cells in hideous durance bound,
Lay groaning reason, dauntless he assail'd,
And hurl'd the massive fabric to the ground.

Rome heard the fall astounded: Britons now
Deride her thunders: may the latest age
Hear Britons' glory in the great event,
And hail "the brutal tyrant's useful rage!"

EDWARD THE SIXTH.

6 years.

5551 1547 Array'd in ev'ry blushing charm of youth,
Who comes in fifteen hundred forty sev'n!
'Tis the sixth Edward; virtuous, learned, mild;
Ah, only shewn, then snatch'd away to heav'n.

MARY.

5 years.

5557 1553 Th' inaudible and noiseless foot of time
O'er fifteen centuries his course had run,
And summers fifty-three, fell Mary then
Her direful reign, sad fury! has begun.

The fury calls, and from, his central gloom
The cruel demon, *Persecution* hies.
Quick o'er her realms his iron whips resound,
His fetters rattle, and his flames arise.

ELIZABETH.

45 years.

5562 1558 Who comes in fifteen hundred fifty-eight,
Begirt with sages and with heroes round?
'Tis great Eliza. Raptur'd fame her praise
Shall to the ears of dying time resound.

From the dread lustre of her piercing eye,
See superstition shrink dismay'd away:
While arts and learning and celestial truth,
Burst on the nation in a flood of day.

On proud Iberia's fleet[a] her vengeful arm
Thunder and terror and destruction hurl'd;
And dauntless Drake, immortal hero, bore
Her awful name around the trembling world.

HOUSE OF STUART, (6 Sovereigns.)

JAMES THE FIRST.

23 years.

5607 1603 Not such her heir; in sixteen hundred three,
Comes Scottish James, (extinct the Tudor line.)
Hark, how vile flatt'ry soothes his pedant ear
"With sapient king" and "king by right divine."

---

a The Spanish Armada.

A. M. A. D.

In action feeble, in the wordy war,
Content is he his prowess to display;
"Content to teach his subject herd how great,
How sacred he, how despicable they."

CHARLES THE FIRST.

23 years.

5629 1625 In sixteen hundred twenty-five, see Charles,
With step secure ascend Britannia's throne;
Taught, unsuspecting, from his infancy,
"Th' enormous faith of many made for one."

Rous'd by oppression to a civil war,
The nation arms. How fall the just and good!
Alas! not all the power ambition brings,
Is worth a Hampden's or a Falkland's blood.

Charles bows his head in stern captivity;
The people hail their liberty restor'd;
But ah! fanatic fury lifts her arm,
And in the monarch's blood she bathes the sword.

CROMWELL.

5657 1653 Five years the fires of civil war had blaz'd:
Cromwell in sixteen hundred fifty-three,
Usurping tyrant! bares his bloody arm;
The shame of pow'r, the scourge of liberty.[a]

5662 1658 Five years he reign'd: his soul in tempests fled.[b]
Richard awhile his father's steps pursued;
But soon resign'd the pow'r he could not wield,
And pass'd his life in rural solitude.

CHARLES THE SECOND.

25 years.

5664 1660 Freed from the tumults of a civil war,
Charles lost in pleasure all his youth's fair fame,
Foe to religion, deaf to honour's voice,
Of royalty at once the pride and shame.

JAMES THE SECOND.

3 years.

5689 1685 His brother York, the second James, ascends—
In sixteen hundred eighty-five, the throne:
Popery show'rs blessings on her bigot son,
And calls the realms of liberty her own.

a The justness of these epithets may be doubted.
He died during a remarkable tempest.

A.M. A.D.

WILLIAM THE THIRD & MARY.

14 years.

5692 1688 In sixteen hundred eighty-eight, behold
Th' invited fleet in triumph's gallant pride,
Fraught with new stores of wealth and freedom, bears
William of Orange o'er the briny tide.

The Constitution.

From hence the *King*, the *Commons* and the *Lords*,
To wield a mutual share of pow'r agree:
From these three states the laws derive their force;
And the king executes the joint decree.

ANNE.

12 years.

5706 1702 Two years o'er seventeen centuries had roll'd
When Anne arose to bless this favour'd land;
Her's was the mildness that could faction soothe,
Her's was each virtue that endears command.

Scotland with England in fair union join'd,
And Britain's fame the wondering nations taught,
From Blenheim's plains to Calpe's[a] rocky height,
"How Anne commanded, and how Marlborough fought."

HOUSE OF BRUNSWICK.

GEORGE THE FIRST.

13 years.

5718 1714 In sev'nteen hundred fourteen Brunswick's line
Bade ev'ry fear and ev'ry tumult cease.
Justice and wisdom George the First combined;
He crush'd rebellion, and he liv'd in peace.

GEORGE THE SECOND.

33 years.

5731 1727 The sev'nteen hundredth year and twenty-sev'nth—
Disclos'd the rise of George the Second's fame.
Anson and Vernon bow'd the Spaniards low:
Both oceans trembled at the British name.

But still to darken the dread gloom of war,
Misguided Stuart drew rebellion's sword:
E'en Derby saw his vaunting banners wave,
And Scottish chieftains hail'd him as their lord.

Ill-fated youth! Culloden's bloody field
Sunk the vain fabric of ambition low;
Press'd with fatigue and hunger long he roamed,
'Mid scenes of danger, and 'mid sights of wo.

---

a Gibraltar.

A.M. A.D.

Britain's victorious streamers Minden saw;
In India, Clive new stores of wealth supplied;
Wolfe pour'd his squadrons o'er Canadian wilds;
The hero fought, he conquered and he died.

GEORGE THE THIRD.

5764 1760 In seventeen hundred sixty, George the Third,
In Britain born, his people's idol, reigns;
Assumes the sceptre by their hands conferr'd,
Twin'd with fresh laurels reaped on Abraham's plains.

5767 1763 Seventeen and sixty-three, great Chatham's name
Hallows to Britons by a glorious peace,
Then rich with honours from the field of fame,
Appeas'd, Britannia bids her thunders cease.

5779 1775 Now had two centuries o'er Columbia roll'd,
And changing seasons saw her states matured;
When the great league, with youthful ardour bold,
Her British parent's ancient rule abjur'd.

5794 1790 But ah! what torches blaze on Gallia's plains;
Seventeen and ninety dates the suffering realm,
See murdered Louis bleeds, and bleeds in vain,
Th' ambitious Corsican grasps the vacant helm.

5816 1812 Now Albion checks alone Napoleon's sway,
Eighteen and twelve the dreary date declare:
Yet unappall'd she holds her steady way,
And arms her sons, Spain's patriot strife to share.

But lo! from realms where winter reigns supreme,
Starts the bold warrior of the invaded soil;
Russia's cold hills with fur-clad patriots teem,
Till crush'd, Napoleon, hides in Elba's isle.

5818 1814 Eighteen fourteen the banished despot saw,
Eighteen fifteen beheld his bold return;
Mistaken France admits once more his law,
Which bloody Waterloo shall see o'erthrown.

LITERARY CHRONOLOGY.

[*From the Companion to the British Almanac for* 1832; *with additions.*]

The following Chronological List of Authors is an extension of the Catalogue furnished in the *Companion* of 1831, differing from it by adding to the name of each author the title of his most important production, or some word expressive of the nature of his works.

In order to show the various literary character of each age the catalogue is divided into three columns: the first containing those authors who have drawn chiefly from their own sources, as poets and novelists; the second those who treat on matters of fact, as history and geography; and the third, the philosophic and scientific writers. Where an author has written in different styles, his name will be found in the column to which his most distinguished productions appertain. The Hebrews having, almost without exception, treated on speculative subjects, the triple division does not extend to them.

The dates of birth and death are appended to each name, where they could be ascertained. In other cases, the situation of the name will show nearly the time when each author has flourished.

HEBREW.

[The words in italics between parentheses are the familiar appellations of the preceding persons; they are formed from the first letters of each word composing their names. For example, the Jews call Maimonides *Rambam*, from the four initial letters of his full name, Rabbi Moses ben Maimon. Jom Tof, in like manner, is called *Ritba*, from the words Rabbi Yom Tof bar Abraham.]

B. C.
1500 Moses, 1572—1452.
Phinehas, supposed author of the book of Joshua.
1100 David, 1085—1015.
1000 Solomon, 1033—975.
800 Jonah, *d.* 761.
Amos.
Hosea.
Joel.
Obadiah,
Micah,
Isaiah, *d.* 681.
Nahum.
700 Habakkuk.
Zephaniah.
Jeremiah.
600 Baruch.
Ezekiel.
Daniel.
Zachariah.
Haggai.
500 Ezra.
Nehemiah, *d.* 430.
Malachi.
300 Jesus, son of Sirach.
100 Nechonia ben Hakkanah, 'Sepher habbahir,' the illustrious book. The most ancient of Rabbinical books. Cabbalistic.
Jonathan, 'Targum,' or Chaldee paraphrase of the Bible.

A. D.
0 Onkelos, 'Targum.'
Josephus, *b.* 35.
100 Akiba, *d.* 120. The Mishna has been incorrectly attributed to him
Shimeon ben Jochai (*Rashbi.*) The 'Zohar,' a celebrated cabbalistic Commentary on the Pentateuch is usually attributed to him, but was composed by his disciples.
Jose ben Chilpheta, 'A History of the World.'
Nathan of Babylon, 'Pirke aboth,' the sayings of the fathers. Ethics.
Eliezer, 'Pirke Eliezer,' the sayings of Eliezer, a History of the World.
Judah Hakkadosh, 'Mishna,' the oral traditions of the Jews, which, with the Gemara or Commentary, constitutes the Babylonian Talmud.
Raf, supposed author of the 'Siphra,' a commentary on Leviticus, and of the 'Siphre,' a commentary on Numbers and Deuteronomy.
200 Ushaya, 'Bereshith Rabba,' a Commentary on the Mishna.
Author of the 'Mechilta,' a Commentary on Exodus.
Jochanan, 'Talmud of Jerusalem.'
300 Rabba bar Nachmon, 'Rabboth,' Commentaries on the Bible.
400 Rabashe, began the 'Gemara,' a Commentary on the Mishna.
Martemar, continued the 'Gemara.'
500 Abina, completed the 'Gemara.'
800 Simeon Hejara, 'Great decisions,' jurid.
Judah bar Nachman (*Riban*,) Compendium of the preceding.
980 Saadia Gaon, 'Philosopher's Stone,' 'Book of Faith,' 'Grammar,' &c.
Sherira, 'The Book of Answers,' history.
1000 Samuel Haccohen, *d.* 1034.

Joseph Ching, Grammarian.
Judah Barzelloni, 'Rights of Women,' juridic.
Joseph ben Gorion (*Ribag*,) 'Compendium of Hebrew History.'
Moses Aben Ezra, *d.* 1080. Grammarian.
Isaac of Cordova, *d.* 1094. 'Chest of Spices.'
1100 Alphes, *d.* 1103. 'Compendium of the Talmud.'
Nathan, *d.* 1106. 'Talmudic and Chaldee Lexicon.'
Solomon Jarchi (*Rashi*,) Grammarian, *d.* 1105. 'Tongue of the Learned.'
Joseph ben Meir (*Ribam*,) *d.* 1141.—'Commentary on Talmud.'
Juda the Levite, 'Sepher Cosri,' philosophical.
Abraham Aben Ezra, very learned Commentaries on the Bible.
Tam. *d.* 117. 'Sepher Hajashar,' the Book of Righteousness.
Samuel Ben Meir (*Rashbam*,) *d.* 1171. 'Commentary on the Talmud.'
Benjamin of Tudela, *d.* 1173. 'Travels.'
Samuel, 'Book of Piety,' Ethics and Theology.
Isaac bar Abba, Grammarian.
Moses Kimhi, Grammarian.
David Kimhi (*Radak*,) Grammarian.
Abraham bar Dior (*Rabad*,) *d.* 1199. Cabbalist.
Abraham ben David (*Rabad*,) Jurist.
Moses ben Maimon (*Rambam*,) 1131-1205. 'Yad Hazaka,' the strong hand, a very celebrated Commentary on the Talmud, &c. (This author is better known by his Latinized name, Maimonides.)
1200 Abraham bar Chasdai, Ethics.
Eliakim, ceremonies.
Baruch Miggarmisa, Laws, Ceremonies.
Eliezer Miggarmisa, Ethics, Commentaries.
Asher, Compendia of Talmud.
Perez Haccohen (*Haraph*,) Cabbalist.
Moses ben Nachman (*Ramban*,) *d.* 1260. 'Law of Man,' a celebrated book on Ceremonies, &c.
Moses Mikkotsi, 'Great Book of Precepts,' 'Compendium of Talmud.'
Isaac ben Solomon, *d.* 1268. 'Proverbs and Fables.'
Nissim, *d.* 1268, 'Book of Homilies.'
Isaac ben Joseph, *d.* 1270. 'Book of Precepts.'
Moses Aben Tybon, Translator of Mathematical and Philosophical works from the Greek and Arabic.
Solomon ben Adras (*Rashba*,) Theology.
Meir, Meditations, on Maimonides.'
Menachem Rekanat, *d.* 1290, 'Reason for the enactment of the Laws of Moses.'
Bechai, 'Commentary on Pentateuch.'
1300 Shimshon, *d.* 1312. 'Intro. to the Talmud.'
Isaac Israeli, 'Foundation of the World,' History.
Judah, son of Benjamin, Ritual.
Mordechai, 'Compendium of Talmud.'
Isaac Dura, 'On Forbidden and Permitted Food.'
Aaron Haccohen, 'The Way of Life.'
Jerucham, 'Book of Rectitude.'
Jacob ben Asher, 'The Four Orders,' a Ritual of much authority.
David Abudraham, astronomy.
Levi ben Gerson (*Ralbag*,) *d.* 1370.—'Commentary on the Law.'
Menachen Aben Serach, *d.* 1375. Ritual.
Isaac ben Sheshat (*Ribash*,) 'Questions and Answers on Various Subjects.'
Moses Haccohen, 'Help of faith.'
Isaac Sprot, 'Aben Bochan,' a polemic work against Christianity.
Jom Tof bar Abraham (*Ritba*,) Commentary on Maimonides.'
Chasdai, *d.* 1396. 'Light of the Lord.' Ethics and Theology.
Simeon bar Zemach, 'Shield of the Fathers.'
1400 Jacob Levi, *d.* 1427. A Ritual.
Joseph Albo, the Divine Philosopher, 'Foundation of Faith.'
Israel Germanus, 'Questions and Answers on the Law.'
Joshua Levita, 'Introd. to the Talmud.'
David Vital, 'Golden Verses.'
Samuel Sirsa, Grammar.
Isaac ben Arama, 'Com. on the Law.'
Elias Misrachi (*Ram*,) Arithmetic.
Abarbinel, 'Commentary on the Bible.'
Isaac Abuhaf, Ethics.
1500 Abraham Seba, 'Bundle of Myrrh,' a Commentary.
Isaac Karro, 'Explanations of the Bible.'
Elias Levi, Grammar.
Solomon ben Virga, 'Hist. of the Jews.
Benjamin Zeef, 'Questions and Answers.'
Abraham Zaccoth, 'Juchasin,' Sacred and Jewish History.
Moses Iserle, Astrology.
Joseph Karro, 'Com. on Maimonides.'
Azarias Edomæus, History and Philology.
Gadaliah, 'Cabbalistic Chain,' History and Chronology.
Leo, *d.* 1592, 'Lion's Whelp,' Grammar.
David Gans, History.
1600 Moses of Trana, 'Book of God.'
1700 Moses Mendelssohn, 1729-1785, Philosophy.

AUTHORS OF THE NEW-TESTAMENT.

A. D.
0 St. Matthew, St. Mark, St. Luke, St. John, Evangelists.
St. Paul, St. Peter, St. James, St. Jude, Epistlers.

GREEK.

Imagination.	*Fact.*	*Speculative & Scientific.*
B. C.	B. C.	B. C.
900 Homer, 'Iliad,' 'Odyssey,' &c. Hesiod, 'Works & Days,' &c.	900	900

Imagination.	*Fact.*	*Speculative and Scientific.*
700 Tyrtæus, Elegies (frgts.) Archilochus, Satires, Elegies (fragments.)	700	700
600 Alcæus, Lyrics (fragm'ts.) Sappho, Lyrics (fragm'ts.) Solon, *d.* 558. Epimenides. Stesichorus, 633-553 Lyrics, (fragments.) Mimnermus, Elegies, (fragments.) Anacreon, Lyrics.	600	600 Pythagoras, Philosophy.
500 Simonides, 556-467, Lyrics. Æschylus, 525-456, Tragedies. Pindar, 518-439, Odes. Bacchylides, Lyrics. Sophocles, 495-405, Tragedies. Euripides, 480-486, Tragedies. Aristophanes, *d.* 338, Comedies.	500 Gorgias, Orations (frgts.) Hecatæus, Hist. (frgts.) Herodotus, *b.* 484, Hist. Thucydides, 471-391, Hist of Peloponnesian War. Antiphon, Orations. Andorides, Orations. Lysias, 458-378, Or..tions.	500 Zeno of Elea, Philosophy. Ocellus Lucanus, Philosophy. Anaxagoras, 500-428, philosophy. Socrates, 468-399, Philosophy.
400 Diphilus, Comedy (frgts.) Menander 342-291, Comedies (fragments.)	400 Cetsias, History (frgts.) Xenophon, 444-359, History, Philosophy, &c. Isæus, Orations. Isocrates, 536-338, Orat'ns Dinarchus, Orations. Lycurgus, Orations. Demosthenes, 382-322, Orations. Æschines, 389-314, Orations.	400 Hippocrates, 460-357, Medicine. Democritus, 460-357, Philosophy. Plato, 429-347, Philosophy. Aristotle, 384-322, Philosophy, Criticism. Theophrastus, *d.* 288, Ethics. Epicurus, 341-270, Philosophy.
300 Bion, Idyls. Moschus, Idyls. Lycophron, 'Cassandra' Callimachus, Hymns and Epigrams. Theocritus, Idyls. Aratus, Poem on Astronomy. Cleanthes, Hymns. Apollonius Rhodius, 'Argonautics.'	300 Manetho, History (frgts.)	300 Euclid, Geometry. Zento of Citium, *d.* 263, Philosophy. Apollonius, Conic Sections. Archimedes, *d.* 212, 'Sphere and Cylinder,' &c. Eratosthenes, Philosophy.
200 Nicander, Theriaca.	200 Polybius, 206-124, Universal History. Apollodorus, 'Bibliotheca,' Mythology.	200
100 Meleager, Epigrams.	100 Conon, Mythology. Scymnus, Poetical Geogr.	100

B. C.	*Imagination.*	B. C.	*Fact.*	B. C.	*Speculative & Scientific.*
100		100	Dionysius Halicarnassus, 'Roman Antiquities.' Dionysius Periegetes, Geography ? Diodorus Siculus, General History.		
0		0	Strabo, Geography. Pausanias, Description of Greece. Plutarch, Biography, Morals, &c. Dion Chrysostom, Orations.	0	Dioscorides, Botany and Medicine. Epictetus, 'Enchiridion,' Philosophy.
A. D. 100	Iamblichus, 'Rhodis and Sinonides,' a novel. Lucian, Dialogues. Oppian, Poems on Hunting and Fishing. Athenæus, *d.* 194, 'Deipnosophistæ,' anecdotes.	A. D. 100	Ælian, *d.* 140. Varieties. Appian, History. Ptolemy, Geog., Astron. Arrian, 'Expedition of Alexander.'	A. D. 100	Justin Martyr, *d.* 163, Theology. Polycarp, *d.* 167. Theol. Galen, 103-193, Medicine. Athenagoras, *d.* 172, 'On the Resurrection.' Phavorinus, Lexicon. Hermogenes, *d.* 161, Rhetoric. Polyænus, Strategy. M. Aurelius Antoninus, Philosophy. Hephæstion, 'On Metres.' Max. Tyrius, Philosophy. Julius Pollux, 'Onomasticon,' Rhetoric.
200		200	Diogenes Laertius, *d.* 222, 'Lives of Philosophers.' Philostratus, *d.* 244, Life of Apollonius. Dion Cassius, History of Rome. Herodian, Hist. of Rome. Porphyrius, 233-304, Life of Pythagoras, Philos.	200	Ammonius, Philosophy. Origen, *d.* 254, Theology. Hesychius, Lexicon. Iamblichus, Philosophy. Longinus, *d.* 273, 'On the Sublime.'
300	Achilles Tatius, 'Clitophon and Leucippe,' novel. Xenophon, 'Anthea and Abrocome,' novel.	300	Eusebius, *d.* 340, Ecclesiastical History. Libanius, Orations and Epistles. Eunapius, 'Lives of Philosophers.'	300	Julian, *d.* 363, Philosophy. Athanasius, 298-371, Theology. Greg. Nazianzen, 318-389. Theology. Gregory Nyssæus, *d.* 396, Theology. Cyril, 315-386, Theology. Diophantus, Mathematics.

Imagination.	*Fact.*	*Speculative & Scientific.*
300 Aristænetus, 'Erotic Letters.' Heliodorus, 'Theagenes & Chariclæa,' novel. Chariton, 'Chæreus and Calirrhoe,' novel.	300	300 Chrysostom, 354-407, Theology.
400 Longus, 'Daphnis and Chloe,' novel. Nonnus, 'Conquest of India by Bacchus.' Stobæus, 'Literary Collections.' Quintus Smyrnæus, (commonly called) Calaber, 'Contin. of Homer. Musæus, Poem of Hero and Leander ? Eumathius, 'Ismenæus & Ismenæa,' novel. Coluthus, Poem on 'Rape of Helen.' Tryphiodorus, Poem on 'Destruction of Troy.'	400 Synesius, Orations and Epistles. Zosimus, 'Hist. of Roman Emperors.' Socrates, 389-446, Ecclesiastical History. Sozomen, *d.* 450, Ecclesiastical History. Theodoret, *d.* 450, Ecclesiastical History.	400 Nemesius, 'Nature of Man,' Philosophy. Cyril, *d.* 443, Homilies. Proclus, *d.* 445, Theology. Proclus, *d.* 500, platonist.
500	509 Stephanus, Geography. Procopius, 'Hist. of Reign of Justinian.' Olympiodorus, 'Hist. of Honorius. Cos. Indicopleustes, Topography. Evagrius, Ecclesiast. Hist. Agathias, Byzantine Hist.	500 Simplicius, 'Comments on Aristotle.' Tribonianus, Jurist.
600	600 Menan. Protector, Chron. Theophanes, Byzant. Hist. Theophylactus Simocatta, Byzantine History.	600 Philoponus, Grammarian.
700	700	700 Damascenus, *d.* 750, Theology.
800	800 Nicephorus, 758-828, Hist. Syncellus, History. John Malalas, History.	800 Theodorus Studites, 759-826, Sermons. Photius, *d.* 891, 'Bibliotheca.'
900	900 Leontius, History. Genesius, History. Const. Porphyrogenneta, 905-959, Hist. Selections. Sim. Metaphrastes, Lives of Saints.'	900 Leo VI., *d.* 911, 'On Christian Faith.'
1000	1000 George Cedrenus, Hist. John Xiphilinus, *d.* 1080, Abridg. of Dion Cassius,	1000

	Imagination.	*Fact.*	*Speculative and Scientific.*
1000		John Scylitza, History.	Theophylactus, Theology. Michael Psellus, Mathematics.
1100	C. Theo. Prodromus, 'Rhodanthe & Dosicles.' novel.	Nicephorus Bryennius, *d.* 1137. Byzant. Affairs. Anna Comnena, Reign of her father Alexius. Const. Manasses, Hist. Zonaras, History of Romans, History of Jews. Will. of Tyre, 1100-1184, History. John Tzetzes, History in Verse. Cinnamus, History.	Euthymius Zygabenus, Theology. Suidas, Lexicon. Eustathius, Commentaries on Homer. Isaac Tzetzes, Commentary on Lycophron.
1200		Joel, History. Michael Glycas History. George Acropolita. Hist. Nicetas Acominatus, Hist. George Pachymer, Hist.	Nicephorus Blemmidas, Theology.
1300	Manuel Philes, 1275-1340. Poems. Maximus Planudes, Anthology. Leo Pilatus, Literature.	Theod. Metochita, *d.* 1312, History. Callistus Xantopulus, Ecclesiastical History. Niceph. Gregoras, Hist. John Cantacuzenus, Hist. George Codinus, Hist. Michael Ducas, History.	
1400	Demet. Pamperes, Tales. Marullus Tarchoniota, d. 1500, Poems.	Theodore Gaza, *d.* 1478. Origin of Turks. Laonicus Chalcondyles, History of Turks. George Phranza, Hist.	Eman. Chrysolorus, *d.* 1415, Grammar. Geo. Gemistius, or Pletho, *d.* 1450, Philosophy. Eman. Moscopulus, Notes on Hesiod. Bessarion, 1395-1472, Theology. Geo. of Trebizond, 1396-1468, Aristotelian. John Argyrophilus, Aristotelian.
1500			Demetrius Chalcondyles, 1453-1513, Philology.
1600			Panagioti, *d.* 1763, Theology.
1700	Kallinikus, Poems. Nicholas Caradza, Translation of Voltaire.	Alexander Maurocordato, History of the Jews. Meletius, Geography.	Dorotheus, Aristotelian. Marcus Tharboures, Mechanics.

Imagination.	*Fact.*	*Speculative and Scientific.*
1700 Riga, *d.* 1796, Lyrics, Natural Philosophy.	1700 Ducas, Translation of Thucydides.	1700 Bulgaris, Mathematics.
1800 N. Piccolo, Tragedy. Christopulus, Anacreontics, Opera. Calvos, Lyrics. Ilarion, Translation of Sophocles.	1800 D. Philippides, *d.* 1827. Hist. of Wallachia, &c. Paliuris, Hist. of Greece. Perrevos, History of Suli and Parga. Gr. Demetrius, Geography	1800 Psalidas, Metaphysics. Coray, Commentaries, Lexicon. Cumas, Dictionary. Neophitus, Bamba, Ethics.

LATIN AND ITALIAN.

[The Latin ceased to be a spoken language about the sixth century, but was in almost universal use throughout Europe as the language of composition until the thirteenth century, when the modern languages began to appear.

As long as the literature of the West was almost exclusively confined to Italy we have arranged all authors who wrote in Latin under the same head; but about the sixth century they will be found under those countries where their works were published, whatever the language in which they wrote.]

Imagination.	*Fact.*	*Speculative and Scientific.*
B. C. 200 M. A. Plautus, Comedies. Q. Ennius, Epics (Fragts.) P. Terentius, Comedies.	B. C. 200	B. C. 200 M. P. Cato, De Re Rustica.
100 T. Lucretius, *b.* 95, De Rerum Natura. Catullus, 86-40, Lyrics. P. Virgilius, 70-19, Eneid. Q. Horatius, 65-8, Odes, Satires. Propertius, 59-16, Elegies. A. Tibullus, 43 B. C.,-17 A. D., Elegies. Ovid, 43 B. C.-17 A. D., Metamorph. Fasti, &c. Hyginus, Poeticon Astronomicon.	100 T. Pomponius Atticus, 110-33, Letters. M. T. Cicero, 107-43, Orator and Philosopher. Julius Cæsar, 98-46, Commentaries. Hirtius Pansa, Gallic War. C. Sallustius, 85-35, Jugurthine War. Corn. Nepos, Biography. T. Livius, 59 B. C.—19 A. D. History of Rome.	100 Varro, 115-28, De Re Rustica, Lingua Latina. Vitruvius, Architecture. Verrius Flaccus, *d.* 4, Fasti Capitolini.
A. D. 0 Phædrus, Fables. Persius, 34-62, Satires. Lucan, 38-65, 'Pharsalia.' Petronius Arbiter, *d.* 67, Satyricon. Valerius Flaccus, Argonautics.	A. D. 0 Vel. Paterculus, 19 B. C.—30 A. D., Hist. of Rome. Pomp. Mela, Geography. Valerius Maximus, Anecdotes of Great Men. Quintus Curtius, History of Alexander.	A. D. 0 C. Celsus, De Medicina. Columella, Agriculture. L. A. Seneca, 12-65, Philosopher, Tragic Poet. Pliny the elder, 23-79, Natural History.

Imagination.	*Fact.*	*Speculative and Scientific.*
0 Silius Italicus, 'Punic War.' Sulpicia, Satires, &c. Statius, *d.* 99, 'Thebais,' 'Achilleis.' Martial, 29-104, Epigrams. Juvenal, 48-128, Satires. Pliny, the younger, 61-113, Epistles.	0	0 Quintilian, Criticism.
100 L. Apuleius, Golden Ass.	100 Tacitus, History. Suetonius, Biography. Florus, History of Rome. Aulus Gellius, Noctes Atticæ. C Jul. Solinus, Polyhistor. Justin, History.	100 Valer. Probus, Grammar. Frontinus, Strategy. Terentianus Maurus, De Arte Metricâ Pompei. Festus, Grammar.
200 Nemesianus, Cynegetica. Jul. Calpurnius, Eclogues.	200	200 Ulpian, *d.* 228, Law. Tertullian, *d.* 220, 'Apology for Christianity.' Minutius Felix, Dialogue in fav. of Christianity. Julius Obsequens, 'De Prodigiis.' Censorinus, 'De Die Natali.' Cyprian, *d.* 258, Theology.
300 Aquilinus Juvencus, Gospel in Verse. M. Victorinus, Hymns. Festus Avienus, Geographical Poem. D. M. Ausonius, Idyls. A. T. Macrobius, Saturnalia. Symmachus, Epistles. C. Claudianus, Poems. A. Prudentius Clemens, Christian Poems.	300 Æl. Spartianus, History. Jul. Capitolinus, Do. Æl. Lampridius, Do. Vul. Gallicanus, Do. Trebellius, Pollio, Do. F. Vopiscus, Do. Aurelius Victor, Do. F. Eutropius, History of Rome. Amm. Marcellinus, Do.	300 Arnobius, 'Adversus gentes.' Lactantius, *d.* 325, Defence of Christianity.' Æl. Donatus, Grammar. F. Maternus, Astronomy, Theology. Ambrosius, Theology. Jerom. 329—420, Version of Bible. Rufinus, *d.* 410, Ecclesiastical History. T. Vegetius Renatus, De Re Militari. Augustin, 354—430, Theology.
400 Sedulius, Poetical Life of Christ. Martianus Capella, De Nuptiis Phil. et Merc. Paulin. Petrocorius, Poem. on Martin of Tours.	400 Vib. Sequester, Geography Sulpitius, Severus, *d.* 420, Sacred History. Orosius Hist. of World.	400

Imagination.	*Fact.*	*Speculative and Scientific.*
400 Sidonius Apollinaris, *d.* 488, Poems. Ennodius, *d.* 521, Christian Poems.	400 Victorius, History of Church in Africa. Idacius, Chronicles to 468	400
500 Boethius, Poet and Philosopher. Arator, 490-556, Acts of Apostles in Verse.	500 Cassiodorus, 481-562 History. Jornandes, Hist. of Goths. Evagrius, Eccl. History.	500 Priscianus, Grammar. Fulgentius, 468-533, Theology. Dionysius Exiguus, *d.* 536, Christian Era. Non. Marcellus, Grammar.
600	600 Secundus, *d.* 615, History of Lombards.	600
700	700 Paul Warnefrid, History of Lombards.	700 Cresconius, Collection Canons, Verses.
800	800 Erchempert, History of Lombards. Anastasius, Lives of Popes.	800
900	900 Luitprand, History of his Times.	900
1000	1000	1000 Papias, Grammar. Lanfranc, *d.* 1089, Theol.
1100 Donizo, Latin Poetry. Ciullo d'Alcamo, Sicilian Poetry.	1100 Falcandus, Hist. of Sicily.	1100 Gratian, Canonist. Campanus, Mathematics.
1200 Guido of Colonna, Poetry, History. Brunetto Latina, *d.* 1294, 'Il Tesoro.' Guido Cavalcanti, *d.* 1300, Poems. John XXII., Poem on Medicine.	1200 Pietro dalle Vigne, *d.* 1249, History. Marco Polo, Travels. G. de Voragine, *d.* 1298, Legends of Saints.	1200 Accursius, 1182-1260, Law. Thomas Aquinas, 1224-1274, Theology. Bonaventura, Scholastic G. Durand, Law. Pietro d Albano, 1250-1315, Astrology Physics. Torregiano Rustechelli, Commentaries.
1300 Dante, 1265-1321, La Divina Commedia. F. Barberino, 1264-1348, Poems. Petrarca, 1304-1374, Sonnets, Epic. Literature. Boccacio, 1313-1375, 'Il Decamerone.'	1300 Ferreti, 1356-1429, History of his Times.	1300 Mon. de Luzzi, Anatomy. Arn. Villanovan, *d.* 1313, Alchemy. Cecco d'Ascoli, *d.* 1327, Astronomy. G. Andreas, *d.* 1348, Canons. Bartolus, Law.

Imagination.	*Fact.*	*Speculative and Scientific.*
	1400 Leonardo Bruni, History of Florence.	1400 Leonard of Pisa, Algebra. Nicholas Tedeschi, Law.
1400 A. Beccadelli, 1374-1471, 'Hermaphroditus.'	Guarino, 1370-1460, Translation of Plutarch	
Poggio, 1380-1459, Literature.		Mich. Savenarola, *d.* 1462, Medicine.
Lorenzo Valla, 1407-1457, Literature.		Bar. Montagnana, *d.* 1460. Baraterius, Law.
D. Burchiello, Sonnets.	B. Accolti, 1415-1466, History of Holy War.	Gianozzo Manetti, 1396-1479, Orientalist.
	Flav. Blondus, 1388-1463, History of Venice, &c.	Paul Toscanello, *d.* 1482, Astronomy.
	Æn. Sylvius, 1405-1464, History, Poetry, &c.	
	John Gobelin, History.	
	Beccat. Panormita, 1393-1471, Biography.	
Pulci, 1432-1487, 'Morgante Maggiore.'	Bart. Platina, 1421-1481, Lives of Popes.	
Franc. Philelphus, 1398-1481, Poetry and Ethics.	F. Buonaccorsi, 1437-1496, Biography.	
Loren. de' Medici, *d.* 1492, Poetry, Literature.	Pomp. Laetus, 1425-1495, Lives of Cæsars, &c.	
Angelo Poliziano, 1454-1494, Poetry, Drama.	Franc. Berlinghieri, Geography.	
Marsilius Ficinus, 1433-1499, Translat. Plato.	G. Pontano, 1426-1503, Wars of Ferdinand I.	Pico de Mirandola, 1463-1494, Metaphysics.
	Bonfinius, *d.* 1502, History of Hungary.	Luca di Burgo, Mathem.
1500	1500 P. Accolti, 1455-1532, History.	1500 Ant. della Torre, *d.* 1512, Anatomy.
		L. da Vinci, 1452-1520, 'Treatise on Painting.'
		G. Abrosi, Astronomy.
G. Rucellai, 1475-1526, 'Le Api.'		A. Acchillini, 1472-1512, Medicine.
Alexander ab Alexandro, 1461-1523, Dies Geniales.		B. Castiglione, 1478-1529, 'The Courtier.'
M. Boiardo, 'Orlando innamorato.'		
Sannazar, 1458-1530, Arcadia.	Machiavelli, 1482-1528, History of Florence, &c.	
Berni, *d.* 1530, Satires.		
Ariosto, 1474-1533, 'Orlando Furioso.'	Guicciardini, 1482-1540, History of Italy.	
F. M. Molza, *d.* 1544, Poems.	Bembo, 1470-1547, History of Venice.	
Trissino, 1478-1550, 'Italy Delivered,' Epic, Tragedy.	L. Alberti, *d.* 1552, History of Bologna.	G. Fracastoro, 1483-1533, Medicine.
		And. Alciato, 1492-1550, Law.
		Nic. Tartaglia, Mathem.
Hier. Vida, *d.* 1566, Latin Poetry.	B. Cellini, 1500-1570, Autobiography.	F. Commandino, 1509-1575, Mathematics.
Mic. Angelo Buonaroti, *d.* 1564, Poems.	B. Varchi, 1503-1566, History of his Times.	Angelo Caninio, *d.* 1557, Orientalist.
Giovanni della Casa, 1503-1556, Il Galateo, &c.		
G. Anguillara, *b.* 1517, Tragedy.		
L. Dolce, 1508-1568, Tragedy, Epic, History.		
Bernardo Tasso, 1493-1575, 'Amadis.'	V. Borghini, 1515-1580, History.	And. Vesalio, 1514-1564, Anatomy.
Greg. Giraldi, 1504-1573, Tragedy.	G. Vasari, 1514-1578, Lives of Painters, &c.	Falopius, 1523-1563, Medicine.

	Imagination.	*Fact.*	*Speculative and Scientific.*
1500		Sperone Speroni, 1500-1588, Orations.	Eustachi, d. 1570, Do.
		S. Ammirato, 1531-1600, History of Florence.	P. Manut Aldus, 1512-1574, Commentaries.
		G. Adriani, 1511-1579, History of his Times.	Cardano, 1501-1576, Mathematics.
	A. F. Grazzini, d. 1583, Comedies.	B. Davanzati, 1529-1606, Hist. Eng. Reformation	P. Launcelloti, 1511-1591, Law.
	Torq. Tasso, 1544-1595, 'Gerusalemme Liberata.'	C. Baronius, 1538-1607, Ecclesiastical Annals.	
	G. Bagnioli, d. 1600, Tragedy.	P. Paruta, 1540-1598, History of Venice.	Andrea Cæsalpino, 1519-1603, Botany.
	Guarini, 1538-1613, 'Il Pastor Fido.'	Possevini, 1533-1611, Description of Muscovy, &c.	U. Aldrovandi, 1522-1605, Natural History.
		P. R. Sarpi, 1552-1623, Hist. of Coun. of Trent.	Orazio Torselline, 1545-1609, Grammar.
	Ottavio Rinuccini, Opera.		
	F. Bracciolini, 1566-1605, 'La Croce Racquistata.'		
	Oraz. Vecchi, Comic Opera		
	G. Marini, 1569-1625, Poems.	E. C. Davila, 1576-1631, Hist. Civil Wars France.	
	C. Achillini, 1577-1640, Poems.		
	A. Tassoni, 1561-1635, 'Secchia Rapita.'		
1600	G. Chiabrera, 1552-1637, Poems.	G. Bentivoglio, 1579-1644, Hist. Civil Wars Flanders.	J. Fabricius, d. 1619, Comparative Anatomy.
			Bellarmino, 1542-1621, Polemics.
			Galileo, 1564-1642, Astron.
			T. A. Campanella, 1568-1693, Philosophy.
			L. Vanini, 1585-1619, Theology.
			B. Castelli, d. 1644, Mathemathics.
			B. Cavalieri, d. 1647, Do.
			Fabio Colonna, 1567-1647, Botany, &c.
		P. della Valle, 1586-1652, Travels.	
		F. Strada, 1571-1649, Hist. of Wars of Flanders.	
	Laur. Lippi, 1606-1664, Comic Poems.	G. B. Nani, 1616-1678, Hist. of Venice.	
	G. Marini, Romances.	Oderic Rainaldi, Ecclesiastical Annals.	
	Salvator Rosa, 1615-1673, Satires.		F. Redi, 1626-1697. Natural History.
	C. M. Maggi, 1630-1699, Poems.	Villani, Hist. Florence.	M. Malpighi, 1628-1694, Anatomy.
			V. Viviani, 1621-1703, Mathematics.
			A. Magliabecchi, 1633-1714, Literature.
	Ben. Manzina, 1646-1704, Art of Poetry, Satires.		
	V. Filicaja, 1642-1707, Poems.		
			G. D. Cassini, 1625-1712, Mathematics, Astron.
			D. Guglielmini, 1655-1710, Mathematics.
1700	Aless. Guidi, 1650-1712, Lyrics.		G. Baglivi, 1668-1706, Medicine.

Imagination.	*Fact.*	*Speculative and Scientific.*
1700 A. Marchetti, 1633-1714, Poems, Philosophy. N. Forteguerra, 1674-1735, Ricciardetto. G. M. Crescembini, 1663-1728, Poetry. Apostolo Zeno, 1669-1750, Operas. S. Maffei, 1675-1755, Tragedy. M. Metastasio, 1698-1782, Operas. C. Goldoni, 1707-1772, Comedies. C. I. Frugoni, 1692-1768, Poems. G. Gozzi, 1713-1786. Satires, Odes. V. Alfieri, 1749-1803, Tragedies.	1700 L. Muratori, 1672-1750, Annals of Italy. B. Giannone, 1680-1748, History of Naples. F. X. Quadrio, 1695-1756, Hist. of the Valteline. B. Buonamici, 1710-1761 History. A. Fabroni, 1732-1802, Biography. G. Tiraboschi, 1731-1794, Hist. of Ital. Literature.	1700 G. V. Gravina, 1664-1718, Law G. Cassini, 1677-1756. Astronomy. G. Morgagni, 1681-1771, Anatomy. A. Genovesi, 1712-1769, Metaphysics. F. Algarotti, 1712-1764, 'Newtonianism.' G. R. Boscowitch, 1711-1787, Mathem. Philol. F. M. Zanetti, 1692-1777, Philosophy. C. Beccaria, 1720-1795, 'Crimes & Punishments.' L. Spallanzani, 1729-1799, Natural History. L. Galvani, 1737-1798, Galvanism. Volta, 1745-1827, Do. G. Filangieri, 1751-1798, Legislation.
1800 Pindemonte, Poems. Monti, Poems. Ugo Foscolo, Drama, Poems.	1800 Denina, History of Italian Revolutions.	1800 Scarpa, Anatomy.

BRITISH, &c.

Imagination.	*Fact.*	*Speculative and Scientific.*
A.D. 500	A. D. 500 Gildas, Conquest of Britain.	A. D. 500
600 Cædmon, Saxon Poems. Aldhelme, *d.* 709, Latin Poems.	600 Nennius, Origin of Britons.	600
700	700 Bede, 673-735, Eccl. Hist. of England.	700 Alcuin, *d.* 804, Theology, History. Poetry.
800 Alfred, 849-901, Saxon Poems, Translations, &c.	800 Asser, *d.* 909, Life of Alfred, Hist. of England.	800 J. Scot Erigena, *d.* 883. 'Of the Nature of Things.'
900	900 Ethelwerd, History of Great Britain.	900

Imagination.	*Fact.*	*Speculative and Scientific.*
1000	1000 Ingulphus, 1030-1109, History of Croyland. Eadmer, Chronicle.	1000
1100 Layamon, Saxon Poetry. Nigellus, Speculum Stultorum. Walter Mapes, Satires, Songs. Jos. of Exeter, Troj. War, War of Antioch, Epics.	1100 Order. Vitalis, 1075-1132, History of England. Florence of Worcester, *d.* 1118, Chron. of England. Geoffry of Monmouth, History of Britain. William of Malmsbury, *d.* 1143, Hist. of Britain. Henry of Huntingdon, Chronicles of England. Simeon of Durham, Chronicles of England. John of Salisbury, *d.* 1181, 'Life of Becket,' &c. G. Cambrensis, Conq. of Ireland, Itin. of Wales. Wm. of Newbury, *b.* 1136, Chron. of England.	1100 Robert Pulleyn, *d.* 1150, Theology. Richard of St. Victor *d.* 1173, Theology. Ralph Glanville, Collection of Laws.
1200 Robert of Glocester, Chronicle in verse. T. Lermont, the Rhymer, Sir Tristrem, Romance.	1200 Roger Hoveden, Chron. of England. Gervase of Canterbury, History of England. Roger of Wendover, Hist. of England. Matthew Paris, *d.* 1259, Hist of England. William Rishanger, History of England.	1200 Alex. Neckham, *d.* 1227 Theology. Robert Grosteste, Natural Philosophy. Alexander Hales, *d.* 1245, Aristotelian. John Peckham, Theology. John Holiwood, *d.* 1256, Astron., Mathematics. Roger Bacon, 1214-1292, Chemistry, Optics, &c. Rich. Middleton, Theology
1300 Adam Davie, Metr. Romance, Life of Alex. Lawrence Minot, *d.* 1352, Historical Poems. John Barbour, 1326-1396, 'The Bruce.' R. Langlande, 'Pierce Plowman,' a Satire. Geof. Chaucer, 1328-1400, 'Canterbury Tales,' &c.	1300 Nicholas Triveth, *d.* 1328, Hist. Physic, Theology. Richard of Chichester, Chron. of England. Ralph Higden, *d.* 1360, Chron. of England. Henry Knighton, *d.* 1370, Chron. of England. Matthew of Westminster, 'Flowers of History.' John Maundeville, *d.* 1372, Travels. John Fordun, Chron. of Scotland.	1300 Albricus, Theology. Duns Scotus *d.* 1308, Philosophy. Walter Burleigh, Philosophy. Gilb. Anglicus, Medicine. R. Aungervile, 1281-1345, Philobiblion. J. Wicliffe, 1324-1384, Theology, Translation of Bible. H. de Bracton, Law.

Imagination.	Fact.	Speculative and Scientific.
1300 John Gower, *d.* 1402, Elegies, Romances, &c.		
1400 John Lydgate, 1380-1440, Poems. James I. of Scotland, 1395-1437, 'King's Quhair,' &c. Harry the Minstrel, 'Sir W. Wallace.' Stephen Hawes, 'Passetyme of pleasure.' John Skelton, *d.* 1529, Satires, Odes.	1400 Andrew of Wyntoun, Chron. of Scotland. T. Walsingham, *d.* 1440, History of Normandy. John Hardyng, Chron. of England. Lord Berners, Trans. of Froissart. W. Caxton, Translations. Douglas of Glastonbury, Chron. of England.	1400 John Fortescue, Laws of England. Thos. Littleton, *d.* 1487, Law.
1500 Wm. Dunbar, 1465-1530, 'Thistle and Rose.' Gawin Douglas, 1475-1522, Trans. Virgil. Thomas More, 1480-1535, 'Utopia.' Thomas Wyatt, *d.* 1541, Sonnets. John Heywood, *d.* 1565, Drama. Earl of Surrey, *d.* 1546-7, Poems. Geo. Gascoigne, *d.* 1577, Drama. Philip Sidney, 1554-1586, 'Arcadia.' Christ. Marlowe, *d.* 1593, Drama. Edmd. Spenser, 1553-1598, 'Faery Queen.' W. Shakspeare, 1564-1616, Drama. John Lylie, 1550-1600. 'Euphues.' John Fletcher, 1576-1625, Drama. F. Beaumont, 1586-1615, Drama.	1500 R. Fabyan, *d.* 1512, Chron. of England and France. T. Halls, *d.* 1547, Hist. of Houses of York and Lancaster. John Leland, *d.* 1552, English Antiquities. W. Cavendish, 1505-1557, 'Life of Wolsey.' J. Bale, 1495-1563, 'Lives of British Writers.' Ralph Hollingshed, *d.* 1581, Chronicles. Geo. Buchanan, 1506-1582, History of Scotland. J. Fox, 1517-1587, Book of Martyrs. N. Fitzherbert, 1550-1612, Biography. John Stowe, 1527-1605, Chronicles, Topography. Sir T. North, Translations of Plutarch.	1500 Thos. Linacre, 1460-1524, Philology. Medicine. Anth. Fitzherbert, Husbandry. Thomas Elyot, Philology. H. Latimer, 1475-1555, Sermons. Roger Ascham, 1515-1568, 'The Schoolmaster.' Thomas Wilson, *d.* 1581, Logic and Rhetoric. Thomas Tusser, *d.* 1580, Husbandry. J. Jewel, 1522-1570, Divinity. R. Hooker, 1553-1600, Ecclesiastical Polity. W. Gilbert, 1540-1603, 'On the Loadstone.' L. Andrews, 1565-1626, Sermons.
1600 John Owen, *d.* 1612, Latin Epigrams.	1600 J. Pitts, 1560-1616, Biog. of Kings, Bishops, &c. Richard Knolles, *d.* 1610, History of the Turks. Wm. Camden, 1551-1623, Antiquities. R. Hackluyt, 1553-1616, Naval Histories. W. Raleigh, 1552-1617, History of the World. Samuel Daniel, 1567-1619, History of England.	1600 Edward Coke, 1550-1634, Law. John Napier, 1550-1617, Logarithms.

Imagination.	*Fact.*	*Speculative and Scientific.*
1600 J. Ford, *b.* 1586, Drama.	1600 John Hayward, *d.* 1627, English history	1600
Ben Jonson, 1574-1637, Drama.	J. Speed, 1555-1629, Hist. of Great Britain.	Robert Burton, 1576-1639, 'Anat. of Melancholy.'
P. Massinger, 1585-1639, Drama.	Henry Spelman, 1562-1641, Antiquities.	Francis Bacon, 1560-1626, Philosophy, History.
J. Harrington, 1561-1612, Trans. Ariosto.	R. B. Cotton, 1570-1631, Antiquities.	Wm. Harvey, 1578-1657, Circulation of Blood.
E. Fairfax, *d.* 1632. Trans. Tasso.	S. Purchas, 1577-1628, Collection of Voyages.	
M. Drayton, 1563-1631, Poems.		John Selden, 1584-1654, Antiquities, Law, Hist.
G. Sandys, 1577-1643, Translations Poems,	Thomas Roe, 1580-1641, Travels in the East.	J. Harrington, 1611-1677, 'Oceana.'
J. Daniel, 1562-1619, Poems.	E.(Ld.)Herbert,1581-1648 History of Henry VIII.	James Usher, 1580-1656, Divinity, Sermons, Hist.
W. Drummond,1585-1649, Poems.	R. Baker, *d.* 1645, Chron. of England.	Thos. Hobbes, 1588-1679, Metaphysics.
John Donne, 1573—1662, Satires, Essays.		W. Dugdale, 1605-1686, Antiquities, History.
Geo. Wither, 1588-1667, Satires.	Thos. Fuller, 1608-1661, History, Biography.	W. Chillingworth, 1602-1644, Theology.
James Shirley, 1594-1666, Drama.	Clarendon, 1608-1673, History of Rebellion.	Isaac Barrow, 1630-1677, Divinity, Mathematics.
Sir J. Suckling, 1609-1641, Poems.	Thomas May, *d.* 1650, History of Parliament.	J. Pearson, 1612-1686. Divinity.
John Denham, 1615-1668, Tragedies,Cooper'sHill.	Izaak Walton, 1593-1683, Biography.	Brian Walton, 1600-1661, Polyglot Bible.
Samuel Butler, 1612-1680, Hudibras.	B. Whitlocke, 1605-1676, History.	Jeremy Taylor, *d.* 1667, Divinity.
John Milton, 1608-1674, 'Paradise Lost.'	Mrs. Hutchinson, Biography.	Alger. Sydney, 1617-1683, 'Discourse on Governmt.'
Edmd. Waller, 1605-1687, Poems.	W. Prynne, 1600-1667, History, Politics.	Thos. Browne, 1605-1682, 'On Vulgar Errors.'
A. Cowley, 1618-1667, Poems.		Edmund Castell, *d.* 1685, Lexicon Heptaglotton.
A. Maxwell, 1620-1678, Poems.		R. Cudworth, 1617-1688, Metaphysics.
		J. Evelyn, 1620-1706, 'Sylva.'
		H. More, 1614-1687, Theology.
Rochester, 1648-1680, Satires.	Wm. Temple, 1629-1710, History.	T. Sydenham, 1624-1689, Medicine.
Roscommon, 1633-1684, Poems.		W. Sherlock, *d.* 1689, Divinity.
N. Lee, 1656-1691, Drama.		J. Tillotson, 1630-1694, Sermons.
John Bunyan,1628-1688, 'Pilgrim's Progress.'		Archbishop Leighton, 1613-1684, Divinity.
John Dryden, 1631-1701, Tragedy,Satire,'Virgil.'		R. Baxter, 1615-1691, 'Saint'sEverlastingRest.'
Thos. Otway, 1651-1685, Tragedy.	R. Brady, *d.* 1700, History of England.	B. Boyle, 1627-1691, Theology, Chemistry.
1700 John Pomfret, 1667-1703, 'The Choice.'	1700 Thomas Rymer, *d.* 1713, Fœdera.	1700
		John Ray, 1628-1705, Botany, Natural History.
		John Locke, 1632-1704, Metaphysics.
		R. South, 1633-1716, Divinity.
John Philips, 1676-1708, 'Splendid Shilling.'		
Thos. Parnell, 1679-1718, 'The Hermit.'	S. Ockley, 1678-1720, Oriental History.	Isaac Newton, 1642-1719, 'Principia.'
Geo. Farquhar, 1678-1707, Comedies.	Thos. Hearne, 1678-1735, History and Antiquities.	J. Flamsteed, 1642-1719, Astronomy.

Imagination.

1700

Matthew Prior, 1664-1721, Poems.

R. Steele, *d.* 1729, Drama, Essays.

Daniel Defoe, 1660-1731, 'Robinson Crusoe.'

Jos. Addison, 1672-1719, 'Spectator,' 'Cato.'

Nich. Rowe, 1673-1718, Tragedy.

J. Vanbrugh, *d.* 1726, Comedy.

W. Congreve, 1672-1728 Comedy.

John Gay, 1688-1732, 'Beggar's Opera,' Fab.

M. W. Montague, 1690-1762, Letters.

Robert Blair, 1699-1746, 'The Grave.'

S. Richardson, 1689-1761, 'Clarissa,' 'Pamela,' &c.

D. Garrick, 1716-1779, Drama.

S. Foote, 1720-1771, Drama.

R. Dodsley, 1703-1764, Drama.

Jona. Swift, 1667-1745, Satires, Tales, &c.

I. Watts, 1674-1748, Hymns.

Ewd. Young, 1681-1765, 'Night Thoughts.'

Alex. Pope, 1688-1744, Poetry.

W. Somerville, 1692-1743, 'The Chase.'

Allan Ramsay, 1696-1758, 'The Gentle Shepherd.'

Richard Savage, 1698-1743, Poems.

Jas. Thomson, 1700-1748, 'Seasons.'

John Dyer, 1700-1758, Poems.

H. Fielding, 1707-1754, 'Tom Jones,' &c.

James Hammond, 1710-1742. Elegies.

Lawr. Sterne, 1713-1768, 'Tristram Shandy,'

W. Shenstone, 1714-1763, Pastorals, &c.

W. Collins, 1720-1756, Odes.

H. Brooke, 1706-1783, 'Fool of Quality.'

Fact.

1700 John Strype, 1643-1737, Eccl. History, Biog.

Gilbert Burnet, 1643-1715, 'History of his Times.'

L. Echard, 1671-1730, History of England.

Thos. Carte, 1686-1754, History of England.

John Potter, 16.4-1747, Antiquities.

Sir W. Petty. 1623-1682, Statistics.

Nathanael Hooke, *d.* 1763, History of Rome.

C. Middleton, 1683-1750, Life of Cicero, &c.

John Swinton, 1703-1767, History, Antiquity.

Lord Lyttleton, 1709-1773, History, Poems, Divinity.

James Granger, *d.* 1776, Biog. Hist. of England.

Sam. Johnson, 1709-1784, Lives of Poets, Dict., &c.

Jonas Hanway, 1712-1786. Travels in the East.

John Blair, *d.* 1782, Chronology.

Speculative and Scientific.

1700 R. Hooke 1635-1702, Philosophy.

B. de Mandeville, 1670-1733, 'Fab. of the Bees.'

Edmd. Halley, 1656-1742, Astronomy.

Hans Sloane, 1660-1753, Natural History.

A. Clark, 1696-1742, Divinity, Philosophy,

D. Waterland, 1683-1740, Divinity.

R. Bentley, 1661-1740, Divinity, Philology.

A. Baxter, 1687-1750, Metaphysics.

Lord Bolingbroke, 1672-1751, Politics, Literature.

G. Berkeley, 1684-1753, Metaphysics, Ethics.

P. Doddridge, 1701-1751, Divinity.

Jas. Bradley, 1692-1762, Astronomy.

F. Hutcheson, 1694-1747, Moral Philosophy.

T. Sherlock, 1678-1761, Divinity.

C. Maclaurin, 1696-1746, Mathematics.

Earl of Chesterfield, 1694-1773, Letters.

Eph. Chambers, *d.* 1740, Cyclopædia.

R. Hoadly, 1676-1761, Polemics.

Bishop Butler, 1692-1752, Divinity.

J. Wesley, 1703-1791, Divinity.

D. Hartley, 1704-1757, 'Observations on Man.'

Soame Jenyns, 1704-1787, Theology.

W. Warburton, 1709-1779, Theology, Criticism.

J. Jortin, 1698-1770, Divinity, Criticism.

Lord Kaimes, 1696-1782, Elements of Criticism.

R. Lowth, 1710-1787, Divinity, Philology.

W. Blackstone, 1723-1780, Laws of England.

	Imagination.		*Fact.*		*Speculative and Scientific.*
1700	M. Akenside, 1721-1770, 'Pleasures of Imagination.'	1700	David Hume, 1711-1776, History of England. Essays, &c.	1700	
	Thos. Gray, 1716-1771, Odes, Elegies.				
	T. Smollet, 1720-1771, Novels.		W. Robertson, 1721-1793, Hist. of Charles V., &c.		Adam Smith, 1723-1790, 'Wealth of Nations.'
	R. Glover, 1712-1789, 'Leonidas.'		Thomas. Warton, 1728-1790, Hist. of England, Poetry, Poems.		J. Harris, 1709-1780, Philology.
	O. Goldsmith, 1731-1774, 'Traveller,' 'Vicar of Wakefield.'				John Hunter, 1728-1793, Medicine.
					F. Balguy, 1716-1795, Divinity.
	W. Mason, 1725-1797, Poems, Biography.		H. Walpole, *d.* 1797, 'Historic Doubts,' 'Royal and Noble Authors.'		
	T. Chatterton, 1752-1770, Poems.		J. Moore, 1730-1802, 'Views of Society and Manners.'		T. Reid, 1710-1796, Metaphysics.
	Ar. Murphy, 1727-1805, Drama.				Sir. J. Reynolds, 1723-1792, Art.
	Wm Cowper, 1731-1800, Poems.		James Bruce, 1730-1794, Travels.		S. Horsley, *d.* 1806, Theol.
	R. Cumberland, 1732-1811, Drama.		W. Gilpin, 1724-1804, Biography. Divinity.		Jos. Priestley, 1733-1804, Metaphysics, Chemistry.
	Eras. Darwin, 1732-1802, 'Botanic Garden.'		E. Gibbon, 1737-1794, Decline and fall of Roman Empire.		Hugh Blair, 1718-1800, Sermons.
	James Beattie, 1735-1803, Poems.				J. Horne Tooke, 1736-1812, Philology.
	R. Ferguson, 1750-1774, Poems.		J. Whitaker, 1735-1808, Hist. of Manchester, &c.		Wm. Jones, 1747-1794, Orientalist.
	Geo. Colman, 1733-1794, Comedies.		Edmd. Burke, 1730-1797, Oratory.		R. Price, 1723-1791, Metaphysics, Divinity.
	J. Wolcot (Peter Pindar,) 1738-1819, Com. Poems.		J. Boswell, 1740-1795, Biography.		Wm. Paley, 1743-1805, Theology.
	Jas. Macpherson, 1738-1796, 'Ossian's Poems.'		J. Milner. 1744-1797, Church History.		Ricd. Porson, 1759-1808, Philology.
	Robert Burns, 1759-1796, Poems.		Joseph Strutt, 1748-1802, Chronology, Antiquities.		Ths. Beddoes, 1760-1808, Medicine.
	J. Home, *d.* 1808, Drama				N. Maskelyne, *d.* 1811, Astronomy.
	Ricd. B. Sheridan, 1751-1816, Drama.				G. L. Staunton, *d.* 1801, Chinese Code.
	Ann Radcliffe, 1764-1823, Novels.		Charles Burney, *d.* 1814, 'History of Music.'		W. Herschell, 1738-1822, Astronomy.
1800	Rob. Bloomfield, *d.* 1823, 'Farmer's Boy.'	1800	J. Macdiarmid, 1779-1808, Biography.	1800	Arthur Young, 1741-1820, Agriculture.
	Mrs. Barbauld, Poems, Tales.				A. Rees, 1743-1825, Cyclopædia.
					Joseph Banks, 1743-1820, Natural History.
			E. D. Clarke, *d.* 1822, Travels.		Dr. Parr, *d.* 1825, Philol.
					D. Ricardo, *d.* 1823, Political Economy.
			C. J. Fox, *d.* 1806, Hist.		
	Lord Byron, 1788-1824, Poems.				C. Hutton, *d.* 1823, Mathematics.
	John Keats, Poems.				John Playfair, *d.* 1819.
	P. B. Shelley, *d.* 1822, Poems.				P. Elmsley, Philology.
			W. Mitford, History of Greece.		T. Wollaston, Chemistry.
	R. C. Maturin, *d.* 1824, Drama.				Thomas Young, Hieroglyphics &c.
					T. Scott, Divinity.
	Miss Austin, Novels.				D. Stewart, Metaphysics.
			R. Heber, Travels, &c.		Archbish. Magee, *d.* 1831, Divinity.
			Major Rennel, Geog.		
					Sir Humph. Davy, *d.* 1829, Chemistry.
					Jer. Bentham *d.* 1832, 'Principles of Legislation.'
	Robt. Pollok, 1798-1827, 'Course of Time.'				
	Geo. Crabbe, *d.* 1832, 'The Borough,' &c.		Sir Jas. Mackintosh, 1766-1832, Hist. of England.		Adam Clarke, 1763-1832, Divinity, Criticism.

GERMAN.

Imagination.	*Fact.*	*Speculative and Scientific.*
800 Walafrid Strabo, *d.* 849, Poems, Theology. Otfried, Harmony of Gospels in rhyme.	800 Eginhard, *d.* 839, Life of Charlemagne, Annals. Nithard, *d.* 853, History of Wars of France.	800 Rabanus Maurus, 776-856, Theology. Gottschalk, *d.* 869, 'On Predestination.'
900 Hroswitha, Let. Comedies. Notger, Trans. of Psalms.	900 Regino, *d.* 915, Chronicles. Witikind, Hist. of Saxons.	900 Batherius, *d.* 974, Theology, Grammar.
1000 Witpo, 'Praise of Henry III.' Biography. Willeram, Francic Poems.	1000 Dithmar, *d.* 1018. Chron. of Saxon Emperors. Hermannus Contractus. Universal History. Mar. Scotus, 1028-1086, Chronicles. Adam of Bremen, Ecclesiastical History. Lambert, General Hist. Sigebert, *d.* 1113, Chron. Kosmas, 1045-1126 History of Bohemia.	1000
1100 Henry of Veldeck, Minnesinger.	1110 Berthold Constantiensis, Universal History. Otto, *d.* 1158, Chronicle. Helmold, *d.* 1170, Chron. of Slavi,	1100 Mangold, Theology.
1200 Günther, Poems. Frederic II., 1196-1254, 'De Arte Venandi.' Freydank, Poems.	1200 Arnold of Lubeck, Chronicle of Slavi.	1200 Epko of Repgow, 'Saxon Mirror,' (Law.) John Semeca, Law. Alb. Magnus, 1193-1280, Natural Philosophy.
300 Rüdger of Manesse, Collection of Ballads. Henry Frauenlob, Songs. Boner, Fables.	1300 Henrich von Rebdorf, Chronicle. Heinrich von Hervorden, Chronicle. Jacob von Königshofen, Chronicle. John Schildberger, History of Timour.	1300 John Tauler, Sermons. John Huss, 1376-1415, Theology.
1400 Felix Hämmerlein, Satires.	1400 Gobelin Persona, General History. Windeck, Life of Sigismund. John Stadweg, Chronicle.	1400 John von Gmünden, Astronomy.

	Imagination.	*Fact.*	*Speculative and Scientific.*
1400	Hans von Rosenplut. Poems. Heinrich von Alkmaar, 'Reinke de Voss.' Conrad Celtes, 1459-1508, Latin Poems, History of Nuremburg. Thos. Murner, 1475-1536, 'Rogues' Guild.'	Peter von Andlo, De Imperio Romano. Mar. Behaim, Geography. Breydenbach, Topogy. Conrad Botho, Chronicle.	Geo. Von. Peurbach, 1423-1461, Theory of Planets. Regiomontanus, 1436-1476, Astron., Mathemat. Nic. von Cusa, Mathemat. Thomas à Kempis, 1380-1471, Theology. Gabriel Brie, *d.* 1495, Theology. John Geyler, 1445-1510, Theology. John Trithemius, 1462-1516. Nat. Philosophy. Reuchlin, 1454-1522, Philology.
1500	Melc. Pfinzing, 1481-1535, 'Theuerdank.' Glareanus (H. L.) 1488-1563, Classics. Hans Sachs, 1494-1574, Poems. John Fischart, 1511-1581, Satires. G. Fabricius, 1516-1571, Lat. Pms. Topography. Rollenhagen, 1542-1609, Froschmäusler. Fr. Taubman, 1565-1613, Latin Poems.	Maximilian, *d.* 1508, Autobiography. Grünbeck, Lives of Emperors. Albert Kranz, *d.* 1517, History of Saxons, &c. B. Pirkheimer, 1480-1530, History, Poetry. John Aventin, 1466-1534, Annals of Bavaria. Con. Peutinger, 1465-1547, History and Geography, John Carion, 1499-1538, Comp. of History. John Sleidan, 1506-1556, Universal History. G. Tschudi, *d.* 1572, Helvetic Chronicle. Gerard Mercator, 1512-1594, Geography. Simon Schard, 1535-1573, Collec. German Hist. John Pistorius, 1544-1607, Collec. German Hist. Marq. Freher, 1565-1614, Hist. Germy & France.	J. Wimpfelingen, 1452-1528., Theol, Poems. Holoander, *d.* 1531, Law. Corn. Agrippa, 1486-1535, Physics, Theology. M. Luther, 1483-1546, Theology. Zwingle, 1484-1531, Theology. Melancthon, 1497-1560, Theology. Paracelsus, 1493-1541, Chemistry. Joac. Camerarius, 1500-1574, Philology. Conrad Gesner, 1516-1565, Natural History. Basil Faber, 1520-1576, Thes. Erud. Schol. Mar. Chemnitz, 1522-1586, Theology, Wm. Xylander, 1532-1576, Philology. Wesenbeck, 1531-1586, Law. Fred. Sylberg 1531-1596, Philology. Theod. Beza, 1519-1609, Theology, Philology. C. Ritterhuis, 1560-1613. Law.
1600	Martin Opitz, 1597-1639, Poems. James Balde, 1603-1668, Poems. A. Gryphius, 1616-1664, Tragedies.	P. Cluvier, 1580-1623, Geography. M. Goldast, 1576-1635, History. G. Calixtus, 1586-1656, Ecclesiastical History. Olearius, 1604-1685, Travels.	C. Schwenkfeld, *d.* 1616, Natural History. J. Buxtorf, 1555-1621, Philology, John Kepler, 1571-1631, Astronomy. B. von Helmont, 1577-1644, Chemistry. C. Scioppius, 1576-1649. Ars Critica. John Bayer, Uranometria, G. Barth, 1587-1658, Philology. Sol. Glass, 1593-1656, Philol. Sacra. Otto Guerike, 1602-1686, Air-Pump, &c.

Imagination.	*Fact.*	*Speculative and Scientific.*
1600 Paul Fleming, 1609-1640, Poems.	1600	1600 Her. Conring, 1606-1681, Antiquities.
	S. von Puffendorf, 1631-1694, History, Law.	Ez. Spanheim, 1629-1702, Numismatology.
Lohenstein, 1638-1683, Poems.	D. G. Morhoff, 1639-1691, Biography, History.	John Schilter, *d.* 1705, Antiquities.
1700 C. Gryphius, 1649-1706, Poems, Hist'y, Philology.	1700 H. Meibomius, 1638-1700, History.	1700 Ludolph, 1649-1711, Philology.
	C. Cellarius, 1638-1707, Geography, Antiq.	Leibnitz, 1646-1716, Mathematics, Metaphysics.
Von Canitz, 1654-1699, Poems.	C. Frankenstein, 1661-1717, History, Biog.	C. Thomasius, 1655-1728, Law.
	J. Arnold, 1665-1714, Ecclesiastical History.	F. Budæus, 1667-1729, Divinity.
	J. G. von Eccard, 1670-1730, General History.	G. E. Stahl, 1660-1734, Chemistry.
	J. A. Fabricius, 1668-1736, Bibliography.	F. Hoffman, 1660-1742, Medicine.
		J. Bernouilli, 1667-1747, Mathematics.
Gunther, 1695-1724, Poems	H. Freyer, Gen. History.	B. Hederick, 1675-1748, Philology.
	B. G. Struve, 1671-1738, History of Germany.	
	J. L. Mosheim, 1695-1755. Ecclesiastical History.	
Liscov, Satires,		J. M. Gessner, 1691-1761, Philology.
J. C. Gottsched, 1700-1766, Poems, Trag., Criticism.		A. G. Baumgarten, 1714-1751, Ethics, Metaph.
Hagedorn, 1708-1754, Fables.		J. J. Gessner, 1707-1787, Numismatology.
Haller, 1708-1777, 'The Alps.'		G. F. Meyer, 1711-1777, Philosophy.
J. E. Schlegel, *d.* 1759, Drama.		F. W. von Gleicken, 1714-1783, Nat. History.
E. C. Kleist, 1715-1759, Idylls.		J. Winkelmann, 1718-1768, Antiquity.
Gellert, 1715-1769, Fables.		Leon. Euler, 1707-1783, Mathematics.
Rabener, 1714-1770, Satir.	A. F. Büsching, 1724-1793, Geography.	
Gleim, *d.* 1803, Songs.	Frank, *d.* 1784, Chronol.	G. J. Zollikofer, 1730-1780. Sermons.
	Walch *d.* 1784, Ecclesiastical History.	J. A. E. Götze, 1731-1786, Entomology.
Klopstock, 1724-1803, 'The Messiah.'		Im. Kant, 1724-1804, Metaphysics.
Zachariæ, 1727-1777, Comic Poems.		
C. F. Weisse, Drama.		
J. G. Zimmerman, 1728-1795, 'On Solitude.'		
Götz, 1721-1781, Pastorals		
Ramler, 1725-1798, Odes.		
Dusch, 1727-1788, Poems,		
G. E. Lessing, 1729-1781, Drama, Fables.		
S. Gessner, 1730-1788, 'Death of Abel.'	C. Gatterer, *d.* 1799, Hist.	
Wieland, 1733-1813, Romances, Poems.		Semler, *d.* 1791, Theology.
Pfeffel, 1736-1809, Fables.	J. W. von Archenholz, 1745-1812, 'Seven Years' War.'	
G. A. Bürger, 1748-1794, Poems.		Pütter, Law of Nations.
I. H. Voss, 1751-1826, Novels.		
F. Schiller, 1750-1805, Drama.	Schröckh, *d.* 1808, Ecclesiastical History.	Adelung, *d.* 1807, Philology.
Kotzebue, 1761-1819, Drama.	Forster, *d.* 1798, Geography.	Lavater, 1741-1801, Physiognomy.
Goethe, 1749-1832, Drama, Tales Poems.	A. L. von Schlözer, *d.* 1809, History.	Werner, Geology.

	Imagination.	*Fact.*	*Speculative and Scientific.*
1800	F. Schlegel, 1773-1829, Novels, Poetry, Hist. &c. Ernst Schultze, 1787-1817, Elegies. E. T. W. Hoffman, *d.* 1822, Tales. A. Lafontaine, 1760-1831, Tales.	J. von Muller, *d.* 1809, Universal History. J. G. Eichhorn, *d.* 1827, History. Von Hammer, Orien. Hist. Körner. Niebuhr.	Herder, 1741-1803, Philosophy of History. Fichte, *d.* 1819, Metaphysics. F. H. Jacobi, *d.* 1819, Metaphysics. Blumenbach, Physiology. Schelling, Metaphysics.

FRENCH.

	Imagination.	*Fact.*	*Speculative and Scientific.*
500	Venan. Fortunatus, Latin Poetry.	Gregory of Tours, 554-595, History.	
600		Marculfe, 'Chartæ Regales,' &c.	
700		Fredegaire, Chronicle.	
800	Theodulph, *d.* 821, Hymns, Theology. Servatus Lupus, *d.* 862, Epistles. Hincmar, *d.* 882, Epistles. Abbon, 'Siege of Paris.'	Ado, *d.* 875, Chronicle.	Agobard, *d.* 840, Theology. Paschasius Radbert, 'Transubstantiation.'
900	Adalberon, *d.* 1030, Poetry.	Flodoard, 896-966, Chron. Dudon, Hist. of Norman Conquest in France.	
1000	Fulbert, *d.* 1029, Epistles.	Aimoin, *d.* 1008, History of France.	Gerbert, *d.* 1003, Geometry, Mathematics, &c. Abon, *d.* 1004, Arithmetic, and Astronomy. Berengarius, *d.* 1088, Theology.
1100	Wm. of Poictiers, 1071-1126, First Troubadour. Hildebert, 1057-1133, Poetry. Bechada, Norman Poetry, 'Gestes de Godefroi.' Geoffroi Gaimar, Anglo-Norm. Chron. in verse. Rob. Wace, 'Roman de Rou.' Fouques, a Troubadour. Alexandre of Bernai, Poetry, Fables.	Guibert, 1053-1124, Hist. of First Crusade. Pierre Theuthode, Hist. of Crusades. Marbodæus, *d.* 1123, Biography. Suger, 1082-1152, Life of Louis le Gros. Hugh de St. Victoire, 1097-1140, Geography, History, and Theology.	Anselm, 1033-1109, Scholastic. Pierre Abelard, 1079-1142, Theology. Bernard of Clairvaux, 1091-1153, Mystic. Peter Lombardus, *d.* 1164, Theology. Alain de l'Isle, *d.* 1202, Theology, Ethics.

Imagination.	*Fact.*	*Speculative and Scientific.*
1200 John Ægidius, Poem on Medicine. William le Breton, 'Deeds of Philip,' in verse. P. Gentier, 'Alexandrieda.' William de Lorris, 'Roman de la Rose.' Jean de Meun, Contin. of 'Roman de la Rose.' Esteve de Bezier, Last Troubadour.	1200 Pierre de Poictiers, Sacred History. Geoffrey de Villehardouin, Conq. of Constantinople Phil. Mouskes, *d.* 1263, Hist. of France in verse. W. Rubruquis, Traveller. Jean de Joinville, 1220-1318, Hist. of Louis IX.	1200 Vincentius of Beauvais, Encyclopædia. Rob. of Sorbonne, *d.* 1271, Theology.
1300 Peter Langtoft, Anglo Norman Chron. Philippe of Vitri, Translation of Ovid.	1300 John Froissart, 1337-1402, Chronicles.	1300 Bernard Gordon, Medicine John of Paris, *d.* 1306, Theology. W. Durand, *d.* 1333, Law. W. Occam, *d.* 1347, Law.
1400 Alain Chartier, *d.* 1458, Poetry Corbeil, Satire. D'Auvergne, *d.* 1508, Poems. Clement Marot, 1463-1525, Poems.	1400 Philip de Comines, 1445-1509, Hist. of his Times.	1400 Peter d'Ailly, 1350-1425, Astronomy. John Gerson, 1363-1429, Scholastic. Raymund de Sebunda, *d.* 1432, Theology. Henry of Balma, *d.* 1439, Mystic. James Lefevre, 1436-1537, Theology. Wm. Budæus, 1467-1540, Jurist.
1500 F. Rabelais, 1483-1553, Satires. J. du Bellay, 1492-1560, Poems. Steph. Jodelle, 1532-1573, Odes, Tragedies, &c. M. A. Muret, 1526-1585, Poems, Criticisms. Mich. de Montaigne, 1533-1592, Essays. Fran. Malherbe, 1556-1628, Odes.	1500 Guill. du Bellay, *d.* 1543, History of his Times. Jaques Amyot, 1514-1593, Translations. J. J. Scaliger, 1540-1609, History, Criticism, &c. J. A. de Thou, 1553-1617, History of France.	1500 J. C. Scaliger, 1484-1558, Philology. Du Bois, 1478-1555, Anat. Rob. Stephens, 1503-1559, Philology. P. Ramus, 1515-1572, Logic Seb. Castellio, 1515-1563, Philology. Jas. Cujacius, 1520-1590, Law. Lambinus, 1516-1572, Commentaries. Hen. Stephens, 1528-1590, Philology. F. Vieta, 1540-1603, Algebra. Pierre Charron, 1543-1603, Theology. Isaac Casaubon, 1559-1604, Philology.
1600 M. Reignier, 1573-1613, Satires.	1600 P. Matthieu, 1544-1621, History of France.	1600

Imagination.	*Fact.*	*Speculative and Scientific.*
1600	An. Du Chesne, 1584-1640, Collections of Histories.	1600 C. Salmasius, 1596-1658, History and Criticisms. Dennis Petau, 1583-1652, Chronology. P. Gassendi, 1592-1655, Philosophy. Des Cartes, 1596-1650, Metaphysics, Mathem,
J. Chapelain, 1595-1674, 'La Pucelle.' P. Corneille, 1606-1684, Drama. St. Evremond, 1613-1703, Literature.	Bochart, 1599-1667, Geographia Sacra.' Henry Spondanus, 1568-1643, History. S. Guicheron, 1607-1664, Hist. of House of Savoy. Henri Valesius, 1603-1696, Ecclesiastical History.	B. Pascal, 1623 1662, Divinity. D'Herbelot, 1626-1695. Orientalist. Cassini, 1625-1712, Astron.
Rochefoucault, 1603-1680, Reflexions. Molière, 1620-1673, Drama. La Fontaine, 1621-1695, Fables, Tales. Segrais, 1624-1701, Idyls. T. Corneille, 1625-1709, Drama. M. de Sevigne, 1626-1694, Letters.	Adr. Valesius, 1607-1692, 'Deeds of the Franks.'	
J. Racine, 1639, 1699, Drama. Boileau, 1636-1711, Satires.	L. Moreri, 1643-1680, Historical Dictionary. Tillemont, 1637-1698, Ecclesiastical History.	Huet, 1630-1721, Philosphy Bourdaloue, 1632-1704, Sermons. La Bruyère, 1636-1696, 'Characters.' Malbranche, 1633-1715, 'Search after Truth.'
1700 Regnard, 1647-1709, Comedies. Galland, 1646-1715, Trans. of Arabian Nights. Fenelon, 1651-1715, 'Telemachus,' &c. Deshoulières, 1638-1694, Elegies.	1700	1700 P. Bayle, 1647-1706, Dictionary. Hardouin, 1646-1729, Criticism. And. Dacier, 1651-1722, Philology. Anne Dacier, 1651-1720, Philology.
	J. Marsollier, 1647-1724, History, various. Fleury, 1653-1723, Ecclesiastical History. G. Daniel, 1649-1728, History of France. Valincourt, 1653-1730, Biography. Vertot, 1655-1735, Hist. Paul Rapin, 1661-1725, History of England.	Tournefort, 1656-1708, Botany. Fontenelle, 1657-1756, 'Plurality of Worlds.' Montfaucon, 1655-1741, Antiquities. Massillon, 1663-1742, Sermons.
J. B. Rousseau, 1671-1741, Odes. Crebillon, 1674-1762, Tragedies. Ren. Le Sage, 1677-1747, 'Gil Blas.' P. N. Destouches, 1680-1754, Comedies. J. B. Grécourt, 1683-1743, Odes, Tales, &c.	Bossuet, 1662-1704, Hist., Sermons. C. Rollin, 1661-1741, Ancient History.	Folard, 1669-1752, Strategy. Saurin, 1677-1730, Sermons.

	Imagination.	*Fact.*	*Speculative and Scientific.*
1700	Marivaux, 1688-1763, Novels. Voltaire, 1695-1778, Tragedy, Poetry, Hist. &c. J. J. Rousseau, 1712-1778, 'Emile,' 'Heloise,' &c. Diderot, 1713-1784, 'Encyclopedie,' Novels. Bernis, 1715-1794, Poems. Favart, *d.* 1762, Comic Operas. Louis Racine, *d.* 1763, Poems. J. J. Barthelemy, 1716-1795, 'Anacharsis.' Marmontel, 1719-1799, Tales. Gresset, *d.* 1777, Elegies. Dorat, *d.* 1780, Novels. Florian, 1755-1794, Tales. Beaumarchais, *d.* 1799, Comedies.	C. I. F. Henault, 1685-1770, Chronicles, History. C. Villaret, 1715-1766, History of France. L. P. Anquetil, 1723-1808, History. Mart. Bouquet, *d.* 1754, Recueil d'Histoireks. A. Goguet, *d.* 1758, 'Origin of Laws, Arts, &c.' Larcher, 1726-1812, Trans. of Herodotus. Crevier, *d.* 1765, Ancient History. Guyot, *d.* 1771, Ecclesiastical History. J. De Guignes, 1721-1800, History of the Huns. D'Anville, 1702-1782, Geography. G. Raynal, 1711-1796, Hist. of East and West Indies. C. F. X. Millot, 1726-1785, History.	Montesquieu, 1698-1755, 'Esprit des Loix.' Réaumur, 1683-1757, Natural History. Houbigant, 1686-1783, Criticism, Philology. Girard, *d.* 1748, 'Synonymes.' Buffon, 1707-1788, Natural History. De Brosses, 1709-1777, Philology, History. Helvetius, 1715-1771, 'De l'Esprit.' D'Aubenton, 1716-1799, Natural History. N. Vattel, *d.* 1770, 'Law of Nations.' D'Alembert, *d.* 1783, 'Encyclopedie.' La Grange, Mathematics. Bailly, 1736-1793, Hist., Astronomy. Lavoisier, 1743-1794, Chemistry. Montucla, 1725-1799, Mathematics. Turgot, Polit. Economy. Mirabeau, Politics. Fourcroi, *d.* 1809, Chem. J. Lalande, *d.* 1807, Astron.
1800	B. St. Pierre, 'Paul and Virginia.' Madme. de Genlis, Novels. Mdme. Cottin, 1772-1807, Tales. Delille, *d.* 1813, 'L'Homme des Champs.' Madame de Staël, 1768-1817, Corinne,' &c.	Denon, *d.* 1825, travels in Egypt.	Volney, 1755-1820, Travels, Philology, &c. Haüy, *d.* 1822, Crystallography. La Place, *d.* 1827, Mathematics. Guyton Morveau, Chem. Cuvier, *d.* 1832, Nat. Hist. Dumont, Legislation. P. L. Courier, Politics.

SPANISH AND PORTUGUESE.

P. *is prefixed for Portuguese.*

	Imagination.	*Fact.*	*Speculative and Scientific.*
500			Anian, Law. Fulgentius Ferrandus, Canon Law. Martin, *d.* 580, Ethics.
600		John of Biclair, *d.* 620, Chronicle. Isidore, *d.* 636, Chron. de Goth.	Ildefonso, *d.* 667, Polemics.
800		Eulogius, *d.* 859, Martyrology. Alvarez, Biog. of Eulogius.	

Imagination.	*Fact.*	*Speculative and Scientific.*
P. 1100 Egas Monez, Songs. P. GonzaloHermiguez, do.	1100	1100
1200 Gonzalo Berceo, Rhymes.	1200 Rodrigo Ximenez, *d.* 1245, History of Spain.	1200 R. De Penafort, 1175-1275, Decretals. Alphonso X., *d.* 1284, Astronomy, Alchemy. Raimund Lullo, 1236-1315, Theology, Chemistry, &c.
1300 Juan Manuel, *d.* 1362, Romances.	1300	1300
1400 Villena, *d.* 1434, Trans. Virgil and Dante. E. de. Villena, 1434, Moral Drama. Juan de Mena, 1412-1456, Poems. L. de Mendoza, 1398-1458, Poems. Perez de Guzman, Lyrics. Juan de la Enzina, Pastoral Dramas.	1400 Diez de Games, Biography R. de Zamora, 1407-1470, History of Spain. Fern. del Pulgas, Biog. of Ferdinand and Isabella	1400 J. de Torquemada, *d.* 1468, Sermons, Criticism. Fras. Ximenes, 1437-1517, Polyglot Bible.
1500 Lope de Rueda, Comedies. Torres Naharro, Comedy. Juan Boscan, *d.* 1544, Sonnets. P. Ber. Ribeyro, Eclogues. Garcilaso de la Vega, 1503-1536, Poems. P. Saa de Miranda, 1495-1558, Lyrics. Juan de la Cueva, Art of Poetry. P. Gil Vicente, *d.* 1557. Comedy. J. de Montemayor, 1520-1561, Romance. Ant. Ferreira, 1528-1569, Elegies. Diego de Mendoza, *d.* 1575, Poems, History. P. Camoens, 1524-1579, 'The Lusiad.' Luis de Leon, 1527-1591, Lyric Poems. Fern. de Herrera, *d.* 1578, Classical Poems. P. Rodriguez Lobo, Romances, Pastorals, &c. P. P. de A. Caminha, *d.* 1595, Epigrams, Pastorals. C. de Castillejo, *d.* 1596, Romantic Poems. A. de Ercilla, 1533-1600, 'Araucana.' Geron. Bermudez, *d.* 1589, Tragedy. L. de Argensola, 1565-1613, Tragedy, History.	1500 P. Damian Goez, History, Travels. P. Joao de Barros, *d.* 1570, 'Hist. Portugu. in India.' A. Zarate, 'Discov. of Peru.' A. de Morales, 1513-1590, History of Spain. J. Acosta, 1547-1600, Hist. of West Indies. Gonzalvo Illescas, *d.* 1580, Lives of the Popes. Luis Marmol, Description of Africa. Jeron. Zurita, 1513-1580, History of Arragon. Estevan Garibay, History of Spain. Juan Mariana, 1537-1624, Hist., Chronology, &c. Blanca, History of Spain.	1500 Perez de Oliva, *d.* 1533, Ethics. J. Luis Vives, 1492-1540, Philosophy, Theology. Ant. de Guevara, *d.* 1544, Ethics, Epistles. P. A. Govea, 1505-1565, Law. Ant. Agostino, 1516-1586, Theology, Law. S. des Brosses, 1523-1600, Grammar. P. D. de Andrada, 1528-1535, Theology. Luis Molina, 1535-1600, Metaphysics. J. Guevara, 1541-1622, Publicist.

Imagination.	*Fact.*	*Speculative and Scientific.*
P. 1500 Jeron. Cortereal, Poems. Cervantes, 1549-1616, 'Don Quixote.'	1500 J. G. de Mendoza, Hist. of China.	1500 J. Valverda, Anatomy.
1600 Bart. de Argensola, 1566-1631, Tragedy, History. F. Quevedo, 1570-1645, Tales, Satires. L. Congora, 1565-1638, Poems. Lope de Vega, 1562-1635, Drama. J. P. de Montalvan, *d.* 1639, Tragedy. M. de Madrigal, Romances. P Man. de Faria e Sousa, *d.* 1649, Pastoral Poems. L. V. de Guevara, *d.* 1646, 'El Diablo Coxuelo.' Vic. Espinel, 1545-1634, Elegies. Calderon, 1601-1667, Drama. L. Ulloa, *d.* 1660, Poems. P. A. B. Bacellar, *d.* 1663, Sonnets. P. Matheo Ribeiro, Romance. M. de Villegas, 1595-1669, Anacreontics. P. F. de Vasconcellos, Poems. P. R. de Macedo, *d.* 1682, do. P. Viol. do Ceo, 1601-1693, do. P. F. da Castanheira, Novel. P. A. Nunhes da Sylva, Sonnets.	1700 Her. y Tordesillas, 1565-1625, History of Spain. P. A. de Meneses, *d.* 1617. History of Augustines. P. F. Andrada, Chronicle of John III. P. B. de Brito, 1570-1617, History of Portugal. P. A. de Andrada, *d.* 1633, Travels in Thibet and Cathay. Fra. de Sandoval, History. Jayme Bleda, History of Moors in Spain. C. Acuna, 1597-1641, 'Descrip. of River Amazon. P. E. de Almeyda, *d.* 1646, History of Ethiopia. P. J. F. de Andrada, 1597-1657, Life of John de Castro, Comic Poetry. Nic. Antonio, 1617-1672, Bibliotheca Hispanica. P. Alb. Coelho, *d.* 1658, 'Wars of Brazil.' Ant. de Solis, 1611-1686, Hist. of Conq. Mexico.	
1700 Fran. Candarno, *d.* 1709, Drama. Ant. de Zamora, Comedy. P. Xav. de Meneses, 1673-1743, 'Henriqueide,' Epic Poem. Ignacio de Luzan, *d.* 1754, Art of Poetry. Tomas de Yriarte, *d.* 1771, Fables, &c. P. A. de Barros Pereira, Poems. P. Manoel da Coste, Poems. V. Garcia de la Huerta, Tragedy. P. P. Correo Garçao, Lyric Poems.	1700 J. Ferreras, 1652-1735, History of Spain. P. Barbosa Machado, Dictionary of Learned Men Velasquez, *d.* 1772, Hist. of Castilian Poetry. P. Figoeireda, Eccl. History. Munoz, Hist. of America.	1700 Feyjoo, 1765, Ethics, Criticism. A. Ulloa, 1716-1795, Mathematician.

Imagination.	*Fact.*	*Speculative and Scientific.*
1700 Leon de Arroyal, Odes. P. Paulino de Vasconcellos, Sonnets. Mel. Valdez, Odes, Lyrics. P. Cathar. de Sousa, Trag'y.	1700 Cavanilles, Annals.	1700 Ruiz, Botany. Pavon, Flora Peruviana. P. J. H. Magalhaens, *d.* 1790, Natural Philosophy. Felix de Azara, Zoology. J. N. de Azara, 1731-1804, Antiquity.
1800 G. Jovellanos, 1744-1811, 'Agrarian Law.' P. Tol. da Almeida, Satires. Fern. de Moratin, *d.* 1828, Comedies. M. Garcia de Villanueva, 'On the Theatre.' J. H. Davila, General Literature.	1800 J. A. Llorente, History of Inquisition. Jose Antonio Conde, History of Moors in Spain.	1800

DUTCH.

Imagination.	*Fact.*	*Speculative and Scientific.*
1200 J. van Maerlant, 1235-1300, Poems, 'Rymbybel.' Melis Stoke, Poetic Chron.	1200	1200
1300 Jan van Helen, Poems, Chronicles. Heij. van Holland, Poems. Claes Willems, Poems.	1300	1300 Gerard Groot, Theology.
1400 J. Wilt, Trans. Bœthius. Dirk van Munster, 'Christian Mirror.' Lambert, Goetman, 'Mirror of Youth.'	1400 Edmund Dinter, *d.* 1448, Chronicles of Brabant. P. vander Heyden, 1393-1473, Chronicles.	1400 J. W. Gansfoet, Theo. Rud. Agricola, 1442-1485, Philosophy, Hist. &c.
1500 A. Byns, Religious Poems. Jan Fruitiers, Poems and Prose. J. Secundus, 1511-1536, Amatory Poems. Dirk Koornhert, 1522-1590, Transl. Homer. P. van Marnix, Odes, Songs. R. Visscher, Epigrams. Hendrick Spieghel, Didactic Poems.	1500 S. Pighius, 1520-1604. 'Roman Annals.' A. Schott, 1552-1629, History of Spain.	1500 Erasmus, 1467-1536, Theology, Literature, &c. J. Heurnius, 1543-1601, Medicine. C. Kiliaan, *d.* 1607, Dictionary. Justus Lipsius, 1547-1606, Philology. Sim. Stevinus, *d.* 1633, Hydrostatics, Mathem. H. Erpenius, 1584-1624, Orientalist.
1600 G. Brederode, 1585-1637, Comedies, &c. D. R. Kamphuizen, 1586-1626, Religious Poems. Daniel Heins, 1580-1655, Poems, Philology.	1600	1600

Imagination.	*Fact.*	*Speculative and Scientific.*
1600 J. Cats, 1577-1660, Drama. P. C. Hooft, 1587-1647, Tragedy, Odes, Hist. of the Netherlands. G. van Baerle, (Barlæus,) 1584-1648, Latin Poems. Just van Vondel, 1587, 1679, Tragedies. M. Visscher, Trans. Tasso. Jan van Heemskerk, 'Arcadia.' J. Westerbaen, 1599-1669, Epigrams. Cons. Huygens, 1596-1687, Epigrams. Jer. Decker, 1610-1666. Elegies. D. Joncktijs, *d.* 1654, Amatory Poems. Nicolas Heins, 1620-1681, Poems, Philology. Jan de Brune, 'Whetstone of Wit.' Jan Vos, Drama, Epigrams Reinier Anslo, 1622-1669, 'Plague of Naples.'	H. de Groot (Grotius.) 1583-1645, Hist., Theology, Poetry, &c. Ger. Brandt, 1626-1685, Hist. of Reformation. Cau, Collec. of Batavian History. J. G. Grævius, 1632-1703, Roman Antiquities. J. Perizonius, 1631-1715, History.	J. Golius, 1596-1667, Orientalist. Voetius, 1589-1676, Polemics. Beverwyk, 1594-1647, Medicine. Diemerbroek, 1609-1674, Anatomy. J.F. Gronovius, 1611-1671, Philology. J. Leusden, 1614-1699, Philology. F. Burmann, 1628-1679, Theology. Chr. Huygens, 1629-1695, Mathem., Mechanics. B. Spinoza, 1632-1677, Theology. Swammerdam, 1637-1680, Natural History. A. Leuwenhoek, 1632-1723. Natural History.
1700 P. Francius, 1645-1704, Latin Poetry. J. A. Vander Goes, 1647, 1684, Drama. Eliz. Wolff, Novels. Loosjes, Novels. Bellamy, 1757-1786, Odes, Klein, Lyrics. Van Alphen, Odes.	1700 J. Gronovius, 1645-1716, Greek Antiquities. P. Bondam, Collection of Batavian History. Simon Styl, History of Netherlands.	1700 F. Ruysch, 1639-1731, Anat. G. Bidloo, 1649-1713, Anat. C. Vitringa, 1659-1722, Theology. Binkershoek, 1663-1743, Law. H. Boerhaave, 1668-1738, Medicine. Hemsterhuis, 1685-1766, Philology. A. Schultens, 1686-1750, Philology. Gravesande, 1688-1742, Mathematics. Chr. Hecht, 1696-1748, Philology. B. S. Albinus, 1683-1771, Anatomy. Oudendorp, 1696-1761, Philology. W. Otto Reiz, 1702-1769, Law. D. Gaubius, 1705-1780, Medicine. Hoogeveen, 1712-1794, Philology. G. van Swieten, 1700-1772, Medicine. P. Camper, 1722-1789, Anatomy. D. Ruhnken, 1723-1798, Philology. Valckenaer, Philology.

Imagination.	*Fact.*	*Speculative and Scientific.*
1800	1800	1800 D. Wyttenbach, *d.* 1808 Philology.
Hincopen, Odes.		
Helmers, *d.* 1831, Poems.		
Nieuwland, Poems.		
Borger, Odes.	Te Water, History.	
Bilderdyk, Dramas, Odes, &c.	Engelberts, Ancient Hist. of Netherlands.	Van Kampen, Statistics.
Tollens, Poems.	Kluits, Hist. of Holland.	De Jonge, Antiquities.
Da Costa, Sacred Poems.	Westendorp, History.	Hamaker, Orientalist.
Wilderbosch, Odes.	Ypey, Ecclesiastical Hist.	Vander Palm, Literature.

SWEDEN, DENMARK, AND ICELAND.

S. Sweden, D. Denmark, Ic. Iceland,

Imagination.	*Fact.*	*Speculative and Scientific.*
Ic. 900 Hjalti, Poems.	900	900
Ic. 1100 Thorwald, Ballads.	1100	1100
	Ic. Aro, *d.* 1148, Annals of Iceland.	
	D. Saxo, Grammaticus, *d.* 1204, Hist. of North. Nations.	D. Sunesen, Jurist.
		D. Axel, Theology.
Ic. Sæmund, *b.* 1156. The Elder Edda.	D. Sueno, Hist. of Denmark.	
Ic. 1200 Snor. Sturleson, *d.* 1241, Younger Edda, Hist. of Norway.	1200	1200
Ic. Suerren, Tales.		
	D. Sturla Thoridsen, History of Norway.	
1400.	1400	S. 1400 Bryn. Karlsson *d.* 1430, Instruction to kings and Princes.
	S. Eric Olai, History of Goths and Swedes.	
1500	S. 1500 John Magnus, *d.* 1544, Hist. of Sweden.	1500
	S. Olaus Magnus, Customs of Northern Nations.	
	S. P. Lagerloof, 1538-1599, History North of Europe.	
	Ic. Arn. Jonas, 1545-1640, Hist. of Iceland &c.	D. Tycho Brahe, 1546-1601, Astronomy.
		D. Ursus, *d.* 1600, Do.
1600	1600	S. 1600 P. Kirsten, 1577-1640, Orientalist.
		D. G. Bartholine, 1585-1629, Anatomy, Theo.
D. Anders Arrebo, *b.* 1587, Religious Poetry.		D. Ole Worm, 1588-1654. Antiquities, Philo.
	D. J. J. Pontanus, 1591-1640, Danish Hist.	
D. Anders Bording, *b.* 1619, Poems.		
S. Stiernhjelm, Epic. Poem, 'Hercules.'		
	Ic. Torfæus, 1639-1720, Hist. of Norway.	
		S. Ol. Rudbeck, 1630-1702 Botany, Anat., &c.
D. 1700 Thos. Kingo, *b.* 1634, Hymns.	1700	D. 1700 J. C. Sturmius, 1635-1703, Phys., Mathem.

	Imagination.		*Fact.*		*Speculative and Scientific.*
1700		S. 1700	John Peringskiold, 1654-1720, History.	1700	
		D.	Arne Magnussen, *b.* 1663, Collec. Hist.		
		D.	Albert Thura, Hist.		
D.	L. Holberg, 1684-1754, Drama, Satire, Hist.	D.	Hans Gram, *d.* 1748, History.		
D.	Ch. Falster, 1690-1752, Satirist.				
		D.	Langebek, *d.* 1775, Collec. Danish Hist.	S.	Linnæus, 1707-1778, Botany.
S.	Olof Dalin, 1708-1763, Poetry, History.	D.	Pontoppidan, *d.* 1764. Origines Havnienses.		
		S.	Lagerbring, *d.* 1781, History.		
D.	Snedorf, 1724-1764, Poems.			S.	Wallerius, *d.* 1785, Mineralogy.
				D.	Oeder, Flora Danica.
D.	Tullin, Lyrics.	D.	P. T. Suhm, 1720-1798, Hist. of Denmark.	S.	Ihre, Dictionary.
D.	John Ewald, 1743-1781, Tragedy, Lyrics.				
D.	J. H. Wessel, Humorous Poems.				
S.	Bellerman, 1741-1796, Lyrics.				
D.	H. Tode, 1736-1806, Dramas, Fables.				
D.	Samsoe, 1759-1796, Tragedies.				
D.	P. A. Heiberg, *b.* 1758, Drama.				
S.	S. Elgström, *d.* 1810, Poems.				
Ic. 1800	Thorlacksen, *d.* 1819, Transl. Milton.	D. 1800	Malte Brun, *d.* 1826, Geography.	1800	
D.	C. L. Sander, Dramas.				
		S.	Thorild, Travels.		
D.	Jens. Baggesen, *d.* 1826, Lyrics.			S.	Berzelius, Chemistry.
				D.	Rask, Orientalist.
D.	Oehlenschlager, Poems.	S.	Afzelius, Iceland Records.	S.	Wotterstadt, 'On Yellow Fever.'
D.	B.S. Ingermann, Lyrics.				
S.	Atterbome, Poems.	S.	Hallenberg, History.	S.	Liliegren, Northern Antiquities.
S.	Tegner, Romances, &c.	S.	Graaberg, Statistics.		
		S.	Blexell, Topography.	S.	Norberg, Orientalist.

POLISH.

	Imagination.		*Fact.*		*Speculative and Scientific.*
1200		1290	Vinc. Kadlubek, *d.* 1226, History of Poland.	1200	
			Boguphalus, *d.* 1253, Chronicle of Poland.		
			Martin Polonus, *d.* 1278, Chronicle of Popes and Emperors.		Vitellio, Optics.
1400		1400	Dlugiossus, 1415-1480, History of Poland.	1400	
1500		1500		1500	N. Copernicus, 1472-1543, Astronomy.
			Cawalenzewski, Chronicles		Lucas Gornicki, Ethics.
			Bielski, do.		Rey of Naglowic, 1515-1568, Ethics.
	Kochanowski, 1530-1584, Dithyrambics.				
			Stryjkowski, Chron. of Poland and Russia.		

Imagination.	*Fact.*	*Speculative and Scientific.*
1600 Sarbiewski, 1595-1640, Latin Poetry.	1600 Ab. Bzovius, 1567-1637, Ecclesiastical Annals. Lubienetski, 1623-1675, Hist. of Reformation.	1600 John Maccov, *d.* 1644, Theology. Przipcov, 1590-1670, Do.
1700 Nartuszewicz, *d.* 1796, Poetry and History.	1700 Dogiel, Coll. Hist. Poland. Mizler, Do.	1700
1800 Krasicki, Poems, Romances. Boguslawski, Drama. Bronikowski, Novels. Bernatowicz, Do. Bulgarin, Do. Mickiewicz, Poems. Odyniec, Drama.	1800 Lach Szmyrna, Travels. Potocki, Do.	1800 Linde, Lexicon.

RUSSIAN.

[The Russian has been in use as the language of literature scarcely more than a century. Almost all books used in Russia were written in the ancient Sclavonic tongue, which does not greatly differ from Russian, but more closely resembles the languages spoken in Servia, and in the other provinces near the Save and Danube. The first printing-office in Russia was established in 1553.]

Imagination.	*Fact.*	*Speculative and Scientific.*
1000	1000 Nestor of Kiew, 1056-1115, Chronicles of Russia.	1000 Yaroslaf, Code of Laws.
1100 The Expedition of Ighor, a celebrated Poem, Author Unknown.	1100 Theodosius, *d.* 1120, Annals. Sylvester, *d.* 1123, Chronicles of Russia. Simeon of Susdal, *d.* 1206, Chronicles of Russia.	1100
1200	1200 John of Novgorod, Hist. of Russia.	1200

[The blank of nearly four centuries arises from the oppression of the Mongols, who held Russia from 1223 to 1477. They destroyed almost all ancient books, and repressed the rising spirit of knowledge which a close connexion with the Greeks was then introducing into Russia.]

Imagination.	*Fact.*	*Speculative and Scientific.*
1500	1500	1500 Sudebnek, Code of Laws.
1600 Simeon of Polotsk, Poems. Spiritual Dramas.	1600	1600 Demetrius of Rostoff, Theo., Spiritual Dramas.
1700 Cantemir, 1708-1744, Satirical Poems. Lomonosoff, 1711-1765, Poetry, Hist., Science. Tredianoffski, Poems. Popofski, Transl. Pope. Sumarokoff, 1718-1777, Drama. Kheraskoff, 1733-1807, 'The Russiad.'	1700 Khilkoff, Hist. of Russia. V. Tatischeff, *d.* 1750. Chronicles of Russia. Cherbatoff, History. Golikoff, Do.	1700 Théophanes, Sermons. Plato, 1737-1812, Sermons.

	Imagination.	*Fact.*	*Speculative and Scientific.*
1700	Kostroff. *d.* 1796, Transl. the Iliad. Petroff, 1736-1799, Transl. the Eneid. Kniajnin, 1742-1794, Drama. J. Khemnitzer, 1744-1784, Fables. Klushin, Comedies. Ephimieff, Comedies. Ablesimoff, Operas. G.R. Derjavin, 1743-1816, Lyric Poetry. H. Bogdanovitch, 1743-1803, 'Dushenka,' Poems. Vizin, 1745-1792, Comedies, Tales. Nicoleff, Tragedies.	1700 Muravieff, 1757-1816, History, Didactics. Eugenius, History.	1700 P. S. Pallas, 1741-1811 Natural History.
1800	Maikoff, Comic Poems. Dmitrieff, Lyrics, Fables. Ozeroff, *d.* 1816, Tragedies. P. Sumarokoff, Poems, Tales. V. A. Jukofski, *b.* 1783, Poems. Milonoff, *d.* 1821, Satires. Batiushkoff, Trans. Tibullus. Gneditch, Trans. Iliad, Odes. Kryloff, Fables.	1800 Karamsin, *b.* 1765, Hist. of Russia. Kachenofski, History. G. Glinka, History. Kotzebue, Voyage of Discovery. Gretch, Hist. of Russian Literature. Timkowski, Journey to China.	1800 Shishkoff, Criticism. Augustin, Sermons.

ARABIAN, PERSIAN, AND TURKISH.

P. Persian. T. Turkish. Those unmarked are Arabian.

	Imagination.	*Fact.*	*Speculative and Scientific.*
600	Mahomet, Koran. Lebid, 622-757, Poems. Zohair, Poems. Kais El Ameri, or Amrulkais, Poems.	600	600 Aharun, Medicine.
700	Abun Massab, Poems. Abunowas, 762-810, Poems. Rehashi, Poems. Abu Obeid, *d.* 838, Fables.	700 Muham. ben Omar, Hist.	700 Jafar, Chemistry, Abu Hanifah, 699-767, Theology.
800	A. Temam, 804-845, Poems. Bochteri, 821-882, Anthol.	Wahab, Travels. Abuzeid, Travels. I. Kotaibah, *d.* 889, Hist. Abu Jafar, 838-922, Hist. Honain ben Isaac, *d.* 874, Translations from Greek.	800 Asmai, 740-830, Theology. Kendi, Philosophy. J. ben Serapion, Medicine. Almamon Astronomical Tables. Bahali. *d.* 835, Etymology. Alfragan, Astronomy. Nasir Khosru, Metaphys. Albumazar, 805-885, Mathematics, Astronomy. Bochari, 810-870, 'The Sahih,' Traditions. Geber, Chemistry.

Imagination.	*Fact.*	*Speculative and Scientific.*
800 Abu Mohammed Abdallah, Literature.		
900 Ibn Doraid *d.* 931, Poems. Almotanabbi, *d.* 965, Poems.	900 Said ben Batrik, 876-937, General History. Eutychius, History. Massudi, *d.* 957, History and Geography. Ibn Haukal, Geography.	900 Albategni, Astronomy. Rases, *d.* 922, Medicine. Ben Musa, Mathematics. Azophi, Astronomy. Alfarabi, *d.* 954, Aristotelian Philosophy. Geuhari, *d.* 998, Aristotelian Philosophy.
P. 1000 Ferdusi, 932-1020, 'Shah Nameh,' epic poem. Abul Ola, 973-1057, Poems.	1000 Almuyadad, History of Saracens in Sicily.	1000 Achmet, Treatise on Dreams. Ibn Mesua, Medicine. Avicenna, 980-1038, Philosophy, Medicine. Abulcasis, Medicine. Jelaleddin, Correction of Calendar. Arzachel, Astronomy.
1100 Tograi, *d.* 1119, Poems. Hariri, 1054-1121, Moral Poems. P. Feleki, *d.* 1181, Poems. P. Khakani, *d.* 1186, Poems. P. Anwari, *d.* 1200, Poems. Jaafar ebn Tofail, *d.* 1198, 'Hai ben Yokdan,' a novel. I. Elfaredh, *d.* 1234, Poems.	1100 Algazel, Antiquities, &c. Ben Idris, *b.* 1099, Geog.	1100 Gazali, 1058-1112, Aristotelian Philosophy. Alhazin, Optics. Tabrizi, *d.* 1136, Commentaries. Alchabit, Optics, Astron. A. Zohar, *d.* 1168, Medic. Averroes, *d.* 1206, Aristotelian Philosophy.
1200 P. Saadi, 1193-1291, 'Gulistan,' 'Bostan.' Elfaragi, Poems.	1200 Bohadin, Life of Saladin. Abdollatif, Topography of Egypt. Abuldem, *d.* 1244, History. El Harawi, Travels. Abulfarage, 1226-1286, Universal History. Elmacin, *d.* 1302, History of Saracens. P. Fadlallah, History of Moguls.	1200 A. Baca, *d.* 1219, Arithm. Caswin *d.* 1274, Natural History. Beithar, *d.* 1246, Botany, Medicine. P. Nasireddin, 1201-1273, Astronomy.
1300	1300 Abulfeda, 1273-1332, Geography, History. Novairi, *d.* 1331, Universal History. Mohammed Ibn Batuta, Travels. Ibn al Wardi, *d.* 1358, Geography.	1300 E. Hajan, *d.* 1344, Gram.

ALPHABETICAL TABLES.

TAB. I.

REFERRING TO THE FOUNDATION AND PROGRESS OF THE PRINCIPAL

KINGDOMS, STATES, CITIES, &c.

[For the present Statistics, see the article under that head. For the names of Sovereigns, &c. see Chronological Table.]

A

Alabama, one of the United States, formerly constituted a part of Western Georgia; made a territory, 1800, divided again, and the eastern part called Alabama, by act of Congress, 1817; admitted into the Union, 1818.

Albany, N. Y., founded by the Dutch, (first called Fort Orange) 1614; incorporated, 1686.

Alexandria, city of, in Egypt, founded by Alexander, 332, B. C.; taken by the Romans, 31. B. C.; by the Turks, A. D. 1515.

Algiers, city of, and Mahometan state; rose into consequence during the middle ages; was attacked by Charles V., 1541; bombarded by the French, 1683; by the Spanish, 1783; by the British, 1816; at war with the United States, 1816; taken by the French, 1830.

America. See Discoveries. Tab. II. &c.

Amsterdam, city of, first mentioned, A. D. 1272.

Annapolis, seaport of Nova Scotia, founded by the French, 1608.

Annapolis, the capital of Maryland, founded, 1692.

Antwerp, first mentioned in history, 517.

Aquitaine, a principality 1362; annexed to France, 1730.

Argos, (in Greece,) the kingdom of, founded by Inachus 1586, B. C.

Arkansas, N. A., first settlement in, by the French, 1685; made a territory of the United States, 1819.

Arragon, a kingdom, (in Spain,) 912; united to Castile, 1479.

Assyrian Empire, was founded either by Nimrod or Ashur, about 2204, B C.; divided into the kingdoms of Babylon and Nineveh, 747, B. C.

Athens, Greece, founded by Cecrops, an Egyptian, 1556, B. C.

Austria, a duchy, 1156; an empire, (See Germany,) 1804.

B

Babylon, founded by Nimrod, 2204, B. C.; taken by Cyrus, 588, B. C.; by Alexander, 333. B. C.

Bagdad, built by Almanzor the Caliph, 762; and is still a place of great trade.

Baltimore, Md., founded, 1729. Population in 1790, 13,503; in 1800, 26,514.

Bavaria, made a duchy, 1180; a kingdom, by Bonaparte, 1805.

Belgium, annexed to Holland, 1813; revolted and became an independent kingdom, 1830.

Berne, in Switzerland, made an imperial city, 1290.

Bohemia, kingdom of, founded, 1630.

Boston, the capital of Massachusetts founded, 1630; evacuated by the British army, March 17, 1776. Population of, in 1800, 24,937; in 1810, 32,250; in 1820, 42,526; in 1830, 61,392.

Bourbon,	made a duchy,	1336
Brabant,	—— ——	1620
Brandenburgh,	—— ——	1526

(the elector became king of Prussia, 1701.)

Brazil, eastern and central part of South America, discovered by Cabral, 24th April, 1500; St. Salvador founded by Souza, the first Portuguese governor, 1549; invaded by the Dutch, 1624; evacuated by them, 1654; gold mines discovered, 1692; Rio de Janeiro taken by the French, 1711; Montevideo founded, 1723; treaty of limits with Spain, 1750; seat of government fixed at Rio, 1763; declared independent of Portugal by the prince regent, afterwards the emperor, Pedro, Dec. 14, 1815; declared an empire but with popular representation, 1822.

Brittany, made a duchy 874; annexed to France, 1150.

Buenos Ayres, country of, S. A., discovered, 1515; city of, founded by Pedro de Mendoza, 1534; Buen Esphranza and Assumption founded, 1536; governments of Pararia and Paraguay separated, 1620; the whole country erected into a vice-royalty, 1787: taken by the British, who kept it one year, 1806; the Argentine Provinces declared themselves independent, and Buenos Ayres made the capital, 1816.

Burgundy, a duchy, 890; a kingdom, 914; united to Germany, 1035; disunited and divided into four sovereignties, 1074; after several revolutions again united, and now forms a part of France and Switzerland.

of the Directory and the two Councils Sept. 22, 1795. Consulate established, (Bonaparte) Nov. 9, 1799. Bonaparte declared emperor, Dec. 2, 1804; abdicated, April 4, 1814; do. a second time, June 22, 1815, when the House of Bourbon was restored; (Louis XVIII.) Revolution of 1830 commenced July 27-29. Louis Philip I. (house of Orleans) *elected* constitutional king.

Geneva, republic of, founded 1512.

Genoa, ——— ——— 1096;—annexed to the French empire 1805; transferred to the king of Sardinia, 1814.

Georgia, one of the United States first settled by a colony under general Oglethorpe, 1733. Constitution ratified May 29, 1798.

Germany was anciently divided into several independent States, which made no figure in history till B. C. 25, when they withstood the attempts to subdue them made by the Romans; who conquered some parts, but were at length expelled, about A. D. 290. A great part of this country was conquered by the Huns from China, 432; but Charlemagne was the first master of the whole, in 800. It was called Allemania from Alleman, i. e. in German, every man, denoting that all nations were welcome there. Dukes being at this time made governors of the provinces, they claimed a right to sovereignty; Hence originated most of the independent, sovereign, and powerful families of Germany. It continued united to the crown of France till 841, Conrad I. was the first *elected* emperor, 912; but we have no authentic account of the imperial electors till 1273, when Rodolph of Hapsburg was chosen emperor by the seven electors. To secure the succession to his son, Henry III. got him elected 'King of the Romans;' a title which continued for several centuries hereditary, like that of the 'Prince of Wales' in England. Charles IV., to procure the election of his son, gave each elector 100,000 ducats, and was forced to mortgage several cities to raise the money, 1376.

Rodolph was the first emperor of the house of **Austria**, which governed the empire till it was succeeded by the house of Lorraine on the marriage of the celebrated Maria Theresa, queen of Hungary and heiress of Austria, with Francis, duke of Lorraine who was elected emperor, 1745.—Francis II. resigned the title of emperor of Germany, and assumed that of 'emperor of Austria,' Aug. 11, 1804.

Grenada, the Moorish kingdom of, in Spain, conquered by Ferdinand, 1492.

Grand Cairo, city of, (in Egypt,) founded by the Saracens, 969; taken by the Turks 1516.

Greek Empire, or *Eastern Empire* of the Romans, finally separated from the Western, 395; usurped by the Latins, 1204; re-conquered, 1261; its final overthrow by the Turks, 1453.

H

Hamburgh, city of, founded 804.

Hanover, ———, walled 1556; incorporated, 1578; made the ninth electorate, 1692; erected into a kingdom, 1814; East Frieeland and Harlingen united to it, 1815; duke of Cambridge appointed lieut. governor of, 1816.

Holland, originally a part of the territory of the Belgæ, conquered by the Romans, B. C. 47. A sovereignty founded by Thierry, first count of Holland, A. D. 868, continued till 1417, when it passed by surrender to the duke of Burgundy. Being oppressed by the bishop of Utrecht, the people ceded the country to Spain, 1534. The Spanish tyranny being insupportable, they revolted and formed the republic now called the United Provinces, 1579. The office of Stadtholder or of captain general of the provinces made hereditary in the prince of Orange's family, 1747; conquered by the French, 1795; erected into a kingdom by Napoleon and given to his brother Louis, 1806; restored to the house of Orange, and Belgium annexed to it, Nov. 1813.

I

Illinois, one of the United States, admitted into the Union 1818.

Indiana, ——— ——— ——— explored by the French, 1690; ceded to England 1763; included in the United States by the treaty of Paris, 1783; made a territory, including Illinois and Michigan, 1801; admitted into the Union as a State, Dec. 1816.

Ireland, is supposed to have been peopled by the Celts, and was formerly divided among several petty sovereigns. It was conquered by the English under Henry II. in 1172. Legislative union with England, Jan. 1, 1801.

Israelitish monarchy founded, B. C., 1095; destroyed B. C. 721.

Italy, kingdom of, began 476; ended, 964.

J

Jerusalem, built B. C. 1800; taken by Nebuchadnezzar, B. C. 588; destroyed by Titus, A. D., 70; re-built by Adrian 130; taken by the Saracens, 637; taken by the Crusaders, July 14, 1099, when seventy thousand infidels are said to have been massacred.

Judah, kingdom of, separated from Israel —, B. C. 975; subverted, B. C. 588.

K

Kentucky explored by Daniel Boone, who established the first colony, 1769—1775; admitted into the Union, June 1, 1792.

L

Liverpool incorporated, 1209.

Lombardy, kingdom of, in Italy, founded A. D. 568; conquered by Charlemagne, 771; annexed to the Austrian dominions, 1814.

London fortified by the Romans 50; walled, and a palace built, 294. The citizens received a charter from king John, to choose a mayor out of their own body, annually, to elect and remove their Sheriffs at pleasure, and their common-councilmen annually, 1208.

Louisiana, one of the United States, ceded by Crozat to the West Company, 1717; ceded by the latter to France, 1731; by France to Spain, 1763; re-ceded to France 1800; purchased by the United States, 1803; admitted into the Union, 1811.

Lubec founded, 1140.

Lucca, republic of, founded, 1450.

Lydia, kingdom of, founded about 1222 B. C. ended, being conquered by Cyrus the Great of Persia, B. C. 548.

M

Macedon, kingdom of, founded B. C. 814; conquered by the Romans B. C. 168.

Madrid built B. C. 936, but remained an obscure village in 1500.

Maine, one of the United States. First permanent settlement, 1635; granted to Sir Ferdinand Gorges 1639; first General Court held at Saco, 1640; claimed as part of Massachusetts and made a county with the name of Yorkshire, 1652; the claim of Gorges extinguished by purchase, 1676, convention at Portland respecting the separation from Massachusetts, 1785. The separation voted for, 1819. Maine admitted into the Union as an independent state, 1819.

Maryland, one of the United States. First settlement on Kent island by Clayborn 1631; granted to lord Baltimore by Charles I. 1632; sent delegates to the continental congress, 1774.

Massachusetts, one of the United States, first settlement at Plymouth, 1620; royal charter obtained 1628; first representative legislature, 1639, from which period to 1692, the two colonies of Massachusetts Bay and Plymouth, were alternately harassed by intestine religious disputes, Indian wars, or in resisting the encroachments of the crown of England. Bloody war with the Indians called 'King Philip's War,' 1674; second charter, uniting the two colonies, 1692. Massachusetts was an actor and sufferer in the several wars between France and Great Britain; contributed to the conquest of Canada; was the first of the colonies in resisting the oppressive measures of the British Government; and proposed the congress of 1774 which led to the union and independence of the States. Constitution adopted 1780, and amended, 1820.

Mexico, republic of, once an Empire under native monarchs; conquered by the Spaniards under Cortez, 1521. Revolution which terminated in its independence of Spain, commenced, 1810; this sanguinary struggle produced the elevation of Iturbide to the throne as emperor; he was expelled, but returned and was tried, condemned, and shot on the 19th October, 1824.

Michigan Territory, N. A., explored by the French, 1648-1650; (Detroit founded 1670.) ceded to Great Britain 1763; to the United States 1783; made a territory under its present name, 1805.

Milan, city of, is said to have been built by the Gauls, B. C. 408;—Conquered by the Romans B. C. 222; formed into a republic, A. D. 121; governed by dukes from 1395 till 1501; given to Austria, 1748; seized by the French, 1796; retaken by the Austrians, 1799; and now forms a part of the Austro-Lombardian Kingdom.

Mississippi, one of the United States, settled near Natches by the French in 1718: conquered by the Spanish 1781; surrendered to the United States, 1798; admitted into the Union, Dec. 1817.

Missouri, one of the United States, admitted into the Union, 1821.

Mogul Empire:—The first conqueror was Genghis Khan, a Tartarian chief, who died 1236. Timur-Bek became Great Mogul by conquest, 1399; the dynasty continued in his family till the conquest by Tamerlane, in the 15th century, whose descendants have kept the throne ever since.

Montreal, city of L. C. founded 1629; taken by the English, 1760; by the Provincials, Nov. 12, 1775, and re-taken by the English, June 15, 1776.

Morocco, empire of, anciently called Mauritania—reduced to a Roman province, A. D. 50; underwent various revolutions till the establishment of the Almovarides; the second emperor of this family built the capital, Morocco. About 1116, Abdallah, the leader of a sect of Mahometans, founded the dynasty of Almahides, which ended in the last sovereign's total defeat in Spain, 1312. Morocco was then seized by the king of Fez; but the Mahometans subdued and again united the three kingdoms, and formed what is at present the empire of Morocco.

Moscow, city of, founded 1156; three fourths of it burnt, 1812.

Munich, in Bavaria, founded 962.

N

Naples, city of, founded B. C. 323.

—— kingdom of, anciently Capua and Campania, founded 1020; underwent various revolutions; given by the pope to the count of Anjou, in exclusion of the right of the heir Conradin, who was beheaded, 1266. Sicily was united to it by Alphonso of Arragon, in 1442; and its sovereigns have since been styled King of the Two Sicilies; Naples was seized by the French and the king was expelled in 1799 and 1806, when Joseph Bonaparte, was created king by Napoleon; transferred to Murat, 1808; restored to Ferdinand, its lawful monarch 1814.

Netherlands declared a free State, 1565;

sovereignty of the House of Orange commenced, 1814. [See Holland.]

New-Hampshire one of the original United States; visited by Capt. John Smith, 1614; granted by the natives to Wheelwright, 1629; received under the protection of Massachusetts, 1640; sent 2 delegates to the continental Congress, 1774.

New-Jersey, one of the original U. States; first settled by the Dutch, 1612; granted by Charles II. to the duke of York, and received its present name, 1664; placed under the government of William Penn, 1682; sent delegates to the congress, 1774; constitution adopted, 1776.

New-Orleans, La., (U. S.,) founded by the French.

New-York, one of the original United States, settled by the Dutch, 1608; taken by the English, 1614; re-taken, 1615; granted by the States General to the West India Company, under the name of New Netherlands, 1621; (its first governor was Wouter Van Twiller, 1629;) recaptured by the English and granted to the duke of York, 1664; zealously opposed the stamp act, &c., and was distinguished in the revolution. Constitution adopted, April 1777. Since the peace of 1783, New-York has made wonderful advances in wealth and population.

New-York, city, originally called Fort Amsterdam, founded by the Dutch, 1608;—population in 1697, was 4,302;—in 1756;—13,040;—in 1790, 33,131;—in 1800, 60,489;—in 1805, 75,770;—in 1810, 96,373;—in 1820, 123,706;—in 1825, 166,086;—in 1830, 203,007.

At this ratio of increase the population will be in 1850, about 330,000;—in 1875, 690,000;—in 1900, 1,398,688;—in 1925, 2,650,000.

Normandy, erected into a dukedom, 876.

Norway, united to Sweden, under Charles XIII., 1814.

O

Ohio, one of the United States; first settlement, at Marietta, 1787; admitted into the Union, 1803.

Ostend, in Flanders, surrendered to the Spaniards after a siege of 3 years, 1604; made a free port, 1781.

P

Paris, city of, founded 357; made the capital of France, 481; the streets first paved, 1186; first lighted 1526.

Pennsylvania, one of the U. States. (This name is derived from the surname of Wm. Penn, and sylva, *woods*; and means, literally Penn's woods.) Granted by Charles II. to Penn, March 4, 1681. The first colonists were chiefly quakers, who still maintain great influence in the state. First assembly was held at Philadelphia in 1683; present constitution adopted, Sept. 2, 1790.

Persian Empire, founded by Cyrus, B. C., 536; conquered by Alexander, B. C., 330.

Petersburgh, in Russia, founded by the czar Peter I. 1703.

Philadelphia, Penn., U. S., founded 1682.

Pisa, republic of, founded, 1403.

Poland, once the country of the Vandals, who left it to invade the Roman empire; made a duchy, 694; a kingdom, under Boleslaus, 1000. Pomerania re-united to it 1465. Augustus abdicated, 1707. The kingdom first divided between Prussia, Russia and Germany, 1772. Revolution and the crown made hereditary in the Saxon family, 1791. The sovereignty abolished, 1795: remainder of the kingdom united to Russia, 1815. Revolt commenced at Warsaw, and the tyrannical regent Constantine expelled, 1830; Warsaw taken, multitudes of the Poles disperse into foreign countries and their country again subjected by the autocrat, 1831.

Portugal, kingdom of, founded by Alphonso I., 1139; united to Spain, 1580; revolted, 1640; the royal family, (house of Braganza,) removed to Brazil, 1807; at war with France, 1808—1811; usurped by don Miguel, uncle of the rightful sovereign, Maria de Gloria, invaded by don Pedro, the father of the latter, 1832.

Prussia, anciently peopled by the Venedi, who were conquered by the Borussi, and from them the country was named: subdued by the Mercian knights, sent by the emperor Frederick II., 1215; revolted to Poland, 1219; made a kingdom 1701; Its king seized a part of Poland, 1772 and 1795.

Rhode Island, one of the U. States, first settled by Roger Williams and his friends. 1636.

Roman Empire, began, B. C., 31; divided, A. D., 364. Western empire ended 476: Eastern, 1453.

Rome, city of, founded by Romulus and Remus the twin brothers, 752, B. C.; kingly government abolished, and succeeded by the consulate, B. C., 509. The republic changed to an empire by Octavius B. C., 31. About this time the revenue of the empire amounted to £40,000,000 Sterling. The city was 50 miles in circumference and its inhabitants exceeded 4,000,000. A. D., 48, it contained 6,900,000. The seat of empire removed to Constantinople, 330. Division of the empire 364. Rome taken and plundered by the Goths, 410; by the Vandals, 455; by the Herulii, 476; conquered by Belisarius, for the eastern emperor, 537; again by Narses, 553; revolted from the Greek emperors and became a free state, governed by a senate, 726; submitted to Charlemagne, who restored the city to the pope, 800; and has since continued under the control of the Pontiff, with the exception of the temporary revolution by the French, in 1798. Its inhabitants in 1780, amounted to 135,184; in this number were included 3,847 monks, 2,397 secular priests, 1910 nuns, 1065 students and 1470 paupers.

Russia, or Muscovy, anciently Sarmatia, and inhabited by the Scythians; remained obscure till the attempt of the natives on Constantinople, 864; (Woldimer was the first Christian king, 981;) conquered by the Poles, 1058; first rose into importance under the czar Peter, who assumed the title of 'Emperor of all the Russias,' introduced the means of education, manufactures and the arts, founded the navy, &c., 1700; Finland annexed to the empire, 1809, and Poland, 1815.

S

Sardinia, island of, conquered by the Spaniards 1303, and remained in their possession till 1708, when it was taken by an English fleet, and given to the duke of Savoy with the title of king; annexed to Italy 1805; restored to Victor Emanuel, with Genoa attached to it, 1814.

Savannah, in Georgia, settled 1732; taken by the British, 1779.

Savoy, a part of Gallia Narbonensis, which submitted to the Romans, 118, B. C., erected into a duchy, 1417; and is now possessed by the king of Sardinia.

Saxony, kingdom of, in Germany, was granted by the emperor Sigismund to Frederick I., as an electorate, 1423; erected into a kingdom by Bonaparte, 1807.

Scotland, anciently Caledonia; tradition says that its first king was Fergus who was sent over from Ireland, B. C., 328; it was inhabited by the two nations of Scots and Picts, united into one monarchy by Kenneth II., the 69th king, and called Scotland, 838; divided into baronies, 1032; dispute for the crown of, between Bruce & Baliol, 1285, referred to the arbitration of Edward I., of England, who took the opportunity to conquer it; the Scotch recovered their independence, 1314. Union of the English and Scotch crowns, 1603; legislative union, 1707. The Scotch boast a line of 115 kings.

Spain, was first visited and civilized by the Phenicians and Carthaginians; made a Roman province, 210; the Goths and Vandals, overturned the Roman power, 569, and continued in the possession of Spain till it was conquered in 711 by the Moors, who kept a part of it till 1093. The Christian kingdom of Asturias founded 758; of Arragon, 1035; of Castile and Leon 1037; the three last united, under the title of the kingdom of Spain, 1479.

Sweden, anciently Scandinavia, kingdom of, founded, 481; united to Denmark and Norway, 1394; the Danes expelled by Gustavus Vasa, in 1525, until which time the crown was elective; had no nobility before 1500; popery abolished and the crown declared to be hereditary, 1544. Charles John Bernadotte the present king elected crown prince 1810; succeeded to the throne 1812.

Switzerland, was formerly inhabited by the Helvetii, who were subdued by Cæsar, 57, B. C; it remained subject to the Romans till 395; became a part of the kingdom of Burgundy, 838; given by the last king of Burgundy to Germany 1032. The Swiss Cantons formed, and declared themselves an independent republic, 1307.

T

Tennessee, one of the United States.—Nashville founded 1780; what is now called Tennessee was conditionally ceded by North Carolina, to the United States, 1789; made a territory 1790; admitted into the Union, and its constitution ratified, 1796.

Troy, city of, founded 1546, B. C., destroyed 1184. B. C.

Turkey, a large empire, now extended over part of Europe, Asia, and Africa. The Turks are of Tartar origin. They founded their empire in Asia, A. D., 1299; in Europe, after taking Constantinople, and overturning the Eastern Empire of the Romans, 1453.

Tuscany, erected into a dukedom, 1530; subdued by the French, 1799; recovered its independence a second time, 1814.

U

United States, of North America, declared their independence of Great Britain, July 4, 1776.

V

Venezuela, South America, became a republic, 1811.

Venice.—The first inhabitants of this country were the Veneti; they were conquered by the Romans, 221, B. C.; by the Gauls, 356, when their kingdom was founded. The islands on which the present city stands, began to be inhabited by Italians, about 421; the first house was erected on the morass by Entinopus, who fled from the Goths; the people of Padua took refuge there also, and were assisted by Entinopus in building the eighty houses which formed the first city, 413; first governed by a *doge*, 697; but the republic was not independent, till 803; its extensive trade almost ruined by the league of Cambray, 1509; the conspiracy on which Otway's play is founded, 1618; its senate dissolved and its government changed by the French, in 1797, when the annual ceremony of "wedding the Adriatic sea," was omitted for the first time since 1173. The French ceded the city with the adjacent country to the emperor of Germany, Oct. 17, 1797; and it now remains subject to Austria.

Vermont, one of the United States; first settled, 1724; claimed as a part of New-York; was declared a free state in 1777, by the people, who petitioned congress for admission into the Union, but were refused. The controversy was terminat- in 1790, Vermont paying to New-York $30,000. Admitted into the Union, Feb. 18, 1791; constitution adopted, July, 1793.

Vienna, made an imperial city in 1136; taken by the king of Hungary, 1490; besieged by the Turks in 1529; again in 1532, 1543, and 1663; taken by the French, 1805, and 1809.

Virginia, the first settled of the United States, was granted by a patent to the London company, 1606; first colony arrived, 1607; captain Smith arrived, 1608. Virginia passed the first resolution against the stamp act. Present constitution adopted July 5, 1776.

W

Wales, peopled by the Britons on their being expelled from England by the Saxons, 685; Griffith the last king died 1137; Wales was united to England, 1536.

Washington City, D. C., U. S., became the seat of government, 1800; incorporated, 1802.

Wurtemberg, erected into a county in 1078; into a duchy, 1495; a kingdom, 1803.

TAB. II.

GEOGRAPHICAL DISCOVERIES, SETTLEMENTS, &c.

A

America—First discovery of land belonging to, (St. Salvador,) by Columbus, in the service of Spain, Oct. 11, 1492;—so named by Americus Vespucius, a Florentine navigator, 1497.

——, *North*, discovered by John and Sebastian Cabot, Venetians, in the service of England, 1497; first permanent English settlement in, at Jamestown, Va. 1607; second do. do. by the Puritans, at Plymouth, Mass., 1620.

——, *South*, by Columbus, April 24, 1500.—(See notices of separate countries.)

[It is remarkable, that with the exception of Martin and Alonzo Pinzon, all the great seamen, who first explored the Atlantic shore of America, were Italians.]

Andreanoffsy isles, between N. America, and Kamschatka, by the Russians, 1760.

Angola, province of, in Western Africa settled by the Portuguese, 1482.

Antigua, island of, W. I., settled by the English, 1632.

Archangel, a sea port in Russia, passage to, discovered by the English, 1553.

Aruba, island of, colonized by the Dutch, 1634.

Azores, or *Western Islands*, discovered by the Portuguese, 1449.

B

Baffin's Bay, separating Greenland from N. America, discovered by Baffin, 1622.

Bahama isles, discovered 1629; taken by the English, 1718.

Barbadoes discovered and settled, 1620.

Batavia, on the Island of Java, founded by the Dutch, 1618.

Bermuda isles discovered 1527; settled 1612.

Botany Bay, New-Holland, first English colony at, 1788.

C

Caledonia, New, disc. by capt. Cook, 1774.

California, —— by Cortes, 1543; taken possession of by Drake, 1578.

Canary isles discovered and granted to Spain 1344.

Cape Breton —— by the English, 1584; yielded to France, 1632; retaken 1745; restored, 1745; again taken 1758, and since retained by England.

Cape de Verde isles discovered, 1447.

Cape of Good Hope discovered, 1487; taken by the British 1795; again 1806.

Cape Horn first sailed round, 1616; Straits discovered, 1643.

Caribbee isles discovered, 1495; war in, between the black and red Caribs, 1772.

Cat-island, one of the Bahamas, supposed by some authors to be the one first seen by Columbus in America, 1492.

Cavendish's first voyage to circumnavigate the globe, 1556.

Cayenne, island of, first planted by the French 1635.

Ceylon, —— discovered by the Portuguese, 1505; taken by the English, 1795.

Charlotte's, queen, islands, discovered by Cartaret, 1767.

Christopher's, St. isle of, discovered 1595; settled by the English, 1626.

Congo, kingdom of, on the western coast of Africa—settled by the Portuguese, 1482.

Cuba, island of, W. I. discovered by Columbus, 1492; invaded by the British, 1762; yielded to Spain, 1763.

Curacoa, settled by the Dutch, 1634.

D

Darien settled, 1700.

Davis' Straits, discovered 1585.

De la Plata, river of, discovered, 1512.

Domingo, St. (the first part of America settled by Europeans,) discovered 1492; city of, founded by Bartholomew Columbus, 1506; colonised by the French, 1650; the negroes revolted and massacred the whites, 1791; and they remain in the independent possession of the island, which is now called *Hayti*.

Dominico, discovered by Columbus, 1493; settled by the French, 1700; taken by the English, 1759; by the French, 1778; restored to England, 1783.

E

East Indies, first discovered by the Romans, the time uncertain; Alexander the Great made extensive conquests in that country; 327 B. C.—Discovered by the Portuguese, 1497; settled by them in 1506. The first settlement was Goa.—The first commercial intercourse of the English with the East Indies was a private adventure of three ships, 1591: only one of them reached India; and after a voyage of three years, the commander, Capt. Lancaster, was brought home in another ship, the sailors having seized his own; but his information gave rise to a capital mercantile voyage. The first East India Company's charter was dated Dec. 31, 1600;—their stock amounted to £72,000;—agreed to pay the government £400,000 per an. for 5 years so they might continue unmolested, Feb. 1769; house built 1726; India Bill passed 1773.—Dutch East India Company formed 1594;—Danish 1612; Swedish, 1731.

F

Falkland Islands discovered, 1592.
Fox island, in the North Pacific Ocean, discovered, 1760.
Frobrisher's Straits, 1578.

G

Gallapagos Isles, Discovered 1700.
Greenland, discovered 1585; settled 1721.
Guadaloupe isle, discovered by Columbus, 1493; planted by the French 1635; taken by the English, 1759, 1779, and 1794.
Guinea coast discovered by the Portuguese, 1482.

H

Helena, St. discovered 1502; settled by the English, 1651.
Hudson's Bay discovered by Capt. Hudson, 1607.

J

Iceland discovered by a Danish pirate, 860.
Jamaica discovered by Columbus, 1494 settled by the Spaniards 1509; taken by the English, 1655.
Japan discovered, 1542.

K

Kamtschatka discov'd by the Russians, 1739.

L

Ladrone islands discovered, 1521.

M

Madagascar, island of, discovered by the Portuguese, 1506.
Madeira, —— ——, 1344 and 1418.
Magellan, straits of, discovered, 1520.

N

Nevis planted by the English, 1628.
Newfoundland, discovered by Cabot 1497; settled 1614.
New-Guinea discovered 1699.
New-Holland, discovered by the Dutch 1627; settled by the English, 1787.
New-Zealand discovered, 1660; explored, 1769.
Nootka Sound on the N. W. coast of America, discovered, 1778.
Nova-Scotia settled, 1622.
Nova Zembla discovered, 1553.

O

Otaheite, discovered, June 18, 1765.
Owhyhe, ———, 1778.

P

Paraguay, discovered, 1525.
Peru. —— 1518.
Philippine isles, —— by the Spaniards, 1521.
Pitt's Straits, in the East Indies, disc. 1760.
Porto Rico, island of, West Indies, 1497.

S

Sandwich Islands, in the Pacific Ocean, discovered 1778.
Sierra Leone, coast of Africa, disc. 1460.
Society Islands, discovered 1765.
Solomon —— 1527.
Somer's Isles, —— 1527.
St. Eustatia isles, settled by the Dutch, 1632.
St. Lawrence River, N. A., discovered and explored by the French, 1508.
St. Salvador, W. I., the first land discovered in America by Columbus, Oct. 11, 1492.
Suwarrow islands discovered by the Russians, 1814.

T

Tobago planted by the Dutch, 1642.
Terceiras isles discovered by the Spaniards, 1583.
Terra Firma settled by the Spaniards, 1521.
Trinidad, island of, discovered, 1498.

TAB. III.

RELIGIOUS ORDERS, SECTS, &c.

Are said to amount to 973, among which are,

Albigenses, originated,.......... A. D. 1160
(opposed to the church of Rome.)

Anabaptists,...................... 1525
(advocate baptism by immersion.)

Anchorites, (Monks.) 1255

Angelites, (See Buck's Dictionary.)...... 494

Antinomians, (founded by I. Agricola,).. 1538
(maintain that the *law* is of no use or obligation under the *gospel* dispensation.)

Antonines, ... 329

Arians, (f. by Arius,)................... 290

Arminians, (f. by Arminius.)............ 1229

Augustines, (a religious order,).......... 389
(had all things in common.)

Baptists, (Buck says) about,............ 1556
(Baptism by immersion.)

Bartholomites, (monks,)................. 1013

Beguines, (nuns,) originated,............ 1208

Behmenists,.......................... 1600

Benedictines, (monks).................. 548

Bereans, (a sect of Protestant dissenters, in Scotland,)

Bethlehemites,........................ 1248

Bohemian Brethren, (Christ. reformers,) 1467

Bridgetines,.......................... 1370
(an order similar to Augustines.)

Brownists,........................... 1660
(a sect among the Puritans.)

Calvinists, founded by J. Calvin,....... 1546
(believe in the doctrines of predestination, conversion by grace, perseverance, &c.)

Canons, (officiated as priests.)........... 400

Capuchins, (of the order of St. Francis,) 1525

Cardinals,............................ 853
(chief governors of the Romish Church.)

Carmelites, (mendicant friars,)......... 1141

Carthusians, a religious order,......... 1084

Catharists, (similar to Manichæans,).... 1373

Celestines, a religious order,........... 1272

Chaplains,........................... 1248

Dominicans, a religious order,.......... 1315

Flagellants, a fanatical sect,...... A. D. 1259
(whipped themselves in public.)

Franciscans, a religious order,......... 1206

Greyfriars,........................... 1122

Greek Church separated from the Latin about,........................ 1050

Hermits,............................ 1257

Holy Trinity, order of, ... 1211

Jesuits, (a religious order of the Romish Church, 1536; expelled England, 1604; Venice, 1606; Portugal, 1759; France, 1602; Spain, 1767; Naples, 1768; Rome and Prussia, 1773; order abolished by the Pope, 1773; restored, 1784—1814.)

Lutherans,.......................... 1517
(Christians who follow the opinions of Martin Luther.)

Mahometans,......................... 622

Manichæans,......................... 343

Methodists,.......................... 1734

Monks, (associated.).................... 328

Moravians, or ***Unitas Fratrum***,......... 1457

Predestinarians,...................... 371

Presbyterians. (Knox,)—about......... 1560

Protestants, (Luther,).................. 1519

Puritans,............................ 1545

Quakers,............................ 1650

Quietists,........................... 1685

Swedenborgians, ... 1780

Trappists,.......................... 1815
(order of monks—inst. in France.)

Trinitarians, order of,.................. 1198

Unitarians,.......................... 1553

Ursulines,........................... 1198

MILITARY ORDERS, TITLES OF HONOUR. &c.

A

Admiral, the first in England, 1297.
Ædiles, first created at Rome, 543, B. C. (They superintended all buildings, baths, &c., and examined weights and measures.)
Alexander, St., order of knighthood, in Russia, 1700.
Aldermen, city magistrates, first appointed in London, 1242.
Andrew, St., order of knighthood, in Scotland, 809; in Russia, 1698.
Anthony, St., order of knighthood, in Germany, 1382.

B

Baron, the title of, first granted by patent, in England, 1388.
Baronet, the title of, granted for £1095, by James I., of England, 1611.
Bath, order of knighthood, instituted in England at the coronation of Henry IV, 1399; renewed, 1725.

C

Censors, whose office was to number the people, regulate the taxes, and watch over morals and manners; at Rome, 413, B. C.
Christian Charity, order of knighthood, in France, 1590.
Cincinnatus, order of, in the U. States, 1783.
Common Council of London, 1208.
Consuls, (who had regal authority for one year,) first at Rome, B. C., 509.
Crescent, order of knighthood, in Naples, 1448.

D

Decemvirs, (ten magistrates of absolute authority,) at Rome, B. C., 450.
Defender of the Faith, the title of, given to Henry VIII., by the pope, 1520.
Dennis, St., order of, in France, 1267.
Dey of Tunis, first appointed, 1570.
Dictator, (a magistrate with regal power) at Rome, B. C., 498.
Duke, title of, first in England, given to Edward son of Edward III., 1336.

E

Earl, title of, first used by king Alfred, 920, as a substitute for that of king.
Electors (of Germany,) title of, first given to the independent princes, who had the power of electing the emperor, 1298.
Eminence, title of, first given to cardinals, 1644.
Esquire, title of, first used to persons of fortune, not attendants on knights, 1345.

G

Garter, order of, instituted by Edward III., 1349, April 23; (It is remarkable that this is the only order which has been granted to foreign princes.)
Gentlemen, the first use of the distinction, 1430.
George, St., order of knighthood, in Carinthia, 1279; in Spain, 1318; in England, 1349; in Austria, 1470.
Golden Fleece, order of knighthood, in Flanders, 1492.
Golden Shield and Thistle, order of, 1370.
Guelphs, order of knighthood, instituted in Hanover, 1816.

H

Holy Trinity, order of knighthood, 1211.
Hospitallers. See Malta.

I

James, St., order of knighthood, in Spain, 1030.
John, St., of Jerusalem. See Malta.

K

King of England title of, first used, 820; of Ireland added to it, 1542; of Great Britain, 1603.
King of France, title of, with the motto "Dieu et mon Droit," assumed by the king of England, 1340; relinquished, 1801.
King of the French, title of, given to Louis Philip I., 1830.
Knighthood, introduced into England, 897; abolished in France, 1791.

L

Legion of Honour, instituted by Bonaparte, 1804; confirmed by Louis XVIII., 1814.

Louis, St., order of knighthood, in France, 1698.

Lord Mayors of London, first appointed annually, 1208.

M

Majesty, the title of, first given to Henry VIII., of England.

Malta, knights of, alias Knights Hospitallers, alias Knights of St. John of Jerusalem. Foundation of the order laid by opening a house for the reception of pilgrims at Jerusalem, 1048; became a regular monastic order, 1099; and a military order, 1118; took Rhodes, and were called Knights of Rhodes, 1310; being expelled from thence by the Turks the emperor Charles V., gave them the island of Malta, 1523, and they were called Knights of Malta; they were expelled from England, 1540: performed great exploits against the Infidels, 1595; conspiracy at Malta to destroy the whole order, for which 125 Turkish slaves suffered death, June 26, 1749.

Marian Knights. See Teutonic Order.

Mark, St., order of, at Venice, 830; revived, 1562.

Maria Theresa, or royal order, for ladies in Spain, 1792.

Martyrs, order of knighthood, in Palestine, 1319.

Merit, order of knighthood, in Prussia, 1730,

Michael, St. order of knighthood, in France, 1469; in Germany, 1618.

N

Noble Passion, order of knighthood in Germany, 1704.

O

Ordo Disciplinarum, order of Knighthood, in Bohemia.

Our Lady and St., George of Montesa, order of knighthood, in Spain, 1317.

P

Passion of Jesus Christ, order of knighthood, in France, 1382.

Patrick, St., order of, in Ireland, 1783.

Poet Laureat, the first in England, 1487.

Pope, title of, first assumed by the bishop of Rome, 154.

R

Round Table, order of knighthood, 516; revived, 1344.

Rupert, St., order of knighthood, in Germany, 1709.

S

Secretaries of State, first appointed in England, 1530.

Sepulchre, order of knighthood, in Palestine, 1092.

Sheriffs, first appointed, 1189.

Sincerity, order of knighthood, in Saxony, 1690.

Slaves of Virtue, order of knighthood, in Germany.

T

Templars, Knights, the first military order, 1118; all of them arrested in France in one day, being charged with enormous crimes and great riches, and 59 of them were burnt alive in Paris, Oct. 13, 1307; order abolished in France, 1342.

Teutonic or Marian order, 1192; abolished, 1322; revived, 1522.

Thistle order, 812.

Tribunes, of the People, at Rome, 495, B. C.

Tribunes, military, with consular power, at Rome, 445, B. C.

V

Virgin Mary, order of knighthood, 1233.

Viscount, the first in England, 1440.

W

Wales, prince of, title of instituted, 1281.

Warfare of Christ, order of knighthood 1325; in Poland, 1705.

TAB. V.

REMARKABLE BUILDINGS.

Adrian's Wall, in Britain, built 121.
Amphitheatre at Rome, (has 14 chapels now within its walls,) built 69.

Babel, tower of, (was 40 years in building,) B. C. 2247.
Bank of England, in London, 1732.
Bastile, at Paris, (b. i i 14 years.) 1369.
Blackfriars Bridge, London, (10 years;—cost £150,840,) 1770.

Capitol of the United States, Washington,
Chinese Wall, 1500 miles in length.
Covent Garden Theatre, London, 1809.
Custom House, London, (first built, 1559,) the present one, 1817.

Drury Lane Theatre, London, (burnt 1809) re-built, 1812.

Eddystone Light House, near Plymouth (destroyed 1703 and 1770,) 1774.
Edinburgh Castle, (first fortified 1074,) 950.
Exeter Castle, 680; *Cathedral*, 1064 and 1485; *Bridge*, 1770.

Guildhall, London, 1416, rebuilt, 1789.

Hampton Court palace, London, 1525
Holt's Hotel, in New-York city, 1832.
Holyrood House, Edinburgh, 1128.

India House, London, 1726.
James St., Palace, London, 1536.
Jupiter Olympus, a temple at Athens, half a mile in circuit.

Kenilworth Castle, Warwickshire, 1120.

London Bridge, (of wood, 1016,) stone, 1209.
Louvre, in Paris, 1552.

Marks, St., Palace at Venice, 450.
———, —, Church, 826.

New-York, City Hall, commenced, 1803; finished, 1811.
New-York, Merchants' Exchange, 1825.
Nottingham Castle, England, 1068.
Notre Dame church, in Paris, 1270.

Pauls, St. in London, built, 610; burnt, 964; rebuilt in 150 years, 1240; burnt, in 1666; present building finished in 35 years, 1710. It cost £1,000,000.
Parthenon, at Athens, burnt by the Persians, 480, B. C.; re-built by Pericles.
Peter's, St. at Rome, began 1514; finished, 1629.
Porcelain Tower, China, 200 feet high.
Pyramid of Cholula and *Temple of the Sun*, Mexico, N. A.

Rheims Cathedral, 840.
Rialto, at Venice, 1591.
Richmond Palace, Eng. 1498.
Royal Exchange, Lond., 1566; re-built, 1670.

Schuylkill Bridge, Philadelphia.
Scone Abbey, near Perth, Scot., 1114.
Somerset House, London, 1776.
Southwark Bridge, —— 1815.
State House, Boston, 1797.

Temple of Belus, in ancient Babylon, half a mile in extent every way.
Tower of London, 1078.
Tremont House, a hotel in Boston, 1827.
Tuilleries, in Paris, 1577.

Versailles Palace, France, (21 years,) 1708.

Warwick Castle, Eng. 1072.
Washington, statue of, (by Chantry,) in Boston, (finished, 1826.)
Westminster Abbey, 914; rebuilt, 1065, and 1269.
——— *bridge* (cost £426,650,) 1741.
——— *hall*, 1098; rebuilt, 1399.
Windsor Castle, England, 1365.

York Cathedral, England, 628.

TAB. VI.

IMPORTANT BATTLES.

(For particulars see *Chronological* Table in this work.)

Marathon,	Gr.	B. C.	490	Blenheim,	Ger.	—	1704
Eurymedon,	—	—	470	Pultowa,	Swe.	—	1709
Leuctra.	—	—	373	Preston,	Eng.	—	1715
Cheronea,	—	—	338	Dettingen,	Ger.	—	1743
Granicus,	Maced.	—	334	Preston Pans,	Eng.	—	1745
Issus,	—	—	333	Culloden,	—	—	1746
Arbela,	—	—	331	Fort du Quesne,	N. A.	—	1755
Issus,	—	—	301	Quebec,	—	—	1759
Cannæ,	Rom.	—	216	Lexington,	—	—	1775
Pharsalia,	—	—	47	Bunker's Hill,	—	—	—
Philippi,	—	—	41	Long Island,	—	—	1776
Actium,	—	—	31	White Plains,	—	—	—
Soissons, Fr,	Fr.	A. D.	481	Brandywine,	—	—	1777
Fontenoy,	—	—	841	Bennington,	—	—	—
Hastings,	Eng.,	—	1066	Saratoga,	—	—	—
Ascalon,	—	—	1191	Monmouth,	—	—	1778
Bannockburn,	—	—	1314	Camden,	—	—	1780
Halidon Hill,	—	—	1346	Guilford,	—	—	1781
Cressy,	—	—	1346	**Yorktown,**	—	—	—
Poictiers,	Eng.	—	1356	Toulon,	Fr.	—	1793
Shrewsbury,	—	—	1403	Lodi,	—	—	1796
Agincourt,	—	—	1415	Acre,	—	—	1799
Towton,	—	—	1461	Marengo,	—	—	1801
Tewksbury,	—	—	1471	Austerlitz,	—	—	1805
Bosworth,	—	—	1485	Wagram,	Fr.	—	1809
Flodden,	—	—	1513	Salamanca,	—	—	1812
Pavia,	Fr.	—	1524	Borodino,	—	—	—
Lutzen,	Ger.	—	1633	Queenstown,	N. A.	—	1813
Marston,	Eng.	—	1644	Pyrenees,	Fr.	—	—
Naseby,	—	—	1645	Leipsic,	—	—	—
Vienna,	Ger.	—	1683	New Orleans,	U. S.	—	1815
Boyne,	Eng.	—	1690	**Waterloo,**	Fr.	—	—
Nara,	Swe.	—	1700				

TAB. VII.

IMPORTANT TREATIES.

Abo, peace of	1743	Belgrade, peace of	1739
Aix la Chapelle, peace of	1668	Berlin, peace of	1742
——— do.	1748	——— decree	1806
Akerman, peace of	1826	——— convention of	1808
Alt Ranstadt, peace of	1706	Breda, peace of	1667
Amiens, peace of	1802	Cambray, league of	1508
Armed neutrality, treaty of	1800	——— peace of	1529
Arras, treaty of	1435	Campo Formio, treaty of	1797
——— do.	1482	Carlowitz, peace of	1699
Augsburg, league of	1686	Carlsbad, congress of	1819
Baden, peace of	1714	Cateau Cambresis, peace of	1559
Barrier Treaty	1715	Chambord, treaty of	1552
Basle, peace of	1795	Chaumont, treaty of	1814
Bayonne, treaty of	1808	Chierasco, treaty of	1631

Cintra, convention of	1808
Closterseven, convention of	1757
Coalition, first against France	1792
———— second do.	1799
———— third do.	1805
———— fourth do.	1806
———— fifth do.	1809
———— sixth do.	1813
Concordat	1801
Conflans, treaty of	1465
Constantinople, peace of	1712
Copenhagen, peace of	1660
Definitive treaty of peace between Great Britain and America	1783
Definitive treaty of peace between Great Britain and Holland	1784
Dresden, peace of	1745
Falezi, peace of	1711
Family Compact	1761
Fontainbleau, peace of	1679
———— treaty of	1785
———— concordat at	1813
Friedwald, treaty of	1551
Fuessen, peace of	1745
Ghent, pacification of	1576
——— peace of	1814
Golden Bull	1356
Grand Alliance	1689
Hague, treaty of the	1659
——— do.	1669
Halle, treaty of	1610
Hamburg, peace of	1762
Hanover treaty	1725
Heilbron, treaty of	1633
Holy Alliance	1815
Hubertsberg, peace of	1763
Interim	1548
Kiel, treaty of	1814
Kutchuk Kainarji, peace of	1774
Laybach, congress of	1821
League	1576
Leipsick, alliance of	1631
Leoben, peace of	1797
Liebau, treaty of	1656
Lisbon, peace of	1668
London, treaty of	1829
Lubeck, peace of	1629
Luneville, peace of	1801
Methuen treaty	1703
Milan decree	1807
Munster, peace of	1648
Naumberg, treaty of	1554
Nice, treaty of	1518
Nimeguen, peace of	1678
Nipchoo, treaty of	1727
Noyon, treaty of	1516
Nuremburg, treaty of	1532
Nystett, peace of	1721
Oliva, peace of	1660
Pacquigni, peace of	1475
Paris, peace of	1763
——— treaty of	1796
——— peace of	1810
——— capitulation of	1814
——— treaty of	1814
——— peace of	1814
——— do.	1815
Paris treaty of	1815
——— do.	1817
Partition, first treaty of	1698
——— second treaty of	1700
Passarowitz, peace of	1718
Passau, treaty of	1552
Petersburg, peace of	1762
———— treaty of	1772
———— do.	1805
Peterswalden, convention of	1813
Pilnitz, convention of	1791
Poland, partition of	1795
Pragmatick Sanction	1439
do.	1713
Prague, peace of	1653
Presburg, peace of	1805
Public Good, league for the	1464
Pyrenees, treaty of the	1659
Quadruple Alliance	1718
Radstadt, peace of	1714
——— congress of	1797
Ratisbon, peace of	1630
Religion, peace of	1555
Rhine, confederation of	1806
Ryswick, peace of	1697
St. Germain, peace of	1570
St. Germain en Laye, peace of	1679
St. Ildefonso, alliance of	1796
Seville, peace of	1792
Siored, peace of	1613
Smalcald, league of	1529
Stettin, peace of	1570
Stockholm, peace of	1719
———— treaty of	1724
———— do.	1813
Temeswar, truce of	1664
Teschen, peace of	1779
Teusin, peace of	1595
Tilsit, peace of	1807
Tolentino, treaty of	1793
Toplitz, treaty of	1817
Triple Alliance	1717
———— of the Hague	1668
Troppau, congress of	1820
Troyes, treaty of	1420
Turkmauchay, peace of	1828
Ulm, peace of	1620
Utrecht, union of	1579
——— peace of	1713
Valencay, treaty of	1813
Verona, congress of	1822
Versailles, peace of	1783
Vienna treaty	1725
——— treaty of alliance of	1731
——— definitive peace of	1737
——— peace of	1809
——— treaty of, March 23	1815
———— May 31	1815
———— June 4	1815
Vossem, peace of	1673
Warsaw treaty of	1768
——— alliance of	1683
Westminster, peace of	1674
Westphalia, peace of	1648
Wilna, treaty of	1561
Worms, edict of	1521
Würzbourg, treaty of	1610

MISCELLANEOUS ITEMS.

Abbeys **and *Monasteries*, pillaged by William the Conqueror, 1069; one hundred suppressed in England by order of council 1414, at a time when general throughout Europe. Dissolved by Henry VIII. of England, to the value of £2,850,000, in 1540—suppressed by the emperor of Germany in 1785; and by France, in 1790.**

Affirmation of the Quakers **first accepted as an Oath, 1702.—Alteration made in it, December 13, 1721. Made legally equal to an oath in most, if not all the states of the United States.**

***Ambassadors and Ministers plenipotentiary*, have been from time immemorial, considered in some measure, privileged characters. Those of king David, about 1030, B. C. being insulted by the king of the Ammonites, led to a war destructive to the aggressors. The Roman ambassadors at Clusium, B. C. 390, mixing with the inhabitants in battle with the Gauls, Brennus, king of the latter, considered their conduct an act of hostility on the part of their country, raised the siege of Clusium, marched towards Rome, defeated the Romans at Allia, and took, plundered and burned Rome. In modern times the privileges of Ambassadors have been more distinctly defined. In England during the protectorship of Oliver Cromwell, Don Pantaleon Sa, brother to the Portuguese ambassador in London, committed a murder in open day, and sought refuge in his brother's house; but the Protector refused to sanction such an asylum in a case of murder, and Sa was seized, confined, tried and hanged, 1653. About twenty years afterwards the prince of Furstenburg was arrested at the diet of Ratisbon for murder, by order of the emperor of Germany, and the case of Sa, given as a justification. In 1709, in England, the Russian ambassador was arrested for debt by a lace merchant, which led to an act of parliament exempting ambassadors, or their immediate suit, from arrest in civil cases. The following table shows the respective salaries paid to the British, and United States' Ambassadors, at the principal states of Europe, amount reduced to dollars, and even numbers:**

	English Ambas.	*U. S. Ambas.*
France	$48,000	$9,000
Spain	52,000	9,000
Holland	52,000	4.500
Russia	52,000	9,000
British in U. S.	26,000	U. S. in Eng. 9000

The first Ambassador from Russia to England, arrived in London 1556. First from India to any part of Europe, was from Tippo Saib to France, 1778. First from the United States was Silas Deane to France, 1776. First from the Ottoman emperor to Great Britain, 1793. First from the new Spanish states of America, were received by the United States, and reciprocated by ministers sent to Buenos Ayres, Mexico, &c.

***Army*, standing, the first in modern times instituted by Charles VII. king of France, 1445. Since that epoch, the whole features of war have changed; most nations have now a regular standing military force. The proportion between the troops in service and men able to bear arms in modern times, has been assumed as 1 to 100—but it is much too low an estimate. In 1828 there were about forty millions of men fit to bear arms in the European and American nations, and though general peace prevails, there is at least one million of men in arms, or about one to forty.**

***Auricular Confession*, first introduced, 1215.**

B

Bible History **ceases 340 years before Christ. Septuagint version made 284; first divided into chapters, 1253. The first English edition was in 1536; the first authorized edition in England was in 1539; the second translation was ordered to be read in churches, 1549; the present translation finished September, 1611; permitted by the pope to be translated into all the languages of the Catholic states, Feb. 28, 1759. The following is a dissection of the Old and New Testament:**

	In Old Testament.	*In the New.*	*Total.*
Books	39	27	66
Chapters	929	260	1,189
Verses	23,214	7,959	31,173
Words	592,493	181,253	773,746
Letters	2,728,100	838,380	3,566,480

The Apocrypha has 183 chapters, 6081 verses, and 125,185 words. The middle chapter, and the least in the Bible, is the 117th Psalm; the middle verse is the 8th of the 118th Psalms; the middle line is the 2d book of the Chronicles, 4th chapter, and 16th verse; the word *and* occurs in the Old Testament 35,535 times; the same word in the New Testament occurs 10,684 times; the word *Jehovah* occurs 6,855 times.

The 21st verse of the 7th chapter of Ezra has all the letters of the alphabet in it.

The 19th chapter of the 2d book of

Kings, and the 37th chapter of Isaiah, are alike.

The book of Esther has 10 chapters, but neither the words Lord nor God is it.

The following is a chronological list of different versions and editions of the scriptures: First translated into the Saxon language 939. Hebrew—first printed Hebrew Bible done at Soncinum in Italy, at Naples, 1487; complete the whole Bible, at Soncinum, 1488: at Venice, by Bomberg, 1518—and at the same epoch in Spain, under Cardinal Ximenes, in 1526—28, the first edition of B. Chaim: Basil, 1534; in 1549, by B. Chaim; in 1572, the royal or Spanish Polyglott 8 vols. at Antwerp: third edition of B. Chaim's Bible, 1618; in 1632, at Venice; Amsterdam, 1724—27; Paris, 1641, 10 fol. vols. London Polyglott, 1757.

Bibles, Hebrew, in quarto—Paris, R. Stephens, 1539—1534; Antwerp, 1571; Geneva, 1619; Amsterdam, 1635, and again 1639; Venice 1639; Amsterdam, by Athias, 1661; and 1667; Frankfort 1677; Berlin 1699; Leusden's last edition of Athias, 1705; Dr. Kennicott's 1776—1780; Parma by De Rossi, 1784—1785—1786.

Bible, Greek, first printed was the Complutersian in Spain, 1514; Venice 1518; Strasberg, 1526; Hamburgh, 1596; Frankfort, 1597; Rome, 1587—1588; Paris, 1628; Oxford, 1707; Franeker, 1709.

Bibles, Latin, see Vulgate.

Bibles, in the modern languages of Europe were first printed in Holland 1478; French 1498; German 1524; Italian 1530; English, by Tindal, 1534—by Miles Coverdale, 1535; Swedish, 1546; Spanish at Ferrara, 1553; Welsh 1588.

Bibles, Oriental, are Samaritan, Chaldee Syriac, Arabic, Coptic, Sahidic or, Upper Egypt, Ethiopic, Armenian, Georgian, Persian, &c.

Bibles, Indian, by the Society for propagating the Gospel in New England, at Cambridge, 1661—1664; in the Natick language; by Elliott at Cambridge in 4to. 1685.

Bibles, first printed in the United States. In consequence of the revolutionary war, bibles became scarce and dear. Robert Aitkin, printer of Philadelphia, September 12th, 1782, published an edition. The Rev. Dr. Wm. White, and the Rev. Mr. Duffield had been appointed to examine it, and reported favourably. Congress itself recommended the book to the people, but neglected to provide for competition in the sales; made peace, and British bibles coming into the market, the meritorious publisher was severely injured.

Bible Societies. See Statistics.

C

China, first voyage to, from the United States, 1784; China porcelain first spoken of in history, 1591.

Cholera, See *Plague*.

Christianity was propagated in Spain, in 36; in Britain, 60; or as others say, in the 5th century; in Franconia and Flanders, in the 7th century; in Lombardy, Thuringia, and Hesse, in the 8th century: in Sweden, Denmark, Poland, and Russia, in the 9th century; in Hungary and Sclavonia, in the 10th century; in Vandalia and Prussia, in the 11th century; in Pomerania and Norway, in the 12th century; in Livonia, Lithuania, and part of Tartary, in the thirteenth century; in Sclavonia, part of Turkey, and the Canary isles, in the 14th century; in Africa, at Guinea, Angola, and Congo, in the 15th century; made great progress in Prussia, both the Indies, and in China, by the Protestant faith, in the 16th century; reinstated in Greece, &c., &c., in the 17th century.

Circumnavigators.—The first was Magellan, or rather by his fleet, (as he was himself slain on the voyage) 1520; Groalva, 1527; Alvaradi, 1537; Mendana, 1567; Sir Francis Drake, 1577; Cavendish, 1586; Lemaire, 1615; Quiros, 1625; Tasman, 1642; Cowley, 1683; Dampier. 1689; Cooke, 1708; Clipperton and Sherlock, 1719; Anson, 1740; Byron, 1764; Wallis 1766; Cook, 1768, 1772, 1776; continued by King, 1780; and since by Portlocke, 1788; Bougainville, 1766; La Peyrouse, 1782; D'Entrecasteaux, 1791.

Colossus of Rhodes, a gigantic brazen statue set up at Rhodes, about 300 B. C.; overthrown by an earthquake, 234; lay on the ground nearly 900 years, and was finally sold by the Saracens when they took the island of Rhodes, A. D. 672. The metal was supposed to have weighed 720,000lbs.

Corfu, a magazine at, was destroyed by fire, when 72,000 pounds of powder, and 600 bomb-shells blew up, and killed 180 men, March 11, 1789; seized by the French, 1797; taken by the Russians, March 3d, 1799.

Corsica, taken from the Moors by the Genoese, A. D., 1115; revolt in, 1730; offered to the British government, 1759; surrendered to France, 1766; put under the British, 1794, but abandoned by them in 1796, and taken again by the French; and afterwards permanently annexed to France.

D

Decameron of Boccacio, a volume in small folio, printed in 1471, was knocked down to the marquis of Blandford, at the sale of the duke of Roxburgh's library, for £2,260, June 17, 1812.

E

Edifices, highest now known, with their elevation.

Name and Situation.	*Eng. Ft.*
Pyramid of Gizeh in Egypt . . .	543
Steeples of the Cathedral at Cologne	501
Steeple of the Minster at Ulm . .	481
Steeple of the Cathedral at Antwerp	476
Steeple of the Minster at Strasburgh	466
Pyramid of Cheops in Egypt . .	452
Steeple of St. Stephen's at Vienna	442
Cupola of St. Peter's at Rome . .	431
Pyramid of Cephrenes in Egypt .	426

Steeple of St. Martin's at Landshut	422
Steeple of the Cathedral at Cremona	396
Steeple of the Minster at Friburg .	395
Cupola of the Cathedral at Florence	384
Steeple of St. Persina in Saxony .	382
Cupola of the Cathedral at Milan .	357
Steeple of the Cathedral at Utrecht	356
Pyramid of Sackkarah in Egypt .	356
Steeples of Notre Dame at Munich	348
Cupola of St. Paul's at London . .	347
Steeple of St Anscharius at Bremen	345
Steeples of the Cathedral at Magdeburg	335
Steeple of St. Mark's at Venice . .	328
Cupola of the Jesuits' church at Paris	314
Assinelli Tower at Bologna . . .	314
Steeple of St. Mary's at Berlin . .	305
Cupola of the Invalids at Paris . .	292

F

Fires, in Boston, March 21st, 1673, castle at the harbour burned; November 27th, 1676, 45 houses, the north meeting house, &c. destroyed; August 8, 1679, 80 houses, 70 warehouses, and a number of vessels destroyed; February 2d, 1798, theatre in Federal-street destroyed; October 4th, 1804, in Beach-street, when two men perished; March 21st, in Fish-street; May 10th, on the Long wharf; December 24th 1816, in several parts of the city; 3d November, 1818, the fine and spacious Exchange consumed.

——, *New-York*, December 29th, 1773, government house destroyed; a great fire by which about 1000 houses were consumed with Trinity church, the Charity school, Lutheran church, &c. September 21st, 1776; 300 houses destroyed, August 7th, 1778; December 9th, 1796, destructive fire at Maiden-lane, between 60 and 70 houses were destroyed; December 18th, fire began at 104 Front-street, about 40 houses, amount of loss estimated at $106,7 0; June 5th, and again on December 15th, 1810; in 1811, on May 19th, October 29th, and November 3rd; the first on Duane and Chatham-streets, 100 houses destroyed; 1813, August 12th. Beekman-street; August 31st, 21 houses destroyed on Dover, and Water-streets, and again same year, 1816; on December 4 and 5, a most ruinous conflagration on Water-street, loss estimated at $200,000; January 15th. 1817, in Chatham-street. From a report presented to the common council of New-York, by the chief engineer, it appears that 131 fires occurred in that city, from the 2nd of January, to the 3d of December, 1828, and the supposed loss of property is estimated at $680,402, including the Bowery theatre, which was burned, May 28, 1828: blocks on Vandam and Charlton-sts., July 4, 1831; on Hudson and Spring-sts., September 1832.

Philadelphia, 1790, March 24th, calico manufactory, S. W. corner of Market and Ninth-streets; 1793, Coates-street; and on the 10th and 11th of the same month and year, destructive conflagration on Third below Chesnut; again same year, September 8th, Dobson's printing office, Chesnut; 1794, December 26th, German Lutheran or Zion church; 27th January, 1797, fire in the printing office and dwelling of Andrew Brown, in Chesnut-street—his wife and three children perished, and he lingered until the 4th of February, when he expired; 1799, December 17th, Ricketts' circus, &c. destroyed; 1803, March 3d, in Whalebone alley, the first in the city, after the establishment of hose companies; 1811, destructive fires on March 1, 5, April 11th, June 15th, August 11th, October 19th, and 23d; of these, that on the 11th of April, on Locust-street, and that of the 19th of October, on Drinker's alley, were very destructive; 1816, on May 8th, July 12th, and December 10th and 24th; that on the 8th of May, on Coates'-street, was very destructive, seven houses being consumed; February 19th, 1817, Gaskill-st., fire overcome with great difficulty, from fire plugs being frozen; October 23d, same year on Arch, between Front and Second.

The most lamentable fire which ever occurred in Philadelphia, was that of the Orphan Asylum, on the very severely cold night betwe n January 23d and 24th 1822 in which twenty-three of the poor orphans perished.

"The great fire in London," 1666.

H

Hurricane, violent winds, particularly in the torrid zone, and in a manner particularly destructive in the West Indies: The following is a list of the most remarkable of these phenomena. 1670, 1674, 1675, Barbadoes; 1691, Antigua; 1700, 1702, Barbadoes; 1707, Carribbee Islands in general; 1712, Jamaica; 1720, Barbadoes; 1722, Jamaica, August 31; 1733, Carribbee Islands in general; 1744, Jamaica: 1764, Martinico, Carthagena, and particularly over some of the Carribbee Islands; 1772, most of the Caribbee Islands; 1780, October 3, Jamaica; 1828, February 18, violent gale at St. Ubes, Portugal, British ship Terror, and 100 men lost.

These gales are also highly destructive along the southern coast of the United States, and have extended with great force as far north as Boston. It is, however, in southern Asia, where the ravages of the wind have been most extensive and ruinous in their effects.

I

Inquisition, court of, began, 1204; abolished in Naples, 1782; in Tuscany, 1785; in Spain, 1811; in Rome, 1809; restored in Spain, 1814.

Joshua, book of, written 1415 B. C.

L

Longevity.—In the year 1772, Mrs. Williams, of Putney, Eng. died at the age of 169. In 1773, Charles M'Findley, of Tipperary; he was a captain in the reign of Charles I, 143. 1776, Mrs. Sarah Brookman, of Glastonbury, 166. 1780, Mr. W. Ellis of Liverpool, 130. 1787,

Mary Brook, Horton, in Staffordshire, 146. 1792, Mrs. Judith Scott, at Islington, 162. 1813, Mrs. Mary Meighan, Donoughmore, 129. 1814, Mary Innes, Glassakilly, Isle of Sky, 127.

—, *Greek.*—Longevity of the learned.—Zenophilus, 169 years of age, died — B. C.; Theophrastus, 106, 288; Zenophanes, 100, 500; Democritus, 100, —; Isocrates, 98, 338; Thales, 92, 348; Carneades, 90, —; Pyrrho, 90, 284; Sophocles, 91, 406; Simonides, 90, 468; Zeno, 97, 264; Pythagoras, 90, 510; Hypocrates, 80, —; Chrysippus, 83, 204; Diogenes, 88, —; Pharycides, 85, —; Solon, 82, 558; Periander, 87, 579; Plato, 81, 348; Thucydides, 80, 391; Zenocrates, 81, 314; Zenophon, 89, 359; Polybius, 81, 124; Socrates *poisoned*, 70, 400; Anaxagoras, 72, 428; Euripides, 76, 407; Æschylus, 70, 456; Aristotle, 63, 322: Anaximander, 64, 547: Pindar, 69, 452—Greek authors, 30—died above 100, 4; 90, 8; 80, 11; 60, 7.

—, *Roman*,—Varro, 87 years of age, died 28 years before Christ; Lucian, 80, —; Epicurus, 73, 168; Cicero, 63, 43; Livy, by a violent death, 67, A. D. 17; Pliny, the elder, 56, 79; Pliny the younger, by a violent death, 52, 113; Ovid, 59, 17; Horace, 57, —; Virgil, 51, B. C. 19.

M

Marriage in Lent forbidden 354; forbidden the priests, 1015; first celebrated in churches, 1226; banns of, first published in churches, about 1200; act of solemnizing it by justices of the peace, 1653; first celebration of a marriage in Virginia, 1608.

Mass first used in Latin, 394; introduced into England, 680; elevation required prostration, 1201.

Massacres, of all the Carthaginians in Sicily, 397 before Christ; 2,000 Tyrians crucified, and 8,000 put to the sword for not surrendering Tyre to Alexander, 331 before Christ. The Jews of Antioch fall upon the other inhabitants and massacre 100,000 for refusing to surrender their arms to Demetrius Nicanor, tyrant of Syria, 154; a dreadful slaughter of the Tuetones and Ambrones, near Aix, by Marius the Roman general, 200,000 being left dead on the spot, 102: the Romans throughout Asia, women and children not excepted, cruelly massacred in one day, by order of Mithridates, king of Pontus, 89: a great number of Roman senators massacred by Cinna, Marius, and Sertorius and several of the patricians dispatched, themselves to avoid their horrid butcheries, 86; again, under Sylla, and Cataline his minister of vengeance, 82 and 79; at Prneste, Octavius Cæsar ordered 300 Roman senators, and other persons of distinction to be sacrificed to the manes of Julius Cæsar, 44; at the destruction of Jerusalem, 1,000,000 Jews were put to the sword, A. D. 70; Cassius, a Roman general, under the emperor M. Aurelius, put to death 37,000 of the inhabitants of Seleucia. 197; at Alexandria, of many thousand citizens, by order of Antoninus, 213; the emperor Probus put to death 700,000 of the inhabitants upon his reduction of Gaul 277; of eighty christian fathers, by order of the emperor Gratian, at Nicomedia; they were put into a ship which was set on fire, and driven out to sea, 370; Thessalonica, when upwards of 7,000 persons, invited into the circus, were put to the sword by order of Theodosius, 390; Belisarius put to death above 30,000 citizens of Constantinople for a revolt on account of two rapacious ministers set over them by Justinian, 532; of the Latins, by Andronicus, 1184 (at Constantinople;) the Sicilians massacred the French throughout the whole island, without distinction of sex or age, on Easter-day, the first bell for vespers being the signal; this horrid affair is known in history by the name of the Sicilian vespers, 1282; at Paris 1418; of the Swedish nobility at a feast, by order of Christian II. 1520; of 70,000 Huguenots, or French protestants, throughout the kingdom of France, attended with circumstances of the most horrid treachery and cruelty; it began at Paris in the night of the festival of St. Bartholomew, August 25, 1572, by secret orders from Charles IX. king of France, at the instigation of the queen dowager, Catharine de Medicis, his mother, which is styled in history the massacre of St. Bartholomew; of the christians in Croatia, by the Turks, when 65,000 were slain, 1592; of a great number of Protestants at Thorn, who were put to death under a pretended legal sentence of the Chancellor of Poland, for being concerned in a tumult occasioned by a popish procession, 1724; at Batavia, where 12,000 Chinese were killed by the natives, October, 1740; in England, 300 English nobles, by Hengist, A. D. 475; of the Danes, in the southern counties of England, in the night of November 13, 1002, and the 23d Etheldred II. at London; it was the most bloody, the churches being no sanctuary; amongst the rest Gunilda, sister of Swein, king of Denmark, left in hostage for the performance of a treaty but newly concluded; of the Jews, (some few pressing into Westminster Hall, at Richard I.'s coronation, were put to death by the people, and a false alarm being given, that the king had ordered a general massacre of them, the people in many parts of England, from an aversion to them, slew all they met; in York, 500, who had taken shelter in the Castle, killed themselves, rather than fall into the hands of the people,) 1189; of the English, by the Dutch at Amboyna, 1624; of the protestants in Ireland, when 40,000 were killed, 1641; of the Macdonalds at Glencoe, in Scotland, for not surrendering in time according to king William's proclamation, though without the king's knowledge, 1692; several dreadful massacres in France during the

revolution, from 1789 to 1794; of 600 negroes by the French at St. Mark's, 1802; Algiers, March 16, 1806; insurrection and dreadful massacre at Madrid, May 2, 1808; of the Mamelukes in the citadel of Cairo, March 1, 1811; of the Greeks in the island of Scio, to the number of twenty or thirty thousand, June 1822, by the Turks; and again by the Greek garrison and inhabitants of the island of Hydra, 1824, which was however most severely retaliated upon the Turks in a few days, a body of Greek troops landing and putting the whole Turkish force to the sword; April 23d, 1826, the inhabitants and garrison of Missilonghi, were murdered under circumstances of accumulated horrors.

—— in the United States, of the first settlers of Virginia, of whom 347 were murdered in one night, 1622, by the savages; at Wilkesbarre by the British and savages, July 3d, 1778; by the British and savages at Cherry Valley, in New-York, Nov. 11th, 1778—both these sanguinary acts were done under the direction of colonel John Butler; of the Moravian Indians, by a party from the western part of Pennsylvania, headed by colonel Williamson, June, 1782; American garrison of Chicago, on their retreat from the place, by the savages, August 15th, 1812; of the American wounded prisoners at Frenchtown, on the river Raisin, January 22d, 1813, by the Indians, with the privity of the British.

N

National Confederation at Paris commemorated, July 14, 1790, in the field of Mars.

National Debt in England, first contracted in Henry VII.'s reign, £14,301; the present national debt commenced, and was near £5,000,000 in 1697; in 1776 one hundred and twenty-three millions; in 1786, two hundred and thirty-nine millions; and at midsummer, 1796, three hundred and sixty millions sterling. See Statistcs.

Money advanced by the bank of England for the public service, and outstanding on the 7th Decem., 1796, £6,777,739, 0s. 9d.

—— ——, and *national income* of the United States. See Statistics.

Navy of England, at the time of the Spanish armada, was only 28 vessels, none larger than frigates. James I. added ten ships of 1400 tons, the largest then ever built.—In 1798, the British navy in commission consisted 140 ships of the line, 22 of 50 guns, 165 frigates, and 317 sloops of war. Number of officers of the rank of lieutenants and upwards, was 2,980; expenditure for the navy this year was £12,591,728, or in dollars, $55,907,272 32c.

P

Paul, St. wrote his first Epistle to the Corinthians, and that to the Galatians, 51; first epistle to the Thessalonians 52; second Epistle, 53; second Epistle to the Corinthians, and that to the Philippians, Ephesians, Colossians, and Philemon, 62; to the Hebrews, 63; first Epistle to Timothy, and that to Titus, 65; second Epistle to Timothy, 66; festival instituted 813.

Pentateuch, or the five books of Moses, written 1452 before Christ.

Pillage, in Italy, by the French, and sent to Paris, consists of 66 pieces of sculpture, and 47 capital Paintings. Among the former are the following celebrated chefs d'œuvre:—the Apollo, the Antinous, the Adonis, the Dying Gladiators, the Laocoon, the Two Sphynxes, and the Tomb of the Muses; among the latter are the principal paintings of Raphael, Perugino, Guerchino, Annibal Carrache, Guido, Titian, and Corregio. In the catalogue of the articles sent to the national library, a manuscript of the antiquities of Josephus on papyrus, a manuscript Virgil of Petrarch, with notes in his handwriting, and 500 of the most curious manuscripts which were in the library of the Vatican.

Plague—The whole world visited by one, 767 before Christ; in Rome, when ten thousand persons died in a day, 78; in Chichester, when 34,000 died, 1772; in Scotland, which swept away 40,000 inhabitants, 954; in England, 1025, 1247, and 1347, when 50,000 died in London, 1500 in Leicester, &c. in Germany, which cut off 90,000 people, 1348; in Paris and London very dreadful, 1367; again, 1379, in London, which killed 30,000 persons, 1407; again when more were destroyed than in fifteen years war before, 1477; again when 30,000 died in London, 1499; again 1548, again 1594, which carried off in London a fourth part of its inhabitants, 1604; at Constantinople, when 200,000 persons died, 1611; at London when 35,417 died, 1625 and 1631; at Lyons, in France, died 60,000, 1632; again at London, which destroyed 68,000 persons in 1665; at Messina, February, 1743; at Algiers, 1755; in Persia, when 80,000 persons perished at Bassorah, 1773; at Smyrna that carried off about 20,000 inhabitants, 1784; and at Tunis, 32,000, 1784; in the Levant, 1786; at Alexandria, Smyrna, &c. 1791; in Egypt, in 1792, where nearly 800,000 died, the yellow fever destroyed 2,006, at Philadelphia, in 1793; on the coast of Africa, particularly at Barbary, 3,000 died daily; at Fez, 247,000 died in June, 1799; 1,800 died at Morocco in 1800, in one day; in Spain and at Gibraltar, where great numbers died in 1804 and in 1805; at Malta, where it committed great ravages, 1813; in lesser Asia, Syria, and the adjacent islands, by which Smyrna is computed to have lost 30,000 persons, 1814; in the kingdom of Naples, where it committed considerable ravages, 1816.

The *Yellow Fever* visited the city of New York, in the years 1741, 1742, 1791, 1795, 1798, 1799, 1800, 1803, 1805, 1819, and 1822. The deaths by that disease were as follows: 732 in 1795; 2086 in 1798; (population 55,000;) 670 in 1803;

280 in 1805; 23 in 1819; 366 in 1822. In 1803, 37,000 of the inhabitants (out of 76,000, the whole population) fled from the city. In 1804, 40 per one died with it at Brooklyn, but New-York escaped.

Philadelphia was nearly desolated by it in 1793, and again in 1798. 4041 persons died in 1793, and 17,000 fled from the city, (population 50,000.) In 1798, the mortality was great, and 50,000, out of 70,000 inhabitants, fled. Several thousand died, and the greatest number of deaths in one day was 117.

Baltimore suffered from this disease in 1798, 1819 and 1821.

New Orleans and Havanna have it annually.

Spasmodic or Asiatic Cholera. The severe epidemic, which under the name of the Cholera, Asiatic Cholera, Malignant Cholera, or Cholera Asphyxia, has within a few years afflicted many parts of the world, is reputed to have originated in August, 1817, at Jessore, the capital of a district in Bengal, lying to the northeast of Calcutta. In the following September it invaded Calcutta, soon after many other cities of Hindostan; and in a short time it extended its ravages into various other countries of Asia. It has been estimated that during the 14 years from its commencement at Jessore, it carried off no less than 18 millions of the inhabitants of Hindostan; and its ravages are said to have been still greater in China. See the "Revue Encyclopedique" for June, 1831. In 1830, it invaded European Russia, and afterwards Poland, Hungary, Germany, Austria, and other countries of Europe. In 1831, October, it broke out at Sunderland, in England; in February, 1832, in London; soon afterwards in various places in the British Empire; in Paris, near the last of March; at Quebec and Montreal in June; and at New-York in July. The mortality in Paris was very great, but the official reports after the first fortnight embraced only a part of the deaths. The number of deaths, as reported, from the 26th of March to the 15th of April, was 8,198; and in France, to the 1st of August, 69,159. The number of cases in England and Scotland, as reported, from the commencement of the disease to the 1st of September, was 47,874; deaths, 17,684; in Ireland, to the 19th of August, 22,865 cases, and 7,119 deaths. During its second appearance in London, no reports were published. The number of cases in Hungary has been stated at 435,330, and of deaths, at 188,000.

The following Table exhibits the Number of Cases of the Cholera and of Deaths in various places which have been visited by it, as reported, and stated in different Journals. *Am. Alm.* 1833.

			Cases.	*Deaths.*
GREAT BRITAIN AND IRELAND.				
Dublin,	. . . .		9,252	2,775
Glasgow,	to Aug.	15	4,164	1,993
Liverpool,	"	31	4,646	1,397
London,	to April	28	2,532	1,334
Cork,			3,305	843
Limerick,			2,497	843
Drogheda,	to July	28	1,202	488
Edinburgh,	"	25	796	467
Paisley,	"	25	638	368
Belfast,			2,559	303
Greenock,	to July	25	531	275
Hull,	"	26	726	250
Leeds,	"	26	544	212
York,	"	25	384	152
Plymouth,	"	26	354	147
Leith,	"	25	194	112
Warrington,	"	26	248	109
Carlisle,	"	25	214	109
CONTINENT OF EUROPE.				
St. Petersburg,			9,247	4,757
Moscow,			8,576	4,690
Lemberg,			4,922	2,589
Vienna,			3,984	1,893
Warsaw,			3,912	1,460
Berlin,			2,2.0	1,401
Prague,			3,234	1,333
Konigsberg,			2,188	1,314
Niznei Novgorod,			1,897	982
Kazan,			1.487	857
Breslau,			1,276	671
Brunn,			1,540	604
Hamburg,			874	455
Magdeburg,			576	346
Elbing,			434	283
Stettin,			366	250
Halle,			303	152
AMERICA.				
Quebec,	to Sept.	1		2,218
Montreal,	"	2	4,385	1,843
New-York,	"	8	5,842	3,197
Do.	Oct.	12		3,471
Philadelphia,	Sept.	1	2,240	740
Baltimore,	Sept.	29		710
Albany,	"	8	1,146	418
Norfolk,	"	11		400
Rochester,	"	3	389	107

Pope, the title of, formerly given to all bishops. The emperor in 666, confined it to the bishops of Rome; Hyginus was the first bishop of Rome that took the title, 154; the pope's supremacy over the christian church established by Boniface III., 607; custom of kissing the pope's toe began 708; pope Stephen III., was the first who was carried to the Lateran on men's shoulders, 752; the pope's temporal grandeur commenced, 755; Sergius II. was the first pope that changed his name on his election, 844; John XIX., a layman, made pope by dint of money. 1024; the first pope that kept an army was Leo IX. 1054. Their assumed authority carried to such excesses as to excommunicate and depose sovereigns, and to claim the presentation of all church benefices, by Gregory VII., and his successors, from 1073 to 1500; pope Gregory obliged Henry IV., emperor of Germany, to stand three days in the depth of winter, bare-footed at his castle gate, to implore his pardon, 1077, pope Celestine III., kicked the emperor

Henry IV's., crown off his head, while kneeling, to show his prerogative of making and unmaking kings, 1191; the pope's authority first introduced into England, 1079; the pope demanded an annual sum for every cathedral and monastery in christendom, but was refused, 1226; collected the tenths of the whole kingdom of England, 1226; residence of the pope removed to Avignon, where it continued seventy years, 1308; their demand on England refused by parliament, 1363; three at one time in 1414; Leo X., made a cardinal at 14 years old; elected pope, March 11, 1513, aged 36; died 1521; Clement VII., began to reign, who brought pluralities to their consummation, making his nephew, Hippolito, Cardinal de Medicis, commendatory universal, granting to him all the vacant benefices in the world, for six months, and appointing him usu-fructuary from the first day of his possession, 1523; Rome sacked and Clement imprisoned, 1527; moved their residence to Avignon, 1531; kissing the pope's toe, and some other ridiculous ceremonies abolished, and the order of Jesuits suppressed by the late pope Clement XIV., 1773; visited Vienna to solicit the emperor in favour of the church, March, 1782; suppressed monasteries, 1782; destitute of all political influence in Europe, 1787.

Post-Office establishment of the United States. The following statement shows the gradual increase and present condition of the post-office department:—

Years.	*Post Offices.*	*Revenue.*	*Miles of Post R.*
1792	195	$67,444	5,642
1797	554	213,998	16,180
1802	1,114	327,045	25,315
1807	1,848	478,763	33,755
1812	2,610	649,208	39,378
1817	3,459	1,002,973	52,009
1823 end'g July 1,	4,498	1,114,344	82,763
1828	7,651	1,598,134	114,536

Potatoes, first brought to England from America, by Hawkins, in 1563; introduced into Ireland by sir Walter Raleigh, in 1586, and were not known in Flanders till 1650.

R

Reformation, began in England, by John Wickliffe, 1370; in Germany, by Huss, and Jerome of Prague; by Luther, 1517; in Hungary by Zirka, 1518; in Swisserland, by Zuinglius, 1519; in Denmark, 1521; in Sweden, 1523; completed in England, under Henry VIII., 1534.

Revolutions, important, in ancient history. See *Chronological Table* in this work, B. C., 1491, 1451, 975, 747, 721, 606, 536, 331, 168, 146, and 31. Modern History, A. D., 364, 476, 800, 823, 1066, 1453. In England, in 1688, Poland, 1772, and 1795; Turkey, in 1730 and 1808; Persia in 1748 and 1753; Russia, 1682, 1740, and 1762; Sweden, in 1772 and 1809; America, in 1775; France, in 1789, and July 27, 1830; Holland, 1795; Venice, May 17, 1797; Rome, February 26, 1797; South America, April 19, 1810; Belgium, 1830; Poland, 1831.

S

Sanctuaries, or cities of refuge, were instituted by the Jews immediately after their establishment in Palestine, about 1400 B. C. Such use or rather abuse, was made of the heathen temples, particularly those of Hercules; Christian churches commenced to be used as such, A. D., 617; abolished in England, 1534.

Swearing on the holy gospel first used, 528.

T

Theatre at Cape d'Istria, in Italy, fell and crushed the performers and audience to death, February 6, 1794.

—— at Mentz, was destroyed by fire during the performance, on the falling in of which many were crushed to death, and above 70 were burnt, August 1796.

—— at Richmond, Va., took fire during the performance, and 70 respectable citizens were burnt to death, 1811.

DISCOVERIES IN THE ARTS, INVENTIONS, &c.

A

Air Guns, invented 1646.

Air Pumps, invented by Otto Guerick, in 1654.

Algebra, or the arithmetic of symbols, invented, it is supposed, in India, was introduced into Europe about A. D. 1300, by the Saracens of Spain. It had become extensively known in 1500.

Almanacs, first published by Martin Ilkus at Buda, 1470: stamps for, in England increased in 1781.

Alphabetic writing introduced into Europe by Cadmus, 1493, B. C.

Anathema, first used by the Christians as a punishment, A. D. 387.

Annuities, or Pensions, first granted in England, 1512, when £20 was given to a lady of the court for services done; and in 1536, £6 13s. 4d. thought sufficient to maintain a gentlewoman: again in 1554, £13 6s. 8d. deemed a competent sum to support a student at law. Annuities for life were regulated by law, 1777.

Arithmetic, by the Arabian figures, introduced into Europe by the Saracens of Spain, in the ninth and tenth centuries of the Christian era.

Arundelian Marbles—These celebrated chronological tables, were brought from Greece to England, in 1627, by Thomas earl of Arundel. They were composed of a large number of marble slabs or blocks, which were, however, mutilated, and in part lost during the civil wars in England, in the middle of the 17th century. Fortunately they have been at different times, and partly whilst the collection was complete, edited by Seldon, Iredeaux, Mattaire, Chandler, &c and though by some their genuineness has been doubted, they are now by the best critics, considered real and invaluable remains of the literature of ancient Greece. They contain a connected chronology in Greek capital letters, from the reign of Cecrops, king of Athens, B. C. 1582, to the Archonship of Astyanax in Paros, and of Diognetus at Athens, B C 264. What remains entire are in the possession of the university of Oxford.

Assassins, a nation or sect of Persia and Phœnicia, which rose into notice about A. D. 891; about 1090, they were settled in Persia. These wretches were the common enemies of mankind, and have given their name to the most atrocious species of murder; they were extirpated about 1258, by Hulacu, the conqueror of Bagdad. Their chief was called "Sheikh Al Jebal" or Old Man of the Mountain.

Astronomy. According to Calisthenes, astronomical observations were made at *Babylon* as early as 2000 years before Christ. The science known to the Chinese, B. C. 1100; lunar eclipses accurately observed at Babylon, 720; spherical form of the earth and the true cause of lunar eclipses taught by Thales about 600; further discoveries in by *Pythagoras*, (who taught the doctrine of celestial motions, and believed in the plurality of habitable worlds, &c. 500; *Dionysius* was the first who found the solar year to consist of 365 days, 5 hours, and 49 minutes, 285; *Hipparchus* began his observations at Rhodes, 167; and made further discoveries, 140, B. C.

The precession of the equinoxes confirmed, and the places and distances of the planets discovered by *Ptolemy*, A. D. 130. After the elapse of several centuries, during which time the science was neglected, it was resumed by the *Arabs*, A. D. 800; brought into Europe by the *Moors*, 1200.—*Copernicus* revived the true doctrine of the planetary motions, 1530; his immortal work the "*Astronomia Instaurata*," was not published till after his death, 1543. *Tycho Brake* made further discoveries in 1600. *Telescopes* invented by *Galileo*, 1610. *Kepler* published his "*Astronomia Nova Celestis*," defining the true laws of the planetary motions, 1626. *Gassendi*, *Richer* and *Huygen's* discoveries followed. *Sir Isaac Newton's* "*Principia*," (consummating what Copernicus and Kepler had begun, explaining the *causes* of the celestial phenomena, and firmly establishing the system as now taught,) published, 1687. Dr. *Herschell*, discovered the Georgium Sidus, (which afterwards received his name,) 1781. *Piazza* discovered Ceres,—1801; Dr. *Olbers* of Bremen, discovered Pallas, 1802, and Vesta, 1807, and Mr. *Harding* discovered Juno, 1804.—*La Place's* "*Mecanique Celeste*" published, 18—. "This immortal monument of human genius" has completed the most sublime of the sciences. It has been translated into English by Dr. *Bowditch*, of Boston, Mass.

Aurora Borealis, first recorded to be seen March 6th, 1716; it had been no doubt occasionally observed from time immemorial.

B

Baize manufacture first introduced into England, at Colchester, 1660.

Balloons, said to have been invented by Gusmac, a Jesuit, 1729. Mr. Lunardi, at London, September 15th, 1784, rose from Moorfields, being the first ascent in England. First experiment with balloons in this country, were made by Dr. Rittenhouse and Francis Hopkinson, December, 1783. They connected several small balloons together, and thus enabled a man to ascend to the height of 100 feet, and to float to a considerable distance. Afterwards an ascent was made by Blanchard, at Philadelphia, January 9, 1793.

Bank, signifying literally a bench, from the custom of Italian merchants, exposing money to lend on a banco or bench, or tables. Banks commenced about the beginning of the ninth century; that of Venice, 1157; of Genoa, 1345; of Amsterdam, 1609; of Rotterdam, 1635; of England, 1640; old Scotch bank, 1649; of Hamburgh, 1710; Royal Bank of Scotland, 1727; of Ireland, 1783. Saving banks, first established in different places in England, 1816.

——, of England was originally projected by a merchant of the name of Patterson, and established, A. D., 1694.

——, of North America, incorporated by congress, December 31, 1781—first at Boston, 1784, and the bank of New-York commenced the same year. The banks of New-Hampshire and South Carolina, incorporated in 1792.

——, of the United States, incorporated March 2, 1791.

"The United States, Bank," with a capital of 35,000,000, of dollars, was chartered for 20 years, April, 1816, and with power to form branches. The mother bank at Philadelphia, went into operation January 1, 1817. It appears, by an official report to congress, 1828, from the treasury department, that the average annual amount of public money in the Bank of the United States and its branches, from 1817 to 1827, inclusive, was 3,554,756 dollars, 50 cents.

Bankers, the first were Lombard Jews, about A. D., 808. In England, the mint was used formerly by merchants to lodge their money in, till the king made free with it in 1640; after which trusting to servants, till too many of them ran to the army, they lodged it with goldsmiths, whose business was to buy and sell plate, and foreign coins; they at first paid fourpence per cent. per diem, but lent it to others at higher interest, and so became the first bankers, 1645.

Barometers, invented 1626; wheel barometers contrived, 1668; phosphoric, 1675; pendant, 1695; marine, 1700.

Battering Ram, invented 441, B. C.

Bayonets, invented at Bayonne, in France, 1670; first used in England, September 24th, 1693.

Bellows, invented 554, B. C.

Bells, invented by Paulinius, bishop of Nola, in Campania, about 400; first known in France, 550; first used in the Greek empire, 864; were introduced into monasteries in the seventh or eighth century. Pope Stephen III., placed three bells in a tower on St. Peter's at Rome. In the churches of Europe they were introduced in 900.

Bills of Exchange first mentioned, 1160; used in England, 1307; the only mode of sending money from England by law, 1381.

Blankets, first made in England 1340.

Blister plasters, invented 60, B. C.

Blue, Prussian, discovered at Berlin, 1704.

Blood, circulation of, through the lungs, first made public by Michael Servetus, a French physician, in 1553; Cisalpinus published an account of the general circulation, of which he had some confused ideas, and improved it afterwards by experiments, 1569; but it was fully confirmed by Harvey, 1628.

Bombs, first invented at Venloo, and used in the siege of Wachtendonch, 1588; first used in the service of France, 1634.

Bomb vessels, first invented in France, 1681.

Books, in the present form, were invented by Attalus, king of Pergamus, about 140 B.C. the first supposed to be written in Job's time; a very large estate given for one on Cosmography, by king Alfred; were sold from 10*l.* to 30*l.* a piece, about 1400; the first printed one was the Vulgate edition of the Bible, 1462; the second was Cicero de Officiis 1466; Cornelius Nepos published at Moscow, being the first classical book printed in Russia, April 29th, 1762; books to the number of 200,000 burnt at Constantinople, by the order of Leo I., 476: above 4,194 412 volumes were in the suppressed monasteries of France in 1790; 2,000,000 were on theology, the manuscripts were 26,000; in the city of Paris alone were 808,120 volumes. See Library.

Bread, made from the flower of gramineous fruits, discovered in very early ages, but not made with yeast by the English until 1650.

Breeches, first introduced into England, 1654.

Breviaries, first introduced in 1080.

Bricks, first used in England by the Romans—the size ordered 1625, by Charles I.

Bridge, the first stone in England, was at Bow near Stratford, 1087.

Building, with stone brought into England by Bennet, a monk, 670; with bricks first introduced by the Romans into their provinces; first in England about 886; reintroduced there by the earl of Arundel 1600, London being then almost entirely built with wood.

C

Calendar, established by Julius Cæsar, 45 B. C.; reformed by pope Gregory, XIII, 1582.

Calico, first imported into England, 1631; first made in Lancashire, 1772; calico-printing and the Dutch loom, first used in England, 1676.

Camera Obscura, invented, 1515.

Canals,—The first regular chain of artificial water inter-communication, of which history has transmitted to us the record, was that between the Nile and Red Sea. This canal route was examined with great care by the French engineers, and several portions found in 1798, in such a state of preservation as only to demand cleansing. It went from Balbeis, on the old Pelusiac branch of the Nile, to Abbaseh, the ancient Thou. It then enters the narrow valley of Arabes—Tomylat, thirty-two or thirty-three feet below the level of the Red Sea; and goes on to Abookesheyd. The original authors of this work have been concealed in the morning darkness of time. The last period at which it was opened was by order of the caliph Omar, A. D. 644, but was again choaked up by order of Jaafar, al Mansur, the second Abasside caliph, 767. The present pacha of Egypt is taking measures to restore this great work.

The system of modern canal improvement may be stated to have commenced in Italy, at Viterbo, 1481, when sluices with double doors were invented, and first used on a large scale, near Milan, by Leonardi da Vinci. The canals of the Delta of the Rhine commenced, it is true, in the dark ages, but it was not before the end of the fifteenth century, that they were planned and constructed with scientific regularity of design. Such, however, has been the progress in the last three centuries, that from the Dollart bay to Ghent, in a distance of about 220 miles, with a mean width of 100 or 22,000 square miles, more than 1400 millions of dollars have been expended on inland navigation. One of the most expensive lines, that from the Holder to Amsterdam, completed, and first navigated in January, 1826.

—— of Languedoc, which joins the Mediterranean and Cantabrian seas, began by Louis XIV.; sixty-four leagues long, supported by 104 sluices.

—— in China, goes from Canton to Pekin, chiefly by the natural channels of rivers, upwards of 806 miles, having 75 locks, and 41 large cities on its banks, with above 10,000 vessels on it; finished in 980; 30,000 men were employed 43 years in making it. In 1355 a canal was dug in Persia, 100 miles long. The Russian chain of inland navigation, began by Peter the Great, in 1708, between the Caspian sea and the Baltic, was not entirely completed till 1780. The line of rivers and canals from the frontiers of China, to Petersburgh, is 4472 miles long, that from Astrachan to Petersburg, 1434 miles long; both of which were began by Peter the Great, who also began some others. In Prussia, a complete chain of inland navigation extends from the Elbe at Magdeberg in part through the channels of Havel, Oder, Netz, Vistula and Nieman, and in part by cuts over the intervening strips of land. This line, including the Elbe, reaches from the North Sea to the Memel, upwards of 800 miles. Besides this great longitudinal series, there are many of lesser note, chiefly constructed by that wonder of human nature, Frederick II. I. Flaven, seventeen miles from the bend of the Havel, near Brandenburgh, to the Elbe, and which shortens the route from Berlin to Magdeburg, 76 miles. II. The canal of Potsdam, a cut to shorten the navigation of the Havel. III. Finaw, 23 miles, uniting the Havel to the Oder. IV. Muhlrose, the oldest canal in Prussia, finished 1688; it is twenty-three miles long, connecting the Spree and Oder, extending from Muhlrose to the Oder, five miles above Frankfort. In Sweden, a project to construct a line of canal navigation from Gothenberg on the Cattegat, to Stockholm, through the Wesmer, and other lakes and rivers was formed as early as 1526, but not prosecuted with any great effect until within this century, and though much advanced is far from complete.

The canal of Kiel in Denmark, is one of the most useful, and in its excavation one of the most perfect canals ever made begun 1777, and finished 1784—length, 22½ miles, admitting vessels of nine feet draught; commencing to the north of Kiel, three English miles, and extends to Rendsberg on the Eyder River. The whole navigation from the North Sea to the Baltic by the Eyder and canal, about 120 miles, whilst the distance round Jutland and through the Danish islands, exceeds five hundred miles.

—— in the United States commenced in Massachusetts. The company formed to construct, what is now called the Middlesex canal, was incorporated 1789; commenced the work 1790: length 29¾ miles, and entire fall 107, by locks; 24 feet wide with four feet water.

The greatest of all works of this nature, yet executed in America, are the two great canals of New-York. The western canal from the Hudson River to Lake Erie, was first suggested by Mr. Gouverneur Morris about 1803: surveys were directed by a resolution of the legislature of New-York, in furtherance of this project, 1808; first board of commissioners organised, 1810, consisting of Gouverneur Morris, Stephen Van Rensselaer, De Witt Clinton, Simeon De Witt, William North, Thomas Eddy, and Peter B. Porter. Law authorizing the actual survey of the ground, passed, April 17th, 1816; this great work was commenced, July 4th, 1817; completed, and the water of Lake Erie let into it, Oct. 26th, 1825; employing 8 years and 144 days. The completion of the Northern, or Lake Champlain Canal, preceded that of Erie, and both taken together consummates the inland communication between the city of New York and the Basin of St. Lawrence. For other canals in the United States, see Statistics.

Candles, of tallow, so great a luxury in England, that splinters of wood were used for light, A. D., 1300—no idea of wax candles until long afterwards.

Candle-light introduced into churches on the continent of Europe, 274.

Canon law, first introduced into England, 1140.

Canonization, first used by papal authority, A. D., 993.

Cards, invented in France, first used for the amusement of Charles VI., 1380; their use was forbidden in Castile in 1387; 128,000 packs were stamped in Englandin 1775.

Cards, for carding cotton and wool, manufactory of, in England; exportation to America prohibited after the revolution, when the manufactory was carried on in several parts of the United States; and about 1800, an American citizen discovered a method of cutting and stamping holes in the leather, bending, cutting, and fixing in the teeth, by machinery, so that the cards, excepting the wood-work, drop completely finished from the machine.

Carriages, first introduced into Vienna, 1515; into London, 1580.

Carving in marble, invented, 772, B. C.

Catalogues, of English printed books, were first published 1595, in Ireland, 1632.

Chain-shot, invented by admiral de Witt, 1666.

Chairs, sedan, first used in London; a fourteen year's patent for selling them granted to Duncombe, 1634.

Cherries brought to Rome, by Lucullus, 70; apricots were first introduced into England, from Epirus; peaches from Persia; the finest plums from Damascus and Armenia; pears and figs from Greece and Egypt; citrons from Media; pomegranates from Carthage, about 114 years before Christ.

Chess, the game of, invented 608, before Christ.

Chest, at Chatham, for the relief of seamen, instituted, 1588.

Chiaro-obscuro, the art of printing in, with three plates, to imitate drawings, first used 1500.

Chimneys first introduced into buildings in England, 1200; only in the kitchen, or large hall, smoky; where the family sat round a large stove, the funnel of which passed through the ceiling, 1300.

China-ware, made in England at Chelsea, in 1752; and in several parts of England, in 1760; by Mr. Wedgewood, 1762; at Dresden, in Saxony, 1706.

Chocolate. introduced into Europe from Mexico, 1520.

Church Music, introduced into worship, 350; choral service. first used in England, at Canterbury, 677; changed throughout England. from the use of St. Paul's to that of Sarum. 1418; first performed in English. May 8, 1559.

Church-Yards, first consecrated, 317; admitted into cities. 740.

Cinnamon trade, first began by the Dutch, 1506; but had been known in the time of Augustus Cæsar, and long before.

Clocks, called water clocks, first used in Rome, 158 B. C.; clocks and dials first set up in churches, 913; clocks made to strike by the Arabians, 801; by the Italians, 1300; a striking clock in Westminster, 1368; the first portable one made 1530; none in England that went tolerably, till that dated 1540, maker's name, N. O., now at Hampton-court palace; clocks with pendulums, &c., invented by one Fromantil, a Dutchman, about 1656; repeating clocks and watches invented by one Barlow, 1676. Till about 1631, neither clocks nor watches were general.

Cloth, coarse woollen, introduced into England, 1191; first made at Kendal, 1390; medleys first made, 1614.

Coaches, first used in England, 1580: an act passed to prevent men riding in coaches as effeminate, in 1601. Began to be common in London, 1605. Hackney chariots, not to exceed 200, licensed 1814.

Coals, discovered near New-Castle, 1234.

Coffee, first brought into England by Nathaniel Conopius, a Cretan, who made it his common beverage, at Baliol college, Oxford, in 1641: first brought to Marseilles, 1644.

Coffee-house, the first in England was kept by Jacob, a Jew, at the sign of the Angel, in Oxford, in 1650.

Coffee-trees were conveyed from Mocha to Holland, in 1616; and carried to the West-Indies in the year 1726; first cultivated at Surinam by the Dutch, 1718; its culture encouraged in the plantations, 1732.

Coin—silver, coined at Rome, 269 B. C.; before then brass money was only used; coin first used in Britain, 25 years B. C.

The Mint of the United States of America, established 1793.

Colleges, as places of public instruction in which academical degrees were granted, were first known at Paris, A. D., 1215, and were completely established there 1231.

The following is a list of the principal colleges or universities in Europe: Cambridge began 626, according to some others, 900; revived, 1110: Dublin, 1591; Edinburgh, founded by James VI. 1580; Frankfort, on the Oder, 1506; Geneva, 1365; Glasgow. Scotland, 1450: Goetingen, Hanover, 1734; Leipsic, Saxony, 1409; Moscow, 1751; Oxford, in England 866; Padua, Italy, 1197; Paris, 792; Petersburgh, Russia, 1747; Sorbonne, France, 1253; Strasburgh, Germany, 1538; Venice, 1592; Vienna, 1236; Utrecht, Holland, 1636; Wurtemburg, Saxony, 1502.

Colleges, or Universities in the United States—See Statistics.

Harvard college, or Cambridge university is the most ancient literary institution in the United States; founded, 1638; first degrees conferred, 1642.

Companies, Societies, Offices, &c., incorporated. See Statistics.

Comedy, the first acted in Athens, on a scaffold, by Susarion and Dolon, 562 B. C.;

those of Terence first acted 154 B. C.; the first in England, 1551.

Compass, or the polarity of magnetised iron, one of the greatest, and as to the *date* of its discovery, most uncertain of human improvements. There is however, good evidence to prove that the mariner's compass was in use in Europe as early as A. D., 1180; variation first observed by Columbus and his companions, 1492; its dip, about 1576.

Copper mines, first discovered in Sweden, 1396; in England, 1561; revived in England, 1689; found in New-York, 1722. The Paris copper mine in Anglesea has a bed of copper ore forty feet thick, and and supplies between 20 and 30,000 tons annually.

Copper mine, discovered in Cornwall, 1806.

Copper is found native in the United States, near the south side of Lake Superior, and in some other places.

Counties, first division of, in England, A. D., 900.

Cow-pox, inoculation by, as a security against the small-pox, introduced into England, by Dr. Jenner, 1800.

Customs, on exports and imports, first collected in England, about 979; amounted to but £14,000 in 1580; to £50,000 in 1592; to £300,000 in 1642; to £4,669,000 in 1786; to £4,965,000 in 1787; to £6,890,000 1790; to £9,973,240 in 1808, and to £11,498,762 in 1823.

D

Decimal Arithmetic, introduced into common use in Europe, about 1600.

Degrees, academical, first granted at Paris, 1213.

Diamonds, first polished and cut at Bruges, 1489.

——, mines discovered in Brazil, 1730; that at Coulour in the East-Indies, 1640; that at Golconda, in 1584; one sent from Brazil for the court of Portugal, weighed 1680 carats, or twelve ounces and a half; valued at 224 millions sterling. Governor Pitt's weighed 127 carats, and 106 after cutting, and sold for £135,000, to the king of France. That which belonged to Aureng Zebe weighed 793 carats. The Mogul's weighed 279 carats, worth £779,244. The grand duke of Tuscany's weighed 139 carats.

Dice, invented 1500 B. C.

Distillation of spirituous liquors began in the 12th century. In Ireland in 1590.

Duelling, introduced into Europe as a public mode of trial, A. D., 1096; became common as a manner of settling points of honour, about 1520.

E

Earthern vessels, first made by the Romans, 715, B. C.; the first made in Italy, 1710; the present improved kind began in 1763, by Mr. Wedgewood.

Electricity, first idea of, given by two globes of brimstone, 1467; electric spark discovered at Leyden, 1746; first known it would fire spirits, 1756; that of the aurora borealis and of lightning in 1769.

Engraving on metal plates, first known in Europe, 584, B. C., by a map on brass brought from Quonia by Anaxagoras of Samos; and yet it was not until A. D., 1423, that impressions were taken on paper from engraved plates; the art of taking impressions from engravings on copper as now used, 1511; in mezzotinto, and improved by prince Rupert, of Palatine, 1648; to represent wash, invented by Barable, a Frenchman, 1761; crayon engraving invented at Paris by Bonnet, 1769.

Engraving on wood, invented in Flanders, 1423; revived by Alb. Durer, 1511; on glass invented 1799, at Paris, by Boudier.

Etching on copper, with aqua fortis, invented, 1512.

Excise, the first used in England, 1643.

F

Fairs, and markets, first instituted in England by Alfred, about 886. The first fairs took their rise from wakes; when the number of people then assembled brought together a variety of traders annually on these days. From these holidays they were called *feriæ*, or fair.

Fans, muffs, masks and false hair, first devised by the harlots in Italy, and brought into England from France, 1572.

Feudal laws, the tenure of land, by suit and service, to the lord or owner of it, introduced into England by the Saxons, about 600; the slavery of this tenure increased under William I. 1068. This was dividing the kingdom into baronies, giving them to certain persons, and requiring those persons to furnish the king with money, and a stated number of soldiers.

Fire engine, to force water, invented, 1663;

—— ships, first invented, 1588.

—— under water, invented, 622.

Fortification, the present mode introduced, about 1500.

G

Gamut, in music, invented by Guy L'Aretin, 1025.

Gardening, introduced into England from the Netherlands, from whence vegetables were imported, till 1509; the pale gooseberry, with salads, garden roots, cabbages &c., brought from Flanders, and hops from Artois, 1520; the damask rose brought by Dr. Linacre, physician to Henry VIII.; pippins brought to England by Leonard Mascal, of Plumstead, in Sussex, 1525; currants or Corinthian grapes, first planted in England, 1555; brought from the isle of Zant, belonging to Venice; the musk rose and several sorts of plums, from Italy, by lord Cromwell; apricots carried there by king Henry VIII's. gardener; tamarask plant from Germany, by archbishop Grindal; at and about Norwich the Flemings first planted flowers unknown in England, as gilliflowers, carnations, the Provence rose, &c. 1567; woad originally from Thoulouse, in France; tulip roots first brought into England from Vienna, 1578; also beans, peas and salads, now in common use, 1660. To which subjoin the following list, with the countries whence they originally came.

Rye and wheat, from Tartary and Siberia, where they are yet indigenous; barley and oats unknown, but certainly not indigenous in England; rice from Ethiopia; buckwheat, Asia; borage, Syria; cresses, Crete; cauliflower, Cyprus; asparagus, Asia; schervil, Italy; fennel, Canary Islands; annise and parsley, Egypt; garlick, the East; shallots, Siberia; horseradish, China; kidney beans, East Indies; gourds, Astracan; lentils, France; potatoes, Brazil; tobacco, America; cabbage, lettuce, &c. Holland.

Jassamine comes from the East Indies; the elder tree from Persia; the tulip from Cappadocia; the daffodil, from Italy, the lily from Syria; the tube-rose from Java and Ceylon; the carnation and pink from Italy, &c.; ranunculus, from the Alps; apples from Syria; apricots, from Epirus; artichokes, from Holland; celery, from Flanders; cherries, from Pontus; currants, from Zant; damask and musk roses, from Damascus, as well as plums; hops, from Artois and France; gooseberries, from Flanders; gilliflowers, carnations, the Provence rose, &c. from Thoulouse, in France; oranges and lemons from Spain; beans and peas, from Spain.

Gas, use of, introduced in London, for lighting shops and streets, 1814; first into the United States, at Baltimore, 1821.

Gazettes, of Venetian origin, and so called from the price being gazetta, a small piece of money; the first published in England, was at Oxford, November 7, 1665; the London Gazette was first published February 5, 1665-6. One was ingeniously forged for a stock-jobbing purpose, November, 1787; the first published at Paris, was in 1723; at Leipzic, in 1715.

Georgium Sidus discovered by Herschell, 1781.

Glass, the art of making it, known to the Romans at least before 79; known to the Chinese about 200; introduced into England by Benedict, a monk, 674; glass windows began to be used in private houses in England, 1180; glass first made in England into bottles and vessels, 1557; the first plate glass for looking glasses and coach windows, made at Lambeth, 1673; in Lancashire, 1773; window glass first made in England, 1557.

Globe of the earth, the first voyage round it was by Sir Francis Drake, 1580; the second by Magellan, 1591; the third by sir Thomas Cavendish, 1586; by lord Anson in 1740; by captain Cook in 1768; and by Peyrouse in 1793—4.

Grammarians, the first regular ones flourished, 276 before Christ.

Greek first introduced into England, 1491.

Gregorian Calendar, first used in the Catholic states of Europe, 1582; in most of the others, 1710; in England and in Sweden, 1752.

Gristmills invented in Ireland, 214.

Gunpowder invented, 1330; first made in England, 1418; first used in Spain, 1344.

Guns, great, invented, 1330; used by the Moors at the siege of Algesiras, in Spain, in 1344; used at the Battle of Cressy, in 1346, when Edward had four pieces of cannon, which gained him the battle; they were used at the siege of Calais, in 1347; in Denmark, 1354; at sea by Venice against Genoa, 1377; first used in Spain, 1406; first made in England of brass, 1635; of iron, 1547; invented to shoot whales, 1731; first used in England, at the siege of Berwick, 1405; bombs and mortars invented, 1634.

H

Handkerchiefs first manufactured at Paisley, in Scotland, 1748, when £15,886 worth were made; in 1784 the manufacture yielded above £164,385.

Harmonicon or Musical Glasses, invented by Francis Hopkinson, of Philadelphia; also attributed to Dr. Franklin. Without knowledge of the preceding facts, Francis Hopkinson Smith, of Baltimore, greatly improved and adapted this simple, rich and delicate instrument, to every key of the gamut, 1825.

Hats invented at Paris, 1404; first made in London, 1510.

Hebrew Points invented, 475.

Hemp and *Flax* first planted in England, 1533. There are 180,000 pounds of rough hemp used in the cordage and sails of a first rate man of war.

Heraldic Lines for colours in coats of arms invented, 1639.

Heraldry had its rise, 1100.

Hour Glasses, were invented in Alexandria, 240, and introduced at Rome, 158 years before Christ.

Hydrostatics taught by Archimedes, 200 years before Christ.

I

Indigo, first produced in Carolina 1747; cultivated in the open air at Vauchuse, in France, 1808.

Inoculation first tried on criminals, 1721.

Insurance on Ships and *Merchandise*, Suetonius conjectures that Claudius was the first contriver of, 43.

——— *on Shipping* began in England, 1560.

——— *Offices* established in London, and its vicinity, 1696.

——— *Policies* were first used in Florence in 1523; first society established at Hanover, 1530; that at Paris, 1740.

Interest first mentioned as legal, 1199, at 10 per cent.; in 1300, at 20 per cent.; in 1558, at 12 per cent.; in 1571, at 10 per cent.; in 1625, at 8 per cent.; in 1749 the funds were reduced from 4 to 3½ and 3 per cent.

Iron discovered by the burning of mount Ida, 1406 B. C.; first cast in England at Backstead, Sussex, 1544; first discovered in America, in Virginia, 1715; bullets first used in England, 1550.

Italian method of book-keeping, published in England, 1569.

Journals of the house of peers, the first taken, 1550.

Jupiter's satellites, discovered by Jansen, 1590.

Juries, first instituted by Ethelred, 979; the plaintiff and defendant in those times used to feed them; whence the common law of denying sustenance to a jury after hearing evidence.

Kingdoms, origin of, by Nimrod, at Babylon, 2204 B. C.

Knitting Stockings, invented in Spain about, 1550.

Knives, first made in England, 1563.

L

Lace, Flanders, more valuable than gold—one ounce of fine Flanders thread has been sold in London for 4*l*. Such an ounce made into lace may be sold for 40*l*. which is ten times the price of standard gold, weight for weight.

Lamp, for preventing explosion by fire-damp in coal mines, invented by sir Humphrey Davy, 1815.

Lanterns, invented by king Alfred, 890.

Library, the first private one, the property of Aristotle, 334 B. C.; the first public library in history was founded at Athens by Hipparchus, 526 B. C.; the second of any note was founded at Alexandria, by Ptolemy Philadelphus, 284. It was burnt when Julius Cæsar set fire to Alexandria, 47 B. C.; (400,000 valuable books in MS. are said to have been lost by this catastrophe.)—The first library at Rome, was established, 167; at Constantinople, founded by Constantine the Great, about A. D., 335; destroyed, 477; a second library formed from the remains of the first at Alexandria, by Ptolemy's successors, and reputed to have consisted of 700,000 volumes, was totally destroyed by the Saracens, who heated the water of their baths for six months, by burning books instead of wood, by command of Omar, caliph of the Saracens, 642; the Vatican at Rome, by pope Nicholas V., 1446; re-built and the library considerably improved by Sixtus V., 1588; the imperial of Vienna, by Maximilian I., about 1500; the royal of Paris, by Francis I., about 1520; the escurial at Madrid, by Philip II., 1557; of Florence, by Cosmo de Medicis, 1560; the Bodleian at Oxford, founded 40 Eliz. 1598; the Cottonian, formerly kept at Cotton-house, Westminster, founded by sir Robert Cotton, about 1600; appropriated to the public use and benefit, 13 William III., 1701; partly destroyed by fire, 1731; removed to the British museum, 1753; the Radcliffeian. at Oxford. founded by the will of Dr. Radcliffe, who left £40,000 to the university for that purpose, 1714; at Cambridge, 1720, to which George I., gave £5,000, to purchase Dr. Moore's collection: in U. S. See Statistics.

Linen, first made in England, 1253; the luxurious wore linen, but the generality woollen shirts. Table linen very scarce in England, 1386.

Lithographic printing, art of, first brought into England, 1801.

Load-stone, polar attraction of, known in France before 1180.

Logwood. first cut in the bay of Honduras and Campeachy by the English, 1662.

Looking-glasses, made only at Venice, 1300.

Looms. the power-loom invented by the Reverend Mr. Cartwright, a clergyman of Kent, in England, 1787.

Lotteries, the first mentioned by historians for sums of money, 1630; established, by law 1693.

M

Magic lantern, first invented by Roger Bacon, 1252.

Magnifying glasses, invented by Roger Bacon, 1260.

Map of England, the first, 1520, by George Lilly; maps and globes invented by Anaximander, 600 B. C.; maps and sea-charts first brought to England by Bartholomew Columbus, to illustrate his brother's theory respecting a western continent, 1489.

Mercators Chart, invented, 1558.

Microscopes, first used, 1621; the double ones, 1624; solar microscopes invented 1740.

Mile, a measure of length common in Europe, but of very unequal length; the subjoined table shows the length in yards of miles, leagues, &c., ancient and modern:—

English and United States' mile, 1760 yards; ancient Roman mile, 1610.348; stadium olympic, or furlong, the 1-8 of a Roman mile, 201,293: stadium, equal to 1-10 of a Roman mile, 161,035: stadium the 1-1100 of a degree of the great circle, 111,2; risin, Jewish, 7½ to a Roman mile, 214,713; leuca, gallic 1½ Roman mile, 2415.522; rast, German or common French league, 4831.044; schoene, Egyptian, 4 Roman miles, 6441.392; league, German or Scandinavian, 9662.088; mile, German, 8239, 846; mile, Arabian, 1½ Roman miles, 2415.522: mile, Roman modern, 1628.466; mile, Greek modern, equal to the Russian werst, 1409.0545; league, modern French, equal to 2500 toises, 5328.75; werst, common of Russia, 1409.0545; league of Spain, 6441.392; league of Spain, large, 8051.74.

Monastery, the first founded, where the sister of St. Anthony retired, 270.

Money, first mentioned as a medium of commerce in the 23d chapter of Genesis, when Abraham purchased a field as a sepulchre for Sarah, in the year of the world, 2139; first made at Argos, 894 B. C.; has increased eighteen times its value from 1290 to 1640; and twelve times its value from 1530 to 1800. Silver has increased thirty times its value since the Norman conquest, viz. a pound in that age was three times the quantity what it is at present, and ten times in value in purchasing any commodity.

Mortars, for bombs, first made in England, 1543.

Musical notes, as now used, 1330.

Muskets, first used in France at the siege of Arras, 1414; in general use 1521.

Muslins, from India, first in England, 1670; first manufactured there 1781.

N

Needles, were first made in England by a native of India, 1545.

New-style, in Chronology, first introduced into Europe, 1582; into Holland and the protestant states, 1700; in England, 1752.

Newspaper, first published in England titled the English Mercury, one of which is remaining in the British Museum, dated, July 28, 1588.

Newspapers, in the United States—the first was the "Boston News Letter," in 1704.

The first printing press in North America, opened at Cambridge, 1639. Among the first books printed were an Indian version of the bible, and Sandy's translation of Ovid. Two licensers were appointed in Massachusetts, 1662; presses were forbidden in Virginia, 1683; the first printer in Connecticut, 1709.

O

Opera, first in London, 1692; by Handel, 1735; opera house burnt, 1789; new one built, 1790; another in the strand, 1816; opera house in Rome, roof fell in January 18, 1762.

Organs were first invented and applied to religious devotion in churches, in the Eastern Empire, 758.

Orrery invented, 1670.

P

Painting, the art of, first introduced at Rome from Etruria by Quintus, who on that account was styled Pictor, 291 B. C.; the first excellent pictures were brought from Corinth to Rome by Mummius, 146 B. C.; in oil, said to have been invented by John Van Eyck, who, with his brother Hubert, were the founders of the Flemish School, 1415; the first picture was an Ecce Homo, 1455; in chiara oscuro, 1500; introduced into Venice by Venetiano, 1450; into Italy by Antonello, 1476.

Paper currency established in America, May 15, 1775.

——— *money* first used in America, 1740.

——— *made of cotton* was in use in 1000; that of linen rags, in 1319; the manufacture of, introduced into England at Dartford, in Kent, 1588; scarcely any but brown paper made in England till 1690; white paper first made in England 1690; made of the asbestos at Danbury, in Connecticut, in North America, by Mr. Beach, who discovered a fine kind there, in 1792; stamped paper first used in Spain and Holland, in 1555; velvet or floss for hanging apartments with, first used, in 1620; made from straw, 1800.

Justinian's Charta Plenaria Securitatis, is one of the most ancient instruments written on Egyptian paper, and was deposited in the library of the late king of France.

The observations of the learned Carmelite Orlando, (noticed in the act. Erudit. Lyps. an. 1724, p. 102) on paper, refers the invention as far back as the eighth century, when Eustatius published his comment on Homer, which is said to have been written on paper. He adds that a MS. of Homer was shown in Geneva in his time, said to be eight hundred years old.

Parchment invented by king Attalus.

Parliament began under the Saxon government; the first regular one was in king John's reign, 1204; the epoch of the house of commons, January 23, 1265.

Patent granted for titles, first used, 1344; first granted for the exclusive privilege of publishing books, 1591.

Pawnbrokers first in business, 1457.

Pens for writing were first made from quills in 635.

Phosphorus, artificial fire, discovered 1699; hermetic phosphorus was made in 1677.

Pins brought from France, 1543, and were first used in England by Catharine Howard, queen of Henry VIII. Before that invention, both sexes used ribbons, loopholes, laces with points and tags, clasps, hooks and eyes, and skewers of brass, silver and gold.

Plaster of Paris, the way first found out for taking a likeness in by And. Verocchio, 1470.

Plays first performed in England, 1378; that by the parish clerks in 1390. Suppressed by parliament, in 1647: restored 1659.

Porcelain and tea from China, first spoken of in history, 1590.

Posts, regular, established between London and most towns of England, Scotland and Ireland, &c., 1635. The emperor Cyrus was the first who erected post-houses throughout the kingdom of Persia; Augustus was the first who introduced this institution among the Romans, and employed post-chaises; Louis XI., first established post houses in France; and they were not settled in England till the 12th of Charles II.

Printing, Chinese mode of, on tables, invented, 930; first performed with wooden blocks, and almost immediately afterwards with separate wooden types, by L. Coster at Harlem, 1430; with metal types, by John Geinsfleich, his brother, Guttenburgh of Mentz, and Faust, 1444: Peter Schæffer, found the method of casting types, 1452; introduced at Oxford, with wooden types by Fr. Corsellis, from Harlem, 1459; brought into England by Wm. Caxton, a mercer of London, 1471, who had a press in Westminster, till 1494, when he died; Aldus Manutius, cast the Hebrew, Greek and Italick characters; the first Greek book printed, 1476; Hebrew book printed, 1478; the number of master printers in London and Westminster limited by the Star Chamber, 1638.

Privy council instituted by Alfred, 896.

Pumps invented 1425.

Q

Quadrant, solar, introduced 290 B. C.

——in Geometry, the fourth part of a circle, containing ninety degrees: also the area or space included between this arc and two radii, drawn from the centre to each extremity. The quadrant, an instrument for taking the altitude of the sun or stars, of great use in navigation and astronomy, originally invented by Godfrey of Philadelphia—falsely claimed in England as Hadley's quadrant, by which name this valuable instrument is now called.

R

Rail Roads, first used near Newcastle upon Tyne, about 1650; wooden rails, four to eight inches square, resting upon transverse sleepers two feet apart, were in use for many years, when rails of the same description, covered with thin plates of iron, were substituted. The usual load for one horse on rail roads of this description, was 42 cwt. Wooden rail roads in pretty general use, to facilitate mining operations, prior to the year 1760. Train roads, with rails of cast iron, first introduced at Colebrook-dale iron works at the instance of Mr. Reynolds, in 1767; at the Sheffield colliery in 1776. Stone props for the support of the rails, substituted for timber in 1797, at Newcastle upon Tyne. Edge rails were brought into use by Mr. Jessop in 1789, at Loughborough. Malleable iron edge rails adopted at Newcastle in 1805, and at Tindale Fell in 1808. The improved malleable edge rail, now in use, was invented by Mr. Birkinsaw in 1820. A locomotive engine, propelled by steam, was employed for the first time on the Merthyn Tydvil rail road, in Wales, in 1804. Blenkinsop's locomotive engine, which operated by means of cog-wheels and rack-rails, was invented and applied on the Leeds rail road in 1811. But the locomotive engine that has obtained the greatest reputation, and been most generally adopted, is that invented by Mr. George Stevenson in 1814. This engine has undergone a variety of improvements since that time, and is deemed more efficient than any of its predecessors.

Rail Roads in the U. States. See Statistics.

Registers, of births, Marriages, and burials, began in 1533.

Revenue, of England at the revolution did not exceed £2,100.000, but in 1786, yielded £12,588,481; in 1787, £12,546,112 in 1791, above £16,000,000.

Rice, was cultivated in Ireland, in 1585; in England 1600; had its first cultivation in South Carolina, by chance, 1702.

S

Sail-cloth, first made in England, 1590; cotton sail-cloth made at Baltimore and at Patterson, N. J., and brought into use in the United States, 1824.

Salt mines, in Staffordshire, discovered, 1670; rock salt was discovered, about 950; in Poland 1289.

Saltpetre. first made in England, 1625.

Scenes first introduced into theatres, 1533.

Sextant. invented by Tycho Brahe, in 1550,

Sheep. the number in England is from 20 to 25 millions. The value of their wool, £3,200.000. Expense in manufacturing it £9.000 000. Exported annually upwards of £3,000,000. Number of persons employed in manufacturing it are above one million. From the wool grower to the consumer, a piece of cloth passes through one hundred different hands. Merino sheep imported into the United States by col. Humphries, the American minister at Spain.

Ship, the first seen in Greece arrived at Rhodes from Egypt, 1485 B. C.; the first double-decked one built in England was of 1000 tons burden, by order of Henry VII., 1509; it was called the Great Harry, and cost £14,000; before this twenty-four gun ships were the largest in the navy, and these had no port holes, the guns being on the upper decks only. Port-holes and other improvements were invented by Decharges, a French builder at Brest, in the reign of Louis XII. 1500: there were not above four merchant ships of 120 tons burden, before 1551.

Shoes, of the present fashion first worn in England, 1633: but the buckle was not introduced till, 1670.

Silk, wrought. brought from Persia to Greece, 325 B. C., From India, A. D. 274; known at Rome in Tiberius's time, when a law passed forbidding men to debase themselves by wearing silk, fit only for women; Heliogabulus first wore a garment all of silk, 220; silkworms were brought to Europe three hundred years later; in 1130, Greek manufacturers of silk brought by Roger, king of Sicily to Europe, settled at Palermo, where they taught the Sicilians, not only to breed up the silk-worms, but to spin and to weave silk; which art was carried afterwards to Italy and to the south of France; Venice inveigled silk weavers from Greece and Palermo, in Sicily, 1207; silk mantles worn by some noblemen's ladies at a ball at Kenilworth castle, in 1286; Silk manufactured in England, 1604; first silk manufacture in France, 1521; silk worms and mulberry-trees propagated by Henry IV., through all France, 1559; broad silk manufacture from raw silk introduced into England,

1620; Lombe's famous silk throwing machine, erected at Derby, in 1719; it contains 26,586 wheels, one water wheel moves the whole, and in a day and a night it works 318,504,960 yards of organzine silk.

Silver Plate, or vessels, first made use of in England, by Welfred, a Northumbrian bishop, 709; silver knives and forks, spoons and cups, 1300.

Slave Trade from Congo and Angola, begun by the Portuguese in 1482; begun with England, 1563; in South America, 1550; Abolished by the Quakers, 1784; by the French convention, 1794; by the British parliament, 1807; by the Prince of the United Netherlands, 1814; in France by Bonaparte, March 29, 1815; abolished in Pennsylvania, 1784; in 1768, there were 104,000 brought in the West-Indies, at £15 each, amounting to £1,582,000, sterling, chiefly by barter; by the French convention, February 4, 1794.

Soap first made at London and Bristol, 1524.

Spectacles invented by Spina, a monk of Pisa 1299.

Sphere invented by Archimedes, of Syracuse 209 B. C.

Spinning-wheel invented at Brunswick, 1530; another invented by Mr. Swindell, at Stockport in Yorkshire, which finishes on each spindle, three lays of thirty hanks to the pound in an hour, 1785.

Standing armies began in France, by Charles VII. in 1445.

Star-chamber court in England, instituted 1487; abolished 1641.

Starching linen first introduced into England, 1552.

Statute miles first ascertained in England, 1593.

Steam engine invented by Savary, for taking ballast or gravel out of rivers, and for raising great quantities of water, and patents granted for, 1618.

Steam-boat, Fulton's (first in America,) succeeded in North River, New-York, October, 1807.

Stereotype printing invented by William Ged, a goldsmith, of Edinburgh, 1725.

Stockings, silk, first worn by Henry II. of France, 1547; Howell says, that in 1560 queen Elizabeth was presented with a pair of black silk knit stockings by her silk woman, and she never wore cloth ones any more; he adds that Henry VIII, wore ordinarily cloth hose, except there came from Spain by great chance a pair of silk stockings, for Spain very early abounded in silk; his son, Edward VI. was presented with a pair of Spanish silk stockings by Sir Thomas Gresham, and the present was then much taken notice of—consequently the invention of knit silk stockings came from Spain; the weaving of them was invented by the Rev. Mr. Lee, of Cambridge, 1589.

Stone buildings first introduced into England, 674.

—— bullets in use in England so late as 1514.

Stops in literature, introduced 1520; the colon 1580; semicolon 1599.

Sugar first mentioned by Paul Eginetta, a physician, 625; produced in Sicily, 1148; first produced in Madeira, 1419; in the Canary islands, 1503; carried to the West-Indies, by the Portuguese and Spaniards, 1510; cultivated at Barbadoes, 1641; sugar refining first discovered by a Venetian, 1503; practised first in England, in 1569.

Sunday-schools first established in Yorkshire, by Robert Raikes, 1784; became general in England and Scotland, in 1789.

Sun-dials, invented, 558 B. C.; the first erected at Rome was that by Papirius Cursor, when time was divided into hours, 308 B. C.; first set up against churches, 613.

Surnames, first introduced into England by the Normans, 1102; became common, 1200.

T

Tariff, or duties on goods imported, estimated amount in the U. S. in 1789, average 7½ per cent.; in 1824, average amount, 25 per cent.; in 1828, average 35 per cent.;

Tea, first brought into Europe by the Dutch East India Company, early in 1591.

Telegraphs, invented, 1687; put into practice by the French, in 1794; by the English, January 28, 1796.

Telescopes, invented by Z. Jansen, a spectacle maker at Middleburgh, 1590; the first reflecting one made on the principles of sir Isaac Newton, 1692.

Theatre, that of Bacchus at Athens, the first ever erected, built by Philos, 420 B. C.; the ruins still exist; first introduced into England, 1566; the first royal license for one in England was in 1574, to James Barbage and four others, servants to the earl of Leicester, to act plays at the Globe, Bankside, or in any part of England; plays were opposed by the Puritans, 1633, and suspended till 1660, when Charles II., licensed two companies, Killigrew's, and Davenant's; till this time boys performed women's parts; Italian opera first introduced in the United States, at the Park Theatre in New-York, with great success, 1825.

Thermometers, first invented by Drebel, a Dutchman, 1620; improved by Reaumur, 1730, and by Fahrenheit, 1749.

Thread, first made at Paisley, in Scotland, in 1722.

Tides, the first theory of, by Kepler, 1596.

Tiles, first used in England, 1246.

Tilts and tournaments, instituted in Germany, 919.

Time, first computed from the christian era, 516; in history, 784; in Spain, 1258; in Arragon and Castile, 1383; in Portugal, 1415.

Time-measure barometer, introduced by Scipio Nasica, 159; king Alfred's time-keeper was six large wax tapers, each twelve inches long; as they burnt unequally, owing to the wind, he invented a lanthorn made of wood and thin-scraped plates of ox-horns, glass being a great rarity, 887. The ancients had three sorts of time measures, hour glasses, sun-dials, and a vessel full of water with a hole in its bottom.

Tin, found in Germany, 1241; in no place before but in Devonshire and Cornwall, in Barbary, 1640; in India, 1740; in New Spain, 1782.

Tithes, given by Moses to the tribe of Levi, 1490 B. C.; first granted to the church in England, 786; established by law by the Lateran council, 1200.

Titles, first creation to by patents, 1344. The following is the succession in which the royal titles swelled in England; Henry IV. had the title of "Grace" conferred on him; Henry VI., that of "Excellent Grace;" Edward IV. that of "High and Mighty Prince;" Henry VII., "Highness;" Henry VIII, "Majesty;" (and was the first and last that was styled "Dread Sovereign;") and James I., that of "Sacred," or "Most Excellent Majesty."

Tournaments, began in 170; instituted by Henry, emperor of Germany, 919.

Tragedy, the first acted at Athens, on a wagon, by Thespis, 585 B. C.

Types, of wood for printing, used, 1470.

Vines, planted in Germany and North Gaul, 276.

Violins, invented about 1477; and introduced in England by Charles II.

Watches, invented at Nuremberg, in Germany, 1477; first used in astronomical observations, 1500.—The emperor Charles V., was the first who had any thing that might be called a watch, though some call it a small table-clock, 1530.—Watches first brought to England from Germany, 1577. Spring pocket ones invented by Hooke, 1658.

Water-mills, for grinding corn, were invented by Belisarius, while besieged in Rome by the Goths, 555. The ancients parched their corn, and pounded it in mortars; afterwards mills were invented, which were turned by men and beasts with great labour; and yet Pliny mentions wheels turned by water.

Weights and measures, invented, 869 B. C.; fixed to a standard in England, 1257; regulated, 1492.

Whale fishery, the first by the Dutch, 1596; by the English at Spitsbergen, 1598.

Whalebone, found by the English ships at Cape Breton, 1521; first mentioned brought home with oil, 1617.

Windows, of glass, first used in England for houses, 1180.

Wines sold by apothecaries as a cordial, 1300; sold at 20*s*. per ton; and the second sort at 13*s*. 4*d*., 1389. In 1790 there were 140,000 pipes of wine made in Portugal.

Wine, from raisins, first made in England, in 1635.

Wood cuts, invented 1460.

Woollen-cloth, manufacturers of, in all civilized countries, and in very remote ages, and probably of linen also. Diodorus Siculus, who wrote in Augustus Cæsar's time, 21 B. C., relates that in the isle of Malta, several mercantile wares were made, particularly very fine cloth. Strabo, speaking of Turtetania, in Lusitania, says, in 34, that cloths were formerly the exports of that country, but that they have now another woollen manufacture of most excellent beauty, such as that of the Corai, a people of Asia, from whence the rams were brought at a talent each, or 100 pounds.

Woollen-cloth manufactories commenced at Sedan in France, 1646; the first made in England, in 1331; medley cloths first made, 1614; greatly improved by the Walloons, 1688; first dyed and dressed in England, in 1667. Its export from Great Britain in 1787, was 3,687,795*l*. 12*s*. 2*d*. value. In 1779, 272,755 pieces of broad cloth, containing 8,806,688 yards, and 180,168 pieces of narrow cloth, containing 6,377,277 yards, were manufactured in the West Riding of Yorkshire, being an increase on the year 1778, a produce of 48,596 pieces, or 1,672,574 yards of broad cloth, and 315,602 pieces or 1,196, 964 yards of narrow cloth.

Z

Zodiac, sign of the, invented by Anaximander, 547 B. C.

TAB. X.

EMINENT AND REMARKABLE PERSONS.

Abbreviations.—*See List in the Introduction.* **Bar.** (*Barbarian,*) *includes several different nations, some not entirely uncivilized.* **f.** *is used for flourished.—In some cases the dates are necessarily left blank.*

NATION.	NAME AND PROFESSION.	BORN.	DIED.
Dan.	Aagesend, Svind, historian,	f. 1188	
Jew.	Aaron, the first high priest,	B. C. 1570	1453
Gr.	Aaron, of Alexandria, physician,	f. 622	
Eng.	Abbot, George, Archbishop of Canterbury and author,	1562	
Fr.	Abelard, Peter, a celebrated scholastic divine,	1079	1142
Sp.	Abenezra, an astron., philos., poet. philologist, &c.,	1119	1174
Eng.	Abercrombie, Sir Ralph, military commander,	1738	1801
Irish	Abernethy John, dissenting minister and author,	1680	1740
Fr.	Ablancourt N. P. D, translator of the classics,	1606	1664
Jew	Abraham, the great progenitor of the Jewish nation,	B. C. 1995	B. C. 1821
Dan.	Absalom, (real name Axel,) archbishop of Den. Sw. and Nor.,	1128	1202
Ara.	Abubeker, father in law and successor of Mahomet,	561	634
Syr.	Abulfeda, the Geographer,	1273	1345
Rom.	Accius, or Attius, a tragic poet, (works not extant,)	B. C. 171	
Ital.	Accursius, or Accorso, an eminent critic,		1229
Gr.	Achilles, one of the leaders in the Trojan war,		f. 1184
Gr.	Achilles Tatius, (of Alexandria) Christian bp. and author,		
Gr.	Acropolita, of Constantinople, statesman and historian,	1220	1282
Eng.	Adam, Alexander, schoolmaster and author,	1741	1809
Eng.	Adam, Robert, an architectural author,	1728	1794
U. S. A.	Adams, Samuel, one of the patriotic founders of the republic,	1726	1806
U. S. A.	——, John, patriot and statesman—2d. pres., U. S.,	1735	1826
Eng.	Addison, Joseph, one of the ornaments of English literature,	1672	1719
Rom.	Adrian, the 15th. emp., (born in Spain,)	76	138
Gr.	Ælian, the historian and rhetorician,	160	
Gr.	Æneas, son of Priam, king of Troy,	f. B. C. 883	
Gr.	Æschines, of Athens, philos.—disciple of Socrates,		
Gr.	—— —— orator,	B. C. 327	B. C. 412
Gr.	Æschylus, —— the great tragic writer,	B. C. 468	B. C. 400
Gr.	Æsop, of Phrygia, the prince of fabulists,	f. B. C. 600	
Rom.	Ætius, mil. com. (defeated Attila,)		454
Rom.	Africanus, Julius, historian,		232
Gr.	Agamemnon, "the king of kings,"		B. C. 904
Gr.	Agathius, historian and poet,	f. 565	
Gr.	Agesilaus II, king of Sparta; (defeats the Per., Egypt., and Gr.,)		B. C. 361
Gr.	Agis IV., the greatest of the Spartan kings,		B. C. 251
Eng.	Aglionby, one of the translators of the bible,		1610
Rom.	Agricola, Cneius Julius, military commander,	40	93
Ger.	Agricola. John, a divine;—founder of the Antinomians,	1490	1566
Rom.	Agrippa, military commander, governor of Judea,	40	94
Fr.	——, Cornelius, philosopher, &c.,	1486	1535
Eng.	Aikin, John, M. D., an elegant writer; editor of poets, &c.,	1747	1822
Eng.	Ainsworth, grammarian and lexicographer,	1660	1743
Tartar.	Akbar, Mohammed, a great Mogul sovereign,	1555	1605
Eng.	Akenside, Mark, a popular poet,	1721	1770
Swe.	Akerblad, philologist,		1819
Bar.	Alaric I., king of the Visigoths,		411
Span.	Alberoni, Julius, (cardinal,) statesman,	1664	1752
Ital.	Alberti, an eminent, writer, paint., sculp., &c.,	1398	1490
Ger.	Albertus Magnus, philosophic writer; tutor of Aquinas,	1205	1280
Bar.	Alboin, the Lombard conqueror,		574
Port.	Albuquerque, (the great,) military commander,	1452	
Gr.	Alcæus, of Lesbos, a lyric poet,	f. B. C. 606	
Ital.	Alciati, of Milan, an eminent civilian and author,	1492	1550
Gr.	Alcibiades, a famous Athenian general and statesman,	B. C. 450	B. C. 404

NATION.	NAME AND PROFESSION.	BORN.	DIED.
Eng.	Alcuinus, (founder of schools at Paris, &c.)		804
Eng.	Aldhelm. St., an eminent scholar and poet,		709
Fren.	Alembert, John le Rond d', math. hist. and philosopher,	1717	1783
Bar.	Alexander, the Great, founder of the Macedonian empire,	B. C. 356	B. C. 323
Rom.	———, Severus, emperor,	209	235
Rus.	———, Nevskoi, a saint and hero;—def. of the Tartars, &c.	1218	1262
Rus.	——— I. emperor, (coalition against Napoleon,)	1777	1825
Greek,	Alexius Commenus, emperor of the east,		1118
Italian,	Alfieri, Victor, an eminent tragic poet,	1749	1803
Eng.	Alfred, justly called the Great, king,	849	900
Italian,	Algarotti, a general scholar, and critic,	1712	1764
Bar.	Ali Bey, gov. of Egypt,—revolted against the Turks,	1728	1773
Bar.	— Tepelini, pacha of Jannina,	1744	1822
U. S. A.	Allen, Ethan, an intrepid officer in the Revolution,		1789
Sar.	Almamon, Caliph,—patron of learning,		833
Sar.	Almansor, caliph,— do do.		775
Span.	Alphonso X., king of Castile, Leon,—and author,	1203	1284
Port.	——— I., Henriquez, founder of the Portuguese monarchy,	1094	1185
Span.	Alva, duke of, celebrated and barbarous mil. com.	1508	1582
Jew.	Amaziah, king of Judah.		B. C. 809
Ital.	Ambrose, St. bishop of Milan;—author,	340	387
Ital.	Americus Vespucius, (of Florence,)—explored the S. Amer. coast,	1451	1512
U. S. A.	Ames, Fisher, a statesman and orator,	1758	1808
Eng.	Amherst, Jeffrey, lord, mil. com. in Amer. &c.	1717	1797
Rom.	Ammianus, Marcellinus, historian,		390
Gr.	Ammonius, a peripatetic philosopher,		B. C. 24
Fr.	Amyot, James, bp. of Auxerre—translator of Plutarch,	1513	1593
Bar.	Anacharsis, a Scythian philosopher, and disciple of Solon, f. B. C.	592	
Gr.	Anacreon, a celebrated poet,		B. C. 474
Gr.	Anastasius,		518
Gr.	Anaxagoras, a philosopher,	B. C. 500	B. C. 428
Gr.	Anaxarchus, a philosopher, companion of Alexander the Great f. B. C.	340	
Gr.	Anaximander of Miletus, an Ionic philosopher,	611	B. C. 547
Gr.	Anaximenes, do do do		B. C. 504
Eng.	Anderson, Sir Edmund, a judge and author,		1605
Scotch,	——— Adam, commercial writer,	1692	1765
Eng.	Andrews, Lancelot, bishop of Winchester,	1555	1626
Gr.	Andronicus of Rhodes, a peripatetic philosopher, flourished, B. C.	63	
Ital.	Anielo, Thomas, (commonly called Masaniello,) a fisherman of Naples who rose to great power,	1623	1646
Gr.	Anna Commena, daughter of the Emperor Alexis I. historian,	1083	1148
Eng.	Annet, Peter, a deistical writer,	1703	1778
Bar.	Annibal, or Hannibal, a celebrated Carthagician general,	B. C. 247	B. C. 183
French,	Anquetil du Perron, a classic scholar, and author,	1731	1805
	Anselm, archbishop of Canterbury—a learned divine,	1033	1109
Eng.	Anson, George, lord, celebrated naval commander,	1697	1762
Rom.	Anthony, Mark, mil. com. and statesman,	B. C. 86	B. C. 30
Egypt,	Anthony, St., the founder of monastic institutions,	251	356
Ital.	———, of Padua, a divine,	1195	1231
	Antigonus, one of the generals of Alexander the Great,		B. C. 301
	Antiochus,		B. C. 164
	Antipater,		B. C. 319
Gr.	Antisthenes, a philos.—founder of the sect of Cynics, before Cchrist,	423	
Rom.	Antoninus Pius, emperor,	86	161
Rom.	———, Marcus Aurelius, emperor—sirnamed the philosopher,	121	180
Pers.	Anveri, a celebrated poet,		1201
Egypt,	Apion, a grammarian, and bitter enemy of the Jews, flourished,	80	
Gr.	Apollonius, surnamed Rhodius, a poet,	B. C. 194	
Gr.	———, Pergamensis, a geometrician, flourished	B. C. 242	
Gr.	———, Tyaneus, a Pythagorean philosopher,		97
Gr.	Appian, an historian, flourished,	143	
Bar.	Apulius, a Platonic philosopher—(African,) flourished,	147	
Italian,	Aquinas, St. Thomas, a celebrated theologian,	1224	1274
Eng.	Aram, Eugene, a learned schoolmaster, executed for murder,	1705	1759
Gr.	Aratus, of Sicyon, mil com. and statesman,	B. C. 273	B. C. 216
Scotch,	Arbuthnot, John, Dr. a poet,		1735
Gr.	Archelaus, Ionic philosopher, flourished,	B. C. 450	
Gr.	Archias, a poet, flourished,	B. C. 719	
Gr.	Archilochus, a poet, flourished,	B. C. 685	
Gr.	Archidemes, a celebrated mathematican,	B. C. 287	B. C. 212

NATION.	NAME AND PROFESSION.	BORN	DIED
Gr.	Archytas, a mathematician,	B. C. 408	B. C. 360
Italian,	Aretino, Guido, inventor of the gamut of music,	995	
Italian,	——, Leonard, an historian,	1369	1444
Italian,	——, Peter, satirist,	1492	156
Spanish,	Argensola, Lupercio, historian and poet,	1565	1613
Spanish,	——, Bartholomew, historian,	1566	1631
Italian,	Ariosto, Lewis, a celebrated poet,	1474	1533
Gr.	Aristarchus, of Samos, mathematician and philosopher, f.	B. C. 280	
Gr.	——, grammarian and critic,	B. C. 160	
Gr.	Aristides, an Athenian statesman,		B. C. 467
Gr.	——, Ælius, an orator and sophist,	129	185
Gr.	——, one of the fathers of the church, flourished,	127	
Gr.	Aristippus, of Cyrene, philoso.—founder of the Cyreniacs,	f. B. C. 392	
Gr.	Aristomenes, a warrior and patriot, flourished	B. C. 662	
Gr.	Aristophanes, an Athenian comic poet,		B. C. 380
Gr.	Aristotle, philosopher—founder of the Peripatetics,	B. C. 384	B. C. 321
Gr.	Arius, of Alexandria, the founder of the Arian sect,		336
Spanish,	—— Montanus, Benedict,—orientalist,	1527	1598
Eng.	Arkwright, Sir Richard, inventor of spinning jennies,	1732	1792
Ger.	Arminius, the deliverer of Germany,		20
Dutch,	——, James, a celebrated divine—founder of a sect,	1560	1610
Eng.	Armstrong, John, M. D.—poet,	1709	1779
Italian,	Arnaud, Daniel,—troubadour,		1220
Fr.	——, Francis Baculard d', dramatist and poet,	1718	1805
Eng.	Arne, Thomas Augustus, musical composer,	1710	1778
Gr.	Arnobius, a defender of Christianity,	f. 303	
Ital.	Arnold, of Brescia, a learned monk; disciple of Abelard,		1155
U. S. A.	—— Benedict, major general—the traitor to his country,		1801
Gr.	Arrian, historian—disciple of Epictetus,	f. 140	
Eng.	Arrowsmith, Aaron, constructer of maps and charts,		1823
Bar.	Arsaces I., the founder of the Parthian monarchy,	f. B. C. 250	
Bar.	Artaxerxes I., King of Persia,		B. C. 425
Bar.	—— founder of the new Persian kingdom,		242
Brit.	Arthur, a prince celebrated in fable,	472	542
Eng.	Arundel, Thomas H., earl of, importer of the Arundelian marbles,		1646
Eng.	Ascham, Roger, a learned writer,	1515	1568
Bar.	Asdrubal, a Carthaginian general,		B. C. 220
Eng.	Asser, John, historian,		909
Gr.	Athanasius, St., one of the fathers of the church,	296	371
Gr.	Athenagoras, philosopher,	f. 177	
Gr.	Athenais, Emp. of the West, and authoress, (called also Eudoxia,)		460
Gr.	Athenæus, a celebrated grammarian,—the Greek Varro,	f. 190	
Bar.	Attalus, found. of the monarchy of Pergamus;—inv. of parchment,		B. C. 198
Gr.	—— Rhodius, mathematician,	f. B. C. 173	
Eng.	Atterbury, Francis, bp. of Rochester, exiled for conspiracy,	1662	1731
Rom.	Atticus, a knight, and author (works lost,)	B. C. 109	B. C. 32
Bar.	Attila, king of the Huns, "the Scourge of God,"		453
Eng.	Auckland, William, lord, statesman,		1814
Fr.	Augereau, duke of Castiglione, mil. com.,	1757	1816
	Augustine, St. a celebrated father of the church,	354	430
	—— the Apostle of the English—1st archbishop of Canterbury,		604
Rom.	Augustulus, Romulus, the last emperor of the West,		476
Rom.	Augustus, Caius Julius Cæsar Octavianus,—1st emperor.,	B. C. 63	14
Rom.	Ausonius, Decimus Magnus, poet,		394
Fr.	Auvergne, Theophilus,—republican—mil. com.,	1743	1800
Ara.	Averroes, philosopher, physician, and author,		1198
Ara.	Avicenna, do do do	980	1037
Eng.	Ayscough, Samuel, Comp. of Index to Shakspeare, &c.		1804

B.

NATION.	NAME AND PROFESSION.	BORN	DIED
Gr.	Bacchylides, lyric poet,	f. B. C. 450	
Port.	Baccellar, a civilian, historian, and lyric poet,	1610	1663
U. S. A.	Backus, Isaac, a divine, and historian,	1724	1806
Eng.	Bacon, Roger, a monk, celebrated for his scientific knowledge,	1214	1292
Eng.	—— Francis, lord Verulam, the celebrated philosopher,	1561	1626
Dan.	Baden, James, one of the founders of Danish literature,	1735	1804
Eng.	Bailey, Nathan, a grammarian and lexicographer,		1742
Fr.	Baillet, a learned theologian, historian, and miscellaneous writer,	1649	1706
Fr.	Bailly, John Silvain, a learned author, and a leader in the rev.	1736	1793
Turk.	Bajazet, sultan; conquered by Tamerlane,		1413

NATION.	NAME AND PROFESSION.	BORN.	DIED.
Fr.	Baldwin, who became emperor of the East,		1206
Swe.	Banier, or Banner, a celebrated military commander,	1596	1641
Eng.	Banks, Sir Joseph, navigator;—president Royal Society,	1743	1820
Pruss.	Baratier, a Hebrew lexicographer before 10 years of age,	1721	1740
Eng.	Barbauld, Anna Letitia, a popular miscellaneous writer,	1743	1825
Turk,	Barbarossa, the celebrated corsair—usurper of Algiers,		1518
Fr.	Barbeyrac, John, miscellaneous writer,	1674	1729
Eng.	Barclay, Robert, the celebrated vindicator of the Quakers,	1648	1690
Ital.	Baretti, Joseph, lexicographer;—author of Travels, &c.	1716	
U. S. A.	Barlow, Joel, a statesman, and poet,	1756	1812
Eng.	Barnes, Joshua, an eminent Greek scholar,	1654	1712
U. S. A.	———, Daniel H., a distinguished conchologist,		1818
Dutch,	Barneveldt, John, statesman, (beheaded),	1547	1619
U. S. A.	Barney, Joshua, a distinguished naval commander,	1759	1818
Fr.	Barras, Paul, count de, mem. of the direct. in the revolution,	1755	1829
Eng.	Barrow, Isaac, a divine, and mathematician,	1630	1677
Fr.	Barthelemy, John James, author of "Anacharsis, &c.,"	1716	1795
U. S. A.	Barton Benj. Smith, M. D. a learned physician and botanist,	1766	1815
U. S. A.	Bartram, John, an eminent botanist,	1701	1777
Gr.	Basil, St., a celebrated father of the Greek church,	326	379
Fr.	Basnage De Beaval, James, historian,	1653	1723
Eng.	Bath, William Pulteney, earl of, statesman,	1682	1764
Eng.	Bathurst, earl of; statesman;—friend of Pope, &c.,	1684	1775
Fr.	Batteux, Charles, rhetorician, and miscellaneous writer,	1713	1780
Eng	Baxter, Richard, an eminent divine, and author,	1615	1691
Fr.	Bayard, Peter, military commander,	1476	1524
U. S. A.	——— James A., a distinguished statesman, and lawyer,	1767	1815
Ger.	Bayer, John, astronomer,		1627
Ger.	——— Theophilus, chronologist, and historian,	1694	1738
Fr.	Bayle, Peter, an eminent philosopher, and critic,	1647	1706
Eng.	Beattie, James L. L. D, poet,	1735	1803
Fr.	Beauharnois, Eugene, son of the empress Josephine, mil. com.—viceroy of Italy, &c.	1780	1824
Fr.	Beaumarchais, P. A. C. de, an eminent dramatist,	1732	1799
Eng.	Beaumont, Francis, dramatic writer,	1555	1616
Fr.	Beauzee, Nicholas, an eminent grammarian,	1714	1789
Ital.	Beccaria, John Baptist, an ecclesiastic, and philosopher,	1716	1781
Ital.	——— Marquis, professor of political economy, and author,	1735	1793
Eng.	Becket, Thomas à, celebrated prelate and statesman,	1119	1170
Brit.	Bede, styled the Venerable, a learned Saxon monk, and historian,	672	735
Eng.	Bedford, John, duke of, military commander,		1435
Ger.	Beethoven, Ludwig Von, celebrated musical composer,	1770	1827
Rom	Belisarius, a celebrated general and conqueror,		565
Scotch,	Bell, John, an eminent surgeon,		1820
U. S. A.	Bellamy, Joseph, D. D., a learned divine and author,	1719	1790
Italian,	Bellarmin, cardinal, the champion of the Roman Catholic Church,	1542	1626
Fr.	Bellau, Remi, poet,	1528	1577
Fr.	Belleisle, Count de, military commander,	1684	1761
Eng.	Beloe, William, a divine and critic;—trans. of Herodotus, &c.		
Fr.	Belon, William, naturalist, and traveller,	1518	1564
Eng.	Belsham, William, historical, political and miscellaneous writer,	1752	1827
Ital.	Belzoni, the celebrated traveller in Egypt,		1823
Ital.	Bembo, cardinal, one of the restorers of literature,	1470	1542
Eng.	Benbow, John, a gallant admiral,	1650	1702
Ital.	Benedict, St., one of the originators of monasteries,	480	547
Ital.	——— XIII. pope;—theological writer,	1649	1728
Ital.	——— XIV. do do do	1675	1758
Fr.	Benezet, Anthony, philanthropist and historian, (d. in America,)	1713	1784
Bar.	Benhadad, king of Syria,	B. C.	895
Fr.	Benserade, Isaac, a wit, and poet,	1612	1691
Eng.	Bentham, Jeremy, political and philosophical writer,		1832
Eng.	Bentley, Richard, an eminent critic and scholar,	1662	1742
Swe.	Bergman, professor of chemistry at Upsal,	1735	1784
Dan.	Behring, a navigator, from whom the strait dividing Asia and America was named,	f. 1730	
Irish,	Berkely, George, bp., an eminent prelate and philosopher,	1684	1753
U. S. A.	——— William, governor of Virginia,		1667
Fr.	Bernard, St., preacher of crusades, and author,	1091	1153
Eng.	——— Edward, a divine, astronomer, and author,	1638	1697
Dutch,	——— John Frederick, a bookseller, editor, and author,		1751

NATION.	NAME AND PROFESSION.	BORN.	DIED
U. S. A.	Bernard, Francis, governor of Massachusetts,		1779
Fr.	Bernardin De Saint Pierre, author of "Studies of Nature," &c.,	1737	1814
Ital.	Berni, poet, (poisoned,)		1536
Swiss,	Bernoulli, James, mathematician,	1654	1705
Bar.	Berosus, the Chaldean historian, f. B. C.	268	
Fr.	Berruyer, a Jesuit, author of a "History of the people of God," in 11 vols. 4to.	1681	1751
Fr.	Berthier, Alexander, a dist. military commander,	1753	1815
Fr.	Berthollet, Claude Louis, an eminent chemist,	1748	1822
Eng.	Berwick, duke of, military commander, (k. at Philipsburg,)	1670	1734
Fr.	Bessieres, duke of Istria, military commander, (k. at Lutzen,)	1769	
Ital.	Bettinelli, Xavier, an elegant miscellaneous writer,	1718	1801
Eng.	Beveridge, William, an eminent theologian, and orientalist,	1638	1708
	Beza, Theodore, an eminent reformer,	1519	1605
Fr.	Bezout, mathematician,	1730	1783
Ital.	Bianchini, Francis, mathematician and author,	1662	1729
Gr.	Bias, one of the seven sages, f. B. C.	606	
Fr.	Bichat, an eminent anatomist, and physiologist,	1771	1802
Eng.	Biddle, John, an eminent Socinian writer,	1615	1662
U. S. A.	———, Nicholas, a captain in U. S. Navy,	1750	1778
Gr.	Bion, pastoral poet,	B. C.	300
Gr.	——— of Borysthenes, philosopher, (Cyreniac,)	B. C.	240
Fr.	Biron, duke of, military commander, (beheaded for conspiracy,)	1561	1602
Scotch,	Bisset, Robert, historian and biographer,		1805
Span.	Bivar, Don Rodrigo, known in history and romance under the name of the Cid,	1040	1099
Eng.	Blackstone, Sir William, an eminent lawyer and author,	1723	1780
Scotch,	Blair, Robert, a divine and poet,	1699	1777
Scotch,	———, John, a chronologist,		1782
Scotch,	———, Dr. Hugh, a divine and rhetorician,	1718	1800
Scotch,	———, James, founder of William and Mary's college in Virginia,	1660	1743
Eng.	Blake, Robert, a celebrated admiral,	1599	1657
Eng.	Bloomfield, Robert, a poet,	1766	1823
Pruss.	Blucher, a celebrated military commander,	1742	1819
Brit.	Boadicea, the warlike queen of the Iceni,		61
Ital.	Boccacio, John, one of the great classic writers of modern Italy,	1313	1373
Ital.	Boccalini, a satirist,	1556	1613
Fr.	Bochart, Samuel, an eminent divine, and orientalist,	1509	1667
Fr.	Bodin, John, a lawyer and author,	1530	1596
Ger.	Bæhmen, Jacob, a fanatic, and author,	1575	1624
Dutch,	Boerhaave, one of the most eminent of modern physicians,	1668	1738
Rom.	Boethius, a statesman, and philosopher,	455	526
	Bohemond, a Norman adventurer,		1111
Fr.	Boileau, Nicholas, an eminent poet,	1636	1711
Fr.	Boissy, Louis de, author of comedies,	1694	1758
Fr.	Boissy, D'Anglas, count de, statesman, and author,	1756	1826
Eng.	Bolinbroke, (Henry St. John,) lord, political and deistical writer,	1678	1751
Colum.	Bolivar, Simon, the heroic deliverer of his country,	1785	1831
Eng.	Bonner, bishop, the persecutor of Protestants,		1569
Swiss,	Bonnet, Charles, a celebrated naturalist,	1720	1793
Eng.	Bonnycastle, John, mathematician,		1821
U. S. A.	Boone, Daniel, the first settler of Kentucky,	1730	1823
Ital.	Borelli, philosopher, and mathematician,		1507
Ital.	Borgia, Cæsar, the infamous pope, Alexander VI.,	1608	1679
Ital.	Borromeo, cardinal, theological writer,	1538	1584
Fr.	Bosc, Louis A. W., naturalist,	1759	1828
Eng.	Boscawen, Edward, a brave and skilful admiral,	1711	1761
Ital.	Boscovich, mathematical, and philosophical writer,	1711	1787
Fr.	Bossuet, James B., a divine, and historian,	1627	1704
Fr.	Bossut, Charles, mathematician,	1730	1814
Scotch,	Boston, Thomas, a divine and author,	1676	1732
Eng.	Boswell, James, the biographer of Dr. Johnson,	1740	1795
Gr.	Botzarris, Mark, a gallant leader in the modern revolution,	1780	1823
U. S. A.	Boudinot, Elias, a statesman, and philanthropist,	1740	1821
Fr.	Boufflers, duke of, military commander,	1644	1711
Fr.	Bourgainville, Louis A., military commander, and author,	1729	1811
Fr.	Bourguer, Peter, mathematician, and hydrographer,	1698	1758
Fr.	Bourlainvilliers, Henry, count de, historian,	1658	1759
Eng.	Boulton, Matthew, an eminent engineer,	1728	1809
Fr.	Bourcet, Peter J. de, an officer and topographer,	1700	1780

NATION.	NAME AND PROFESSION.	BORN.	DIED.
Fr.	Bourdalone, Louis, a noted preacher,	1632	1704
Fr.	Bourignon, Antoinetta, a fanatical author,	1616	1680
Eng.	Bourne, Vincent, an elegant Latin poet,		1747
Fr.	Bousmard, M. de, a military engineer,		1807
Eng.	Bowdler, Thomas, editor Shakspeare, &c.	1754	1825
U. S. A.	Bowdoin, James, L. L. D. philosopher and statesman,	1727	1790
U. S. A.	——— James, (son of the last,) ambassador to Spain,	1752	1811
U. S. A.	Boylston, Zabdiel, an eminent physician,	1680	1776
Scotch,	Boyd, Mark Alexander, a poet,	1562	1601
Irish,	Boyle, Robert, an eminent philosopher,	1626	1691
Eng.	Bradley, Dr. James, astronomer and mathematician,	1692	1762
Eng.	Bradwardine, Thomas, mathematician and theologian,		1349
Eng.	Brady, Robert, physician, and historian,		1700
U. S. A.	Bradford, Wm. second governor of Plymouth colony,	1588	1657
U. S. A.	——— William, attorney general of the United States,	1755	1795
Dan.	Brahe, Tycho, a celebrated astronomer,	1546	1601
Ger.	Brandes, John Christian, actor and dramatist,	1735	1799
U. S. A.	Brainard, David, Missionary to the Indians,		
U. S. A.	Brainard, J. G. C., a poet,	1797	1826
Ger.	Breitkopf, John G. E., an eminent printer and type-founder,	1719	1794
Bar.	Brennus, the leader of the Gauls, f. B. C.	390	
Eng.	Bridgewater, duke of, introducer of canals in England,	1736	1803
Eng.	Briggs, Henry, mathematician,	1536	1630
Fr.	Brisson, Mathurin James, naturalist,	1723	1806
Fr.	Bissot, John Peter, a revolutionist and author,	1757	1793
Irish,	Brooke, Henry, miscellaneous writer,	1706	1783
U. S. A.	Brooks, John, L. L. D., governor of Massachusetts,	1752	1825
Fr.	Brotier, G., a Jesuit,—editor of Tacitus,	1723	1789
U. S. A.	Brown, Arthur, a distinguished scholar, and barrister,		1805
U. S. A.	Brown, Charles Brockden, a novelist,	1771	1810
Eng.	Brown, John, D. D., miscellaneous writer,	1715	1766
Scotch,	Brown, John, a divine and author,	1722	1787
Scotch,	Brown, Dr. Thomas, metaphysician and poet,	1777	1820
Eng.	Browne, Sir Thomas, a physician and writer,	1605	1682
Irish,	Browne, George, count de, an officer in the Russian service,	1698	1792
Eng.	Browne, William George, a traveller in Africa, &c.		1814
Scotch,	Bruce, Robert, the deliverer of his country,		1329
Eng.	Bruce, James, a celebrated traveller,	1730	1794
Fr.	Brueys, Francis Paul, admiral,	1750	1798
Fr.	Brumoy, Peter, a jesuit and author,	1688	1742
Fr.	Brune, William Mary Ann, marshal and revolutionist,	1763	1815
Fr.	Bruno, St., founder of the Carthusian order,	1377	1444
Ger.	Brunswick, Ferdinand, duke of, military commander,	1721	1792
Ger.	Brunswick Luneuburg, Charles, Wm. Fer. duke of, mil. com.	1735	1806
Rom.	Brutus, Lucius Junius, founder of the republican government,		B. C. 505
Rom.	——— Marcus Junius, conspirator against Cæsar,		B. C. 42
Fr.	Bruyere, John de la, a celebrated writer,	1644	1697
Dutch,	Bruyn, Cornelius le, traveller,	1652	
Eng.	Bryant, Jacob, a philologist, and antiquary,	1715	1804
Fr.	Buat Nancay, Louis G. count de, a learned writer,		
Fr.	Bucer, Martin, one of the fathers of the reformation,	1491	1551
Scotch,	Buchan, William, a physician and author,	1729	1791
Scotch,	Buchanan, George, an eminent writer,	1506	1582
Scotch,	———, Claudius, a divine,	1766	1805
Eng.	Buckingham, George Villiers, duke of, statesman,	1592	1628
Eng.	do do do son of the former,	1627	1688
Polish,	Buffier, Claude, a jesuit, and miscellaneous writer,	1661	1737
Fr.	Buffon, George L., le Clerc, count of, celebrated naturalist,	1707	1788
Swiss,	Bullinger, Henry, reformer and author,	1504	1575
Eng.	Bunyan, John, author of "Pilgrim's Progress,"	1628	1688
Swiss,	Burckhardt, John Louis, oriental traveller,	1784	1815
Ger.	Burckhardt, John Charles, mathematician,	1773	1815
Eng.	Burgoyne, John, military commander and author,		1792
Irish,	Burke, Edmund, a great statesman and writer,	1730	1797
Eng.	Burleigh, William Cecil, lord, eminent statesman,	1520	1598
Dutch,	Burman, Peter, critic and editor,	1668	1741
Scotch,	Burnet Gilbert, a divine and historian,	1643	1715
Eng.	Burney, James, admiral and author,	1739	1820
Eng.	———, Charles, a doctor of music,	1726	1814
Scotch,	Burns, Robert, a popular and national poet,	1759	1796

NATION.	NAME AND PROFESSION.	BORN.	DIED.
Eng.	Burton, Robert, author of the "Anatomy of Melancholy,"	1576	1639
Ger.	Busching, Anthony Frederick, philos. and geog. writer,	1721	1793
Eng.	Bute, John Stuart, earl of, statesman,	1738	1792
Eng.	Butler, Samuel, a humorous poet,	1612	1680
Eng.	——, Joseph, bishop, an eminent prelate and author,	1692	1752
U. S. A.	——, Richard, colonel, an officer in the revolution,		1791
Ger.	Buxtorf, John, a Hebrew, and Chaldaic lexicographer,	1564	1629
Ger.	——, do (son of the preceding) do	1599	1664
Eng.	Byng, honourable John, admiral,	1704	1757
Eng.	Byron, honourable John, admiral,	1723	1786
Eng.	Byron, George Gordon, lord, a popular poet,	1788	1824

C

NATION.	NAME AND PROFESSION.	BORN.	DIED.
Ital.	Cabot, Sebastian, (son of John,) navigator,	1477	
Port.	Cabral, Pedro Alvarez, navigator,	f. 1500	
Fr.	Cadet De Grassicourt, Charles L., chemist and philosopher,	1769	1821
Ital.	Cadamosta, Louis da, navigator,	f. 1456	
Rom.	Cæsar, Caius Julius, warrior, statesman and author,	B. C. 100	B. C. 44
Ital.	Cajetan, Cardinal, diplomatist and author,	1510	1593
Gr.	Calaber, Quintus, poet,	f. 250	
Span.	Calderon de La Barca, don Pedro, dramatist,	1600	1687
Ital.	Calepino, Ambrose, author of a Lexicon in 11 languages,	1435	1511
Gr.	Calippus, astronomer and mathematician,	f. B. C. 330	
Gr.	Callimachus, a poet,	f. B. C. 150	
Gr.	Callisthenes, philosopher and historian,		B. C. 328
Fr.	Calmet, Augustine, an erudite divine and author,	1672	1757
Ital.	Calogera, Angelo, a learned monk and author,	1699	1768
Fr.	Calonne, Charles Alex. de, minister of state,	1734	1802
Fr.	Calvin, John, one of the apostles of the Reformation,	1509	1564
U. S. A.	Calvert, Leonard, first governor of Maryland,		1676
Fr.	Cambaceres, John J. R., distinguished revolutionist,	1753	1824
Eng.	Camden, Wm., an eminent antiquary and historian,	1551	1623
Rom.	Camillus, Marcus Furius, a distinguished dictator,		B. C. 365
Port.	Camoens, Louis, the most eminent poet of his country,	1517	
Scotch,	Campbell, George, a divine and author,	1709	1796
Scotch,	Campbell, John, D. D., a multifario s writer,	1709	
Ger.	Camper, Peter, an eminent naturalist,	1722	1789
Fr.	Campiston, John G. de, dramatist,	1656	1723
Fr.	Cange, Charles Dufresne, Sieur du, historian,	1610	1688
Eng.	Canning, George, statesman, orator and poet,	1770	1827
Span.	Capmany, Don Antonio, historian,	1754	1810
Rom.	Caracalla, Marcus Aurelius Antoninus, emperor,	188	217
Brit.	Caractacus, prince of the Silures, a brave warrior,	(ab.) 100	
Ital.	Cardan, Jerom. philosopher, mathematician and physician,	1501	1576
Fr.	Cardonne, Dennis D., an eminent orientalist,	1720	1 83
Eng.	Carey, Henry, earl of Monmouth, translator,	1596	1661
Ital.	Carissimi, James, musical composer,	1600	
Irish	Carleton, Sir Guy, military commander, and gov. of Canada,	1724	1808
Ital.	Carli, John Rinaldo, count de, author,	1720	1795
Gr.	Carneades, philosopher, founder of the 3d. Academy,	B. C. 218	B. C. 128
Fr.	Carnot, Lazarus Nicholas, revolutionist,	1753	1823
Eng.	Carter, Elizabeth, a learned translatress, &c.,	1717	1806
U. S. A.	——, Nathaniel H., a scholar and traveller,		1830
Eng.	Cartwright, major John, parliament reformer,	1740	1824
U. S. A.	Carver, Jonathan, traveller and author,	1732	1780
U. S. A.	——, John, first governor of Plymouth colony,		1621
Span.	Casas, Bartholomew de las, philanthropist and, historian,	1474	1564
Fr.	Cassini, John Dominic, astronomer,	1625	1712
Ital.	Cassiodorus, Marcus Aur., statesman and historian,	470	516
Rom.	Cassius Longinus, Caius, conspirator against Cæsar,		B. C. 42
Eng.	Castell, Edmund, divine and lexicographer,	1606	1685
Ital.	Castiglione, Balthasar, statesman and author,	1468	1529
Eng.	Catesby, Mark, naturalist,	1680	1749
Russ.	Catherine II., a powerful and profligate empress,	1729	1796
Rom.	Catiline, Lucius Sergius, patrician conspirator,		B. C. 62
Fr.	Catinat, Nicholas, military commander,	1637	1712
Rom.	Cato, Marcus Portius, the Censor, statesman and author,	B. C. 232	B. C. 147
Rom.	Cato, Marcus Porcius, "of Utica," statesman,	B. C. 95	B. C. 46
Rom.	Catullus, Caius Valerius, poet,	B. C. 86	

NATION.	NAME AND PROFESSION.	BORN.	DIED.
Fr.	Caussin, Nicholas, a Jesuit, author of "the Holy Court,"	1583	1651
Eng.	Cavendish, Sir Wm., courtier and writer,	1505	1557
Eng.	———, Thomas, navigator,		1591
Eng.	Caxton, Wm., the introducer of printing into England,	1410	1492
Fr.	Cazales, James A. M. de, an eloquent orator,	1752	1805
Fr.	Caylus, A. C. P., count de, miscellaneous writer,	1720	1765
Rom.	Celsus, Aurelius Cornelius, a celebrated physician,	f. 30	
Gr.	———, an Epicurean philosopher,	f. 150	
Rom.	Censorinus, a critic and grammarian,	f. 240	
Irish.	Centlivre, Susanna, dramatic writer,	1667	1723
Span.	Cervantes, Saavedra Michael, author of "Don Quixotte,"	1547	1617
Ital.	Cesarotti, Melchior, a voluminous author,	1730	1808
Scotch,	Chalmers, George, miscellaneous writer,	1744	1826
Eng.	Chambers, Sir Wm., an architect,		1796
Eng.	Chapman, George, poetical translator,	1557	1634
Eng.	Chapone, Hester, miscellaneous writer,	1727	1801
Fr.	Charles Martel, statesman and warrior,		741
Fr.	Charlemagne, emperor of the west, and king of France,	742	814
Swed.	Charles XII., king, a celebrated warrior,	1682	1718
Fr.	Charlevoix, Peter F. X. de, a Jesuit historian,	1682	1761
Eng.	Chatham, Wm. Pitt. earl of, statesman,	1708	1778
Eng.	Chatterton, Thomas, famed for precocious talent,	1752	1770
Eng.	Chaucer, Geoffrey, the Father of English poetry,	1328	1400
U. S. A.	Chauncey, Charles, D. D., president of Harvard College,		1671
Eng.	Cheselden, Wm., an eminent anatomist,	1688	1752
Eng.	Chesterfield, Philip D. Stanhope, earl of, statesman and writer,	1694	1773
Gr.	Chilo, Ephorus of Sparta—one of the 7 wise men,	f. B. C. 598	
Swed.	Christina, queen, (daughter of G. Adolphus,)	1626	1689
Afric.	Christophe, a slave—afterwards king of Hayti,	1767	1820
Gr.	Chrysippus, a Stoic philosopher,	B. C. 280	B. C. 207
Gr.	Chrysostom, St. John, Christian father and orator,	344	407
Eng.	Churchill, Charles, a satirical poet,	1731	1764
U. S. A.	Church, Benjamin, military commander,	1639	1718
Eng.	Cibber, Colley, tragic and comic actor and poet,	1671	1757
Roman,	Cicero, Marcus Tullius, one of the greatest of orators,	B. C. 105	B. C. 43
Italian,	Cimarosa, Dominic, dramatic and music composer,	1754	1801
Gr.	Cimon, an Athenian general,		B. C. 449
Rom.	Cincinnatus, Lucius Quinctius, the patriot, flourished,	B. C. 456	
Rom.	Cinna, Lucius Cornelius, partizan of Marius, flourished,	B. C. 87	
Ital.	Cirillo, Dominic, a botanist and physician,	1734	1799
U. S. A.	Clair, Arthur, St. a distinguished officer in the revolution,		1818
Fr.	Clairaut, Alexis Claude, geometrician,	1713	1765
Scotch,	Clapperton, Hugh, traveller in Africa,	1788	1827
Eng.	Clarendon, Edw. Hyde, earl of, statesman and historian,	1608	1674
Eng.	Clarke, Samuel, Dr. theologian and philosopher,	1675	1729
Eng.	———, Dr. Edw. Danl., traveller and mineralogist,	1767	1821
Eng.	———, Dr. Adam, a celebrated theologian, and commentator,	1760	1832
U. S. A.	Clap, Thomas, president of Yale College,	1703	1767
U. S. A.	Clayton, John, an eminent physician and botanist,	1705	1773
Gr.	Cleanthes, a Stoic philosopher, flourished,	B. C. 260	
Gr.	Cleobulus, one of the seven wise men, flourished,	B. C. 559	
Egypt,	Cleopatra, a voluptuous queen,		B. C. 30
U. S. A.	Clinton, George, gov. of New-York, and 4th vice pres. of U. S.	1739	1812
U. S. A.	———, Dewitt, governor and benefactor of New-York,	1769	1828
Eng.	Clive, Robert, lord, military commander,	1725	1774
U. S. A.	Coddington, William, a distinguished patriot of Rhode-Island.		
Eng.	Cogan, Thomas, phys. and misc. writer,	1736	1818
Eng.	Coke, Sir Edward, a learned judge,	1549	1634
Fr.	Colbert, John Baptist, an eminent statesman,	1619	1683
U. S. A.	Colden, Cadwallader, an eminent botanist, astronomer, &c.	1688	1776
Eng.	Collier, Jeremy, a divine and miscellaneous writer,	1630	1726
Eng.	Collingwood, Cuthbert, lord, admiral,	1748	1810
Eng.	Collins, William a popular poet,	1720	1756
Eng.	Coleman, George, dramatic writer,	1733	1784
U. S. A.	———, Benjamin, a learned divine, (in Boston,)	1673	1747
Ital.	Columbus, Christopher, the discoverer of America,	1441	1506
Fr.	Conde, Louis II. of Bourbon, Protestant mil. com.	1621	1686
Fr.	Condillac, Stephen Bonnot de, metaphysical writer,	1715	1780
Chinese,	Confucius, a celebrated philosopher,	B. C. 550	
Eng.	Congreve, William, a comic dramatist,	1670	1728

NATION.	NAME AND PROFESSION.	BORN	DIED.
Gr.	Conon, an Athenian general,	B. C.	390
Gr.	Constantine (the Great,) the first Christian emperor,	274	337
Gr.	———, VII. (Porphyrogenitus,) emperor and author,	905	959
Gr.	———, (Paleologus,) the last of the Greek emperors,	1403	1453
Eng.	Cook, James, a celebrated circumnavigator,	1728	1779
Eng.	Cooke, Thomas, editor and translator,	1702	1756
Eng.	———, George F. an eminent actor,	1756	1812
U. S. A.	Cooper, Samuel, D. D. a divine, and political writer,	1725	1783
Irish,	Coote, Sir Eyre, military commander in India,	1726	1783
Pruss.	Copernicus, Nicholas, a celebrated astronomer,—the reviver of the Pythagorean system of the universe,	1473	1543
Gr.	Corinna, a poetess, flourished, in the fifteenth century, before Christ.		
Rom.	Coriolanus, Caius Marcius, a warrior,	B. C.	488
Ital.	Cornaro, Lewis, a noble,—author of a book on temperance,	1467	1565
Fr.	Corneille, Peter, an eminent dramatic writer,	1606	1684
Eng.	Cornwallis, Charles, marquis, military commander,	1738	1805
Fr.	Cornelli, Mark, Vincent, a Venetian geographer and historian,		1718
Port.	Cortereal, Gaspar, a navigator, flourished,	1500	
Span.	Cortes, Ferdinand, the brutal conqueror of Mexico,	1485	1554
Dutch,	Coster, John Laurence, one of the supposed inventors of printing,	1370	
Fr.	Cottin Sophia, madame, a novelist,	1773	1807
U. S. A.	Cotton, John, (of Boston,) a learned divine,	1585	1652
Fr.	Coulomb, Charles, Augustine de, philosopher,	1736	1806
Fr.	Courier, Paul Louis, political writer,	1774	1825
Fr.	Court de Gebelin, Anthony, an antiquarian and author,	1725	1784
Fr.	Cousin, Louis, historian,	1627	1707
Eng.	Cowley, Abraham, poet,	1618	1667
Eng.	Cowper, William, poet,	1731	1800
Eng.	Coxe, William, traveller and historian,	1747	1828
Ger.	Cramer, John Andrew, miscellaneous writer,	1723	1788
Eng.	Cranmer, Thomas, a celebrated reformer,	1489	1556
Rom.	Crassus, Marcus, Lucinius, (the Rich,) military commander,	B. C.	53
Fr.	Crebillon, Prosper Jolyott de, tragic poet,	1674	1762
Fr.	Crevier, John Baptist Lewis, historian,	1693	1765
Eng.	Cromwell, Thomas, earl of Essex, successor of Wolsey,	1490	1540
Eng.	———, Oliver, military commander and statesman,	1599	1658
Scotch,	Cruden, Alexander, author of a Concordance to the Bible,	1701	
Eng.	Cudworth, Ralph, philosopher,	1617	1688
Scotch,	Cullen, William, an eminent physician,	1712	1790
Eng.	Cumberland, William Augustus, duke of, military commander,	1721	1765
Eng.	Cumberland, Richard, a multifarious writer,	1732	1811
Irish,	Curran, John Philpot, a celebrated barrister and orator,	1750	1817
Rom.	Curtius, Rufus Quintus, history,		
Fr.	Cuvier, baron, one of the greatest of naturalists,	1769	1832
	Cyprian, bishop of Carthage, an eminent father of the church,		258
	Cyril, St., the apostle of the Sclavi,		822

D

Fr.	Dacier, Andrew, a critic and translator,	1651	1722
Fr.	———, Anne, a celebrated classical scholar,	1651	1720
Swed.	Dalin, Olaus Von, the father of Swedish poetry,	1708	1763
U. S. A.	Dallas, James Alexander, secretary treasury U. S.	1759	1817
Ger.	Damm, Christian Tobias, Greek lexicographer,	1699	1778
Eng.	Dampier, William, an eminent navigator,	1652	1711
Ital.	Dante Alighieri, "the sublimest of the Italian poets,"	1265	1321
Eng.	Darwin, Erasmus, a poet, physician and botanist,	1721	1802
Aust.	Daun, Leopold Joseph Mary, count de, military commander,	1705	1766
U. S. A.	Davidson, Lucretia M., a youthful poetess of uncommon genius,	1808	1825
U. S. A.	Davies, Samuel, president of Princeton college,—an author,	1724	1761
Ital.	Davila, Henry Catharine, an historian,	1576	1631
Eng.	Davis, John, a navigator—discoverer of "Davis' Straits,"		1605
	Davy, Sir Humphrey, the most eminent of chemists,	1778	1829
U. S. A.	Deane, Silas, minister of the U. S. to France,	1758	1789
U. S. A.	Dearborn, Henry, a distinguished officer of the American wars,	1751	1829
Fr.	Debrue, William Francis, a bookseller, and bibliographer,	1731	1782
U. S. A.	Decatur, Stephen, a gallant commodore, in the U. S. navy,	1779	1820
Eng.	Defoe, Daniel, miscellaneous writer,	1661	1731
Fr.	Delambre, John Baptist Joseph, astronomer,	1749	1822
Fr.	Delille, James, a celebrated poet,	1738	1813

NATION.	NAME AND PROFESSION.	BORN.	DIED.
Fr.	Delisle, Joseph Nicholas, an eminent astronomer, . .	1688	1768
Gr.	Democritus, a celebrated philosopher, . .	B. C. 460	
Gr.	Demosthenes, one of the greatest of orators, . .	B. C. 381	B. C. 322
Eng.	Denham, lieut. colonel Dixon, an enterprising traveller,	1786	1828
Ital.	Denina, Charles John Maria, an historian, . .	1731	1813
Russ.	Derzhavine, Gabriel, R., a poet and statesman, . . .	1743	1816
Fr.	Desaix, Louis Charles Anthony, military commander, .	1768	1800
Fr.	Descartes, Rene, an eminent philosopher, . . .	1596	1650
Afr.	Dessalines, John James,—emperor of Hayti, .		1806
Fr.	Destouches, Philip Nericault, dramatic writer, .	1680	1754
Dutch,	Deurhoff, William, founder of a sect, and an author, .	1650	1717
Dutch,	De Witt, John, an eminent statesman, .	1625	1672
Port.	Diaz Bartholomew, discoverer of the Cape of Good Hope,		1500
Eng.	Dibdin, Charles, a dramatic and musical composer, .	1748	1814
Fr.	Diderot, Denis, first editor, of "the Encyclopedia," &c. .	1713	1784
Fr.	Didot, Francis A., a celebrated printer and type-founder,	1730	1804
Egypt,	Didymus, who wrote from 3000 to 6000 works,	f. B. C. 30	
Span.	Diez, John Martin, a patriotic military commander, .	1775	1825
Maced.	Dinocrates, an architect—(built Alexandria, &c.) .	f. B. C. 350	
Gr.	Dion Cassius, author of Roman history, .		
Gr.	Dio Chysostom, a rhetorician and philosopher,	f. 30	
Gr.	Diodorus, Siculus, a historian, .		
Gr.	Diogenes, the Cynic, a philosopher,	B. C. 413	B. C. 323
Gr.	Diogenes, Laertius, biographer, .		
Gr.	Dionysius, of Halicarnassus, critic and historian, .		52
Gr.	Dionysius, a geographer, ...	f. 140	
Eng.	Dodd, Dr. William, miscellaneous writer, . . .	1729	1777
Eng.	Doddridge, Phillip, a gifted and pious divine and writer, .	1702	1756
Ital.	Doria, Andrew, the deliverer of his country, (Genoa,)	1468	1560
Scotch,	Douglas, Gawin, a poet and translator, . .	1474	1521
Gr.	Draco, an Athenian legislator, . . .	f. 623	
Eng.	Drake, Sir Francis, a celebrated circumnavigator, .	1545	1596
Dutch,	Drebbel, Cornelius Van, inventor of the thermometer, .	1572	1634
Eng.	Dryden, John, an eminent poet, . .	1631	1700
Fr.	Duchesne, Andrew, an historian, . .	1584	1640
Fr.	Duclos, Charles Pineau, an historian, . .	1704	1772
Fr.	Duguesclin, Bertrand, military commander, . .	1314	1380
Fr.	Dumont, John, traveller, and political writer, .		1726
Fr.	Dumourier, Charles Francis Duperier, military commander,	1739	1823
Scotch,	Dunbar, William, a poet, .	1465	1535
Scotch,	Duncan, William, logician and translator,	1717	1760
Scotch,	——— Adam, viscount, a successful admiral, .	1731	1804
Fr.	Dupin, Louis Ellies, an ecclesiastical historian, .	1637	1719
Fr.	Duquesne, Abraham, a gallant admiral, .	1610	1688
Fr.	Duroc, Michael, duke of Friuli, military commander, .	1772	1813
U. S. A.	Dwight, Dr. Timothy, an eminent divine and writer, .	1752	1817

E

NATION.	NAME AND PROFESSION.	BORN.	DIED.
Ger.	Eckhard, John George, an antiquary and historian, . .	1674	1730
Eng.	Edward, the Black Prince, a warrior, . .	1330	1376
U. S. A.	Edwards, Jonathan, an able divine and metaphysician, .	1703	1757
Eng.	———, Bryan, an historian, . . .	1743	1800
Gr.	Eginhard, an historian, ...		839
Eng.	Elizabeth, queen, ...	1533	1603
U. S. A.	Elliot, John, "the apostle to the Indians," .	1604	1690
U. S. A.	Ellsworth, Oliver, a distinguished chief justice of the U. S.	1745	1807
Eng.	Emerson, William. an eminent mathematician, .	1701	1782
Irish,	Emmet, Thomas Addis, an eminent lawyer and orator, .	1764	1827
Ger.	Empedocles, a Pythagorean philosopher, . .		
Eng.	Enfield, William, miscellaneous writer, . .	1741	1797
Fr.	Eon De Beaumont, Chevalier, an eccentric writer, . .	1728	1810
Gr	Epaminondas, an illustrious Theban general, .		B. C. 363
Gr.	Epictetus, a Stoic philosopher, . .	f. 40	
Gr.	Epicurus, founder of the Epicurean sect of philosophers,	B. C. 342	B. C. 271
Dutch,	Erasmus, Desiderius, a celebrated scholar and author, .	1467	1536
Span.	Ercilla, Don Alonzo, a poet, . . . ,	1525	1595
Span.	Ericeira, Ferdinand, a statesman and historian, .	1614	1699
Eng.	Erigena, John Scotus, a learned man of the 9th century,		
Ger.	Ernesti, John, Augustus, an eminent critic, .	1707	1781
Scotch,	Erskine, Thomas, lord, a celebrated forensic orator, .	1750	1823

NATION.	NAME AND PROFESSION.	BORN.	DIED.
Span.	Escobar Y Mendoza, Anthony, a celebrated casuist,	1589	1669
Eng.	Essex, Robert Devereux, earl of, a warrior,	1567	1601
Ger.	Euclid, an eminent geometrician, f. B. C.	300	
Fr.	Eugene, Francis, prince, a great warrior, (in the German service,)	1663	1736
Swiss,	Euler, Leonard, an eminent mathematician,	1707	1783
Bar.	Eumenes, one of Alexander's generals,		B. C. 315
Gr.	Euripides, a celebrated tragic poet,	B. C. 480	
Gr.	Eusebius, bishop of Cæsarea, a learned father of the church, and ecclesiastical historian,		340
Rom.	Eutropius, an historian,		
Rom.	Eutyches, an ecclesiastic, founder of a sect,		
Eng.	Evelyn, John, miscellaneous writer,		1651

F

NATION.	NAME AND PROFESSION.	BORN.	DIED.
Rom.	Fabius, Quintus M. V., a skilful warrior,		B. C. 204
Ger.	Fabricius, John Albert, a critic and bibliographer,	1668	1736
Ger.	———, John Christian, a celebrated entomologist,	1742	1807
Ital.	Fabroni, Angelo, a learned biographer,	1732	1803
Pruss.	Fahrenheit, Gabriel Daniel, an experimental philosopher,	1686	1736
Eng.	Fairfax, Thomas, lord, a general in the civil war,	1611	1671
Eng.	Falconer, Wm., a poet,	1730	1769
Ital.	Faliero, Marino, doge of Venice, (beheaded)		1355
Port.	Faria Y Souza, Manuel, an historian and poet,	1588	1647
Irish.	Farquar, George, a dramatist,	1678	1707
Ger.	Faust, John, one of the inventors of printing,		1466
Eng.	Fawkes, Francis, a poet and translator,	1721	1777
Fr.	Fayette, Mary, M., countess of, miscellaneous writer,	1632	1693
Fr.	Fenelon, Francis de Salignac de la Motte, an able writer and one of the most virtuous of men,	1651	1715
Swed.	Ferber, John James, an eminent mineralogist,	1743	1790
Eng.	Ferguson, James, a self-educated astronomer, philosopher &c.,	1710	1776
Eng.	———, Adam, an historian and moral philosopher,	1724	1816
Span.	Ferreras, John de, a celebrated historian,	1652	1735
Span.	Feyjoo Y Montenegro, an able miscellaneous writer,	1701	1764
Ital.	Ficino, Marsilius, a Platonic philosopher,	1433	1499
Eng.	Fielding, Henry, a humorous novelist and dramatist,	1707	1754
Ital.	Fiesco, John Louis, the conspirator against Doria,		1547
Eng.	Flavel, John, an eminent non-conformist divine,	1627	1691
Fr.	Flechier, Esprit, a celebrated prelate,	1632	1710
Eng.	Fletcher, John, a dramatist,	1576	1625
Fr.	Fleury, Claude, a divine and historian,	1640	1722
Fr.	———, Andrew Hercules de, a cardinal and statesman,	1653	1743
Fr.	Florian, John Peter Claris de, miscellaneous writer,	1755	1794
Fr.	Fontenelle Bernard le Bovier de, miscellaneous writer,	1657	1757
Eng.	Foote, Samuel, a comic writer and actor,	1721	1771
Ital.	Forcellini, Giles, a Latin lexicographer,	1688	
Eng.	Ford, John, an early dramatic writer,	1586	1639
Fr.	Fouche, Joseph, duke of Otranto, a brutal revolutionist,	1763	1820
Eng.	Fox, John, a divine, author of the Book of Martyrs,	1517	1587
Eng.	——, George, the founder of the society of friends or quakers,	1624	1690
Eng.	——, Charles James, one of the greatest of statesmen and orators,	1748	1806
Irish,	Francis, Sir Philip, political writer,	1740	1818
U. S. A.	Franklin, Benj. a celebrated philosopher and statesman,	1706	1790
Pruss.	Frederick II., the Great, king, an able general and author,	1712	1786
Eng.	Frobisher, Sir Martin, a celebrated navigator,		1594
Fr.	Froissart, John, a chronicler and poet,	1333	1400
Eng.	Fuller, Thomas, a divine and historian,	1608	1661
Eng.	———, Andrew, an eminent Baptist minister,	1754	1815
U. S. A.	Fulton, Robert the introducer of steamboats in America,	1767	1815
Fr.	Furitiere, Antony, a philologist,	1620	1688

G

NATION.	NAME AND PROFESSION.	BORN.	DIED.
Fr.	Gagnier, John, an orientalist and author,	1670	1740
Fr.	Gaillard, Gabriel Henry, miscellaneous writer and historian,	1728	1806
Fr.	Galen, Claudius, a celebrated ancient physician,	131	
Ital.	Galileo, an illustrious philosopher and astronomer,	1564	1642
Ger.	Gall, John Joseph, a celebrated physiologist and founder of the science of phrenology,	1758	1828

NATION.	NAME AND PROFESSION.	BORN.	DIED
Ital.	Galvani, Louis, a physician and experimental philosopher, discoverer of galvanic electricity,	1737	1798
Port.	Gama, Vasco de, navigator, first who doubled the Cape of Good Hope . . .		1524
Span.	Garcias Lasso, de la Vega, "the Prince of Spanish Poetry,"	1503	1536
Eng.	Garrick, David, a celebrated actor and dramatist, .	1716	1779
Eng.	Gascoigne, Sir Wm., the Judge who imprisoned Henry prince of Wales for a misdemeanor, . . .	1350	1413
Fr.	Gassendi, Peter, a celebrated philosopher, ...	1592	1655
U. S. A.	Gates, Horatio, a distinguished officer in the revolution, .	1728	1806
Eng.	Gay, John, a popular poet, ...	1688	1732
Ger.	Gellert, Christian Furchtegott, a poet and miscellaneous writer,	1715	1769
Tar.	Genghis Khan, a celebrated conqueror, . . .	1164	1227
Fr.	Genlis, Stephania Felicity, countess de, miscellaneous writer	1746	1830
Eng.	Geoffrey of Monmouth, an historian of the 12th century, .		
Rom.	Germanicus, Tiberius Drusus Cæsar, military commander,		19
Fr.	Gerson, John Charlier de, an ecclesiastic and author, . . .	1363	1429
Swiss,	Gesner, Conrad, an eminent naturalist, . . .	1516	1565
Ger.	Gesner, John Matthias, a philologist, . . .	1691	1761
U. S. A.	Gerry, Elbridge, a distinguished patriot, vice pres., U. S.,		1814
Ital.	Giannone, Peter, an historian, ...	1676	1758
Eng.	Gibbon, Edward, one of the greatest of English historians,	1737	1794
U. S. A.	Gibson, Col. John, and Col. Geo., both officers in the Revolution,		
Eng.	Gifford, William, a critic and poet, ...	1757	1826
Eng.	———, John, an historical and political writer, . .	1758	1818
Eng.	Gilbert, Sir Humphrey, one of the earliest adventurers in America, ...		
Eng.	Gill, John, a divine, oriental scholar and author, . .	1697	1771
Swed.	Gmelin, John Frederick, a chemist, . . .	1748	1805
Fr.	Godfrey of Bouillon, a celebrated leader in the Crusades, .		1100
U. S. A.	Godman, John, M. D., a distinguished naturalist, &c., .		1830
Ger.	Goethe, a celebrated dramatist, ...		1831
Ital.	Goldoni, Charles, "the Italian Moliere," . . .	1707	1793
Irish,	Goldsmith, Oliver, a celebrated poet and miscellaneous writer,	1731	1774
Dutch,	Golius, James, an orientalist and lexicographer, . .	1596	1667
Span.	Gonsalvo of Cordova, a celebrated warrior, . . .	1443	1515
Gr.	Gorgias, an orator and sophist, f. B. C. 5th century,		
Eng.	Gower, John, one of the earliest English poets, . .		1402
Rom.	Gracchus, Tiberius Sempronius, a celebrated democrat, .		B. C. 133
Rom.	———, Caius Sempronius, ...		B. C. 121
Ger.	Græfe, or Grævius, an erudite classic writer, . .	1632	1703
Scotch,	Grahame, James, a poet, ...	1765	1811
Eng.	Granville, John Carteret, earl, a statesman, . . .	1690	1763
Ital.	Gratian, a monk, compiler of the canon law, f. 12th century,		
Irish,	Grattan, Henry, a distinguished orator and statesman, .	1750	1820
Dutch,	Gravesande, Wm. Jacob, a geometrician and philosopher,	1688	1742
Eng.	Gray, Thomas, a poet, ...	1716	1771
	Gregory Nazianzen, St., Christian writer, . . .	328	389
	Gregory of Nyssa, St., do. . . .	331	396
Fr.	Gregory (of Tours,) St., an historian, . . .	544	593
Fr.	Gregory I., the Great, pope, an author, . . .	544	604
Ital.	———, VII., ——— (Hildebrand,) a celebrated despot,		1085
Scotch,	———, James, a philosopher and mathematician, . .	1648	1685
Scotch,	———, David, do. . . .	1661	1710
Irish	———, George, D. D., a miscellaneous writer, . .	1754	1808
U. S. A.	Greene, Nathaniel, maj. gen., distinguished in the Revolution,	1741	1786
Eng.	Grey, lady Jane, the accomplished victim of another's ambition,	1537	1554
Ger.	Griesbach, John James, an eminent theologian, . . .	1745	1812
Dutch,	Gronovius, James, an erudite critic, . . .	1645	1716
Dutch,	Grotius, or De Groot, Hugh, an eminent scholar, . .	1583	1645
Ger.	Gryph, Andrew, a dramatist, ...	1616	1664
Ital.	Guarini, John Baptist, a poet, ...	1537	1612
Ger.	Guericke, Otto, exp. philos.,—inventor of the air-pump, .	1602	1686
Ital.	Guicciardini, Francis, an historian, ...	1482	1540
Nor.	Guiscard, Robert, a Norman warrior, . . .	1015	1085
Fr.	Guise, Francis of Lorraine, duke of, a celebrated warrior,	1519	1563
Fr.	———, Charles of, Cardinal, a bigoted and ambitious statesman,	1525	1574
Fr.	———, Henry of Lorraine, duke of, an ambitious warrior,	1550	1588
Eng.	Gunter, Edmund, a mathematician—inventor of the "Gunter's scale," &c.	1581	1619

NATION.	NAME AND PROFESSION.	BORN.	DIED.
Swe.	Gustavus Adolphus, king of Sweden, an able warrior,	1594	1633
Scotch,	Guthrie, William, author of a history of England, Scotland, &c.	1708	1770
Ger.	Guttemberg, John, one of the inventors of printing,	1400	1468
	H		
Pers.	Hafiz, Mohammed, a poet—the Anacreon of Persia,		1389
Ger.	Hahn, Simon Frederick, an historian,	1692	1729
Eng.	Hakluyt, Richard, author of voyages, &c. of the English,	1553	1616
Eng.	Hale, Sir Matthew, an eminent and incorruptible judge,	1609	1676
Eng.	Hall, Robert, an eminent divine,		1831
Swiss,	Haller, Albert Von, miscellaneous writer,	1708	1777
Eng.	Halley, Edmund, an eminent astronomer and mathematician,	1656	1741
U. S. A.	Hamilton, Alexander, a statesman—first sect'y of treasury, U. S.	1757	1804
Irish,	Hamilton, Elizabeth, a talented miscellaneous writer,	1758	1816
Eng.	Hampden, John, a celebrated patriot,	1594	1643
U. S. A.	Hancock, John, a distinguished patriot—president of Congress,	1737	1793
Ger.	Handel, Geo. Frederick, one of the greatest musical composers,	1684	1758
Eng.	Harley, Robert, earl of Oxford, a celebrated statesman,	1661	
Sar.	Haroun Al Raschid, caliph, a patron of learning,		808
Eng.	Harris, James, compiler of the first Cyclopedia, &c.	1670	1719
U. S. A.	Harvard, John, founder of Harvard College,		
Eng.	Harvey, William, discoverer of the circulation of the blood,	1569	1658
Eng.	Hastings, Warren, governor-general of British India,	1733	1818
Eng.	———, marquis of, military commander,	1754	1825
Fr.	Hauy, Renatus Justus, mineralogist,	1742	1822
Eng.	Hawke, Edward, lord, a brave and successful admiral,	1713	1781
Eng.	Hawkesworth, Dr. John, miscellaneous writer,	1715	1773
Eng.	Hawkins, Sir John, a navigator—originator of the slave trade,	1520	1595
Ger.	Hayden, Joseph, a celebrated musical composer,	1732	1809
Eng.	Hayley, William, a poet and miscellaneous writer,	1745	1820
Eng.	Hazlitt, William, a miscellaneous writer,		1830
Eng.	Heber, Reginald, a divine, and poet,	1783	1826
Ger.	Hederich, Benjamin, a lexicographer,	1675	1748
Ger.	Hedwig, John, a physician and botanist,	1730	1799
	Heliodorus, (of Emessa,) the first romance writer, flourished in the 4th century.		
Ger.	Helvicus, Christopher, a chronologist,	1581	1617
Fr.	Henry IV., an able and popular monarch,	1553	1610
Eng.	Henry, Robert, an historian,	1718	1790
U. S. A.	———, Patrick, an orator and patriot,	1736	1799
Gr.	Heraclitus, a philosopher, flourished before Christ	504	
Ger.	Herder, John Godfrey, a philosophical writer,	1744	1803
Gr.	Hermogenes, a rhetorician, flourished,	180	
Gr.	Herodian, an historian,		
Gr.	Herodotus, the earliest of the Greek historians whose works are extant,	B. C. 484	
Span.	Herrera, Anthony, an historian,	1559	1625
Eng.	Herrick, Robert, a poet,	1591	
Eng.	Herschel, sir Wm., one of the greatest of astronomers,	1738	1822
Eng.	Hervey, James, a pious and amiable divine and writer,	1713	1758
Gr.	Hesiod a poet, a contemporary of Homer, flourished,	B. C. 907	
Ger.	Heyne, C. G. a learned critic and writer,	1729	1812
Eng.	Hickes, George, a theologian and philologist,	1642	1715
Eng.	Hill, sir John, a botanist and multifarious writer,	1716	1775
Jew.	Hillel, the elder, one of the compilers of the Talmud,	B. C. 112	
Gr.	Hipparchus, one of the greatest ancient astronomers,		
Gr.	Hippocrates, the father of medicine, before Christ,	460	
Eng.	Hoadley, William, a celebrated prelate and author,	1676	1761
U. S. A.	Hobart, John Henry, bishop of New-York,	1776	1830
Eng.	Hobbes, Thomas, a philosopher and translator,	1588	1679
Fr.	Hoche, Lazarus, military commander,	1768	1797
Swiss,	Hofer, Andrew, a Tyrolian Patriot,	1765	1810
Dan.	Holberg, Louis, baron de, an historian,	1685	1754
Eng.	Holcroft, Thomas, a dramatist and miscellaneous writer,	1744	1809
Eng.	Holingshed, a chronicler,		1568
Eng.	Holland, Philemon, a translator,	1551	1636
Scotch,	Home, John, a divine, dramatist and historian,	1724	1808
Gr.	Homer, the "greatest of poets," [supposed to have] flourished,	B. C. 907	
Eng.	Hood, Samuel, viscount, a naval officer,	1724	1816
Dutch,	Hoogvliet, Arnold, a poet,	1687	1763
Eng.	Hook, Robert, a mathematician,	1635	1702

NATION.	NAME AND PROFESSION.	BORN.	DIED.
Eng.	Hooke, Nathaniel, author of a Roman History,		1763
Eng.	Hooker, Richard, an eminent divine,	1553	1600
Eng.	Hoole, John, a poet and translator,	1717	1803
Eng.	Hooper, John, one of the first Protestant martyrs,	1495	1555
Eng.	Hope, Thomas, a miscellaneous writer,		1831
U. S. A.	Hopkins, Samuel, an eminent divine and author,	1721	1803
Rom.	Horace, Quintus Flaccus, an eminent poet,	B. C. 65	B. C. 8
Eng.	Horne, George, a learned prelate,		
Eng.	Horsley, Samuel, a prelate and Mathematician,	1733	1806
Eng.	Howard, John, a celebrated philanthropist,	1726	1790
Eng.	Hudson, Henry, discoverer of "Hudson river,"	f. 1609	
Fr.	Huet, Peter Daniel, an erudite prelate and author,	1630	1721
Scotch,	Hume, David, an historian and philosopher,	1711	1776
	Hunniades, John, a celebrated warrior,		1456
Eng.	Huskisson, Rt. hon. Wm., an able statesman,		1830
Ger.	Huss, John, the great Bohemian reformer,	1376	1416
Irish,	Hutcheson, Francis, a philosophical writer,	1694	1747
U. S. A.	Hutchinson, Thomas, a distinguished governor of Massachusetts, and historian,	1711	1780
Scotch,	Hutton, Charles, a geologist and philosopher,	1726	1797
Eng.	Hutton, Samuel, an eminent mathematician,	1737	1823
Dutch,	Huygens, Christian, a scientific author,	1629	1705
Ind.	Hyder Ali, a celebrated warrior,		1782

I

Gr.	Ibycus, a lyric poet,		
Span.	Ignatius De Loyola, the founder of the Jesuits,	1491	1556
Eng.	Inchbald, Elizabeth, a dramatist and novelist,	1756	1821
Gr.	Isæus, an orator,	B. C. 418	
Gr.	Isocrates, an orator,	B. C. 436	
Mex.	Iturbide, emperor of Mexico,		1824

J

Dutch,	Jacquin, Nicholas Joseph, a botanist,	1727	1817
Ger.	Jahn, John, an eminent oriental scholar,		1817
Dutch,	Jansen, Cornelius, founder of a sect,	1585	1638
U. S. A.	Jay, John, a distinguished patriot and statesman,	-	18—
U. S. A.	Jefferson, Thomas, a patriotic statesman, 3d pres. U. S.,	1743	1826
Eng.	Jenner, Edward, introducer of the vaccine inoculation,	1749	1823
Eng.	Jenyns, Soame, a poet and miscellaneouswriter,	1704	1787
	Jerome, St., one of the Fathers of the church,		420
Ger.	Jerome, of Prague, a reformer, companion of Huss,		1416
Eng.	Jewel, John, a learned prelate and author,	1522	1571
Fr.	Joan of Arc, "the greatest of heroines,"	1410	1431
Eng.	Johnson, Samuel, a divine and writer in the cause of liberty,	1649	1703
Eng.	———, Samuel, "the colossus of English literature,"	1709	1800
Ital.	Jomelli, Nicholas, a dramatic and musical composer,	1714	1774
Eng.	Jones, Inigo, an eminent architect,	1572	1652
Eng.	——, William, a divine and author,	1726	1800
Eng.	——, Sir William, an eminent poet, scholar, and lawyer,	1746	1794
Scotch,	——, John Paul, a captain in the navy of the United States,	1736	1792
Eng.	Jonson, Benjamin, a celebrated poet and dramatist,	1574	1637
Eng.	Jortin, Dr. John, a learned theologian and author,	1698	1770
	Josephine, empress of the French, (born in Martinico,)	1761	1814
Jew.	Josephus, a celebrated historian and warrior,	37	95
Ger.	Juan, or John, of Austria, don, a warrior,	1546	1578
Jew.	Judah, Hakkadosh, a famous rabbi and Talmudist,	120	194
Dan.	Juel, Nicholas, a celebrated admiral,	1629	1697
	Julian, Flavius Claudius, a Roman emperor and author,	331	363
Ger.	Junge, Joachim, Philosopher,	1587	1657
Dutch,	Junius, Adrian, a voluminous writer,	1512	1575
Fr.	Junot, Andoche, duke d' Abrantes, military officer,	1771	1813
	Justin the Martyr, one of the fathers of the Church,		165
Rom.	Juvenal, Decius Junius, the most vehement of Satirists,		128

K

Ger.	Kæmpfer, a naturalist, traveller and historian,	1651	1716
Ger.	Kæstner, Abraham Gothelf, a mathematician and astronomer,	1719	1799

NATION.	NAME AND PROFESSION.	BORN.	DIED.
Fr.	Kalb, baron de, who generously aided the American cause,		1780
Scotch,	Kames, Henry Home, lord, a judge and author,	1696	1782
Russ.	Karamsin, Nicholas M. historiographer of the empire,	1765	1826
Eng.	Keats, John, a poet,	1796	1821
Scotch,	Keith, James, an officer in the Russian and Prussian service,	1696	1758
Irish,	Kelly, Michael, a composer and singer,	1762	1826
Eng.	Kemble, John Philip, a celebrated tragedian,	1757	1823
French,	Kempis, Thomas à, supposed author of the "Imitation of Christ,"	1380	1471
Eng.	Kennet, White, a learned prelate and author,	1660	1728
Eng.	Kennicott, Benjamin, a divine and biblical critic,	1718	1783
Ger.	Kepler, John, an Eminent Astronomer,	1571	1630
Scotch,	Kerr, Robert, a miscellaneous writer,		1814
Eng.	Kitchiner, William, writer on cookery,		1827
Fren.	Kleber, John Baptist, military officer,	1754	1800
Ger.	Klopstock, "the Milton of Germany,"	1724	1803
Scotch,	Knox, John, the great champion of the reformation,	1505	1572
Eng.	———, Dr. Vicesimus, a divine and miscellaneous writer,	1752	1821
U. S. A	Knox, Henry, military officer and statesman,	1750	1806
Ger.	Koch, Christopher William, an historian,	1737	1813
Polish,	Kosciusko, Thaddeus, a warrior and patriot,	1746	1817
	(Served in the American army during the revolution.)		
Ger.	Kotzebue, Augustus Frederick, Fer. Von, an historian, &c.	1761	1819
Russ.	Kutosoff, Michael L. G., field marshal,	1745	1813
	L		
Fr.	Lacepede, Bernard G. S. de la Ville, count de, naturalist,	1756	1825
	Lactantius, L. C., a father of the church; styled the Christian Cicero,		325
Fr.	Laennec, R. T. H., an eminent physician,	1781	1826
Fr.	Lafontaine "an inimitable fabulist,"	1621	1695
Italian,	Lagrange, Joseph Louis, an able mathematician,	1736	1813
Fr.	La Harpe, John Francis de, a dramatist, critic, &c.	1739	1793
Fr.	Lalande, Joseph J. le Francis de, astronomer,	1732	1807
Fr.	Lamarque, a general of the revolution of 1789,	1770	1832
Fr.	Landon, C. P., author of works on the fine arts,		1826
Ital.	Langfranc, a learned archbishop of Canterbury,	1005	1089
Eng.	Langton, Stephen, cardinal, and archbishop of Canterbury,		1228
Eng.	Lansdown, Henry Petty, marquis of,—premier,	1737	1805
Fr.	Laplace, marquis Peter Simon, an eminent astron. and geom.	1749	1827
Eng.	Lardner, Nathaniel, a learned dissenting divine,	1684	1768
Eng.	Latimer, Hugh, a prelate—martyred for being a reformer,	1470	1555
Eng.	Laud, William, a prelate, famed for his tyranny and superstition,	1573	1645
U. S. A.	Laurens, Henry, a patriot and statesman,		1792
Swiss,	Lavater, John Caspar, a celebrated physiognomist,	1741	1801
Fr.	Lavoisier, Anthony L. a celebrated chemist,	1743	
Fr.	Lebrun, Pontius D. E., a poet,	1729	1807
	Leclerc, John, an eminent critic,	1657	1736
U. S. A.	Ledyard, John, an intrepid and enterprising traveller,		1788
U. S. A.	Lee, Charles, an officer in the revolution,		1782
U. S. A.	——, Richard Henry, president of congress,	1732	1794
U. S. A.	——, Arthur, M. D. a statesman,	1740	1782
Ger.	Leibnitz, Godfrey William, an able and learned philosopher,	1646	1716
Scotch,	Leighton, Robert, an able prelate,	1613	1684
Eng.	Leland, John, an eminent divine, and author,	1691	1766
Irish,	———, Thomas, ——— ——— ———,	1772	1785
Eng.	Lempriere, John, a biographer and lexicographer,		1824
Ital.	Leo X., pope, (John de Medici,) a patron of injustice and the arts,	1475	1521
Gr.	Leonidas I., King of Sparta—the Hero of Thermopylæ, f. B. C.	491	
Fr.	Lesage, Alain Rene, a novelist and dramatist,	1668	1747
Fr.	Levizac, John P. B. L. de, a grammarian,		1813
Eng.	Lewis, Matthew Gregory, miscellaneous writer	1773	1818
Ger.	Lichtenberg, George C., experimental philosopher,	1742	1799
Eng.	Lightfoot, John, a learned divine and author,	1602	1675
Dutch,	Ligne, Charles Joseph, military officer, and author,	1735	1814
Dutch,	Limborch, Philip, a theologian and author,	1633	1712
French,	Linguet, Simon N. H., political writer, and historian,	1736	1794
Swed.	Linnæus, Charles Von, the most celebrated of naturalists,	1707	1778
Eng.	Liverpool, Robert Banks Jenkinson, earl of, premier,	1770	1828
Rom.	Livius, or Livy, Titus, a celebrated historian,		17
U. S. A.	Livingston, William, a poet,	1723	1790

NATION.	NAME AND PROFESSION.	BORN.	DIED.
Eng.	Locke, John, an eminent philosopher, and metaphysician,	1632	1704
Russ.	Lomonosoff, Michael V., a poet and historian,	1711	1765
Irish,	Londonderry, Robert Stewart, marquis of, a statesman,	1769	1822
Gr.	Longinus, Dionysius Cassius, a critic and philosopher,		
Span.	Lope De Vega Carpio, Felix, a poet and dramatist,	1562	1635
Eng.	Lowth, Robert, an eminent divine and author,	1710	1787
	Lucan, Marcus Annæus, a Latin poet,		37
Gr	Lucian, a celebrated writer,	120	210
Rom.	Lucilius, the earliest Roman satirist,	B. C. 148	B. C. 191
Rom.	Lucretius, Caius Titus, an eminent poet,	B. C. 95	
Rom.	Lucullus, a wealthy warrior,	B. C. 115	B. C. 49
Ger.	Luther, Martin, the parent of the protestant reformation,	1484	1546
Fr.	Luxemburg, duke of, a military officer,	1628	1695
Gr.	Lycurgus, the Spartan legislator,	B. C. 898	
Gr.	Lysander, a famous Spartan general,		B. C. 395
Gr	Lysias, an orator,	B. C. 459	
Eng.	Lyttleton, George, lord, a poet and historian,	1709	1763
	M.		
Italian,	Machiavel, Nicholas, a celebrated writer,	1469	1527
Scotch,	Mackenzie, Henry, "the Addison of the North,"	1745	1831
Eng.	Mackintosh, Sir James, a celebrated literary character,		1832
Scotch,	Macknight, James, a divine and author,	1721	1800
Scotch,	Maclaurin, Colin, a mathematician,	1698	1746
Scotch,	Macpherson, James, a miscellaneous writer,	1738	1796
Rom.	Mæcenas, Caius C., the minister of Augustus, and patron of lit.,		B. C. 9
Port.	Magellan, Ferdinand, a celebrated navigator,		1521
Sar.	Mahomet, or Mohammed, the founder of the religion which bears his name,	569	632
Turkish,	Mahomet II., 7th Turkish sultan,—conqueror of Constantinople,	1430	1481
Fr.	Maimbourg, Louis, an historian,	1610	1686
Jew.	Maimonides, Moses, a celebrated rabbi,	1131	1204
Fr.	Maintenon, Frances d' Aubigne, queen,	1635	1719
Eng.	Maittaire, Michael, a bibliographer, &c.,	1668	1747
Eng.	Malmesbury, William of, an historian,		1143
Eng.	Malone, Edward, a dramatic commentator,	1741	1812
Ital.	Malpighi, Marcellus, a naturalist, and anatomist,	1628	1694
Ger.	Malte-Brun, Conrad, a poet and geographer,	1775	1826
Pers.	Manes, or Manichæus, founder of the Manichæan sect,	239	274
Ger.	Mansfield, Ernest of, a warrior,	1585	1626
Ital.	Manutius, Aldus, a celebrated printer and author,	1447	1515
Fr.	Marat, John Paul, an infamous revolutionist,	1744	1793
Span.	Mariana, John, a celebrated historian,	1537	1624
U. S. A.	Marion, Francis, a distinguished officer in the revolution,		1795
Rom.	Marius, Caius, a famous general and demagogue,	B. C. 153	B. C. 86
Eng.	Marlborough, John Churchill, duke of, an able warrior,	1650	1722
Fr.	Marmontel, John Francis, a celebrated writer,	1723	1799
Rom.	Martial, Marcus Valerius, an epigrammatist,	40	100
Ital.	Martyr, Peter, a reformer and theologian,	1500	1561
Eng.	Mason, John, a divine and author,	1706	1763
Eng.	——, William, a divine and poet,	1725	1797
U. S. A.	——, John, M., an eminent divine,	1770	1829
Fr.	Massena, Andrew, one of the ablest of Napoleon's marshals,	1758	1817
Fr.	Massilon, John Baptist, an eloquent divine,	1663	1742
Eng.	Massinger, Philip, a dramatist,	1584	1639
U. S. A.	Mather, Cotton, a divine,	1663	1728
Irish,	Maturin, Charles Robert, a divine, dramatist and poet,	1782	1825
Fr.	Maupertius, Peter L. M. a geometrician and astronomer,	1698	1759
Fr.	Maury, John Siffrein, a cardinal and statesman,	1746	1817
Eng.	Mawe, Joseph, a mineralogist,	1755	1829
Fr.	Mazarin, Julius, cardinal, an able statesman,	1602	1661
	Mazeppa, John, prince of the Cossacks,		1709
Ital.	Medici, Lorenzo d', a poet,—governor of Florence, and patron of the arts,	1448	1492
Ger.	Meiners, Christopher, an historian,	1747	1810
Ger.	Melancthon, Philip, a celebrated reformer,	1497	1560
Gr.	Menander, a comic poet,	B. C. 342	B. C. 290
Ger.	Meninski, Francis M., a learned orientalist,	1623	1698
Dutch,	Mercator, Gerard, a geographer,	1512	1594
Ital.	Metastasio, Peter B., a celebrated poet,	1698	1782

NATION.	NAME AND PROFESSION.	BORN.	DIED.
Dutch,	Meursius, John, an erudite critic,	1579	1639
Fr.	Mezerai, Francis, Eudes de, an historian,	1610	1683
Ger.	Michaelis, John David, a learned orientalist and critic,	1717	1791
Eng.	Middleton, Conyers, a divine, and an elegant writer,	1683	1750
Fr.	Millevoye, Charles Hubert, a poet,	1782	1816
Fr.	Millin, Aubin Louis, a naturalist, &c.,	1759	
Fr.	Millot, Claude Francis Xavier, an historian,	1726	1785
Eng.	Mills, Charles, an historian,	1788	1826
Eng.	Milner, Joseph, author of Church History,	1744	1797
Gr.	Miltiades, an illustrious Athenian general,		B. C. 489
Eng.	Milton, John, the Homer of Britain,	1608	1674
U. S. A.	Mitchell, Samuel L., celebrated physician and naturalist,	1763	1831
Fr.	Mirabeau, H. G. Riquetti, count de, a celebrated character in the Revolution, and author,	1749	1791
Span.	Miranda, Francis, a revolutionary general,	1750	1816
Eng.	Mitford, William, an historian and philologist,	1734	1827
	Mithridates, king of Pontus, a warrior,	B. C. 123	B. C. 64
Sar.	Mohammed Ben Abd Al Wahab, Shiek, founder of the sect of Wahabites,	flourished 1650	
Fr.	Moleville, Anthony F. de Bertrand, count de, an historian,	1754	1817
Fr.	Moliere, John Baptist, a celebrated comic writer,	1622	1673
Fr.	Monge, Gaspar, an eminent geometrician,	1746	1818
Eng.	Monk, George, duke of Albemarle, military officer,	1608	1670
U. S. A.	Monroe, James, a statesman, 5th president U. S.	1759	1831
Fr.	Monstrelet, Enguerrand de, a chronicler,	1390	1453
Eng.	Montagu, lady Mary Wortley, an elegant writer,	1690	1762
Fr.	Montaigne, Michael de, an eminent essayist,	1533	1592
Fr.	Montebello, John Lannes, duke of, marshal,	1769	1809
Ger.	Montecuculi, Raymond, a warrior,	1609	1681
Fr.	Montesquieu, Charles, baron de, an able writer,	1689	1755
U. S. A.	Montgomery, Richard, an intrepid military officer,	1737	1775
Ital.	Monti, Vincent, a poet,	1753	1828
Fr.	Montmorenci, Anne de, marshal,	1493	1567
Eng.	Moore, Sir John, General,	1761	1809
Eng.	Moore, Sir Thomas, chancellor,	1480	1535
Fr.	Moreau, John Victor, a celebrated general,	1763	1813
U. S. A.	Morris, Robert, a signer of the Dec. Ind., and a financier,	1703	1806
U. S. A.	——, Governeur, a distinguished statesman,	1752	1816
U. S. A.	Morse, Jedidiah, a geographer and statistical writer,	1761	1827
Gr.	Moschus, a bucolic poet,		
Ger.	Mosheim, John Laurence, an ecclesiastical historian,	1695	1755
	Mouradgea D'Ohsson, an Armenian historian,	1740	1807
Ger.	Mozart, John C. W. T., an eminent composer,	1756	1792
Swiss,	Mullen, John Von, a celebrated historian,	1752	1809
Fr.	Murat, Joachim, an intrepid marshal, and king of Naples,	1771	1815
Ital.	Muratori, Louis Anthony, an historian,	1672	1750
Irish,	Murphy, Arthur, a dramatist and translator,	1727	1805
Eng.	Murray, Lindley, a grammarian,	1745	1826
Scotch,	Murray, Alexander, a self taught linguist,	1775	1813
U. S. A.	——, William Vans, a statesman,	1761	1803
Gr.	Musæus, an Athenian poet,	f. B. C. 1243	

N

Pers.	Nadir Shah, or Thamas Kouli Khan, a warrior and king,	1688	1747
Scotch,	Napier, John, baron, inventor of logarithms,	1550	1617
Fr.	Napoleon I., (Bonaparte,)	1769	1821
Pers.	Narses, a warrior, in the service of Justinian I., the emperor,		567
Dutch,	Nassau, prince Maurice of, an able general,	1567	1625
Pers.	Nassir Eddyn, a celebrated astronomer,	1201	1274
Eng.	Neal, Daniel, author of History of the Puritans, &c.,	1678	1743
Fr.	Necker, James, an eminent financier and statesman,	1732	1804
Eng.	Neele, Henry, a poet and miscellaneous writer,	1798	1828
Eng.	Nelson, Horatio, viscount, a celebrated admiral,	1758	1805
Rom.	Nepos, Cornelius, an historian,		
Eng.	Newton, Sir Isaac, the greatest of philosophers,	1642	1727
Eng.	——, Thomas, a learned prelate,	1704	1782
Eng.	——, John, a Calvinistic divine and writer,	1725	1807
Fr.	Ney, Michael, marshal, "the bravest of the brave,"	1769	1815
Eng.	Nicholson, William, writer on nat. philosophy and chemistry,	1753	1815
Ger.	Nicolai Chris., Fred., a bookseller and author,	1733	1811

NATION.	NAME AND PROFESSION.	BORN.	DIED.
Ger.	Niebuhr, Carsten, a celebrated traveller,	1733	1815
Ger.	———, B. G., a statesman and historian,		1830
Eng.	North, Frederick, lord, prime minister,	1732	1792
Eng.	Nott, John, a poet and translator,	1751	1826

O

NATION.	NAME AND PROFESSION.	BORN.	DIED.
Eng.	Oates, Titus, the infamous pretender of the "Popish Plot,"	1619	1705
Eng.	Ockley, Simon, an orientalist,	1678	1720
Arab.	Odenatus, a warrior, the husband of Zenobia,		267
Gr.	Oppian, a poet,	f. 150	
Dutch,	Orange, William of Nassau, prince of; the founder of the Dutch republic,	1533	1584
Dutch,	Origen, one of the fathers of the church,	185	253
Eng.	Orme, Robert, an historian,	1728	1801
Eng.	Ormond, James Butler, duke of, a statesman,	1610	1688
Gr.	Orpheus, a poet, sometimes styled "the father of poetry,"		
Port.	Osorio, Jerome, a philosopher, historian, and theological writer,	1506	1580
U. S. A.	Otis, James, a patriot and statesman,	1725	1772
Eng.	Otway, Thomas, a celebrated dramatist,	1651	1685
Rom.	Ovid, Publius Naso, a poet,	B. C. 43	17
Eng.	Owen, John, an eminent divine,	1765	1822

P

NATION.	NAME AND PROFESSION.	BORN.	DIED.
Eng.	Paine, Thomas, a political and deistical writer,	1736	1809
Eng.	Paley, William, an eminent divine and author,	1745	1805
Fr.	Pallisset De Montenoy, Charles, a satirist,	1730	1815
Pruss.	Pallas, Peter Simon, traveller and naturalist,	1741	1811
	Paoli, Pascal, a Corsican patriot and general,	1726	1807
	Papinian, Æmilius, a civil lawyer,	145	212
Swiss,	Paracelsus, A. P. T. B. de H, an alchemist,	1493	1541
Eng.	Paris, Matthew, an historian,		1259
Scotch,	Park, Mungo, a celebrated traveller,	1771	1804
Eng.	Parkes, Samuel, a chemist and author,	1759	1825
Eng.	Parkhurst, John, Hebrew and Greek lexicographer,	1723	1797
Ital.	Parma, Alexander Farnese, duke of, a warrior,		1592
Fr.	Pascal, Blaize, eminent as a geometrician and writer,	1623	1662
Rom.	Paterculus, Caius Velleius, an historian,		
Gr.	Pausanias, an orator and historian.		
Brit.	Pelagius, a monk, founder of a sect,	354	
Gr.	Pelopidas, an illustrious Theban general,		B. C. 364
Eng.	Penn, William, the founder and legislator of Pennsylvania,	1644	1718
Fr.	Perefixe, Hardouin de Beaumont de, historian,	1605	1670
Gr.	Pericles, an able Athenian orator and statesman,	B. C. 490	B. C. 429
Fr.	Perrier, M. Cassimir, a statesman,		1832
Fr.	Perouse, John F. Galaup, de la, a navigator,	1741	1788
Rom.	Persius Flaccus, Aulus, a satirist,	34	62
Swiss,	Pestalozzi, Henry, introducer of a new system of education,	1745	1827
Fr.	Peter the Hermit, the first mover of the Crusades,		1115
Russ.	Peter I., the Great, a warrior and statesman,	1672	1725
Eng.	Peterborough, Charles Mordaunt, earl of, a warrior,	1658	1735
	Petion, Alexander, a mulatto, president of Hayti,	1770	1818
Ital.	Petrarch, Francis, one of the four greatest of Italian poets,	1304	1374
Rom.	Phædrus, a fabulist,		
	Philip II., king of Macedon, a warrior,	B. C. 383	B. C. 336
Gr.	Philopœmen, a celebrated general,	B. C. 253	B. C. 183
Gr.	Phocion, an eminent Athenian,	B. C. 400	B. C. 318
	Photius, a learned patriarch of Constantinople,		891
Fr.	Picard, Louis Benedict, a dramatist and novelist,	1769	1824
Fr.	Pichegru, Charles, an eminent general,	1761	1804
U. S. A.	Pickering, Timothy, a distinguished statesman,	1746	1829
Gr.	Pindar, the greatest of lyric poets,	B. C. 522	B. C. 442
Scotch,	Pinkerton, John, a fertile and eccentric author,	1758	1826
U. S. A.	Pinkney, William, a distinguished orator and diplomatist,	1765	1822
Span.	Pinzon, Vincent Yanez, a navigator, discovered Brazil,	f. 1500	
Fr.	Piron, Alexis, a poet, dramatist and wit,	1689	1773
Gr.	Pisistratus, sovereign of Athens,		B. C. 527
Eng.	Pitt, Christopher, a poet and translator,	1699	1748
Eng.	——, William, a celebrated statesman,	1759	1806
Gr.	Pittacus, of Mitylene, one of the seven sages,	B. C. 650	B. C. 570

NATION.	NAME AND PROFESSION.	BORN.	DIED.
Span.	Pizarro, Francis, the conqueror of Peru,	1475	1541
Gr.	Plato, an illustrious philos.—founder of the academic sect.	B. C. 430	B. C. 347
Rom.	Plautus, a comic poet,	B. C. 227	B. C. 184
Scotch,	Playfair, John, an eminent mathematician and natural philos.,	1749	1819
Rom.	Pliny, the elder, or C. P. Secundus, author of Natural History,	23	79
Rom.	——, the younger, a warrior and author,	61	115
Egypt.	Plotinus, a Platonic philosopher,	203	270
Gr.	Plutarch, a celebrated biographer,	50	120
Eng.	Pole, Reginald, a cardinal, and statesman,	1500	1558
Fr.	Polignac, Melchior de, a cardinal and statesman,	1611	1741
Ital.	Polo, Mark, a celebrated Venetian traveller,	1250	1523
Gr.	Polybius, an eminent historian,	B. C. 205	B. C. 123
Rom.	Pompey, Cneus, a statesman and warrior,	B. C. 106	B. C. 48
Pol.	Poniatowski, Joseph, prince, an able general,	1763	1814
Eng.	Pool, Matthew, an able divine and author,	1624	1679
Eng.	Pope, Alexander, a celebrated poet,	1688	1744
	Porphyry, a Platonic philosopher,	233	304
Eng.	Porson, Richard, an eminent hellenist and critic,	1759	1808
Ital.	Porta, John Baptist, a natural philosopher,	1540	1615
Eng.	Porteus, Beilby, an eminent prelate,	1731	1808
Eng.	Potter, Robert, a divine, poet and translator,	1721	1804
Eng.	Prideaux, Humphry, a learned divine,	1648	1724
Eng.	Priestley, Joseph, an eminent philosopher and writer,	1733	1804
Eng.	Prior, Matthew, a poet and statesman,	1664	1721
Gr.	Proclus, a platonic philosopher,	410	487
Gr.	Procopius, an historian,		560
Rom.	Propertius, Sextus Aurelius, a poet,	B. C. 52	B. C. 12
Egypt.	Ptolemy, Claudius, an eminent astronomer and geographer,	70	
Ger.	Puffendorf, Samuel, a publicist and historian,	1632	1694
Ital.	Pulci, Louis, a Poet,	1432	1487
U. S. A.	Putnam, Israel, a distinguished officer in the revolution,	1718	1790
Gr.	Pyrrho, a philosopher, founder of the Skeptic sect,	f. B. C. 300	
Gr.	Pythagorus, a celebrated philosopher,	B. C. 586	B. C. 497

Q

Span.	Quevedo De Villegas, Francis, a poet,	1580	1645
Fr.	Quinault, Philip, a lyrical dramatist,	1635	1666
Rom.	Quintilian, Marcus Fabius, a celebrated orator,	42	122

R

Fr.	Racine, John, an eminent dramatist,	1639	1699
Eng.	Radcliffe, Anne, a celebrated romance writer,	1764	1823
Eng.	Raleigh, or Ralegh, Sir Walter, "a man illustrious in arms and literature,"	1552	1618
Scotch,	Ramsay, Allan, a poet,	1685	1758
U. S. A.	Ramsay, David, an historian,	1749	1812
U. S. A.	Randolph, Peyton, first president of Congress,	1723	1775
Eng.	Ray, John, a naturalist and author,	1628	1705
Fr.	Raynal, William Thomas Francis, an historian and philosopher,	1713	1796
Eng.	Reed, Isaac, a critic and editor,	1742	1807
Eng.	Rees, Dr. Abraham, editor of an enclycopedia, &c.	1743	1825
Eng.	Reeve, Clara, a novelist,	1723	1803
Fr.	Regnard, John Francis, a comic writer,	1647	1709
Scotch,	Reid, Thomas, a celebrated metaphysician,	1710	1796
Eng.	Rennie, John, an eminent engineer,	1761	1821
Fr.	Retz, John F. P. de Gondi, cardinal de, a demagogue,	1614	1679
Eng.	Ricaut, Sir Paul, a traveller and historian,		1700
Eng.	Richardson, Samuel, an eminent novelist,	1689	1761
French,	Richelieu, A. J. du Plessis, cardinal and duke, a statesman,	1585	
Ger.	Richter, John Paul Frederick, a novelist, &c.	1763	1825
Span.	Riego Y Nunez, Raphael del, a patriot,	1783	1825
Ital.	Rienzi, Nicholas Gabrino de, a political reformer,		1354
U. S. A.	Rittenhouse, David, a philosopher and astronomer,	1731	1796
Eng.	Robertson, William, a celebrated historian,	1721	1793
Fr.	Robespierre, F. M. J. I the "terrorist" of the Revolution,	1759	1794
Fr.	Rochefoucauld, Liancourt, F. A. F. duke de la,	1747	1827
Fr.	Rochejaquelein, H. de la, a royalist leader,	1773	1794
Eng.	Rodney, George Brydges, lord, an able admiral,	1717	1792

NATION.	NAME AND PROFESSION.	BORN.	DIED.
Fr.	Roland de la Platriere, J. M. a revolutionist and author,	1732	1793
Fr.	Rollin, Charles, a celebrated historian,	1661	1741
Eng.	Romaine, William, a divine and author,	1714	1795
Rom.	Romulus, the founder and first king of Rome,		B. C. 716
Eng.	Rooke, Sir George, an admiral,	1650	1708
Rom.	Roscius, Quintus, an actor of proverbial talent,		B. C. 61
Eng.	Roscoe, William, a biographer and miscellaneous writer,	1751	1831
Fr.	Rosseau, John Baptist, a poet,	1670	1741
Fr.	———, John James, an eloquent and paradoxical writer,	1712	1778
Eng.	Rowe, Nicholas, a poet and dramatist,	1673	1718
U. S. A.	Rumford, Benjamin Thompson, count, an officer, (in foreign service,) and philosopher,	1753	1814
Ger.	Rupert, prince, a warrior,	1619	1682
U. S. A.	Rush, Benjamin, an eminent physician and author,	1745	1813
Eng.	Russel, lord, William, one of the martyrs of liberty,	1641	1683
Eng.	———, lady Rachael, (wife of the last,) author of "Letters."		1723
Eng.	Russell, William, an historian,	1746	1794

S.

Pers.	Sadi, or Saadi, a poet,		1296
Ital.	Saint Real, Cæsar Vichard, abbe de, an historian,	1639	1692
Eng.	Saint Vincent, John Jervis, earl of, admiral,	1734	1823
	Saladin, Sultan of Egypt and Syria, a celebrated warrior,	1137	1193
Eng.	Salisbury, Robert Cecil, earl of, a statesman,	1550	1612
Rom.	Sallust, Caius Crispus, an historian,	f. B. C. 86	B. C. 35
Fr.	Salmasius, Claudius, a scholar and author,	1588	1653
Eng.	Sandwich, Edward Montague, earl of, naval officer,	1623	1672
Fr.	Sanson, Nicholas, a geographer and engineer,	1600	1667
Gr.	Sappho, a poetess, flourished,	B. C. 606	
Ital.	Sarpi, Peter, known as father Paul, a patriot and author,	1552	1623
Fr.	Saurin, James, a divine and sermon writer,	1677	1730
Pruss.	Saxe, Maurice, count de, a celebrated general in the French service,	1696	1750
Ger,	Saxe-Weimar, Bernard, duke of, a warrior,	1600	1639
Ital.	Scaliger, Julius Cæsar, a learned critic,	1484	1558
	Scanderbeg, (real name George Castriot,) an Albanian prince and warrior,	1404	1467
Ger.	Scapula, John, a lexicographer,		1600
Swed.	Scheele, Charles William, an eminent chemist,	1742	1786
Pruss.	Schill, Ferdinand Von, an intrepid and patriotic officer,	1773	1809
Ger.	Schiller, John Frederic C. an eminent historian and dramatist,	1759	1805
Ger.	Schmidt, Michael Ignatius, an historian,	1736	1794
Dutch,	Schomberg, Armand Frederick, a warrior,	1619	1690
Dutch,	Schrevelius, Cornelius, a lexicographer,	1615	1667
Ger.	Schulembourg, John Matthias, a warrior,	1661	1747
U. S. A.	Schuyler, Philip, an officer in the revolution,		1804
Ger.	Scioppius, Gaspar, a philologist and grammarian,	1576	1649
Rom.	Scipio, Publius Cornelius, surnamed Africanus, an able warrior,		B. C. 183
Rom.	———, Æmilianus, Publius, ———		B. C. 129
Scotch,	Scott, Michael, a philosopher—supposed magician,		1291
Eng.	——, Thomas, a divine, and biblical commentator,	1747	1821
Scotch,	——, Sir Walter, one of the most eminent, voluminous, and popular writers of modern times,		1832
Eng.	Secker, Thomas, an eminent prelate,	1693	1768
Fr.	Segur, count Louis de, a diplomatist and writer,	1753	1830
Rom.	Seneca, Lucius Annæus, a celebrated philosopher, statesman and moralist,	B. C. 2	65
Span.	Sepulveda, John Ginez de, an historian,	1490	1572
Roman,	Sertorius, Quintus, a warrior,		B. C. 73
Fr.	Sevigne, Mary de, marchioness of, an epistolary writer,	1627	1696
Eng.	Shaftesbury, Anthony Ashley Cooper, earl of, a statesman,	1621	1683
Eng.	Shakespeare, William, the greatest of dramatic poets,	1564	1616
Eng.	Sharpe, Granville, a philanthropist,	1734	1813
Eng.	Shaw, George, a naturalist,	1751	1813
Eng.	Shelly, Percy Bysshe, an eminent poet and atheist,	1792	1822
Eng.	Shenstone, William, a poet,	1714	1763
Eng.	Sheridan, Thomas, an actor and author,	1721	1788
Eng.	———, Richard Brinsley, a dramatist and orator,	1751	1816
Eng.	Sherlock, Thomas, a prelate,	1678	1761
U. S. A.	Sherman, Roger, a patriot and self-taught statesman,	1721	1793

NATION.	NAME AND PROFESSION.	BORN.	DIED.
Eng.	Shovel, Sir Cloudesley, an able naval officer,	1650	1705
Eng.	Siddons, Sarah, the most eminent of tragic actresses,	1755	1831
Eng.	Sidney, Sir Philip, an accomplished officer and author,	1554	1586
Eng.	——, Algernon, a martyr of liberty and an author,	1620	1683
Eng.	Simpson, Thomas, a mathematician,	1710	1761
Eng.	——, Robert do	1687	1768
Ger.	Sleidan, John Philipson, an historian,	1506	1556
Eng.	Sloane, Sir Hans, an eminent naturalist,	1660	1752
Eng.	Smart, Christopher, a poet and translator,	1722	1770
Eng.	Smeaton, John, an eminent civil engineer,	1724	1792
Scotch,	Smellie, William, a naturalist,	1740	1795
Eng.	Smith, William, a divine and translator,	1711	1787
Scotch,	——, Adam, a celebrated writer, on morals and political economy,	1723	1790
Eng.	——, Charlotte, a poetess.	1749	1806
Eng.	Smollet, Dr. Tobias, a novelist and historian,		1771
Pol.	Sobieski, John III., king of Poland, a warrior,	1629	1696
Ital.	Socinus, Faustus, founder of the Socinian sect,	1539	1594
Gr.	Socrates, one of the greatest of ancient philosophers,	B. C. 470	B. C. 400
Gr.	Solon, the illustrious legislator of Athens,	flourished B. C. 598	
Gr.	Sophocles, an eminent tragic poet,	B. C. 495	404
Eng.	South, Robert, an eminent, divine,	1638	
Eng.	Southcott, Joanna, a fanatic, (her sect not yet extinct,)	1750	1814
Eng.	Spencer, Edmund, an eminent poet,	1553	1598
Span.	Spinola, Ambrose, marquis de, a warrior,	1571	1630
Ger.	Spurzheim, Dr., a celebrated Phrenologist, (d. at Boston,)	1776	1832
Fr.	Stael, Madame de, a talented writer,	1693	1750
Eng.	Stackhouse, Thomas, a divine and author,	1680	1752
Fr.	Stael-Holstien, Anne L. G., baroness de, an authoress,	1766	1817
Eng.	Stanhope, Charles, earl, a politician and inventor,	1753	1816
U. S. A.	Stark, John, a distinguished officer in the revolution,	1728	1822
Irish,	Steel, Sir Richard, an essayist and dramatist,	1671	1729
Irish,	Sterne, Lawrence, a miscellaneous writer,	1713	1768
Pruss.	Steuben, Fred. W. A., baron, who generously sided the Am. cause,		1794
Scotch,	Stewart, Dugald, an eminent philosopher and writer,	1753	1828
Gr.	Strabo an eminent geographer,		
Eng.	Strafford, Thomas Wentworth, earl of, a statesman,	1593	1641
Eng.	Stuart, James, an architect and author,	1713	1788
Scotch,	——, Gilbert, an historian,	1742	1786
Fr.	Suchet, Louis Gabriel, a celebrated marshal,	1772	1826
Rom.	Suetonius, Tranquillus Caius, an historian,		
Rom.	——, Paulinus, a warrior,	37	
Dan.	Suhm, Peter Frederick, an eminent historian,	1728	1798
	Suidas, a Greek lexicographer,		
Fr.	Sully, Maximilian de Bethune, a warrior and statesman,	1560	1641
Eng.	Surrey, Henry Howard, earl of, a poet,	1515	1547
Russ.	Suvaroff, or Suwarrow) prince Alexander, a celebrated and cruel warrior,	1730	1800
Swed.	Swedenborg, Emanuel, founder of a sect,	1689	1772
Irish,	Swift, Jonathan, a celebrated satirist,	1667	1745
Rom.	Sylla, Lucius Cornelius, a warrior, and a brutal usurper,	B. C. 137	B. C. 78

T

NATION.	NAME AND PROFESSION.	BORN.	DIED.
Rom.	Tacitus, Caius Cornelius, an eminent historian,	56	135
Fr.	Talma, Francis Joseph, one of the greatest of actors,	1763	1826
	Tamerlane, Timur Beg, or Timour, a celebrated Tartar prince and conqueror,	1336	1405
Ital.	Tasso, Bernardo, a poet,—author of Amadis de Gaul,	1493	1569
Ital.	——, Torquato, one of the greatest of Italian poets,	1544	1595
Eng.	Taylor, Jeremy, a prelate and eloquent writer,	1613	1667
Swiss,	Tell, William, one of the champions of Swiss liberty,		1354
Eng.	Temple, Sir William, a statesman and writer,	1628	1698
Rom.	Terence, or Terrentius, a comic writer,	B. C. 192	
	Tertullian, Q. S. F., one of the most learned of the fathers of the church,	160	245
Gr.	Thales, one of the seven sages—founder of the Ionic school of philosophy,	B. C. 639	B. C. 543
Gr.	Themistocles, an illustrious Athenian,	B. C. 535	B. C. 470
Gr.	Theocritus, a pastoral poet,	flourished B. C. 285	
Rom.	Theodosius, Flavius, a Roman emperor and warrior,	346	395
Gr.	Theophrastus, a celebrated philosopher,	B. C. 371	

NATION.	NAME AND PROFESSION.	BORN.	DIED.
Gr.	Thespis, a poet, said to be the inventor of tragedy,	B. C. 576	
Eng.	Thompson, James, a popular poet,	1700	1748
Gr.	Thucydides, an historian,	B. C. 469	B. C. 400
Rom.	Tiberius, Claudius Drusus Nero, a warrior and emperor,	B. C. 34	37
Rom.	Tibullus, Aulus Albius, an elegiac poet,	f. B. C. 30	
Eng.	Tillotson, John, an eminent prelate,	1630	1694
	Tippoo Saib, Sultan of Mysore India, a warrior,	1749	1799
Rom.	Titus, Sabinus, Vespasianus Flavius, an emp. the father of his people,	40	81
Eng.	Tomline, George, a prelate and writer,	1750	1787
Eng.	Tooke, John Horne, a politician and philologist,	1736	1812
Eng.	——, William a miscellaneous writer,	1744	1820
Eng.	Toplady, Augustus M., an eminent divine,	1740	1778
Rom.	Trajan, Marcus U. C., an able emperor and warrior,	52	117
Pruss.	Trenck, Frederick, baron de, celebrated for his adventures,	1726	1794
Dutch,	Tromp, Martin H., a celebrated admiral,	1597	1653
U. S. A.	Trumbull, Jonathan, a statesman,		1809
U. S. A.	———, John, a poet; born in Connecticut,	1750	1831
Eng.	Tucker, Abraham, a metaphysical writer,	1705	1774
Fr.	Turenne, viscount de, an eminent warrior,	1611	1675
Fr.	Turgot, Anne Robert James, a statesman,	1727	1781
Eng.	Tyrrel, James, an historian,	1642	1718
Gr.	Tyrtæus, a poet,		
Scotch,	Tytler, William, an historical and miscellaneous writer,	1711	1792
Scotch,	——, Alexander Fraser, ——— ———	1747	1813

U

NATION.	NAME AND PROFESSION.	BORN.	DIED.
Span.	Ulloa, don Anthony de, a navigator and author,	1716	1795
Irish,	Usher, James, a learned divine and historian,	1580	1656

V

NATION.	NAME AND PROFESSION.	BORN.	DIED.
Fr.	Vaillant, Sebastian, an eminent botanist,	1669	1722
Dutch,	Valckenaer, Louis, Gasper, an able philologist and critic,	1715	1785
Fr.	Valdo, Peter, founder of the sect of Waldenses, f. in 12th century.		
Rom.	Valerius Maximus, an historian,		
Ital.	Valla, Laurence, an eminent philologist,	1406	1457
Eng.	Vancouver, George, a navigator,	1750	1798
Eng.	Vane, Sir Henry, an advocate of republicanism,	1612	1662
Rom.	Varro, Marcus T. "the most learned of the Romans,"	B. C. 116	B. C. 27
Ger.	Vater, John Severinus, an eminent philologist,	1771	1826
Fr.	Vauban, S. le P. de, marshal, a military engineer,	1633	1707
Fr.	Vendome, Louis Joseph, duke of, a warrior,	1654	1712
Eng.	Vernon, Edward, admiral,	1684	1759
Fr.	Vertot, Rene Aubert, abbe de, an historian,	1655	1735
Rom.	Vespasian, Titus Flavius, a warrior and emperor,		79
Ital.	Vespucius, Americus, a navigator whose name was unjustly given to the new world,	1451	1516
Ital.	Vida, Mark Jerome, a Latin poet,	1490	1566
Fr.	Villars, Louis Hector, duke of, an able general,	1653	1734
Eng.	Vince, Samuel, an eminent mathematician,		1821
Rom.	Virgil, or Pub., Virgilius Maro, the greatest of the Roman poets,	B. C. 70	B. C. 19
Fr.	Volney, count de, a celebrated writer,	1757	1820
Fr.	Voltaire, Mary Arouet de, ———	1694	

W

NATION.	NAME AND PROFESSION.	BORN.	DIED.
Eng.	Wakefield, Gilbert, a scholar and critic,	1756	1801
Eng.	Walker, John, a lexicographer,	1732	1807
Scotch,	Wallace, William, a patriot and hero,	1276	1305
Ger.	Wallenstein, A. V. E., a celebrated general,	1583	1634
Eng.	Waller, Sir William, a parliamentary general,	1597	1668
Eng.	——, Edmund, an elegant poet,	1603	1687
Eng.	Walpole, Robert, earl of Orford, a statesman,	1676	1745
Eng.	———, Horace, ——— an author,	1718	1797
Eng.	Walsingham, Sir Francis, a statesman,	1536	1590
Eng.	Walton, Izaak, an angler and biographer,	1593	1683
Eng.	——, Brian, a divine and orientalist,	1600	1661
Eng.	Warburton, William, an eminent prelate and writer,	1698	1779
U. S. A.	Ward, Artemas, an officer in the revolution,	1746	1800

NATION.	NAME AND PROFESSION.	BORN.	DIED.
Eng.	Warren, Sir John Borlase, a naval officer, ...	1754	1822
Eng.	Warton, Joseph, a poet and critic, ...	1722	1800
Eng.	——, Thomas, ...	1728	1790
U. S. A.	Washington, George, the father of his country, .	1732	1799
Scotch,	Watson, Robert, an historian, ...	1730	1780
Eng.	——, Richard, an eminent prelate and writer, .	1737	1816
Scotch,	Watt, James, a celebrated natural philosopher and engineer,	1736	1819
Scotch,	——, Robert, a bibliographer, ...	1774	1819
Eng.	Watts, Dr. Isaac, a pious and highly gifted divine, poet and miscellaneous writer, ...	1674	
Ger.	Weber, Carl Martan Von, an eminent composer . .	1786	1826
Eng.	Wells, Edward, a theologian and scholar, . . .	1663	1727
Ger.	Werner, Abraham Theophilus, a mineralogist, . . .	1750	1817
Ger.	——, Fred L. Z., a poet and dramatist, . . .	1768	1823
Eng.	Wesley, John, the founder of the Methodist Society, .	1703	1791
Eng.	Whiston, William, a divine, mathematician and translator,	1667	1752
Eng.	Whitby, David, a learned divine, ...	1638	1726
Eng.	White, Henry Kirke, a poet, ...	1785	1806
Eng.	Whitefield, George, founder, of the Calvinistic Methodists,	1714	1770
Eng.	Wickliffe, or Wiclif, John, the morning star of the reformation,	1324	1384
Ger.	Wieland, Christopher M., an able and fertile writer, .	1733	1813
Eng.	Wilkes, John, a celebrated political character, . .	1717	1797
Eng.	Williams, Helen Maria, a miscellaneous, writer, . .	1762	1827
U. S. A.	Wilson, Alexander, a celebrated naturalist, . .		1813
Eng.	Windham, William, a statesman, ...	1750	1810
U. S. A.	Wistar, Caspar, an eminent physician and anatomist, .	1761	1818
U. S. A.	Witherspoon, John, an able divine and patriot, . .	1722	1794
U. S. A.	Wolcott, Oliver, a patriot—signer dec. Ind., . .	1727	1797
Eng.	——, John, known as Peter Pindar, a poet, . .	1738	1819
Eng.	Wolfe, James, a distinguished general, . . .	1726	1759
Ger.	Wolff, John Christian, a philosopher and mathematician, .	1679	1754
Eng.	Wollaston, William Hyde, an experimental philosopher, .	1766	1828
Eng.	Wolsey, Thomas, cardinal, a celebrated statesman, . .	1471	1530
Eng.	Wren, Sir Christopher, a celebrated architect, . .	1632	1723
U. S. A.	Wythe, George, an eminent lawyer, statesman and patriot, .		1806

X

Fr.	Xavier, St. Francis, "the Apostle to the Indies," . . .	1506	1552
Gr.	Xenocrates, a philosopher, ... B. C.	406 B. C.	314
Gr.	Xenophenes, a philosopher,—founder of the Eleatics, flourished		
Gr.	Xenophon, a celebrated philosopher, historian and general, B. C.	446 B. C.	360
Span.	Ximenes, Francis, cardinal, an eminent statesman, .	1457	1517

Y

Eng.	Young, Edward, a poet and miscellaneous writer, . .	1681	1765
Eng.	——, Arthur, an agricultural writer, . . .	1741	1820
Eng.	——, Thomas, a physician and philosopher, . . .	1774	1829
	Ypsilanti, prince Alexander, a leader in the modern Greek revol.		1821
Spanish,	Yriarte, don Thomas de, an eminent poet, ...	1750	1790

Z

Ital.	Zaccaria, Francis A., a voluminous writer, . . .	1714	1795
Gr.	Zeno, of Elea, a philosopher, ... B. C.	463	
Gr.	——, the founder of the sect of Stoics, . . . B. C.	362 B. C.	264
Ital.	——, Apostolo, an eminent writer, ...	1668	1750
	Zenobia, Septimia, queen of Palmyra, a conqueror, and patroness of the arts, ...		300
Swiss,	Zimmerman, John George, a miscellaneons writer, . .	1728	1795
Swiss,	Zuinglius, Ulric, an enlightened reformer, . . .	1484	1531

TAB. XI.

HEATHEN DEITIES, AND OTHER FABULOUS PERSONS,

WITH THE

HEROES AND HEROINES OF ANTIQUITY.

A

Ab'aris, a Scythian, priest of Apollo.
Abeo'na, a goddess of voyages, &c.
Abreta'nus, a surname of Jupiter.
A'bron, a very voluptuous Grecian.
Aby'la, a famous mountain in Africa.
Acan'tha, a nymph beloved by Apollo.
Acas'tus, the name of a famous hunter.
Ace'tus, one of the priests of Bacchus.
Achæ'menes, the first king of Persia.
Acha'tes, a trusty friend of Æneas.
Ach'eron, a son of Titan and Terra, changed into a river of hell for assisting the Titans in their war against Jupiter.
Achil'les, son of Peleus, king of Thrace, and Thetis, a goddess of the sea, who, being dipped by his mother in the river Styx, was invulnerable in every part except his right heel, by which she held him; after signalizing himself at the siege of Troy, for his valour, as well as cruelty, he was at length killed by Paris with an arrow.
Acid'alia, and *Arma'ta*, names of Venus.
Acida'lus, a famous fountain of Bœotia.
A'cis, a Sicilian shepherd, killed by Polyphemus, because he rivalled him in the affections of Galatea.
Ac'mon, a famous king of the Titans.
Ac'ratus, the genius of drunkards at Athens.
Ac'tæon, a celebrated hunter, who, accidentally discovering Diana bathing, was by her turned into a stag, and devoured by his own hounds.
Adme'tus, a king of Thessaly.
Ado'nis, the incestuous offspring of Cinyras and Myrrha, remarkably beautiful, beloved by Venus and Proserpine.
Adras'tea, the goddess Nemesis.
Æ'acus, one of the infernal judges.
Æ'ga, Jupiter's nurse, daughter of Olenus.
Æge'us, a king of Attica, giving name to the Ægean sea by drowning himself in it.
Ægi'na, a particular favourite of Jupiter.
Æ'gis, a Gorgon, whom Pallas slew.
Æ'gle, one of the three Hesperides.
Æ'gon, a wrestler famous for strength.
Ægyp'tus, son of Neptune and Lybia.
Æl'lo, one of the three Harpies.
Ænе'as, son of Anchises and Venus.
Æo'lus, the god of the winds.
Æo'us, oneof the four horses of the sun.
Æscula'nus, a Roman god of riches.
Æscula'pius, the god of physic.
Æthal'ides, a son of Mercury.
Æ'thon, one of the four horses of the sun.
Æt'næus, a title of Vulcan.
Æto'los, a son of Endymion and Diana.
Agamem'non, a brother to Menelaus, chosen captain-general of the Greeks at the siege of Troy.
Aganip'pe, daughter of the river Permessus, which flows from mount Helicon.
Age'nor, the first king of Argos.
Ageno'ria, the goddess of industry
Agelas'tus and *Agesi'laus*, names of Pluto.
Agla'ia, one of the three graces.
A'jax, one of the most distinguished princes and heroes at the siege of Troy.
Albu'nea, a famous sybil of Tripoli.
Alci'des, a title of Hercules.
Alci'nous, a king of Corcyra.
Alci'oneus, a giant slain by Hercules.
Alci'ope, a favourite mistress of Neptune.
Alcme'na, the wife of Amphitryon.
Alec'to, one of the three Furies.
Alec'tryon, or *Gal'lus*, a favourite of Mars.
Al'mus, and *Alum'nus*, titles of Jupiter.
Alo'a, a festival of Bacchus and Ceres.
Alæ'us, a giant who warred with Jupiter.
Amalthæ'a, the goat that suckled Jupiter.
Amberva'le, a spring sacrifice to Ceres.
Ambro'sia, the food of the gods.
Am'mon, a title of Jupiter.
Amphiara'us, son of Apollo and Hypermnestra, a very famous augur.
Amphime'don, one of the suitors of Penelope.
Amphi'on, a famous musician.
Amphitri'te, the wife of Neptune.
Amyntor, a king of Epirus.
Ana'tis, the goddess of prostitution.]
Ancæ'us, a king of Arcadia.
Androgeus, the son of Minos.
Androm'ache, the wife of Hector.
Androm'eda, the daughter of Cepheus and Cassiope, who, contending for the prize of beauty with the Nereides, was by them bound to a rock and exposed to be devoured by a sea monster; but Perseus slew the monster, and married her.

Ange'rona, the goddess of silence.
An'na, the sister of Pygmalion, and Dido.
Antæ'us, a giant son of Neptune and Terra; he was squeezed to death by Hercules.
An'teros, one of the names of Cupid,
Antever'ta, a goddess of women in labour.
An'thia, and *Argi'va*, titles of Juno.
Anu'bis, an Egyptian god with a dog's head.
Aon'ides, a name of the muses
Apatu'ria, and *Aphrodi'tis* titles of Venus.
A'pis, son of Jupiter and Niobe, called also, Serapis, and Osiris: he first taught the Egyptians to sow corn and plant vines; after his death they worshipped him in the form of an ox, a symbol of husbandry.
Arach'ne, a Lydian princess, turned by Minerva, into a spider, for presuming to vie with her at spinning.
Arethu'sa, the daughter of Nereus.
Argenti'nus, and *Æscula'nus*, gods of wealth.
Ar'go, the ship that conveyed Jason and his companions to Colchis, and reported to have been the first man of war.
Ar'gonauts, the companions of Jason.
Ar'gus, son of Aristor, said to have had a hundred eyes; also an architect, who built the ship Argo.
Ariad'ne, daughter of Minos, who, from love, gave Theseus a clue of thread to guide him out of the Cretan labyrinth: being afterwards deserted by him, she was married to Bacchus, and made his priestess.
Arimas'pi, a warlike people of Scythia.
Ari'on, a lyric poet of Methymna.
Aristæ'us, son of Apollo and Cyrene.
Aristome'nes, a cruel Titan.
Aristoph'anes, a comic poet, born at Lindus, a town of Rhodes.
Arte'mis, the Delphic cybil; also Diana.
Ascle'pia, festivals of Æsculapius.
Asco'lia, feasts of Bacchus, celebrated in Attica.
Aste'ria, daughter of Ceus.
Astrapæ'us, and *Ataby'rus*, Jupiter.
Astræ'a, the goddess of justice.
Astrol'ogus, a title of Hercules.
Asty'anax, the only son of Hector.
Astypalæ'a, daughter of Phœnix.
A'te, the goddess of revenge.
Atlan'tes, a savage people of Ethiopia.
At'las, a king of Mauritania.
At'ropos, one of the three Fates.
Aver'nus, a lake on the borders of hell.
Averrunc'us, a god of the Romans.
Auge'as, a king of Elis whose stable of 3000 oxen was not cleansed for 30 years, yet Hercules cleansed it in one day.
A'vistuper, a title of Priapus.
Au'rea, a name of Fortuna.
Auro'ra, the goddess of morning.
Auto'leon, a general of the Crotonians.
Autum'nus, the god of fruits.

B

Bac'chus, the god of wine.
Bap'ta, the goddess of shame.
Barba'ta, a title of Venus and Fortuna.
Bas'sareus, a title of Bacchus.

26

Bat'tus, a herdsman, turned by Mercury into a loadstone.
Bau'cis, an old woman, who, with her husband Philemon, entertained Jupiter and Mercury, travelling over Phrygia, when all others refused.
Bellero'phon, son of Glaucus, king of Ephyra, who underwent numberless hardships for refusing an intimacy with Sthenobœa, the wife of Prœtus, king of Argos.
Bello'na, the goddess of war.
Berecyn'thia Ma'ter, a title of Cybele.
Bereni'ce, a Grecian lady, who was the only person of her sex permitted to see the Olympic games.
Ber'gion, a giant, slain by Jupiter.
Bib'lia, the wife of Duillius, who first instituted a triumph for naval victory.
Bi'ceps, and *Bi'frons*, names of Janus.
Bisul'tor, a name of Mars.
Bi'thon, a remarkably strong Grecian.
Boli'na, a nymph rendered immortal for her modesty and resistance of Apollo.
Bo'na De'a, a title of Cybele, and Fortuna.
Bo'nus Dæ'mon, a title of Priapus.
Bo'reas, son of Æstræus and Heribeia, generally put for the north wind.
Bre'vis, a title of Fortuna.
Bri'areus, a monstrous giant, son of Titan and Terra: the poets feign him to have had a hundred arms and fifty heads.
Bri'mo, and *Bu'bastis*, names of Hecate.
Brise'is, daughter of Brises, priest of Jupiter, given to Achilles upon the taking of Lyrnessus, a city of Troas, by the Greeks.
Bron'tes, a maker of Jupiter's thunder.
Bro'theus, a son of Vulcan, who threw himself into mount Ætna, on account of his deformity.
Bruma'lia, feasts of Bacchus.
Bubo'na, the goddess of oxen.
Busi'ris, a son of Neptune, and a most cruel tyrant; he was slain by Hercules.
Byb'lis, the daughter of Miletus.

C

Cabar'ni, priests of Ceres.
Cabi'ri, priests of Cybele.
Ca'brus, a god of the Phaselitæ.
Ca'cus, a son of Vulcan.
Cad'mus, son of Agenor and Telephessa, who, searching in vain for his sister, built the city of Thebes, and invented 16 letters of the Greek alphabet.
Cadu'ceus, Mercury's golden rod or wand.
Cæ'ca, and *Conserva'trix*, titles of Fortuna.
Cæc'ulus, a robber, son of Vulcan.
Cæ'neus, a title of Jupiter.
Cal'chas, a famous Greek soothsayer.
Calis'to, the daughter of Lycaon.
Calli'ope, the muse of heroic poetry.
Calyp'so, daughter of Oceanus and Thetis, who reigned in the island of Ogygia, where she entertained and became enamoured of Ulysses, on his return from Troy.
Cam'bles, a gluttonous king of Lydia.
Camby'ses, the son of Cyrus, and king of the Medes and Persians.
Camæ'na, and *Carna*, goddess of infants.
Ca'nes, a title of the furies.

Can'opus, an Egyptian god.
Car'dua, a household goddess.
Carmen'ta, a name of Themis.
Car'na, a Roman goddess.
Carya'tis, a title of Diana.
Cas'pii, a people of Hyrcania, who were said to starve their parents to death when 70 years old, and to train up dogs for war.
Cassan'dra, a daughter of Priam, and Hecuba, endowed with the gift of prophecy by Apollo.
Castal'ides, the Muses, from the fountain Castalius, at the foot of Parnassus.
Cas'tor, son of Jupiter and Leda, between whom and his brother Pollux immortality was alternately shared.
Ca'tius, a tutelar god to grown persons.
Ce'crops, the first king of Athens.
Celæ'no, one of the three Harpies.
Cen'taurs, children of Ixion, half men, half horses, inhabiting Thessaly.
Cepha'lus, the son of Mercury and Hersa.
Ce'pheus, a prince of Arcadia and Ethiopia.
Cerau'nius, a title of Jupiter.
Cer'berus, a dog with three heads and necks, who guarded the gates of hell.
Cerea'lia, festivals in honour of Ceres.
Ce'res, the goddess of agriculture.
Ce'rus, or *Serus*, the god of opportunity.
Chal'cea, festivals in honour of Vulcan.
Char'ites, a name of the graces.
Cha'ron, the ferryman of Hell.
Chi'mera, a strange monster of Lycia, which was killed by Bellerophon.
Chi'ron, the preceptor of Achilles.
Chro'mis, a cruel son of Hercules.
Chrysao'rius, a surname of Jupiter.
Chry'sis, a priestess of Juno at Argos.
Cir'ce, a famous enchantress.
Cir'rha, a cavern of Phocis, near Delphi, whence the winds issued which caused a divine rage, and produced oracular responses.
Cithæ'rides, a title of the Muses.
Clau'sina, a name of Venus.
Clau'sius, or *Clu'sius*, a name of Janus.
Cleo'medes, a famous wrestler.
Cli'o, the muse presiding over history, and patroness of heroic poets.
Clo'tho, one of the three Fates.
Clytemnes'tra, daughter of Jupiter and Leda, killed by her son, Orestes, on account of her adultery with Ægisthus.
Cocy'tus, a river of hell, flowing from Styx.
Colli'na, the goddess of hills.
Compita'lia, games of the household gods.
Co'mus, the god of festivals and merriment.
Concor'dia, the goddess of peace.
Conserva'tor, and *Cus'tos*, titles of Jupiter.
Con'sus, a title of Neptune.
Corti'na, the covering of Apollo's tripos.
Coryban'tes, and *Cure'tes*, priests of Cybele.
Cre'on, a king of Thebes.
Cri'nis, a priest of Apollo.
Crinis'sus, a Trojan prince, who could change himself into any shape.
Crœ'sus, a rich king of Lydia.
Cro'nia, festivals in honour of Saturn.
Ctes'ibus, a famous Athenian parasite.
Cu'nia, the goddess of new-born infants.
Cu'pid, son of Mars and Venus, the god of love, smiles, &c.
Cy'clops, Vulcan's workmen, with only one eye in the middle of their forehead.
Cyb'ele, the wife of Saturn.
Cyc'nus, a king of Liguria; also a son of Neptune, who was invulnerable.
Cylle'nius, and *Camil'lus*, names of Mercury.
Cynoceph'ali, a people of India, said to have heads resembling those of dogs.
Cyn'thia, and *Cyn'thius*, Diana, and Apollo.
Cyparisse'a, a title of Minerva.
Cyp'ria, *Cythere'a*, titles of Venus.

D

Deda'lion, the son of Lucifer.
Ded'alus, an artificer of Athens, who formed the Cretan labyrinth, and invented the auger, axe, glue, plumbline, saw, and masts and sails for ships.
Da'mon, the sincere friend of Pythias.
Da'mon Be'nus, *Dithyram'bus*, and *Dionys'ius*, titles of Bacchus.
Da'nae, the daughter of Acrisius, king of Argos, seduced by Jupiter in the form of a golden shower.
Dana'ides, or *Be'lides*, the fifty daughters of Danaus, king of Argos, all of whom except Hypermnestra, killed their husbands, the sons of their uncle Ægyptus, on the marriage night: they were therefore condemned to draw water out of a deep well with sieves, so that their labour was without end or success.
Daph'ne, a nymph beloved by Apollo.
Darda'nus, the founder of Troy.
Da'res, a very ancient historian who wrote an account of the Trojan war.
De'a Syr'ia, a title of Venus.
De'cima, a title of Lachesis.
Deiani'ra, the wife of Hercules.
Deida'mia, a daughter of Lycomedes, king of Scyros, by whom Achilles had Pyrrhus, while he lay concealed in woman's apparel in the court of Lycomedes, to avoid going to the Trojan war.
Deiope'a, a beautiful attendant on Juno.
Deiph'obe, the Cumean sybil.
Deiph'obus, a son of Priam and Hecuba.
De'lia, *De'lius*, Diana and Apollo.
De'los, the island where Apollo was born.
Del'phi, a city of Phocis, famous for a temple and an oracle of Apollo.
Del'phicus, *Didymæ'us*, titles of Apollo.
Dem'ades, an Athenian orator.
Der'bices, a people near the Caspian Sea, who punished all crimes with death.
Deuca'lion, son of Prometheus, and king of Thessaly, who, with his wife Pyrrha, was preserved from the general deluge, and re-peopled the world.
Dever'ra, the goddess of breeding women.
Diag'oras, a Rhodian, who died for joy, because his three sons had on the same day gained prizes at the Olympic games.
Dia'na, the goddess of hunting, &c.
Di'do, daughter of Belus, the founder and queen of Carthage, whom Virgil fables to

have burnt herself through despair, because Æneas left her.
Di'es, and *Dies'piter*, titles of Jupiter.
Din'dyme, *Dindyme'ne*, titles of Cybele.
Diome'des, a king of Ætolia, who gained great reputation at Troy, and, accompanied by Ulysses, carried off the Palladium; also, a tyrant of Thrace.
Dio'ne, one of Jupiter's mistresses.
Dionys'ia, feasts in honour of Bacchus.
Dioscu'ri, a title of Castor and Pollux.
Di'ræ, a title of the furies.
Dis, a title of Pluto.
Discor'dia, the goddess of contention.
Domidu'ca, a title of Juno.
Domidu'cus, and *Domi'tius*, nuptial gods.
Dom'ina, a title of Proserpine.
Dry'ades, nymphs of the woods and forests.

E

Echi'on, a companion of Cadmus.
Ec'ho, daughter of Aer and Tellus, who pined away for love of Narcissus.
Edon'ides, priestesses of Bacchus.
Edu'ca, a goddess of new born infants.
Ege'ria, a title of Juno; also a goddess.
Elec'tra, the daughter of Agamemnon and Clytemnestra, who instigated Orestes to revenge their father's death on their mother and her adulterer Ægisthus.
E'leus, and *Eleuthe'rius*, titles of Bacchus.
Eleusin'ia, feasts in honour of Ceres and Proserpine.
Elo'ides, nymphs of Bacchus.
Empu'sæ, a name of the Gorgons,
Endym'ion, a shepherd of Caria, who, for insolently soliciting Juno, was condemned to a sleep of 30 years; Luna visited him by night in a cave of mount Latmus.
Enia'lius, a title of Mars.
En'yo, the same as Bellona.
Epe'us, the artist of the Trojan horse.
Epig'ones, the sons of the seven worthies who besieged Thebes, a second time.
Epila'nea, sacrifices to Bacchus.
Epistro'phia, and *Eryci'na*, titles of Venus.
Epizeph'rii, a people of Locris, who punished those with death that drank more wine than physicians prescribed.
Era'to, the muse of love poetry.
Er'ebus, an infernal deity, son of Chaos and Nox: a river of hell.
Er'eane, a river whose waters inebriated.
Eriotho'nius, a king of Athens, who, being lame and very deformed in his feet, invented coaches to conceal his lameness.
Erin'nys, a common name of the furies.
E'ros, one of the names of Cupid.
Eros'tratus, the person who, to perpetuate his name, set fire to the celebrated temple of Diana at Ephesus.
Ete'ocles, and *Poly'nices*, sons of Oedipus, who violently hated, and, at last killed each other.
Evad'ne, daughter of Mars and Thebe, who threw herself on the funeral pile of her husband Cataneus, from affection.
Euc'rates, a person remarkable for shuffling, duplicity, and dissimulation.
Eumen'ides, a name of the Furies.
Euphros'yne, one of the three Graces.
Euro'pa, the daughter of Agenor, who, it is said, was carried by Jupiter, in the form of a white bull into Crete.
Eury'ale, one of the three Gorgons.
Euryd'ice, the wife of Orpheus.
Eurym'one, an infernal deity.
Euter'pe, the muse presiding over music.
Euthy'mus, a very famous wrestler.

F

Fab'ula, the goddess of lies.
Fabuli'nus, a god of infants.
Fa'ma, the goddess of report, &c.
Fas'cinum, a title of Priapus.
Fates, the three daughters of Nox and Erebus, Clothos, Lachesis, and Atropos, entrusted with the lives of mortals, &c.
Fau'na, and *Fat'ua*, names of Cybele.
Fau'nus, the son of Mercury and Nox, and father of the Fauns, rural gods.
Feb'rua, *Flor'ida*, *Fluo'nia*, titles of Juno.
Feb'rua, a goddess of purification.
Feb'ruus, a title of Pluto.
Feli'citas, the goddess of happiness.
Fer'culus, a household god.
Fere'trius, and *Fulmina'tor*, titles of Jupiter.
Fero'nia, a goddess of woods.
Fesso'nia, a goddess of wearied persons.
Fid'ius, the god of treaties.
Flam'ines, priests of Jupiter, Mars, &c.
Flo'ra, the goddess of flowers.
Fluvia'les, or *Potamides*, nymphs of rivers.
For'nax, a goddess of corn and bakers.
Fortu'na, or *For'tune*, the goddess of happiness, &c., said to be blind.
Fu'ries, or *Eumen'ides*, the three daughters of Nox and Acheron, named Alecto, Megæra, and Tisiphone, with hair composed of snakes, and armed with whips, chains, &c.

G

Galate'a, daughter of Nereus and Doris, passionately beloved by Polyphemus.
Gal'li, castrated priests of Cybele.
Gal'lus, or *Alec'trion*, a favourite of Mars, and changed by him into a cock.
Game'lia, a title of Juno.
Gan'ges, a famous river of India.
Gany'mede, the cup-bearer of Jupiter.
Gelasi'nus, the god of mirth and smiles.
Gelo'ni, a people of Scythia, who used to paint themselves in order to appear more terrible to their enemies.
Ge'nii, guardian angels.
Ge'nius, a name of Priapus.
Ger'yon, a king of Spain, who fed his oxen with human flesh, and was therefore killed by Hercules.
Glauco'pis, a name of Minerva.
Glau'cus, a fisherman made a sea god by eating a certain herb: also the son of Hippolochus, who exchanged his arms of gold for the brazen ones of Diomede.
Gnos'sis, a name of Ariadne.
Gor'dius, a husbandman but afterwards king of Phrygia, remarkable for tying a knot of cords on which the empire of Asia

depended, in so very intricate a manner, that Alexander the great, unable to unravel it, cut it to pieces.

Gor'gons, the three daughters of Phorcys and Ceta, Medusa, Euryale, and Stheno, who could change into stone those whom they looked on; Perseus slew Medusa, the principal of them.

Gorgoph'orus, a title of Pallas.

Gra'ces, Aglaia, Thalia, and Euphrosyne, the daughters of Jupiter and Eurynome; attendants on Venus and the Muses.

Gradi'vus, a title of Mars.

Gy'ges, a Lydian, to whom Candaules, king of Lydia, showed his queen naked, which so incensed her that she slew Candaules, and married Gyges; also a shepherd, who by means of a ring could render himself invisible.

H

Ha'des, a title of Pluto.

Hamaxo'bii, a people of Scythia, who lived in carts, and removed from place to place, as necessity required.

Harmo'nis, a famous artist of Troy.

Harpal'yca, a very beautiful maid of Argos.

Har'pies, three monsters, Aello, Celœno, and Ocypete, with the faces of virgins, bodies of vultures, and hands armed with monstrous claws.

Harpoc'rates, the Egyptian god of silence.

He'be, the goddess of youth.

He'brus, a river in Thrace.

He'calius, a title given to Jupiter by Theseus.

Hec'ate, Diana's name in hell.

Hec'tor, a son of Priam and Hecuba, and the most valiant of all the Trojans.

Hec'uba, the wife of Priam.

Hegesius, a philosopher of Cyrene, who described the miseries of life with such a gloomy eloquence, that many of his auditors killed themselves through despair.

Hel'ena, the wife of Menelaus, the most beautiful woman in the world, who, running away with Paris, occasioned the Trojan war.

Hel'enus, a son of Priam and Hecuba.

Hel'icon, a famous mountain of Bœotia, dedicated to Apollo and the Muses.

Hera'ia, sacrifices to Juno.

Her'cules, the son of Jupiter and Alcmena, remarkable for his numerous exploits and dangerous enterprises.

Heribe'ia, the wife of Astreus.

Her'mæ, statutes of Mercury.

Her'mes, a name of Mercury.

Hermi'one, a daughter of Mars and Venus, married to Cadmus; also a daughter of Menelaus and Helena, married to Pyrrhus.

He'ro, a beautiful woman of Sestos, in Thrace, priestess of Venus; Leander, of Abydos, loved her so tenderly that he swam over the Hellespont every night to see her; but being at length unfortunately drowned, she threw herself into the sea, through despair.

Herod'otus, a very famous historian of Halicarnassus.

Heroph'ila, the Erythræan sybil.

Hersili'a, the wife of Romulus.

Hes'perus, or *Vesper*, the evening star.

Hesperides, the daughters of Hesperus; Ægle, Arethusa, and Hesperethusa, who had a garden bearing golden apples, watched by a dragon, which Hercules slew, and bore away the fruit.

He'sus, a name of Mars among the Gauls.

Hip'pias, a philosopher of Elis.

Hippocam'pi, Neptune's horses.

Hip'pocrene, a fountain at the bottom of mount Helicon, dedicated to Apollo.

Hippol'ytus, the son of Theseus and Antiope or Hyppolite, who refused intimacies with his stepmother Phædro. At the request of Diana, Æsculapius restored him to life, after he had been thrown from his chariot, and dragged through the woods till he was torn in pieces.

Hippo'na, the goddess of horses and stables.

Histo'ria, the goddess of history.

Hortex'sia, a name of Venus.

Ho'rus, a title of the sun.

Hostili'na, a goddess of corn.

Hy'ades, the seven daughters of Atlas and Æthra; Ambrosia, Eudora, Coronis, Pasithoe, Plexaris, Pytho, and Tyche.—They were changed by Jupiter into seven stars.

Hy'bla, a mountain in Sicily, universally famous for its thyme and bees.

Hy'dra, a serpent, which had seven heads or as some say, nine, others fifty, killed by Hercules in the lake Lerna.

Hyge'ia, the goddess of health.

Hyl'lus, the son of Hercules and Dejanire.

Hy'men, the god of marriage.

Hype'rion, a son of Cœlus and Terra.

Hypsip'yle, a queen of Lemnos, who was banished for preserving her father when all the other men of the island were murdered by their kindred.

I

Iac'chus, a name of Bacchus.

Ian'the, the beautiful wife of Iphis.

Iape'tus, a son of Cœlum and Terra.

Iar'bas, a cruel king of Mauritania.

Ica'rius, the son of Oebalus, who having received from Bacchus a bottle of wine, went into Atticá, to show men the use of it; but, making some shepherds drunk, they thought he had given them poison, and therefore threw him into a well.

Ica'rus, the son of Dædalus, who, flying with his father out of Crete into Sicily, and soaring too high, melted the wax of his wings, and fell into the sea, thence called the Icarian sea.

I'da, a mountain near Troy.

Idæ'a Mater, a name of Cybele.

Idæ'i Dact'yli, a priest of Cybele.

Ida'lia, a name of Venus.

Id'mon, a famous soothsayer.

Ido'thea, Jupiter's nurse.

Ili'one, the eldest daughter of Priam.

Ilis'sus, a river in Attica.

I'lus, the son of Tros and Callirrhoe, from whom Troy was called Ilium.

Impera'tor, a name of Jupiter.
In'achis and *I'ses*, names of Io.
I'no, daughter of Cadmus and Hermiones, and wife of Athamas.
Intercido'na, a goddess of breeding women.
Interdu'ca, and *Ju'ga*, names of Juno.
In'uus, and *Inc'ubus*, names of Pan.
I'o, daughter of Inachus, transformed by Jupiter, into a white heifer; but afterwards resuming her former shape, was worshipped as a goddess by the Egyptians, under the name of Isis.
Iph'iclus, the twin brother of Hercules.
Iphige'nia, daughter of Agamemnon and Clytemnestra, who, standing as a victim ready to be sacrificed to appease the rage of Diana, was, by that goddess transformed into a white hart, carried to Tauris, and made her priestess,
I'phis, a prince of Cyprus, who hanged himself for love; also a daughter of Lygdas.
Iph'itus, son of Praxonides, who instituted Olympic games to Hercules.
I'ris, the daughter of Thaumas; she was Juno's favourite companion, and her messenger on affairs of discord, &c.
I'tys, the son of Tereus and Progne, murdered and served up by his mother at a banquet before Tereus, in revenge for his having violated her sister Philomela.
Ixi'on, the son of Phlegyas, who was fastened in hell to a wheel perpetually turning round, for boasting that he had lain with Juno.

J

Jan'itor, and *Juno'nius*, titles of Janus.
Ja'nus, the first king of Italy, son of Apollo and Creusa.
Ja'son, a Thessalian prince, son of Æson, who by Medea's help brought away the golden fleece from Colchis.
Jocas'ta, the daughter of Creon, who unwittingly married her own son Œdipus.
Ju'no, the sister and wife of Jupiter.
Ju'no, Infer'na, a name of Proserpine.
Juno'nes, guardian angels of women.
Ju'piter, a son of Saturn and Ops—the supreme deity of the heathen.
Ju'piter Secun'dus, a name of Neptune.
Ju'piter Ter'tius, Infer'nus, or *Sty'gius*, several appellations given to Pluto.
Juven'ta, a goddess of youth.

L

La'chesis, one of the three Fates.
Lacin'ia, and *Lucil'ia*, titles of Juno.
Lactu'ra, or *Lactuci'na*, a goddess of corn.
Læstrig'ones, cannibals of Italy, who roasted and ate the companions of Ulysses.
La'ius, a king of Thebes, killed unwittingly by his own son Œdipus.
La'miæ, a name of the Gorgons.
Laoc'oon, a son of Priam and high-priest of Apollo: he and his two sons were killed by serpents for opposing the reception of the wooden horse into Troy.

26*

La'pis, or *Lapid'eus*, titles of Jupiter.
La'res, sons of Mercury and Lara, worshipped as household gods.
Latera'nus, a household god.
Laver'na, a goddess of thieves.
Lean'der, see Hero.
Le'da, daughter of Thestias, and wife of Tyndarus, seduced by Jupiter in the shape of a swan.
Lemoni'ades, nymphs of meadows, &c.
Le'næ, priestesses of Bacchus.
Ler'na, a marsh of Argos, famous for a Hydra, killed there by Hercules.
Le'the, a river of hell, whose waters caused a total forgetfulness of things past.
Leva'na, a goddess of new born infants.
Libiti'na, the goddess of funerals.
Li'nus, son of Apollo and Terpsichore.
Luben'tia, the goddess of pleasure.
Lu'cifer, son of Jupiter and Aurora, made the morning star.
Lu'na, Diana's name in heaven.
Luper'calia, feasts in honour of Pan.
Luper'ci, priests of Pan.
Lyca'on, a king of Arcadia, turned by Jupiter into a wolf.

M

Ma'ia, loved by Jupiter, and by him turned into a star to avoid Juno's rage.
Manugene'ta, a goddess of women in labour.
Matu'ra, a goddess of corn.
Matur'na, and *Me'na*, nuptial goddesses.
Mari'na, *Mel'anis*, *Mer'etrix*, *Migoni'tis*, and *Mur'cia*, titles of Venus.
Mars, the god of war.
Mauso'lus, a king of Caria, who had a most magnificent tomb erected to him by his wife Artemisia.
Mede'a, daughter of Ætes, king of Colchis, a famous sorceress, who assisted Jason to obtain the golden fleece.
Meditri'na, a goddess of grown persons.
Medu'sa, the chief of the three Gorgons.
Megæ'ra, one of the three Furies.
Megalen'sia, festivals in honour of Cybele.
Mega'ra, the wife of Hercules.
Melani'ra, a name of Venus.
Me'liæ, Nymphs of the fields.
Me'lius, a name of Hercules.
Melo'na, the goddess of honey.
Melpom'ene, the muse of tragedy,
Mem'non, a king of Abydos.
Menala'us, a famous Centaur,
Menela'us, the husband of Helena.
Men'tha, a mistress of Pluto.
Men'tor, the governor of Telemachus.
Mer'cury, the messenger of the gods, inventor of letters, and god of eloquence, merchandise, and robbers.
Mero'pe, one of the seven Pleiades.
Mi'das, a king of Phrygia, who entertained Bacchus, or, as some say, Silenus, had the power given him of turning whatever he touched into gold.
Mi'lo, a wrestler of remarkable strength.
Mimal'lones, attendants on Bacchus.
Miner'va, the goddess of wisdom,

Mi'nos, a king of Crete, made, for his extraordinary justice, a judge of hell.
Min'otaur, a monster, half man, half beast.
Min'ye, a name of the Argonauts.
Mnemos'yne, the goddess of memory.
Mo'mus, the god of raillery, wit, &c.
Mone'ta, a title of Juno.
Mor'pheus, the god of sleep, dreams, &c.
Mors, the goddess of death.
Mul'ciber, a title of Vulcan.
Mu'ses, nine daughters of Jupiter and Mnemosyne, born on mount Pierius, mistresses of all the sciences, presidents of musicians, and poets, and governesses of the feasts of the gods; Calliope, Clio, Erato, Euterpe, Melpomene, Polyhymnia, Terpsichore, Thalia, and Urania.
Mu'ta, the goddess of silence.

N

Nænia, the goddess of funeral songs.
Na'iades, nymphs of rivers, &c.
Narcis'sus, a very beautiful youth, who, falling in love with his own shadow in the water, pined away into a daffodil.
Na'tio, and *Nundi'na*, goddesses of infants.
Nemæ'a, a country of Elis, famed for a terrible lion killed there by Hercules.
Nem'esis, the goddess of revenge.
Nep'tune, the god of the sea.
Ne'reides, sea nymphs.
Ne'rio, the wife of Mars.
Niceph'orus, a title of Jupiter.
Ni'nus, the first king of the Assyrians.
Ni'obe, daughter of Tantalus, and wife of Amphion, who preferring herself to Latona, had her 14 children killed by Diana and Apollo, and wept herself into a statue.
No'mius, a name of Apollo.
Nox, the most ancient of the deities; she was even reckoned older than Chaos.

O

Ob'sequens, a title of Fortuna.
Occa'tor, the god of harrowing.
Oce'anus, an ancient sea god.
Ocyp'ete, one of the three Harpies.
Œd'ipus, son of Laius and Jocasta, and king of Thebes, who solved the riddle of the Sphinx, unwittingly killed his father, married his mother, and at last ran mad, and tore out his eyes.
Om'phale, a queen of Lydia, with whom Hercules was so enamoured, that she made him submit to spinning and other unbecoming offices.
Oper'tus, a name of Pluto.
Opi'gena, a name of Juno.
Ops a name of Cybele.
Orbo'na, a goddess of grown persons.
Ores'tes, the son of Agamemnon.
Ori'on, a great and mighty hunter.
Or'pheus, son of Jupiter and Calliope, who had great skill in music, and was torn in pieces, by the Mænades, for disliking the company of women after the death of his wife Eurydice,
Orythi'a, a queen of the Amazons.
Osi'ris. See Apis.

P

Pac'tolus, a river of Lydia, with golden sands and medical waters.
Pæ'an, and *Phæ'bus*, names of Apollo.
Pa'les, the goddess of shepherds.
Palil'ia, feasts in honour of Pales.
Palla'dium, a statue of Minerva, which the Trojans imagined fell from heaven, and that their city could not be taken whilst that remained in it.
Pal'las, and *Py'lotis*, names of Minerva.
Pan, the god of shepherds.
Pando'ra, the first woman made by Vulcan, and endowed with gifts by all the deities; Jupiter gave her a box containing all manner of evils, war, famine, &c. with hope at the bottom.
Pan'ope, one of the Nereides.
Pa'phia, a title of Venus.
Par'cæ, a name of the Fates.
Par'is, or *Al'exander*, son of Priam and Hecuba, a most beautiful youth, who ran away with Helena, and occasioned the Trojan war.
Parnas'sus, a mountain of Phocis, famous for a temple of Apollo, and being the favourite residence of the Muses.
Par'tunda, a nuptial goddess.
Pastoph'ori, priests of Isis.
Pat'areus, a title of Apollo.
Pateli'na, a goddess of corn.
Patula'cius, a name of Janus.
Patule'ius, a name of Jupiter.
Paven'tia, and *Poli'na*, goddesses of infants.
Peg'asus, a winged horse belonging to Apollo and the Muses.
Pello'nia, a goddess of grown persons.
Pena'tes, small statues or household gods.
Penel'ope, daughter of Icarus, celebrated for her chastity and fidelity during the long absence of Ulysses.
Per'seus, son of Jupiter and Danae, who performed many extraordinary exploits by means of Medusa's head.
Phacasia'ni, ancient gods of Greece.
Pha'eton, son of Sol (Apollo) and Climene, who asked the guidance of his father's chariot for one day, as a proof of his divine descent; but unable to manage the horses, set the world on fire, and was therefore struck by Jupiter with a thunderbolt into the river Po.
Phal'lica, feasts of Bacchus.
Philam'mon, a skilful musician.
Philome'la, daughter of Pandion, king of Athens, who was ravished by her brother-in-law, Tereus, and was changed into a nightingale.
Phin'eas, son of Agenor, and king of Paphlagonia, who had his eyes torn out by Boreas, but was recompensed with the knowledge of futurity; also king of Thrace, turned into a stone by Perseus, by the help of Medusa's head.
Phleg'ethon, a boiling river of hell.
Phle'gon, one of the four horses of Sol.

Phleg'yæ, a people of Bœotia, destroyed by Neptune, on account of their piracies and other crimes.
Phæ'bas, the priestess of Apollo.
Phæ'bus, a title of Apollo.
Phæ'nix, son of Amyntor, who being falsely accused of having attempted the honour of one of his father's concubines, was condemned to have his eyes torn out; but was cured by Chiron, and went with Achilles to the siege of Troy.
Picum'nus, a rural god.
Pilum'nus, a god of breeding women.
Pin'dus, a mountain of Thessaly.
Pi'tho, a goddess of eloquence.
Ple'iades, the seven daughters of Atlas and Pleione; Maia, Electra, Taygete, Asterope, Merope, Halcyone, and Celœno; they were changed into stars.
Plu'to, the god of hell.
Plu'tus, the god of riches.
Pol'lux. See Castor.
Polyd'amas, a famous wrestler.
Polyd'ius, a famous prophet and physician.
Polyhym'nia, the muse of rhetoric.
Polyphe'mus, a monstrous giant, son of Neptune, with but one eye in the middle of his forehead.
Pomo'na, the goddess of fruits and autumn.
Pose'idon, a name of Neptune.
Prænesti'na, a name of Fortuna.
Præs'tes, a title of Jupiter and Minerva.
Praxit'eles, a famous statuary.
Pri'am, son of Laomedon, and father of Paris, Hector, &c.; he was the last king of Troy.
Prog'ne, wife of Tereus, king of Thrace, and sister of Philomela; she was turned into a swallow.
Prome'theus, son of Iapetus, who animated a man that he had formed of clay, with fire, which, by the assistance of Minerva, he stole from heaven, and was therefore chained by Jupiter to mount Caucasus, with a vulture continually preying on his liver.
Propy'læa, a name of Hecate.
Pros'erpine, the wife of Pluto.
Pro'teus, a seagod, who could transform himself into any shape.
Psy'che. a goddess of pleasure.
Pyl'ades, the constant friend of Orestes.
Pyr'amus, and *This'be*, two lovers of Babylon, who killed themselves with the same sword, and occasioned the turning the berries of the mulberry-tree, under which they died, from white to red.
Pyrœ'tis, one of the four horses of the Sun.
Pyr'rhus, son of Achilles, remarkable for his cruelty at the siege of Troy.
Py'thon, a huge serpent, produced from the mud of the deluge which Apollo killed, and, in memory thereof, instituted the Pythian games.
Pythonis'sa, the priestess of Apollo.

Q

Quad'rifrons, a title of Janus.
Qui'es, a goddess of grown persons.
Quieta'lis and *Quie'tus*, names of Pluto.
Quinqua'tria, feasts of Pallas.

R

Rec'tus, a title of Bacchus.
Re'dux, and *Re'gia*, titles of Fortune.
Regi'na, a title of Juno.
Rhadaman'thus, one of the three infernal judges.
Rhe'a, a title of Cybele.
Rhe'a-syl'via, the mother of Romulus.
Robi'gus, a god of corn.
Romu'lus, the first king of Rome.
Rumi'na, a goddess of new born infants.
Runci'na, the goddess of weeding.
Rusi'na, a rural deity.

S

Saba'zia, feasts of Proserpine.
Sa'lii, the 12 frantic priests of Mars.
Salmone'us, a king of Elis, struck by a thunderbolt to hell for imitating Jupiter's thunder.
Sa'lus, the goddess of health.
Sanc'us, a god of the Sabines.
Sa'tor, and *Serri'tor*, rural gods.
Saturna'lia, feasts of Saturn.
Satur'nus, or *Sat'urn*, the son of Cœlum and Terra.
Sat'yrs, the attendants of Bacchus, horned monsters, half men, half goats.
Scy'ron, a famous robber of Attica.
Se'ia, and *Sege'tia*, goddesses of corn.
Sel'li, priests of Jupiter.
Sen'ta, a goddess of married women.
Sera'pis. See *Apis*.
Sile'nus, the foster-father and companion of Bacchus, who lived in Arcadia, rode on an ass, and was drunk every day.
Si'nis, a famous robber, killed by Hercules.
Sis'yphus, the son of Æolus, killed by Theseus, and doomed incessantly to roll a huge stone up a mountain in hell for his perfidy and numerous robberies.
Sol, a name of Apollo.
Som'nus, the god of sleep.
Sphinx, a monster, born of Syphon, and Echidna, who destroyed herself because Œdipus solved the enigma she proposed.
Sta'ta, a goddess of grown persons.
Sten'tor, a Grecian, whose voice is reported to have been as strong and as loud as the voices of 50 men together.
Sthe'no, one of the three Gorgons.
Styx, a river of hell.
Sua'da, a nuptial goddess.
Summa'nus, a name of Pluto.
Sylva'nus, a god of woods and forests,
Sy'rens, seamonsters.

T

Ta'cita, a goddess of silence.
Tanta'lus a king of Paphlagonia, who, serving up to table the limbs of his son Pelops, to try the divinity of the gods, was plunged to the chin in a lake of hell, and doomed to everlasting thirst and hunger, as a punishment for his barbarity and impiety.
Tarta'rus, the place of the wicked in hell.
Tau'rus, the bull, under whose form Jupiter carried away Europa.
Telchi'nes, priests of Cybele.

Telema'chus, the only son of Ulysses.
Tem'pe, a most beautiful valley in Thessaly, the resort of the gods.
Ter'minus, the god of boundaries.
Terpsicho're, the muse of music, &c.
Ter'ror, the god of dread and fear.
Tha'lia, the muse of comedy.
The'mis, the daughter of Cœlum and Terra, the goddess of laws, oracles, &c.
Thes'pis, the first tragic poet.
The'tis, daughter of Nereus and Doris, and goddess of the sea.
Thyr'sus, the rod of Bacchus.
Ti'phys, the pilot of the ship Argo.
Tisiph'one, one of the three Furies.
Ti'tan, son of Cœlum and Terra, and the elder brother of Saturnus, or Saturn.
Tma'rius, a title of Jupiter.
Tri'ton, Neptune's trumpeter.
Tri'tonia, a name of Minerva.
Tro'ilus, a son of Priam and Hecuba.
Troy, a city of Phrygia, famous for holding out a siege of ten years against the Greeks, but they at last captured and destroyed it.
Tuteli'na, a goddess of corn.
Ty're, one of the Nereids.

U

Ulys'ses, son of Laertes and Anticlea, and king of Ithaca, who, by his subtlety and eloquence, was eminently serviceable to the Greeks in the Trojan war.
Unx'ia, a title of Juno.
Ura'nia, the muse of astronomy.

V

Vacu'na, the goddess of idle persons.
Vagita'nus, a god of little infants.
Vallo'nia, a goddess of valleys.
Veni'lia, a wife of Neptune.
Ve'nus, the goddess of love, and beauty.
Vergil'ia, a name of the Pleiades.
Verticor'dia, a name of Venus.
Vertum'nus, the god of the spring.
Ves'ta, the goddess of fire.
Via'les, deities of the highways.
Vibil'ia, the goddess of wanderers.
Virgmen'sis, a nuptial goddess.
Vir'go, a name of Astrea and Fortune.
Viri'lis, and *Visca'ta*, titles of Fortune.
Viri'placa, an inferior nuptial goddess, who reconciled husbands to their wives; a temple, at Rome, was dedicated to her, whither the married couple repaired after a quarrel, and returned together friendly.
Vitu'la, the goddess of mirth.
Volu'sia, a goddess of corn.
Vul'can, the god of subterraneous fire.

X

Xan'thus, one of the horses of Achilles, born of the harpy Celœno, a river near Troy, called also Scamander.

Z

Za'greus, a title of Bacchus.
Zeph'yrus, son of Æolus and Aurora, who passionately loved the goddess Flora, and is put for the west wind.
Ze'tes, and *Ca'lais*, sons of Boreas and Orythia, who accompanied the Argonauts, and drove the Harpies from Thrace.
Ze'tus, a son of Jupiter and Antiope, very expert in Music.
Ze'us, a title of Jupiter.

TAB. XII.

EMINENT LIVING CHARACTERS.

A

NATION.	NAME AND PROFESSION.
Fr.	Angouleme, Louis A., de Bourbon, son of Charles X. born 1773,
	B
Eng.	Bathurst, Henry, earl of, late secretary of State, b. 1762.
	Bernadotte, John Baptist Julius, now Charles XIV., king of Sweden;—b. at Hau, in Berne, 1764.
Eng.	Bickersteth, Rev. Edward, author of several theological works.
	Bonaparte, Joseph,—b. in Corsica, 1768; proclaimed king of Naples by his brother Napoleon, 1806; king of Spain, 1808; retreated from there, 1815; came in 1815 to America and resided at Bordentown, New Jersey, until 1832, when he went to England.
	———, Lucien, b. 1775, quarrelled with Napoleon, and was banished from France. He now resides at Rome.

NATION.	NAME AND PROFESSION.
	———, Louis, third brother of Napoleon, b. 1778; became king of Holland in 1806, and governed with mildness and wisdom; resigned the throne at Napoleon's command. He has published a work relating to his reign in Holland.
	———, Jerome, b. 1784, visited the U. S., and married a young lady of Baltimore, 1801; made king of Westphalia, 1807.
Eng.	Brewster, David, "one of the most learned natural philosophers in Great Britain," b. about 1785. He is the editor of the much esteemed Edinburgh Encyclopedia &c. &c.
Eng.	Brougham, Henry, now lord chancellor of Great Britain, b. in London, 1779; "Pre-eminent as a man of science, a literary man, a statesman, lawyer and orator," he necessarily occupies a large space in the public eye.

C

Scotch,	Campbell, Thomas, b. 1777:—a distinguished poet—now editor of "The Metropolitan" magazine, London.
Eng.	Carey, William, L. L. D., Baptist missionary in Bengal.
Ital.	Catalini, Angelica, a celebrated vocalist, b. 1782.
Scotch,	Chalmers, Alexander, D. D., an eminent divine and author.
Fr.	Charles X. b. 1777; became king 1824; dethroned July, 1830.
Fr.	Chateaubriand, Francis Augustus, viscount de, a distinguished statesman, and author; b. 1769; visited the United States, 1790; became one of Napoleon's ministers, and on the restoration of the Bourbons was created a viscount and sent as minister to Berlin; resigned soon after, and has since lived in private. He is the author of "*Travels*," "*Essay* on *Ancient and Modern Revolutions*;" "*Genius of Christianity*," and other works, most of which have been translated into English.
Eng.	Clarkson, Thomas, a distinguished philanthropist; author of several works against the *Slave trade*, b. 1761.
Eng.	Cobbett, William, a talented writer, and advocate of the "people's rights," visited America in 1792, and 1817.
Eng.	Congreve, Sir William, a scientific writer, inventor of the *Congreve Rockets*.
Eng.	Cooper, Sir Astley Paston, F. R. S., a celebrated surgeon and medical writer.
Eng.	Croly, Rev. George, a poet: author of a *Life of George IVth*, &c.

D

Eng.	Dick, Thomas, author of "The Christian Philosopher," &c.
Scotch,	Douglas, James, author of several popular essays.

E

Irish,	Edgeworth, Maria, one of the most eminent of female novelists, and writers on education.
Eng.	Eldon, earl of, late lord chancellor of Great Britain, b. 1750.

F

Eng.	Faber, George Stanley, author of Dissertations on the Prophecies, on Romanism, on Infidelity, &c.
Fr.	Fesch, cardinal, uncle of Napoleon Bonaparte, b. 1763; became successively archbishop of Lyons, ambassador of his imperial nephew to Rome, grand almoner of France, and arch-chancellor of the German empire.
Eng.	Foster, Rev. John, an essayist.
Eng.	Fry, Mrs. Elizabeth, a lady distinguished for her benevolence, b. 1780,

G

Scotch,	Galt, John, author of a life of Benjamin West, and of cardinal Wolsey, &c. b. 1779.
Eng.	Gillies, John, author of "History of Ancient Greece," "History of the World from Alexander to Augustus," &c. b. 1750.
Eng.	Gisborne, Rev. T., a writer on, Moral Philosophy &c.
Eng.	Godwin, Wm. author of "Life of Chaucer," "Caleb Williams," "Fleetwood," &c.
Eng.	Grafton, duke of, a Whig Stateman, b. 1760.

H

Ger.	Hardenberg, prince, an able statesman;—now prime minister of the king of Prussia, b. 1750.
Eng.	Hallam, Henry, author of a History of England, and of "Europe during the Middle Ages."
Eng.	Hazlett, William, a poetical editor and critic.
Eng.	Hemans Mrs. Felicia, a popular poetess.
Eng.	Hoffand, Mrs., author of works for children.

NATION.	NAME AND PROFESSION.
Scotch,	Hogg, James, the Ettrick Shepherd, a poet.
Pruss.	Humboldt, Frederick, baron, a celebrated and intelligent traveller, author of a "History of New Spain," &c., b. at Berlin, in 1769.
	J
Ger.	Jahn, John, author of "Biblical Archæology," "History of the Hebrew Commonwealth," &c.
Scotch,	Jeffrey, Francis, a celebrated literary character,—formerly editor of the Edinburgh Review, b. 1773.
Fr.	Jordan, marshal, count, a celebrated military commander; b. 1762; chosen president of the council of 500, in 1797.
	K
Eng.	Kett, Rev. Henry, author of "Elements of General Knowledge," &c.
	L
Fr.	Lacroix, M. Sylvester, an eminent mathematician.
Fr.	La Fayette, Gilbert Mottier, marquis de, the distinguished general, and philanthropist, b. Sept. 1757; came to America and fought in the cause of freedom, 1777; gave $11,000 to aid the American Army; was elected president of the States General of France in 1789; commanded the national guards; taken and imprisoned by the Austrians at Olmutz, 1792; liberated, 1799; visited the United States, 1824; commanded the national guards in the Revolution of 1830; now resides at La Grange.
Fr.	Lameth, Alexander, count de, a general distinguished in the revolution of 1789.
Fr.	Las Cases, count de, the secretary and biographer of Napoleon.
Fr.	Lavalette, count de, an officer in the French revolution; b. 1769.
Eng.	Lingard, John, a Roman Catholic clergyman—author of a History of England.
Scotch,	Lockhart, John G., a popular miscellaneous writer, b. 1792.
	M
Ger.	Malte Brun, M., a celebrated geographer
Fr.	Manuel, M., an eloquent and intrepid defender of liberty.
Aust.	Maria Louisa, princess of Parma, late empress of France, b. 1787.
Fr.	Marmont, duke of Ragusa, a general who deserted from Bonaparte, b. 1790.
Irish,	Maturin, Rev. C. R., a miscellaneous writer, b. 1782.
Aust.	Metternich-Winebourg, prince, prime minister of the emperor of Austria.
Eng.	Millman, Rev. Henry H., a poet,—author of "The fall of Jerusalem," History of the Jews, &c.
Span.	Mina, Don Francisco Esposy, an able and patriotic general.
Scotch,	Montgomery, James, a popular poet, b. 1771.
Scotch,	———, Robert, do
Irish,	Moore, Thomas. a celebrated poet.
Eng.	More, Mrs. Hannah, the veteran authoress of several excellent and popular moral and religious works, b. 1750.
Span.	Morillo, Don Pablo, the general who fought against Bolivar in S. A. in 1815.
	O
Eng.	Opie, Mrs. Amelia, a prose and poetical writer, b. 1771.
	P
	Paez, general, one of the liberators of Colombia, b. 1787.
Eng.	Parry, Edward William, noted for his polar voyages, b, 1790.
Eng.	Porter, Jane and Anna Maria, (sisters) novelists. Jane has written "Thaddeus of Warsaw," "The Scottish Chiefs," &c.
	R
Eng.	Rogers, Samuel, an eminent poet,—author of "Italy," "Pleasures of Memory," &c.
Ger.	Rosenmueller, a Biblical scholar and commentator.
	S
S. A.	San, Martin, Don Juan, general, one of the champions of South American Indep.

NATION.	NAME AND PROFESSION.
Ger.	**Senefelder, Alois, the inventor of *lithography*, b. at Munich.**
Eng.	**Southey, Robert, poet laureate, a prolific miscel. writer. b. at Bristol in 1774.**

T

Fr.	**Talleyrand, Perigord, prince de, a celebrated statesman, b. 1754; an active character in the revolution—friend of Bonaparte, and his minister for foreign affairs; reinstated in his office by Louis XVIII.; appointed ambassador to Great Britain by Louis Philippe I., 1831.**

W

Irish,	**Wellington, Arthur Wellesley, duke of, a celebrated military and political character—late prime minister of Great Britain, b. 1769.**
Eng.	**Wilberforce, William, a distinguished philanthropist—one of the first effectual opposers of the slave trade, b. 1759.**
Eng.	**Wordsworth, William, an eminent poet, b. 1770.**

TAB. XIII.

EMINENT PAINTERS, ENGRAVERS, SCULPTORS, &c.

[P. *Painter.* S. *Sculptor,* E. *Engraver,* A. *Architect.*]

A

NATION.	NAME AND PROFESSION.		BORN.	DIED.
Gr.	Agatharcus, the inventor of perspective scenery in theatres,		B. C.	480
Gr.	Ageldas,	S. f.	B. C. 5th C.	
Gr.	Agesander, (sculptor of "Laocoon and his Children,")	S.	B. C. 5th C.	
Ital.	Albano, Francis, ("the painter of the Graces,")	P.	1578	1660
Ital.	Alberti, Leo Baptist, a Florentine,	P. S. & A.	1400	1490
Ital.	Albertinelli, Mariotto,	P.		1520
Ital.	Angelo, Michael, (Buonarotti,) a pre-eminent	P. S. & A.	1474	1563
Ital.	——, ——, (Caravaggio,	P.	1569	1609
Gr.	Apelles, the most celebrated of ancient painters, f. B. C.			
Gr.	Apollodorus, an Athenian painter,	f. B. C.	408	
Fr.	Audran, Gerard, a celebrated historical engraver,		1640	1703

B

NATION.	NAME AND PROFESSION.		BORN.	DIED.
Ital.	Baccio, Della Porta, (known as San Marco,)	P.	1469	1517
Eng.	Bacon, John,	S.	1740	1799
Flem.	Balen, Henry Van,	P.		1632
Ital.	Bandinelli, Baccio,	S.	1487	1559
Irish,	Barry, James,	P.	1741	1806
Ital.	Batoni, Pompey,		1708	1787
Ital.	Bella, Stephano Della, a Florentine engraver,		1610	1684
Dutch,	Both, John and Andrew,			1650 & 56
Fr.	Bourdon, Sebastian,	P. & E.	1616	1671
Swiss.	Bourgeoise, Sir Francis, (born in London,)	P.	1756	1811
Eng.	Boydell, John, (a printseller, and lord-mayor of London.)	E.	1719	1804
Ital.	Bramante D' Urbino, Francis L., (1st of St. Peter's Church,)	A.	1444	1514
Dutch,	Brentel, Francis,	P. f.	1635	
Dutch,	Brill, Matthew,		1550	1584
Dutch,	Bruges, John of, or John Van Eyck,		13.0	1441
Dutch,	Buonarotti, See Angelo,			

C

NATION.	NAME AND PROFESSION.		BORN.	DIED.
Ital.	Cagliari, Paul, (known as Paul Veronese) a celebrated painter,		1532	1588
Ital.	———, Benedict, Carletto and Gabriel, brothers, and sons of Paul,			
Ital.	Cambiaso, Lucus, a Genoese,	P.	1527	1585
tal.	Canaletto, Anthony, a Venetian, (landscape,)		1697	1718
Ital.	Canova, Antonio, one of the greatest of sculptors,		1757	1822
Ital.	Caravaggio, See Angelo.			

NATION.	NAME AND PROFESSION.		BORN.	DIED.
Ital.	Carpi, Hugh di, discoverer of the art of printing in Chiaro-obscuro, with 3 plates—to imitate drawings,		1486	
Fr.	Cassas, Louis Francis,	P. &. A	1756	1827
Span.	Castillo Y. Saavedra, Anthony,	P.	1603	1667
Ital.	Cavendone, James, (fresco,)	P.	1577	1660
Ital.	Cellini, Benvenuto, a Florentine engraver and sculptor,		1500	1570
Flem.	Champagne, Philip de,	P.	1604	1674
Eng.	Chantry, Francis, (Statue of Washington,) &c.	S.		
Fr.	Chaudet, Anthony Denis,	P.	1763	1810
Ital.	Cimabue, John a Florentine painter,		1240	1300
Ital.	Claude Lorraine,	P.	1600	1682
Gr.	Cleomenes, an Athenian, (The Medicean Venus,)	S. f. B. C.	180	
Eng.	Cooper, Samuel, (miniature)	P.	1609	1676
U. S. A.	Copley, John Singleton, (born in Boston,)	P.	1738	1815
Ital.	Corregio, Anthony, (founder of the Lombard school,	P.	1490	1534
Ital.	Cortona, Pietro da, a Tuscan, painter,		1596	1669
Eng.	Cosway, Richard, miniature painter,			1826
Fr.	Courtois, James, (known as Il Borgognone,)	P.	1621	1673
Fr.	Coustou, Nicholas, (also, his brother William,)	S.	1658	1731

D

Fr.	David, James Louis, a celebrated painter,		1750	1825
Ger.	Denner, Balthasar, portrait painter,		1685	1747
Gr.	Dinocrates, a Macedonian, (builder of Alexandria,) &c.,	A.		
Ital.	Dolci, Carlo, (scripture,)	P.	1616	1686
Ital.	Domenichino, (excelled in expression,)	P.	1581	1641
Ital.	Donatello, or Donato, a Florentine, sculptor,		1383	1466
Fr.	Dufresnoy, Charles Alphonso,	P.		
Ger.	Durer, Albert, (and author,)	P. E. S. & A.	1471	1528

E

Eng.	Eginton, Francis, (restorer of the art of painting on *glass*,)	P.	1737	1805
Dutch,	Eyck, John, Van, (said to have invented painting in *oil*,)	P.	1370	1441

F

Eng.	Flaxman, John,	S.	1755	1826
Swiss	Fuseli, Henry, (resided in England,)	P.	1739	1825

G

Ital.	Ghiberti, Laurence, a Florentine sculptor,		1738	1456
Ital.	Giorando, Luke, (The Proteus of painting,)	P.	1629	1704
Ital.	Giorgione,	P.	1477	1511
Ital.	Giotto,	P. S. &. A.	1276	1336
Fr.	Giraldon, Francis,	S.	1630	1715
Fr.	Girodet—Trioson, Anne Louis,	P.	1767	1824
Fr.	Gougon, John, ("The French Phidias,")	S.		1572
Ital.	Guercino, (real name Francis Barbieri,)	P.	1590	1666
Ital.	Guido Reni, (excelled in beauty, of expression and grace,)	P.	1574	1642

H

Eng.	Harlow, George Henry,	P.	1787	1819
Eng.	Hogarth, William, one of the most original of painters,		1697	1764
Swiss,	Holbein, Hans, a celebrated portrait and historical painter,		1498	1554
Ger.	Hollar, Wenceslaus, (executed 2400 plates,)	E.	1607	1677
Dutch,	Houbraken, Jacob, (600 portraits,)	E.	1698	1780
Fr.	Houdon, (executed statue of Franklin,)	S.	1746	1828
Fr.	Houel, John, (Picturesque Travels, &c.,)	P. & E.	1735	1813

J

Eng.	Jones, Inigo,	A.		
Ital.	Julio Romano,	P. & A.	1492	1546

K

	Kauffman, M. A. Angelica C., poetical painter,		1747	1807
Ger.	Kneller, Sir Godfrey, (resided in England,)	P.	1648	1723

NATION.	NAME AND PROFESSION.	BORN.	DIED.
	L		
Dutch,	Lairesse, Gerard, (excelled in expedition,)	P. & E. 1640	1711
Fr.	Landon, C. P. (more eminent as an author of works on the fine arts,)	P.	1826
Fr.	Lebrun, Charles, (painter to Louis XIV.,)	P. 1619	1690
Ger.	Lely, Sir Peter, (painter to Charles II., of England,)	P. 1618	1680
Fr.	Lesuer, Eustace, (the French Raphael)	P. 1617	1655
Fr.	Leyden, Lucas, Dammesz,	P. & E. 1494	1533
	M		
Flem.	Matsys, Quintin,	P. 1460	1529
Ital.	Mazzuolo, Francis, (inventor of *etching*,)	P. 1503	1540
Ger.	Mengs, Anthony R., (the Raphael of Germany,)	P. 1729	1779
	Miguard, Peter,	P. 1610	1695
Span.	Murillo, Bartholomew S.,	P. 1618	1682
	O		
Eng.	Opie, John,	P.	
	P		
Fr.	Pajou, Augustin,	S. 1730	1809
Ital.	Palladio, Andrew,	A. 1518	1580
Span.	Palomino de Castro Y Velasco, A. A.,	P. 1653	1726
Fr.	Perrault, Claudius, (designed the front of the Louvre,)	A. 1613	1688
Ital.	Perugino, Peter, (the master of Raphael,)	P. 1446	1524
	Petitot, John, (excelled in enamel,)	P. 1607	1691
Gr.	Phidias, (the most famous of ancient sculptors,)	498 B. C.	431
Fr.	Picart, Bernard,	E. 1663	1733
Fr.	Pigalle, John Baptist,	S. 1714	1785
Fr.	Piles, Roger de, (an author and painter,)	1635	1709
Ital.	Piranesi, John Baptist, (16 vols. folio,)	E. 1707	1778
Gr.	Polycletus, (statue of Juno at Argos,)	S. 480 B. C.	
Dutch,	Potter, Paul, (unequalled in *animal* painting,)	1625	1654
Fr.	Poussin, Nicholas, (excelled in landscape painting,)	1594	1665
Ital.	———, Gaspar, landscape painting,		1675
Gr.	Praxiletes,	S. f. 350 B. C.	
Fr.	Puget, Peter,	S. P. & A. 1622	1694
	R		
Ital.	Raphael, (real name Sanzio,) a pre-eminent painter,	1483	1520
Ital.	Rembrant, Paul,	P. 1606	1647
Eng.	Reynolds, Sir Joshua,	P. 1723	1792
Fr.	Roland, Philip L., (Homer in the Louvre,)	S. 1746	1816
Eng.	Romney, George,	1734	1802
Ital.	Rosa, Salvator, (scenes of gloom,)	P. 1614	1673
Eng.	Rowlandson, Thomas, (caricature—Dr. Syntax, &c.,)	P. & E.	
Eng.	Rubens, Peter Paul, a celebrated painter,	1577	1640
Dutch,	Ruysdael, Jacob, (landscape) painter,	1636	1681
Dutch,	———, Solomon,	P. 1616	1670
Eng.	Rysbrach, John Michael, (works in Westminster Abbey,)	S. 1694	1770
	S		
Ital.	Sanmicheli, Michael,	A. 1484	1559
Ital.	Scamozzi, Vincent,	A. 1550	1616
Ital.	Schadow, Zono Ridolpho, (a Roman) sculptor,		
Dutch,	Schalken, Godfrey, (candlelight scenes,)	P. 1643	1706
Gr.	Scopas,	S. 460 B. C.	
Eng.	Sharp, William,	E. 1740	1824
Eng.	Sherwin, John Keyse,	E.	1790
Flem.	Snyders, Francis, (landscape and animal) painting,	1579	1657
Fr.	Soufflot, J. G., (church of St. Genevieve at Paris,)	A. 1714	1781
Dutch,	Spaendonck, Geradvan, (flower) painter,	1746	1822
Scotch,	Strange, Robert,	E. 1721	1792

NATION.	NAME AND PROFESSION.	BORN.	DIED.
Eng.	Strutt, Joseph, an author and painter,)	1749	1802
Eng.	Stuart James, (author of the "Antiquities of Athens,")	A. 1713	1788
U. S. A.	Stuart, Gilbert, celebrated as a portrait painter, (born at Newport, Rhode Island,)—was a pupil of Benjamin West,	1755	1828

T

Flem.	Teniers, David, the elder, (pupil of Rubens,)	P. 1582	1649
	———, ———, the younger, do	P. 1610	1694
Ital.	Tintoretto, (a Venetian—pupil of Titian,)	P. 1512	1594
Ital.	Titian, (the greatest painter of the Venetian school,)	1480	1576

V

Eng.	Vanbrugh, Sir John (Blenheim and Castle Howard,)	A. 1672	1726
Dutch,	Vandervelde, William, (marine and battle) painter,	1610	1693
Dutch,	——— ———, ———, the young, do	1633	1707
Dutch,	——— Adrian, (landscape) painter,	1639	1672
Dutch,	Vanderwerf, Adrian, (historical) painting,	1654	1718
Flem.	Vandyck, Sir Anthony, (the greatest of portrait) painters,	1598	1641
Ital.	Vannucchi or Andrew del Sarto,	P. 1488	1530
Ital.	Van Vitelli, Louis, a Neapolitan architect,	1700	1773
Ital.	Vasari George (a biographer of artists.)	A. & P. 1512	1574
Sic.	Vasi, Joseph, a designer and engraver,	1710	1782
Span.	Velasquez, Carlos Rodrigo de Sylva Y,	P. 1599	1660
Fr.	Vernet, Joseph,	P. 1714	1789
Ital.	Verrochio, Andrea, (inventor of the method of taking the features in a plaster mould,)	S. 1422	1488
Ital.	Veronese, Paul, (See Cagliari,)		
Eng.	Vertue, George, 500 plates,	E. 1684	1756
Ital.	Vignola, James, (Caprarola Palace and St. Peters,)	A. 1507	1573
Ital.	Vinci, Leonardo da, a celebrated painter,	P. 1452	1519
Ital.	Volpato, John,	E. 1733	1802
Fr.	Vouet, Simon,	P. 1562	1649

W

Fr.	Wailly, Charles de,	A. 1729	1798
Eng.	Warren, Charles, (perfecter of engraving on *steel*,)	E.	1823
U. S. A.	West, Benjamin, a [illegible] painter,	1738	1820
Eng.	Wilkie, David, familiar life painter,		
Eng.	Wilson, Richard,	P. 1714	1782
Eng.	Woollett, William,	E. 1735	1785
Dutch,	Wouvermans Philip,	P. 1620	1668
Eng.	Wren, Sir Christopher, (St. Pauls, &c.)	A. 1632	1723
Eng.	Wyatt, James, (Pantheon, Kew Palace, &c.,)	A. 1743	1813

Z

Ital.	Zabblia, Nicholas,	A. 1674	1750
Gr.	Zeuxis, a celebrated ancient painter,	490 B. C.	400
Ger.	Zincke, an enamel portrait painter,	1684	1767

STATISTICS.

Part I.

STATISTICS OF THE WORLD.

[*From the "Balance Politique du Globe," en* 1828, *by M. Adrien Balbi.*]

The French are in the habit of bestowing very minute attention upon this interesting branch of inquiry; and some of their men of letters have devoted themselves to the preparation of Tables of reference, which may show, from time to time, the progress and actual condition of the various states of the world. Amongst others, M. Adrien Balbi has applied himself for twenty years to these important labours, and he has recently published a Chart, entitled "Balance Politique du Globe, en 1828," which is considered the most correct work of its kind, and which the author states is the result of a long period of the most laborious investigation. The late distinguished geographer, M lte-Brun, mentions this production, which was nearly completed before his death, as a most valuable abstract, of which he intended to insert a part in his concluding volume.

From this Chart of M. Balbi, the following Table has been compiled. The geographical division is that of M. Walkenaer. The surface of the earth, has been estimated at 148,522,000 square miles, of 60 to the equatorial degree (geographical miles.) of which nearly three-fourths, or 110,489,000 square miles are covered by the Ocean and the interior Seas;—the remainder, consisting of 37,673,000 square miles, forming the five parts of the world, called Europe, Asia, Africa, America, and Australasia, (or Oceania.) The square geographical mile has been retained in the following Tables, instead of the English square mile being adopted, as the former is used in most works on geography, particularly in those of France and Germany. The English square mile is about three-fourths of the area of the square geographical mile; that is, four English square miles are nearly equal to three geographical.

The table contains in successive columns, the names of countries, extent in square miles, population, reigning sovereign, or head of government, capital cities, with their population, principal religious denominations, revenue in pounds sterling, debt in pounds sterling, army, navy.

The particulars relating to each State are carried across two pages, and the figures prefixed to each are repeated in the last column of the right hand page, to assist the reference. For those States which have Colonial Possessions, a second line is given, showing the total extent of their power:—Example 1.—"*French Monarchy*, 154,000 square miles, 32,000,000 population"—gives the area and population of France itself; but the second line, "*Total of French Monarchy*," includes the amount of France and all its possessions and dependencies. Wherever this mark (?) is attached to a sum, or stands in the place of one, the information is considered questionable or is not to be obtained.

Companion to the British Almanac.

STATES AND TITLES.	Surface in Geogra. Sq. Miles.	Population.	Reigning Sovereign, or Head of Government.
EUROPE.			
Surface 2,793,800 Geographical Sq. Miles. Population 227,700,000 inhabitants.			
CENTRAL STATES.			
WESTERN DIVISION.			
1 French Monarchy . . .	154,000	32,000,000	Louis Philippe, 1830
Total of *French Monarchy* .	168,000	32,554,000	
2 Austrian Empire . . .	194,500	32,000,000	Francis I., 1792 .
3 Prussian Monarchy, . .	80,450	12,464,000	Frederic William III., 1797
4 Monarchy of the Netherlands, .	8,396	2,302,000	William I., 1815 .(Stat-holder. 1806,) .
5 Belgium	9,708	3,840,000	Leopold I., 1830 . .
6 Swiss Confederation . . .	11,200	1,980,000	Al. Am. Rhyn, Landmann . .
GERMANIC CONFEDERATION.			
7 Kingdom of Bavaria . .	22,120	4,070,000	Louis I., 1825 . .
8 Kingdom of Wirtemberg .	5,720	1,520,000	William I., 1816 .
9 Kingdom of Hanover . .	11,125	1,550,000	William IV., 1830 .
10 Kingdom of Saxony . .	4,341	1,400,000	Anthony, 1827 .
11 Grand Duchy of Baden . .	4,480	1,130,000	Ch. Leopold, Fr. 1830
12 Grand Duchy of Hesse .	2,826	700,000	Louis, 1830 . .
13 Electorate of Hesse . .	3,344	592,000	William II., 1821 .
14 Grand Duchy of Saxe Weimar	1,070	222,000	Charles Frederick, 1828
15 Do. of Mecklenberg-Schwerin	3,582	431,000	Francis, 1785 . .
16 Do. of Mecklenberg-Strelitz	578	77,000	George, 1816 . .
17 Do. of Holstein-Oldenburgh	1,840	241,000	Augustus, 1829 .
18 Duchy of Nassau . .	1,446	337,000	William, 1816 . .
19 Duchy of Brunswick . .	1,126	242,000	William, 1831 . .
20 Duchy of Saxe-Coburg-Gotha	731	143,000	Ernest, 1826 . .
21 Duchy of Saxe Meiningen .	691	130,000	Bernard, 1803 . .
22 Duchy of Saxe Altenburgh	397	104,000	Frederic, 1780 . .
23 Duchy of Anhalt-Dessau .	261	56,000	Leopold, 1817 . .
24 Duchy of Anhalt-Berneburgh	253	38,000	Alexis, 1796 . .
25 Duchy of Anhalt-Koethen .	240	34,000	Ferdinand, 1818 .
26 Princip. of Schwarz-Rudolstadt	306	57,000	Guther Frederic, 1807
27 Prin. of Schwarz-Sondershausen	270	48,000	Guther Fred. Charles, 1794 . .
28 Principality of Reuss-Greitz	109	23,000	Henry, XIX, 1817 .
29 Principality of Reuss-Schleitz	156	28,000	Henry LXII., 1818 :
30 Pr. of Reuss Lobenst.-Ebersdorf	182	26,000	Henry LXXII., 1822
31 Prin. of Lippe-Detmold .	330	72,000	Leopold, 1802 . .
32 Prin. of Lippe-Schaubenburg	157	26,000	George William, 1787
33 Prin. of Waldeck . . .	347	54,000	George, 1813 . .
34 Pr. of Hohenzollern Sigmaringen	293	38,000	Anthony, 1785 . .
35 Pr. of Hohenzollern Hechingen	82	15,000	Frederic, 1810 .
36 Prin. of Liechten-tien .	40	6,000	John, 1805 . . .
37 Landgrave of Hesse Homburgh	125	20,000	Louis, 1829 . .
38 Republic of Francfort . .	69	52,000	D. Malapert (Burgomaster) . . .
39 Republic of Bremen . .	51	49,000	Grœning, Schmidt, Nowen, & Dantze, (Burg.)
40 Republic of Hamburgh . .	114	148,000	Amsink, Heise, Bartels, and Koch, (Burgo.)
41 Republic of Lubeck .	88	41,000	Beneke, Kindler, Boeg, & Evers, (Burgom'rs.)
42 Lordship of Kniphausen .	13	2,859	Wm. Gusta. Fred. 1825

* Of this number, 50 are ships of the line, 51 frigates, and 213 inferior vessels.

Capital Cities, with their Population.	Principal Religious Denominations.	Revenue £ Sterling.	Debt £ Sterling.	Armies.	Ships.	
Paris, 890,000	Catholic, Calvinist	39,560,000	164,000,960	231,560	323*	1
Vienna, 300,000	Catholic, Greek, Calvinist, Lutheran	14,000,000	58,400,000	271,400	72†	2
Berlin, 220,000	Protestant, (Lutheran, Calvinist,) Cath.	8,600,000	29,067,200	162,600	1	3
Amsterdam, 201,000	Catholic, Calvinist, Lutheran			26,000	101	4
Brussels,	——			47,000		
Zurich, 10,000	Calvinist, Catholic	400,000	?	33,760	. .	5
Munich, 70,000	Catholic, Protestant	3,164,000	9,568,000	35,800	. .	6
Stuttgard, 32,000	Lutheran, Catholic	950,440	2,260,000	13,950	. .	7
Hanover, 28,000	Lutheran, Catholic	1,040,000	2,560,000	13,050	. .	8
Dresden, 70,000	Lutheran	1,120,000	2,800,000	12,000	. .	9
Karlsrhue, 19,000	Catholic, Lutheran	814,120	1,560,000	10,000	. .	10
Darmstadt, 20,000	Lutheran, Cath. Cal.	628,560	1,080,000	6,190	. .	11
Cassel, 26,000	Protestant, Catholic	620,000	263,200	5,680	. .	12
Weimar, 10,000	Lutheran	196,520	651,640	2,100	. .	13
Schwerin, 12,000	Lutheran	240,000	980,000	3,590	. .	14
N. Strelitz, 5,000	Lutheran	52,000	120,000	720	. .	15
Oldenburgh, 6,000	Lutheran, Catholic	155,160		1,650	. .	16
Wiesbaden, 7,000	Protestant, Catholic	240,000	432,000	3,000	.	17
Brunswick, 36,000	Lutheran	252,000	320,000	2,100		18
Gotha, 11,000	Lutheran	98,280	280,000	1,400	. .	19
Meiningen, 5,000	Lutheran	77,560	80,000	1,270	. .	20
Altenburgh, 10,000	Lutheran	61,040	100,000	1,030	.	21
Dessau, 10,000	Calvinist, Lutheran	73,440	82,760	530	. .	22
Berneburgh, 5,000	Calvinist, Lutheran	46,560	82,760	370	. .	23
Koethen, 6,000	Calvinist, Lutheran	33 080	124,120	320	. .	24
Rudolstadt, 3,000	Lutheran	33,600	37,760	540	. .	25
Sondershausen, 3,000	Lutheran	20,680	12,200	450	. .	26
Greitz, 6,000	Lutheran	14,480	20,680	200	. .	27
Schleitz, 5,000	Lutheran	13,440	} 72,400?	280	. .	28
Ebersdorf, 1,000	Lutheran	24,840	}	260	. .	29
Detmold, 2,000,	Calvinist	50,680	72,400	690	. .	30
Buckeburg, 2,000	Lutheran	22,240	41,360	240	. .	31
Corbach, 2,000	Lutheran	41,360	124,120	520	. .	32
Sigmaringen, 800	Catholic	31,040	155,160?	320	. .	33
Hechingen, 3,000	Catholic	12,400	51,720	150	. .	34
Liechtenstien, 700	Catholic	140,000	312,000	55	. .	35
Homburgh, 3,000	Calvinist, Lutheran	18,600	46,560	200	. .	36
Francfort, 48,000	Lutheran	78,600	827,440	470	. .	37
Bremen, 38,000	Lutheran, Calvinist	41,360	312,000	380	. .	38
Hamburgh, 112,000	Lutheran	224,000	1,880,000	1,300	. .	39
Lubeck, 22,000	Lutheran	41,360	360,000	400	. .	40
Kniphausen, 100	Lutheran	15,520	?	28	. .	41

†3 ships of the line, 8 frigates, and 61 inferior vessels.

STATES AND TITLES.	Surface in Geogra. Sq. Miles.	Population	Reigning Sovereign, or Head of Government.
WESTERN DIVISION.			
SOUTHERN STATES.			
42 Republic of Andora (Spain) .	144	15,000	Magis. of the Republic
ITALY.			
43 Republic of San Marino. .	17	7,000	2 Quarterly Chiefs .
44 Duchy of Massa . . .	71	29,000	Maria Beatrice, 1814
45 Duchy of Modena . .	1,500	350,000	Francis IV., 1814 .
46 Principality of Monaco .	38	6,500	Honorius, 1819 .
47 Duchy of Lucca . . .	312	143,000	Charles, 1824 . .
48 Duchy of Parma . .	1,660	440,000	Maria Louisa, 1814
49 Grand Duchy of Tuscany .	6,324	1,275,000	Leopold II., 1824 .
50 Kingdom of Sardinia .	21.000	4,300,000	Charles Emanuel, 1831
51 State of the Church . .	13,000	2,590,000	Gregory XVI., 1831 .
52 Kingdom of the Two Sicilies	31,800	7,420,000	Ferdinand II., 1830
53 Spanish Monarchy . . .	137,400	13,900,000	Ferdinand VII., 1808
Total of the Spanish Monarchy	214,400	17,9[illegible]8,000	. . . . .
54 Portuguese Monarchy . . .	29,150	3,530,000	Miguel, 1828 . .
Total of the Portuguese Monarchy	430,000	5,607,000	
NORTHERN STATES.			
55 Monarchy of Sweden and Norway	223,000	3,866,000	Charles XIV., 1818 .
56 Danish Monarchy . . .	16,500	1,950,000	Frederic VI., 1808
Total of the Danish Monarchy .	341,000	2,125,000	. . . .
57 British Monarchy . . .	90,948	23,400,000	William IV., 1830 .
Total of the British Monarchy	4,457,598	140,450,000	. . . .
EASTERN DIVISION.			
58 Russian Empire. . . .	1,499,000	52,625,000	Nicholas I., 1826 .
Kingdom of Poland . .	36,700	3,900,000	. . . .
Total of the Russian Empire .	5,912,000	60,000,000	[Wodzicky, 1824
59 Republic of Cracow . .	373	114,000	Count Stanislaus, of
60 Ottoman Empire . .	155,000	9,500,000	Mahmoud II., 1808 .
Total of the Ottoman Empire	1,078,000	25,000,000	. . . .
61 Republic of the Ionian Isles.	754	176,000	Prince Anthony Comuto (President.) .
ASIA.			
Surface 12,118,000 Geographical Sq. Miles. Population 390,000,000 Inhabitants ?			
62 Chinese Empire	4,070,000	170,000,000	Tao Kouang, 1820 .
63 Empire of Japan	180,000	25,000,000	Bounoaw, 1804 .
64 Empire of An-nam	270,000?	14,000,000	Minh Mea, 1820 .
65 Kingdom of Siam	124,000?	3,000,000	Kroma Chiat, 1824
66 Birman Empire	140,000	3.500.000	Madou Tchen, 1818 .
67 British Indian Empire . . .	849,650	114,430,000	. . . . .
East Indian Company's Territory .	349,000	80,800,000	Ld. William Bentinck,
East India Company's Dependencies	485,000	32,800,000	. [1827, Gov. Gen.
Island of Ceylon	15,650	830,000	. . . . .
68 Kingdom of Sindia	29,760	4,000,000	Dijunkadji Rao, 1827
69 Kingdom of Nepaul	40,000	2,500,000	Bickram Djah, 1816 .
70 Confederation of the Sikhs . .	66,000	5,500,000	Son of Runjit Sin., 1827
71 Triumvirate of Sindhy . . .	40,000	1,000,000	Son of Mir Gholaum Ali,
72 ingdom of Cabaul	172 000	6,500,000	. . . [1812
73 Confederation of the Beloutchis .	110,000?	2,000,000	Mahomet, 1795 .
74 Kingdom of Herat (Eastern Korassan)	50,000?	1.500,000	. . . . .
75 Kingdom of Persia	350,000	9,000,000	Feth Ali Schah, 1796
76 Khanate of Boukhara	173,000	2,500,000?	Mir Batyr, 1827 . .
77 Khanate of Khiva	145,000	800,000	Rhaman Kouli Khan,
78 Khanate of Khokhan	100,000?	1,000,000	Emir Khan [1826
79 Imanate of Yemen	40,000?	2,500,000	. . . .
80 Imanate of Mascate	39,000?	1,600,000?	Bidou Ebn Saaf, 1806
81 Ottoman Asia	556,000	12,500,000	. . . . .
82 Russian Asia	4,006,000	3,445,000	. . . . .
83 Portuguese Asia	3,700	500,000	. . . . .
84 French Asia	400	179,000	. . . . .

* 10 ships of the line, 16 frigates, 30 inferior. † 4 ships of the line, 6 do. 37 do. ‡ 4 do. 7 do. 18 do.

Capital Cities with their Population.	Principal Religious Denominatians.	Revenue £ Sterling	Debt £Sterling.	Armies.	Ships.	
Andorra, 2,000 .	Catholic . .	?	?	?	. .	42
San Marino, 4,000	Catholic . .	2,800	?	40	. .	43
Massa, 7.000 .	Catholic . .	20,000	} 60,000?	100	. .	44
Modena, 27,000 .	Catholic . .	140,000	}	1,680	. .	45
Monaco, 1,000 .	Catholic . .	16,000	?		. .	46
Lucca, 22,000 .	Catholic . .	76,000	?	800	. .	47
Parma, 30,000 .	Catholic . .	184,000	180,000	1,320	. .	48
Florence, 80,000	Catholic . .	680,000	. .	4,000	. .	49
Turin, 114,000	Catholic . .	2,600,000	4,000,000?	26,000	1	50
Rome, 154,000 .	Catholic . .	1,200,000	24.000,000?	6,000	8?	51
Naples, 364,000 .	Catholic . .	3,360.000	20.000,000?	30,000	27?	52
Madrid, 201,000,	Catholic . .	4,320,000?	160,000,000	50,000	56*	53
Lisbon, 260,000	Catholic . :	2,163,840	6,400,000	26,630	47†	54
Stockholm, 78,000	Lutheran . .	1,680,000	8,000,000	45,200	261	55
Copenhagen, 109,000	Lutheran . .	1,600,000	10,800,000	38,820	29‡	56
London, 1,350,000 [(a)	Protest., Episcopal., Pres., Catholic	62,306,214	777,476,892	102,280	606‖	57
St. Petersburgh [320,000?	Greek, Cath., Luth., Mahometan .	16,000,000	52,000,000	1,039,000	130¶	58
Cracow, 25,000 .	Catholic . .	34,440	?	80	. .	59
Constantinople, [600,000?	Greek, Mahometan	10,000,000	4,000,000	278,000	285**	60
Corfu, 14,000 .	Greek . . .	146,240	?	1,200		61
Pekin, 1,300,000?	{ Budhists, disci. of Confucius, &c. }	30,000,000?	.	{ 914,000 1500000w	? ?	62
Jeddo, 1,300,000?	Lintorist, Budhist	12,000,000	. .	120,000	?	63
Phuxuan, 100.000?	Budhist . .	3,600,000	. .	80,000	150?	64
Bancock, 90,000?	Budhist . . .	1,600,000?	. .	80,000w	?	65
New Ava, 50,000?	Budhist . .	1,800,000?	. .	150,000w	?	66
Calcutta, 500,000?	Brah., Mah., Nanekist	21,089,440	39,000,000?	210,000	18	67
Ougein, 100,000 .	Brahmin, Mahometan	1,040,000	. .	20,000	. .	68
Katmandou, 12,000?	Brah., Boud., Lam.	520,000	. .	17,000	. .	69
Amretsir, 40,000 .	Nanekist, Brah., Mah.	2,000,000	. .	250 000w	. .	70
Heider Abad, 15,000	Mahometan, Brahman	520,000	. .	50,000w	. .	71
Cabaul, 80,000 .	Mahometan, Brahman	1,800.000	. .	150,000w	. .	72
Kelat, 20,000 .	Mahometan .	40,000	. .	150,000w	. .	73
Herat, 100,000 .	Mahometan . .	320,000?	. .	8,000	. .	74
Teheran, 150,000	Mahometan .	3,200,000	. .	80,000	. .	75
Boukhara, 80,000?	Mahometan . .	480,000	. .	25,000	. .	76
Khiva, 10,000 .	Mahometan .	?	. .	100,000w	. .	77
Khokhan, 60,000?	Mahometan . .	?	. .	100,000w	. .	78
Szanna, 20,000 .	Mahometan .	480,000?	. .	5,000?	. .	79
Mascate, 60,000	Mahometan . .	160,000?	. .	1,000	34	80
Koutahich, 50,000	Mah., Armenian, Gr.	. .	. .	. .	. .	81
Tobolsk, 25,000	Gr., Mah., Fetichist	. .	. .	. .	. .	82
Goa, 18,000 .	Catholic . .	. .	. .	. .	. .	83
Pondicherry, 40,000	Brahman, Catholic	. .	. .	. .	. .	84

‖165 ships, 117 frigates, 324 inferior. ¶ 50 do. 30 do. 50 do. ** Before the Battle of Navarino. (a) This is an *estimated* increase upon the returns of 1821.

STATES AND TITLES.	Surface in Geogra. Sq. Miles.	Population	Reigning Sovereign, or Head of Government.
AFRICA.			
Surface 8,516,000 Geograph. Sq. Miles. Population 60,000,000 Inhabitants.?			
85 Empire of Morocco	130,000	4,500,000	MuleiAbderrahman1822
86 Algiers	70,000	1,500,000	Houssan, 1818
87 State of Tunis	40,000	1,800,000	Sidi Hassan, 1824
88 State of Tripoly	208,000	660,000	Yousof, 1795
89 Kingdom of Tigre	130,000	1,500,000?	
90 Kingdom of Amharra	48,000?	1,000,000?	
91 Empire of Bornou	100,000?	2,000,000?	Schumin el Kanemy
92 Empire of the Felatahs	120,000?	3,000,000?	Bello
93 Kingdom of Upper Bambarra	50,000?	1,500,000?	
94 Republic of Fouta Toro	15,000?	700,000?	
95 Empire of Ashantee	100,000?	3,000,000?	
96 Kingdom of Dahomey	40,000?	900,000?	
97 Kingdom of Benin	63,000?	1,500,000?	
98 Kingdom of Changamera	70,000?	840,000?	Changamera
99 Kingdom of Madagascar	100,000?	2,000,000?	Radama
100 Ottoman Africa	367,000	3,000,000	Mahomet-Aly, 1805
101 Portuguese Africa	389,000	1,440,000	
102 English Africa	91,000	270,000	
103 Spanish Africa	2,430	208,000	
104 French Africa	3,000?	135,000	
AMERICA, or the New World.			
Surface 11,046,000 Geograph. Sqr. Miles. Population 39,000,000 Inhabitants.			
105 Empire of Brazil	2,313,000	5,000,000	Pedro II. 1831.
106 United States of North America	1,570,000?	12,856,171	Andrew Jackson, 1829, President
107 United States of Mexico	1,242,000	7,500,000	Bustamente, V. P.
108 United States of Central America	139,000	1,650,000	Morazan, President,
109 Republic of Colombia	828,000	2,800,000	Santander, President
110 Republic of Venezuela			Paez
111 Republic of Peru	373,000	1,700,000	Gamarra, President,
112 Republic of Bolivia	310,000?	1,300,000	Santa Cruz, President
113 Republic of Chili	129,000	1,400,000	Prieto, President,
114 Republic of Buenos Ayres	683,000	700,000	Rosas, President
115 Republic of Hayti	22,100	950,000	Boyer, 1820 President
116 Directorate of Paraguay	67,000	250,000?	Francia, 1809, Dictator
117 Or. Republic of Uraguay			Lavalleja, President.
118 English America	1,930,000?	2,290,000	
119 Spanish America	35,400	1,240,000	
120 French America	30,000?	240,000	
121 Danish America	324,000?	110,000	
122 American Netherlands	30,000?	114,000	
123 Russian America	370,000?	50,000	
AUSTRALASIA.			
Surface 3,100,000 Geograph. Sqr. Miles. Population 20,300,000 Inhabitants.			
124 Kingdom of Siak (Sumatra)	320,000?	600,000?	
125 Kingdom of Achees (Sumatra)	16,600?	500 000?	
126 Kingdom of Borneo	20,000?	260,000?	
127 Kingdom of Solou	11,000?	300,000?	
128 Kingdom of Mindanao	12,000?	360,000?	
129 Kingdom of Sandwich Islands	5,100	130,000	Kaukianti, 1824
130 Java, Sumatra, &c. (Dutch)	203,000	9,360,000	
131 Philippine Islands, &c. (Spanish)	39,000	2,640,000	
132 Australia, or New Holland	1,496,000	60,000	
133 Island of Timor, part of, (Portuguese)	8,000	137,000	

* 7 Ships of the line, 12 frigates, 19 inferior.

Capital Cities with their Population.	Principal Religious Denominations.	Revenue £ Sterling.	Debt. £Sterling.	Armies.	Ships.	
Mequinez, 70,000 .	Mahometan . .	880,000	. .	36,000	15	85
Algiers, 50,000 . .	Mahometan . .	160,000	. .	20,000	25	86
Tunis, 100,000 . .	Mahometan . .	280,000	. .	6,000	18	87
Tripoli, 15.000 . .	Mahometan . .	80,000	. .	4,000	17	88
Chelicut, 8,000? .	Copt	. .	. .	48,000	. .	89
Gondar, 40,000? . .	Copt	. .	. .	25,000	. .	90
Bornou, 30,000 . .	Fetichist, Mahometan	. .	. .	70,000	. .	91
Sakkatoo, 80,000? .	Fetichist, Mahometan	. .	. .	100,000	. .	92
Sego, 30,000 . .	Mahometan, Fetichist	. .	. .	. .	. .	93
Tjiloga?, 4,000? . .	Mahometan, Fetichist	. .	. .	. .	. .	94
Coumassie, 15,000 .	Fetichist . .	. .	. .	100,000	. .	95
Abomey, 24,000 .	Fetichist . .	. .	. .	30,000	. .	96
Benin, 60,000? . .	Fetichist . .	. .	. .	50,000	. .	97
Zimbaoe, ...	Fetichist . .	. .	. .	30,000	. .	98
Emirne, 30,000 . .	Fetichist, Mahometan	. .	. .	30,000	. .	99
Cairo, 260,000 . .	Mahometan . .	. .	. .	. .	. .	100
St. Paul de Loanda	Fetichist, Catholic	. .	. .	. .	. .	101
The Cape, 18,000 .	Calvinist, Cath., Ch. of England, Fetichist	. .	. .	. .	. .	102
Ceuta, 7,000 . . .	Catholic . .	. .	. .	. .	. .	103
Fort St. Louis, 10,000	Mahometan, Catholic	. .	. .	. .	. .	104
Rio de Janeiro, [140,000? .	Catholic . .	2,500,000	9,320,000	30,000	101	105
Washington, 18,827 [(a)	Congregationl., Pres., Ep., Lu., Cath., Meth.	5,539,600	5,475,000	5,779	35*	106
Mexico, 180,000 .	Catholic . .	2,950,280	20,340,000	22,750	16	107
New Guatem., 40,000	Catholic . .	400,000	3?0,000	3,500	2	108
Bogota, 30,000 . .	Catholic . .	1,712,000	9,160,000	32,370	17	109
Caraccas, 30,000	. . . .	. .	. .	. .	7	110
Lima, 80,000 . .	Catholic . .	1,200,000	5,899,520	7,500	. .	111
Chuguisaca . .	Catholic . .	440,000	640,000	?		112
Santiago, 60,000 .	Catholic . .	600,000	6,440,000	8,000	6	113
Buenos Ayres, 80,000	Catholic . .	600,000	5,360 000	10,000	16	114
Port-au-Prin., 30,000	Catholic . .	1,200,000	6 000,000	45,000	6	115
Assumption, 12,000?	Catholic . .	200,000	. .	5,000	2	116
Monte Video, 10,000	. .	. .	. .	. .	. .	117
Quebec, 22,000 . .	Ch. of En., Cal., Cath.	. .	. .	. .	. .	118
Havannah, 130,000 .	Catholic . .	. .	. .	. .	. .	119
Fort-Royal, 9,000 .	Catholic . .	. .	. .	. .	. .	120
Raikiavik, 500 . .	Lutheran . .	. .	. .	. .	. .	121
Paramaribo, 20,000	Calvinist . .	. .	. .	. .	. .	122
St. Paul, 600 . .	Fetichist . .	. .	. .	. .	. .	123
Siak, 8.000? [15,000?	Mahometan . .	. .	. .	. .	. .	124
Telosancaouay, .	Mahometan . .	. .	. .	. .	. .	125
Borneo, 15,000? .	Mahometan . .	. .	. .	. .	. .	126
Bevan, 6,000 . .	Mahometan . .	. .	. .	. .	. .	127
Selangan, 10.000 .	Mahometan . .	. .	. .	. .	. .	128
Hanarura, 6,000? .	Fetichist, Methodist,	. .	. .	. .	11?	129
Batavia, 46,000 .	Mahometan . .	. .	. .	. .	. .	130
Manilla, 140,000 .	Catholic, Mahometan	. .	. .	. .	. .	131
Sydney, 10,000 . .	Ch., of En., Prs., Cath.	. .	. .	. .	. .	132
Dille, 2,000 . . .	Catholic, Fetichist,	. .	. .	. .	. .	133

(a) Washington is the seat of government in the United States, and is therefore the nominal Capital. The Capitals of several of the individual states are superior in population and importance.

TOTAL POPULATION OF THE EARTH

A summary of the preceding table gives the following results for the surface of the habitable globe (in geographical square miles,) and the amount of population.

	Surface.	Inhabitants.
Europe	2,793,000	227,700,000
Asia	12,118,000	390,000,000
Africa	8,516,000	60,000,000
America	11,046,000	39,000,000
Australasia	3,100,000	20,300,000
Total	37,573,000	737,000,000

INHABITANTS OF THE EARTH, DIVIDED ACCORDING TO THEIR RELIGIOUS BELIEF.

The two following estimates are according to the geographers, Malte-Brun and Hassel.

	Malte-Brun.	Hassel.
Catholics	116,000,000	134,000,000
Greek Church	70,000,000	62,000,000
Protestants	42,000,000	55,000,000
Total of Christians	228,000,000	251,000,000
Jews	4,000,000	3,000,000
Mahometans,	100,000,000	120,000,000
Pagans	310,000,000	550,000,000
Total Inhabitants of the Globe	642,000,000	924,000,000

Part II.

UNITED STATES.

1. EXECUTIVE GOVERNMENT.

The government of the United States is a confederated republic, each State being independent, with its own executive, legislature, &c. for conducting local affairs.

For the management of foreign affairs, and commerce, and to provide for the general welfare, a general government exists, consisting of a President, Vice President, Congress, and Judiciary, or Supreme Court. The President is entrusted with the executive power of the nation, and is chosen by electors selected in each state, according to the number of members of Congress, once in four years. The legislative power is vested in a Congress, composed of a Senate and House of Representatives. (*See Pages 327 & 328.*) The President has a cabinet, consisting of the Secretaries of State, of the Treasury, of War, and of the Navy, the Postmaster General, and Attorney General. Besides the power of nominating to office, he has the privilege of placing his *veto* on acts of Congress, which cannot then become laws, unless two thirds of both houses agree to pass them.

SALARIES OF THE PRINCIPAL OFFICERS.

President	$25,000	Secretary of War	$6,000
Vice President	5,000	Secretary of the Navy	6,000
Secretary of State	6,000	Post Master General	6,000
Secretary of the Treasury	6,000	Attorney General	3,500

SIGNERS OF THE DECLARATION OF INDEPENDENCE.

Names.		*Where and when born.*		*Age in 1776.*	*Died.*	*Age.*
Josiah Bartlett,	N. H.	N. Hampshire,	1729	47	May 19, 1795	66
William Whipple,	N. H.	Maine,	1730	40	Nov. 28, 1785	55
Matthew Thornton,	N. H.	Ireland,	1714	62	June 24, 1803	89
John Hancock,	Ms.	Massachusetts,	1737	39	Oct. 8, 1793	56
Samuel Adams,	Ms.	Massachusetts,	Sept. 22, 1722	54	Oct. 2, 1803	81
John Adams,	Ms.	Massachusetts,	Oct. 19, 1735	41	July 4, 1826	91
Robt. Treat Paine,	Ms.	Massachusetts,	1731	45	May 11, 1814	83
Elbridge Gerry,	Ms.	Massachusetts,	July 17, 1744	32	Nov. 23, 1814	70
Stephen Hopkins,	R. I.	Rhode Island,	March 7, 1707	69	July 13, 1785	78
William Ellery,	R. I.	Rhode Island,	Dec. 22, 1727	49	Feb. 15, 1820	93
Roger Sherman,	Ct.	Massachusetts,	April 19, 1721	55	July 23, 1793	72
Saml. Huntington,	Ct.	Connecticut,	July 2, 1732	44	Jan. 5, 1796	64
William Williams,	Ct.	Connecticut,	April 8, 1731	45	Aug. 2, 1811	81
Oliver Wolcott,	Ct.	Connecticut,	1726	50	Dec. 1, 1797	71
William Floyd,	N. Y.	Long Island,	Dec. 17, 1734	42	Aug. 4, 1821	87
Philip Livingston,	N. Y.	New-York,	Jan. 15, 1716	60	June 12, 1778	62
Francis Lewis,	N. Y.	South Wales,	1713	63	Dec. 30, 1803	90
Lewis Morris,	N. Y.	New-York,	1726	50	Jan. 1798	72
Richard Stockton,	N. J.	New-Jersey,	Oct. 1, 1730	46	Feb. 28, 1781	51
John Witherspoon,	N. J.	Scotland,	Feb. 5, 1722	54	Nov. 15, 1794	72
Francis Hopkinson,	N. J.	Pennsylvania,	1737	39	May 8, 1791	54
John Hart,	N. J.	New-Jersey,			1780	
Abraham Clark,	N. J.	New-Jersey,	Feb. 5, 1726	50	1794	68
Robert Morris,	Pa.	England,	Jan. 1733	43	May 8, 1806	73
Benjamin Rush,	Pa.	Pennsylvania,	Dec. 24, 1745	31	April 19, 1812	67
Benjamin Franklin,	Pa.	Massachusetts,	Jan. 17, 1706	70	April 17, 1790	84
John Morton,	Pa.	Delaware,	1724	52	1777	53
George Clymer,	Pa.	Pennsylvania,	1739	37	Jan. 23, 1813	74
James Smith,	Pa.	Ireland,			1806	
George Taylor,	Pa.	Ireland,	1716	60	Feb. 23, 1781	65
James Wilson,	Pa.	Scotland,	1742	34	Aug. 28, 1798	56
George Ross,	Pa.	Delaware,	1730	46	July 1779	49
Cæsar Rodney,	Del.	Delaware,	1730	46	1783	53
George Read,	Del.	Maryland,	1734	42	1798	64
Thomas M'Kean,	Del.	Pennsylvania,	March 19, 1734	42	June 24, 1817	83
Samuel Chase,	Md.	Maryland,	April 17, 1741	35	June 19, 1811	70
William Paca,	Md.	Maryland,	Oct. 31, 1740	36	1799	59
Thomas Stone,	Md.	Maryland,	1740	36	Oct. 5, 1787	47
Charles Carroll,	Md.	Maryland,	Sept. 8, 1737	39	1832	95
George Wythe,	Va.	Virginia,	1726	50	June 6, 1806	80
Richard H. Lee,	Va.	Virginia,	Jan. 20, 1732	44	June 19, 1794	62
Thomas Jefferson,	Va.	Virginia,	April 2, 1743	33	July 4, 1826	83
BenjaminHarrison,	Va.	Virginia,			April 1791	
Thomas Nelson,	Va.	Virginia,	Dec. 26, 1738	38	Jan. 4, 1789	51
Francis L. Lee,	Va.	Virginia,	Oct. 14, 1734	42	April, 1797	63
Carter Braxton,	Va.	Virginia,	Sept. 10, 1736	40	Oct. 10, 1797	61
William Hooper,	N. C.	Massachusetts,	June 17, 1742	34	Oct., 1790	48
Joseph Hewes,	N. C.	New-Jersey,	1730	46	Nov. 10, 1779	49
John Penn,	N. C.	Virginia,	May 17, 1741	35	Sept., 1788	47
Edward Rutledge,	S. C.	South Carolina,	Nov. 1749	27	Jan. 23, 1800	51
Thomas Heyward,	S. C.	South Carolina,	1746	30	March, 1809	63
Thomas Lynch,	S. C.	South Carolina,	Aug. 5, 1749	27	About 1780	31
Arthur Middleton,	S. C.	South Carolina,	1743	33	Jan. 1, 1787	44
Button Gwinnett,	Geo.	England,	1732	44	May 27, 1777	45
Lyman Hall,	Geo.	Connecticut,	1731	45	About 1790	69
George Walton,	Geo.	Virginia,	1740	36	Feb. 2, 1804	64

PRESIDENTS OF THE CONTINENTAL CONGRESS.

John Hancock, May 24th, 1775, to October 29th, 1777; Henry Laurens, Nov. 1st, 1777, to December 9th, 1778; John Jay, Decem. 9th, 1778, to September 28th, 1779; Samuel Huntingdon, September 28th, to July 10th, 1780; Thomas McKean, July, 10th, 1780; John Hanson, 1781; Elias Boudinot, 1782; Thomas Mifflin, 1783; Richard Henry Lee, 1784; Nathaniel Gorham, 1786; Arthur St. Clair, 1787. Cyrus Griffin, 1788.

SUCCESSIVE ADMINISTRATIONS.

First Administration;—1789 to 1797;—8 years.

George Washington,	Virginia,	April 30, 1789.	President.
John Adams,	Massachusetts,	do. 1789.	Vice President.
		Appointed.	
Thomas Jefferson,	Virginia,	Sept. 26, 1789.	Secretaries of State.
Edmund Randolph,	do.	Jan. 2, 1794.	
Timothy Pickering,	Pennsylvania,	Dec. 10, 1795.	
Alexander Hamilton,	New-York,	Sept. 11, 1789.	Secretaries of the Treasury.
Oliver Wolcott,	Connecticut,	Feb. 3, 1795.	
Henry Knox,	Massachusetts,	Sept. 12, 1789.	Secretaries of War.
Timothy Pickering,	Pennsylvania,	Jan. 2, 1795.	
James M'Henry,	Maryland,	Jan. 27, 1796.	
Samuel Osgood,	Massachusetts,	Sept. 26, 1789.	Post Masters Gen.
Timothy Pickering,	Pennsylvania,	Nov. 7, 1791.	
Joseph Habersham,	Georgia,	Feb. 25, 1795.	
Edmund Randolph,	Virginia,	Sept. 26, 1789.	Attorneys General.
William Bradford,	Pennsylvania,	Jan. 27, 1794.	
Charles Lee,	Virginia,	Dec. 10, 1795.	

Speakers of the House of Representatives.

Frederick A. Muhlenberg,	Pennsylvania,	1st Congress,	1789.
Jonathan Trumbull,	Connecticut,	2d do.	1791.
Frederick A. Muhlenberg,	Pennsylvania,	3d do.	1793.
Jonathan Dayton,	New Jersey,	4th do.	1795.

Second Administration;—1797 to 1801;—4 years.

John Adams,	Massachusetts,	March 4, 1797.	President.
Thomas Jefferson,	Virginia,	1797.	Vice President.
		Appointed.	
Timothy Pickering,	Pennsylvania, (*continued in office.*)		Secretaries of State.
John Marshall,	Virginia,	May 13, 1800.	
Oliver Wolcott,	Connecticut, (*continued in office.*)		Secretaries of the Treasury.
Samuel Dexter,	Massachusetts,	Dec. 31, 1800.	
James M'Henry,	Maryland, (*continued in office.*)		Secretaries of War.
Samuel Dexter,	Massachusetts,	May 13, 1800.	
Roger Griswold,	Connecticut,	Feb. 3, 1801.	
George Cabot,*	Massachusetts,	May 3, 1798.	Secretaries of the Navy.
Benjamin Stoddart,	Maryland,	May 21, 1798.	
Joseph Habersham,	Georgia, (*continued in office.*)		Post Master Gen.
Charles Lee,	Virginia, (*continued in office.*)		Attorney General.

Speakers of the House of Representatives.

Jonathan Dayton,	New Jersey,	5th Congress.	1797.
Theodore Sedgwick,	Massachusetts,	6th Do.	1799.

Third Administration;—1801 to 1809;—8 years.

Thomas Jefferson,	Virginia,	March 4, 1801.	President.
Aaron Burr,	New-York,	do. 1801.	Vice Presidents.
George Clinton,	New-York,	do. 1805.	
		Appointed.	
James Madison,	Virginia,	March 5, 1801.	Secretary, of State.
Samuel Dexter,	Mass. (*continued in office.*)		Secretaries of the Treasury.
Albert Gallatin,	Pennsylvania,	Jan. 26, 1802.	
Henry Dearborn,	Massachusetts,	March 5, 1801.	Secretary of War.

* *Mr. Cabot* declined the appointment. The *Navy Department* was established in 1798.

Benjamin Stoddert,	Md. (*continued in office*)		Secretaries of the Navy.
Robert Smith,*	Maryland,	Jan. 26, 1802.	
Joseph Habersham,	Georgia, (*continued in office.*)		Post Masters General.
Gideon Granger,	Connecticut,	Jan. 26, 1802.	
Levi Lincoln,	Massachusetts,	March 5, 1801.	Attorneys General.
John Breckenridge,	Kentucky,	Dec. 23, 1805.	
Cæsar A. Rodney,	Delaware,	Jan. 20, 1807.	

Speakers of the House of Representatives.

Nathaniel Macon,	North Carolina,	7th	Congress.	1801.
Joseph B. Varnum,	Massachusetts,	8th	do.	1803.
Nathaniel Macon,	North Carolina,	9th	do.	1805.
Joseph B. Varnum.	Massachusetts,	10th	do.	1807.

FOURTH ADMINISTRATION ;—1809 to 1817 ;—8 years.

JAMES MADISON,	Virginia,	March 4, 1809.	President.
George Clinton,	New-York, 1809, (*died April*	20, 1812.	Vice Presidents.
Elbridge Gerry,	Mass., 1813, (*died Nov.*	23, 1814.	

Appointed.

Robert Smith,	Maryland,	March 6, 1809.	Secretaries of State.
James Monroe,	Virginia,	Nov. 25, 1811.	
James Monroe,†	Virginia,	Feb. 25, 1815.	
Albert Gallatin,	Pennsylvania (*continued in office.*)		Secretaries of the Treasury.
George W. Campbell,	Tennessee,	Feb. 9, 1814.	
Alexander J. Dallas,	Pennsylvania,	Oct. 6, 1814.	
William Eustis,	Massachusetts,	March, 7, 1809.	Secretaries of War.
John Armstrong,	New-York,	Jan. 13, 1813.	
James Monroe,	Virginia,	Sept. 27, 1814.	
William H. Crawford,	Georgia,	March 2, 1815.	
Paul Hamilton,	South Caroiina,	March 7, 1809.	Secretaries of the Navy.
William Jones,	Pennsylvania	Jan. 12, 1813.	
Benj. W. Crowninshield,	Massachusetts,	Dec. 19, 1814.	
Gideon Granger,	Connecticut, (*continued in office.*)		Post Masters General.
Return J. Meigs,	Ohio,	March 17, 1814.	
Cæsar A. Rodney,	Delaware, (*continued in office.*		Attorneys General.
William Pinkney,	Maryland,	Dec. 11, 1811.	
Richard Rush,	Pennsylvania,	Feb. 10, 1814.	

Speakers of the House of Representatives.

Joseph B. Varnum,	Massachusetts,	11th	Congress,	1809.
Henry Clay,	Kentucky,	12th	do.	1811.
Henry Clay,	Kentucky,	13th	do.	1812.
Langdon, Cheves,	South Carolina,			1814.
Henry Clay,	Kentucky,	14th	do.	1815.

FIFTH ADMINISTRATION ;—1817 to 1825 ,—8 years.

JAMES MONROE,	Virginia,	March 4, 1817.	President.
Daniel D. Tompkins,	New-York,	do. 1817.	Vice President.

Appointed.

John Q. Adams,	Massachusetts,	March 5, 1817.	Secretary of State.
William H. Crawford,	Georgia,	March 5, 1817.	Secretary of Treas.
Isaac Shelby‡	Kentucky,	March 5, 1817.	Secretaries of War.
John C. Calhoun,	South Carolina,	Dec. 16, 1817.	
Benj. W. Crowninshield,	Massachusetts, (*continued in office.*)		Secretaries of the Navy.
Smith Thompson,	New-York,	Nov. 30, 1818.	
Samuel L. Southard,	New-Jersey,	Dec. 9, 1823.	
Return J. Meigs.	Ohio, (*continued in office.*)		Post Masters General.
John McLean,	do.	Dec. 9, 1823.	
Richard Rush,	Pennsylvania, (*continued in office.*)		Attorneys General.
William Wirt,	Virginia,	Dec. 16, 1817.	

* *Robert Smith* was appointed Attorney General, and *Jacob Crowninshield* of Massachusetts, Secretary of the Navy, on the 2d of March, 1805, but they both declined these appointments; and *Mr. Smith* continued in the office of Secretary of the Navy, till the end of Mr. Jefferson's administration.

† James Monroe was recommissioned, having for some time acted as Secretary of War.

‡ Isaac Shelby declined the appointment.

Speakers of the House of Representatives.

Henry Clay,	Kentucky,	15th	Congress,	1817.
Henry Clay,	Kentucky,	16th	do.	1819.
John W. Taylor,	New-York,			1820.
Philip P. Barbour,	Virginia,	17th	do.	1821.
Henry Clay,	Kentucky,	18th	do.	1823.

SIXTH ADMINISTRATION;—1825 to 1829;—4 years.

JOHN Q. ADAMS,	Massachusetts,	March 4, 1825.	President.
John C. Calhoun,	South Carolina	do. 1825.	Vice President.

Appointed.

Henry Clay,	Kentucky,	March 8, 1825,	Secretary of State.
Richard Rush,	Pennsylvania,	March 7, 1825,	Secr'y of the Treas.
James Barbour,	Virginia,	do. 1825,	Secretaries of War.
Peter B. Porter,	New-York,	May 26, 1828,	
Samuel L. Southard,	New Jersey, (*continued in office.*)		Secr'y of the Navy.
John McLean,	Ohio, *continued in office,*)		Post Master Gen.
William Wirt,	Virginia, (*continued in office.*)		Attorney General.

Speakers of the House of Representatives..

John W. Taylor,	New-York,	19th	Congress,	1827.
Andrew Stephenson,	Virginia,	20th	do.	1828.

SEVENTH ADMINISTRATION;—1829.—

ANDREW JACKSON,	Tennessee,	March 4, 1829.	President.
John C. Calhoun,	South Carolina,	do. 1829.	Vice President.

Appointed.

Martin Van Buren,	New-York,	March 6, 1829.	Secretaries of State.
Edward Livingston,	Louisiana,	1831.	
Samuel D. Ingham,	Pennsylvania,	March 6, 1829.	Secretaries, of the Treasury.
Louis McLane,	Delaware,	1831.	
John H. Eaton,	Tennessee,	March 9, 1829.	Secretaries of War.
Lewis Cass,	Ohio,	1831.	
John Branch,	North Carolina,	March 9. 1829.	Secretaries of the Navy.
Levi Woodbury,	New Hampshire,	1831.	
William T. Barry,	Kentucky,	March 9, 1829.	Post Masters Gen-
John McP. Berrien,	Georgia,	March, 9, 1829.	Attorneys General.

Speakers of the House of Representatives.

Andrew Stevenson,	Virginia,	21st Congress.	1829.
Andrew Stevenson,	Virginia.	22d Congress.	1831.

Note. The dates of the appointments of the principal executive officers, in the several administrations, above exhibited, are the times when the several nominations, made by the Presidents, were confirmed by the Senate, as stated in the "Journal of the Executive Proceedings of the Senate of the United States."

DEPARTMENT OF STATE.

The Department of State was created by an act of Congress of the 15th of September, 1789: by a previous act of the 27th of July, 1789, it was denominated the Department of Foreign Affairs; and it embraces what in some other governments are styled the Department of Foreign Affairs and the Home Department.

The Secretary of State conducts the making of all treaties between the United States and Foreign Powers, and corresponds, officially, with the Public Ministers of the United States at Foreign Courts, and with the Ministers of Foreign Powers resident in the United States. He is intrusted with the publication and distribution of all the acts and resolutions of Congress, and of all treaties with Foreign Powers and Indian Tribes; preserves the originals of all laws and treaties, and of the public correspondence growing out of the intercourse between the United States and Foreign Nations; is required to procure and preserve copies of the statutes of the several states; grants passports to American citizens visiting foreign countries; preserves the evidence of copy rights, and has control of the office which issues patents for useful inventions. He has the charge of the Seal of the United States, but cannot affix it to any commission until signed by the President, nor to any instrument or act without the special authority of the President.

TREASURY DEPARTMENT.

The Treasury Department was created by an act of Congress of the 2d of September, 1789. The Secretary of the Treasury superintends all the fiscal concerns of the government, and, upon his own responsibility, recommends to Congress measures for improving the condition of the revenue.

All the accounts of the government are finally settled at the Treasury Department; and for this purpose it is divided into the office of the Secretary (who has a general superintendence of the whole,) the offices of two Comptrollers, five Auditors, a Treasurer, a Register, and a Solicitor. The Auditors of the public accounts are empowered to administer oaths or affirmations to witnesses in any case in which they may deem it necessary for the due examination of the accounts with which they are charged.

WAR DEPARTMENT.

The war department was created by an act of Congress of the 7th of August, 1789, and at first embraced not only military, but also naval affairs.

The Secretary of War superintends every branch of military affairs, and has, under his immediate direction, a Requisition Bureau, a Bounty-Land Office, a Pension Bureau, a Bureau of Indian affairs, an Engineer Office, an Ordnance Office, an Office for the Commissary General of Subsistence, a Paymaster-General's office, and a Surgeon-General's Office.

This department has the superintendence of the erection of fortifications, of making topographical surveys, of surveying and leasing the national lead mines, and of the intercourse with Indian tribes.

NAVY DEPARTMENT.

The Office of the Secretary of the Navy was created by the act of Congress of the 30th of April, 1798. The Secretary issues all orders to the Navy of the United States, and superintends the concerns of the Navy establishment generally.

GENERAL POST-OFFICE.

The Post-Master General has the sole appointment of all the Post-Masters throughout the United States, the making of all contracts for carrying the mails, and the direction of every thing relating to the Department.

The revenue arising from the General Post-Office has been principally expended upon the extension and improvement of the establishment, by which means the regular conveyance, by mail, of letters, newspapers, pamphlets, &c. has been extended to the inhabitants of every part of the Union, even to the remotest territorial settlements.

Post-Offices	in	1790,	75;	Extent of	Post-Roads	in	miles		1,875
Do.	do.	1800,	903;	Do.	do.	do.	do.		20,817
Do.	do.	1810,	2,300;	Do.	do.	do.	do.		36,406
Do.	do.	1820,	4,500;	Do.	do.	do.	do.		72,492
Do.	do.	1830,	8,450;	Do.	do.	do.	do.		115,176

[The information respecting the duties of the executive officers has been chiefly derived from the "National Calendar."]—*American Almanac.*

---

2. LEGISLATURE, OR CONGRESS.

The Congress of the United States consists of a Senate and House of Representatives, and must assemble, at least, once every year, on the first Monday of December, unless it is otherwise provided by law.

The Senate is composed of two members from each State; and of course the present regular number is 48. They are chosen by the Legislatures of the several states, for the term of six years, one third of them being elected biennially.

The Vice-President of the United States is the President of the Senate, in which body he has only a casting vote, which is given in case of an equal division of the votes of the senators. In his absence, a President *pro tempore* is chosen by the Senate.

The House of Representatives is composed of members from the several states, elected by the people for the term of two years. The representatives are apportioned among the different states according to population; and in accordance with an act of Congress of the 3d of March, 1823, one representative is now returned for every 40,000 persons, computed according to the Constitution. The present number is 216, including 3 delegates.

Since the 4th of March, 1807, the compensation of each member of the Senate and House of Representatives, has been $8 a day, during the period of his attendance in Congress, without deduction in cases of sickness, and $8 for every twenty miles' travel, in the usual road, in going to and returning from the seat of government. The compensation of the President of the Senate pro tempore, and the Speaker of the House of Representatives, is $16 a day.

3. THE JUDICIARY.

The Chief Justices and Associate Justices of the Supreme Court of the United States since 1789, with the dates of their appointment, as stated in the "Journals of the Executive Proceedings of the Senate."

CHIEF JUSTICES.

John Jay,	N. Y.	Sept. 26, 1789	Oliver Elsworth,	Mass.	March 4, 1796
John Rutledge,*	S. C.	July 1, 1795	John Jay,†	N. Y.	Dec. 19, 1800
William Cushing,	Mass.	Jan. 27, 1796	John Marshall,	Va.	Jan. 27, 1801

ASSOCIATE JUSTICES.

John Rutledge,	S. C.	Sept. 26, 1789	Brockh. Livingston,	N. Y.	Dec. 17, 1806
William Cushing,	Mass.	do do do	Thomas Todd,	Va.	March 2, 1807
R. H. Harrison,	Md.	do do do	Levi Lincoln,†	Mass.	Jan. 3, 1811
James Wilson,	Pa.	do do do	John Q. Adams,†	do	Feb. 22, 1811
John Blair,	Va.	do do do	Gabriel Duval,	Md.	Nov. 18, 1811
James Iredell,	N. C.	Feb. 10, 1790	Joseph Story,	Mass.	do do
Thomas Johnson,	Md.	Nov. 7, 1791	Smith Thompson,	N. Y.	Dec. 9, 1823
William Patterson,	N. J.	March 4, 1793	Robert Trimble,	Ken.	May 9, 1826
Samuel Chase,	Md.	Jan. 27, 1796	John McLean,	Ohio.	March 7, 1829
Bush. Washington,	Va.	Dec. 20, 1798	Henry Baldwin,	Pa.	Jan. 6, 1830
William Johnson,	S. C.	March 24, 1804			

The judicial power of the United States is vested in one Supreme Court and in such inferior courts as Congress may, from time to time, establish. The present judicial establishment of the United States, consists of a Supreme Court, thirty-one District Courts, and 7 Circuit Courts, which are thus organized: the Supreme Court is composed of one Chief Justice, and six Associate Justices, who hold a court in the city of Washington, annually; besides which, each of these Justices attends in a certain circuit, comprising two or more districts appropriated to each, and, together with the judge of the district, composes a Circuit Court, which is held in each district of the circuit.

4. FOREIGN INTERCOURSE.

Ministers Plenipotentiary receive an annual salary of $9,000, besides 9,000 for an outfit. A Chargé d'Affairs receives a salary of $4,500, and a Secretary of Legation one of $2,000. These several officers are appointed by the President, by and with the advice and consent of the Senate.

5. THE ARMY AND NAVY.

The standing army of the Union in time of peace, is generally few in number. At present it consists of about 6,500 men, who are principally located in forts and on the frontiers. The militia of the several states, however, amounted by the returns of 1830, to 1,262,315 men. At West Point, in the state of New-York, is a National Military Academy, established in 1802, where are constantly about 240 young men, who are educated for the army and for engineers. The navy consists of seven ships of the line, ten frigates, fifteen sloops of war, and eight schooners; besides five ships of the line, and seven frigates, now building.

6. FINANCES IN 1831.

RECEIPTS.		EXPENDITURES.	
Balance on hand from 1830,	$6,014,539. 75	Civil list, Foreign Intercourse, &c.	$3,064,646. 10
Customs,	24,224,441. 77	Military Service, &c.	6,943,238. 25
Lands,	3,210,815. 00	Naval Service,	3,856,183. 07
Dividends in Bank Stock,	490,000. 00	Public Debt,	16,174,378. 22
First and second instalments under convention with Denmark,	449,249. 53	Balance to 1832,	4,502,914. 45
Incidental,	152,314. 04		
	$34,541,360. 09		$34,541,360. 09

Total, expenses of government, foreign intercourse, army and navy, in 1831, $13,864,067 42.

7. MINT.

The mint of the United States, for the purpose of a national coinage, was established by the act of 2d April, 1792, in the city of Philadelphia, where it has since been continued.

The coinage effected within the year 1831, amounts to $3,923,473 60, comprising $714,270 in gold coins, $3,175,600 in silver, and $33,603 60 in copper, and consisting of 11,792,284 pieces of coin. Of the amount of gold coined within 1831, about 130,000 dollars were derived from Mexico, South America, and the West Indies, $27,000 from Africa, $518,000 from the gold regions of the United States, and about $39,000 from sources not ascertained.—"*The National Calendar.*"

*Appointed by the President, July 1, 1795; nominated to the Senate Dec. 10, 1795; but not confirmed. †Declined the appointment.

COMMERCE OF THE UNITED STATES, 1831.

From Williams' Gazetteer.

Commerce of the United States, exhibiting the value of every description of Imports from and Exports to, each Foreign Country, during the year ending 30th September, 1831.

COUNTRIES.	Value of imports	Value of Exports. Domestic produce.	Foreign produce.	Total.
Russia	$ 1,608,328	$ 114,852	$ 347,914	$ 462,766
Prussia	50,970	27,043		27,043
Sweden and Norway	901,812	190,511	86,519	277,030
Swedish West Indies	218,918	251,937	11,111	263,048
Denmark.	575	178,333	176,883	355,216
Danish West Indies	1,651,641	1,421,075	224,502	1,645,577
Netherlands	989,837	1,707,292	212,860	1,920,152
Dutch West Indies,	343,799	370,857	45,274	416,131
Dutch East Indies	319,395	128,884	631,442	760,326
England	41,854,323	28,841,430	2,367,439	31,208,869
Scotland	1,977,830	1,185,142	5,567	1,190,709
Ireland	261,564	589,941		589,941
Gibraltar	150,517	429,087	165,786	594,873
British African Ports		6,064		6,064
British East Indies	1,544,273	132,442	675,390	807,832
British West Indies	1,303,301	1,417,291	23,962	1,441,253
Newfoundland, &c.				
British American Colonies	864,909	4,026,392	35,446	4,061,838
Other British Colonies				
Hanse towns	3,493,301	1,812,241	779,931	2,592,172
France on the Atlantic	12,876,977	4,963,557	3,228,452	8,192,009
France on the Mediterranean	1,188,766	671,867	300,926	972,793
French West Indies	671,842	704,833	13,044	717,877
Spain on the Atlantic	566,072	235,584	63,428	299,012
Spain on the Mediterranean	709,022	75,121	7,198	82,319
Teneriffe and the other Canaries	125,159	34,931	3,446	38,377
Manilla and Philippine Islands	348,995	15,994	16,830	32,824
Cuba	8,371,797	3,634,144	1,259,698	4,893,842
Other Spanish West Indies	1,580,156	261,801	53,245	315,046
Portugal	124,446	39,149	2,356	41,505
Madeira	177,369	171,563	5,728	177,291
Fayal and the other Azores	32,092	10,549	6,049	16,598
Cape de Verd Islands	63,643	45,432	13,557	58,989
Italy	1,704,264	371,515	323,010	694,525
Sicily	144,047	2,369		2,369
Trieste, &c.	161,062	276,561	262,808	539,369
Turkey	521,598	38,503	298,304	336,807
Hayti	1,580,578	1,126,698	191,677	1,318,375
Mexico	5,166,745	1,091,489	5,086,729	6,178,218
Central Republic of America	198,504	141,179	165,318	306,497
Colombia	1,207,154	375,319	282,830	658,149
Honduras	44,463	46,233	13,732	59,965
Brazil	2,375,829	1,652,193	423,902	2,076,095
Argentine Republic	928,103	415,489	244,290	659,779
Cisplatine Republic				
Peru	917,788	8,560	7,616	16,176
Chili	413,758	849,493	518,662	1,368,155
South America, generally	4,924	19,922	15,731	35,653
Cape of Good Hope				
China	3,083,205	244,790	1,046,045	1,290,835
Asia, generally	77,861	48,268	251,126	299,394
East Indies, generally	10,691	628,153	7,474	635,627
West Indies, generally		25,702	15	25,717
Europe, generally	148,932	175,166	69,891	245,057
Africa, generally	51,186	16,910	8,963	25,873
South Seas	67,635	27,206	51,420	78,626
Northwest Coast of America	11,168			
Uncertain				
Total	103,191,124	61,277,057	20,033,526	81,310,583

9. NAVIGATION OF THE UNITED STATES, 1831.

A Table,—showing the Tunnage of American and Foreign Vessels arriving from, and departing to, each Foreign Country, during the year ending 30th September, 1831.

COUNTRIES.	American tunnage.		Foreign tunnage.	
	Entered into U. S.	Departed from U. S.	Entered into U. S.	Departed from U. S.
Russia	$ 8,931	4,310	577	
Prussia	700	387		
Sweden and Norway	11,346	3,232	2,999	472
Swedish West Indies	4,793	7,199	262	552
Denmark		3,060		
Danish West Indies	27,501	41,730	2,827	2,708
Netherlands	24,076	23,168	349	1,994
Dutch West Indies	11,296	11,430	312	194
Dutch East Indies	2,533	6,498		
England	223,345	235,345	84,324	83,461
Scotland	5,674	6,312	11,008	9,102
Ireland	4,388	7,838	7,020	2,306
Gibraltar	3,599	11,703		256
British African ports		121		
British East Indies	5,342	6,481		
British West Indies	38,046	40,922	23,760	17,903
Newfoundland, &c	275	277	736	
British American Colonies	92,672	79,364	82,557	94,776
Other British Colonies	248	434		
Hanse towns	15,934	17,147	12,175	17,487
France on the Atlantic	40,849	48,022	8,666	3,722
France on the Mediterranean	13,774	15,459	493	1,477
French West Indies	26,704	35,334	2,793	2,254
Spain on the Atlantic	6,760	4,598		1,068
Spain on the Mediterranean	9,583	1,905		536
Teneriffe and the other Canaries	1,963	1,418		
Manilla and Philippine Islands	2,938	249		
Cuba	132,830	132,222	19,639	17,816
Other Spanish West Indies	24,060	8,272	3,117	1,051
Portugal	5,043	1,598	1,451	
Madeira	2,514	5,163		131
Fayal and the other Azores	660	475	397	251
Cape de Verd Islands	875	1,200		236
Italy	10,683	9,120	159	
Sicily	2,080	378		
Trieste, &c.	1,920	4,215		
Turkey	3,918	2,935		
Hayti	26,446	27,807	699	1,006
Mexico	22,377	22,303	11,498	10,019
Central Republic of America	2,821	3,315		
Colombia	9,174	7,188	56	
Honduras	1,456	1,449	600	223
Brazil	29,805	36,892	1,360	203
Argentine Republic	9,652	8,169		
Cisplatine Republic	274	356		
Peru	2,577	523		
Chili	3,729	11,145		
South America, generally	703	1,013	94	242
Cape of Good Hope	929	891		
China	4,316	5,061		
Asia, generally	1,171	2,447		
East Indies, generally		669		
West Indies, generally	2,903	17,839		400
Europe, generally	4,169	560	2,090	
Africa, generally	2,511	5,098		148
South Seas	29,581	39,470		
Northwest Coast of America	375	783		
Uncertain	80			
Total	922,952	972,504	281,948	271,994

10. NUMBER OF VESSELS, SEAMEN, AND TUNNAGE OF THE U. STATES.

Statement of the number of vessels, with the amount of tunnage and the number of seamen employed in navigating the same, (including their repeated voyages,) which entered into, and departed from each state and territory, in the year ending on the 30th Sept., 1830.

STATES AND TERRITORIES.	Number of Vessels.	Amount of Tunnage.		Number of Seamen employed.
		Entered.	Departed.	
Maine,	535	69,363	91,629	2,949
New-Hampshire,	38	9,416	4,632	284
Vermont,	121	29,741	19,290	871
Massachusetts,	912	168,243	148,124	9,118
Rhode Island,	87	16,676	14,094	836
Connecticut,	93	16,171	18,285	1,103
New-York,	1,382	298,434	229,341	14,298
New-Jersey,	3	586	627	23
Pennsylvania,	365	72,009	63,022	3,907
Delaware,	9	1,691	962	81
Maryland,	90	55,317	55,020	908
District of Columbia,	54	10,458	13,803	448
Virginia,	93	25,997	43,715	843
North-Carolina,	235	27,757	36,592	1,482
South-Carolina,	115	50,859	52,464	927
Georgia,	79	19,249	50,394	772
Alabama,	66	10,490	22,277	484
Louisiana,	451	83,270	106,017	4,323
Florida,	15	1,444	1,366	93
Ohio,	1	56	56	3
Michigan	1		50	3
	4,745	967,227	971,760	43,756

11. COMMERCE OF EACH STATE AND TERRITORY IN THE U. STATES.

Statement of the Commerce of each state and territory, commencing on the first day of October, 1830, and ending on the 30th day of September, 1831.

STATES AND TERRITORIES.	Value of Imports.	Value of Exports.			Tunnage Entered.
		Domestic Produce.	Foreign Produce.	Total.	
Maine,	941,407	799,748	5,825	805,573	101 454
New-Hampshire,	146.205	109,456	1,766	111,222	7,198
Vermont,	166,206	925,127	. .	925,127	20,201
Massachusetts,	14,269,056	4,027,201	3,706,562	7,733,763	192,219
Rhode-Island,	562,161	348,250	19,215	367,465	23,945
Connecticut,	405,066	482,073	810	482,883	17,750
New-York,	57,077,417	15,726,118	9,809,026	25,535,144	393,691
New-Jersey,	. .	11,430	. .	11,430	369
Pennsylvania,	12,124,083	3,594,302	1,919,411	5,513,713	80,058
Delaware,	21,656	34,514	. .	34,514	3,736
Maryland,	4,826,577	3,730,506	578,141	4,308,647	65,826
District of Columbia	193,555	1,207,517	13,458	1,220,975	5,668
Virginia,	488,522	4,149,986	489	4,150,475	32,918
North-Carolina,	196,356	340,973	167	341,140	18,502
South-Carolina,	1,238,163	6,528,605	46,596	6,575,201	53,390
Georgia,	399,940	3,957,245	2,568	3,959,813	29,034
Alabama,	224,435	2,412,862	1,032	2,413,894	29,166
Mississippi,	. .	. .	. .	. .	. .
Louisiana,	9,766,693	12,835,531	3,926,458	16,761,989	131,772
Ohio,	617	14,728	. .	14,728	229
Florida Territory,	115,710	28,493	2,002	30,495	4,931
Michigan Territory	27,299	12,392		12,392	43
Total.	103,191,124	61,277,057	20,033,526	81,310,583	1,204,900

12. PRODUCTS OF THE UNITED STATES, EXPORTED IN 1831.

Summary Statement of the value of the exports of the growth, produce, and manufacture of the United States, during the year commencing on the first of October, 1830, and ending on the 30th day of September, 1831.

THE SEA.	*Dollars.*
Fisheries—	
Dried fish, or cod fisheries	625,393
Pickled fish, or river fisheries, herring, shad, salmon, mackerel	304,441
Whale and other fish oil	554,440
Spermaceti oil	53,526
Whalebone	133,842
Spermaceti candles,	217,830
	1,889,472
THE FOREST.	
Skins and furs	750,938
Ginseng	115,928
Product of wood—	
Staves, shingles, boards, and hewn timber	1,467,065
Other lumber	214,105
Masts and spars	7,806
Oak bark and other dies	99,116
All manufactories of wood	275,219
Naval stores, tar, pitch, rosin, and turpentine	397,687
Ashes, pot and Pearl	935,613
	4,263,477
AGRICULTURE.	
Product of animals—	
Beef, tallow, hides, and horned cattle	829,982
Butter and Cheese	264,796
Pork, (pickled,) bacon, lard, live hogs	1,501,644
Horses and mules	218,015
Sheep	14,499
Vegetable food—	
Wheat	523,270
Flour	9,938,458
Indian corn	396,617
Indian meal	595,434
Rye meal	71,881
Rye, oats, and other small grain and pulse	132,717
Biscuit or ship bread	250,533
Potatoes	41,147
Apples	31,148
Rice	2,016,267
All other agricultural products—	
Tobacco	4,892,388
Cotton	25,289,492
Indigo	
Flaxseed	216,376
Hops	26,664
Brown sugar	10,105
	47,261,423
MANUFACTURES.	
Soap and tallow candles	643,252
Leather, boots and shoes	290,937
Household furniture	229,231
Coaches and other carriages	49,490
Hats	353,013
Saddlery	39,440
Wax	114,017
Spirits from grain, beer, ale and porter	141,794
Snuff and tobacco	292,475
Lead	7,068
Linseed oil and spirits of turpentine	54,092
Cordage	6,109
Iron, pig, bar, and nails	62,376
—— castings	21,827
—— all manufactures of	149,438
Spirits from molasses	34,569
Sugar refined	215,794
Chocolate	1,965
Gunpowder	102,033
Copper and brass	55,755
Medicinal drugs	104,760
Wearing apparel	59,749
Combs and buttons	120,217
Brushes	3,947
Billiard tables and apparatus	2,343
Umbrellas and parasols	29,580
Leather and morrocco skins not sold per pound	58,146
Printing presses and type	8,713
Musical instruments	10,906
Books and maps	35,609
Paper and other stationary	55,121
Paints and varnish	22,022
Vinegar	7,178
Earthen and stone ware	7,378
Fire engines and apparatus	5,630
Manufactures of glass	102,736
Manufactures of tin	3,909
Manufactures of pewter and lead	6,422
Manufactures of marble and stone	3,588
Manufactures of gold and silver, and gold leaf	3,464
Gold and silver coin,	2,058,474
Artificial flowers and jewelry	11,439
Molasses	948
Trunks	5,326
Brick and lime	4,412
Salt	26,848
Cotton piece goods—	
Printed or coloured	96,931
White	947,932
Nankeens	2,397
Twist, yarn, and thread	17,221
All other manufactures of	61,832
Flax and Hemp—	
Cloth and thread	231
Bags and manufactures of	2,589
	7,878,996
Articles not enumerated—	
Manufactured	394,681
Other articles	715,311
	1,109,992
Total	61,277,057

13. ARTICLES IMPORTED INTO THE UNITED STATES IN 1831.

Summary Statement of the value of goods, wares, and merchandise, imported into the United States in American and Foreign Vessels, during the year ending the 30th Sept., 1831.

VALUE OF MERCHANDISE FREE OF DUTY.	*Dollars.*
Articles imported for the use of the United States.	292
Articles especially imported for incorporated philosophical societies.	
Philosophical apparatus and instruments	10,917
Books, maps, and charts	15,733
Statuary, busts, casts, and specimens of sculpture	721
Paintings, drawings, etchings, and engravings	2,478
Medals, and collections of Antiquity	5
Specimens of botany	6,458
Models of invention and machinery	11
Anatomical preparations	1,839
Antimony, regulus of	20,487
Lapis calaminaris, teutenegue, spelter or zinc	29,723
Burr-stones, unwrought	40,744
Brimstone and sulphur	36,634
Cork tree, bark of,	1,264
Clay, unwrought	10,711
Rags of any kind of cloth	276,617
Furs of all kinds	417,038
Hides and skins, raw	3,057,543
Plaster of Paris	119,444
Barilla	43,560
Wood—die	308,957
—— unmanufactured mahogany	332,111
Animals for breed	18,563
Pewter, old	1,543
Tin in pigs and bars	134,380
Brass old	2,429
Copper in pigs and bars	530,682
—— in plates suited to the sheathing of ships	560,609
——for the use of the mint	14,735
——old, fit only to be manufactured	119,281
Bullion—gold	166,191
——silver	686,283
Specie—gold	765,838
——silver	5,687,633
All other articles	35,171
Total	13,456,625

VALUE OF MERCHANDISE SUBJECT TO DUTIES AD VALOREM.	*Dollars.*
Manufactures of—	
Wool—or of which wool is a component material—not exceeding 50 cents per square yard	1,317,645
——Exceeding 50 cts. and not exceeding 100 cts. per yard	2,405,770
——Exceeding 100 cts. and not exceeding 250 cts. per yard	2,303,511
——Exceeding 250 cts. and not exceeding 400 cts. per yard	85,998
——Exceeding 400 cts. per yard	8,518
——Blankets	1,180,478
——Hosiery, gloves, mits, and bindings	325,856
——Bombasins	461,898
——Worsted stuff goods	3,392,037
——All other manufactures of	490,651
Cotton—printed or coloured	10,046,500
——White	4,285,175
——Hosiery, gloves, mits, and bindings	887,957
——Twist, yarn, and thread	393,414
Cotton—Nankeens	114,076
——All other manufactures of	363,102
Silks from India—piece goods	1,803,239
——sewing silk, hosiery, and other manufactures	53,766
Silks, from other places—piece goods	6,155,739
——sewing silk, hosiery, and other manufactures	2,891,649
Lace—Thread, silk, or cotton	1,369,465
——Coach	5,068
Flax,—Linens, bleached, and unbleached	3,145,797
——checks and stripes	18,159
——Other manufactures of	626,155
Hemp—Ticklenburgs, osnaburgs, and burlaps	514,645
Hemp,—Sheeting, brown	275,059
——white	76,440
——All other manufactures of	122,009
Clothing, ready made	108,242
Hats, caps, and bonnets—Leghorn, straw, chip, &c.	255,893
——Fur, wool, leather, or silk	70,156
Iron, and iron and steel—Side arms and fire arms, other than muskets and rifles	214,194
——Drawing knives, axes, adzes, and socket chisels	30,183
——Bridle bits of every description	80,637
——Steelyards, scale beams, and vices	67,609
——Cutting knives, sickles, scythes, reaping hooks, &c.	118,743
——Wood screws	112,545
——Other articles not specified	3,735,010
Copper, vessels of	8,170
——All other manufactures of	42,117
Gold and silver—Lace	4,043
——Watches, and parts thereof	445,977
——Articles composed of pearls	85,582
Glass ware not subject to specific duties	235,909
China or porcelain ware	108,169
Earthern and stone ware	1,516,435
Japanned ware	71,658
Plated ware	189,419
Gilt ware	105,429
Brass	630,687
Tin	20,472
Pewter and lead, except shot	34,843
Wood, including cabinet wares	147,750

ARTICLES IMPORTED INTO THE UNITED STATES IN 1831. Continued.

VALUE OF MERCHANDISE SUBJECT TO DUTIES AD VALOREM.	Dollars.
Leather, including saddles, bridles, and harness	811,251
Plated saddlery, coach and harness furniture	94,512
Marble, and manufactures of	7,747
Square wire used for umbrella stretchers	29,050
Cyphering slates	14,024
Prepared quills	19,087
Black lead pencils	5,129
Paper hangings	88,467
Brushes of all kinds	16,741
Hair seating	36,748
Bolting cloths	52,203
Copper bottoms, cut round, raised to the edge	20,609
Quicksilver	411,079
Brass in plates	17,153
Tin in plates	588,417
Crude salt petre	282,115
Lead ore	
Opium	176,736
Unmanufactured raw silk	88,557
Articles not specially enumerated, subject to duty from 12½ to 50 per ct.	5,215,693
Total	61,534,966

VALUE OF MERCHANDISE PAYING SPECIFIC DUTIES.	Dollars.
Manufactures of wool	$ 695,660
Carpeting—Brussels, Turkey, and Wilton	170,718
——Venetian and Ingrain	249,980
——All other of wool, flax, hemp or cotton	401
Patent printed or stained floor cloths	18,962
Oil cloth, other than patent floor cloth	2,800
Furniture oil cloth	3,015
Floor matting, of flags or other materials	4,225
Sail duck	470 030
Cotton bagging	18,966
Wines—Madeira	202,027
——Sherry	91,030
——Red, of France and Spain	227,927
——of France, Spain and Germany not enumerated	609,591
——of Sicily and other countries, not enumerated	542,483
Foreign spirits, from grain	242,137
——other materials	795,600
Molasses	2,432,488
Beer, ale and porter	57,271
Vinegar	6,692
Oils	200,408
Teas	1,418,037
Coffee	6,317,666
Cocoa	152,134
Chocolate	2,444

VALUE OF MERCHANDISE PAYING SPECIFIC DUTIES.	Dollars.
Sugar—Brown	4,220,993
——White clayed, &c.	689,884
——Candy and loaf	20,899
——Other refined	48
Fruits	554,307
Spices	279,095
Candles—Spermaceti or wax	117
——Tallow	1,559
Cheese	7,277
Soap	9,640
Tallow	10,266
Lard	451
Beef and Pork	6,690
Bacon	2,506
Butter	104
Saltpetre	22
Camphor	13,705
Salts	6
Tobacco, manufactured, other than snuff and cigars	24
Snuff	2,265
Indigo	759,012
Cotton	33,475
Gunpowder	20,043
Bristles	74,776
Glue	9,528
Ochre, dry	18,205
——in oil	53
White and red lead	6,762
Whiting and Paris white	630
Litharge	10
Orange mineral	26
Sugar of lead	16,779
Lead—bar, sheet, and pig	52,120
——shot	290
Cordage, tarred, and cables	33,522
——untarred and yarn	6,344
Twine, packthread and seines	71,172
Corks	31,455
Copper rods and bolts	3,906
——nails and spikes	1,542
Fire arms—muskets	2,946
——rifles	193
Iron—iron and steel wire	67,718
——Tacks, brads, &c.	4,297
——Nails	52,597
——Spikes	3,175
——Cables and chains, or parts thereof	51,341
——Mill cranks and mill iron, of wrought iron	3
——Mill saws	16,160
——Anchors	2,287
——Anvils	64,064
——Hammers and sledges	4,249
——Castings, vessels, and all others	32,143
——Braziers' rods, or round iron	13,660
——Nail or spike rods, slit	4,585
——Sheets and hoops	151,909
——Slit or rolled, &c.	724
——Pig	160,681
——Bar and bolt, rolled and hammered	1,804,830

ARTICLES IMPORTED INTO THE UNITED STATES IN 1831. Continued.

VALUE OF MERCHANDISE PAYING SPECIFIC DUTIES.	Dollars.	VALUE OF MERCHANDISE PAYING SPECIFIC DUTIES.	Dollars.
Steel	399,635	Glass ware—Cut not specified	7,813
Hemp	295,706	—— ——All other	102,075
Flax unmanufactured	6,472	Glass—Apothecaries' vials	1,260
Wool do	1,288,909	—Bottles	81,877
Alum	13	—Demijohns	17,851
Copperas	30	—Window	59,576
Wheat flour	14	Fish	49,421
Salt	535,138	Shoes	11,954
Coal	108,250	Boots and bootees	2,868
Wheat	685	Cigars	433,457
Oats	333	Playing cards	118
Potatoes	7,818	Roofing slates	70,349
Paper	212,994		
Books	175,049	Total	28,199,533

SUMMARY.	American vessels.	Foreign vessels.	Total.
Total value of merchandise paying specific duties	25,589,520	2,610,013	28,199,533
do do do ad valorem	56,698,042	4,836,924	61,534,966
do do free of duty	11,674,548	1,781,077	13,456,625
Total	93,962,110	9,229,014	103,191,124

14. TUNNAGE OF THE UNITED STATES.

Comparative View of the Registered, Enrolled, and Licensed Tunnage of the United States, from 1815 *to* 1830, *inclusive.*

Years	Registered Tunnage.	Enrolled & Licensed.	Total Tunnage.	Years	Registered Tunnage.	Enrolled & Licensed.	Total Tunnage.
1815	854,294	513,833	1,368,127	1823	630,920	696,644	1,336,565
1816	800,759	571,458	1,372,218	1824	669,972	719,190	1,389,163
1817	809,724	590,186	1,399,911	1825	700,787	722,323	1,423,111
1818	606,088	609,095	1,225,184	1826	737,978	796,212	1,534,190
1819	612,930	647,821	1,260,751	1827	747,170	873,437	1,620,607
1820	619,047	661,118	1,280,166	1828	812,619	928,772	1,741,391
1821	619,096	679,062	1,298,956	1829	650,142	610,654	1,260,977
1822	628,150	696,548	1,324,699	1830*	576,475	615,301	1,191,776

* *Omitted*, cancelled, 89,307 tuns, sold and lost; making the *actual increase* this year 20,286 tuns.

15. COTTON WOOL IMPORTED INTO GREAT BRITAIN FROM 1821 TO 1830.

Statement of the quantity of Packages of Cotton Wool imported into Great Britain for Ten Years, from 1821 *to* 1830 *inclusive, and from what country.*

From	1821	1822	1823	1824	1825		1829	1830
America.	301,945	329,052	449,866	282,773	424,688		461,569	613,185
Brazil	122,062	144,176	148,475	142,559	198,034		139,939	192,267
W. Indies	37,471	40,548	31,197	31,837	34,614		20,808	12,648
E. Indies	30,369	19,263	38,535	50,846	60,502		80,522	35,212
Egypt			2,000	33,745	103,412	32,855	24,712	13,596
Total	491,847	533,039	670,073	541,760	821,250	749,588	747,449	871,908

A Comparative View of the amount of Imports and Exports from 1822 to 1831 inclusive.

Years.	Imports.	Exports.	Years.	Imports.	Exports.
1822	$83,241.541	$72,160,281	1827	$79,484,068	$82,324,827
1823	77,579,267	74,699,030	1828	88,509,824	72,264,686
1824	80,549,007	75,986,657	1829	74,492,527	72,358,671
1825	96,340,075	99,535,388	1830	70,876,920	73,849,508
1826	84,974,477	77,595,322	1831	103,191,124	81,310,583

16. POPULATION ACCORDING TO 5 OFFICIAL ENUMERATIONS.

States and Territories.	1st Census. Pop. 1790.	2d Census Pop. 1800.	3d Census. Pop. 1810.	4th Census. Pop. 1820.	5th Census Pop. 1830.	Per. cent. 10 years.
Maine	96,540	151,719	228,705	298,335	399,462	33,9
New Hampshire	141,885	183,858	214,460	244,161	269,533	10,4
Vermont	85,539	154,465	217,895	235,764	280,679	19,0
Massachusetts	378,787	422,845	472,040	523,287	610,014	16,6
Rhode Island	68,825	69,122	76,931	83,059	97,210	17,0
Connecticut	237,946	251,002	261,942	275,248	297,711	8,2
New-York	340,120	586,050	959,049	1,372,812	1,913,508	39,4
New-Jersey	184,139	211,149	245,562	277,575	320,779	15,6
Pennsylvania	434.373	602,545	810,091	1,049,313	1,347,672	28,4
Delaware	59,096	64,273	72,674	72,749	76,739	5,5
Maryland	319,728	345,824	380.546	407,350	446,913	9,7
Virginia	747,610	880,200	979,622	1,065,366	1,211,272	13,7
North Carolina	393,951	478,103	555,500	638,829	738,470	15,6
South Carolina	249,073	345,591	415,115	502,741	581,458	15,7
Georgia	82,548	162,686	252,433	340,989	516,567	51,5
Alabama }				127,901	308,997	141,6
Mississippi }	. . .	8,850	40,352	75,448	136,806	80,1
Louisiana	. . .	. . .	76,556	153,407	215,575	40,7
Tennessee	. . .	105,602	261,727	420,813	684,822	62,7
Kentucky	73,677	220,959	406,511	564,317	688,844	22,1
Ohio	. . .	45,365	230,760	581,434	937,679	61,2
Indiana	. . .	4,651	24,520	147,178	341,582	132,1
Illinois	. . .	215	12,282	55,211	157,575	185,4
Missouri	. . .	. . .	19,783	66,586	140,074	110,4
D. of Columbia	. . .	15,093	240,23	33,039	39,858	20,1
Michigan Ter.	. . .	551	4,762	8,896	31,260	250,1
Arkansas Ter.	. . .	. . .	1,062	14,273	30,383	113,3
Florida Territory	. . .	. . .	. . .	. . .	34,729	
Total	3,929,328	7,239,603	7,239,903	9,638,166	12,856,171	33,4

SLAVES, ACCORDING TO FIVE OFFICIAL ENUMERATIONS.

States.	Slaves 1790.	Slaves 1800.	Slaves 1810.	Slaves 1820.	Slaves 1830.
Maine	0	0	0	0	0
New Hampshire	158	8	0	0	0
Vermont	16	0	0	0	0
Massachusetts	0	0	0	0	0
Rhode Island	948	380	108	48	14
Connecticut	2,764	951	310	97	23
New-York	21,324	20,613	15,017	10,088	46
New-Jersey	11,423	12,422	10,851	7,557	2,246
Pennsylvania	3,737	1,706	795	211	386
Delaware	8,887	6,153	4,177	4,509	3,305
Maryland	103,036	108,554	111,502	107,398	102,878
Virginia	292,627	346,968	392,518	425,153	469.724
North Carolina	100,572	133,296	168,824	205,017	246,462
South Carolina	107,094	146,151	196,365	258,475	315,665
Georgia	29,264	59,699	105,218	149,656	217,470
Alabama				41,879	117,294
Mississippi	.	3,489	17,088	32,814	65,659
Louisiani			34,660	69,064	109,631
Tennessee		13,584	44,535	80,107	142,382
Kentucky	12,430	40,343	80,561	126,732	165,350
Ohio	3,417	0	0	0	0
Indiana		135	237	190	.0
Illinois			168	917	746
Missouri			3,011	10,222	24,990
District of Columbia			5,395	6,377	6,050
Michigan Territory			24	0	27
Arkansas Territory				1,617	4,578
Florida Territory					15,510
	697,697	896,849	1,191,364	1,538 061	2,010,436

Comparative view of Cities, Towns, and Villages in the United States, the population of each of which exceeds 5,000 *from the census returns of* 1820 *and* 1830.

N. B. This list is intended to comprise only compact settlements.

		1830.	1820.			1830.	1820.
New York,	N. Y.	202,589	123,706	Newport,	R. I.	8,010	7,319
Philadelphia,	Penn.	167,811	108,116	New-Brunswick,	N. J.	7,831	6,764
Baltimore,	Md.	80,625	62,738	Paterson,	N. J.	7,731	1,578
Boston,	Mass.	61,392	43,288	Lancaster,	Penn.	7,704	6,663
New-Orleans,	Lou.	46,310	27,176	New-Bedford,	Mass.	7,592	3,947
Charleston,	S. C.	30,289	24,780	Troy,	Mass.	7,590	1,594
Cincinnati,	Ohio.	24,831	9,642	Savannah,	Geo.	7,303	7,520
Albany,	N. Y.	24,209	12,630	Nantucket,	Mass.	7,202	7,266
WASHINGTON,	D. C.	18,827	13,247	Middletown,	Conn.	6,892	6,479
Providence,	R. I.	16,832	11,767	Springfield,	Mass.	6,784	3,914
Richmond,	Va.	16,060	12,046	Augusta,	Geo.	6,696	4,000
Salem,	Mass.	13,886	12,731	Wilmington,	Del.	6,628	5,268
Portland,	Me.	12,601	8,581	Lowell,	Mass.	6,474	
Pittsburg,	Penn.	12,542	7,248	Newburyport,	Mass.	6,388	6,852
Brooklyn,	N. Y.	12,403	7,175	Buffalo,	N. Y.	6,321	1,100
Troy,	N. Y.	11,556	5,261	Lynn,	Mass.	6,138	4,515
Newark,	N. J.	10,953	6,507	Lexington,	Ky.	6,104	5,267
New-Haven,	Conn.	10,678	7,147	Cambridge,	Mass.	6,071	3,295
Louisville,	Ken.	10,352	4,012	Taunton,	Mass.	6,045	4,590
Norfolk,	Va.	9,816	8,478	St. Louis,	Mo.	5,852	4,598
Hartford,	Conn.	9,789	6,901	Reading,	Penn.	5,839	4,332
Rochester,	N. Y.	9,269	1,502	Nashville,	Tenn.	5,566	3,500
Charlestown,	Mass.	8,787	6,591	Dover,	N. H.	5,449	2,871
Georgetown,	D. C.	8,441	7,360	Hudson,	N. Y.	5,392	5,310
Utica,	N. Y.	8,323	2,972	Wheeling,	Va.	5,221	1,500
Petersburg,	Va.	8,322	6,690	Norwich,	Conn.	5,169	3,634
Alexandria,	D. C.	8,263	8,218	Marblehead,	Mass.	5,150	5,630
Portsmouth,	N. H.	8,082	7,327	Poughkeepsie,	N. Y.	5,023	3,401

17. SEATS OF GOVERNMENT OF THE SEVERAL STATES, &c.

Maine,	Augusta,	3,980	South-Carolina,	Columbia,	3,310
New-Hampshire,	Concord,	3,727	Georgia,	Milledgeville,	1,599
Massachusetts,	Boston,	61,392	Alabama,	Tuscaloosa,	1,600
Vermont,	Montpelier,	1,193	Mississippi,	Jackson,	1,000
Rhode-Island,	Newport,	8,010	Tennessee,	Nashville,	5,566
	Providence,	16,832	Kentucky,	Frankfort,	1,680
Connecticut,	Hartford,	9,789	Ohio,	Columbus,	2,437
	New-Haven,	10,678	Indiana,	Indianapolis,	1,200
New-York,	Albany,	24,209	Illinois,	Vandalia,	606
New-Jersey,	Trenton,	3,925	Missouri,	Jefferson,	600
Pennsylvania,	Harrisburg,	4,311	*Territories.*		
Delaware,	Dover,	1,200	Florida,	Tallahassee,	1,500
Maryland,	Annapolis,	2,623	Michigan,	Detroit,	2,227
Virginia,	Richmond,	16,060	Arkansas,	Little Rock,	1,000
North-Carolina,	Raleigh,	1,700	District of Columbia,	WASHINGTON,	18,827

18. LENGTH OF THE PRINCIPAL RAIL ROADS IN THE UNITED STATES.

Rail Roads.	*miles*	*Rail Roads.*	*miles*
From Baltimore, to the Ohio river, at or near Wheeling, Va.	270	Hollidaysburg to Johnstown, Penn. over the Allegany mountains	37
Charleston, S. C. to Hamburgh, on the Savannah river . . .	135	Ithaca, N. Y. to Owego, on the Susquehannah river	29
Philadelphia to Pottsville, Pennsylvania, through Germantown, &c.	100	Boston to Lowell, Mass.	25
Philadelphia to Columbia, on the Susquehannah river	81	Saratoga and Schenectady, N. Y. .	22
Lexington to Louisville, Ky. . .	75	Lackawaxen; from Honesdale, to Carbondale, Pennsylvania . .	16
Camden, opposite Philadelphia, to Amboy, N. J.	60	Frenchtown, Md. to Newcastle, Del.	16
Baltimore to the Susquehannah river	48	Albany to Schenectady, N. Y. .	14
Boston to Providence, R. I. . . .	43	Mauch Chunk, Pennsylvania . .	9
		Harlem, N. Y.	7
		Quincy, Mass. to Boston Harbor .	6
		New-Orleans to Lake Ponchartrain .	5

19. COLLEGES IN THE UNITED STATES.

NAMES.	WHERE SITUATED.	Founded.	Instructors	No. of Alumni.	Under graduates.	Volumes in College Library.	Vols. in Students' Libraries.
Bowdoin,	Brunswick, Me.	1794	7	392	137	8000	4300
Waterville,	Waterville, Me.	1820	5	60	45	1800	600
Dartmouth,	Hanover, N. H.	1770	9	2250	153	6000	8000
Vermont University,	Burlington, Vt.	1791	4	182	36	1000	500
Middlebury,	Middlebury, Vt.	1800	5	509	99	1846	2322
Harvard University,	Cambridge, Mass.	1638	24	5621	236	35000	4600
Williams,	Williamstown, Mass.	1793	7	721	115	2550	2000
Amherst,	Amherst, Mass.	1821	10	208	188	2380	4515
Brown University,	Providence, R. I.	1764	6	1182	95	6100	6000
Yale,	New-Haven, Conn.	1700	15	4428	346	8500	9000
Washington,	Hartford, Conn.	1826	9	25	70	5000	1200
Wesleyan University,	Middletown, Conn.	1831	5				
Columbia,	New-York city,	1754	6	880	124	8000	6000
University of New-York,	New-York city,	1832					
Union,	Schenectady, N. Y.	1795	10	1373	205	5150	8450
Hamilton,	Clinton, N. Y.	1812	7	189	77	2900	3000
Geneva,	Geneva, N. Y.	1823	6	15	31	500	900
College of New-Jersey,	Princeton, N. J.	1746	10	1930	105	8000	4000
Rutgers,	New-Brunswick, N. J.	1770	5		70		
University of Pennsylvania,	Philadelphia, Penn.	1755	9		125		
Dickinson,	Carlisle, Penn.	1783	4		21	2000	5000
Jefferson,	Canonsburg, Penn.	1802	7	341	120	700	1800
Western University,	Pittsburg, Penn.	1820	4	45	53		50
Washington,	Washington, Penn.	1806	4	143	47	400	525
Allegany,	Meadville, Penn.	1815	3	9	6	8000	
Madison,	Union Town, Penn.	1829	5		70		
Baltimore,	Baltimore, Md.						
St. Mary's,	Baltimore, Md.	1799	18		147	10000	
University of Maryland,	Baltimore, Md.	1812	11				
St. John's,	Annapolis, Md.	1784	5	636	76	2100	
Mount St. Mary's,	Near Emmitsburg, Md.	1830	25	12	130	7000	
Columbian,	Washington, D. C.	1821	4		50	4000	
Georgetown,	Georgetown, D. C.	1799	19		140	7000	
William and Mary,	Williamsburg, Va.	1693	7		60	3600	600
Hampden Sydney,	Prince Edward Co. Va.	1774	6		54		
Washington,	Lexington, Va.	1812		380	23	700	1500
University of Virginia,	Charlottesville, Va.	1819	9	538	130	8000	
University of North-Carolina,	Chapel Hill, N. C.	1791	9	434	69	1800	3000
Charleston,	Charleston, S. C.	1785	7	27	61	3000	1000
College of South-Carolina,	Columbia, S. C.	1801	9	490	111	7000	
University of Georgia,	Athens, Geo.	1785	7	256	95	2000	2250
Alabama University,	Tuscaloosa, Ala.	1820	6		65	1000	
Jefferson,	Washington, Mi.	1802	10		160		
Louisiana,	Jackson, La.						
Greenville,	Greenville, Tenn.	1794			32	3500	
University of Nashville,	Nashville, Tenn.	1806	4	93	95	2500	750
East Tennessee,	Knoxville, Tenn.		2		21	340	200
Transylvania University,	Lexington, Ky.	1798	6		93	2350	1500
Centre,	Danville, Ky.	1822	4	19	66	1258	108
Augusta,	Augusta, Ky.	1823	7		98	1500	550
Cumberland,	Princeton, Ky.	1825	3	13	57	1000	600
St. Joseph's,	Bardstown, Ky.	1819	15	37	150	1300	
Georgetown,	Georgetown, Ky.	1830			32		
University of Ohio,	Athens, Ohio.	1802	4	60	57	1000	1000
Miami University,	Oxford, Ohio.	1824	11	51	82	1000	1200
Western Reserve,	Hudson, Ohio.	1826	4		25	1000	100
Kenyon,	Gambier, Ohio.	1828	4		80		
Franklin,	New Athens, Ohio.	1824	3		40		
Indiana,	Bloomington, In.	1827	3	4	51	182	50
Illinois,	Jacksonville, Il.	1830	3		35	600	
St. Louis,	St. Louis, Mo.	1829	6		125	1200	

20. THEOLOGICAL SEMINARIES.

Name.	Place.	Denomination.	Com. operation.	No. educated.	Stud. in 1831.	Vols. in Library.	No. Prof.
Bangor Theol. Sem.	Bangor, Maine,	Cong.	1816	50	14	1,200	
Theol. Seminary,	Andover, Mass.,	Cong.	1808	514	139	10,000	4
Theological School,	Cambridge, do	Cong. Unit.	1824	87	33		4
Mass. Epis. Theol. Sch.,	Do do	Episcopal,	1831				4
Theological Institution,	Newton, do	Baptist,	1825	25	22	1,020	2
Theol. Dep. Yale College,	New-Haven, Ct.	Cong.	1822	70	48		3
Theol. Ins. Epis. Ch.	New-York, N. Y.	Prot. Epis.	1819	134	28	3,600	4
Theol. Sem. of Auburn,	Auburn, do	Presbyterian	1821	157	51	4,000	3
Hamilton Lit. and Th. In.	Hamilton, do	Baptist,	1820	100	80	1,600	4
Hartwick Seminary,	Hartwick, do	Lutheran,	1816				
Th. Sem. Du. Ref. Ch.	N. Br'wick. N. J.	Dutch Ref.			24		
Th. Sem. Pr. Ch. U. S.	Princeton, do	Presbyt.	1812	537	111	6,000	3
Sem. Luth. Ch. U. S.	Gettysburgh, Pa.	Evang. L.	1826		43	6,200	2
German Reformed,	York, do	Gr. Ref. Ch.	1825	11	14		2
West. Theol. Seminary,	Alleghany, do	Presbyt.	1828		22	3,964	2
Epis. Theol. School Va.	Fairfax Co. Va.	Prot. Epis.			19	1,500	3
Union Theol. Seminary,	Pr. Edw. Co. Va.	Presbyt.,	1824	30	42	3,000	3
South. Theol. Seminary,	Columbia, S. C.	Do.	1829		9		2
South West. Th. Sem.	Maryville, Ten.	Do.	1821	41	22	5,500	3
Lane Seminary,	Cincinnatti, Oo.	Do.	1829				
Rock Spring Seminary,	Rock Spring, Il.	Baptist,	1827		5	1,200	1

There are *Roman Catholic* Theological Seminaries at *Baltimore* and near *Emmittsburg*, Md., at *Charleston*, S. C., at *Bardstown*, and in *Washington County*, Ky., in *Perry County*, and *St. Louis*, Mo., and at *Cincinnati*, Ohio.

21. MEDICAL SCHOOLS.

Name.	Place.	Lectures commence.	Prof	Stud
Maine Medical School,	Brunswick,	February,	4	99
Warterville Medical School,	Waterville,	1st, Th., March,	4	28
New Hampshire Medical School,	Hanover,	2 weeks after Com.	3	98
Vermont Medical School University, Vt.	Burlington,	2d Wednesday, Sept.,	3	40
Vermont Academy of Medicine,	Castleton,	3d Thurs., in August.	6	62
Mass. Med. School, Harvard University,	Boston,	3d Wed., October,	5	95
Berkshire Medical Inst. Wms. College.	Pittsfield,	1st Thurs. September,	6	85
Medical School, Yale College,	New Haven	Lastweek in October,	5	69
College Physicians and Surgeons, N. Y.	New-York,	1st Mond., November,	7	180
College Phys. and Surg. West. Dist.	Fairfield,		5	170
Medical Dep. Jef. Col. Canonsburg,	Philadelphia,	1st Mond., November	5	121
Medical Dep. University Pennsylvania,	Philadelphia,		9	410
Medical Department University, Md.	Baltimore,	Last Mond., October,	7	
Medical Department Columbian College,	Dist. Columbia,	1st Mond., November,	7	
Medical Department, Univ. Virginia,	Charlott'sville,	September,	3	
Medical College, Charleston, S. C.,	Charleston,	2d Mond., November,	7	150
Medical College, Trans. University,	Lexington,		6	211
Medical College of Ohio,	Cincinnati,	1st Mond., November,	8	113

22. LAW SCHOOLS.

At *Cambridge*, Mass., 2 professors and 41 students; at *New Haven*, Ct., 2 professors and 44 students; at *Litchfield*, Ct.: at *Philadelphia*, Pa.; at *Baltimore*, Md., 22 students; at *Williamsburg* and *Staunton*, Va.; and at *Lexington*, Ken., 24 students.

[*From the "Annals of Education."*]

23. TABULAR VIEW OF EDUCATION IN THE UNITED STATES AND EUROPE.

The number of *Academical* Students in the United States is here estimated at 3,475; Theological Students, 663; Legal, 88; Medical, not far from 2,000. They belong to the several States as here apportioned. For want of data, however, the Medical and Legal Students were divided among the various States according to their respective population.

American States

	No. of Stud.	Proportion to Inhabitants.	
Massachusetts,	770	1	792
Connecticut,	327	1	960
New-Hampshire,	241	1	1,118
Vermont,	186	1	1,509
Maine,	238	1	1,611
New-Jersey,	193	1	1,661
South Carolina,	325	1	1,789
Pennsylvania,	688	1	1,928
New-York,	986	1	1,940
Rhode Island,	50	1	1,944
Maryland,	175	1	2,554
Virginia,	457	1	2,650
Kentucky,	249	1	2,766
Georgia,	173	1	2,985
Mississippi,	45	1	3,040
North Carolina,	233	1	3,170
Tennessee,	211	1	3,245
Ohio,	285	1	3,290
Louisiana,	46	1	3,335
Delaware,	23	1	3,336
Alabama,	84	1	3,634
Missouri,	28	1	5,003
Indiana,	65	1	5,101
Illinois,	28	1	5,624

European Countries.

	No. of Stud.	Proportion to Inhabitants	
Scotland,	3,249	1	683
Baden,	1,399	1	816
Saxony,	1,360	1	1,040
England,	10,549	1	1,132
Hanover,	1,203	1	1,303
Bavaria,	2,593	1	1,312
Tuscany,	900	1	1,402
Spain,	9,867	1	1,414
Prussia,	6,236	1	1,470
Wirtemberg,	887	1	1,731
Sweden and Norway	2,687	1	1,732
Portugal,	1,604	1	1,879
Netherlands,	2,998	1	1,979
Sardinia,	1,722	1	2,420
Switzerland,	767	1	2,655
Denmark,	578	1	3,342
Naples and Sicily,	2,065	1	3,590
Austria,	8,584	1	3,760
France,	6,196	1	5,140
Ireland,	1,254	1	5,767
Russia,	3,626	1	15,455

Sections of the United States.

Eastern States,	1,748	1	1,118
Middle States,	1,995	1	1,844
Southern States,	1,483	1	2,612
Western States,	957	1	3,516
United States,	6,185	1	2,078

European Countries.

England,	10,549	1	1,132
Portugal,	1,604	1	1,879
Switzerland,	767	1	2,655
Naples and Sicily,	2,065	1	3,590
Western Europe,	69,634	1	2,285

Proportion of Pupils in Common Schools to the whole Population.

Wirtemberg, 1 pupil to 6 inhabitants, Canton Vaud, Switzerland, 1 to 6.6, Bavaria, 1 to 7, Prussia, 1 to 7, Netherlands, 1 to 9.7, Scotland, . to 10, Austria, 1 to 13, England, 1 to 15.3, France, 1 to 17.6, Ireland, 1 to 18, Portugal, 1 to 88, Russia, 1 to 367.

New-York, 1 to 3 9, Massachusetts, Maine, Connecticut, estimated 1 to 4, all New-England, at least 1 to 5, Pennsylvania, New-Jersey, 1 to 8, Illinois, 1 to 13, Kentucky 1 to 21.

24. RELIGIOUS DENOMINATIONS.

Denominations.	Min.	Ch. or Cong	Communicants	Populat'n *Estimate*
Calvinistic Baptists,	2,914	4,384	304,827	2,743,453
Methodist Episcopal Church,	1,777		476,000	2,600,000
Presbyterian, *General Assembly*,	1,801	2,253	182,017	1,800,000
Congregationalists, *Orthodox*,	1,000	1,381	140,000	1,260,000
Protestant Episcopal Church,	558	922		600,000
Universalists,	150	300		500,000
Roman Catholics,		784		800,000
Lutherans,	205	1,200	44,000	400,000
Christians,	200	800	25,000	275,000
German Reformed,	84	400	17,400	200,000
Friends, or Quakers,		462		200,000
Unitarians, *Congregationalists*,	160	193		176,000
Associate and other Methodists,	350		35,000	175,000
Free-will Baptists,	300	400	16,000	150,000
Dutch Reformed,	159	602	17,888	125,000
Menonnites,	200		30,000	120,000
Associate Presbyterians,	74	144	15,000	100,000
Cumberland Presbyterians,	50	75	8,000	100,000
Tunkers,	40	40	3,000	30,000
Free Communion Baptists,	30		3,500	30,000
Seventh day Baptists,	30	40	2,000	20,000
Six-Principle Baptists,	25	30	1,800	20,000
United Brethren, or Moravians,	23	23	2,000	7,000
Millennial Church, or Shakers,	45	15		6,000
New Jerusalem Church,	30	28		5,000
Emancipators, *Baptists*,	15		600	4,500
Jews, and others not mentioned,		150		50,000

25. BENEVOLENT SOCIETIES.

NAME.	FORMA.	INCOME, 1829–30	NAME.	FORMA.	INCOME, 1829–30
Connecticut Miss. Societ.	1798	$3,013 06	Dutch Reformed Miss. Soc.	1822	$4,604 00
Philadelphia Bible Society	1808		Amer. S. School Union,	1824	70,521 70
American Board For. Miss.	1810	106,928 26	Baptist General Tract Soc.	1824	5,536 39
Am. Bap. Brd. For. Miss.	1814	20,000 00	Prison Discipline Society,	1825	3,353 52
Am. Tract Society, *Bost.*	1814	11,102 06	Mass. Sunday School Union,	1825	1,465 46
Am. Education Society,	1816	30,710 14	American Tract Society,	1825	60,210 00
Am. Asy. Deaf and Dumb,	1816		Am. Temperance Society,	1826	
American Bible Society,	1816	170,067 55	Am. Home Miss. Society,	1826	33,929 00
Presby. Br. Am. Ed. Soc.	1817	12,632 00	Am. Seamens' Friend Soc.	1826	4,159 87
Board Miss. Gen. Assembly,	1818	12,632 43	Mass. Miss. Society, *reorg.*	1827	
Methodist Miss. Society,	1819	13,128 00	American Peace Society.	1828	495 85
Board Edu. Gen. Assembly,	1819		African Education Society,	1830	
Am. Colonization Society,	1819	20,295 00			584,084 29

26. NUMBER OF INDIANS WITHIN THE UNITED STATES.

Within		Within	
New England and Va.	2,573	Michigan Peninsula,	9,340
New-York,	4,820	Arkansas Territory,	7,200
Pennsylvania,	300	Florida Territory,	4,000
North-Carolina,	3,106	North-west or Huron Territory,	20,200
South-Carolina,	300	Between the Mississippi, and the Rocky Mountains, exclusive of the States of Louisiana and Missouri, and Arkansas Territory,	94,300
Georgia,	5,000	Within the Rocky Mountains,	20,000
Tennessee,	1,000	West of the Rocky Mountains, between Lat. 44° and 49°,	80,000
Alabama,	19,200	Total within the United States,	312,130
Mississippi,	23,400		
Louisiana,	939		
Ohio,	1,877		
Indiana,	4,050		
Illinois,	5,900		
Missouri,	5,631		

Part III.

STATISTICS OF EUROPE.

[From the American Almanac.]

I. SWEDEN AND NORWAY.

The Swedish monarchy comprises Sweden and Norway, two of the least fertile and least populous countries in Europe; and excepting Russia, it possesses a greater extent of territory than any other European sovereignty.

In 1808, Sweden lost Finland, which was conquered by Russia; but in 1814, this loss was repaired by the acquisition of Norway.

Sweden comprises three general divisions, Gothland, Sweden Proper, and Norrland, which are now divided into 26 laus or governments; and Norway, formerly divided into the four dioceses, or governments, of Aggerhuus, Christiansand, Bergen, and Drontheim, is now formed into 18 divisions.

GOVERNMENT.

Sweden and Norway have different Constitutions, though they are under the government of one and the same king, who is, of all constitutional monarchs of Europe, one of the most limited. The monarchical power is hereditary; but females are excluded. The liberty of the press is secured by a fundamental law. The king appoints to all employments, and has the right of conferring pardons; but he cannot make any new laws, or interpret old ones, raise taxes, or declare war, without the consent of the States, which he alone has the power of convoking. The Senate, or Court of Peers, is composed of 22 members; and 12 counsellors of the crown form a Council of State.

The legislative body, styled the Diet, or States General, consists of four orders; 1st, nobles, in which order each noble family has its representative; 2dly, clergy, represented by the bishops, and also by pastors chosen in each chapter; 3dly, burgesses, who are chosen by the principal towns; 4thly, peasantry, chosen by themselves in their assemblies. Each deputy must be of one of these orders, profess the Protestant religion, and be 25 years of age. Each order deliberates and votes separately. The States assemble every five years, except in extraordinary cases.

They have the right of legislation and taxation, and the superintendence of the finances: but the king has an unconditional *veto*.

The Constitution of Norway combines the principles of monarchy and democracy. Nobility is abolished; and the legislative body or Diet, called the *Storthing*, consists of two houses.

KING AND ROYAL FAMILY.

Gustavus IV., Adolphus, the deposed king, was born Nov. 1778, and on the death of his father Gustavus III., March 29, 1792, was proclaimed king of Sweden. He remained 4½ years under the guardianship of his uncle, Charles, Duke of Sudermannland, then regent, and ascended the throne Nov. 1, 1796. In 1809, he was deposed for his violent conduct; his heirs also were excluded from the throne by an act of the Diet; and his uncle, the late regent, assumed the government, under the title of *Charles XIII.* On the 18th of August, 1810, king Charles proposed *Marshal Bernadotte* for his successor, who was elected, August 21, by the estates, on condition that he should embrace the Lutheran religion, which having done, he was, by an act of November 5, 1810, adopted by the king, assumed the name of *Charles John*, and took the oath as *Crown Prince* and heir to the throne. In 1818, on the death of Charles XIII., the Crown Prince succeeded to the throne, under the title of *Charles XIV.*

CHARLES XIV., king of Sweden and Norway; born at Pau, in France, Jan. 26, 1764; succeeded to the throne Feb. 5, 1818; m. Aug. 16, 1798, EUGENIE BERNARDHINE DE CLARY, b. Nov. 8, 1781;—Issue:—

Joseph Francis OSCAR, *Prince Royal*, Viceroy of Norway; born July 4, 1799; m. June 19, 1823, to Princess *Josephine* of Leuchtenberg, b. March 14, 1807:—Issue:—

1. *Charles Louis Eugene*, Duke of Scania; b. May 3, 1826.
2. *Francis Gustavus Oscar*, Duke of Upland; b. June 18, 1827.
3. *Oscar Frederick*, Duke of East Gothland; b. Jan. 21, 1829.
4. *Charlotte Eugene Augusta Amelia Albertine*; b. Nov. 8, 1831.

II. RUSSIA.

The empire of Russia, which includes the most of the north of Europe and all the north of Asia, is the most extensive on the globe, and is more than twice as large as all Europe; but the principal part of it is very thinly inhabited. The Asiatic part is far the larger in extent; but the European part is far the more populous; though this is much less populous than the middle and south of Europe.

The political importance of this empire, which is now one of the most powerful sovereignties of Europe, is of recent origin. The foundation of its greatness was laid by *Peter the Great*; and its dominions were subsequently very much extended during the reigns of *Catharine II.* and *Alexander*.

GOVERNMENT.

The government of Russia is an absolute hereditary monarchy; and in the succession to the throne, Females are not excluded. The government is conducted by a Council of the Empire, the Ministry, and a Senate; but there is no representative body. The late Emperor Alexander gave the Senate the right of remonstrating against any ukase or edict contrary to law. It is a body partly deliberative and partly executive, and forms the highest judicial tribunal of the empire. It is divided into nine departments or sections, of which six, comprising 62 members, hold their sittings at St. Petersburg, and three sections, with 26 members at Moscow. The ministers of the great departments are responsible to the Senate. The established religion is that of the Greek Church, but all others are tolerated.

EMPEROR AND IMPERIAL FAMILY.

NICHOLAS, Emperor of all the Russias, and King of Poland; b. July 6, 1796; m. July 13, 1817, ALEXANDRA (formerly *Charlotte*,) daughter of the king of Prussia, b. July 13, 1798; succeeded his brother *Alexander* Dec. 1, 1825, (his elder brother *Constantine*, b. May 8, 1779, having renounced his right to the throne—died 1831:)—Issue:—

1. ALEXANDER *Hereditary Prince*; b. April 29, 1818.
2. *Mary*; b. August 18, 1819.
3. *Olga*; b. Sept. 11, 1822.
4. *Alexandra*; b. June 24, 1825.
5. *Constantine*; b. Sept. 21, 1827.
6. *Nicholas*, b. August 8, 1831.

Princes of the Blood.

Maria, Princess of Saxe-Weimar; b. Feb. 16, 1786.

Anne, Princess of Orange: b. Jan. 18, 1795.

Michael, Grand Duke; b. Feb. 9, 1798; m. Feb. 20, 1824, *Paulina*, niece of the King of Wirtemberg, b. Jan. 9, 1807;—Issue; *Maria* (b. 1825,) *Elizabeth* (b. 1826,) *Catharine* (b. 1827,) and *Alexandra* (b. 1831.)

III. DENMARK.

Denmark is a small kingdom, composed of the peninsula of Jutland, the Duchy of Sleswick, and several islands in the Baltic, the largest of which are Zealand and Funen: to this kingdom also belong the German Duchies of Holstein and Lauenburg, the Faroe Islands, and the large, dreary island of Iceland: it also possesses Greenland in North America, the islands of Santa Cruz, St. Thomas, and St. John's in the West Indies, Tranquebar and Serampore in Hindostan, and a settlement in Guinea, in Africa.

KING AND ROYAL FAMILY.

FREDERICK VI, King of Denmark, Duke of Pomerania; b. Jan. 28, 1768,; declared co-regent with his Father, *Christian VII.*, April 14, 1784, succeeded to the throne March 13, 1808; m. July 31, 1790, SOPHIA FREDERICA, niece of the Elector of Hesse-Cassel, b. Oct. 28, 1767; Issue:—

1. *Caroline*, Princess Royal; b. Oct. 28, 1793; m. to Prince Frederick Ferdinand, Aug. 1, 1829.
2. *Wilhelmina*; b. Jan. 17, 1808; m. to Prince Frederick Charles Christian, Nov. 1, 1828.

Sister of the King.

Louisa Augusta, Princess Dowager of Holstein Sonderburg-Augustenburg; b. July 7, 1771.

Cousins of the King.

Christian Frederick, b. Sept. 18, 1786; proclaimed King of Norway, May 19, 1814, abdicated Aug. 15, 1814; m. (I.) Feb. 18, 1806, Charlotte Frederica of Mecklenburg-Schwerin; (II.) m. May 22, 1815, Caroline Amelia, Princess of Holstein-Sonderburg-Augustenburg;—Issue of the first marriage;—

1. *Frederick Charles Christian*, b. Oct. 6, 1808; m. Nov. 1, 1828, Wilhelmina Maria, daughter of the king.
2. *Julianne*; b. Feb. 18, 1788.
3. *Louisa Charlotte*; b. Oct. 30, 1789.
4. *Frederick Ferdinand*, b. Nov. 22, 1792; m. Aug. 1, 1829, Caroline princess Royal of Denmark.

IV. BELGIUM.

OUTLINES OF THE CONSTITUTION.

The legislative power is exercised collectively by the king, the Chamber of Representatives, and the Senate. The *initiative* pertains to each of the three branches of the legislative power; nevertheless every law relating to the revenue and expenditure of the state, or to the contingent of the army, must be first voted by the Chamber of Representatives.

THE KING.

LEOPOLD, king of the Belgians, formerly prince Leopold of Saxe-Coburg, brother of the present duke of Saxe-Coburg-Gotha; b. Dec. 16, 1790; m. (I.) May 2, 1816, the daughter of George IV., of England, who died Nov. 6, 1817; elected king of the Belgians, June 4, 1831; took the oath to the constitution, July 21, 1831; m. (II.) Aug. 9. 1832, LOUISE, daughter of Louis Philip, king of France, b. April 3, 1812.

V. HOLLAND.

Holland, a small commercial kingdom, comprises the country formerly styled the Republic of the Seven United Provinces, and often also the Republic of Holland.

In 1579, the Seven United Provinces revolted from Philip II., king of Spain, and established their independence, which they maintained till after the French Revolution; and they became distinguished for their commercial enterprise and prosperity.

These provinces were, for a few years united to the French empire; but, after the downfall of Bonaparte, the Dutch and Belgic provinces, together with the German grand duchy of Luxemburg, were formed, by the Congress of Vienna, into a kingdom, and placed under the government of William, prince of Orange, who received the title of king of the Netherlands and Grand duke of Luxemburg.

In 1830, the Belgic Provinces revolted from the government of William, and declared their independence, which has been acknowledged by the five great powers of Europe.—*See Belgium.*

KING AND ROYAL FAMILY.

WILLIAM, king of Holland (lately of the Netherlands,) prince of Orange-Nassau; b. Aug. 24, 1772; succeeded his father in his hereditary possessions in Germany, April 9, 1806; declared Sovereign prince of the Netherlands, Dec. 3, 1813; assumed the crown, March 15, 1815; m. Oct. 1, 1791, WILHELMINA, sister of the king of Prussia, b. Nov. 18, 1774: Issue:—

1. WILLIAM, *Prince Royal* and *Prince of Orange;* b. Dec. 6, 1792; m. Feb. 21, 1816, *Anne*, sister of the emperor of Russia, b. Jan. 18, 1795; —Issue; *William*, b. Feb. 19, 1817; *Alexander*, b. Aug. 2, 1818; *Frederick*, b. June 13, 1820; *Sophia*, b. April 8, 1824.
2. *Frederick;* b. Feb. 28, 1797; m. May 21, 1825, *Louisa*, 3d daughter of the king of Prussia:—Issue: *Wilhelmina*, b. Aug 5, 1828.
3. *Marianne;* b. May 9, 1810; m. Sept. 14, 1830, to Albert of Prussia.

VI. GREAT BRITAIN.

The United Kingdom of Great Britain and Ireland consists of the two Islands of Great Britain (comprising England, Wales, and Scotland) and Ireland; together with various small neighbouring islands; it also possesses the fortress of Gibraltar, and the islands of Malta and Heligoland, in Europe, and has possessions of vast extent in America, Asia, and Africa.

	Sq. m.	Pop. 1821.	Capitals.	Pop.
England and Wales	58,345	11,977,663	LONDON	1,225,694
Scotland	30,234	2,092,014	Edinburgh	112,235
Ireland	30,000	6,846,949	Dublin	185,881
Gibraltar, Malta and Heligoland		110,000		
Total		21,026,626		

POSSESSIONS IN THE EAST INDIES.

	Sq. m.	Population.
Bengal	328,000	52,500,000
Madras	154,000	15,000,000
Bombay	71,000	10,500,000
Territory of Allies	550,000	40,000,000
Arracan	11,000	100,000
Tavay, Tenaserim, Marguia, and Ye	21,000	51,000
Assam and Garrow	45,000	150,000
Malacca	800	22,000
Singapore	210	14,712
Island of the Prince of Wales	160	51,207
Total	1,181,170	123,388,926

Thus the East India Company possess a territory of more than 1 million square miles, upon which there is a population of more than 123 millions, The *English* inhabitants amount to about 40,000, of which 2,000 are attached to the government, 300 to the judiciary, 7,000 are merchants and seamen; the rest belong to the army, which is composed, in great part, of natives, and comprises 300,000 men. The revenue of Bengal, Madras, and Bombay amounted, in 1822, to more than 213 millions of florins.

GOVERNMENT.

The government of England is a constitutional hereditary monarchy, in which the power of the sovereign is controlled by the influence of the aristocracy in the House of Peers, and by that of the democracy in the House of Commons. The executive authority is vested in the king; the legislative, in the king and Parliament. The king has the power of appointing all the great officers of state, and all the executive acts of the government are performed in his name; but his ministers only are responsible for them.

PARLIAMENT.

The Parliament of Great Britain is the great council of the nation, constituting the legislature, which is summoned by the king's authority, to consult on public affairs, and enact and repeal laws. It consists of Lords Spiritual and Temporal, called the Peers, or Upper House; and knights, citizens or burgesses, who are comprehended under the name of the Commons or Lower House. The duration of Parliament was formerly for three years; but the Septennial Act in 1715, extended the duration to seven years, unless dissolved by the king; but it seldom happens that Parliament sits out this period.

The union with Ireland was carried into effect, January 1, 1801, and the Parliament, which met the same month, and which included the members from Ireland, is styled the *First Imperial Parliament*, or the *First Parliament of the United kingdom.*

The House of Lords is composed of all the five orders of nobility of England, dukes marquesses, earls, viscounts, and barons, who have attained the age of 21 years, and labour under no disqualification; of 16 representative peers from Scotland; 28 representative peers from Ireland; 2 English archbishops and 24 bishops; and 4 representative Irish bishops:—the number of each in 1832, being as follows:

Dukes (4 Royal Dukes)	23	Representative Peers of Scotland,	16
Marquesses,	21	Representative Peers of Ireland,	28
Earls,	106	English Archbishops and Bishops,	26
Viscounts,	19	Irish Representative Bishops,	4
Barons,	182		
		Total of the House of Peers,	425

The lords temporal are peers of the Realm, and are hereditary counsellors of the crown; their honours, immunities, and privileges are hereditary. A peer may vote by proxy: when sitting in judgment he gives his vote not on *oath*, like a commoner, but upon his *honour*. The persons of peers are for ever sacred and inviolable from arrest and imprisonment for debts, trespasses, &c. They cannot be outlawed in any civil action; nor can any attachment lie against their persons; and they are possessed of various other privileges and immunities.

The number of the lords temporal is indefinite, and may be increased at the pleasure of the crown. The ancient nobility sit in the house by *descent*; the new-made peers, by *creation*; the 16 representative peers for Scotland, and the 28 representative peers for Ireland, by *election*; the former are elected for each parliament; the latter for life.

HOUSE OF COMMONS.

The house of commons consists of knights, citizens, and burgesses, respectively chosen by counties, cities and boroughs. It is not accurately and satisfactorily ascertained at what precise period the parliament, as it is now constituted, was formed; that is when the commons first began to compose a distinct assembly from the lords; but the generally received opinion is, that the parliament was on the whole, much the same as it now is, so long ago as the 17th year of king John, A. D. 1215. (See "New Edinburgh Encyclopedia," Vol. VIII. p. 616.) The first Speaker certainly known was Petrus de Mountford, chosen in 1260, in the reign of Henry III.

Classification of the members of the House of Commons, dissolved April 22, 1831.

Landholders	358	Engaged in Trade and Manufactures,	51
Military Officers	83	Connected with the W. India Trade,	34
Placemen and Pensioners,	63	Bankers,	33
Of the profession of the Law,	62	Naval Officers,	24
Connected with the East India Co.,	62		

EDUCATION.

England has two richly endowed Universities, Oxford and Cambridge. The number of members on the books (including undergraduates,) and of the undergraduates, is here given for 1832.

	Professors.	Members.	Undergraduates.
Oxford,	29	5,274	1,417
Cambridge,	24	5,361	1,700

Some of the other literary institutions are the London University, with 29 professors and (in 1829) 437 students; King's College, London, with 23 professors; the East India College; Halebury, with 9 professors; St. David's college, Lampter, with 5 professors; Eton College; and Winchester College. According to returns, made in 1818, there were 4,167 endowed schools, with a revenue of £3,000,525; and 14,282 unendowed schools. Common schools have been much increased within a few years; but England is still behind Scotland with respect to the general diffusion of education. The number of Sunday Schools in England and Wales, connected with the Sunday School Union, reported in 1831, was 5,775; teachers 83,860; scholars, 778,612.

ENGLISH BENEVOLENT SOCIETIES.

Name.	Date	Income. 1828-9	1829-30	Name.	Date	Income. 1828-9	1829-30
British & Foreign Bib.	1801	86,259	84,982	Hibernian	1806	7,595	9,228
Prom'g Chr. Knowl.	1799	72,486	60,000	Sund. School Union	1803	5,276	6,323
Wesleyan Missionary		50,005	55,565	Home Missionary	1819		5,782
London Missionary	1795	41,803	48,526	Missions Unit. Breth.	1732	8,930	4,021
Church Missionary	1800	53,675	47,328	Naval and Milit. Bible	1780	3,771	3,396
Propagating the Gosp.	1701	27,582	29,168	British Reformation	1827	1,741	3,000
Religious Tract	1799	22,469	24,973	Pra'er B'kand Homily	1813	2,189	2,207
National School	1810	20,102	20,000	Anti-Slavery	1823	1,787	2,134
London Jews'	1808	13,129	12,272	Brit. and For. School	1805	2,615	2,038
Baptist Missionary	1792	10,393	11,300	Peace	1816	612	628

KING AND ROYAL FAMILY OF GREAT BRITAIN.

WILLIAM IV. king of the United Kingdom of Great Britain and Ireland, and king of Hanover; b. Aug. 21, 1765; m. July 11, 1818, ADELAIDE, sister of the duke of Saxe-Meiningen, b. Aug. 13, 1792; succeeded his brother *George IV.*, June 26, 1830.

Brothers and Sisters of the King, with their Annual Parliamentary Allowance.

1. *Augusta Sophia*; (£13,000;) b. Nov. 3, 1768.
2. *Elizabeth*; b. May 22, 1770: m. April 7, 1818, to *Frederic Joseph Lewis*, Landgrave of Hesse-Homburg, who died April 2, 1823.
3. *Ernest-Augustus*, duke of Cumberland; (£25,000;) b. June 5, 1771; m. May 29, 1815, *Frederica Sophia Carolina*, sister of the duke of Mecklenberg-Strelitz, and widow of Frederic William, Prince of Solms-Braunfels, b. March 20, 1778;—Issue; *George Frederick*, b. May 27, 1819.
4. *Augustus Frederick*, duke of Sussex; (£21,000) b. Jan. 27, 1773.
5. *Adolphus Frederick*, duke of Cambridge; (£27,000;) b. Feb. 24, 1774; m. May 7, 1818, *Augusta Wilhelmina Louisa*, neice of the Landgrave of Hesse, b. July 25, 1797;—Issue; 1. *George William*, b. March 26, 1819: 2. *Augusta Carolina*, b. July 19, 1822.
6. *Mary* Duchess of Gloucester; (£13,000;) b. April 25,1776; m. July 22, 1816, to her cousin the duke of Gloucester.
7. *Sophia*; (£13,000;) b. Nov. 3, 1777.

Niece of the King.

ALEXANDRINA VICTORIA, *Heiress Presumptive*, (daughter of the late *Prince Edward, duke of Kent*,—b. Nov. 2, 1767, died Jan. 23, 1820,—by *Victoria Maria Louisa* (£12,000) sister of the duke of Saxe-Coburg-Gotha, and of Leopold, king of Belgium; b. Aug. 17, 1786;) b. May 24, 1819.

Cousins of the King.—Issue of the late duke of Gloucester.

Sophia Matilda, (£7,000;) b. May, 23, 1773.

William Frederick, duke of Gloucester; (£14,000;) b. Jan. 15, 1776; m. July 22, 1816, his cousin the *Princess Mary*.

THE KING'S MINISTERS.

Earl Grey was appointed in 1833 First Lord of the Treasury, and Premier. The other members of the cabinet were—Viscount Althorp, Lord Brougham, Marquess of Lansdowne, Lord Durham, Viscount Melbourne, Viscount Palmerston, Viscount Goderich, Rt. Hon. Sir Jas. R. G. Graham, bt., Lord Auckland, Rt. Hon. Charles Grant, Duke of Richmond, Lord Holland, Lord John Russel, Rt. Hon. Edward G. S. Stanley, Earl of Carlisle.

VII. FRANCE.

GOVERNMENT.

The government of France is a constitutional monarchy. The legislative power is vested in the King, a Chamber of Peers, nominated by the king, and a Chamber of Deputies elected by the people.

Chamber of Peers. The rights of the Peers were formerly hereditary; but, in 1831, their hereditary rights were abolished by an act which was passed in the Chamber of Deputies, on the 18th of October, by a vote of 386 to 40: and in the Chamber of Peers, on the 28th of December, by a vote of 103 to 70. The Peers are now nominated by the king, and hold their office for life; their number is unlimited. The Chamber of Peers, as stated in "Almanach National pour l'Anne 1832," consists of 259 members, including princes, dukes, Marquesses, Counts, Viscounts, and Barons. There are besides, 33 Peers, who have not taken their seats; 13 who abdicated their seats on the 9th of January, 1832; and 49 who had before taken their seats, but refused to take the oath required by the law of the 31st August, 1830.

The *Chamber of Deputies* is composed of 430 members. The members of the present Chamber were elected, in July 1831, under the new electoral law, by which every Frenchman who pays a direct tax of 200 francs is authorized to vote.

KING AND ROYAL FAMILY.

LOUIS PHILLIP, king of the French; of the branch of Orleans, and descended from a brother of Louis XIV.; b. Oct. 6, 1773; king of the French, Aug. 9, 1830; m. Nov. 25, 1809, Maria Amelia, daughter of Ferdinand, late king of the Two Sicilies, b. April 26, 1782: Issue:—

1. Ferdinand; Duke of Orleans, *Prince Royal;* b. Sept. 3, 1810.
2. *Louise;* b. April 3, 1812; m. Aug. 9, 1832, *Leopold*, king of Belgium.
3. *Maria;* b. April 12, 1813.
4. *Louis Charles*, duke of Nemours; b. Oct. 25, 1814.
5. *Clementina;* b. June 3, 1817.
6. *Francis*, Prince of Joinville; b. Aug. 14, 1818.
7. *Henry*, Duke of Aumale; b. Jan. 16, 1822.
8. *Anthony*, Duke of Montpensier; b. July 31, 1824.

Sister of the King.

Eugenia Adelaide Louisa, Mad. d'Orleans; b. Aug. 23, 1777.

The king and family *excluded by the Declaration of the Chamber of Deputies of the 7th of August*, 1830.

CHARLES X., King of France and Navarre; most christian majesty; b. Oct. 9, 1757; succeeded his brother *Louis XVIII.* Sept. 16, 1824; crowned at Rheims, May 29, 1825; m. Nov. 6, 1773, *Maria Theresa*, sister of the king of Sardinia, who died at Gratz, June 2, 1805: Issue;—

Louis Anthony, duke of Angouleme, *Dauphin;* b. Aug. 6, 1775; m. June 10, 1799, *Maria Theresa* (*Dauphiness*,) daughter of Louis XVI., b. Dec. 19, 1778.

Louisa Maria Theresa, (daughter of the late duke of Berri, next brother to the Dauphin;) b. Sept. 21, 1819.

Henry, duke of Bordeaux (a posthumous son of the late duke of Berri;) b. Sept. 29, 1820.

VIII. PRUSSIA.

Prussia, which was first erected into a kingdom in 1701, was originally a small state; but it was much enlarged during the long reign of Frederick the Great; and it has since received large additions, particularly at the time of the settlement of the affairs of Europe by the congress of Vienna, in 1815; since which period, it has ranked as one of the five Great Powers of Europe.

The Prussian States consist chiefly of two parts, entirely separated from each other, the larger one lying in the northeast of Germany, and the smaller one in the west. The kingdom is divided into ten provinces. The two provinces of East Prussia and West Prussia comprise Prussia Proper; the province of Posen is formed of the Prussian part of Poland; the other seven provinces are all included within the limits of the late German Empire. The western part of the kingdom includes the three provinces of Westphalia, Cleves-Berg, and Lower Rhine.

KING AND ROYAL FAMILY.

FREDERICK WILLIAM III., king of Prussia, Margrave of Brandenburg, and Sovereign duke of Silesia; b. Aug. 3, 1770; succeeded his father *Frederick William II.*, Nov. 16, 1797; m. Dec. 24, 1793, *Louisa Augusta*, princess of Mecklinburg-Strelitz, who died July 19, 1810. [m. (II.) (by private marriage, *mariage marganatique*) Nov. 9, 1824, to *Augusta*, princess of Liegnitz, b. Aug. 30, 1800:]—Issue by the first marriage:—

Frederick William, *Prince Royal;* b. Oct. 15, 1795; m. Nov. 29, 1823, *Elizabeth Louisa*, sister of the king of Bavaria, b. Nov. 13, 1801.

2. *William Louis;* b. March 22, 1797; m. June 11, 1829, *Augusta*, daughter of the duke of Saxe-Weimar, b. Sept. 30, 1811.

3. Charlotte, (*Empress of Russia*,) b. July 13, 1798; m. July 13, 1817.

4. *Charles;* b. June 29, 1801; m. May 26, 1827, *Maria*, daughter of the duke of Saxe-Weimar, b. Feb. 3, 1808:—issue, *Frederick*, b. March 28, 1828; *Maria*, b. March 1, 1829.

5. *Alexandrina;* b. Feb. 23, 1803; m. May 25, 1822, to prince *Frederick* of Mecklenburg-Schwerin.

6. *Louisa:* b. Feb. 1, 1808; m. May 21, 1825, to *Frederick* of Orange.

7. *Albert;* b. Oct. 4, 1809; betrothed to *Marianne* of Orange, Nov. 7, 1829.

IX. SAXONY.

Saxony, situated towards the northeast of Germany, comprising a part of the late circle of Upper Saxony, is the smallest kingdom in Europe. It was formerly an electorate, but was erected into a kingdom, in 1806, by Bonaparte by the treaty of Posen. It was greatly reduced by the congress of Vienna, the northern and eastern parts, containing a population of 850,000, being separated from the kingdom and transferred to Prussia.

KING AND ROYAL FAMILY.

ANTHONY, king of Saxony; b. Dec. 27, 1755; succeeded his brother *Frederick Augustus*, the first king of Saxony, May 12, 1827; m. MARIA THERESA, sister of the Emperor of Austria.—Sept. 9, 1830, a commotion took place at Dresden; a few days after which, the king resigned his authority to his nephew *Frederick Augustus* (*Maximilian* having renounced his right to the succession,) and Frederick Augustus was appointed *Regent*.

MAXIMILIAN, brother of the king; b. April 13, 1759; m. (I.) *Caroline*, of Parma, May 9, 1799; m. (II.) *Maria Louisa*, sister of the duke of Lucca, Nov. 7, 1825;—Issue by the first marriage:—1. *Amelia*, b. Aug. 10, 1794;—2. *Maria*, b. April 27, 1796;—

3. FREDERICK AUGUSTUS, appointed *Regent* Sept. 13, 1830; b. May 18, 1797; m. Oct. 7, 1819, *Caroline* of Austria:—4. *Anne*, b. Nov. 15, 1799; —5, *John*, b. Dec. 12, 1801, m. 1822, *Amelia*, of Bavaria:—Issue, *Maria*, b. Jan. 22, 1827; *Albert*, b. April 23, 1828; *Elizabeth*, b. Feb. 4, 1830; *Ernest*, b. April 5, 1831.

X. WIRTEMBURG.

Wirtemburg, a small kingdom, situated in the southwest part of Germany, comprises a part of the late circle of Swabia. It was formerly a dukedom; but in 1803, *Frederick*, duke of Wirtemburg, was raised to the rank of an *Elector*, and in 1806, to that of *King*, by Bonaparte.

KING AND ROYAL FAMILY.

WILLIAM, king of Wirtemburg, duke of Swabia and Teek; b. Sept. 27, 1781; succeeded his father *Frederick*, the first king of Wirtemburg, Oct. 30, 1816; m. (I.) Jan. 24, 1816, *Catharine*, sister of the emperor of Russia and widow of the duke of Oldenberg, b. May 21, 1788, d. Jan. 9, 1819:—m. (II.) April 15, 1820, PAULINA, daughter of his uncle, duke Alexander, b. Sept. 4, 1800:—Issue by the first marriage:—

1. *Maria*; b. Oct. 30, 1816.—2. *Sophia*; b. June 17, 1818.—Issue by the second marriage: —3. *Catharine*; b. Aug. 24, 1821.—4. CHARLES, *Prince Royal*; b. March 6, 1823:—5. *Augusta*; b. Oct. 4, 1826.

XI. BAVARIA.

Bavaria, composed of the greater part of the late circles of Bavaria and Franconia, was erected into a kingdom, in 1805, under *Maximilian Joseph* (formerly elector of Bavaria,) on whom Bonaparte conferred the title of king, and caused it to be ceded to him at the peace of Presburg, the same year. Maximilian Joseph died in 1825, and was succeeded by his son *Louis*, the present king.

KING AND ROYAL FAMILY.

Louis, king of Bavaria; b. Aug. 25, 1786; succeeded his father *Maximilian Joseph*, Oct. 13, 1825; m. Oct. 12, 1810, THERESA, daughter of the duke of Saxe-Altenberg, b. July 8, 1792:—Issue:—

1. MAXIMILIAN, *Prince Royal*; b. Nov. 28, 1811.
2. *Matilda*; b. Aug. 30, 1813.
3. OTHO; elected king of Greece; b. June 1, 1815.
4. *Leopold*; b. March 14, 1821.
5. *Adeline*; b. March 19, 1823.
6. *Hildegarde*; b. June 1, 1825.
7. *Alexandrina*; b. Aug. 26, 1826.
8. *Albert*; b. July 19, 1828.

XII. AUSTRIA.

Austria was erected into an empire in 1804, by *Francis II.*, Emperor of Germany, who assumed the title of Hereditary Emperor of Austria. In 1806, Francis II. resigned his title of Emperor of Germany, and the German empire was dissolved.

The Austrian Empire is composed of several states or countries, which are situated towards the south of Europe, and which are inhabited by different nations, speaking different languages. The empire is more extensive in territory than the kingdom of France, and the number of inhabitants about equal.

EMPEROR AND IMPERIAL FAMILY.

FRANCIS (the last emperor of Germany and the first emperor of Austria,) emperor of Austria, king of Hungary, Bohemia, Lombardy, and Venice, and president of the German Confederation; b. at Florence, Feb. 12, 1768; succeeded his father *Leopold II.*, as emperor of Germany, July 7, 1792; declared himself hereditary emperor of Austria, Aug. 11, 1804, and resigned his title of Emperor of Germany, Aug. 6, 1806; m. (I.) Jan. 6, 1788, *Elizabeth* of Wirtemburg, who died 1790; m. (II.) Aug. 14, 1790, *Maria Theresa*, daughter of Ferdinand IV. of Sicily, who died April 13, 1807; m. (III.) Jan. 9, 1808, *Maria Louisa Beatrix*, daughter of the duke of Modena, who died April 7, 1816; m. (IV.) Nov. 10, 1816, CAROLINE AUGUSTA, daughter of the King of Bavaria, b. Feb. 8, 1792:—Issue by the second marriage:—

1. MARIA LOUISA, b. Dec. 12, 1791; m. April 2, 1810, to the emperor Napoleon Bonaparte:—created duchess of Parma, May 30, 1814.

2. Ferdinand, *Prince Imperial*; b. April 19, 1793; m. Feb. 27, 1831, to Anna, daughter of the late king of Sardinia.
3. *Maria Clementina*, b. March 1, 1798; m. July 28, 1817, Leopold, Prince of Salerno.
4. *Carolina Ferdinanda*; b. April 8, 1801; m. Oct. 7, 1819, to Frederick Augustus, prince regent of Saxony.
5. *Francis Charles Joseph*, viceroy of Bohemia; b. Dec. 7, 1802; m. Nov. 4, 1824, Sophia, sister of the king of Bavaria.
6. *Maria Anne Frances*; b. June 8, 1804.

Brothers of the Emperor.

1. *Archduke Charles*, field-marshal, governor and captain-general of Bohemia; b. 1771.
2. *Archduke Joseph*, palatine, governor, and captain-general of Hungary; b. Mar. 9, 1776.
3. *Archduke Anthony*, G. M. of the Teutonic order; b. Aug. 31, 1779.
4. *Archduke John*, general of cavalry; b. Jan. 20, 1782.
5. *Archduke Renier*, viceroy of Lombardy and Venice; b. Sept. 30, 1783.
6. *Archduke Louis*, field-marshal and director-general of artillery; b. Dec. 13, 1784.

XIII. SWITZERLAND

is divided into twenty-two Cantons.

GOVERNMENT.

Each Canton is an independent republic. In some of the cantons the form of government is a democracy; but in most of them, an oligarchy. But for the general security, the cantons are confederated together, and the regulation of affairs which concern the whole confederation, is entrusted to a Diet composed of deputies from the 22 cantons, who assemble commonly on the first Monday in July at Zurich, Berne, or Lucerne, the place of meeting being changed in rotation every two years; and the deputy of the canton in whose capital the diet assembles presides. In 1833 and 1834, the diet meets at Zurich; in 1835 and 1836, at Berne; and in 1837 and 1838, at Lucerne.

XIV. SPAIN.

Spain, a mountainous country, comprising the most of a great peninsula lying in the south west of Europe, is advantageously situated, and two centuries ago it was the most formidable power in Christendom; but it is now comparatively weak, and is backward with respect to agriculture, manufactures, the arts and education.

It is divided into fourteen large provinces, and subdivided into thirty-one smaller ones.

Ecclesiastics.—The whole number of ecclesiastics, in Spain, in 1826, is stated at 148,696 of whom 61 were archbishops and bishops; 2,363 canons; 61,327 men in convents, and 31,400 women in convents.

GOVERNMENT.

Spain is governed by an absolute hereditary monarch, though several unsuccessful attempts have been made to establish a constitutional government. It has been governed by the Bourbon family since 1700. The succession was limited to the male line till April 6, 1830, when, by a royal ordinance, females were rendered capable of succeeding to the throne.

KING AND ROYAL FAMILY.

FERDINAND VII., king of Spain and the Indies; Most Catholic; b. Oct. 14, 1784; succeeded to the throne on the abdication of his father *Charles IV.*, March 19, 1808; m. (I.) Sept. 29, 1816, *Isabella Maria*, infanta of Portugal, b. May 19, 1797, d. Dec. 26, 1818; m. (II.) *Maria Josephina*, niece of the king of Saxony, d. May, 1829; m. (III.) Dec. 4, 1829, Maria Christina, daughter of the king of the Two Sicilies:—Issue; *Maria Isabella, Infanta*, b. Oct. 12, 1830.

Brothers and Sister of the King.

Charles Isidore, Infant; b. March 29, 1788; m. *Frances* of Portugal, Sept. 22, 1816.
Maria Isabella, widow of Francis I. of the Two Sicilies; b. June 6, 1789.
Francis de Paul; b. March 10, 1794; m. June 12, 1819, to *Louisa Charlotte* of the Two Sicilies.

XV. PORTUGAL.

Portugal, the most westerly state of Europe, is a small kingdom, once distinguished as a maritime power, but its prosperity long since declined; and it is now one of the most backward European countries with regard to agriculture, manufactures, education and the arts.

KING AND ROYAL FAMILY.

MIGUEL, king of Portugal and the Algarves; 2d son of *John VI.* of Portugal; b. Oct. 26, 1802; affianced at Vienna, Oct. 29, 1826, by proxy to his niece *Maria da Gloria*, who was declared Queen of Portugal; took the oath Feb. 26, 1828, as Regent of Portugal; was proclaimed King, by the Cortes, June 26, 1828, and formally assumed the title of King of Portugal and the Algarves, July 4, 1828.

[MARIA DE GLORIA, eldest daughter of *Pedro*, ex-emperor of Brazil, eldest son of *John VI.* of Portugal, b. April 4th 1819; declared queen of Portugal in consequence of the abdication of her father, May 2, 1826.—Pedro having become emperor of Brazil, under the conditions of the constitution of that country by an act of May 2, 1826, abdicated the throne of Portugal in favour of his daughter, promulgated a constitution for the kingdom with a cortes, and appointed his brother Don Miguel regent, during the minority of his daughter. Miguel, after having sworn to the constitution renounced it, assumed absolute sovereignty in his own right, and has since reigned as king of Portugal.].

Sisters of Miguel.

1. *Maria Theresa*, princess of Beira; born April 29, 1793; widow of Peter Charles of Spain.—2. *Maria Frances*; b. April 22, 1800; m. Sept. 29, 1816, to Charles Isidore of Spain.—3. *Isabella Maria*; b. July 4, 1801.—4. *Maria de l'Assomption*: b. July 25, 1805. —5. *Maria Anne Jesus*; b. Dec. 23, 1806; m. Dec. 1, 1827, to the Marquis de Loule.

XVI. KINGDOM OF SARDINIA.

The Kingdom of Sardinia comprises Piedmont, including the county of Nice, the duchy of Montferat, and the Sardinian Milanese; Savoy, Genoa, and the island of Sardinia. This kingdom dates from 1718. Genoa, which was once a republic, was annexed to it in 1815.

KING AND ROYAL FAMILY.

CHARLES EMANUEL, king of Sardinia, duke of Savoy, Piedmont, and Genoa; b. Aug. 16, 1800, succeeded his uncle *Charles Felix*. April 27, 1831; m. Sept. 30, 1817, THERESA, sister of the grand duke of Tuscany, b. March 21, 1801:—Issue: 1. VICTOR EMANUEL; b. March 14, 1820;—2. *Ferdinand*: b. Nov. 15, 1822.

XVII. THE TWO SICILIES.

The kingdom of the Two Sicilies, comprising Naples and the island of Sicily, have formed a separate independent monarchy since the year, 1735, under the government of the House of Bourbon.

KING AND ROYAL FAMILY.

FERDINAND II. king of the Two Sicilies; b. Jan. 12, 1810; succeeded his father *Francis*, Nov. 8, 1830.

Queen *Mother*.—Maria Isabella, sister of the king of Spain; b. July 6, 1789.

Brothers and sisters of the king.

1. *Maria Caroline*; b. Nov. 5, 1798; m. Feb. 14, 1816, duke of Berri.—2. *Louisa Charlotte*; b. Oct. 24, 1804; m. June 12, 1819, Don Francis of Spain.—3. *Maria Christina*, queen of Spain; b. April 27, 1806.—4. *Charles*, Prince of Capua; b. Dec. 10, 1811.—5. *Leopold*, Count of Syracuse; b. May 22, 1813.—6. *Marie Antoinette*; b. Dec. 19, 1814.—7. *Antonio*, count of Lecce; b. Sept. 23, 1816.—8. *Maria Amelia*; b. Feb. 25, 1818.—9. *Caroline*; b. Feb. 28, 1820.—10. *Theresa*, b. March 14, 1822.—11. *Louis*, Count of Aquila; b. July 19, 1824.—12. *Francis*, Count of Trapani; b. Aug. 13, 1827.

XVII. TURKEY.

Moldavia and Wallachia are not governed directly by the Porte; but by Hospodars or princes who are of the Greek religion.

GOVERNMENT.

The government is absolute monarchy; the sovereign who is styled Sultan, Grand Seignor, Emperor, is the sole fountain of honour and office, and is the absolute master of the property and lives of his subjects. His cabinet council is Styled the *Divan*; his court, the *Porte* or *Sublime Porte*.

THE SULTAN AND HIS FAMILY.

MAHMOUD II., grand seignor and sultan of the Ottoman empire; b. July 20, 1785; called to the throne July 28, 1808:—Issue:—

1. Salyha; b. June 16, 1821. 2. Abdul-Meschid; b. April 20, 1823. 3. Hadidscha; b. Sept. 5, 1825. 4. Adila; b. May 21, 1826. 5. Abdul-Aziz; b. Feb. 8, 1830. 6. Harie; b. Jan. 23, 1831.

XVIII. GREECE.

OTHO, sovereign Prince of Greece, (son of the king of Bavaria.)

The Greeks revolted from the Turkish domination in 1821, asserted independence, and established a republican government. The Turks attempted to reduce them to subjection; a destructive war ensued, which lasted several years; at length the governments of Russia, France, and Great Britain interfered; and the Sultan of Turkey was induced to consent to the independence of Greece. In 1827, *Count Capo d'Istra* was elected president of Greece for the term of seven years; in January, 1828, he entered upon the duties of his office, and he has succeeded in establishing an efficient administration, and in gaining the confidence and affection of the people.

In February, 1830, the plenipotentiaries of Great Britain, France, and Russia, appointed *Prince Leopold* of Saxe-Coburg to be the hereditary sovereign of Greece, with the title of "Sovereign Prince." The prince accepted the appointment; but on learning the actual condition of the country, and the feelings of the people in regard to an appointment in which they had no voice, he afterwards resigned it.

The young Prince Otho, of Bavaria, was subsequently chosen—and assumed the government in 1832.

The government was reorganized by the fourth national Congress, which met at Argos in the summer of 1829, Capo d'Istra still remaining at its head. The *Panhellenium*, a Council of 27 members, was replaced by another body consisting also of 27 members, called the *Gerousia*, senate or congress. This body gives its opinion on matters of legislation; but has not the power of a negative upon the decisions of the president. Besides the senate, there is a ministry, consisting of four departments, each having a secretary, viz: the Home Department; Foreign Affairs, including commerce; the Judiciary; and public education and ecclesiastical affairs.

The country of Greece, which is liberated, comprises the Morea, the most of the continent lying south of ancient Thessaly and Epirus, the island of Negropont and most of the smaller islands in the Archipelago, leaving Candia, Samos, and Scio in the possession of the Turks. The total area is not far from 16,000 square miles. "The Peloponnesus contains about 280,000 inhabitants; the islands about 175,000; and continental Greece, includ- Acarnania and Ætolia, about 180,000,—in all 635,000 souls.—*See Anderson's "Observations upon the Peloponnesus and the Greek Islands, made in* 1829.

SUPPLEMENTARY ITEMS TO THE GENERAL CHRONICLE.

1832.

Aug. 9. Married, at Compeigne:—Leopold, king of the Belgians, to Louise, daughter of the king of the French.

Oct. 10. France:—New ministry formed, under the direction of Marshal Soult, president of the council.

Nov. Gt. Britain.—Sir Thomas Denman appointed lord chief justice of the court of king's bench, in place of lord Tenterden, deceased.

—— 7. France:—Arrest of the duchess of Berri, at Nantes.

—— 13. Belgian Chambers opened by the king in person, who announced the recognition of Belgium as an independent state, by the leading powers of Europe.

—— —— The French army under Marshal Gerard enters Belgium and encamps before the citadel of Antwerp, which is garrisoned by Dutch troops under general Chasse.—Hostilities commence on the 30th.

—— 18. Violent Eruption of mount Etna: the Town of Bronte, containing 10,000 people, destroyed, but with little loss of life.

—— 19. France: The king fired upon. M. Dupin, chosen president of the Chambers.

Dec. 3. Great Britain.—Parliament dissolved by proclamation, and a new parliament summoned.

—— 24. Belgium:—Surrender of the citadel of Antwerp, to the French besieging army. The king of Holland refusing to give up the other three Belgian fortresses in his possession, gen. Chasse and the garrison are marched into France as prisoners of war, and the invaders retire.

1833.

Jan. 29. Great Britain:—Meeting of the new Parliament,—C. M. Sutton re-elected speaker of the Commons.

Feb. 6. Greece:—King Otho arrives at Napoli, and publishes a proclamation of his good intentions, &c.

—— Turkey:—Ibrahim Pacha, the celebrated rebel viceroy of Egypt takes posses sion of Smyrna and the surrounding country. The Turkish Sultan, alarmed for the safety of his capital and the remainder of his empire, engages the assistance of Russia.

—— 25. United States:—The bill introduced by Henry Clay, (usually styled *The Compromise* Tariff Bill,) for "*gradually* reducing the duties onforeign articles to the *revenue standard*," passes the House of Representatives of the United States by a vote of 120 to 85.

—— 27. West Indies:—The Cholera breaks out at Havanna.

March 1. United States:—"The *Enforcing* Bill," providing for collection of the United States revenue, passes the House, 149 to 47.

—— 2. —— Closing of the 2d session of 22d Congress.

—— 4. —— Andrew Jackson re-inaugurated president of the United States.

—— 10. Portugal:—Sartorious, the commander of Don Pedro's fleet, having resigned the office, Capt. Crosbie is appointed to succeed him; but the latter instead of re-

CPSIA information can be obtained
at www.ICGtesting.com
Printed in the USA
LVOW13*1445120218
566240LV00021B/1097/P

9 780331 532906